# International Economics

## FOURTH EDITION

## James Gerber

### San Diego State University

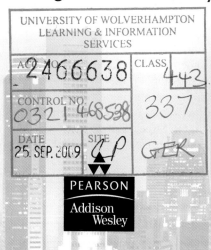

PEARSON
Addison
Wesley

Boston  San Francisco  New York
London  Toronto  Sydney  Tokyo  Singapore  Madrid
Mexico City  Munich  Paris  Cape Town  Hong Kong  Montreal

*For Monica and Elizabeth.*

| | |
|---|---|
| Publisher | *Greg Tobin* |
| Editor in Chief | *Denise Clinton* |
| Sponsoring Editor | *Noel Kamm* |
| Editorial Assistant | *Margaret Beste* |
| Managing Editor | *Nancy Fenton* |
| Senior Production Supervisor | *Meredith Gertz* |
| Cover Designer | *Charles Spaulding* |
| Supplements Editor | *Heather McNally* |
| Media Producer | *Bridget Page* |
| Senior Marketing Manager | *Roxanne Hoch* |
| Senior Prepress Supervisor | *Caroline Fell* |
| Senior Manufacturing Buyer | *Carol Melville* |
| Production Coordination, Composition, Text Design, and Illustrations | *Gillian Hall, The Aardvark Group* |
| Copyeditor | *Kathleen Cantwell, C4 Technologies* |
| Proofreader | *Holly McLean-Aldis* |
| Indexer | *Jack Lewis* |
| Cover Image | *© 2007 Glen Allison/The Image Bank/ Getty Images* |

ISBN-13: 978-0-321-46853-6
ISBN-10: 0-321-46853-8

If you purchased this book within the United States or Canada you should be aware that it has been wrongfully imported without the approval of the Publisher or the Author.

1 2 3 4 5 6 7 8 9 10—CRW—11 10 09 08 07

# International Economics

## FOURTH EDITION

# The Addison-Wesley Series in Economics

**Abel/Bernanke/Croushore**
*Macroeconomics*

**Bade/Parkin**
*Foundations of Economics*

**Bierman/Fernandez**
*Game Theory with Economic Applications*

**Binger/Hoffman**
*Microeconomics with Calculus*

**Boyer**
*Principles of Transportation Economics*

**Branson**
*Macroeconomic Theory and Policy*

**Bruce**
*Public Finance and the American Economy*

**Byrns/Stone**
*Economics*

**Carlton/Perloff**
*Modern Industrial Organization*

**Caves/Frankel/Jones**
*World Trade and Payments: An Introduction*

**Chapman**
*Environmental Economics: Theory, Application, and Policy*

**Cooter/Ulen**
*Law and Economics*

**Downs**
*An Economic Theory of Democracy*

**Ehrenberg/Smith**
*Modern Labor Economics*

**Ekelund/Ressler/Tollison**
*Economics*

**Fusfeld**
*The Age of the Economist*

**Gerber**
*International Economics*

**Ghiara**
*Learning Economics*

**Gordon**
*Macroeconomics*

**Gregory**
*Essentials of Economics*

**Gregory/Stuart**
*Russian and Soviet Economic Performance and Structure*

**Hartwick/Olewiler**
*The Economics of Natural Resource Use*

**Hoffman/Averett**
*Women and the Economy: Family, Work, and Pay*

**Holt**
*Markets, Games and Strategic Behavior*

**Hubbard**
*Money, the Financial System, and the Economy*

**Hughes/Cain**
*American Economic History*

**Husted/Melvin**
*International Economics*

**Jehle/Reny**
*Advanced Microeconomic Theory*

**Johnson-Lans**
*A Health Economics Primer*

**Klein**
*Mathematical Methods for Economics*

**Krugman/Obstfeld**
*International Economics*

**Laidler**
*The Demand for Money*

**Leeds/von Allmen**
*The Economics of Sports*

**Leeds/von Allmen/Schiming**
*Economics*

**Lipsey/Ragan/Storer**
*Economics*

**Melvin**
*International Money and Finance*

**Miller**
*Economics Today*

**Miller**
*Understanding Modern Economics*

**Miller/Benjamin**
*The Economics of Macro Issues*

**Miller/Benjamin/North**
*The Economics of Public Issues*

**Mills/Hamilton**
*Urban Economics*

**Mishkin**
*The Economics of Money, Banking, and Financial Markets*

**Mishkin**
*The Economics of Money, Banking, and Financial Markets, Alternate Edition*

**Murray**
*Econometrics: A Modern Introduction*

**Parkin**
*Economics*

**Perloff**
*Microeconomics*

**Perman/Common/McGilvray/Ma**
*Natural Resources and Environmental Economics*

**Phelps**
*Health Economics*

**Riddell/Shackelford/Stamos/Schneider**
*Economics: A Tool for Critically Understanding Society*

**Ritter/Silber/Udell**
*Principles of Money, Banking, and Financial Markets*

**Rohlf**
*Introduction to Economic Reasoning*

**Ruffin/Gregory**
*Principles of Economics*

**Sargent**
*Rational Expectations and Inflation*

**Scherer**
*Industry Structure, Strategy, and Public Policy*

**Stock/Watson**
*Introduction to Econometrics*

**Studenmund**
*Using Econometrics*

**Tietenberg**
*Environmental and Natural Resource Economics*

**Tietenberg**
*Environmental Economics and Policy*

**Todaro/Smith**
*Economic Development*

**Waldman**
*Microeconomics*

**Waldman/Jensen**
*Industrial Organization: Theory and Practice*

**Weil**
*Economic Growth*

**Williamson**
*Macroeconomics*

# Brief Contents

Preface    xvi

**PART 1    Introduction and Institutions    1**

chapter 1    The United States in a Global Economy    2
chapter 2    International Economic Institutions
                since World War II    17

**PART 2    International Trade    37**

chapter 3    Comparative Advantage and the Gains from Trade    38
chapter 4    Comparative Advantage and Factor Endowments    60
chapter 5    Beyond Comparative Advantage    90
chapter 6    The Theory of Tariffs and Quotas    116
chapter 7    Commercial Policy    136
chapter 8    International Trade and Labor and Environmental
                Standards    155

**PART 3    International Finance    177**

chapter 9    Trade and the Balance of Payments    178
chapter 10   Exchange Rates and Exchange Rate Systems    209
chapter 11   An Introduction to Open Economy Macroeconomics    248
chapter 12   International Financial Crises    273

**PART 4    Regional Issues in the Global Economy    301**

chapter 13   Economic Integration in North America    302
chapter 14   The European Union: Many Markets into One    332
chapter 15   Trade and Policy Reform in Latin America    364
chapter 16   Export-Oriented Growth in East Asia    394
chapter 17   China and India in the World Economy    423

**Suggested Readings    445**
**Glossary    457**
**Index    469**

# Contents

**Preface    xvi**

## PART 1    Introduction and Institutions    1

### chapter 1    The United States in a Global Economy    2

Introduction: The Re-Emergence of International
Economic Integration                                                  2

Globalization in Perspective                                           3

    The Growth of World Trade                      4
    Capital and Labor Mobility                     5
    New Features of the Global Economy              7
    Trade and Economic Growth                       9

Twelve Issues in the International Economy                            11

    The Gains from Trade (Chapters 3, 4, and 5)                      11
    Wages, Jobs, and Protection (Chapters 3, 6, 7, and 8)           11
    Trade Deficits (Chapters 9 and 11)                              11
    Regional Trade Agreements (Chapters 2, 13, and 14)              12
    The Resolution of Trade Conflicts (Chapters 2, 7, and 8)        12
    The Role of International Institutions (Chapters 2 and 12)       12
    Exchange Rates and the Macroeconomy (Chapters 10 and 11)        13
    Financial Crises and Global Contagion (Chapter 12)              13
    Capital Flows and the Debt of Developing Countries
        (Chapters 2, 9, and 12)                13
    Crisis and Reform in Latin America (Chapter 15)                 14
    Export-Led Growth in East Asia (Chapter 16)                     14
    The Integration of India and China into the World Economy
        (Chapter 17)                           14

*Vocabulary 15  •  Study Questions 15*

chapter 2     **International Economic Institutions
since World War II    17**

Introduction: International Institutions and Issues
    since World War II                                                          17
    International Institutions                                                  17
    A Taxonomy of International Economic Institutions                          18

The IMF, the World Bank, and the WTO                                            19
    The IMF and World Bank                                                      19
    The GATT, the Uruguay Round, and the WTO                                    20
    **CASE STUDY:** The GATT Rounds                                            22

Regional Trade Agreements                                                       23
    Four Types of Regional Trade Agreements                                    23
    **CASE STUDY:** Prominent Regional Trade Agreements                        24

The Role of International Economic Institutions                                 26
    The Definition of Public Goods                                             27
    Maintaining Order and Reducing Uncertainty                                 28
    **CASE STUDY:** Bretton Woods                                             29

Criticism of International Institutions                                         31
    Sovereignty and Transparency                                              31
    Ideology                                                                   32
    Implementation and Adjustment Costs                                        33

*Summary 34 • Vocabulary 35 • Study Questions 36*


**PART 2** **International Trade    37**

chapter 3     **Comparative Advantage and the Gains from Trade    38**

Introduction: Absolute Advantage and the Gains from Trade                       38
    Adam Smith and the Attack on Economic Nationalism                          38
    A Simple Model of Production and Trade                                     39
    Absolute Productivity Advantage and the Gains from Trade                   40
    **CASE STUDY:** The International Market for Crude Oil                      42

Comparative Productivity Advantage and the Gains from Trade                     44

The Production Possibilities Curve                                              44
    Relative Prices                                                            45
    The Price Line or Trade Line                                               46
    The Gains from Trade                                                       47
    Domestic Prices and the Trade Price                                        49

Absolute and Comparative Productivity Advantage Contrasted                      50

Gains from Trade with No Absolute Advantage             50

Comparative Advantage and "Competitiveness"            51

Economic Restructuring                                 53
    **CASE STUDY:** Changing Comparative Advantage in the Republic
    of Korea, 1960–2000                                55

*Summary 57  •  Vocabulary 57  •  Study Questions 58*

### chapter 4     Comparative Advantage and Factor Endowments     60

Introduction: The Determinants of Comparative Advantage    60

Modern Trade Theory                                    60
    The Heckscher-Ohlin (HO) Trade Model               61
    Gains from Trade in the HO Model                   62

Trade and Income Distribution                          65
    The Stolper-Samuelson Theorem                      66
    The Specific Factors Model                         68
    **CASE STUDY:** Forecasts of Winners and Losers under NAFTA    70

Empirical Tests of the Theory of Comparative Advantage    72

Extension of the Heckscher-Ohlin Model                 73
    The Product Cycle                                  73
    Foreign Trade versus Foreign Investment            75
    **CASE STUDY:** United States–China Trade          77
    Outsourcing                                        79
    Migration and Trade                                80

The Impact of Trade on Wages and Jobs                  82

*Summary 84  •  Vocabulary 85  •  Study Questions 86*

**APPENDIX:** Finding Trade Data                       87

### chapter 5     Beyond Comparative Advantage     90

Introduction: More Reasons to Trade                    90

Intraindustry Trade                                    91
    Measures of Intraindustry Trade                    91
    Characteristics of Intraindustry Trade             92
    The Gains from Intraindustry Trade                 94
    **CASE STUDY:** United States and Canada Trade     95

Trade and Geography                                    96
    External Economies of Scale                        97
    Trade and External Economies                       98

Industrial Policy                                      100
    Industrial Policies and Market Failure             101

Strategic Trade                                                                     103
Industrial Policy Tools                                                             105
Problems with Industrial Policies                                                   106

U.S. Industrial Policies                                                            108
CASE STUDY: Subsidizing Commercial Aircraft                                         110

*Summary 112 • Vocabulary 113 • Study Questions 113*

APPENDIX: A Graphical Illustration of Prices and Costs
with Monopolistic Competition                                                       114

chapter 6    **The Theory of Tariffs and Quotas    116**

Introduction: The Impact of Tariffs                                                 116
Analysis of a Tariff                                                                116
Consumer and Producer Surplus                                                       117
The Effect of a Tariff on Prices, Output, and Consumption                           118
The Effect of a Tariff on Resource Allocation and Income
    Distribution                                                                    120
Other Potential Costs                                                               122
The Large Country Case                                                              123
Effective versus Nominal Rates of Protection                                        124
CASE STUDY: A Comparison of Tariff Rates                                            126

Analysis of Quotas                                                                  128
Types of Quotas                                                                     128
The Effect on the Profits of Foreign Producers                                      129
Hidden Forms of Protection                                                          131
CASE STUDY: Intellectual Property Rights and Trade                                  131

*Summary 133 • Vocabulary 134 • Study Questions 134*

chapter 7    **Commercial Policy    136**

Introduction: Commercial Policy and Jobs                                            136

Protection in the European Union, Japan, and the United States                      136
Direct Costs and Jobs Saved in Agriculture, Clothing, and Textiles                  137
The Logic of Collective Action                                                      140
CASE STUDY: The Uruguay and Doha Rounds                                             141

Why Nations Protect Their Industries                                                142
The Labor Argument                                                                  143
The Infant Industry Argument                                                        143
The National Security Argument                                                      144
The Retaliation Argument                                                            145
CASE STUDY: Economic Sanctions                                                      146

The Politics of Protection in the United States                                     148
Countervailing Duties                                                               148

|  |  |
|---|---|
| Antidumping Duties | 149 |
| Escape Clause Relief | 150 |
| Section 301 and Special 301 | 151 |
| **CASE STUDY:** Agricultural Subsidies | 151 |

*Summary 153 • Vocabulary 153 • Study Questions 154*

**chapter 8    International Trade and Labor and Environmental Standards    155**

| | |
|---|---|
| Introduction: Income and Standards | 155 |
| Setting Standards: Harmonization, Mutual Recognition, or Separate? | 156 |
| **CASE STUDY:** Income, Environment, and Society | 157 |
| Labor Standards | 159 |
| Defining Labor Standards | 160 |
| **CASE STUDY:** Child Labor | 160 |
| Labor Standards and Trade | 163 |
| Evidence on Low Standards as a Predatory Practice | 164 |
| **CASE STUDY:** The International Labor Organization (ILO) | 165 |
| Trade and the Environment | 167 |
| Transboundary and Non-Transboundary Effects | 167 |
| **CASE STUDY:** Trade Barriers and Endangered Species | 169 |
| Alternatives to Trade Measures | 170 |
| Labels for Exports | 171 |
| Requiring Home Country Standards | 172 |
| Increasing International Negotiations | 173 |

*Summary 173 • Vocabulary 174 • Study Questions 175*

**PART 3    International Finance    177**

**chapter 9    Trade and the Balance of Payments    178**

| | |
|---|---|
| Introduction: The Current Account | 178 |
| The Trade Balance | 178 |
| The Current Account Balance | 179 |
| Introduction to the Financial and Capital Accounts | 181 |
| Types of Financial Flows | 184 |
| Limits on Financial Flows | 188 |
| **CASE STUDY:** The Mexican Sexenio Crisis | 189 |
| The Current Account and the Macroeconomy | 190 |
| The National Income and Product Accounts | 190 |

Are Current Account Deficits Harmful? 196
**CASE STUDY:** Current Account Deficits in the United States 197

International Debt 199
**CASE STUDY:** Odious Debt 201

The International Investment Position 203

*Summary 204 • Vocabulary 205 • Study Questions 205*

**APPENDIX A:** Measuring the International Investment Position 206
**APPENDIX B:** Balance of Payments Data 207

chapter 10 **Exchange Rates and Exchange Rate Systems** 209

Introduction: Fixed, Flexible, or In-Between? 209

Exchange Rates and Currency Trading 209
Reasons for Holding Foreign Currencies 211
Institutions 212
Exchange Rate Risk 213

The Supply and Demand for Foreign Exchange 214
Supply and Demand with Flexible Exchange Rates 214
Exchange Rates in the Long Run 216
Exchange Rates in the Medium Run and Short Run 220
**CASE STUDY:** The Largest Market in the World 224

The Real Exchange Rate 226

Alternatives to Flexible Exchange Rates 228

Fixed Exchange Rate Systems 229
**CASE STUDY:** Dollarization and Currency Boards 232

Choosing the Right Exchange Rate System 235
**CASE STUDY:** The End of the Bretton Woods System 238

Single Currency Areas 239
Conditions for Adopting a Single Currency 241
**CASE STUDY:** Is the NAFTA Region an Optimal Currency Area? 242

*Summary 244 • Vocabulary 245 • Study Questions 245*

**APPENDIX:** The Interest Rate Parity Condition 247

chapter 11 **An Introduction to Open Economy Macroeconomics** 248

Introduction: The Macroeconomy in a Global Setting 248

Aggregate Demand and Aggregate Supply 249

Fiscal and Monetary Policies 254
Fiscal Policy 254

Monetary Policy                                                            255
**CASE STUDY:** Fiscal and Monetary Policy during the Great
    Depression                                                            257

Current Account Balances Revisited                                        260
Fiscal and Monetary Policies, Interest Rates, and Exchange Rates          261
Fiscal and Monetary Policy and the Current Account                        262
The Long Run                                                              264

Macro Policies for Current Account Imbalances                             265
The Adjustment Process                                                    266
**CASE STUDY:** The Adjustment Process in the United States               267

Macroeconomic Policy Coordination in Developed Countries                  268

*Summary 269 • Vocabulary 270 • Study Questions 271*


chapter 12  **International Financial Crises   273**

Introduction: The Challenge to Financial Integration                      273

Definition of a Financial Crisis                                          274

Two Types of International Financial Crises                               275
Crises Caused by Macroeconomic Imbalances                                275
Crises Caused by Volatile Capital Flows                                  277
**CASE STUDY:** The Mexican Peso Crisis of 1994 and 1995                 278

Domestic Issues in Crisis Avoidance                                       281
Moral Hazard and Financial Sector Regulation                             282
Exchange Rate Policy                                                     283
Capital Controls                                                         284
**CASE STUDY:** Chilean Taxes on Capital Inflows                         286

Domestic Policies for Crisis Management                                   287
**CASE STUDY:** The Asian Crisis of 1997 and 1998                        288

Reform of the International Financial Architecture                        292
A Lender of Last Resort                                                  293
Conditionality                                                          294
Reform Urgency                                                          296

*Summary 297 • Vocabulary 299 • Study Questions 299*


PART 4  **Regional Issues in the Global Economy   301**

chapter 13  **Economic Integration in North America   302**

Introduction: Expanding Economic Relations                                302
Economic and Demographic Characteristics of North America                 302

The Canada-U.S. Trade Relationship                                    305
    The Auto Pact of 1965                                             306
    The Canadian-U.S. Trade Agreement (CUSTA) of 1989                307

Recent Mexican Economic History                                      310
    The Slowdown in Economic Growth                                  310
    The Lost Decade of the 1980s                                     311
    Economic Policy Reforms in the Mexican Economy                   312
    **CASE STUDY:** Mexico's Export Processing Industry              313

The North American Free Trade Agreement (NAFTA)                       315

The NAFTA Debate in the United States                                316
    Labor Issues                                                     317
    Environmental Issues                                             318
    Immigration                                                      320

Jobs, Politics, and the Future                                       322
    The Expansion of NAFTA                                           325
    The Future of NAFTA: A North American Community?                 326
    **CASE STUDY:** Doing Business in Canada, Mexico,
      and the United States                                         328
    *Summary 329 • Vocabulary 330 • Study Questions 331*

**chapter 14**   **The European Union: Many Markets into One**   **332**

Introduction: The European Union                                     332

The Size of the European Market                                      333

Before the European Union                                            336
    The Treaty of Rome                                               336
    Institutional Structure of the EEC                               337

Deepening and Widening the Community in the 1970s
    and 1980s                                                        340
    Before the Euro                                                  340

The Second Wave of Deepening: The Single European Act                343
    **CASE STUDY:** The Schengen Agreement                           343
    The Delors Report                                                344
    Forecasts of the Gains from the Single European Act             345
    Problems in the Implementation of the SEA                        346

The Third Wave of Deepening: The Maastricht Treaty                   350

Monetary Union and the Euro                                          351
    Costs and Benefits of Monetary Union                             352
    The Political Economy of a Single Currency                       353
    Implementation of the Single Currency                            354

Widening the European Union                                                    355
    Central and Eastern Europe                                                 356
    Turkey                                                                     358
    **CASE STUDY:** Spain's Switch from Emigration to Immigration              358
The Demographic Challenge of the Future                                        360
*Summary 361 • Vocabulary 362 • Study Questions 363*

chapter 15 **Trade and Policy Reform in Latin America    364**
Introduction: Defining a "Latin American" Economy                             364
Population, Income, and Economic Growth                                        365
Import Substitution Industrialization                                          367
    Origins and Goals of ISI                                                   369
    Criticisms of ISI                                                          371
    **CASE STUDY:** ISI in Mexico                                             373
Macroeconomic Instability and Economic Populism                               375
    Populism in Latin America                                                  375
The Debt Crisis of the 1980s                                                   376
    Proximate Causes of the Debt Crisis                                        376
    Responses to the Debt Crisis                                               377
Economic Policy Reform and the "Washington Consensus"                          380
    Stabilization Policies to Control Inflation                                380
    Structural Reform and Open Trade                                           383
    **CASE STUDY:** Regional Trade Blocs in Latin America                      386
    The Washington Consensus                                                   388
    The Next Generation of Reforms                                             389
*Summary 391 • Vocabulary 392 • Study Questions 393*

chapter 16 **Export-Oriented Growth in East Asia    394**
Introduction: The High-Performance Asian Economies                            394
Population, Income, and Economic Growth                                        395
General Characteristics of Growth in the HPAEs                                 399
    Shared Growth                                                              399
    Rapid Accumulation of Physical and Human Capital                           401
    Rapid Growth of Manufactured Exports                                       402
    Stable Macroeconomic Environments                                          402
The Institutional Environment                                                  403
    Fiscal Discipline                                                          404
    Business-Government Relations                                              404

**CASE STUDY:** Deliberation Councils in the Ministry
of International Trade and Industry (MITI)                              405
Avoiding Rent Seeking                                                   406
**CASE STUDY:** Were East Asian Economies Open?                        407

The Role of Industrial Policies                                        410
Targeting Specific Industries in the HPAEs                             410
Did Industrial Policies Work?                                          411
**CASE STUDY:** HCI in Korea                                           413

The Role of Manufactured Exports                                       414
The Connections between Growth and Exports                             414
Is Export Promotion a Good Model for Other Regions?                    416
**CASE STUDY:** Asian Trade Blocs                                      417

Is There an Asian Model of Economic Growth?                            418

*Summary 421 • Vocabulary 421 • Study Questions 422*

chapter 17 **China and India in the World Economy    423**

Introduction: The Challenges of Openness                               423

Demographic and Economic Characteristics                               424
Economic Reforms in China and India                                    426
The Reform Process in China                                            426
Indian Economic Reforms                                                428
Remaining Issues                                                       429
**CASE STUDY:** Why Did the USSR Collapse and China Succeed?           430

China and India in the World Economy                                   432
Chinese and Indian Trade Patterns                                      432

The Challenges of India and China in the World Economy                 435
Unresolved Issues                                                      438
The Choices Ahead                                                      441

*Summary 442 • Vocabulary 443 • Study Questions 443*

**Suggested Readings    445**

**Glossary    457**

**Index    469**

# Preface

*International Economics* is designed for a one-semester course covering both the micro and macro components of international economics. The Fourth Edition continues the approach of the first three editions by offering a principles-level introduction to the core theories, together with policy analysis and the institutional and historical contexts of our world's increasingly international economic integration. My goal is to make economic reasoning about the international economy accessible to a diverse group of students, including both economics majors and nonmajors.

Several features of *International Economics* distinguish it from the many excellent texts in the field:

- First, the approach is broader than the theoretical apparatus used by economists. Economic theory is covered and its mastery is essential, but it is my belief that most readers grasp theory more completely when it is presented along with real-world applications. To this end, I have supplemented economic theory with case studies and other content ranging from the role of economic institutions and the analysis of international economic policies, to the recent history of the world economy.

- Second, the objective of covering both the micro and macro sides in a one-semester course necessitates paring back the coverage of theory in order to focus on the central concepts. As all instructors are aware, many theoretical topics are of secondary or tertiary importance, which can pose a problem for students who may lack the needed breadth and depth of understanding to rank topics by their relative importance.

- Third, *International Economics* provides richer historical and institutional detail than most other texts. This material illuminates the relationships between economic theory and policy, and between economics and the other social sciences.

- Fourth, I have organized Part 4 of the book into five chapters, each focused on a geographic area as follows: North America, the European Union, Latin America, East Asia, and China and India. These chapters offer students the chance to broaden their understanding of world trends and to observe the intellectual power of economic theory in practice.

## New to the Fourth Edition

This Fourth Edition of *International Economics* preserves the organization and coverage of the Third Edition and adds a number of updates and enhancements. New to this edition:

- All tables and graphs have been updated.
- Chapter 2 presents a new discussion of points raised by the critics of international institutions.
- Chapter 3 includes a fully developed example of the gains from trade when a country has no absolute advantage.
- Chapter 4 contains a new discussion of outsourcing and migration.
- The discussion of nontariff measures in Chapter 6 now includes a case study of intellectual property rights.
- A new case study in Chapter 9 analyzes the risks posed by the large current account deficit in the United States.
- Chapter 13 provides a more in-depth discussion of the Mexican migration issue; it also introduces the World Bank's Doing Business Web site in the context of a comparison between Canada, Mexico, and the United States.
- Chapter 14 includes the recent expansion of the EU to include Bulgaria and Romania, along with a discussion of the challenge posed by Turkey's possible accession.
- The EU's demographic future is also discussed in Chapter 14, along with a case study examining Spain's shift from an emigrant country to a destination for immigrants.
- Chapter 16 looks at the degree of openness in East Asia, and has a new case study examining East Asia's many new regional trade agreements.
- Chapter 17 is an entirely new chapter that examines the integration of China and India into the world economy.

## Flexibility of Organization

A book requires a fixed topical sequence because it must order the chapters one after another. This is a potential problem for some instructors, as there is a wide variety of preferences for the order in which topics are taught. The Fourth Edition strives for flexibility in allowing instructors to find their own preferred sequence.

Part 1 includes two introductory chapters that are designed to build vocabulary, develop historical perspective, and provide background information about the different international organizations and the roles that they play in the world economy. Some instructors prefer to delve into the theory chapters immediately, and reserve this material for later in the course. There is no loss of continuity with this approach.

Part 2 presents the micro side of international economics, while Part 3 covers the macro side. These two parts can easily be reversed in sequence if desired.

Part 2 includes six chapters that cover trade models (Chapters 3–5) and commercial policy (Chapters 6–8). A condensed treatment of this section could focus on the Ricardian model in Chapter 3, and the analysis of tariffs and quotas in Chapters 6 and 7. Chapter 8 on labor and environmental standards can stand on its own, although the preceding chapters deepen student understanding of the trade-offs.

Part 3 covers the balance of payments, exchange rates, open-economy macroeconomics, and international financial crises. Chapter 11 in Part 3, on open economy macroeconomics, is optional. It is intended for students and instructors who want a review of macroeconomics, including the concepts of fiscal and monetary policy, in a context that includes current accounts and exchange rates. If Chapter 11 is omitted, Chapter 12 remains accessible, as long as students have an understanding of the basic concepts of fiscal and monetary policy. Chapter 12 relies most heavily on Chapters 9 (balance of payments) and 10 (exchange rates and exchange rate systems).

Part 4 presents five chapters, each focused on a geographic area. These chapters use theory presented in Chapters 3–12 in a similar fashion to the economics discussion that students find in the business press, congressional testimonies, speeches, and other sources intended for a broad civic audience. Where necessary, concepts such as the real rate of exchange are briefly reviewed. One or more of these chapters can be moved forward to fit the needs of a particular course.

## Supplementary Materials

The following supplementary resources are available to support teaching and learning.

### Companion Website: www.aw-bc.com/gerber

- Jeff Sarbaum of the University of North Carolina, Greensboro, has prepared a Web-based PowerPoint presentation comprising lecture notes and all of the text's tables and figures.

- In recognition of the importance of the Internet as a source of timely information, the Companion Website offers Web links, also prepared by Jeff Sarbaum, for each chapter of *International Economics*. These links, complete with descriptions of the content available at each site, provide easy access to relevant, current data sources.

### Other Supplements

Laura Wolff of Southern Illinois University, Edwardsville, has updated the Study Guide, which offers handy review and study aids as well as practice problems and tests. Laura has also revised and improved the Instructor's Manual/Test Bank and brought it up to date with the text. Among other teaching resources, each chapter of this supplement provides thumbnail sketches of the text coverage; student learning goals; suggested assignments; the answers to the end-of-chapter questions; and a rich set of multiple-choice questions. Also available is a convenient Instructor's Resource Disk (CD) containing the PowerPoint resources mentioned above, plus the Instructor's Manual and a computerized Test Bank.

## Acknowledgments

All books are team efforts, even single-authored books. I owe a debt of gratitude to a large number of people, not the least of whom are my wife, Joan Wilkinson, and my two daughters, Monica and Elizabeth.

At San Diego State University, I have benefited from the opportunity to teach and converse with a wide range of students. My colleagues in economics and other disciplines, both here in San Diego and across the border in Mexico, have been extremely helpful. Their comments, together with the day-to-day conversations we have shared, constantly push me to think about the core economic ideas that should be a part of a college student's education, and to search for ways to explain the relevance and importance of those ideas with greater clarity and precision. Any failure in this regard is, of course, mine alone.

I am deeply grateful to Noel Kamm, Sponsoring Editor; Meredith Gertz, Senior Production Supervisor; Roxanne Hoch, Senior Marketing Manager; Charles Spaulding, Cover Designer; Heather McNally, Supplements Editor; and Bridget Page, Media Producer.

Finally, my gratitude goes to the numerous reviewers who have played an essential role in the development of *International Economics*. Each of the following individuals reviewed the manuscript, many of them several times, and provided useful commentary. I cannot express how much the text has benefited from their comments.

Mary Acker
*Iona College*

Jeff Ankrom
*Wittenberg University*

David Aschauer
*Bates College*

H. Somnez Atesoglu
*Clarkson University*

Mohsen Bahmani-Oskooee
*University of Wisconsin, Milwaukee*

Richard T. Baillie
*Michigan State University*

Eugene Beaulieu
*University of Calgary*

Ted Black
*Towson University*

Bruce Blonigen
*University of Oregon*

Lee Bour
*Florida State University*

Byron Brown
*Southern Oregon University*

Laura Brown
*University of Manitoba*

Albert Callewaert
*Walsh College*

Tom Carter
*Oklahoma City University*

Srikanta Chatterjee
*Massey University, New Zealand*

Jen-Chi Cheng
*Wichita State University*

Don Clark
*University of Tennessee*

Raymond Cohn
*Illinois State University*

Peter Crabb
*Northwest Nazarene University*

David Crary
*Eastern Michigan University*

Al Culver
*California State University, Chico*

Joseph Daniels
*Marquette University*

Alan Deardorff
*University of Michigan*

Craig Depken II
*University of Texas, Arlington*

John Devereaux
*University of Miami*

K. Doroodian
*Ohio University*

Noel J. J. Farley
*Bryn Mawr College*

Lewis R. Gale IV
*University of Southwest Louisiana*

Ira Gang
*Rutgers University*

Amy Jocelyn Glass
*Texas A & M University*

Joanne Gowa
*Princeton University*

Gregory Green
*Idaho State University*

Thomas Grennes
*North Carolina State University*

Winston Griffith
*Bucknell University*

Jane Hall
*California State University, Fullerton*

Seid Hassan
*Murray State University*

F. Steb Hipple
*East Tennessee State University*

Paul Jensen
*Drexel University*

George Karras
*University of Illinois at Chicago*

Kathy Kelly
*University of Texas, Arlington*

Abdul Khandker
*University of Wisconsin, La Crosse*

Jacqueline Khorassani
*Marietta College*

Sunghyun Henry Kim
*Brandeis University*

Vani Kotcherlakota
*University of Nebraska at Kearney*

Corrine Krupp
*Michigan State University*

Kishore Kulkarni
*Metropolitan State College of Denver*

Farrokh Langdana
*Rutgers University*

Daniel Y. Lee
*Shippensburg University*

Mary Lesser
*Iona College*

Susan Linz
*Michigan State University*

Marc Lombard
*Macquarie University, Australia*

Thomas Lowinger
*Washington State University*

Nicolas Magud
*University of Oregon*

Bala Maniam
*Sam Houston State University*

Mary McGlasson
*Arizona State University*

Joseph McKinney
*Baylor University*

Judith McKinney
*Hobart & William Smith Colleges*

Howard McNier
*San Francisco State University*

Michael O. Moore
*George Washington University*

Stephan Norribin
*Florida State University*

William H. Phillips
*University of South Carolina*

Frank Raymond
*Bellarmine University*

Donald Richards
*Indiana State University*

John Robertson
*University of Kentucky Community College System*

Jeffrey Rosensweig
*Emory University*

Marina Rosser
*James Madison University*

Raj Roy
*University of Toledo*

George Samuels
*Sam Houston State University*

Craig Schulman
*University of Arizona*

William Seyfried
*Winthrop University*

Eckhard Siggel
*Concordia University*

David Spiro
*Columbia University*

Richard Sprinkle
*University of Texas, El Paso*

Ann Sternlicht
*Virginia Commonwealth University*

Leonie Stone
*State University of New York at Geneseo*

Rebecca Summary
*Southeast Missouri State University*

Jack Suyderhoud
*University of Hawaii*

Kishor Thanawala
*Villanova University*

Henry Thompson
*Auburn University*

Cynthia Tori
*Valdosta State University*

Edward Tower
*Duke University*

# Introduction and Institutions

# 1

# The United States in a Global Economy

##  Introduction: The Re-Emergence of International Economic Integration

During the summer of 1997, an economic crisis hit East Asia, beginning first in Thailand and then spreading to Indonesia, Malaysia, the Philippines, and South Korea. Currency values fell, stock markets crashed, and credit dried up. Several countries appealed to the International Monetary Fund (IMF) for emergency loans and by the fall of 1997 the IMF was spelling out the terms and conditions for its assistance. There was a sense of urgency in addressing the problem because the crisis was spreading globally. Japanese and European banks were heavily exposed with a large number of loans to the region, North and South American stock markets felt pressures from nervous investors, and American firms prepared for a wave of cheap imports brought on by the depreciated Asian currencies. While the crisis posed a threat to global economic stability, in fact it was only the latest in a series of episodes over the last decades. The Mexican peso collapse in 1994, speculation against the European Monetary System in 1992, the overvalued U.S. dollar in the mid-1980s, and the onset of the third-world debt crisis in 1982 all posed equally serious challenges to global financial stability.

Over the last few years, the world economy has been relatively crisis free, at least by comparison to the instability generated during the Asian crisis. Nevertheless, individual countries have experienced domestic crises related to their international economic networks (Argentina, Turkey, Russia, and others), and worries over the possibility of regional or global problems never disappear completely. For example, the large U.S. trade imbalances in the first decade of the new millennium worry many analysts. National economies are no longer as isolated as they once were, but are linked through extensive networks of financial and commercial relations. These networks bring many good things, such as lower prices and innovative technologies, but they also make it more likely that a crisis will spread from one part of the world to another.

The sudden appearance of the Internet and of instantaneous information flows in the 1990s tends to make the economic integration of regions and countries seem like an entirely new development. From a long-term historical perspective, however, many of the main features of globalization are not new. International flows of people and goods, the transmission of financial crises, and the spread of new technologies have taken place for centuries, if not millennia. Our twenty-first-century technology has reduced the time it takes to communicate and travel over great distances, but at the margin, technological changes in the late 1800s may have had a greater impact on commerce and politics. The nations and regions of our contemporary world are much more economically integrated than in the recent past, but even these changes are not without precedent. By the 1880s, farmers in North and South America, Europe, and parts of Asia were sensitive to commodity price movements around the world.

The market integration that transpired over the second half of the 1800s and the first part of the 1900s began to erode with the onset of World War I. From then until the end of World War II, nations erected trade barriers, cut their capital flows abroad, and limited immigration. World trade declined dramatically and nations became far less economically integrated than they were in 1900. In effect, much of the growth in world trade that began after 1950 simply brought the world back to where it was at the time of World War I.

#  Globalization in Perspective

There is no doubt that the economy of the United States is more integrated with other national economies than at any time in the last 60 or 70 years. It is tempting to say that global economic integration is greater than at any time in history, yet that fact is less certain than it may seem. In the age of the Internet, e-mail, and fax machines, it is easy to lose sight of the fact that most of what we buy and sell never makes it out of our local or national markets. We are aware of the fact that the parts in our cars are made in a dozen or more countries, but we should not forget that haircuts, restaurant meals, gardens, health care, education, financial services, utilities, most entertainment, and many other goods and services are domestic products. In the United States, about 83.8 percent of goods and services are produced domestically and imports are equal to about 16.2 percent of total economic output (2005). In 1890, the United States made about 92 percent of its goods and services, a larger share than today, but not radically different.

Imports and exports constitute one criterion by which we can judge the importance of the international economy, but it is not the only one. Integrated economies are also linked by the movement of capital and labor. Consider, for example, the 50 states of the United States. No one could claim that they are fully integrated if workers and investment flows were not free to move across state lines. This is also true of national economies where the degrees of freedom in the movement of capital and labor are indicators of the depth of integration. Another marker of economic integration is the movement of prices in different markets. When economies become linked to each other, price differences across markets should shrink as goods and services move freely across international boundaries. Each of these indicators—trade flows, factor movements, and similarity of prices—are measures of the degree of international economic integration.

## The Growth of World Trade

Since the end of World War II, world trade has grown much faster than world output. World output, which is equivalent to world income, has risen about six-fold over the last 50 years, while world trade has grown about twelvefold. As a result, trade has become a larger share of most national economies. One measure of the importance of international trade in a nation's economy is the sum of exports plus imports, divided by the **gross domestic product (GDP)**, where GDP is a measure of total production. Specifically, it is the value of all final goods and services produced inside a nation during some period, usually one year. The ratio of trade to GDP is called the **index of openness**, represented as follows:

$$\text{Index of Openness} = (\text{Exports} + \text{Imports}) \div \text{GDP}$$

Openness does not tell us about a country's trade policies and countries with higher openness measures do not necessarily have lower barriers to trade, although that is one possibility. In general, large countries are less dependent on international trade because their firms can reach an optimal production size without having to sell to foreign markets. Consequently, smaller countries tend to have higher measures of openness.

Figure 1.1 shows the openness index for six countries between 1913 and 2000. The decline in trade between the onset of World War I and 1950 is clearly visible in each country, as is the subsequent increase after 1950. Another pattern shown in Figure 1.1 is the smaller indexes for the United States and Japan, which have the largest populations, and the much higher index for the Netherlands, which has the smallest population in the sample. In general, smaller countries trade more than larger ones since they cannot efficiently produce as wide a range of goods and must depend on trade to a greater extent. For example, if the Netherlands were to produce autos solely for its own market, it would lack economies of scale and could not produce at a competitive cost, whereas the very large U.S. market can absorb a very large share of U.S. output. Hence, the openness index measures the relative importance of international trade in a nation's economy, but it does not provide any direct information about trade policy or trade barriers.

Figure 1.1 gives an historical overview of the decline and subsequent return of international trade after World War II, but it obscures important changes in the composition of trade flows from early in the twentieth century to those at the end of the century. Prior to World War I most trade consisted of agricultural commodities and raw materials, while current trade is primarily manufactured consumer goods and producer goods (machinery and equipment). Consequently, today's manufacturers are much more exposed to international competition than was the case in 1900. Furthermore, with the telecommunication advances of the

**FIGURE 1.1** ● **Openness Index for Six Countries, 1913–2000**

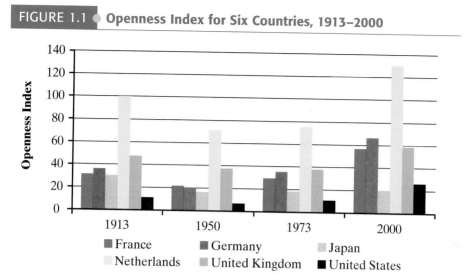

*Source*: Maddison, A. (1991) "Dynamic Forces in Capitalist Development" and World Bank (2006), "World Development Indicators."

1990s, outsourcing of services has become an important trend and a variety of service companies now face growing international competition as well. In sum, manufacturing and some services are now far more affected by world trade than the bars of Figure 1.1 imply.

## Capital and Labor Mobility

In addition to exports and imports, factor movements are also an indicator of economic integration. As national economies become more interdependent, labor and capital should move more easily across international boundaries. Labor, however, is less mobile internationally than it was in 1900. Consider, for example, that in 1890 approximately 14.5 percent of the U.S. population was foreign born, while in 2004, the figure was 12 percent. In 1900, many nations had open door immigration policies, and passport controls, immigration visas, and work permits were exceptions rather than rules. In the 1920s, the United States sharply restricted immigration and international labor mobility declined. These restrictions lasted until the 1960s, when changes in immigration laws once again encouraged foreigners to migrate to the United States.

On the capital side, measurement is more difficult, since there are several ways to measure capital flows. The most basic distinction is between flows of financial capital representing paper assets such as stocks, bonds, currencies, and bank accounts, and flows of capital representing physical assets such as real estate, factories, and businesses. The latter type of capital flow is called **foreign direct investment (FDI)**. To some extent, the distinction between the two is immaterial because both types of capital flows represent shifts in wealth across national boundaries and both make one nation's savings available to another.

When we compare today's trends to those of a century ago, we should keep two points in mind. First, if there were a single world capital market, then the investment rates (Investment/GDP) of any particular country would not need to be correlated with its saving rates (Saving/GDP). Financial capital would flow to the countries that offered the highest (risk-adjusted) rates of return. Since capital is abundant in high-income countries and relatively scarce in developing countries, we should expect to see higher risk-adjusted returns in developing countries and enormous flows into them. While capital flows to developing countries have grown significantly over the last decades, it is still true, however, that the level of investment in any country is highly correlated with its level of saving. As a result, low-saving countries have low investment levels, high-saving countries have high investment levels, and national saving rates are a far more important determinant of a nation's investment than are global capital flows.

The second point to keep in mind is that technological improvements increased trade and capital flows in the 1800s just as they are doing today. For example, in 1866, the first transatlantic cable linked New York to the world's largest financial market in London, decreasing the time required to obtain market information and conclude a transaction from about three weeks to just one day. One effect was that the gap in interest rates and asset prices between New York and London decreased significantly.

Capital flows at the end of the nineteenth century also increased from the construction of railroads and mines in the colonies and former colonies of the European powers. Large financial flows were made possible by the development of financial institutions such as Wall Street and stock, bond, and commodity exchanges. In the late nineteenth and early twentieth centuries, Great Britain supplied 5 to 10 percent of its GDP to world capital markets annually and at its peak invested as much abroad as it did domestically. Today, countries with large flows of foreign investment (all kinds) rarely supply more than 2 to 3 percent (net) of their GDP to world capital markets. As in the case of labor and trade flows, capital mobility was also reduced by the two world wars and the Great Depression. Industrial countries began to restrict capital flows during the 1920s, and in most cases, capital mobility did not begin to recover until the 1970s and 1980s.

Today, capital flows are different from earlier periods in at least three ways. First, there are many more financial instruments available now than there were a century ago. They range from relatively mundane stocks and mutual funds to relatively exotic instruments such as derivatives, ADRs, currency swaps, and others. In aggregate, they represent a wide variety of instruments that can be tailored to nearly every level of income and risk tolerance. Many of these new financial instruments are complex, specialized tools designed to meet very narrow objectives in an innovative and more open global economy. By contrast, at the turn of the twentieth century, there were only a few hundred stocks listed on the New York Stock Exchange, and most international financial transactions involved the buying and selling of bonds. The financial innovation of the late twentieth century is a sign that flows of financial capital are probably much larger than they were in the nineteenth century. According to the Bank for International Settlements in Geneva, Switzerland, *daily* foreign exchange transactions in 2004 were equal to $1.88 *trillion*, whereas in 1973, they were $15 billion.

The increase in financial transaction involving currency exchanges is related to the second major difference between capital flows today and those of a hundred years ago. In 1900, the world operated on a fixed exchange rate standard with less day-to-day risk of losses due to a decrease in value of the foreign currency. By comparison, protecting against exchange rate risk is a key component of today's international financial markets and accounts for a significant share of the day-to-day international transactions of financial institutions.

The third major difference in capital flows is that the costs of foreign financial transactions have fallen significantly. Economists refer to the costs of obtaining market information, negotiating an agreement, and enforcing the agreement as **transaction costs**. They are an important part of any business's costs, whether it is a purely domestic enterprise or a company involved in foreign markets. Due to sheer distance, as well as differences in culture, laws, and languages, transaction costs are often higher in international markets than in domestic ones. Today's lower transaction costs for foreign investment means that it is less expensive to move capital across international boundaries.

The occasional extremely volatile movement of financial capital across international boundaries is often mistakenly regarded as a new feature of the international economy. Speculative excesses and overinvestment, followed by capital flight and bankruptcies, have occurred throughout the modern era, going back at least to the 1600s and probably earlier. U.S. history shows a number of such cases. During the fifty years after 1890, at least four episodes of overspeculation and crisis hit the U.S. economy: 1890 to 1893 (speculation in silver stocks), 1907 (coffee futures and trust companies), 1920 to 1921 (agricultural land), and 1929 (U.S. stocks). As long as enough people cling to a get-rich-quick dream, and as long as domestic policymakers are subject to human error, the world will probably continue to experience episodes of volatile capital flows and speculative excess. One of the challenges of economic policymaking is to tame this type of excess without making things worse by destroying the beneficial effects of capital flows.

## New Features of the Global Economy

While international economic integration has been rapid, it does not appear to be historically unprecedented. Trade, as measured by the openness index, is about 50 percent more important to the U.S. economy than it was in 1890. Labor is less mobile than previous episodes in U.S. history, but capital is somewhat more mobile. Prices in many U.S. and foreign markets tend to be similar, although there are still significant differences (for example, the price of a pair of jeans in the United States and Europe). Given these patterns, other than the size of capital flows and the increased amount of trade, is anything fundamentally different about today's economy? The answer is "Yes."

**New Issues in International Trade and Investment.** Most high-income, industrial countries have few barriers to imports of manufactured goods. There are exceptions (for example, processed foodstuffs, textiles, and apparel), but as a general rule, import tariffs are low and other forms of protection are uncommon. Low trade barriers are the result of a process that began at the end of World War II and that has had a slow cumulative effect in rolling back the high levels of protection that were implemented in the 1920s and 1930s. The relative absence of tariffs outside of agriculture and apparel manufacturing does not mean that there are no barriers to trade, however. As countries gradually eliminate their formal restrictions on imports, various domestic policies become barriers to further increases in trade flows. These policies include sensitive issues such as labor conditions, environmental policy, the rules of fair economic competition, limits on investment, and government support for specific industries.

Negotiations between nations can be difficult in these areas because the rules and laws are complex and because they represent fundamental elements of domestic policy. Reducing a tax on imports is simple by comparison, particularly if other nations agree to similar cuts. When nations open their markets symmetrically through simultaneous reductions in import taxes, the change is easily understood by the electorate and appeals to their sense of fairness. A similar symmetry in changing labor standards or investment rules is more difficult to define. When restrictive investment rules are eliminated, for example, it may seem that there is no reciprocal action, and that foreign influence has undermined national sovereignty.

Economists refer to the elimination of **tariffs** (taxes on imports) and **quotas** (quantitative restrictions on imports) as **shallow integration**, or integration at the border. By contrast, the elimination or reduction of trade barriers caused by non–trade-related domestic policies is referred to as **deep integration**.

The issues of deep integration take up a sizable part of the dialogue between nations over matters related to foreign trade and investment. Economically, it is not necessary and is often undesirable that nations should adopt the same or similar policies. Nevertheless, small countries fear that they will be forced to adopt the standards of the United States or some other industrial economy, and large countries such as the United States worry that their domestic policies will be determined by the collective action of small countries. An international dialogue on these issues is a relatively new experience.

**The Role of International Organizations.** At the end of World War II, the United States, Great Britain, and their allies created a number of international organizations that were given active roles in maintaining international economic and political stability. Although the architects of these organizations could not envision the challenges and issues they would confront over the next 50 years, the organizations were given significant flexibility and they continue to play an important and growing role, in part as a forum for addressing the issues of deep integration.

The International Monetary Fund (IMF), the World Bank, the General Agreement on Tariffs and Trade (GATT), the United Nations (UN), the World

Trade Organization (WTO began operation in 1995, but grew out of the GATT), and a host of smaller organizations have broad international participation. They serve as forums for discussing and establishing rules, as mediators of disputes, and as organizers of actions to resolve problems. All of these organizations are controversial and have come under increasing fire from critics who charge that they promote unsustainable economic policies that often destroy the environment and protect the interests of wealthy elites. Many critics argue that they are also tools of the United States and other rich nations, while critics in the United States sometimes argue that they are unnecessary foreign entanglements that severely limit the scope for national action (Chapter 2 examines this issue in detail). Nevertheless, these organizations are attempts to create internationally acceptable rules for trade and commerce and to deal with potential disputes before they spill across international borders. Without a doubt, they are an entirely new element in the international economy.

**Regional Trade Agreements.** Agreements between groups of nations are not new. Free-trade agreements and other forms of preferential trade have existed throughout history. What is new is the significant increase in the number of **regional trade agreements** that have been signed in the last twenty years, especially in the 1990s. It is too early to say if this is a new trend or simply a phenomenon that will soon disappear.

The formation of preferential trade agreements is controversial. Trade opponents dislike the provisions that expose more of the national economy to international competition, whereas some trade proponents dislike the preferential nature of these agreements, which invariably favors regions included in the agreement at the expense of regions outside the agreement. The North American Free Trade Agreement (NAFTA), the European Union (EU), the Mercado Común del Sur (MERCOSUR), and the Asia Pacific Economic Cooperation (APEC) are the largest alliances, but they are only the tip of the iceberg of regional economic alliances.

## Trade and Economic Growth

It is not surprising that many people are more than a little apprehensive about increased international economic integration. The list of potential problems is a long one. More trade may give consumers lower prices and greater choices, but it also means more competition for firms and workers. Capital flows make more funds available for investment purposes, but they also increase the risk of spreading financial crises internationally. Rising immigration means higher incomes for migrants and lower labor costs for firms, but also it means more competition in labor markets and inevitably, greater social tensions. International organizations may help resolve disputes, but they may also reduce national sovereignty by putting pressure on countries to make operational changes. Free-trade agreements may increase trade flows, but again, that means more competition and more pressure on domestic workers and firms. Given the pluses and minuses, it seems appropriate to ask whether these changes are worth it.

In general, economists remain firmly convinced that the benefits of trade outweigh the costs. There is disagreement over the best way to achieve different goals (for example, how to protect against the harmful effects of sudden flows of capital), but the general belief that openness to the world economy is a superior policy to closing off a country is quite strong. To support this stance, economists can point to the following kinds of evidence:

- Casual empirical evidence of historical experience
- Evidence based on economic models and deductive reasoning
- Evidence from statistical comparisons of countries

While no one of these is conclusive by itself, together they provide solid support for the idea that open economies generally grow faster and prosper sooner than closed ones.

The historical evidence examines the experiences of countries when they tried to isolate themselves from the world economy. There are the experiences of the 1930s, when most countries tried to protect themselves from world events by shutting out flows of goods, capital, and labor. This did not cause the Great Depression of the 1930s, but worsened it, and ultimately led to the misery and tragedy of World War II. There are also the parallel experiences of countries that were divided by war, with one side becoming closed to the world economy, and the other side open. Germany and Korea are the best examples, but all of Eastern Europe stands in stark contrast to the prosperity and cleaner environments of Western Europe after World War II. There are also the experiences of Latin America and East Asia in the 1960s, 1970s, and 1980s. It is perhaps not too much of a generalization to say that East Asia integrated itself into the world economy and watched growth take off, while Latin America partially closed its doors and realized mediocre growth and a decade of depression and crisis in the 1980s.

The logic of economic theory generally supports these examples by suggesting the causal mechanisms that lead from trade to faster growth. Trade theory also points to cases where the costs of trade may outweigh the benefits (see Chapter 5), but generally, the benefits of increased innovation and access to new technologies and ideas that are fostered by trade are seen as positive factors. Trade increases the quality and quantity of machinery and equipment, and leads to more output. On the consumer side, it provides a greater variety of goods and offers them at lower prices. Both the variety and cost factors are real increases in consumer income.

The statistical evidence of the benefits of more open economies comes from comparisons of large samples of countries over different periods. While the statistical tests of the relationship between trade policy and economic growth suffer from their own technical shortcomings (usually problems of measuring trade policy), the results consistently show that more open economies grow faster. These results cannot be viewed as absolutely conclusive, but based on historical evidence, trade theory, and statistical tests taken as a whole, it would be unreasonable to believe that trade is generally bad for the economy.

# Twelve Issues in the International Economy

The following chapters examine twelve international economy issues. Each theme raises a number of important issues for the international economy. In some cases, international economics provides a relatively straightforward method of analysis for understanding the issues. In other cases, the themes are overlapping, multisided, and interdisciplinary. International economics cannot claim the final word on these issues, yet in the following chapters you will find that it provides an analytically powerful and logically consistent approach. It would be a huge mistake to dismiss the economic analysis of these issues.

## The Gains from Trade (Chapters 3, 4, and 5)

Why is international trade desirable? We have briefly addressed this issue, and we will consider additional points as we continue. Given that economic analysis clearly demonstrates that the benefits of international trade outweigh the costs, it is not surprising that virtually all economists support open markets and increased trade. Recent polls of economists put the level of agreement on this issue at around 98 percent, when a general question is asked about the desirability of closed versus open markets. The benefits were first analyzed in the late 1700s, and are perhaps the oldest and strongest finding in all of economics. Given the certainty of the benefits from trade, why do many non-economists oppose it?

## Wages, Jobs, and Protection (Chapters 3, 6, 7, and 8)

International trade benefits the majority of people in a national economy, but it does not usually benefit every member of society. Workers in firms that cannot compete may be forced to find new jobs or to take pay cuts. The fact that consumers pay less for the goods they buy, or that exporters hire more workers, may not help them. Increased awareness of the international economy has heightened the fears of people who feel vulnerable to changes in the international economy. They are concerned that wages in high-income countries must fall in order to compete with workers in low-wage countries, and that their jobs may be moved overseas. The solution, according to some, is to keep foreign goods out— particularly goods that are made by laborers who are paid less than American, European, or Japanese workers. One of the key issues challenging policymakers is to find the right mix of domestic policies so that the nation benefits from trade without creating a backlash from those individuals and industries that are hurt.

## Trade Deficits (Chapters 9 and 11)

In 1980, a comprehensive measure of trade accounts in the United States showed that there was a slight surplus of $2.3 billion. It was all downhill from there and by 2005 the same measure had fallen to a deficit of $791.5 billion. Each year that a country runs a trade deficit, it must borrow from abroad, essentially selling a piece of its future output in order to obtain more goods and services today. Among other things, large trade deficits have been known to cause currencies to collapse and to generate severe crises in financial systems, usually followed by deep recessions. The impact of large trade imbalances is uncertain, however, and the conditions that cause one country's deficits to disappear and another's to turn into a deep recession, are imperfectly understood.

## Regional Trade Agreements
## (Chapters 2, 13, and 14)

As the world economy becomes more integrated, some regions are running ahead of the general trend. Western Europeans, for example, have eliminated many of the economic barriers separating their nations, and are creating a broad political and economic union. With implementation of NAFTA in 1994, the United States, Canada, and Mexico became a free-trade area while the largest countries in the Pacific Basin, including China, Japan, and the United States, have agreed to turn the Pacific region into another free-trade area by 2020. The NAFTA nations expanded in 2005 to include countries in Central America and the Dominican Republic, and the United States continues to negotiate free trade agreements with a number of South American countries. In 2004, ten Central and East European nations joined the European Union, followed by two more in 2007, The Association of South East Asian Nations (ASEAN) has moved toward the creation of a free-trade zone among its member states and has signed an agreement with China to provide greater market access.

## The Resolution of Trade Conflicts
## (Chapters 2, 7, and 8)

Commercial conflicts between nations cover a wide variety of issues and complaints. In one sense these conflicts are routine, as the WTO provides a formal dispute resolution procedure that has the assent of most of the world's nations. The WTO process does not cover all goods and services, however, nor does it say much about a large number of practices that some nations find objectionable. The ability of nations to resolve conflicts without resorting to protectionist measures is one key to maintaining a healthy international economic environment. Disputes can become acrimonious, so it is imperative that differences of opinion are not permitted to escalate into a wider disagreement. Trade wars are not real wars, but they are harmful nonetheless.

## The Role of International Institutions
## (Chapters 2 and 12)

The organization with the greatest responsibility for resolving trade disagreements is the World Trade Organization. The WTO came into existence in 1995 and was an adaptation of the General Agreement on Tariffs and Trade (GATT), which was created shortly after World War II. Resolving trade disputes is only one of the new roles played by international organizations. Various organizations offer development support, technical economic advice, emergency loans in a crisis situation, and other services and assistance. These organizations perform services that were not offered before World War II (development support), or that were done by a single country (lending in a crisis)—usually the world's greatest military power. They exist today only through the mutual consent and cooperation of participating nations, and without that cooperation, they would dissolve. Their abilities are limited, however. They cannot prevent crises, and they cannot make poor countries rich. They are also controversial and are viewed by some as tools of the United States or as a threat to national independence. They are very likely to grow in function, however, as many international problems cannot be solved by individual nations alone.

## Exchange Rates and the Macroeconomy (Chapters 10 and 11)

Thirteen of the members of the European Union have adopted the euro as common currency and ten more are planning to give up their national currency by 2010. Three Latin American nations (Panama, Ecuador, and El Salvador) have adopted the dollar while countries around the world are searching for the best exchange rate system. Floating rates, fixed rates, and crawling pegs each have important implications for domestic economic policy and all serve as a two-way communication link between the domestic and world economies. When exchange rate systems develop problems, nations sometimes fall into deep recessions.

## Financial Crises and Global Contagion (Chapter 12)

As trade and investment barriers decline, and as fax, e-mail, and satellite communication systems grow, it becomes easier to move capital across international borders. This trend is bolstered by lower transaction costs for foreign investment and increased availability of different types of financial assets. The increase in international capital flows has created an impression that the global economy is more unstable today than it was in the past. As discussed earlier, financial crisis is an old story, but the increase in global capital flows during the 1990s has led to discussions about techniques for reducing volatile capital flows across international borders. In particular, how do countries tame the capital flows that add to instability without stopping those that create valuable new investment? Given that the volatility of international capital flows is not likely to disappear, this issue will continue to be a topic of discussion and investigation.

## Capital Flows and the Debt of Developing Countries (Chapters 2, 9, and 12)

In 1996, the World Bank and the International Monetary Fund began a debt relief program for a group of 42 countries labeled the Highly Indebted Poor

Countries (HIPC). Thirty-four of these countries are in Africa. At the same time, non-governmental groups such as Jubilee 2000 began to lobby successfully for a reduction in the debts of poor countries and for changes in the lending policies of rich countries. In many parts of the world, problems of extreme poverty are compounded by large foreign debts that are unlikely to be repaid and often require a constant supply of new loans to pay interest on the old ones. The search for workable solutions is complicated in the borrowing countries by economic shocks, corruption, and unsustainable economic policies. Common problems in the lending countries include unwise loans to corrupt dictators and loans for some expensive and unnecessary goods sold by rich countries.

## Crisis and Reform in Latin America (Chapter 15)

Beginning in the early 1980s, many of the nations of Latin America entered into a crisis brought on by high levels of debt owed to banks and governments outside the region. The crisis was characterized by deep recessions, high interest rates, bankruptcies, falling wages, and increasing poverty. Throughout the region, the 1980s came to be called the Lost Decade, a name that symbolized the absolute lack of progress in meeting economic development needs. Beginning in the mid-1980s, a series of policy reforms emerged out of the debt crisis and spread across Latin America. Economies that had been sheltered from international competition were opened, and the region gave up its traditional, inward-looking policies dating from the 1930s. The shift in national policies, from inward- to outward-looking perspectives, is unfinished, but remains one of the most interesting and significant stories in the contemporary international economy.

## Export-Led Growth in East Asia (Chapter 16)

Throughout the late 1980s and into the 1990s, it was hard to ignore the East Asian "miracle." While some economists point out that it was not really a miracle—just a lot of hard work and sound economic policies—the growth rates of the "high-performance Asian economies" were unique in human history. Rates of growth of real GDP *per person* commonly reached 4 to 5 percent per year, with 6 to 8 percent not unusual. In 1997, an economic and financial crisis hit the region hard. Although there were lingering effects, by 2000, the economies of the region's developing countries were growing at more than 7 percent a year. One of the dominant traits of the countries in East Asia is the extent to which they are outward looking and dependent on the growth of their manufactured exports.

## The Integration of India and China into the World Economy (Chapter 17)

China and India are the most populous countries in the world. In 2005, China's 1.31 billion people plus India's 1.08 billion accounted for over 37 percent of the world's population of 6.45 billion. Throughout most of the twentieth century, both countries had limited economic ties with other nations and made very little impact on the world economy. This began to change in 1978, when China began a dramatic shift away from isolationism. Reforms in China's economy led to an ever-growing presence of foreign investment, more exports and imports, fewer restrictions on privately owned enterprises, and in 2001, membership in the World Trade Organization. India's transformation from a relatively closed economy toward greater openness began later, in 1991, and has proceeded at a slower pace. Nevertheless, its sheer population size coupled with the technical excellence of its scientists and engineers and its developing high technology sector have turned it into a growing force in the world economy. Low wages and competitive firms and technologies in China and India have caught the attention of nearly all developing and developed nations, and have generated a variety of fears and opportunities, both realistic and unrealistic.

## Vocabulary

deep integration

foreign direct investment (FDI)

gross domestic product (GDP)

index of openness

quotas

regional trade agreement

shallow integration

tariffs

transaction costs

## Study Questions

1. How can globalization and international economic integration be measured?

2. In what ways is the U.S. economy more integrated with the world today than it was a century ago? In what ways is it less integrated?

3. What is "openness"? How is it measured? Does a low openness indicator indicate that a country is closed to trade with the outside world?

4. Describe the pattern over the last century shown by the openness index for leading industrial economies.

5. Trade and capital flows were described and measured in relative terms rather than absolute terms. Explain the difference. Which terms seem more valid—relative or absolute? Why?

6. The relative size of international capital flows may not be much greater today than they were 100 years ago, although they are certainly greater than they were 50 years ago. Qualitatively, however, capital flows are different today. Explain.

7. What are the new issues in international trade and investment? In what sense do they expose national economies to outside influences?

8. Describe the three kinds of evidence that economists use to support the assertion that open economies grow faster than economies that are closed to the world economy.

# International Economic Institutions since World War II

 ## Introduction: International Institutions and Issues since World War II

As World War II was drawing to a close, representatives from the United States, Great Britain, and other allied nations met in the small New Hampshire town of Bretton Woods. The outcome of these meetings was a series of agreements that created an exchange rate system (which lasted until 1971), the International Bank for Reconstruction and Development (IBRD), also known as the **World Bank**, and the International Monetary Fund (IMF). In 1946, two years after Bretton Woods, twenty-three nations including the United States and Great Britain began talks on reducing their trade barriers, leading to the **General Agreement on Tariffs and Trade (GATT)**, which began operation in 1948.

This chapter focuses on these global economic institutions, their history, their role in the world economy, and controversies surrounding their activities. Institutions that do not have a primary economic role, such as the General Assembly of the United Nations or the North Atlantic Treaty Organization (NATO), are not included.

### International Institutions

International economic institutions are an important feature of the world economy. When social scientists try to explain the increasing integration of national economies after World War II, one of the key explanations must be the increased stability and reduced uncertainty that these institutions help to create. Nevertheless, as international economic integration has increased, these organizations have come under more scrutiny and received much criticism. Before we look at their impact and some of the criticisms levied at them, we should define what we mean by an *institution*.

When most people hear the word **institution**, they probably think of a formal organization. However, economists tend to define institutions more abstractly. For example, the "New Institutionalists," led by economist Douglas North, have argued that organizations are not institutions in themselves, but are rather the rules that govern behavior—telling us what is permissible and what is not and acting as constraints that limit our actions.

Institutions can be formal or informal. A formal institution is a written set of rules that explicitly state what is and is not allowed. The rules may be embodied in a club, an association, or a legal system. An informal institution is a custom or tradition that tells people how to act in the same way that a law does, but without legal enforcement. For example, informal institutions include the rules of socializing, gift exchange, table manners, e-mail etiquette ("netiquette"), and so on. In this chapter, the term *institution* refers to rules and organizations.

## A Taxonomy of International Economic Institutions

International economic institutions come in many shapes and sizes. They can be lobbying groups for a particular commodity or an international producer's association; the joint management by several nations of a common resource; trade agreements or development funds for a select group of nations; or even global associations. Although this chapter's focus is on global economic institutions, it is useful to look at a taxonomy of international economic institutions, from the most limited and specific, to the most general. Table 2.1 shows five main types.

| TABLE 2.1 ● A Taxonomy of International Economic Institutions, with Examples | |
|---|---|
| Type | Examples |
| Commodity- or industry-specific organizations:<br>　These range from trade associations to international standards setting bodies to powerful cartels | • Oil Producing and Exporting Countries (OPEC)<br>• International Telecommunications Union (ITU)<br>• International Sugar Organization<br>• International Lead and Zinc Study Group |
| Commissions and agencies for managing shared resources | • International Boundary and Water Commission (IBWC)<br>• Lake Chad Basin Commission<br>• Mekong River Commission |
| Development funds and banks | • Inter-American Development Bank (IDB)<br>• North American Development Bank (NADBank)<br>• Asian Development Bank<br>• Islamic Development Bank |
| International trade agreements involving a few nations (regional trade alliances or trade blocs) | • North American Free Trade Agreement (NAFTA)<br>• US-Israel Free Trade Agreement<br>• Mercado Común del Sur (MERCOSUR)<br>• Asia-Pacific Economic Cooperation (APEC) |
| Global organizations for trade, development, and macroeconomic stability | • International Monetary Fund (IMF)<br>• World Bank<br>• World Trade Organization (WTO) |

# The IMF, the World Bank, and the WTO

Three global organizations play a major role in international economic relations and are central to this book: the International Monetary Fund (IMF), the World Bank, and the **World Trade Organization (WTO)**. The IMF and the World Bank date from the end of World War II; the WTO began in 1995 and grew out of the General Agreement on Tariffs and Trade (GATT), which it deepens and broadens. Accordingly, it is useful to know the history and function of the GATT as well as the WTO.

## The IMF and World Bank

During World War II, the United States and Great Britain (and a few other Allies) held regular discussions about the shape of the postwar international economic order. They wanted to avoid the mistakes of the 1920s and 1930s, when a lack of international cooperation led to the complete collapse of economic relations. The culmination of these talks was the **Bretton Woods conference** held in July 1944, where the Allies created the outlines of the **International Monetary Fund (IMF)** and the International Bank for Reconstruction and Development (World Bank).

The IMF began operation on December 27, 1945, with a membership of twenty-nine countries. Its success is indicated by the fact that by the year 2003, it had grown to 184 members. The IMF provides loans to its members under different programs for the short, medium, and long term. Each member is charged a fee, or **quota**, as the price of membership. The size of the quota varies with the size of the nation's economy and the importance of its currency in world trade and payments. In 2006, the IMF had over $315 billion in quotas. Important decisions within the IMF are made by vote with the weight of each nation's vote proportional to its quota. This gives the high-income countries of the world a voting power that is disproportionate to their population. For example, the United States alone controls 17 percent of the total votes, and the the seven largest industrial economies (Canada, Italy, France, Germany, Japan, the United Kingdom, and the United States) control almost 45 percent. Some votes on IMF policy require a "super majority" of 85 percent, giving the United States a veto power on those particular issues. The size of the quota also determines a country's access to loans.

The most visible role for the IMF is to intercede, by invitation, whenever a nation experiences a crisis in its international payments. For example, if a country imports more than it exports, then it may run out of foreign exchange reserves. **Foreign exchange reserves** are dollars, yen, pounds, euros, or another currency (or gold) that is accepted internationally. In addition, the IMF has its own currency, called an SDR, or special drawing right. SDRs are based on a country's quota and are a part of their international reserves. If a country lacks reserves, it cannot pay for its imports, nor can it pay the interest and principal it owes on its international borrowings. This is one scenario that warrants a call to the IMF. The IMF makes loans to its members, but it usually extracts a price above and beyond the interest it charges. The price is an agreement by the borrower to change its policies so that the problem cannot recur. If simple economic reforms such as a cut in the value of the currency, or limits on the central bank's creation of credit, are insufficient to solve the problem permanently, then the IMF usually requires a borrower to make fundamental changes in the relationship between government and markets in order to qualify for IMF funds. These requirements are known as **IMF conditionality**. For example, during the crisis of 1997–1998, the IMF was the main provider of funds and expertise to East Asia, again, with a great deal of controversy over the advice it gave and the conditions it imposed.

The World Bank was founded in 1944 at the same time as the IMF. In 2006, there were 184 members. Members buy shares in the Bank and as with the IMF, shareholding determines the weight of each member in setting the Bank's policies and practices. Originally, the World Bank was known as the International Bank for Reconstruction and Development, or IBRD. The name reflected the fact that it was primarily created to assist in the reconstruction of the war-torn areas. As the capital requirements for reconstruction grew, however, it soon became apparent that the IBRD lacked sufficient funds to do the job and in 1948, to assist Europe, the United States created the parallel program known as the Marshall Plan.

By the 1950s, the field of development economics had begun to take off. Several leading economists were able to make credible arguments that the world's less economically developed regions could grow much faster if they could get around the constraints imposed by a lack of investment capital, and the IBRD was encouraged to lend to developing economies. Today, the IBRD is one of five separate organizations that make up the World Bank. The role of the IBRD is to lend money for specific development projects such as dams, highways, and schools, and to support major adjustments in government policies that change the way they manage the economy. Other organizations in the World Bank are focused on the very poor, private sector development, and loan guarantee programs. Only developing countries can borrow from the World Bank.

## The GATT, the Uruguay Round, and the WTO

At the end of World War II, a third global economic organization was proposed to be named the International Trade Organization (ITO). If it had been implemented, the ITO's job would have been to establish rules relating to world trade, business practices, and international investment. U.S. opposition killed the idea of the ITO, however, and no such organization was created until 1995. Nevertheless, in 1946, while they were still considering the idea of the ITO, twenty-three countries opened negotiations over tariff reductions. These negotiations led to some 45,000 tariff reductions affecting $10 billion, or one-fifth of world trade. In addition, a number of agreements were made on rules for trade, with the expectation that the rules would become a part of the ITO. Both the tariff reductions and the rules were implemented in 1948; when the possibility of an ITO died in 1950, the agreements on tariffs and trade rules remained in force as a separate agreement, known as the General Agreement on Tariffs and Trade (GATT). The GATT has been very successful in bringing down trade barriers gradually. One indicator is that international trade has grown more than 6 percent per year over the last fifty years, which is much faster than before the war and faster than growth in the world's total output.

The GATT functions through a series of **trade rounds** in which countries periodically negotiate a set of incremental tariff reductions. Gradually, through the Kennedy Round in the mid-1960s and the Tokyo Round of the 1970s, trade rules other than tariffs began to be addressed, including the problems of dumping (selling in a foreign market below cost or below a fair price), subsidies to industry, and nontariff barriers to trade. As tariffs came down, these nontariff issues became more prominent.

The GATT intentionally ignored the extremely contentious sectors of agriculture, textiles, and apparel. In addition, trade in services was ignored because it was not important. The accumulation of unresolved issues in these sectors, however, along with the increased importance of nontariff trade barriers, led to the demand for a new, more extensive set of negotiations. These demands culminated in the **Uruguay Round** of trade negotiations that began in 1986 and concluded in 1993. In 1994, the new agreement was signed by 125 countries, and by 2006, its membership had grown to 149 members, with approximately another 32 in the process of negotiating to join.

The WTO continues trade talks and sector-specific discussions between comprehensive rounds of negotiations. For example, in 1997, 69 countries signed an agreement to open their telecommunication sectors, and another 70 agreed to significant opening in their financial services sectors. In addition, every two years, trade ministers from the member countries meet to set the WTO's policy objectives. In 2001, trade ministers meeting in Doha, Qatar, agreed to launch a new round of trade negotiations emphasizing issues of importance to developing countries. The round came to be called the **Doha Development Agenda** and led to five years of negotiations before talks were suspended in July 2006. The negotiating stances of the United States, the European Union, and large emerging economies such as India and Brazil, were too far apart and there was little progress toward a compromise agreement. The Doha Round is not the first set of trade talks to fall apart—the Uruguay Round was also suspended at one point, but ultimately it reached a successful conclusion. Issues in the Doha Round that are the most contentious include U.S. farm subsidies, European Union tariffs on agricultural imports, and developing country tariffs on manufactured imports.

The foundation of all WTO and GATT agreements are the principles of **national treatment** and **nondiscrimination**. National treatment is the requirement that foreign goods are treated similarly to the same domestic goods once they enter a nation's markets. Nondiscrimination is embodied in the concept of **most-favored nation (MFN) status**. MFN requires all WTO members to treat each other as well as they treat their most-favored trading partner. In effect, this is a prohibition against discrimination. Somewhat contradictorily, MFN allows trade agreements such as the North American Free Trade Agreement (NAFTA) and the European Union (EU) even though every trade agreement causes countries to discriminate in favor of each other and implicitly against nonmembers. In theory, the WTO permits such agreements as long as they do not harm the overall level of international trade, and in practice, the WTO has never challenged the validity of a trade agreement between member countries.

## CASE STUDY

# The GATT Rounds

Agreements in the GATT forum to reduce trade barriers take place in rounds of negotiations. Counting the first round, there have been nine rounds of negotiations, with the Doha Round still in progress. Originally, the GATT was an international agreement and not an organization. The failure to create the International Trade Organization in 1950, however, resulted in the gradual conversion of the GATT into a *de facto* organization by 1960, with a permanent secretariat to manage it from Geneva. Table 2.2 lists the various rounds of negotiations.

The first five rounds were organized around product-by-product negotiations. Beginning with the Kennedy Round, negotiations were simplified as countries negotiated an across-the-board percentage reduction in all tariffs for a range of industrial products. One effect is that tariffs have never been uniform across countries. The goal has been to bring them all down, but not necessarily to create the same tariff for all countries.

The Tokyo Round is notable because it was the first round to begin to establish rules regarding subsidies. Subsidies give an industry a competitive advantage, since the national government pays part of the cost of production, either through direct payment or indirectly through subsidized interest rates, artificially cheap access to foreign currency, or some other way. The Tokyo Round began the laborious process of creating rules in this area, one of the most important being the agreement to prohibit subsidies for exports of industrial goods (but not agricultural goods or textiles and apparel).

The subsidy issue of the Tokyo Round was carried forward into the Uruguay Round, where subsidies were defined in greater detail. The Uruguay Round accomplished many other things as well, not the least of which was the creation of the World Trade Organization as a formal organization to oversee and administer the GATT. Additional accomplishments are described in Chapter 7, which explores trade policy and trade barriers in more detail.

| TABLE 2.2 • The GATT Rounds | | |
| --- | --- | --- |
| Round | Year | Number of Participants |
| Geneva I | 1947 | 23 |
| Annecy | 1949 | 13 |
| Torquay | 1951 | 38 |
| Geneva II | 1956 | 26 |
| Dillon | 1960–1961 | 26 |
| Kennedy | 1964–1967 | 62 |
| Tokyo | 1973–1979 | 102 |
| Uruguay | 1986–1993 | 105 |
| Doha (WTO) | 2001– | 149 |

 # Regional Trade Agreements

Trade agreements between two or more countries constitute another important type of institutional structure in the world economy. Many of these have familiar names—NAFTA, the EU, and so on—but basic differences in the common types of agreements are less familiar. These regional agreements are usually classified into one of four categories of trade agreements, but they often include more than trade, and they do not fit very neatly into nonoverlapping categories. Reality is far messier than a classification scheme, and most formal agreements between nations combine incomplete elements from two or more of the categories. In addition, it is useful to recognize a fifth type of agreement, a **partial trade agreement**, which does not rise to the level of the first category. With a partial trade agreement, two or more countries agree to liberalize trade in a selected group of categories. This type of agreement has become common, particularly among developing countries, whenever there is a reluctance to open the economy completely to a set of trading partners, but all partners desire free trade for a limited group of commodities. With a partial trade agreement, for example, two countries might agree to free trade in certain manufactured goods, but maintain protectionist barriers in other areas.

## Four Types of Regional Trade Agreements

As more goods are included in the partial trade agreement, it begins to look more like a **free trade area**. One example is NAFTA, but there are many others, such as the European Free Trade Area (EFTA) and the U.S.-Israel Free Trade Agreement. In a free trade area, nations are allowed to trade goods and services across international boundaries without paying a tariff and without the limita-

## CASE STUDY

# Prominent Regional Trade Agreements

Each of the four levels of integration is an example of a different kind of **regional trade agreement (RTA)**, or **trade bloc**. The question naturally arises as to how many agreements there are and whether they are beneficial or harmful for the world economy. The simple question of how many is difficult to answer precisely. Many of the agreements do not fit neatly into any of the four categories, so it is not clear they should be counted. That is, should all partial agreements be counted when they are not quite free-trade areas, yet they have elements of free trade, customs unions, and even common markets? In addition, many of the agreements exist either on paper only (have no real effect), or have yet to be fully negotiated and/or implemented. Until there is substantial implementation, there is always the possibility that the agreement will collapse, because opening an economy inevitably generates opposition from uncompetitive sectors.

Countries that have signed the GATT are obligated to notify the GATT secretariat when they form an RTA. According to the WTO, since the implementation of the GATT in 1948, they have been notified about more than 250 RTAs. Some of these are defunct, but over 197 are still operating in 2006. Most of the agreements that are still functioning were started in the 1990s, with 164 agreements entering into force since 1992. Europe accounts for about 65 percent of the RTAs currently in force, and about 78 percent of all RTAs involve developed countries only (43 percent) or developed and developing countries (35 percent).

The answer to the second question above—are they beneficial or harmful?—is even more difficult to ascertain. A 1995 study by the WTO concluded that in most cases "regional and multilateral integration initiatives are complements rather than alternatives." Broadly speaking, the WTO sees these agreements as helping it to reduce trade barriers further. This view is not shared by all economists, however, as any regional agreement must favor the interests of its members over the interests of outsiders. In other words, there is an element of discrimination that goes against the WTO's fundamental principle of equal treatment (most favored nation). Preferential treatment for members of the trade agreement causes most regional trade agreements to destroy some of the trade between their members and nonmembers. The WTO recognizes this problem, but argues that as long as a regional agreement creates more new trade than it destroys, the net result is beneficial. In addition, the WTO sees the regional trade agreements as places where countries can try out new arrangements, some of which will be eventually incorporated into the larger, global agreement.

Nearly all WTO members belong to at least one RTA, and many countries belong to several. For example, Mexico is a member of NAFTA (Canada-Mexico-United States) but in 2000 it entered a free trade agreement with the European Union. It has also signed free trade and other agreements with other countries, including Chile, Japan, Israel, and Costa Rica, among others. Table 2.3 lists some of the RTAs currently in force. Among the best known are the European Union, the European Free Trade Association, the North American Free Trade Agreement, MERCOSUR in South America, the ASEAN Free Trade Area in Southeast Asia, and COMESA in eastern and southern Africa. There are many more, however, ranging from tariff agreements on a subset of output to common markets and economic unions. The dates in parentheses are the dates of implementation of the agreements.

### TABLE 2.3 ● Prominent Regional Trade Blocs

| Region/Trade Bloc | Objective |
| --- | --- |
| **Africa** | |
| COMESA—Common Market for Eastern and Southern Africa (1993) | Common market |
| ECCAS—Economic Community of Central African States (1992) | Common market |
| ECOWAS—Economic Community of West African States (1975) | Common market |
| **Asia** | |
| AFTA—ASEAN Free Trade Arrangement (1992) | Free-trade area |
| ANZCERTA—Australia–New Zealand Closer Economic Relations (1983) | Free-trade area |
| APEC—Asia-Pacific Economic Cooperation (1989) | Free-trade area |
| **Europe** | |
| CEFTA—Central European Free Trade Arrangement (1992) | Free-trade area |
| EEA—European Economic Area (1994) | Common market |
| EFTA—European Free Trade Association (1960) | Free-trade area |
| EU—European Union (1957) | Economic union |
| **Middle East** | |
| ACM—Arab Common Market (1964) | Customs union |
| AMU—Arab-Maghreb Union (1989) | Economic union |
| GCC—Gulf Cooperation Council (1981) | Common market |
| **Western Hemisphere** | |
| ANCOM—Andean Common Market (1969) | Common market |
| CACM—Central American Common Market (1961) | Customs union |
| CARICOM—Caribbean Community (1973) | Common market |
| MERCOSUR—Southern Cone Common Market (1991) | Common market |
| NAFTA—North American Free Trade Area (1994) | Free-trade area |

*Sources*: Harmsen, Richard, and Michael Leidy, "Regional Trading Arrangements," in *International Trade Policies: The Uruguay Round and Beyond. Volume II: Background Papers*. Washington, DC: International Monetary Fund, 1994.

The WTO, "Regionalism." Geneva: The World Trade Organization.http://www.wto.org/english/thewto_e/whatis_e/ tif_e/ bey3_e.htm. Accessed October 6, 2000.

tions imposed by quotas, which are direct limits on imports. In reality, however, most free trade areas such as NAFTA do not allow completely free trade. Nations usually reserve some restrictions for particularly sensitive items. For example, as part of its efforts to protect its culture, Canada limits the number of U.S. television programs that Canadian television stations may purchase. With a free-trade area, nations usually keep their own health, safety, and technical standards, and may deny entry of imports if they do not meet national standards. For example, the United States does not allow Mexican avocados to enter California (where they are grown) because farmers claim that they contain a seed weevil that could destroy the U.S. crop.

The next level of integration is called a **customs union**. A customs union is a free-trade area plus a **common external tariff** toward nonmembers. Between the mid-1970s and the early 1990s, the European Union was a customs union, and in today's economy, MERCOSUR (Brazil, Argentina, Uruguay, Paraguay, and Venezuela) is one. This means that the five members have free trade with each other and the same tariff on imports from nonmembers, for example American computers. As with free-trade areas, many items are usually left out of the agreement. In the European case, each nation retained its own tariffs and quotas with respect to Japanese autos. Common markets are the next level beyond customs unions. A **common market** is a customs union plus an agreement to allow the free mobility of inputs, such as labor and capital. The clearest example is the European Union in the 1990s. Soon after his election in 2000, Vicente Fox, the president of Mexico, indicated that he would like to see the NAFTA countries move toward becoming a common market, but the problems associated with the free mobility of labor have stymied this idea. Nevertheless, the three NAFTA countries have elements of a common market (without the common external tariff) because they allow capital to move freely around the region. NAFTA also grants relatively free movement to certain types of white-collar labor, such as architects, business consultants, and others.

The final level of economic integration is an **economic union**. An economic union is a common market with substantial coordination of macroeconomic policies, including a common currency, and harmonization of many standards and regulations. The clearest examples are the states of the United States or the provinces of Canada. The BENELUX Union of Belgium, the Netherlands, and Luxembourg is an example of separate nations that have formed a union, and the European Union is in the process of becoming an economic union, with the euro as its common currency, and at some point, with a common defense policy and common citizenship rights.

 ## The Role of International Economic Institutions

In every part of the world, people rely on institutions to create order and reduce uncertainty. By defining the constraints or limits on economic, political, and social interactions, institutions define the incentive system of a society and help to create stability. The provision of order and the reduction of uncertainty are so important that when they are absent, economies cannot develop. Within a nation, the formal rules of behavior are defined by the various levels of government. In the United States, for example, this includes cities, counties, special districts, states, and the federal government. In the international sphere, however, there are no corresponding sets of government. The establishment of rules for international trade and international macroeconomic relations are dependent on the voluntary associations of nations in international economic organizations.

The primary difference between international economic organizations and the government of a single nation is that the former have limited enforcement power. National and local governments have police powers that they can use to enforce their rules; international organizations have no police power, but they have more subtle powers for encouraging cooperation. For example, the IMF and World Bank can withdraw lines of credit to developing countries. The withdrawal of IMF credit and its stamp of approval raises a red flag for private lenders and makes it more costly for uncooperative nations to gain access to capital in private markets. Likewise, the WTO can legitimize retaliatory sanctions against nations that fail to honor their trade obligations. Basically, however, international organizations rely on moral suasion and the commitments of individual nations to remain effective. If nations choose to withdraw their support from an international organization, it dies.

The provision of order and the reduction of uncertainty are services that everyone values. This is why we pay police officers, judges, and legislators. Although public order and the lessening of uncertainty are intangibles, they are desired and valued in the same sense that more tangible material objects are. Their economic characteristics are different from most goods and services however, and they fall into the category known as **public goods**.

## The Definition of Public Goods

By definition, public goods are **nonexcludable** and **nonrival** or **nondiminishable**. Nonexcludability means that the normal price mechanism does not work as a way of regulating access. For example, when a signal is broadcast on the airwaves by a television station, anyone with a TV set who lives in its range can pick it up. (Of course, this is not the case with cable stations, which are granted permission to scramble their signals. Signal scrambling is a clever technological solution to the problem of nonexcludability.)

The second characteristic of public goods is that they are nonrival or nondiminishable. This refers to the attribute of not being diminished by consumption. For example, if I tune in to the broadcast signal of a local TV station, my neighbors will have the same signal amount available to them. Most goods get smaller, or diminish, when they are consumed, but public goods do not.

Private markets often fail to supply optimal levels of public goods because of the problem of **free riding**. Free riding means that there is no incentive to pay for public goods because people cannot be excluded from consumption. Given this characteristic, public goods will not be produced optimally by free markets unless institutional arrangements can somehow overcome the free riding. In most cases, governments step in as providers and use their powers to tax as a means to force people to pay for the goods.

## Maintaining Order and Reducing Uncertainty

Two of the most important functions of international economic institutions are to maintain order in international economic relations and to reduce uncertainty. Together, these functions are often instrumental in the avoidance of a global economic crisis. Furthermore, if a national crisis threatens to become global, international institutions often help to bring it to a less costly end and to prevent nations from shifting the cost of national problems to other countries.

The maintenance of order and the reduction of uncertainty are general tasks that require specific rules in a number of areas of international economic interaction, although economists do not completely agree on the specific rules or the specific types of cooperation that should be provided. Nevertheless, the proponents of international institutions, such as economist Charles Kindleberger, have noted several areas where institutions are needed in order to strengthen cooperation and prevent free riding in the provision of international public goods. Among these items are the four public goods listed in Table 2.4.

Kindleberger and others have argued that the absence of a set of rules for providing one or more of these public goods has usually been a key part of the explanation of historical crises such as the worldwide Great Depression of the 1930s. The specific items in Table 2.4 may be debatable, but the basic point is sound. If no international institutions are available to help nations overcome the tendency to free ride, then international economic stability grows more fragile. As an illustration, consider the first item listed. During recessions, politicians begin to feel enormous pressure to close markets in order to protect jobs at home. During the 1930s, for example, most nations enacted high tariffs and restrictive quotas on imports. This set in motion waves of retaliation as the nations that lost their foreign markets followed suit and imposed their own tariffs and quotas. In the end, no one benefited and international trade collapsed.

**TABLE 2.4** • **Four Examples of International Public Goods**

| Public Good | Purpose |
|---|---|
| Open markets in a recession | To prevent a fall in exports from magnifying the effects of a recession. |
| Capital flows to less-developed countries (LDCs) | To assist economic development in poor countries. |
| International money for settlement of international debts | To maintain a globally accepted system for paying debts. |
| Last-resort lending | To prevent the spread of some types of financial crises. |

In essence, each nation was free riding. In a recession, free riders want to close their markets to reduce imports and create more jobs. At the same time, however, they want all other nations to stay open so that they do not lose any export markets. These motives are inconsistent, and the effect of free riding behavior is that all countries retaliate by closing their markets, international trade collapses, and everyone is worse off than before. Kindleberger shows that the shift in trade policies toward high tariffs and restrictive quotas helped to intensify and spread the Great Depression of the 1930s.

Kindleberger also argues that the sudden decline in capital flows to developing countries in the 1930s and the complete absence of a **lender of last resort** deepened the Great Depression and provides further historical evidence for the importance of international institutions. The lack of a lender of last resort was particularly critical because a number of countries with temporary financial problems soon passed into full-blown financial collapse. As it became impossible for them to pay their foreign debts, the crisis spread from the indebted nations to the lending nations.

No one has tried to measure the frequency of potentially disastrous international economic events. Their occurrence is not infrequent, however, and it is relatively easy to list a number of recent events that have had the potential to turn into major global problems: the debt crisis in many developing countries in the early 1980s, the collapse of the Mexican peso in 1994, the transition to capitalism by the socialist countries, the Asian crisis of 1997, Russia's default on its debt in 1998—the list is fairly long.

In each crisis or potential crisis, international institutions play an important role by preventing free riding. Lacking much in the way of formal enforcement mechanisms, they overcome the free rider problem by changing each nation's expectations about every other nation. For example, if all countries are committed to open markets in good times and bad, then during a worldwide recession no country expects its trading partners to close their markets. As another example, if each country pays a share of the IMF's operating funds, then it overcomes the problems that arise when each country waits for the others to make risky loans during a crisis. The effectiveness of international institutions depends on the credible commitment of the world's nations. If a country agrees to a set of rules, but has a reputation for breaking its agreements, then its commitment is not credible. Institutions cannot overcome the free rider problem under those circumstances.

## CASE STUDY

# Bretton Woods

After World War I, the United States retreated into a relative isolationism under the mistaken belief that noninvolvement in European affairs would protect the country from entanglement in disastrous European conflicts such as World War

I. The rise of Hitler, Japanese aggression in the Pacific, and the start of World War II showed that this policy would not work.

The United States began to realize its mistake in the 1930s as it watched Hitler take over a large part of the European continent. U.S. and British cooperation and planning for the postwar era began before the United States entered the war in December 1941, and long before the outcome was known. President Roosevelt and Prime Minister Churchill met on a battleship off the coast of Newfoundland in August 1941. Soon after, they announced the Atlantic Charter, a program for postwar reconstruction that committed both nations to working for the fullest possible economic collaboration among all nations after the war. Concurrent with the Atlantic Charter, the United States and Britain began discussing the kinds of international institutions that might be proposed.

All parties agreed that in any postwar order, the United States would have to be the political, military, and economic leader. The United States had surpassed Great Britain in wealth and size several decades earlier, and its leadership during the war gave it prestige and credibility. In addition, the physical infrastructure of the United States was not damaged by the war, and it was the only industrial nation able to provide the financial capital and physical material needed to repair the war damage.

Looking back to the 1920s and 1930s, the postwar planners recognized four serious problems that they should guard against: (1) the worldwide depression; (2) the collapse of international trade; (3) the collapse of the international monetary system; and (4) the collapse of international lending. Discussions during World War II were mainly devoted to rules, agreements, and organizations that could be created to avoid these problems. The following international institutions were viewed as central for the achievement of these goals:

- An international organization to help stabilize exchange rates and to assist nations that are unable to pay their international debts
- Agreements to reduce trade barriers
- An international organization for providing relief to the war-damaged nations, and to assist with reconstruction

Plans for the postwar period were finalized at a conference held in July 1944, in Bretton Woods, New Hampshire. The Bretton Woods institutions include the International Monetary Fund, the World Bank, and the Bretton Woods exchange rate system. Although it was conceived separately, the General Agreement on Tariffs and Trade is sometimes included because it embodies the goals and ideas of the Bretton Woods planners with respect to international trade. Together, these institutions are an historically unique set of international economic institutions, and each, in its own area, has played a key role in the history of the international economy since 1945.

The founding principles of the Bretton Woods institutions are relatively simple. First, trade should open in all countries, not just in the United States alone, or in the United States and the United Kingdom together. In economic terms, this was a call for multilateral opening, as opposed to unilateralism (one-sided opening) or bilateralism (two-sided opening). Second, nations should not discriminate against other nations. Whatever tariffs and quotas the United Kingdom or the United States might levy against another country, they should be the same ones imposed on everyone. Third, in order to ensure the ability of importers to purchase goods abroad, countries should not limit the buying and selling of currency when its purpose is to pay for imports. Fourth, exchange rates should be fixed but with the possibility for periodic adjustment. These principles formed the cornerstones of the institutions.

#  Criticism of International Institutions

The World Bank, IMF, WTO, and various regional trade agreements have provided financial resources for development, technical assistance for crisis management, and mechanisms for opening markets. Not everyone agrees that these efforts are positive on balance, however, and even those who view their actions favorably would agree that there is room for improvement. The range of criticism covers a wide spectrum, from public demonstrations against trade ministers meeting under the auspices of the WTO to the well-informed criticisms by leading economists such as Nobel Laureate Joseph Stiglitz. The underlying question is whether the IMF, World Bank, and WTO are fostering development and economic security, or generating greater economic inequality and compounding the risks to vulnerable groups.

In general, most analysts probably agree that some types of international institutions are necessary due to the international public goods discussed earlier. The IMF, World Bank, and WTO were created in response to real historical events and for the explicit purposes of avoiding crises and promoting growth. Economic changes such as transportation and communication revolutions, the integration of new markets in Europe, East Asia, and Latin America, and technological innovations have increased the need for institutions by reducing the isolation of nations and creating more interactions and spillovers among them. While there is a widely recognized need for a set of agreements covering the international economic policies practiced by individual nations, there is less consensus regarding the content of the agreements and how they should be implemented.

## Sovereignty and Transparency

**Sovereignty** covers the rights of nations to be free from unwanted foreign interference in their affairs. One of the strongest complaints about international institutions is that they violate national sovereignty by imposing unwanted domestic economic policies. For example, when a country experiences a financial crisis, the IMF is often the only potential source of outside help. Once engaged, however, the IMF imposes conditions that sometimes amount to a complete rearrangement of national economic policies. Specific examples include IMF requirements that countries cut government spending, privatize their publicly owned enterprises, and open their financial sector to the free movement of capital. Each of these may go against public preferences. For example, when a country is in the midst of a financial crisis, cuts in government spending can increase the depth of a recession and often have a disproportionately large impact on the middle class and the poor. Aside from the potential benefits or costs, often it appears that governments are coerced by the international financial community. In response to this perception, some argue that if countries avoid financial crises, they do not need to ask for help. Furthermore, it would be harmful to everyone if the IMF lent money unconditionally. Still, the issue of how hard international institutions should be allowed to push countries to change their policies is an open debate.

Closely related to the issue of sovereignty is the issue of transparency. Transparency concerns are based on questions about the decision making that occurs within international institutions. As noted earlier, the IMF and the World Bank have voting structures based on the size of the quotas or dues paid by each country. This gives the United States in particular, and developed country interests in general, control over these bodies and makes it difficult for them to differentiate U.S. or EU interests from the interests of client countries. For example, a client country may be told to open its financial markets because it will increase foreign capital inflows and investment, but the main beneficiaries are banks and financial firms in the United States or the European Union. Some critics conclude that IMF and World Bank policies are explicitly designed to benefit special interests in developed countries and do not serve the interests of the world economy.

The governing structure of the WTO is not based on quotas or dues, but the fact that developing countries lack the armies of lawyers, trade association lobbyists, and industry specialists that the United States and the European Union can muster during a round of negotiations puts them at a disadvantage. A specific example is the Uruguay Round deal on agriculture and intellectual property rights. Developed countries pushed a comprehensive and strict set of enforcement policies for protecting intellectual property rights (copyrights, trademarks, patents, brand names, and so on). In return, developing countries thought that they would face fewer barriers to selling agricultural products in industrial country markets. In fact, their access to developed country agricultural markets was much less than anticipated, and the costs of enforcing intellectual property rights turned out to be higher than expected.

## Ideology

Issues of sovereignty and transparency are compounded by questions about the value of the technical economic advice given by the IMF and other institutions. Some of the sharpest criticisms come from economists who strongly favor international economic integration but argue that the advice and technical assistance provided to developing countries are a reflection of the biases and wishes of developed country interests. For example, critics charge that the IMF views financial sector interests as preeminent, often to the harm and neglect of other sectors. When polled, the vast majority of professional economists favor more open trade over protectionism, but there is no consensus whether developing countries are better off with the free movement of capital. Some economists favor free capital movement as a means of ensuring adequate investment, while others favor limits on capital flows in order to reduce the risk of financial crisis. There are strong arguments on both sides of this debate but the IMF has consistently favored free capital flows in its policy advice.

Similarly, the IMF and World Bank have been major proponents of privatization. Privatization of publicly owned enterprises can have a number of benefits, but it can also impose high costs. When countries lack regulatory structures or when local institutions are easily captured by powerful economic interests, privatization may trade a public monopoly for a much more predatory private one. Similar criticisms have been voiced about the lending practices of the World Bank. Some critics view its loans and development programs as frequently driven by ideological goals that are out of touch with local conditions, and therefore unlikely to achieve the intended development outcomes. These critics share a deep skepticism about grand schemes for "fixing a country" all at once with a universal set of policies that can be applied anywhere. (We will return to the issue of the technical advice administered by the IMF when we look at financial crises in more detail in Chapter 12.)

It is important to note that international institutions are often blamed for outcomes that they did not promote. They are easy targets and more than one national government has blamed them as a way to deflect criticisms of unpopular policies. "The IMF made me do it" can be an easy way out of a difficult domestic political situation. Furthermore, our understanding of fundamental processes and events such as economic development and financial crises is not perfect and there are many areas where there is no consensus on the best policy. Our ignorance about the best course of action is compounded by the problems of an asymmetric distribution of political, economic, and military power, and the complexity of creating systems of international decision making that are accepted as legitimate.

## Implementation and Adjustment Costs

Trade agreements and the WTO are a major focus of complaints by the critics of economic integration. In particular, when agreements combine developing and developed countries, asymmetries in negotiating skills and the ability to absorb the costs of implementation and adjustment are singled out for criticism. An often cited example is the previously mentioned case of the Uruguay Round agreement on intellectual property rights. In order to implement this part of the agreement, developing countries have to create or improve their patent systems and copyright and trademark enforcement mechanisms. The latter step would entail cutting down on pirated drugs, videos, CDs, software, and so on. The opportunity cost of implementing this part of the agreement is substantial, particularly for a developing country with very limited resources.

Once in place, trade agreements always impose costs in the form of adjustments to the new opportunities and challenges. Some markets will expand while others will contract. In general, the costs of adjusting to the new incentives are less significant than the benefits, but for some developing countries the adjustment costs may be quite large. Developing countries tend to have higher unemployment rates, which means that workers in contracting industries may spend more time searching for jobs. They also tend to have less diversified economies so that the impact of a contraction in one or two sectors can have large effects on a substantial share of the economy. In order to take advantage of the opportunities presented by greater access to foreign markets, countries may need to construct new infrastructures, for example, roads and ports for moving fresh produce. The ability of developing countries to build infrastructures is more limited than for developed countries, as is the access to credit by entrepreneurs in developing countries.

Issues of sovereignty and transparency, ideological biases, and the costs of implementation and adjustment are only a partial catalog of the concerns raised by the critics of international institutions. In general, however, there is widespread agreement among professional economists that there are theoretical and practical reasons for their existence. Nevertheless, beyond a basic consensus about need, many issues remain subject to debate, particularly issues of governance and the amount of authority that should be vested in international organizations. Still, in spite of these uncertainties, it is safe to say that if these international institutions did not exist, we would create them.

## Summary

- Institutions are the "rules of the game." They can be formal, as in a nation's constitution, or informal, as in a custom or tradition. In both cases, we depend on institutions as mechanisms for creating order and reducing uncertainty. Global institutions have played an important role in fostering the growth of international trade and investment during the last 50 years. They have defined a set of rules that have helped avoid trade wars and the problems of the 1930s.

- The "Big 3" of international economic organizations are the International Monetary Fund, the World Bank, and the World Trade Organization. The latter grew out of the General Agreement on Tariffs and Trade. The IMF, World Bank, and the GATT were created at the end of World War II with the purpose of avoiding a return to the destructive economic conditions of the interwar years (between World War I and World War II).

- Regional trade agreements are another important type of international institution, although they are not global in scope. Formally, there are four types of regional trade agreements. In order, from less integrated to more integrated, they are free-trade areas, customs unions, common markets, and economic unions. Each level is cumulative and incorporates the features of the previous level. The real world is messier than this, however, and actual trade agreements usually combine features from two or more types.

- International economic institutions are an attempt to overcome the problem of free riding by individual nations in the sphere of providing international public goods. The most important public goods are order and a reduction in uncertainty. Some economists believe that these goods are best provided when there are agreements that help keep markets open in recessions and in boom periods; when there is an international lender of last resort; when there are sufficient lenders of capital to developing nations; and when there is an adequate supply of money for international payment.

- Most analysts agree that some forms of international institutions are necessary as a precaution against crises and to promote growth, but there is significant disagreement over the design of governance structures and the scope of their responsibilities.

- Primary areas of criticism are in sovereignty, transparency, ideological bias, and implementation and adjustment costs.

## Vocabulary

Bretton Woods conference

common external tariff

common market

customs union

Doha Development Agenda

economic union

foreign exchange reserves

free riding

free trade area

General Agreement on Tariffs and Trade (GATT)

IMF conditionality

institution

International Monetary Fund (IMF)

lender of last resort

most-favored nation (MFN) status

national treatment

nondiminishable

nondiscrimination

nonexcludable

nonrival

partial trade agreement

public goods

quota

regional trade agreement (RTA)

sovereignty

trade bloc

trade rounds

Uruguay Round

World Bank

World Trade Organization (WTO)

**Study Questions**

1. What is an institution? Give examples of formal and informal institutions. Explain how they differ from organizations.

2. What are the arguments in favor of international organizations? What are the arguments against? Which do you think are stronger?

3. What are public goods and how do they differ from private ones? Give examples of each.

4. What are the main tasks or functions of each of the following:
   - The International Monetary Fund
   - The World Bank
   - The General Agreement on Tariffs and Trade
   - The World Trade Organization

5. When nations sign the GATT agreement, they bind their tariffs at their current level, or lower. Tariff binding means that they agree not to raise the tariffs except under unusual circumstances. Explain how tariff binding in the GATT prevents free riding during a global slowdown.

6. Kindleberger's study of the Great Depression of the 1930s led him to believe that market economies are sometimes unstable and that nations can get locked into prolonged downturns. Other economists are not convinced. Suppose that you disagree with Kindleberger and that you believe that market-based economies are inherently stable. How would you view the need for international institutions to address the provision of each of the public goods listed in Table 2.4?

7. What are the four main types of regional trade agreements and what are their primary characteristics?

8. Critics of the global institutions have a variety of complaints about the WTO, the IMF, and the World Bank. Explain the main categories of complaints.

# International Trade

# 3 Comparative Advantage and the Gains from Trade

## Introduction: Absolute Advantage and the Gains from Trade

This chapter introduces the theory of comparative advantage. A simple model is used to show how nations maximize their material welfare by specializing in goods and services that have the lowest relative costs of production. The improvement in national welfare is known as the **gains from trade**. The concepts of comparative advantage and the gains from trade are two of the oldest and most widely held ideas in all of economics, yet they are often misunderstood and misinterpreted. Therefore, it is worth the effort to develop a clear understanding of both.

### Adam Smith and the Attack on Economic Nationalism

The development of modern economic theory is intimately linked to the birth of international economics. In 1776, Adam Smith published *An Inquiry into the Nature and Causes of the Wealth of Nations*, a work that became the first modern statement of economic theory. In the process of laying out the basic ground rules for the efficient allocation of resources, Smith initiated a general attack on **mercantilism**, the system of nationalistic economics that dominated economic thought in the 1700s. Mercantilism stressed exports over imports, primarily as a way to obtain revenues for building armies and national construction projects. Although Smith successfully established modern economics, he did not end mercantilist thinking, which persists today as economic nationalism.

The key mistake in mercantilist thinking was the belief that trade was a **zero sum** activity. In the eighteenth century the term *zero sum* did not exist, but it is a convenient expression for the concept that one nation's gain is another nation's loss. A moment's reflection should be enough to see the mistake in this belief, at least as it applies to voluntary exchange. When you buy a gallon of milk, do you lose and the store wins? Why would you buy the milk if that were true? If the store loses, why would they sell it? Voluntary exchange is positive sum. Both sides must gain, or else one or both sides would withdraw from the exchange. In trade, the most accurate metaphor is not football or poker or some other zero sum competitive game, but rather rock climbing or dancing, which are positive sum activities.

No one in the 1770s thought that they were living in the midst of an industrial revolution, but Smith was observant enough to perceive that many improvements in the standard of living had occurred during his lifetime as a result of increasing specialization in production. When he analyzed specialization, he made one of his most important contributions to economics: the discovery that specialization depends on the size of the market.

A contemporary example may be helpful. If General Motors was permitted to sell its cars and trucks only in Michigan, they would have much less revenue and would sell many fewer vehicles. They would hire fewer employees, and each person would be less specialized. As it is, GM's market is so large (essentially, the world) that it can hire engineers who are completely specialized in small, even minuscule, parts of a car—door locks, for example. Your door lock engineer will know everything there is to know about the design, production, and assembly of door locks and will be able to help GM put them into cars most efficiently. A firm that was limited to the Michigan market could never afford to hire such specialized skills in every area of vehicle manufacture.

One of the keys to Smith's story of wealth creation is access to foreign markets. If no one is willing to import, then every company is limited by the size of the national market. In some cases, that may be large enough (the United States or China), but in most cases, it is not. Small- and medium-sized countries cannot efficiently produce every item they consume. Holland, for example, has always imported a large share of its goods and has depended on access to foreign markets in order to earn money to pay for imports.

Smith was highly critical of trade barriers because they decreased specialization, technological progress, and wealth creation. He also recognized that imports enable a country to obtain goods that it cannot make or cannot make as cheaply, while exports are made for someone else and are useful only if they lead to imports. The modern view of trade shares Smith's dislike of trade barriers for mostly the same reasons. Although international economists recognize that there are limitations to the application of theory, most economists share a strongly held preference for free and open markets. In Chapters 6 and 7 we will examine trade barriers in greater detail, but at this point we will develop a deeper understanding of the gains from trade by means of a simple algebraic and graphical model.

## A Simple Model of Production and Trade

We will begin with one of the simplest models in economics. The conclusion of this analysis is that a policy of free trade maximizes a nation's material well-being. Later, we will examine some of the cases where real-world conditions do not conform to the assumptions of the model and where the optimality of free trade is questionable.

The basic model is often referred to as a Ricardian model, since it first took form in the analysis of David Ricardo. The model begins by assuming that there are only two countries, producing two goods, using one input (labor). More complex models can be built with *n* countries producing *m* goods and using *k* inputs, but other than adding a layer of mathematical sophistication, the final outcome is almost the same. The Ricardian model assumes that firms are price takers, or, in other words, markets are competitive, and no firm has market power. The model is static in the sense that it assumes that technology is constant and there are no learning effects of production that might make firms and industries more productive over time. We will relax both of these assumptions in the coming chapters. Ricardo assumed that labor is perfectly mobile and can easily move back and forth between industries, another simplifying assumption that will be dropped in Chapter 4. In this chapter, we assume that labor is mobile between industries, but not across national boundaries.

## Absolute Productivity Advantage and the Gains from Trade

To begin, we define *productivity* in the Ricardian model. Productivity is the amount of output obtained from a unit of input. Since labor is the only input, we can define **labor productivity** as follows:

(units of output) / (hours worked)

If, for example, two loaves of bread can be produced in 1 hour, then productivity is as follows:

(2 loaves) / (1 hour)

or 2 loaves per hour. If 4 loaves are produced in 2 hours, then productivity is still as follows:

(4 loaves) / (2 hours) = 2 loaves per hour

Suppose that there are two goods, bread and steel, and two countries, the United States and Canada. Suppose also that each produces according to the productivities shown in Table 3.1.

The values in Table 3.1 shows that productivity in the making of bread is greater in Canada than in the United States, and that productivity in steel is greater in the United States. Canada has an **absolute productivity advantage** in bread because it produces more loaves per hour worked (3 versus 2 in the United States). Using the same logic, the United States has an absolute productivity advantage in steel production.

The basis of Adam Smith's support for free trade was the belief that every country would have an absolute advantage in something, and that the source of the advantage did not matter. Whether it was due to special skills in the labor force, climate and soil characteristics of the country, or the temperament of its

| TABLE 3.1 ● **Output per Hour Worked** | | |
| --- | --- | --- |
| | United States | Canada |
| **Bread** | 2 loaves | 3 loaves |
| **Steel** | 3 tons | 1 ton |

Canada is more productive than the United States in bread production, but the United States is more productive in steel production.

people, there would be goods that each country could manufacture, grow, or dig out of the ground more efficiently than its trading partner. Consequently, every country could benefit from trade.

In the numerical example outlined in Table 3.1, each loaf of bread costs the United States 1.5 tons of steel. Put another way, the **opportunity cost** of bread is 1.5 tons of steel, since each unit of bread produced requires the economy to move labor out of steel production, forfeiting 1.5 tons of steel that it could have produced instead. This follows from the fact that each hour of labor can produce either 2 loaves of bread or 3 tons of steel. We can write this ratio as the barter price of bread as follows:

$$P_{us}^{b} = \frac{3 \text{ tons}}{2 \text{ loaves}} = 1.5 \left( \frac{\text{tons}}{\text{loaves}} \right),$$

where $b$ is bread and $us$ is the country. Similarly, we can write the U.S. price of steel as the inverse as follows:

$$P_{us}^{s} = \frac{2 \text{ loaves}}{3 \text{ tons}} = 0.67 \left( \frac{\text{loaves}}{\text{tons}} \right).$$

You should be able to verify that the Canadian price of bread will be 0.33 (tons/loaf) and that steel will cost 3 (loaves/ton).

If the United States can sell a ton of steel for more than 0.67 loaves of bread, it is better off. Similarly, if Canadians can obtain a ton of steel for fewer than 3 loaves of bread, they are better off. Each country will gain from trade if the United States agrees to sell steel for fewer than 3 loaves of bread but more than 0.67 loaves. Anywhere in that range, both Canadians and Americans will benefit. In the end, trade will occur at a price somewhere between these two limits as follows:

$$3.0 \left( \frac{\text{loaves}}{\text{tons}} \right) > P_{w}^{s} > 0.67 \left( \frac{\text{loaves}}{\text{tons}} \right),$$

where $P_{w}^{s}$ = the world price of steel (the trade price). Without knowing more details about the demand side of the market, it is impossible to say whether the price will settle closer to 3.0 (the Canadian opportunity cost of steel) or 0.67 (the U.S. opportunity cost). The closer the price is to 0.67, the more Canada benefits from trade, and the closer it is to 3.0, the more the United States benefits. Regardless of which country benefits more, as long as the price is between these two limits, both countries benefit from trade.

## CASE STUDY

# The International Market for Crude Oil

Natural resources are a source of comparative advantage in many countries. Chile has copper, Botswana has diamonds, and Saudi Arabia has oil. Crude oil is probably the most important geopolitical resource today, and it is certainly the largest resource market. In fact, other than currency trading, international trade in crude oil exceeds the volume and value of any other good or service. According to the U.S. Department of Energy, worldwide daily export of crude oil in 2003 was 52.8 million barrels. At an average price of around $27 per barrel, that is equivalent to more than $1,400 million per day. (As large as it is, oil trading is still less than one-tenth the size of the world's currency markets.)

Comparative advantage in crude oil production depends largely on a country's endowment of oil, and as everyone is aware, countries in the Middle East have a majority of the world's proven reserves of crude oil. Table 3.2 shows the world's regional distribution of oil reserves, along with an estimate of the number of years the current reserves will last at current rates of production (R/P).

Proven oil reserves are defined as the quantity of oil that can be profitably recovered given current geological and technological information and existing

| TABLE 3.2 • **Proven Oil Reserves, 2005** | | | |
| --- | --- | --- | --- |
| Region | Billions of Barrels | World Share (%) | R/P |
| Middle East | 742.7 | 61.9 | 81.0 |
| South and Central America | 103.5 | 8.6 | 40.7 |
| Europe and former Soviet Union | 140.5 | 11.7 | 22.0 |
| Africa | 114.3 | 9.5 | 31.8 |
| North America, including Mexico | 59.5 | 5.0 | 11.9 |
| Asia-Pacific | 40.2 | 3.4 | 13.8 |
| **Total** | 1,200.7 | 100 | 40.6 |

Source: *Quantifying Energy: BP Statistical Review of World Energy June 2006.*

Note: R/P is Reserves/Production. This is the number of years of reserves given current production levels.

market conditions. Proven oil reserves have grown by about 55 percent since 1985. Some growth has occurred from new discoveries of oil while in other cases, technological advances have allowed oil producers to extract more oil from each well. Market conditions also influence proven reserves since the world price of oil determines whether it is economically feasible to extract a particular pool of oil. In most cases, less than half of the oil in a reservoir is labeled proven reserves because the majority is too expensive to recover.

The cost of extracting oil has many components but it is largely dependent on the geologic characteristics of the oil field. The cheapest way to obtain oil is to let the natural pressure inside the oil reservoir push it to the surface. Over time, however, natural pressure diminishes and alternative techniques must be used, such as pumping oil out, forcing water down the well to push it out, or using chemicals or steam to push it out. Obviously, the more energy and other resources required to push the oil out, the more expensive it is to obtain. Countries with easily accessible oil with a lot of natural pressure inside the reservoir will have a lower cost of production and a greater absolute advantage.

The actual price of oil depends on a number of additional factors—on the supply side and on the demand side. Supply side factors include exploration costs as well as extraction costs, and since most refining is done near consumer markets, there are significant transportation costs involved in moving the crude oil to refineries where it can be processed into gasoline and other products. This means that oil of similar quality will sell for similar or equal price, but transportation costs will play a major role in determining regional differences in actual delivery prices. Generally speaking, crude oil moves to the nearest market. That is, most countries obtain their supplies of oil from the nearest available source. For example, the United States obtains more than 50 percent of its oil from the Western Hemisphere where transportation times are less than one week, and another 25 percent from the Atlantic Basin (North Sea and West Africa) where transportation takes two to three weeks. Most of Asia's oil comes from the Middle East, while Europe purchases over 40 percent of its imports from the former Soviet Union and another 24 percent from the Middle East.

While non-market factors such as politics play an important role in the oil market, it is still a world market. Hence, it is a mistake to think that if a country does not buy oil from the Middle East, it is not affected by political turmoil and a disruption in Middle Eastern supplies. When Saudi Arabia or another large producer (for example, Iraq) reduces its production, the world price is affected, regardless if the oil comes from Latin America, Canada, or Africa.

It is also a mistake to believe that natural resources are a guaranteed path to success. Major oil exporters do not tend to be among the richest countries of the world, and those that are, tend to be relatively minor players in world oil markets. One of the disadvantages of owning a valuable natural resource such as oil is that it raises economic returns to its extraction and production, causing labor and capital to be concentrated in that activity alone. In other words, it is difficult to develop a diversified and highly educated labor force if one activity is dominant.

# Comparative Productivity Advantage and the Gains from Trade

At this point, the obvious question to ask is what happens if a country does not have an absolute productivity advantage in anything. It is not hard to imagine an extremely poor, resource-deficient nation with low literacy and scarce capital. What can these countries produce more efficiently than the United States or Germany? Why would a rich country want to trade with them when they are inefficient at everything? The answer is that even if a country lacks a single good in which it has an absolute productivity advantage, it can still benefit from trade. Perhaps even more surprising, rich, high-productivity countries also benefit from the trade. In other words, the idea that nations benefit from trade has nothing to do with whether a country has an absolute advantage in producing a particular good. In order to see this, first we must develop a few more basic concepts.

## The Production Possibilities Curve

The **production possibilities curve (PPC)** shows the trade-offs a country faces when it chooses its combination of bread and steel output. Figure 3.1 illustrates a hypothetical PPC for the United States. Point B on the PPC is an efficient point of production because it utilizes existing resources to obtain the maximum possible level of output. The assumption of full employment is equivalent to assuming that the United States is operating at a point like B that lies on its PPC. At point A, the economy is inside its production curve and is operating at an inefficient level of output because it is not obtaining the maximum possible output

**FIGURE 3.1** • **A Production Possibilities Curve for the United States**

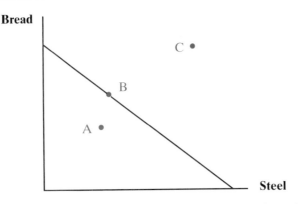

In a model with only two goods, the production possibilities curve shows the trade-offs between them.

from its available inputs. At point A, there is waste in the economy, since a greater quantity of bread and steel could be produced with the existing labor supply. Point C is infeasible because resources do not permit the production of bread and steel in the combination indicated.

The PPC shown in Figure 3.1 is a straight line because it is assumed that the trade-off between bread and steel does not change. This follows from the assumption that labor is homogeneous and that no group of workers is more skilled than another group. The trade-off between bread and steel is another way to refer to the opportunity cost of steel. This follows from the definition of opportunity cost as the best forgone alternative: in order to produce a ton of steel, the United States gives up two-thirds of a loaf of bread. In Figure 3.2, the slope of the PPC is 0.67, the number of loaves of bread forgone (Δbread) divided by the quantity of steel obtained (Δsteel)—written as follows:

$$\text{Slope of the PPC} = (\Delta\text{bread output}) / (\Delta\text{steel output})$$
$$= \text{opportunity cost of steel}$$

## Relative Prices

Suppose that the slope of the PPC is –0.67, as shown in Figure 3.2. If the United States does not trade, it gives up 0.67 loaves of bread for an additional ton of steel. This trade-off is called the **relative price** of steel or the opportunity cost of steel. The term *relative price* follows from the fact that it is not in monetary units, but rather in units of the other good. If no trade takes place, then the relative price of a good must be equal to its opportunity cost in production.

**FIGURE 3.2** ● **Opportunity Costs and the Slope of the PPC**

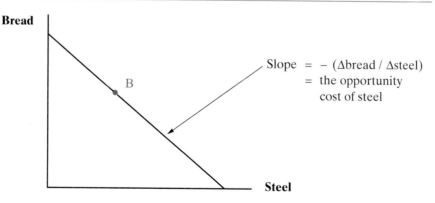

The slope of the PPC is the opportunity cost of the good on the horizontal axis. This follows from the definition of the slope as the ratio of the vertical change to the horizontal change moving along the PPC.

It is easy to convert the relative price of steel into the relative price of bread: simply take the inverse of the price of steel. In other words, if 0.67 loaves of bread is the price of one ton of steel in the United States, then 1.5 tons of steel is the price of one loaf of bread. By the same reasoning, 1.5 tons of steel is the opportunity cost of one loaf of bread in the United States when production is at point B in Figure 3.2.

## The Price Line or Trade Line

The complete absence of trade is called **autarky**, and in this situation, both the United States and Canada are limited in their consumption to the goods that they produce at home. Suppose that autarky prevails and the opportunity cost of steel in Canada is 3 loaves of bread per ton, and in the United States it is 0.67 loaves per ton (as given in Table 3.1). In this case, both countries can raise their consumption levels if they trade. In particular, for trade to be desirable, the price of steel must settle somewhere between the opportunity costs in Canada and in the United States. That is, the countries benefit if the following is true:

$$3.0 \text{ (loaves / ton)} > P_w^s > 0.67 \text{ (loaves / ton)}$$

Suppose that the price settles at 2 loaves per ton. In the United States, the pre-trade price was 0.67 loaves per ton. This is illustrated in Figure 3.3, where the PPC for the United States is shown with the production point at A. The trading possibilities for the United States are illustrated by line TT, the **price line** or **trade line**. The slope of TT is −2, which is the relative price of steel, or the rate at which bread and steel can be traded for each other. TT passes through point A because this is the combination of steel and bread that is available to trade if the United States produces at A. If the United States chooses to trade, it could move up TT,

**FIGURE 3.3** • **Production and Trade before Specialization**

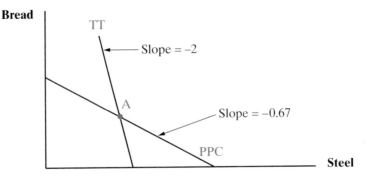

If the United States produces at A and the trade price of steel is 2, then it can trade steel for bread and move its consumption bundle outside its PPC.

trading each ton of steel for two loaves of bread. This is a better trade-off than it gets if it tries to make more bread, since along its PPC each ton brings only two-thirds more loaves of bread. While it is always impossible to produce outside the PPC, in effect, the United States can consume outside it by trading steel for bread.

## The Gains from Trade

You should wonder why the United States would choose to make bread at all, since a ton of steel not produced brings in only two-thirds of a loaf of bread. If the United States were to specialize in steel production and trade for bread, it could do much better, since it would get 2 loaves for each ton. This possibility is shown in Figure 3.4. Here, the pre-trade production point for the United States is at A. This is also its consumption point, since in the absence of trade, consumption must equal production. Point B in Figure 3.4 represents production that is completely specialized in steel. With the opening of trade, production could occur at B, and the United States could trade up along TT′, which has a slope of −2, the same as TT. If the United States produces at B and moves up TT′, it can reach a point like C, which is unambiguously superior to the consumption bundle available when production is at point A. C is superior because it represents more of both bread and steel than is available at A. Similarly, for any combination of bread and steel that is available along the PPC, or along TT if the United States produces at A and trades, there is a consumption bundle on TT′, which represents more of both goods.

The most important thing to note about production point B is that it maximizes U.S. income. This follows from the fact that it makes available the greatest

## FIGURE 3.4 ● Production to Maximize Income

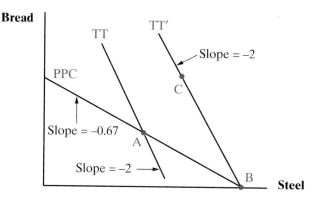

By specializing production at B and trading for bread, the United States obtains the largest possible consumption bundle.

combinations of bread and steel. To see this, consider that no other point of production puts the United States on a price line that lies farther out from the origin. Every other production point on the United States' PPC lies below TT', and every trade line with a slope of −2 that passes through the PPC at a point other than B also lies below TT'. In other words, given the United States' PPC and a relative steel price of 2, the largest bundle of consumption goods is obtained when the United States specializes in steel and trades for its bread.

The United States benefits from trade, but does Canada? Unequivocally, the answer is yes. Consider Figure 3.5 where point A is Canada's pre-trade production point. Along Canada's PPC, the opportunity cost of steel is 3 loaves of bread per ton. After trade, the price settles between 0.67 and 3.00, at 2 loaves per ton. With a trade price of 2 (price line TT), Canada maximizes its income by moving along its PPC to where it is completely specialized in bread production. Then it can trade bread for steel at a trade price that is more favorable than its domestic trade-off of 3 loaves per ton. Canada, too, can consume at a point on TT that is outside its PPC and above and to the right of its pre-trade equilibrium at point A. Canada, like the United States, is better off because with trade it gets a larger combination of both goods than it can produce for itself.

A numerical example will help clarify the existence of gains from trade. Suppose the relative price of steel is 2 loaves per ton. When the United States increases its steel output by 1 ton, it gives up 0.67 loaves of bread output, but it can trade the steel for 2 loaves, leaving a net gain of 1.33 loaves (2 − 0.67 = 1.33). In order to meet U.S. demand for 2 more loaves of bread, Canada must give up 0.67 ton of steel production. It trades the 2 loaves for 1 ton of steel, however, leaving a net gain of 0.33 ton (1 − 0.67 = 0.33). Hence, both countries benefit from the trade.

**FIGURE 3.5** • **Canada's Gains from Trade**

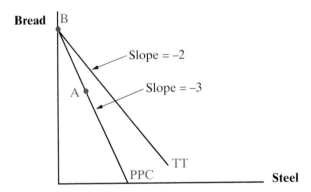

By specializing production at B and trading for steel, Canada obtains the largest possible consumption bundle.

## Domestic Prices and the Trade Price

Now we know that as long as the trade price is between the pre-trade domestic prices in Canada and the United States, both countries can gain from trade. What ensures that the trade price actually settles within this range, 3.0 (loaves/ton) > $P_w^s$ > 0.67 (loaves/ton)? What would happen if, for example, $P_w^s$ were equal to 4, or 0.5?

Consider the first case when the trade price is 4 loaves per ton of steel. At $P_w^s = 4$, the trade price of steel is greater than the production cost in each country. Clearly, the United States would want to continue to specialize in steel and trade it for bread. Nothing has changed with regard to the U.S. strategy for maximizing its consumption bundle, or income. The only difference now is that the United States gets 4 units of bread for each unit of steel, instead of 2 as before. In Canada's case, the higher price of steel makes it profitable for Canadian producers to switch to steel production. This follows because the production opportunity cost of steel is 3 loaves of bread, but each ton produced can trade for 4 loaves. By specializing in steel production and trading for bread, Canada maximizes its consumption bundle.

Finally, it should be obvious that both countries are specialized in steel production and that no one is producing bread. Both Canada and the United States will bring their excess steel to market looking to trade it for bread, but neither country has any to trade. There is a bread shortage and a glut of steel. Consequently, bread prices rise, and steel prices fall. This goes on at least until the trade price of steel falls below the opportunity cost of production in Canada, the higher-cost country. Once $P_w^s$ is less than 3, Canadian producers switch back to bread, steel production goes down, bread is up, and trade can resume.

In the second case, where $P_w^s$ is less than 0.67, Canada continues to specialize in bread, and the United States switches. Bread is the surplus good, steel is in short supply, and a similar dynamic causes the price to move in order to ensure that both goods are produced. The equilibrium trade price, then, has to be within the range we specified earlier, between the opportunity costs in the two countries. In our case, this is between 0.67 and 3.0 loaves per ton.

At the extreme, the trade price could be equal to the opportunity cost in one country; for example, if the trade price of steel is 0.67 loaves per ton, then the United States is indifferent about trading. It cannot be hurt by trading, but it does not gain either, since all the gains go to Canada. Similarly, if the trade price is equal to Canada's opportunity cost, then Canada is indifferent and all the gains accrue to the United States.

Without more information we cannot say much more about the trade price. Will it be close to 0.67 or to 3.0? The answer depends on the strength of demand for each good in both countries, but we have not explicitly included demand in our model, so we cannot say. We do know that if the price is closer to 0.67, then the gains from trade are larger for Canada, and if it is closer to 3.0, the United States benefits more. Nevertheless, both countries gain as long as the price is between the two opportunity costs, and economic forces determine that the price must be in that range.

## Absolute and Comparative Productivity Advantage Contrasted

Absolute productivity advantage is defined as having higher labor productivity. We saw that if each country has an absolute productivity advantage in one of the goods, they can both benefit by specializing in that good and trading it for the other good. Note, however, that the gains from trade we saw did not depend in any way on each country having an absolute advantage. In fact, it was the pre-trade opportunity costs of bread and steel in each country that mattered. The opportunity costs were derived from the productivities, but since they are a ratio, vastly different levels of productivity can lead to the same trade-off.

A country has a **comparative productivity advantage** in a good, or simply a comparative advantage, if its opportunity costs of producing a good are lower than those of its trading partners. The concept of comparative advantage is based on the idea that nations maximize their material well-being when they use their resources where they have their highest value. In order to know the highest-valued usage for any resource, we must compare alternative uses. If, by comparison to that of the United States, Canada's opportunity cost of bread is lower, then it should produce more bread and trade for steel.

The distinction between absolute and comparative productivity advantages is one of the most important in economics. It is also one of the least well understood, in spite of the fact that it is relatively simple. For example, it is common to read or hear comments about competitiveness that assume that if a country does not have an absolute advantage, it will not be able to sell its products abroad. Our model explains why this logic is erroneous and why even the least productive nations export some goods.

## Gains from Trade with No Absolute Advantage

Consider the case shown in Table 3.3. Japan has an absolute advantage in both cars (2 > 0.5) and steel (2 > 1), yet it can still gain from trade, as can Malaysia, even though it lacks an absolute advantage in either good. If Japan does not trade, it is limited to its own production possibilities, which require it to give up

| TABLE 3.3 ● **Output per Hour Worked** | | |
|---|---|---|
| | Japan | Malaysia |
| **Cars** | 2 | 0.5 |
| **Steel** | 2 tons | 1 ton |

1 ton of steel for each car it produces. In Malaysia, each car costs 2 tons of steel. Hence, there is scope for a mutually beneficial exchange.

Japan's opportunity cost of steel production is greater than Malaysia's even though it has a higher absolute rate of productivity in steel. Therefore, if it follows its comparative advantage and maximizes its income, it will specialize in cars, the sector where its opportunity cost is lower than Malaysia's. Once trade opens, the world price of cars will be between 1 and 2 tons of steel per car, the opportunity costs of production in Japan and Malaysia as follows:

$$1\left(\frac{\text{tons}}{\text{car}}\right) < P_w^c < 2\left(\frac{\text{tons}}{\text{car}}\right)$$

Let the price be 1.5 tons of steel per car. If Japan moves to specialize in cars with the opening of trade, it gives up 1 ton of steel for each additional car it produces. With the additional car, it can trade for 1.5 tons of steel, which is a net gain of 0.5 tons over its own production. Similarly, Malaysia gives up 0.5 cars produced for each additional ton of steel it manufactures, but it gains 0.67 cars from each ton of steel traded. Both countries benefit and both countries are able to consume a greater amount of both goods than they could if they relied on their national production alone.

This is a very simplified example of the gains from trade, but it illustrates a fundamental principle. What matters most for the purposes of trade is not a country's absolute advantage, but rather its comparative advantage. This is a central point of international economics: differences in absolute advantage do not eliminate gains from trade. Furthermore, although both countries gain from trade, it does not imply that their living standards or income are equal. Malaysia's income will be less than Japan's because it produces less per hour. In effect, an hour of work in Malaysia returns the equivalent of 1 ton of steel or, through trade, 0.67 cars. Japanese workers produce 2 cars per hour worked, which is equivalent to 3 tons of steel through trade. As a result of higher absolute productivity, incomes in Japan are quite a bit higher, with or without trade.

# Comparative Advantage and "Competitiveness"

The rhetoric of "competitiveness" is so common in our public discourse that it is useful to consider its relationship to comparative advantage. In the analysis so far, comparative advantage resulted from productivity differences between nations in autarky. In our simple model of a barter economy, wages, prices, and exchange rates were omitted. Real businesses do not barter steel for bread, however, and they cannot pay their workers by dividing up the firm's output.

In general, by ignoring money wages, money prices, and exchange rates, we assumed that all goods and labor were correctly priced. In other words, we assumed that the prices of outputs and inputs are an accurate indication of their relative scarcity. In this case, there is no difference between a nation's comparative advantage in a good and the ability of its firms to sell the good at a price that is competitive. That is, if all markets correctly value the price of inputs and outputs, then a nation's commercial advantage is determined by its comparative advantage.

Unfortunately, markets sometimes fail to produce optimal outcomes, and at times, outputs and inputs are incorrectly priced. Sometimes, undervaluation or overvaluation of a good stems from inherent difficulties in measuring its true value or in measuring its true cost of production. For example, we usually ignore the costs of air pollution when we measure the costs of driving a car. Other times, undervaluation or overvaluation may result from government policies, as when prices are maintained at an artificially high or low level. In either case, the fact that a market price may not accurately reflect the economic value of an input or an output means that a wedge is driven between commercial or **competitive advantage** and comparative advantage.

It is often (incorrectly) argued that nations should pursue commercial advantages for their firms even if it means a misallocation of resources. In effect, this means a country follows policies that lower living standards by failing to maximize the value of national output. In terms of Figure 3.4 and Figure 3.5, this is equivalent to asserting that the United States and Canada should each remain at a point like A, where the United States overestimates the value of producing its own bread and Canada overestimates the value of steel. Both countries end up with consumption bundles that are suboptimal from the standpoint of national welfare.

Consider a real-world example. Indonesia tried to develop an aircraft industry in spite of the fact that it lacks a comparative advantage in aircraft production. Nevertheless, through a combination of government policies (some of which paid people to buy the planes!) the price to foreigners was competitive at times. From the perspective of Indonesian national welfare and the optimal use of scarce Indonesian resources, this was a mistake. From the perspective of a business, however, Indonesian policies have made it profitable to make airplanes, even though it means using resources in ways that are suboptimal from the national perspective.

This case illustrates the common mistake of equating nations with business enterprises. Indonesian plane manufacturers care about their subsidies and any other policy that makes them profitable. The national interest, however, is to achieve the most efficient allocation of resources possible within the framework of the nation's laws and values. It is possible to make individual firms highly profitable through subsidies or protection from international competition, while at the same time and through the same policies cause the nation's overall standard of living to be lower than it would be otherwise. Businesses are not designed to ensure that resources are efficiently allocated at the national level. If they can legally tip the playing field in their direction, they will not hesitate.

Another important distinction between nations and business enterprises is that nations do not compete with each other in any normal sense of the word. Economic relations between the United States and Canada, or any pair of nations, are not equivalent to the commercial competition that exists between companies such as Coke and Pepsi. If Canada grows, the United States does not go out of business or suffer in any identifiable way. In fact, Canadian growth would be a stimulus to U.S. growth and would create spillover benefits for Americans. Cola companies fight over a relatively static market size, but nations can all simultaneously increase their incomes.

#  Economic Restructuring

**Economic restructuring** refers to changes in the economy that may require some industries to grow and others to shrink or even disappear altogether. For example, the United States has seen a dramatic decrease in the size of its steel industry and, some years later, a rebirth of a new industry based around smaller, more specialized steel mills. In any dynamic economy, some types of economic activity will be growing, and others will be scaling back or dying. In some cases, these changes are a direct consequence of increased openness to foreign competition. For example, the influx of Japanese cars has played a major role in the reorganization and restructuring of the U.S. auto industry.

In our simple Ricardian model, after the opening of trade the United States was able to maximize its well-being by shifting workers out of bread production and into steel production. Even though this restructuring of the economy improved overall economic welfare, it does not mean that it benefited every individual—a nation's gains from trade may be divided in different ways, and it is usually the case that some individuals benefit while others are hurt by trade. If there are net gains from opening trade (which are measured by an increase in the consumption bundle), then it means that the economic gains of the winners are greater than the economic losses of the losers, and therefore the nation as a whole is better off. Nevertheless, opening an economy to increased foreign competition is rarely painless and usually generates a number of new problems. In the model used in this chapter, it is likely that bread producers may not know much about steel production. They may not know where to go to find work, and they may leave behind a community that is dying as its most mobile and economically active citizens find work elsewhere.

When the U.S. auto industry was in its least competitive position against the Japanese in the early 1980s, our overly simplified model of comparative advantage would have counseled laid-off autoworkers to leave Michigan and move to California where they could find jobs in the booming computer and defense industries. Obviously, this is not realistic advice for most autoworkers. The fact that the U.S. economy was open to Japanese auto manufacturers certainly made consumers and firms that bought cars better off. It increased the selection of automobiles and enabled us to buy higher quality cars at lower prices. It is another matter, however, for the U.S. autoworkers who lost their jobs.

Most economists would agree that this trade-off is worth it because the availability of Japanese cars, or foreign made goods in general, increases our choices as consumers, lowers the cost of inputs for producers, increases competition and innovation, and enables us to obtain a greater bundle of goods. It also leads to the diffusion of technological change, which benefits all of us. No one would argue, for example, that if a German drug company invented a cure for AIDS or cancer that we should prohibit its importation because it may hurt the income of a lot of doctors and perhaps lead to the closing of some clinics. The gain to the nation would vastly outweigh the losses to those adversely affected by the changes in medicine.

While it is easy to show that trade barriers are a suboptimal solution to the social problems of economic change that are caused by trade, it is uncertain what the optimal policies are. To a large extent, political assumptions about the way the world works will color the solutions offered by economists, political scientists, and other social scientists. For example, some ardent believers in less government intervention into the economy would argue that government should not have any policies for handling unemployment or the economic collapse of communities that is caused by the rapid growth of imports. They maintain that unemployment is a self-correcting problem; laid-off workers will look for new jobs and will, if necessary, accept lower wages. The argument that government cannot efficiently deal with these sorts of problems, and that it creates inefficient, bureaucratic programs that live on long after they become unnecessary, is also frequently heard. Others make a value judgment that this sort of social problem should not be a governmental concern and that it should be left up to the private economy and individual initiative.

An alternative to this "do nothing" approach to economic restructuring is for the government to look for ways to get the winners to compensate the losers. The proponents of this view justify it on several grounds. First, the nation as a whole benefits from trade, so there are newly added resources to the economy that make compensation possible. Second, many people believe they have an ethical obligation to assist people hurt by economic change. And third, compensation reduces the incentives for those that oppose trade to organize against imports. If industries or workers think they are unable to compete, they may organize to restrict trade. Promises of financial assistance and help in finding another job may weaken this urge. In this view, compensation is a useful tool for undermining the antitrade position.

The practice of offering **trade adjustment assistance (TAA)** is common in many countries, including the United States. Usually these programs take the form of extended unemployment benefits and worker re-training, along with a temporary imposition of a tax on imports in order to create some breathing room for an industry suffering from a sudden surge in imports. For example, the U.S. government created a special program of benefits for workers who are hurt by trade with Mexico due to the signing of the North American Free Trade Agreement (NAFTA). In 1994, the first year of NAFTA, 17,000 workers qualified for TAA under the NAFTA provision. Generally, in order to qualify for the benefits, workers must demonstrate that they were laid off as a result of imports from Mexico or Canada or because their firm relocated to one of those countries.

Needless to say, it is sometimes difficult to establish a direct link between imports and job loss; a poorly managed firm may have been on its way out of business with or without imports.

The important point is that trade creates change, and it may be difficult for some people, industries, or communities to deal with it. When a nation moves along its PPC toward a different mix of industries, there is a period of transition that is painful for some. Economic restructuring does not happen overnight, and although it is desirable for the higher living standard it brings, change and transformation cost time and money.

## CASE STUDY

# Changing Comparative Advantage in the Republic of Korea, 1960–2000

Few countries began life with a more limited set of possibilities than the Republic of Korea (South Korea). Liberated from its 40 years of colonial status (1905–1945) by the defeat of Japan in World War II, Korea was soon wracked by civil war (1950–1953) and divided it into two nations. Many observers were pessimistic about the future of noncommunist South Korea. The industrial capacity of the country was mostly located in communist controlled North Korea, and South Korea had little to offer besides the dedication and hard work of its people. Yet, over the following 50 years, few countries have grown faster. The Republic of Korea is an economic success story that is worth studying.

From 1960 to the present, per capita income in the Republic of Korea grew at the rate of 5.95 percent per year, in real terms (Table 3.4). At this rate, per capita income doubles every 12 years, and over the span of one generation, average incomes increase nearly four times. Behind the rising incomes is an equally impressive growth in productivity, which increased by a factor of 8 over the 40 year span from 1960 to 2000.

Korea's economic strategy for the first few years after the Korean War was to limit imports and concentrate on producing import substitutes, a common

| TABLE 3.4 ● Indicators of the Korean Economy | | | | | |
|---|---|---|---|---|---|
| | 1960 | 1970 | 1980 | 1990 | 2000 |
| **GDP per capita, US$(2000)** | 1,571 | 2,777 | 4,830 | 9,959 | 15,881 |
| **Output per worker (1960 = 100)** | 100 | 170 | 277 | 534 | 824 |
| **Openness** | 4.52 | 14.94 | 35.21 | 43.01 | 86.31 |

*Source*: Penn World Tables, author's calculations.

strategy for developing countries in the 1950s. Korea was one of the first to recognize its limitations and to change its policies. In 1960 and 1961, political changes led to a change in economic policies and a more aggressive engagement with the world economy. Korea removed many of its restrictions on imports and began to promote export oriented industries. Between 1960 and 2000, its openness index increased more than 19-fold, from 4.52 to 86.31.

Initially, Korea's export efforts were limited to the commodities on hand, mostly minerals, a few agricultural and marine products (for example, seaweed) and very simple consumer goods. Over several decades after 1960, its export industries evolved several times, from simple products requiring few skills and little capital to products that required more skills and greater capital. After its first few years of exploring its comparative advantage, Korea developed competitive sectors in wigs, textiles, shoes, and plywood. With the increase in income came increases in skills and financial capital. This permitted the development of more skill and capital intensive industries such as steel, shipbuilding, household appliances, and electronic subassemblies. Eventually, these were followed by cars, computers, and electronics. In the first decade of the new millennium, Korea is a high income industrial economy and is capable of exporting the most technologically advanced products available in several fields. Clearly, its history demonstrates that comparative advantage is not unchangeable, and that it can be a vehicle for raising incomes and promoting development.

An increasing share of Korea's output was sold in world markets. Consequently, production was not limited to the growth in its own domestic market. In addition, its goods had to be competitive in quality and price. Its ability to obtain imports at world prices was also important, but standing behind Korea's competitiveness was its rapid increases in productivity. Without more output per hour of work, incomes could not have risen as fast as they did and Korea's ability to shift its comparative advantage from low skill to increasingly higher skill products could not have gone forward. In turn, productivity increases require a host of complementary changes, ranging from the development of universities and research institutes to organizational changes and the raising of financial capital for investing in new machinery and equipment.

In the process of promoting exports and raising productivity, Korea encountered a number of obstacles including its own bureaucratic inflexibility, problems in marketing to foreign markets that are radically different from Korea, and a shortage of technical management and industrial expertise.

The Korean experience is an example of a country that used its comparative advantage to develop export markets. At the same time, it also used the competitive pressures of foreign competition to raise its own productivity and quality standards, which in turn raised the incomes of its citizens. Korea's success was a joint product of efforts by its government, the private sector, and a number of public-private organizations. The role that each of these played is still hotly debated. Is Korea's success due to the wise guidance of government policies, or did those policies play a secondary (or even negative) role to markets and competition?

# Summary

- The single most important determinant of trade patterns is the opportunity cost of producing traded goods. Countries that sacrifice the least amount of alternative production when producing a particular good have the lowest opportunity cost, or a comparative advantage. The idea of comparative advantage has been one of the most enduring concepts of economic thought and has been a central theme in international economic policy since the mid-1800s.

- Nations that produce according to their comparative advantage are maximizing the benefits they receive from trade and, consequently, their national welfare. This is the same as maximizing their gains from trade.

- Comparative advantage is often confused with absolute advantage. The latter refers to the advantage a nation has if its absolute productivity in a particular product is greater than its trading partners. It is not necessary to have an absolute advantage in order to have a comparative advantage.

- One common fallacious argument against following comparative advantage is that workers in other countries are paid less than workers at home. This argument neglects the issue of productivity. Developing-country wages are lower because the value of output from one hour of labor is less. Labor productivity is less because workers are generally less skilled, they have less capital on the job, and they have less capital in the surrounding economy to support their on-the-job productivity.

- Business people look at the issue of trade differently than economists do because they have different objectives in mind. Business people are often concerned about their ability to compete—that is, to sell a particular item in a given market at the lowest price. Their perspective is that of the firm. Economists focus on the efficient use of resources at the national or global level. The perspective is that of all firms taken together.

# Vocabulary

| | |
|---|---|
| absolute productivity advantage | opportunity cost |
| autarky | price line |
| comparative productivity advantage | production possibilities curve (PPC) |
| competitive advantage | relative price |
| economic restructuring | trade adjustment assistance (TAA) |
| gains from trade | trade line |
| labor productivity | zero sum |
| mercantilism | |

## Study Questions

1. Use the information in the following table on labor productivities in France and Germany to answer the questions a through f.

**Output per hour worked**

|  | France | Germany |
|---|---|---|
| **Cheese** | 2 kilograms | 1 kilogram |
| **Cars** | 0.25 | 0.5 |

a.  Which country has an absolute advantage in cheese? In cars?

b.  What is the relative price of cheese in France if it does not trade? In Germany?

c.  What is opportunity cost of cheese in France? In Germany?

d.  Which country has a comparative advantage in cheese? In cars? Explain your answer.

e.  What are the upper and lower bounds for the trade price of cheese?

f.  Draw a hypothetical PPC for France and label its slope. Suppose that France follows its comparative advantage in deciding where to produce on its PPC. Label its production point. If the trade price of cars is 5 kilos of cheese per car, draw a trade line showing how France can gain from trade.

2. Suppose that the table in Study Question 1 looks as follows. Use the information to answer questions a through f.

**Output per hour worked**

|  | France | Germany |
|---|---|---|
| **Cheese** | 1 kilogram | 2 kilograms |
| **Cars** | 0.25 car | 2 cars |

a.  Which country has an absolute advantage in cheese? In cars?

b.  What is the relative price of cheese in France if it does not trade? In Germany?

c.  What is opportunity cost of cheese in France? In Germany?

d.  Which country has a comparative advantage in cheese? In cars? Explain your answer.

e.  What are the upper and lower bounds for the trade price of cheese?

f.  Draw a hypothetical PPC for France and label its slope. Suppose that France follows its comparative advantage in deciding where to produce on its PPC. Label its production point. If the trade price of cars is 5 kilos of cheese per car, draw a trade line showing how France can gain from trade.

3. Explain how a nation can gain from trade even though as a result not everyone is better off. Is this a contradiction?

4. Economic nationalists in developed countries worry that international trade is destroying the national economy. A common complaint is that trade agreements open the economy to increased trade with countries where workers are paid a fraction of what they earn at home. Explain the faulty logic of this argument.

5. Many people believe that the goal of international trade should be to create jobs. Consequently, when they see workers laid off due to a firm's inability to compete against cheaper and better imports, they assume that trade must be bad for the economy. Is this assumption correct? Why, or why not?

6. Suppose that Germany decides to become self sufficient in bananas and even to export them. In order to accomplish these goals, large tax incentives are granted to companies that will invest in banana production. Soon, the German industry is competitive and able to sell bananas at the lowest price anywhere. Does Germany have a comparative advantage? Why, or why not? What are the consequences for the overall economy?

# 4 Comparative Advantage and Factor Endowments

 ## Introduction: The Determinants of Comparative Advantage

The theory presented in Chapter 3 did not consider the determinants of comparative advantage. It was assumed that countries had different levels of productivity, but the reasons why one country might be more productive than another in a particular line of production was not analyzed. In this chapter, the idea of comparative advantage is examined in more detail, beginning with the factors that determine it. We will also examine the impact of trade on income distribution. In the simple model discussed in Chapter 3, it was assumed that everyone that wanted a job could find one and that after trade began, anyone laid off from the shrinking industry found employment in the expanding one. The opposition to expanded trade, however, often comes from people who fear that increased trade will downsize their industry, and they do not view themselves as having options for employment in the expanding sectors. We also saw that trade causes the price of the export good to rise and the price of the import good to fall, making the nation as a whole better off. In reality, we consume both export and import goods, and the fact that the nation is better off may not reflect individual circumstances if consumption is heavily weighted toward the export good.

 ## Modern Trade Theory

In Chapter 3, comparative advantage depended on each country's relative productivity, which was given by assumption at the start of the exercise. Smith and Ricardo thought that each country would have its own technology, its own climate, and its own resources, and that differences among nations would give rise to productivity differences. In the twentieth century, several economists have developed a more detailed explanation of trade in which the productivity differences of each country depend on the country's endowments of the inputs (called factors of production, or simply, factors) that are used to produce each good. The theory has various names: the Heckscher-Ohlin theory (HO), the Heckscher-Ohlin-Samuelson theory, or the Factor Proportions theory. They all refer to the same set of ideas.

## The Heckscher-Ohlin (HO) Trade Model

The HO trade model begins with the observation that nations are endowed with different levels of each input (factors). Furthermore, each output has a different "recipe" for its production and requires different combinations and levels of the various inputs. Steel production, for example, requires a lot of iron ore, coking material, semiskilled labor, and some expensive capital equipment. Clothing production requires unskilled and semiskilled workers with rudimentary capital equipment in the form of sewing machines.

In order to analyze how the availability of inputs creates productivity differences, first we define **factor abundance** and **factor scarcity**. Table 4.1 illustrates the concepts with a numerical example. The capital-labor ratio of the United States ($K_{us} / L_{us}$) is $^{50}/_{150}$, or $^1/_3$. Canada's ($K_{can} / L_{can}$) is $^2/_{10}$, or $^1/_5$. Because the United States' capital-labor ratio is higher than Canada's ($K_{us} / L_{us} > K_{can} / L_{can}$), the United States is the capital-abundant country and Canada is the labor-abundant country. Note that Canada's absolute labor endowment is less than that of the United States, but Canada it is still considered labor-abundant because it has more labor relative to its capital.

Relative abundance of a factor implies that its relative cost is less than in counties where it is relatively scarcer. Conversely, relatively scarce resources are more expensive. Consequently, capital is relatively cheap in the United States and labor is relatively expensive. It follows that economies have relatively lower costs in the production of goods where the "recipe" calls for greater quantities of the abundant factor and smaller quantities of the scarce factor. In this example, Canada will have a lower opportunity cost in production that uses relatively more labor and relatively less capital, while the United States will have a lower opportunity cost in production that uses relatively more capital and less labor.

The **Heckscher-Ohlin (HO) trade theory** makes this point exactly. It asserts that a country's comparative advantage lies in the production of goods that use relatively abundant factors. In other words, comparative advantage is determined

**TABLE 4.1** • **An Example of Factor Abundance**

|  | United States | Canada |
|---|---|---|
| **Capital** | 50 machines | 2 machines |
| **Labor** | 150 workers | 10 workers |

The United States is capital abundant and Canada is labor abundant.

by a nation's factor endowment, and once this is determined, it should be possible to predict the goods a country exports and imports.

To clarify, consider the United States. It is richly endowed with a wide variety of factors. It has natural resources in the form of rich farmland and extensive forests. It has highly skilled labor, such as scientists, engineers, and managers. Although savings rates are not very high, the wealth of the nation has enabled it to create an abundance of physical capital, both public and private. Its exports, therefore, should include agricultural products, particularly those requiring skilled labor and physical capital, and all sorts of machinery and industrial goods that require intensive input of physical capital and scientific and engineering skills.

One leading U.S. export is commercial jet aircraft—a product that requires a vast array of physical capital and scientific, engineering, and managerial talent. The United States is also a major exporter of grains and grain products, such as vegetable oils. These are produced with relatively small labor inputs, very large capital inputs (combines, tractors, and so on), farmland, and a great deal of scientific research and development that has produced hybrid seeds, pesticides, herbicides, and other agricultural inputs.

## Gains from Trade in the HO Model

In the Ricardian model we assumed that each country faced a constant set of trade-offs: 2 loaves of bread for 3 tons of steel (United States) or 3 loaves of bread for 1 ton of steel (Canada). The constant costs of the Ricardian model stemmed from the fact that there was one homogeneous input: labor. Labor could be used to make bread or steel. Workers did not vary in their skills, and since there was no capital input, each worker was as productive as the next. Consequently, when labor was reallocated from bread to steel, or vice versa, the trade-off was always at a constant rate.

In the HO model, we have a multiplicity of inputs—labor, capital, farmland—so each worker may be equipped with a different quantity of supporting inputs, such as capital. Obviously, at the end of the day, a worker with a $5 shovel will have dug a smaller hole than one equipped with a $150,000 earth moving machine. Furthermore, the quality of labor and capital can vary. Some labor is skilled, and some is unskilled. Certain jobs require scientific or other technical training, while others require basic literacy or even less. Similarly, capital can be low- or high-tech, and resources such as farmland have different fertility and climate characteristics. In effect, each important qualitative difference can be treated as a key characteristic of a separate input, so unskilled and skilled labor can be considered different factors.

If a country has multiple inputs with various suitabilities for different tasks, we can no longer assume a PPC with constant costs. Rather, the economy is assumed to have increasing costs, which implies that each country has a rising opportunity cost for each type of production. Consequently, as the United States or Canada moves labor, capital, and land into bread production, each additional unit of bread leads to a greater loss of steel output than the one before. The reason is straightforward: if more bread is wanted, resources must be taken out of steel. The optimal strategy is to move resources that are relatively good at bread production, but poor at steel production. This leads to the greatest gain in bread with the smallest loss of steel. The next shift in production, toward more bread, cuts deeper into the stock of resources used for steel production, and in all likelihood there will not be resources to move that are as good at bread and as poor at steel as the previous production shift. Consequently, in order to get the same increase in bread, more steel must be given up than before. This result is symmetric, so shifts going the other way, toward more steel, cause the opportunity cost of steel to rise with each shift. Figure 4.1 illustrates a PPC with increasing costs.

As with constant costs, the trade-off between bread and steel is equal to the slope of the PPC. Since the PPC is curved, its slope changes at every point, and we must measure the trade-off at the point of production. For example, in Figure 4.2, if the United States is producing at point A, then the opportunity cost of an additional ton of steel is equivalent to the slope of the PPC at point A. Since the PPC is a curve rather than a straight line, the slope is measured by drawing a tangent line at the point of production and measuring its slope.

Most of the analysis of the gains from trade discussed in Chapter 3 carries over into the HO model. In order to demonstrate this, assume that point A is the U.S. production point in autarky and that at point A the opportunity cost of steel is 0.67 loaves of bread. This means that the slope of the tangent at A is −0.67. Also assume that Canada's opportunity cost of steel is above that of the United States at 3 loaves of bread per ton, the same as before. Also assume that after trade begins, the world price, or trade price, is 2 loaves of bread per ton of steel, the same as the example shown in Chapter 3. After trade opens, the United

**FIGURE 4.1** ● **The United States' Production Possibilities Curve with Increasing Costs**

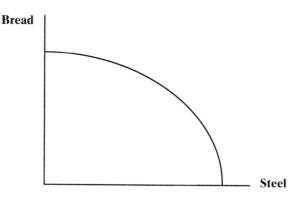

Moving from left to right, the opportunity cost of another unit of steel increases.

## FIGURE 4.2 ● Opportunity Costs and the Slope of the PPC

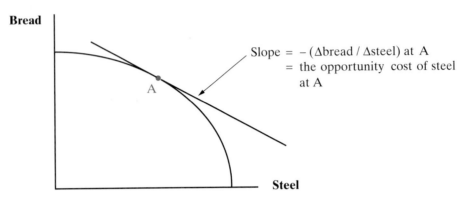

The opportunity cost of steel is measured by the slope of the tangent at the point of production.

States can continue to produce at A and not trade, or it can produce at A and trade. Trade line TT shown in Figure 4.3 illustrates the possibilities if the United States stays at point A on its PPC.

TT is the price line with a slope of −2 passing through A and showing the combinations of bread and steel that are available when production is at A and trade is possible. In Figure 4.3, TT′ is a trade line that is tangent to the PPC at

## FIGURE 4.3 ● Gains from Trade in the HO Model

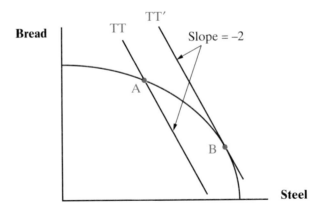

TT is the trade line if production is at A. Production at B maximizes income.

point B, an alternative production point to the right of A and closer to the steel axis. If the United States exploits its comparative advantage and shifts toward increased steel production, increasing costs come into play, which is the same as saying that the marginal cost of steel output is rising. As production rises, the gap between the opportunity cost of production and the trade price narrows, until finally, they are equal at point B. Further increases in steel production would push the cost above its value in trade; therefore, they are not warranted.

At point B, the opportunity cost of steel equals its trade price. Since the model is symmetric and the opportunity cost and trade price of bread are the inverse of the steel, the same equivalency holds for bread. To the left of B, the opportunity cost of steel (bread) is less (greater) than the trade price, so more (less) production is warranted. To the right of B, the opportunity cost of steel (bread) is greater (less) than the trade price, so less (more) production is warranted. Only at point B does the opportunity cost equal the trade price. Since no other changes can make the United States better off, point B is the production combination that maximizes income.

Graphically, the superiority of point B can be seen by first comparing B to A. Point B is clearly superior to A in terms of the consumption possibilities because for every point along TT there is another point on TT′ that offers more of both goods. That is, TT′ lies above and to the right of TT. Since a greater combination of both goods is available if the United States produces at B and trades, B is superior to A. Furthermore, when the trade price is 2, every other production point along the PPC leads to smaller consumption bundles. That is, at any other production point, a trade line with a slope of −2 that passes through the point will lie below and to the left of TT′, representing smaller combinations of steel and bread. Consequently, point B maximizes income by creating the largest possible consumption bundle.

The notion of gains from trade in the HO model is nearly the same as the Ricardian model. The only significant difference is that specialization is not complete in the HO model. The United States continues to make some bread, and Canada makes some steel.

##  Trade and Income Distribution

Recall that in the Ricardian model of comparative advantage, the nation as a whole gained from trade, and, by assumption, we ruled out the potentially harmful effects of trade on some members of society. When trade began, the economy shifted from one point on its production frontier to a different point. Workers that were affected by the production shift simply moved out of the declining industry and into the expanding one. Everyone had the same skills, and each type of production required only labor, so everyone had access to a job, and everyone benefited from both the fall in the price of the imported good and the rise in the price of the exported one.

The Heckscher-Ohlin trade model is a more sophisticated way to analyze the gains and losses from trade because it drops these unrealistic assumptions. Labor can be divided into two or more skill categories, other types of inputs can be included, and industries can require different mixes of the various inputs. Under these more realistic assumptions, it can be shown that while trade benefits the nation as a whole, some groups within the nation benefit more than others, and some will actually be harmed. Furthermore, it can be shown that there is a systematic relationship between the factor endowments of a country and the winners and losers from trade. Opening the discussion to an analysis of winners and losers adds an important and necessary element of realism. We are all aware that not everyone favors increased trade, and without an analysis of trade's income distribution effects, we have no basis for understanding the opposition to increased trade.

## The Stolper-Samuelson Theorem

The analysis begins by recognizing that everyone's income depends on the inputs he or she supplies to the economy. Labor earns wages that may be high or low, depending on the skill level; owners of capital earn profits; landowners earn rents. The amount of income earned per unit of input depends on the demand for the inputs as well as their supply. The demand for a particular input is sometimes referred to as a **derived demand** because it is derived indirectly from the demand for the output it is used to produce. If the output is in high demand, and consequently its price is high, then the inputs that are used to produce it will benefit by receiving higher returns.

In general, any change in the economy that alters the price of outputs will have a direct impact on incomes. We have seen that trade causes output prices to change. Specifically, the price of the export good rises, while the price of the import falls. The movement of prices causes a change in the demand for each factor and leads to a change in the returns paid to each factor. Hence, trade affects income distribution.

When trade begins and output prices change, resources leave the sector that produces imported goods and move into the sector that produces exports. In the HO model, unlike the simple Ricardian model, different goods are produced with different combinations of inputs, so the movement along the production possibilities frontier causes a change in the demand for each input. Factors that are used intensively in the imported goods sector will find that the demand for their services has shrunk—and so has their income. Conversely, factors used intensively in the export sector will experience an increase in the demand for their services and in their incomes. In sum, when trade begins, incomes of the factors used intensively in the import sector fall, and incomes of the factors used intensively in the export sector rise.

These effects are summarized in the **Stolper-Samuelson theorem**, which is derived from the HO theory. The Stolper-Samuelson theorem says that an increase in the price of a good raises the income earned by factors that are used intensively in its production. Conversely, a fall in the price of a good lowers the income of the factors it uses intensively.

Figure 4.4 illustrates these tendencies. Suppose that the United States and Canada can make bread or steel, using capital and labor. Also suppose that bread is the labor-intensive product, shown as follows:

$$K^b / L^b < K^s / L^s$$

and that the United States is relatively well endowed with capital, compared to Canada, as follows:

$$K_{can} / L_{can} < K_{us} / L_{us}.$$

According to the HO theory, the United States will have a comparative advantage in steel, which it will export in return for Canadian bread. In Figure 4.4, after trade begins, the United States moves along its PPC toward the steel axis from point A to point B.

As the United States shifts along its PPC, the change in the mix of goods produced leads to lower demands for labor and higher demands for capital. The steel industry will pick up some of the labor laid off in the bread industry, but since it is not as labor intensive as bread, its increase in labor demand is less than the fall in labor demand in the bread industry. The net result is that labor experiences a fall in demand, leading to a fall in wages and income earned. Note that Stolper-Samuelson does not state that all factors used in the export industries are better off, or that all factors used in the import competing industry get hurt. Rather, the abundant factor that is used to determine comparative advantage and exports is favored, and the scarce factor sees a decline in its income, regardless of industry.

**FIGURE 4.4** ● **The Stolper-Samuelson Theorem**

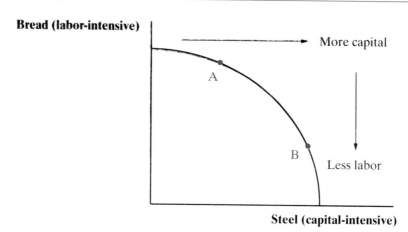

Movement along the PPC from A to B reduces the economy's demand for labor and increases its demand for capital.

The Stolper-Samuelson theorem is a starting point for understanding the income distribution effects of trade, but it tells only part of the story. An extension of the theorem, called the **magnification effect**, shows that the change in output prices has a magnified effect on factor incomes. For example, if after opening trade, bread prices declined by 75 percent, then the fall in labor income will be greater than 75 percent. Similarly, if the price of an export good (steel) rises by 50 percent, for example, incomes earned by the intensively used factors in the export sector (capital) rise more than 50 percent.

The ultimate effects on income of an opening of trade depend on the flexibility of the affected factors. If labor is stuck in bread production and unable to move to the steel sector, it could be hurt much worse than if it were completely flexible to move. Another example illustrates this point: within the debate over U.S.-Mexico free trade, there is a small, but intense controversy surrounding avocado production. Mexico has a comparative advantage in avocados because it is well endowed with the necessary inputs (a particular quality of land and climate, together with unskilled labor and a little capital). If free trade were to open in the avocado market, the owners of avocado orchards in California would find their investments in land, equipment, and avocado trees worthless. Why would anyone pay $1 or more per avocado when Mexican ones sell for 25¢ or less? However, many of the California avocado groves are located in the suburbs of sprawling metropolitan regions, and presumably, if the land were worthless for avocado production, it could be put to valuable use in another line of production—for example, as housing developments. Consequently, the income of the landowners may not decline in the long run, although in the short run, they may be unable to put their land to an alternative use. In order to build these considerations into a trade model, we must turn to a short-run version of the HO model.

## The Specific Factors Model

In the short run, the ability of factors to move between different output sectors is more limited. For example, suppose stiffer competition in the world steel industry causes American steelworkers to take pay cuts, and perhaps some to lose their jobs. In the long run, most of the laid-off steelworkers will find jobs outside of the steel sector, but in the short run, they are stuck with cuts in pay and layoffs. Similarly, physical capital is usually dedicated to a particular use and cannot be converted into producing a different product, and, as we have seen, land is usually tied up in a particular use and cannot be switched to something else instantaneously. In the long run, however, plants and equipment can be redirected to a different line of production, land can be put to different uses, and workers find jobs doing something else.

In order to highlight the ability of labor and other factors to find alternative employment in the long run but not in the short run, sometimes economists add conditions to the HO model. Suppose there are three factors—land, labor, and capital—and two goods—steel and bread. Assume that the production of steel takes capital and labor, while bread takes land and labor. In this version of the HO model, labor is the variable factor because its use varies between both goods.

Land and capital are the specific factors because their use is specific to bread and steel, respectively.

The model just described is an example of the **specific factors model**, a special case of the HO model. The HO model assumes that factors migrate easily from one sector to another—from steel to bread, for example. In the specific factors model (Table 4.2), each good is produced with a specific factor, whose only use is in the production of that good, and a variable factor, which is used to produce both goods. The specific factors (land and capital) are immobile and cannot move between bread and steel, while the variable factor (labor) is completely mobile between industries.

The determinants of comparative advantage with a specific factors model are similar to the analysis with an HO model. As with HO, comparative advantage depends on factor endowments. The main difference in the two models is that the specific factor plays a critical role. Suppose that Canada is relatively well endowed with land and that the United States is relatively well endowed with capital. Then Canada exports bread, and the United States exports steel. The reasoning is the same as with the HO model. Since Canada is well endowed with the specific factor used to make bread, its opportunity cost of bread production is lower than it is in the United States, where land is relatively less abundant. Similarly, steel uses capital, which is abundant in the United States and relatively scarce in Canada.

The analysis of the income distribution effects of trade is straightforward. When trade opens, each country follows its comparative advantage and moves toward greater specialization. The shift in production alters the demand for the specific factor that is used in the industry that shrinks. In each country, the specific factor in the declining industry experiences a fall in income. For example, Canada cuts back on steel production in order to concentrate on bread, which it exports for steel. Canadian owners of capital are hurt, since the structure of the economy changes from the production of capital-intensive steel, while Canadian landowners experience precisely the opposite effect. Their incomes rise as the demand for land to produce bread exports rises. In the United States, landowners lose and capital owners win.

| Inputs | Bread | Steel |
|---|---|---|
| **TABLE 4.2 • A Specific Factors Model** | | |
| | **Outputs** | |
| Specific factors | Land | Capital |
| Variable factors | Labor | Labor |

The specific factors of land and capital can be used to produce only one good. The variable factor of labor is used in both bread and steel production.

In this example, the income distribution effects of trade on labor, the variable factor, are indeterminate. Since labor is mobile, workers laid off in the declining sector find employment in the expanding sector. Canadian workers find that steel is cheaper, so they are better off to the extent that they consume products that embody steel. On the other hand, the fact that the world price of bread is above the price Canadians paid in autarky means that they are worse off to the extent that their income goes to buy bread. The net effect on Canadian labor depends on which effect is strongest, rising bread prices or falling steel prices. U.S. workers face rising steel prices and falling bread prices, and, again, the net effect is ambiguous and depends on their consumption patterns.

## CASE STUDY

# Forecasts of Winners and Losers under NAFTA

When the United States, Mexico, and Canada began negotiations over the North American Free Trade Agreement (NAFTA), one of the major issues in the United States was the effect of free trade on the livelihood of various groups. The Heckscher-Ohlin trade model, the Stolper-Samuelson theorem, and the specific factors model were each used to analyze this effect.

Since the United States and Canada are similarly endowed with labor, capital, and land, and since they began a free-trade arrangement in 1989 (the Canadian–United States Trade Agreement, or CUSTA), NAFTA was not expected to significantly affect U.S.-Canadian trade. Mexico, however, was a different case. Where the United States and Canada have relatively abundant supplies of skilled labor, including scientists, engineers, managers, technicians, and professionals, Mexico has shortages of skilled labor and an abundant supply of unskilled and semiskilled labor. In addition, capital is relatively abundant in the United States and Canada and relatively scarce in Mexico. Finally, Mexico's climate and soils make it a good location to produce many kinds of fruits and vegetables, but it is a poor location for grains.

Given these simple observations, it was relatively straightforward to estimate the winners and losers in a U.S.-Mexico trade agreement. Mexican industries that were expected to pose the greatest challenge to the United States were the ones that combined the experience of Mexico's relatively scarce entrepreneurs and managers with its abundant supply of unskilled and semiskilled labor. To the extent that these industries could avoid large inputs of capital, they were likely to be even more competitive.

One of the first industries that was expected to gain was Mexico's small, but significant, apparel industry. Clothing manufacturing requires little capital, some managerial expertise to obtain orders for clothing and ensure their timely delivery to purchasers, and an abundant supply of relatively less-skilled labor. (The fashion design industry is another matter. The focus here is on basic, standardized apparel, such as undershirts and socks.) In the United States, large sections of this industry existed only as a result of U.S. quotas on imports. Consequently, many long-run forecasts of the impacts of NAFTA on U.S. garment workers were negative. Unions in the apparel industry were cognizant of this fact, and they formed one of the strongest bases of opposition to NAFTA. In effect, labor in the apparel industry viewed itself as a specific factor that, given their skills and location, was unable to shift to another line of employment.

Industries that are similar to clothing manufacturing are leather goods, furniture, and building materials (stone, clay, and glass manufacturers). Each requires some material inputs (wood, cloth, leather, stone, and so on), less capital than in more advanced manufacturing processes, and a lot of basic labor.

In the area of agriculture, it was forecast that some labor-intensive fruit and vegetable crops would expand into Mexico and contract in the United States. These included frozen vegetables such as broccoli and cauliflower, and citrus crops such as oranges for frozen juice. Not surprisingly, Florida citrus growers and California avocado growers opposed the agreement. As owners of specific factors (citrus and avocado groves), they had no alternative uses for their land.

On the other hand, U.S. crops that were capital intensive rather than labor intensive were expected to benefit. Notable examples are cereals (for human and animal consumption) and oilseeds. These crops use enormous quantities of agricultural machinery, together with extensive land inputs and a favorable climate to produce grains and legumes at prices that are competitive with the best in the world. In Mexico, producers of corn opposed the agreement.

A second type of industry that feared more open competition with Mexico was intermediate and basic manufacturing, such as automobiles, some kinds of industrial machinery (for example, pumps, diesel engines, and electrical motors), and fabricated metal products, such as screws and fasteners. The capital requirements for production are higher in these areas, but the products are well established. Scientific research or product development can be done in the United States if necessary, while production can move to Mexico.

Many autoworkers feared that under the terms of a more open North American market, U.S. automakers would relocate their capital to Mexico where unskilled and semiskilled labor are relatively abundant and inexpensive. Autoworkers viewed alternatives to their current employment as dismal, and therefore, they formed one of the strongest blocs against NAFTA.

In reality, the net effect of trade opening in basic and intermediate manufacturing is ambiguous. Mexico's ability to compete depends on a number of additional factors in the wider economy. For example, auto assembly requires delivery to the factory of thousands of parts. If they must come all the way from Detroit or Windsor, Ontario, it may be uneconomical to assemble cars in Mexico. (Forecasts were that the Mexican car industry will grow over time, but there is a debate as to whether this will be at the expense of U.S. and Canadian producers or at the expense of European and Japanese firms.) In addition to parts suppliers, these more capital-intensive manufacturing processes depend on reliable, low-cost transportation and communication systems, along with overall infrastructure, such as power systems, water delivery, and waste disposal.

In the United States and Canada, the industries that were expected to benefit included the very capital-intensive grain and oilseeds industries. In addition, it was expected that a wide variety of more advanced manufacturing industries, including telecommunications, computing, aircraft, measuring and control devices, chemicals, and so on, would see growing markets. Furthermore, a number of skilled, high-wage service industries were also expected to expand, including banking, insurance, business services, engineering services, and others. Like advanced manufacturing, each of these service industries requires highly skilled, well-educated labor.

Two good summaries of these issues are *North American Free Trade: Issues and Recommendations* (1992), by Jeffrey Schott and Gary Clyde Hufbauer, and *North American Free Trade: Assessing the Impact* (1992), edited by Nora Lustig, Barry P. Bosworth, and Robert Z. Lawrence. For a recent overview after ten years of implementation, see *NAFTA Revisited* (2005) by Gary Clyde Hufbauer and Jeffrey J. Schott.

# Empirical Tests of the Theory of Comparative Advantage

All the popular theories of trade are variations on the idea of comparative advantage. In addition, each theory makes predictions about the goods that a country will export and import. Therefore, it should be relatively straightforward to test each theory by holding its predictions up to actual trade flows and seeing if the two match. Unfortunately, empirical tests of trade theories are more difficult to conduct than they are to describe. Part of the problem is that it is difficult to measure variables such as factor endowments and prices in autarky.

The trade theories presented here and in Chapter 3 are the two most widely accepted by economists—the Ricardian theory of trade, based on relative productivities, and the Heckscher-Ohlin theory, based on factor endowments. In the Ricardian theory discussed in Chapter 3, comparative advantage depended on relative productivity. This model is easier to test because it is easier to measure labor productivity than factor endowments. Therefore, it is not surprising that statistical tests of the Ricardian theory have been more successful. In general, they have confirmed the hypothesis that trade patterns between pairs of countries are determined to a significant degree by the relative differences in their labor productivities. More specifically, as labor productivity in a particular industry increases, the greater the likelihood the country becomes a net exporter of the good.

Tests of the Heckscher-Ohlin theory of trade have been mixed. One of the problems for researchers in this area is that it is difficult to obtain a uniform set of measurements of factor endowments. In the presentation of the model in this chapter, only two inputs were considered, although we expanded that to three when we covered the specific factors model. In reality, there are many more than three factors. There are different kinds of labor (unskilled, semiskilled, managerial, technical, and so on), and there are many varieties of natural resources and capital. None of these categories has standardized definitions, and consequently each type of labor, capital, and natural resource is measured differently in each country. As a result, formal statistical analyses of tests of the HO theory have concluded that measurement errors in the data are a major problem.

Nevertheless, the consensus among economists seems to be that endowments matter, although they are far from the whole story. Even if it were possible to measure factor endowments accurately, technological differences between countries would not be captured, and these can be a significant source of productivity differences. In addition to technology, other important determinants of trade patterns not considered by the factor endowment theory are economies of scale, corporate structure, and economic policy.

While the theory of trade based on factor endowments receives mixed empirical support, nevertheless, it remains the foundation of most economists' thinking about trade. This may seem curious, but there is actually a good reason for it. While factor endowments cannot explain all of the world's trade patterns, they do explain a significant part of it. Therefore, it is useful to begin with factor endowments and to supplement this view with other ideas. Perhaps most importantly, the factor endowment schema is a useful way to categorize the income distribution effects of trade. For both these reasons, the HO model and its variations remain at the core of international economics.

 # Extension of the Heckscher-Ohlin Model

Several alternative trade models are popular in the literature. Both of the models presented next focus on an attribute of production in an industry or group of industries that makes them unlike the simple models assumed by the Ricardian and HO models. Both, however, are elaborations of the theory of comparative advantage. In Chapter 5 we will leave the comparative advantage framework and look at cases where trade is not determined by productivity differences or factor endowments.

## The Product Cycle

The **product cycle** model of trade was developed by Raymond Vernon. The model is an insightful analysis that incorporates ideas about the evolution of manufactured goods and technology. One of its greatest strengths is that it can explain exports of sophisticated manufactured goods from countries that have shortages of skilled labor and capital.

Vernon pointed out that many manufactured products, such as automobiles, VCRs, and semiconductors, go through a product cycle in which the inputs change over time. Initially, when these goods are brand new, there is a great deal of experimentation in both the characteristics of the final product and its manufacturing process. For example, when video machines were first developed for the home market, there was a wide variety of different forms to choose from. There were laser discs, Betamax, and VHS, each of which had different sets of options, often even within the same technology. That is, while Betamax differed from VHS, the features on a VHS machine were not standardized either.

In this early stage of production, manufacturers need to be near a high-income market, where consumer feedback is greatest. Experimentation with basic design features requires information about the market's reaction. Consequently, there must be a consumer base with substantial income and skilled marketing to advertise information about the product. In addition, on the input side, experimentation and improvement in design and manufacturing require scientific and engineering inputs, along with capital that is willing to risk failure and an initial period of little or no profits. Both the consumption side and the production side necessitate that product research, development, and initial production take place in industrial countries.

Over time, however, the product begins to leave the early phase of its development and production and enters the middle phase (see Figure 4.5 and Figure 4.6). The product itself begins to be standardized in size, features, and manufacturing process. Experimentation with fundamentally new designs begins to wane as product development shifts toward incremental improvements in a basic design. In the middle phase, production begins to shift to countries with low labor costs. Standardized manufacturing routines are increasingly common, using low-skilled and semiskilled labor in assembly type operations.

Countries reach the late phase of the product cycle when consumption in high-income nations begins to exceed production. At this point, an increasing share of the world's output is moving to developing countries where abundant

FIGURE 4.5 ● **The Product Cycle in High-Income Countries**

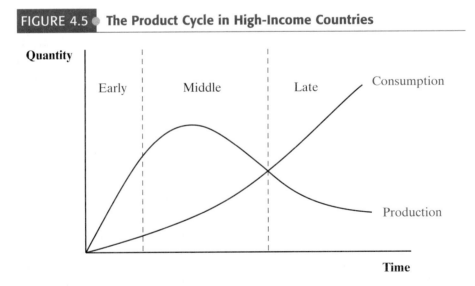

Many manufactured goods experience a product cycle of innovation, stabilization, and standardization.

**FIGURE 4.6** ● **The Product Cycle in Low-Income Countries**

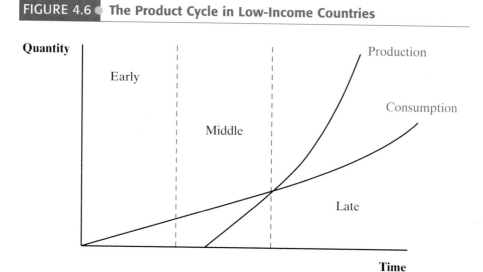

Low-income countries begin producing during the middle period when product design and production techniques begin to stabilize.

unskilled and semiskilled labor keeps labor costs low. The pressure on high-income countries in the late phase is to turn toward innovation of new products, which starts the cycle over again.

The product cycle is a more elaborate story about technology than either the Ricardian or HO models. It may seem to differ fundamentally from those models, but in fact it is very similar. At its core is a story about opportunity costs. As manufacturing processes become standardized, they can be performed by relatively unskilled labor. In effect, the blend of inputs changes over time, from highly skilled scientific, engineering, and marketing elements to basic unskilled and semiskilled labor. Consequently, the opportunity cost of production in developing countries becomes lower than the cost in high-income countries. In essence, it's the Ricardian story once again.

## Foreign Trade versus Foreign Investment

In the product cycle, firms invest abroad instead of exporting, and some of the output may be imported back into the home country. This pattern is very different from the simple Heckscher-Ohlin model where countries export one good and import another. First, it implies that under the conditions outlined in the product cycle, firms prefer to invest abroad rather than to export. That is, they substitute foreign investment for foreign trade. Second, the part of the output that they ship from their foreign operation back into the home country is international trade, but it is handled entirely within a single firm. That is, they engage in **intra-firm trade**: international trade between a parent company and a foreign-owned affiliate.

Intra-firm trade is difficult to measure, but in the mid-1990s, it was estimated that about one-third of U.S. merchandise exports and two-fifths of merchandise imports were intra-firm. Most foreign investment, however, is not for the purpose of exporting, but rather is intended to supply the market where the foreign investment is located. Whether for trade purposes or not, the selection of foreign investment instead of foreign trade poses a number of questions for economists and business scholars. Why do firms sometimes prefer to set up foreign-based operations instead of buying imports directly from a separate company located overseas? Or, if the foreign investment is for the purpose of selling in the foreign market, why don't companies export directly to the market instead of producing there? In essence, the questions are the same because both ask about the circumstances that cause foreign investment rather than foreign trade.

The product cycle provides one answer to these questions, but it is an incomplete answer, because it does not explain why a firm would invest in China instead of in Mexico. If labor costs are the only reason, then Africa would have the most foreign investment instead of the least of any continent. Furthermore, the product cycle is unable to explain why the greatest proportion of foreign investment goes to developed, industrial countries in Europe and North America where the comparative advantages are the same as or similar to those of the countries that supply the most foreign investment. According to World Bank data, developing countries (low- and middle-income) received just 11.4 percent of the world's foreign investment in 2000, with the developed world receiving the other 88.6 percent. While the share of developing countries varies from year to year, it rarely exceeds 30 percent.

Research into the trade-offs between investing abroad versus exporting from a home base acknowledges the importance of both the microeconomic characteristics of firms and the macroeconomic characteristics of countries that attract foreign investment. Microeconomic factors look at the internal constraints and opportunities of individual firms, while macroeconomic factors take into account the conditions inside countries that cause them to be suitable locations for a foreign firm to invest. The analytical framework that combines both sets of characteristics is known as the **OLI theory** of foreign direct investment. Its founder, John Dunning, offered it as an eclectic theory combining many different microeconomic and macroeconomic elements.

OLI is an acronym for *ownership-location-internalization*. In Dunning's analysis, firms investing abroad own an asset that gives them a competitive advantage in the world market (ownership). The asset may be something tangible, such as a patent, an innovation, a blueprint, or a trade secret. Or it may be something intangible, such as a trademark or the firm's reputation. In either case, ownership of a valuable asset confers a potential advantage on the firm. Second, the firm will seek a production location that offers them advantages (location). These may be in the form of low input costs, a large customer base, or an ability to produce a better product more efficiently due to the surrounding economic environment. Cheap labor is only one possibility, and if it does not come with a good infrastructure of roads and utilities, does not supply the skills that employers need, or is too far from the product's final market, then the fact that wages are low will not overcome the country's disadvantages.

Third, and most abstractly, the firm that invests abroad tries to capture within itself all the advantages that ownership of its asset confers (internalization). A firm that invests abroad can, if it chooses, simply sell the rights to its asset and let a foreign firm do the production—and in fact, many firms operate this way. That is, as an alternative, the investing firm can sell a license to its technology or its trademark or its trade secrets. Some firms, however, choose to take on the added costs of setting up production in a foreign location. There are many potential reasons for this choice, including the fear of theft or copy of its technology, the problem of monitoring and enforcing a contract with a foreign firm, and the concern that production mistakes by the foreign firm may hurt the reputation or trademark of the home country firm. Whatever the reason, the investing firm decides that it benefits more if it internalizes the advantages of asset ownership within itself rather than sells those advantages to another firm.

Dunning's analysis has been added to and extended by a large number of scholars who have found it to be a robust and adaptable description of the behavior of many firms. It is not a theory of trade, because it describes the circumstances that motivate firms to invest abroad rather than to engage in trade, but it does not contradict trade theory. Rather, it simply states that firms are internationally mobile and will use the comparative advantages they find in different locations. In this sense, it demonstrates how those advantages motivate individual firms to adapt their own behavior.

## CASE STUDY

# United States–China Trade

China is the world's most populous nation, with more than 1.3 billion people in mid-2000, according to the U.S. Census Bureau. The World Bank puts its GNP per capita at the equivalent of $1,500 (at market exchange rates, 2004). About 5 percent of China's men and 13.5 percent of its women are estimated to be illiterate.

China's economy was substantially closed to the outside until 1978, when it began significant economic reforms. Initially, the reforms were limited to agriculture, but they quickly incorporated a number of special economic zones in the coastal regions (see Chapter 17). China's proximity to Hong Kong, along with large populations of Chinese in Taiwan, Hong Kong, Singapore, and other regions of East Asia, enabled it to attract huge amounts of foreign investment once it became receptive to capital inflows. The net result is that its economy and, especially, its exports have grown rapidly over the last two decades.

China's resource endowment includes a huge population of unskilled and semiskilled labor and a relative scarcity of scientific and engineering talent. It is not surprising, therefore, that its exports are heavily weighted toward labor-intensive manufactured goods. Table 4.3 lists the top ten Chinese exports to the United States in 2002. The major items are simple manufactured goods that use China's abundant labor together with a little capital: toys, shoes, plastic items, and so on. In the top ten, items 2, 4, 5, 9, and 10 fall into this category. Items 7 and 8 might also be categorized as producing a relatively unsophisticated product with labor-intensive manufacturing.

Items 1, 3, and 6, however, appear to be different. These are high-technology items related to telecommunications and computing (data processing), and they also illustrate the product cycle. These Chinese exports originate in assembly operations, many of which have been set up with capital from outside China. A telephone manufacturer, for example, decides to take advantage of low wages by producing a standardized product in China. Once the assembly plant is built, only a handful of skilled workers are required to keep it running. Most workers can be quickly trained to fasten pieces and to perform simple diagnostic tests on the product. The result is that China exports telecommunications equipment and appears to have a developing high-technology sector. Very little design, research, or industrial engineering take place there, however.

Similarly, not too long ago, CD and DVD players (item 7) were exclusively products of industrial countries. They became standardized, along with the methods for producing them, and production migrated to places where unskilled labor was relatively more abundant. In sum, China's successful export drive has utilized two forces: a shift toward its comparative advantage and the product cycle.

| TABLE 4.3 • Top 10 Chinese Exports to the United States, 2004 | |
|---|---|
| Item | Value, Millions of US$ |
| 1. Automatic data processing machines | 24,461 |
| 2. Toys and sporting goods | 17,569 |
| 3. Telecommunications equipment | 12,097 |
| 4. Footwear | 11,351 |
| 5. Furniture and bedding accessories | 10,910 |
| 6. Parts for office machines data processing machines | 9,266 |
| 7. Sound recorders and TV recorders | 7,605 |
| 8. Household electric and nonelectric equipment | 4,546 |
| 9. Articles of plastic | 4,264 |
| 10. Trunks, suitcases, vanity cases, and briefcases | 4,044 |

China's labor endowment and the product cycle explain its exports to the United States.

*Source*: U.S. Department of Commerce, *United States Foreign Trade Highlights, 2005*. http://www.ita.doc.gov/td/industry/otea/usfth/top80cty/china.html (August 2006).

# Outsourcing

**Outsourcing** is the relocation of service industry functions to another country. What makes it distinctive and a recent topic for popular discussion is the services element, which is a relatively new development. Historically, most services have been consumed at the point of production, but with growing trade in services, largely driven by developments in communication technologies, it has become possible to relocate some service production away from the point of consumption. For example, a doctor in the United States or Europe might consult a colleague in India who is specialized in reading a particular type of x-ray. The Internet and increased efficiencies in telephony make it possible for doctors in both places to see the same image and to communicate with each other easily and cheaply.

Economists have just begun to analyze outsourcing and most government agencies have not yet begun to collect the kinds of statistics that are necessary in order to have a clear picture of its consequences and its extent. Nevertheless, the first generation of research and analysis points toward a conclusion that is consistent with our traditional understanding of trade and comparative advantage — there is no obvious reason why trade in services should be different from trade in goods. If an automaker decides to import a particular auto part because the combination of cost and quality favor foreigner producers, then the theory of comparative advantage shows how the nation is a little better off than it would be if we made the part at home. Services imports and exports should not be any different in this regard, and specialization and trade should provide the same or similar gains for services as they do for goods.

The concern over outsourcing probably stems from the fact that services are historically traded less across borders. Service trade statistics mainly reflect consumption abroad (for example, expenditures by foreign tourists), or the delivery of services by a foreign firm with a local presence (for example, shipping), or through the travel of a service provider to a foreign country (for example, business consulting). Until recently, however, it was much less common for the service provider to be located in a different country from the service consumer. But with the Internet, inexpensive long distance phone service, fax machines, video conferencing, and other advances in telecommunications, it is possible for companies to locate some of their service industry functions abroad. If a Pakistani or Indian firm can provide a cheaper service, then the home-based company benefits by lowering its costs and consumers benefit from lower prices.

The main focus of debate about outsourcing is the issue of job loss. Outsourcing is particularly unsettling for workers who have felt immune from international trade, and it seems to be another instance of creeping globalization making life less certain. Nevertheless, the first generation of research and analysis of outsourcing raises a number of questions about the assumptions behind this concern. For example, it appears that in many instances, outsourcing is complementary to home production rather than a substitute. Consequently, outsourcing is often associated with an expansion of jobs and production rather than a contraction.

It seems safe to assume that outsourcing will continue to grow, as overall services trade has recently grown at a slightly faster pace than goods trade and technological changes favor increased flexibility for the location of service consumption and production. Given that outsourcing is likely to increase, its policy implications are important to consider. As in the case for expanded goods trade, expanded trade in services implies a need to consider expanded trade assistance for displaced workers and to ensure strong overall job growth. Some economists, however, have argued that a loosening of immigration restrictions would work best, since rather than sending work abroad, it might be more efficient to bring workers to the home economy.

## Migration and Trade

According to the World Bank, in the year 2000 there were over 176 million international migrants spread around the world. More than half (55 percent) were located in high-income countries, and nearly 20 percent (19.7 percent) were in the United States. The presence of large numbers of international migrants stands in stark contrast to the assumptions of the HO model and the assumption of a fixed supply of each input, including labor. The basic model considers labor and other factors as mobile between sectors, moving from bread to steel and back as necessary and implicitly moving within a country if that is required. Although the HO model does not make any assumptions about the physical location of production, migration within a country is assumed to occur if necessary. International migration, on the other hand, is ruled out since it alters the labor endowment and, potentially, a country's comparative advantage.

Economists have long studied migration, as have sociologists, demographers, political scientists, and other social scientists. Each discipline brings its own tools of analysis and contributes another piece to our understanding of the determinants and effects of migration. Sociologists and anthropologists, for example, have helped to clarify that the decision to migrate is often a family decision or, in some cases, a community decision to send one of its members abroad. Political scientists have helped to clarify how migration policies are set and enforced, or not enforced, as the case may be. The economic view of migration tends to understand it in terms of the individual migrant and the underlying incentives to migrate. In this view, economic incentives play a major role by determining the factors that cause migrants to leave and the factors that attract them to a particular destination.

Economists refer to **supply-push factors** as the forces inside a country that cause people to think about leaving. Push factors include recessions, long-run structural changes that cause job dislocations, wars, natural disasters, and anything else that makes life difficult at home. Examples of structural changes include the recent transformations of central European economies, Latin American economic reforms, and industrial development in many parts of the globe. In the near future, we can expect large migrations from changing agricultural patterns and the inundation of coastal areas as a result of climate change. Any factor that makes it difficult to continue in the same line of work or to remain in the same location will cause some residents to leave or to send a family member where they can earn a better income and contribute to the family's survival. **Demand-pull factors** are the forces that pull migrants to a particular country or place within a country. Key factors include the cost of reaching a particular destination, the probability of finding a job, and the wage that will be earned. The wage gap between developed countries and developing countries explains a large share of the flow of migrants, but other factors are important as well. The business cycle in the receiving country, its migration policies, and the overall set of opportunities encountered by foreign workers are all important demand-pull factors. A third factor determining migration is the existence of **social networks**. Migrants do not scatter randomly around a desirable destination, but instead congregate in certain places. This is partly due to job opportunities, but it also reflects the fact that migration is hard and expensive and the presence of family or community members makes it a little easier. The supply of information about the new locale is better if there are already migrants who can report home on conditions, and who can help newcomers become established with a place to live, a job, and familiar faces to ward off loneliness.

In theory, if the endowment of a particular factor increases, then the relative abundance of the factor and, potentially, its comparative advantage also change. In practice, labor inflows are often used to produce services that are not traded. For example, the three countries with the largest percentages of foreigners in their population are Qatar (76.0 percent), United Arab Emirates (70.4 percent), and Kuwait (63.4 percent). A large share of the foreign workers in those countries are Filipinos, Palestinians, and other migrants who work as domestics, providing cleaning, cooking, day care, and other services that cannot be traded. These migrants do not have a direct impact on the host countries comparative advantage since the labor is not used to produce tradable goods (although they free up citizens to work in the export sector). However, many migrant workers are also engineers and business specialists, who provide technical expertise to the oil and gas industry. Without some high-skilled migrant labor, it is possible that production in these three oil and gas producing countries would be much more limited.

Most international migration is from developing to developed countries. For example, in the 1980s and 1990s, civil wars in Central America produced large outflows of Salvadorian and Guatemalan immigrants to the United States, many of whom settled in California where some found employment in apparel manufacturing. California's apparel sector added over 40,000 jobs between 1983 and 1997 (a growth of almost 50 percent), largely based on the availability of low wage, unskilled immigrant workers. Given that apparel is a declining sector in the United States, immigrant labor appears to have postponed the decline of the industry in California for about a decade. In the long run, however, apparel continues to decline as the immigrants are assimilated into the U.S. economy. Other U.S. examples of where immigration influences comparative advantage include certain agricultural crops that depend on abundant supplies of immigrant labor and the tourism industry. Over the long run, however, assimilation occurs and the children or grandchildren of migrants (if not the migrants themselves) become similar to non-migrants, both in terms of their skills and their wages.

 # The Impact of Trade on Wages and Jobs

Since the 1960s, manufacturing in North America and Europe has become a smaller part of the economy when measured as a share of GDP and as a share of overall employment. In Europe, the assumption that a shrinking manufacturing sector is a significant problem has been emphasized by high rates of overall unemployment and very slow growth in the total number of new jobs created. At the same time, wage inequality has increased, rather slowly at first, then more rapidly in the 1980s. Wage inequality has been particularly severe in the United States and has primarily affected younger workers and workers with less education or fewer skills.

Does trade with low-wage countries cause wages to fall in high-wage countries? Are industrialized countries losing jobs to developing countries? Organized opposition to trade is usually premised on these points. It is probably no surprise that U.S. public opinion about the impact of trade on wages and jobs is divided along educational and skill lines, with more highly educated and more skilled workers favoring reduced trade barriers, and less skilled and less educated workers opposing. These are average characterizations, however, and it is not hard to find highly educated workers who oppose freer trade and poorly educated workers who support it.

One issue is whether trade has a negative impact on the number of jobs available to workers in high-wage countries. Economic theory offers some evidence on this issue. In the medium run and long run, the absolute number of jobs depends mainly on factors such as the age and size of the population, rules governing the hiring and firing of employees (labor market policies), and the generosity of the social safety net (incentives to work). In the short run, one of the primary determinants of the number of jobs is the government's macroeconomic policies, which determine variables such as interest rates, taxes, and overall government expenditures. While trade may have a short-run effect as well, particularly if firms cannot compete against imports, or if sudden opportunities for export expansion appear, these impacts are usually outweighed by macroeconomic policies affecting the entire domestic economy. By comparison, changes in trade flows usually affect one or two manufacturing industries and a small share of overall GDP. Trade will certainly affect the composition of jobs, but it is unlikely to have much impact on the overall number of jobs.

The last point is worth emphasizing. Trade definitely causes some firms to shut down. In sectors where competition from imports is particularly intense, it is not unusual to read about factories that close their doors as a result of competition from developing countries. Import competition is especially fierce, for example, in apparel, certain types of electrical machinery, motor vehicle manufacturing, footwear, some types of textiles, and toys and sporting goods. In these industries, there are numerous examples in industrial countries of plant closures due to a loss of competitiveness

The problem of persistently high unemployment in some European countries, such as Spain and France, cannot be caused by trade. In those cases, the inability of laid-off workers to find new jobs must be attributed to labor market policies that restrict job creation or macroeconomic policies that restrict overall economic growth. Ten or fifteen years of high unemployment, which has been the norm in many European countries, is a long enough time for even the most radical restructuring to occur. The fact that unemployment remains high means that new jobs are not created elsewhere in the economy.

A majority of the reductions in manufacturing employment in all industrial countries appears to have resulted from productivity gains, not trade. Manufacturing is easier to automate than services and as a consequence has much faster rates of productivity growth than services. Because productivity grows so fast in manufacturing, it takes fewer and fewer people to produce the products we consume. Many services, on the other hand, have stagnant or very slow rates of productivity growth. Often, the same number of workers is required today as it was centuries ago; one haircut, for example, still takes one barber (who may or may not be faster), and modern musicians are no more "productive" at playing Bach's Brandenburg Concertos than they were in the 1700s. When incomes rise, we consume more services and more manufactured goods, but because the services require more or less the same number of workers per unit made, and manufactured goods can be made with fewer workers per good, a growing share of our total employment ends up in services.

The second issue concerns the impact of trade with less-developed countries (LDCs) on the wages of workers in the advanced industrial economies. This question has been studied by many economists, and the general consensus is that trade may have caused some of the decline in wages for the less skilled (and, hence, some of the increase in wage inequality), but it is responsible for only a small share of the overall changes. The primary culprit seems to be technological changes that have reduced the role of unskilled and semiskilled labor in manufacturing.

The Stolper-Samuelson theorem predicts that if the United States and other industrial countries have relatively scarce supplies of unskilled labor (by comparison to less-developed countries), then trade will cause the wages of unskilled workers to fall. Over the years, however, firms can alter their use of inputs to take advantage of cheaper unskilled labor and to conserve on more expensive skilled labor. The key is that the time frame must be sufficiently long so that firms can alter their capital and other inputs. In the case of skilled and unskilled labor the reverse has happened. As skilled labor has become more expensive, firms have used relatively more, and as unskilled labor has become cheaper, they have used less. This trend has gone on for over two decades, so firms have had plenty of time to alter their production technologies if they can. One explanation is that technology has created larger roles for skilled labor and smaller ones for the unskilled.

While it seems the consensus of professional economic opinion is that technological change and not trade is responsible for the lion's share of both the decline in manufactured jobs and the growth of wage inequality, there is also a widespread recognition that economists really aren't sure. A small number of economists continue to argue that trade has played a far larger role in the growth of wage inequality than is generally recognized. If they are correct, the policy conclusions are likely to be the same. In both cases, where trade is responsible for inequality and where it is not, there is a need for education and training programs targeted at the less skilled. Chapters 6 and 7 will show that blocking trade to protect jobs is extraordinarily expensive, and doing so to protect wages will actually make things worse in the long run.

 # Summary

- The Heckscher-Ohlin (HO) model hypothesizes that comparative advantage is based on national differences in factor endowments. Countries export goods that have production requirements that are intensive in the nation's relatively abundant factors. They import goods that require intensive input from the nation's relatively scarce factors.

- The Heckscher-Ohlin model has implications for the income distribution effects of trade. The opening of trade favors the abundant factor and reduces the use of the scarce factor. Consequently, the income or returns earned by the abundant factor rises, while it falls for the scarce factor. A corollary to the Heckscher-Ohlin model, called the Stolper-Samuelson theorem, describes these effects.

- In the specific factors model, some factors of production are assumed to be immobile between different outputs. Consequently, when trade expands the production of it, the specific factor used to produce it experiences a rise in the demand for its services, and its income increases. The specific factor used to produce the import good experiences a fall in the demand for its services, and its income declines. The specific factors model can be viewed as a short- to medium-run version of the HO model.

- Empirical tests of the theory of comparative advantage give mixed results. While underlying productivity differences explain a significant share of trade, national differences in factor endowments are less successful at explaining trade patterns.

- Several alternative trade models have been hypothesized. Most are elaborations of the theory of comparative advantage. Two of the most popular alternative trade theories are the theory of the product cycle and the theory of intra-firm trade. The product cycle focuses on the speed of technological change and the life history of many manufactured items through periods of innovation, stabilization, and standardization. The theory of intra-firm trade allows a role for comparative advantage but also has industrial organization elements. It is impossible to state a general rule about the determinants of intra-firm trade.

- Outsourcing is the relocation of service industry functions to another country. Advances in telecommunications enable production of an increasing number of services to be located away from their place of consumption. The same analysis that is used for trade in goods applies to trade in services, including the conclusion of gains from trade.

- International migration can alter a country's comparative advantage, although in practice most countries do not receive enough migrants or a sufficiently long enough flow of migrants to cause long-run changes. Migrants are motivated by supply-push factors in their home country, demand-pull factors in the receiving country, and social networks that provide information and resources for settling in the new country.

- In the medium to long run, trade has little or no effect on the number of jobs in a country. The abundance or scarcity of jobs is a function of labor market policies, incentives to work, and the macroeconomic policies of the central bank and government. In the short run, trade may reduce jobs in an industry that suffers a loss in its competitiveness, just as it may increase jobs in an industry with growing competitiveness.

- The consensus among economists is that trade between developing and high-income countries may have contributed slightly to the decline in real wages for unskilled workers in the industrial economies. This is consistent with the predictions of the Stolper-Samuelson theorem. The main cause of increasing wage inequality is thought to be technological changes that have reduced the demand for unskilled labor and increased it for skilled, highly educated labor. This point is not settled, however, and continues to receive a significant amount of empirical investigation.

# Vocabulary

| | |
|---|---|
| demand-pull factors | OLI theory |
| derived demand | outsourcing |
| factor abundance | product cycle |
| factor scarcity | social networks |
| Heckscher-Ohlin (HO) trade theory | specific factors model |
| intra-firm trade | Stolper-Samuelson theorem |
| magnification effect | supply-push factors |

## Study Questions

1. According to the following table, which country is relatively more labor-abundant? Explain your answer. Which country is relatively capital-abundant?

|  | United States | Canada |
| --- | --- | --- |
| **Capital** | 40 machines | 10 machines |
| **Labor** | 200 workers | 60 workers |

2. Suppose that the United States and Canada have the factor endowments in the preceding table. Suppose further that the production requirements for a unit of steel are two machines and eight workers, and the requirement for a unit of bread is one machine and eight workers.

   a. Which good, bread or steel, is relatively capital-intensive? Labor-intensive? Explain your answer.

   b. Which country would export bread? Why?

3. Suppose that before trade takes place, the United States is at a point on its PPC where it produces 20 loaves of bread and 20 units of steel. Once trade becomes possible, the price of a unit of steel is two units of bread. In response, the United States moves along its PPC to a new point where it produces 30 units of steel and 10 units of bread. Is the country better off? How do you know?

4. Given the information in Study Questions 1 and 2, explain what happens to the returns to capital and labor after trade begins.

5. Suppose that there are three factors: capital, labor, and land. Bread requires inputs of land and labor, and steel requires capital and labor.

   a. Which factors are variable, and which are specific?

   b. Suppose Canada's endowments are 10 capital and 100 land and the United States' are 50 capital and 100 land. Which good does each country export?

   c. How does trade affect the returns to land, labor, and capital in the United States and in Canada?

6. Describe the changes in production requirements and location of production that take place over the three phases of the product cycle.

7. Does intra-firm trade contradict the theory of comparative advantage? Why or why not?

8. General Motors is a U.S.-based multinational, but it is also one of the largest car manufacturers in Europe and South America. How might Dunning's OLI theory explain the trade-offs GM faced as it decided whether to export to those two markets or to produce in them?

9. Many domestically owned apparel manufacturers buy their garments overseas, sew their labels into them, and then sell them abroad or back into the home market. What are some of the considerations that a clothing manufacturer might go through to choose this strategy instead of producing at home and exporting?

10. Suppose Spain was to open its borders to the large number of unskilled Africans seeking to immigrate. In general, what effects would you expect to see in Spain's trade patterns and its comparative advantage?

## APPENDIX

# Finding Trade Data

## U.S. Data

Data on U.S. trade in individual commodities are easy to find. The problem for the first-time user of U.S. data is to make sense of the classifications used to categorize goods and services. Export and import statistics are initially collected and compiled into 8,000 and 14,000 commodity classifications, respectively. These classifications conform to a standard for classifying goods known as the Harmonized Commodity Description and Coding System, or the Harmonized System (HS). The HS was developed by the Customs Cooperation Council in Brussels, Belgium, and included participants from the United States, Canada, Western Europe, and Japan. A source of confusion is that the description of U.S. data in HS format bears the names TSUSA (Tariff Schedule for the United States, Annotated) for imports and Schedule B for exports.

A second system of classifying goods is also used by the United States, the United Nations, and many other nations. This is the Standard International Trade Classification (SITC). The SITC is on its third revision, so it is sometimes called the SITC-Rev. 3. The Harmonized System and the SITC are interrelated, and in effect, the SITC scheme is an aggregation of the HS. For example, the United States takes its 8,000 HS categories of exports and summarizes them into 3,000 SITC categories, which it calls Schedule E. The HS categories for imports are rearranged in SITC codes and called Schedule A. The SITC system is useful for international comparisons and is the form in which the most commonly available U.S. publications present their data.

Table 4.4 lists the names used by U.S. publications to label imports and exports, classified according to the HS or SITC system. For example, reading across the row labeled Exports, we see that HS export data is called Schedule B and that Schedule E is the rearrangement of the data into SITC format.

Three other commodity classifications are in use, and although they are of lesser importance worldwide, they are relevant for research on the United States. One is another summarization of the HS into what is called the End Use Commodity Category. It consists of 6 principal categories and 140 broad category definitions. Several of the more commonly found U.S. publications use these commodity definitions to summarize reported data. Another classification scheme is the Standard Industrial Classification (SIC) code, which is used to classify industries. The SIC code and the associated trade data have been replaced with the North American Industrial Classification System (NAICS), which is a harmonization of the codes of Canada, Mexico, and the United States. The SIC and its replacement, the NAICS, are the primary systems for reporting information about industries. Having the trade data on the same basis allows comparisons to be made between industries and for the trade data to be linked up with the characteristics of particular industries. A complete description with additional detail can be found on the International Trade Administration's (ITA) Web site: http://www.ita.doc.gov/td/industry/otea/trade_data_basics.html.

Free online data is also available from the ITA (http://www.ita.doc.gov). *Trade Stats Express* is a quick way to download national U.S. data and state level data. It is available at http://tse.export.gov. In addition, *United States Foreign Trade Highlights* provides a large amount of product and country specific data spanning several years: http://www.ita.doc.gov/td/industry/otea/usfth/. You can find trade by region, by commodity (under the HS, SITC, and SIC classification schemes), and by country. In addition, the ITA site shows exports by state and city.

## International Data

Most international data are presented in the SITC-Rev. 3 format. The following are leading sources:

1. *The World Trade Organization* provides trade statistics for all its member countries. Its databases can be found at http://www.wto.org/english/res_e/ statis_e/statis_e.htm.

2. *International Trade Centre (ITC)* (http://www.intracen.org). The ITC is a partnership between the UN and the WTO. It provides a wide variety of free, online trade data, including export profiles of individual countries, an index of online trade data from commercial and noncommercial sources, and five years of trade statistics for most of the world's nations, classified in SITC-Rev. 3 format.

| TABLE 4.4 • U.S. Names for Trade Data Classifications Schemes | | |
| --- | --- | --- |
| | Harmonized System (HS) | Standard International Trade Classification (SITC) |
| **Exports** | Schedule B | Schedule E |
| **Imports** | Tariff Schedule of the United States, Annotated (TSUSA) | Schedule A |

**3.** *International Trade Statistics Yearbook.* The *Yearbook* is published by the United Nations, along with the more general *Statistical Yearbook.* The *Yearbook* of trade statistics is more detailed in its treatment of commodity flows. Goods are classified on the basis of SITC-Rev. 3 codes. It is useful for historical data. The United Nations also provides data online through the United Nations Statistics Division: http://unstats.un.org/unsd/databases.htm. The UN COMTRADE database is an extensive database for 140 countries. It is available online by subscription only.

**4.** *Direction of Trade Statistics (DOTS). DOTS* is one of several sister publications of the International Monetary Fund. *DOTS* is an easy-to-use source of information on trade between pairs of countries. It has annual data for the most recent seven or eight years, along with percentage changes. *DOTS* does not disaggregate the data by commodity.

# 5 Beyond Comparative Advantage

##  Introduction: More Reasons to Trade

The idea of comparative advantage is the foundation of our understanding of the gains from trade and its potential income distribution effects. Unfortunately, trade models built exclusively on the idea of comparative advantage have a mixed record when it comes to predicting a country's trade patterns. This is an important failure since we tend to think that if we accurately measure a country's comparative advantage, we should be able to predict import and export patterns. In addition, if we know in advance what specific products an economy could produce at the lowest relative cost, it would give policymakers and entrepreneurs a definite advantage in deciding what to produce. The problem, however, is that it is exceedingly difficult to measure a country's comparative advantage. This problem is compounded by the fact that there are many potential products an economy might export that use the same comparative advantage, and there is no way to determine which specific products will dominate. Furthermore, and perhaps most seriously, a large share of international trade is not based on comparative advantage. This chapter takes up two important exceptions to the models of the previous chapters, and examines how and why many countries try to select and plan the development of their export industries.

The first section tries to make sense of the fact that an important share of world trade consists of countries exporting the same thing they import. Canada and the United States, for example, have the largest trade relationship in the world, and a large share of it is based on both countries exporting cars and car parts to each other. This pattern is clearly at odds with the bread-for-steel examples shown in Chapters 3 and 4. In the second section of the chapter, we examine industrial clustering. Many traded goods and services that are essential parts of a country's exports are produced in regional clusters. For example, the U.S. advantage in entertainment products (music, television programming, and movies) largely reflects the output of a handful of regions such as Hollywood and Nashville. Software reflects clusters in Silicon Valley, Seattle, and a few other spots, and biotechnology is in San Francisco,

San Diego, and a handful of other places. Surprisingly, international trade can play an important role in this type of clustering and may, under certain conditions, prevent new clusters from forming.

The issue of regional clusters leads directly into a discussion of industrial policies in the third section of the chapter. Industrial policies are used to address the challenge of trying to plan an advantage in a particular industry or a group of products. Can countries pick the items they will export and successfully build a strong export industry? What are the costs and benefits of the policies they follow? At bottom, we are asking if comparative advantage is mutable and how nations can use their policies to shape its development.

 # Intraindustry Trade

The models of comparative advantage developed in Chapters 3 and 4 are built on the foundation of country differences. In those models, differences in productivity (Chapter 3) or factor endowments (Chapter 4) make it possible for countries to raise their living standards by specializing their production and trading. The point of these models is not to paint a detailed portrait of economic life, but rather to create a simplified abstract model of the economy that is focused on key economic relations in the area of trade. To that end, unnecessary details are omitted, and rare or exceptional cases are ignored.

Sometimes it happens that rare or exceptional cases become more important over time. Such is the case with the increasing importance of **intraindustry trade** (the prefix "intra" means *within*). Intraindustry trade is the international trade of products made within the same industry, for example steel-for-steel, or bread-for-bread. The opposite of intraindustry trade is **interindustry trade** (the prefix "inter" means *between*). Interindustry trade is international trade of products between two different industries (for example, bread-for-steel). The growing importance of intraindustry trade has forced economists to develop a new set of models in order to explain the reasons why countries often export the same goods they import, and to explain the benefits from this type of trade.

## Measures of Intraindustry Trade

Intraindustry trade between industrial countries is common. Empirical measures of the importance of intraindustry trade vary, however, because of the fundamental problem of defining an industry. For example, if computers are defined as office machinery, then computers and pencil sharpeners are in the same industry and a country that exports computers and imports pencil sharpeners would engage in intraindustry trade. In general, the broader the definition of an industry, the more trade appears to be intraindustry. Conversely, the more detailed the definition, the less trade is defined as intraindustry. Intraindustry trade is measured for each industry with the following statistic called the **Grubel-Lloyd (GL) index**:

$$GL_i = 1 - \frac{|X_i - M_i|}{X_i + M_i}$$

The equation says that the index for any industry (industry "i") is calculated by taking the absolute value of the trade balance for the industry, $|X_i - M_i|$, dividing it by exports plus imports from the same industry, $X_i + M_i$, and subtracting the ratio from 1. If exports of a domestic industry are equal to the value of imports from the same industry ($X_i = M_i$), then the numerator in the ratio is equal to 0 and the index equals 1. In that case, all of the industry's trade is intraindustry. Conversely, if a country only exports or only imports, then either $X_i$ or $M_i$ will be 0. In that case, the numerator equals the denominator, the index is 0, and none of the industry's trade is intraindustry. In order to calculate the index for the whole economy and not just for one industry, both the numerator and the denominator of the ratio are summed over all industries before calculating the ratio, and the result is subtracted from 1.

Estimates of the share of total U.S. merchandise trade that is intraindustry range between one-third and two-thirds, depending on the narrowness of the definitions of industry. When narrow definitions are used, so that goods are classified together only when they are very similar, U.S. intraindustry trade is more than 50 percent of total merchandise trade (excluding services and food). This pattern is repeated for most industrial countries, and probably more than 40 percent of total world trade is intraindustry. Evidence suggests that intraindustry trade is greater in high technology industries where the rapid generation of new products leads to greater product differentiation, and is greater in countries with few barriers to trade. Intraindustry trade also grows in importance as a nation's income rises.

## Characteristics of Intraindustry Trade

In the models of comparative advantage-based trade presented in Chapters 3 and 4, production costs are either constant (Chapter 3) or increasing (Chapter 4). Accordingly, each additional unit of bread produced led to the loss of a fixed or increasing amount of steel. The production of many goods, however, is characterized by economies of scale, or decreasing costs, over a relatively large range of output. Economies of scale can be either **internal economies of scale** or **external economies of scale**. Internal economies are defined as falling average costs over a relatively large range of output. In practice, this leads to larger firms because size confers a competitive advantage in the form of lower average costs. One of the distinguishing features of intraindustry trade is the presence of internal economies of scale. In the case of external economies, larger firms have no inherent advantage over smaller firms, but average costs decline for all firms as the size of the industry increases. Unlike internal economies of scale, with external economies, the size or scale effects are located in the industry and not in the firm. We will examine external economies when we look at industrial clustering later in the chapter.

| TABLE 5.1 • **Increasing Returns to Scale for a Single Firm** | | |
| --- | --- | --- |
| Output | Total Cost | Average Cost |
| 100 | 1000 | 10 |
| 200 | 1400 | 7 |
| 300 | 1500 | 5 |
| 400 | 1600 | 4 |
| 500 | 1650 | 3.5 |
| 600 | 1950 | 3.25 |

As production increases, total costs rise, but the cost per unit falls. Bigger firms are more efficient than smaller firms.

Table 5.1 illustrates a firm's cost structure when it experiences increasing returns to scale. More output leads to higher costs, but the cost per unit, or average cost, declines. In most cases, with increasing production levels, average cost eventually begins to rise. In a few cases, such as commercial jet aircraft discussed later in the chapter, the output level at which average cost starts to rise is equal to a large share of the entire world market and, consequently, large firms have enormous advantages. Increasing returns are usually based on the inherent development, engineering, or marketing aspects of production and are associated with products that have a large fixed cost component. Car companies, software, and popular household brand name products, to name a few, tend to have large fixed costs. These occur for various reasons, such as the cost of constructing a large production plant, large R&D budgets, or large marketing expenditures. Software, for example, requires large up-front expenditures on R&D to develop a product, and the more units a firm can sell, the more it can spread out those fixed R&D costs.

Internal economies of scale have important implications for the type of market that prevails. In Chapters 3 and 4, it is assumed that firms operate in competitive markets where no one firm can influence prices or overall industry output. When larger firms are more competitive, however, it reduces the number of firms in a market and leads to one of several types of market structures. In an **oligopoly**, a handful of firms produce the entire market output. In this case, the pattern of production and trade is very difficult to predict because each firm uses predictions about the actions of its competitors as it formulates its own profit-maximizing strategy. This type of response means that each firm alters its output level as it sees what its competitors are doing, and production levels and trade become less predictable. An example is presented later in the chapter when we discuss industrial policies and strategic trade theory.

Often, internal economies lead to the relatively common market structure called **monopolistic competition**. Recall that in a pure monopoly, one firm produces the entire industry output. In monopolistic competition, there is competition among many firms, but their competition is attenuated by the practice of **product differentiation**. With product differentiation, each firm produces a slightly different product. This gives rise to the monopoly element of monopolistic competition, in that each firm is the sole producer of its products. For |example, only Ford can sell Ford Explorers. Unlike a pure monopoly, however, every other firm produces a close substitute and this introduces a real element of competition.

In monopolistic competition, the level of competition among firms increases whenever new firms enter the market. This has two effects. On the one hand, heightened competition will lead to lower prices because products are substitutes for each other and in the struggle to capture sales, downward pressure is placed on prices. On the other hand, when more firms divide the market, on average each firm sells fewer units of output, and so costs rise. This follows directly from the internal economies of each firm. As long as prices are above costs, more firms will enter the market, and whenever prices are below costs, firms exit.

The presence of internal economies of scale is the reason why firms want to enter export markets. Any firm that exports has a competitive advantage since it will have higher sales and be able to take advantage of the cost-reducing effects of its internal economies of scale. For any given number of firms, average costs are lower in a larger market. This follows from the economies of scale that each firm experiences and the fact that if the number of firms is held constant, each firm sells more as the size of the market expands.

## The Gains from Intraindustry Trade

Intraindustry trade also creates gains from trade. While the increase in the size of the market leads to lower costs through the effect of scale economies, competition among firms forces them to pass on their lower costs to consumers in the form of lower prices. Lower prices for exports and imports stands in marked contrast to the case of comparative advantage-based trade. Recall that in the trade models of Chapters 3 and 4, each country's consumers benefit from a reduction in the price of the good it imports, but at the same time, the price of the export rises. With intraindustry trade, however, prices for imports and exports decline, leading to unambiguous benefits for consumers in both countries. Trade enables firms to produce for a larger market and at a higher level of efficiency. That raises everyone's real income through the reduction in prices.

The expansion of the market that occurs with trade ultimately leads to an increase in the number of firms. This follows from the fact that exports create a situation where costs are below prices, attracting new firms into the market until excess profits are competed away. It is indeterminate if the increase in the number of firms comes about through an increase in domestic or foreign firms, or how the increase might be divided between the two. While it is safe to say that the combined foreign and domestic industry will expand, the location of the expansion is indeterminate. It is even conceivable that foreigners might expand disproportionately and leave the domestic industry smaller than it was initially. While this cannot be ruled out, in general, intraindustry trade is usually perceived as less threatening to jobs and firms than comparative advantage-based trade. This difference is primarily due to the decline of the import sector in comparative advantage-based trade, and the need for some or all of its workers to look for work in the expanding export sector. By contrast, in intraindustry trade, there is a significant likelihood that trade expands the number of domestic firms and the quantity of domestic output. At the very least, domestic firms have an opportunity to expand, and it would be expected that well-run firms would take heed of the larger market available to them. This makes intraindustry trade inherently less threatening and less likely to lead to complaints about fairness or that foreigners are taking advantage of lower labor or environmental standards in order to expand their production. Recall also that intraindustry trade is primarily between countries of similar income and factor endowments, which also reduces the tendency toward protectionist pressure.

In addition to lower prices (higher real income) and the potential expansion of production, another benefit from intraindustry trade is that it increases consumer choices. Without trade, consumers are limited to the goods produced in the domestic market. This is not necessarily a limitation for some people, but a scan of the highways should be enough to convince anyone that many consumers prefer foreign made goods over their domestic substitutes. The value of added choices is not easy to measure in dollar terms, but it is clearly a significant benefit for most people.

## CASE STUDY

# United States and Canada Trade

In 1965, the United States and Canada implemented a free-trade policy that covered autos and auto parts. The results were dramatic, particularly on the Canadian side of the border. Prior to the Auto Pact, Canada required most cars sold domestically to be made inside the country. The relatively small market in Canada meant that only a few different car models were produced, each in small batches that cost more to make since automakers could not take full advantage of economies of scale in production. After the Auto Pact, automakers refocused production on a smaller number of models that were produced for the combined Canadian and U.S. market. Canadian productivity in the automobile industry rose dramatically as the scale of production increased. In addition, as imports from the United States increased, Canadian consumers had many more models to choose from.

Overall, the automobile industry began to integrate production in the United States and Canada completely. Trade between the two countries rose dramatically, and eventually grew into the largest bilateral trade relationship of any two countries in the world. Table 5.2 illustrates the importance of intraindustry trade.

Four of the top five U.S. exports to Canada and two of the top five imports are motor vehicles or related products. In terms of value, an overwhelming share of the top five exports and imports are car related. Clearly, intraindustry trade is fundamental to the U.S.-Canadian trade pattern.

It is also interesting to note that the top five U.S. imports include a number of Canadian exports that take advantage of its natural resource endowment. This part of the trade relationship illustrates comparative advantage-based trade built around differing factor endowments. As a result, U.S.-Canadian trade is partly intraindustry, partly interindustry comparative advantage-based.

| TABLE 5.2 • U.S.-Canadian Merchandise Trade, 2004 (Billions of US$) | | | |
|---|---|---|---|
| Top 5 U.S. Exports | Value | Top 5 U.S. Imports | Value |
| Motor vehicle parts* | 17.8 | Motor vehicles* | 36.2 |
| Motor vehicles* | 10.8 | Natural gas | 19.5 |
| Internal combustion engines* | 6.7 | Crude oil | 19.0 |
| Special-purpose vehicles* | 6.4 | Motor vehicle parts* | 11.5 |
| Data processing machinery | 5.4 | Miscellaneous unclassified transactions | 9.7 |

Cars and car parts are the largest component of U.S.-Canadian trade.

*Related to motor vehicle manufacturing.

*Source*: Department of Commerce, *United States Foreign Trade Highlights, 2005*.
http://www.ita.doc.gov/td/industry/otea/usfth/top80cty/canada.html (September 2006).

 **Trade and Geography**

The telecommunications revolution has reduced the size of geographical barriers and lessened the importance of distance. Satellites, fiber optics, cell phones, and e-mail have dramatically reduced the cost of communicating over vast distances and enabled firms to coordinate production that is spread around the globe. At the same time, and in a somewhat contradictory manner, discussion of these developments often assumes a critically important role for geographical concentrations of technology such as Silicon Valley or the Research Triangle. Clearly, distance still matters for some things. High-tech startups may be able to locate anywhere, but a lot of them still want to be in Silicon Valley, even though housing and other costs are ridiculously high and freeways are congested. The concentration of software design, biotechnology, carpet manufacturing, and a number of other industries in just a few locations tells us that geography and distance have not been completely conquered by the recent advances in telecommunications. The fact that firms are willing to take on the higher costs of locating in Silicon Valley, for example, is strong evidence that for some types of firms there are large financial benefits to geographical clustering.

It may be obvious that the incentives for some firms to form regional concentrations, or **agglomerations**, are still very strong in spite of the recent advances in telecommunications and transportation, but it is probably not too clear what it has to do with trade and trade patterns. There are two key connections between geography and trade. First, as trade barriers come down, there are powerful incentives for some industries to reallocate production to take advantage of lower trade costs. For example, Mexico used to require firms to make cars inside the country if they wanted to sell them there, but as the North American car market became more integrated following the opening of the Mexican economy, a different pattern of automobile production emerged. Automakers now look at the entire continent as a single market, both for production and for sales. Decisions about production location and trade flows are made in response to regional variations in demand, the location of supplier industries, and the quality of transportation infrastructure, instead of in response to barriers imposed by Mexican, U.S., or Canadian policies.

A second connection between trade and geography occurs when geographical concentration gives an industry a competitive advantage. When a firm joins a regional industrial cluster it may obtain certain advantages for itself, but it may also enhance the competitiveness of the other firms in the cluster and strengthen the country's export performance. When a country is the first to develop a particular industrial concentration, it may gain a competitive advantage over all other potential rivals and actually prevent the development of competing industries in other nations. In this case, the ability of the firms in the agglomeration to export at a low price prevents a similar concentration from developing in other countries. Cheap imports remove the incentive for new firms to enter the market, and trade actually closes the door on potential developments. In the next section, we look at the mechanisms that lead to industrial clustering.

## External Economies of Scale

Geographical concentrations of industries are not a new, high-tech, phenomenon. In the twentieth century, Detroit emerged as a center of automobile production, and before that there were geographical concentrations of steel producers, textile firms, pottery manufacturers, financial service providers, and so on down a long list of economic activities. In some cases, the motivating factor behind the agglomerations was a plentiful supply of raw materials or good access to inexpensive water power, but in other cases, geographical concentration conferred advantages on the individual firm through the mechanism of external economies of scale.

External economies of scale differ from internal economies in that the advantage of larger size does not apply to the firm, but rather to the whole industry. When external economies are present, a larger industry creates advantages for individual firms but the firms themselves have no incentive to grow so large that they can influence markets. External economies can occur in one or more ways. First, if the firms in a region produce similar products, then there are likely to be knowledge spillovers that help keep all firms abreast of the latest technology and newest developments. Close physical proximity enhances knowledge spillovers because it creates more opportunities for information exchange through formal and informal networks of people. Regional industry associations can be important, but so can soccer teams, churches, Girl Scouts, and other civic organizations that bring together people that work in different firms. Knowledge spillovers are particularly important in frontier industries undergoing rapid technological change, and they seem to be very sensitive to the face-to-face contact that is impaired by geographical distance.

A second form of external economies of scale occurs when the presence of a large number of producers in one area helps to create a deep labor market for specialized skills. If an industry is large enough to attract a steady stream of potential employees with specialized skills, it reduces the search costs of firms and also offers them the best available skills. This advantage is particularly important in industries that demand highly technical or scarce skills.

A third potential advantage to a large geographical concentration is that it can lead to a dense network of input suppliers. Manufacturers of intermediate inputs prefer to locate near the market for their products since it holds down transportation costs and may keep them better informed. In high-tech sectors, a large number of nearby supplier firms will lower the cost of finding a producer of a specialized input and will also create a wider and deeper selection of input goods and services. All of these effects hold down producer costs. The linkage from producers back to their suppliers can also occur in the other direction. If the concentrated industry manufactures intermediate goods or services, it may attract firms that use its products to make a final good or service. This gives firms more information about their market and may also lead to closer collaboration between suppliers and purchasers of intermediate inputs.

## Trade and External Economies

One of the essential features of geographical concentration is that it is self reinforcing. For example, as firms attract skilled workers or specialized input suppliers, the increase in the availability of high-quality inputs creates feedback leading to more firms in the same industry locating in the area. In turn, this leads to a stronger pull for workers and input suppliers. In effect, each of the elements acts on each other to propel the system forward. At some point, as a region grows beyond its ability to provide adequate housing or other infrastructure, the high monetary cost of living in the region and the discomfort of crowding and congestion will put an end to further development, but it is probably safe to say that few regions reach this point.

One implication of these features is that small differences in initial conditions may lead to large differences in outcome. That is, a region with a small head start or other small initial advantage in attracting firms may develop significant scale economies before other regions. Once the scale advantages become significant, the gap between the lead region and its competitors can widen, and may turn into a permanent competitive advantage. The source of the initial advantage can be anything, including historical accident. For example, during World War II, as jet engines were being developed in Great Britain, the Allies decided to locate production in the United States on the West Coast where it minimized the probability that the Axis powers could destroy the factories with air raids. Ultimately, this led to a supplier industry around the major jet aircraft manufacturers (Boeing, Lockheed, and McDonnell-Douglas), and helped in the development of specialized labor skills such as aerospace engineering. As a result of an historical accident and the Allies' decisions during the war, the United States dominated the commercial jet aircraft industry for several decades, until a consortium of European governments used large subsidies and other interventions to foster a European competitor, Airbus.

Once the U.S. lead was established, then other countries with essentially the same technological ability as the United States could never catch up, even though in theory they had the capacity to achieve the same level of efficiency. The development of U.S. regional agglomerations (for example, the concentration of specialized aerospace manufacturing firms in the Seattle and Southern California regions) gave the United States a head start and a competitive advantage that could not be easily overcome. U.S. planes were always available at lower prices than a newer, less developed, industry could offer. In this instance, trade stifles the development of an industry that may be as competitive as existing producers.

In theory, it is possible that the outcome is even worse than described: trade may stifle the development of a new industry that is more efficient than the existing one. Suppose, for example, that Europeans are potentially more efficient at making commercial aircraft than Americans. Their potential can only be realized, however, after a period of experimentation and development. The initial problem they face is that the efficiency advantage goes to the United States because of its better developed linkages between suppliers and producers. In this case, trade and the initial availability of U.S. planes at a lower cost remove the incentive for Europeans to invest in their industry and prevent the development of what would be a more efficient industry. As long as U.S. planes are available at a lower price than European planes, there is no economic reason why anyone would buy European, and the lack of an initial market for their planes guarantees the Europeans a period of financial losses, thereby discouraging investment. In effect, the historical accident of locating jet aircraft production in the United States in order to avoid Hitler's bombers is locked in by trade.

The aircraft example is instructive because it illustrates a case in which trade may not be beneficial. In every other case we've examined so far, trade is beneficial. However, under the circumstances outlined above, it is potentially harmful since, in this hypothetical case, it reduces global efficiency by concentrating world production in the less efficient producer. The aircraft example also illustrates how small initial differences can cascade into large differences in outcome and how with external economies, trade patterns can be a result of completely unpredictable accidents of history.

#  Industrial Policy

Faced with a more competitive U.S. aircraft industry, what can Europeans do to get their own industry off the ground? This was the question asked several decades ago by the governments of Britain, France, Germany, and Spain. Their answer was to pool the resources of their domestic aircraft and aerospace firms to provide generous subsidies from the four governments to help the consortium absorb the initial losses and to develop their own industry. The result was Airbus, the large European challenger to the U.S.-based Boeing company.

The creation of Airbus is a prime example of governments using **industrial policies** to direct economic activity explicitly. As the name and example imply, industrial policies are government policies designed to create new industries or to support existing ones. Industrial policies are widely pursued around the globe by developed and developing countries and they can have profound impacts on trade and trade patterns. Airbus, for example, now exports commercial aircraft around the world and is a serious competitive force.

It should not be a surprise that industrial policies are controversial, so much so, that recent international agreements limit the scope of action that countries can take to support their industries. In addition, it is clear that in some cases they are politically motivated and end up wasting huge amounts of money. Brazil and Indonesia, for example, have also used industrial policies to develop regional commercial jet aircraft industries, targeted at the 20- to 100-passenger plane market. While Brazil has had commercial success, the Indonesian industry wasted billions of tax dollars and used a large number of engineers and other skilled workers whose talents could have been put to work developing the Indonesian economy. In the European case, however, it is clear that there are small differences between the United States and Europe. Both regions have a comparative advantage in aircraft, while Indonesia does not.

There is no doubt that comparative advantage can change, and someday Indonesia may have a comparative advantage in aircraft production as educational attainment rises, as the infrastructure of roads and ports improve, and as capital becomes more abundant. Comparative advantage is not immutable but it is a leap of reason to argue that a country can successfully pick the specific industry it wants to develop. Aircraft are beyond the reach of Indonesia at this time, and large-scale commercial jetliners may be beyond the reach of Brazil, but how should a country decide which industries it can successfully develop? And, even more basic, why should countries target any particular industry at all? Why not provide the basic components of a well functioning economy, such as education, stable institutions, the rule of law, and so on, and let the market decide whether to produce aircraft, high-speed trains, or some other product?

## Industrial Policies and Market Failure

When the private market economy fails to deliver an optimal quantity of goods and services, it is called a **market failure**. Market failure is one of the main theoretical justifications for industrial policies. An optimal quantity is one where the full value of the goods to private consumers and society is equal to its full cost of production. It follows that too little or too much of a good is a market failure. There are many different ways to approach this concept, but one of the clearest is to view market failures as a divergence between **private returns** and **social returns**. A frequent cause of a divergence between private and social returns is that some of the costs or benefits of an activity are externalized, or outside the area of concern of the economic agents engaged in the activity. For obvious reasons, economists refer to the market failure that results from the externalization of costs or benefits as an **externality**. The idea behind the concept of externalities is that not all the costs or benefits of an action go to the people or companies engaged in the economic activity. That is, they externalize the costs or benefits. For example, a steel mill that pollutes a river imposes a cost on inhabitants downstream, and parents who vaccinate their child create a benefit for their neighbor's children. In an accounting sense, the private returns are the cost and benefits to the steel mill or the parents with the vaccinated child, while the social returns include the private costs and benefits, but also take into account the costs and benefits to the rest of society—the downstream inhabitants or the neighbor's children. Note that externalized costs or benefits do not mean that they disappear and are of no consequence. From an economic viewpoint, they are as important as any other costs or benefits even though they do not fall on the individuals or firms that created them.

There are two simple rules for analyzing cases of market failure. First, when social returns are greater than private returns, a free-market economy produces less than the optimal amount. This follows from the fact that not all the benefits are captured by individuals or firms that produce the benefits, so naturally they do not consider the entire set of benefits when they decide how much to produce. The second rule is that when social returns are less than private returns, a free-market economy produces more than the optimal amount. In this case, economic agents do not take into account the costs that spill over onto others and that reduce the value to society of the good or service.

The divergence between private and social returns is shown in Figure 5.1. Supply and demand are plotted for a competitively produced good that generates external benefits when it is produced. The supply curve $S_{priv}$ is a normal market supply curve, embodying all of the private costs encountered by firms that engage in production. It is labeled with the subscript "priv" to indicate that only the private costs, the costs paid by the firms producing the good, are taken into account. Since production entails some external benefits to members of the soci-

## FIGURE 5.1 ● Market Failure: Externalities

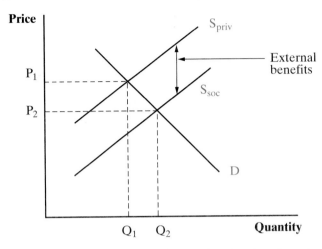

When social returns exceed private returns, markets produce less than the optimum and sell it at too high a price.

ety (who are not specified in this model), we can offset some of the costs of production with the external benefits. These are subtracted from the supply curve to derive the social supply curve, $S_{soc}$, which embodies the private costs minus the external benefits. The supply curve $S_{soc}$ is more comprehensive than $S_{priv}$ since it takes into consideration all the costs and benefits to society, not simply the private ones.

As can be seen in Figure 5.1, private markets lead to output $Q_1$ at price $P_1$. From the standpoint of the social optimum, however, the price is too high and the quantity is too low. The social optimum, at $P_2$ and $Q_2$, takes into account the costs and benefits that are external to the producing firms and their internal costs and benefits. In effect, private agents earn less than the social return, which includes the external benefit that firms cannot capture. As a result, there is less than the socially optimal amount of investment in the activity generating the returns. For advocates of industrial policies, the solution is activist government intervention to increase the level of the desirable activity. The tools and problems associated with this type of intervention are discussed next.

There are many reasons why social returns and private returns may differ. Knowledge spillovers are a common example and are often cited as a reason for industrial policies. Social and business interactions among workers in different firms can spread knowledge about new products and new processes. In this case, the social return to the new knowledge is greater than the private return because some of the value of the knowledge spills over from the firm that created it into other firms. An important case of knowledge spillovers comes from the first entrant into a particular industry. The first firm in an industry provides valuable information about the feasibility of the industry. The first firm may also leak marketing and technological information to other firms, and again, under any of these circumstances, the social returns are higher than the private ones.

A related knowledge spillover occurs in the area of research and development (R&D). Firms that develop new technologies may create breakthroughs that pay handsome profits. Often, before too much time goes by, the new product will be taken apart and improved upon by a competitor. In essence, the competitor benefits from the original research and development by being able to copy and improve upon it. Although the original innovator is unable to capture the full monetary benefit of its R&D, the benefits are not lost since other elements in society capture them. A variation of the effect of R&D is the problem of obtaining existing information. Often, existing technology may provide a solution to a common problem, but information about the technology may lie buried, for example, in a government research lab or in a Japanese technical journal. Firms could pay to search these sources for technical information, but once they find the answer to their problem, there is a high probability that all their competitors will be able to copy it because it is difficult to keep information secret within a single firm.

Another source of divergence between private and social returns is capital market imperfections. According to this argument, new firms may have difficulty attracting sufficient start-up capital. The same applies to existing firms that need to borrow to develop new products or processes. If banks and other lenders in the financial system lack the information they need to make loans, many solid prospects may not receive funding. Imperfect capital markets may also lead to market failure when economies of scale are involved. Proponents of industrial policies cite the fact that many large-scale projects require a set of interdependent investments to be made all at once. For example, a potentially competitive steel industry may require simultaneous investment in port and rail linkages. By itself, each piece may be unprofitable, but taken together the result would be a large, competitive, sector.

## Strategic Trade

In addition to addressing market failures, a second justification for industrial policies is **strategic trade policy**. The two essential ingredients for strategic trade policy are that an industry has economies of scale and firms in the industry have market power that enables them to earn higher than normal profits. Strategic trade policy is the selective use of trade barriers and industry subsidies in order to capture some of the profits of foreign firms. Setting aside for a minute the practical difficulties of enacting strategic trade policy, in theory it is possible to convince foreign firms to leave the industry by starting a well-publicized and credible system of subsidies to new domestic firms. The size of the subsidy should be sufficient to enable the home country firms to earn profits. As long as home country firms gain a market share, their presence reduces the output of their competitors and, due to economies of scale, drives up the costs of production for foreign firms.

The following example illustrates these ideas. We return to the case of aircraft production. Regional commercial jet aircraft are smaller than the behemoths produced by Boeing and Airbus, and are used for shorter trips, with 20- to 100-seat planes often flying between destinations inside a country. Approximately 90 percent of the world's production is evenly split between Canada's Bombardier and Brazil's Embraer. Given that these firms can satisfy 90 percent of world demand, it can be assumed that there are significant economies of scale in production. The Brazilian firm, Embraer, is the younger of the two. It started in 1969 as a government-owned firm producing aircraft for the Brazilian military, and has moved into the commercial jet business, where it has several current planes, and several more under development. In 1994, the company was privatized, but the Brazilian government retains stock shares and veto power over certain business decisions.

This example imagines a time before the entry of Embraer, when Bombardier (actually its predecessor) was a dominant firm. The problem faced by the Brazilian firm was that the capital investment required to enter the market was enormous, in the tens of billions of dollars, and it was too much to risk in a speculative venture that would certainly run into stiff competition from an already established and profitable Canadian firm.

Table 5.3 presents a set of hypothetical payoffs to Embraer and Bombardier as the younger firm contemplates entering the market. As the Brazilian firm surveys its options, it notes that it has a choice of entering the market and losing −10, or staying out and losing 0. Obviously, staying out of the market is the better choice, given that the Canadian firm is already in the market and is not likely to leave. The dominant strategy under these circumstances is that Bombardier stays in the market and Embraer stays out. Suppose, however, that the Brazilian government decides to offer a subsidy. The subsidy should be enough to keep its company profitable regardless of whether the Canadian company leaves the market or stays in it. Let's say that the governments offer a subsidy of 15 if

**TABLE 5.3 ● A Hypothetical Payoff Matrix**

| Canada's Bombardier (CB) | Brazil's Embraer (BE) | |
| --- | --- | --- |
| | Enter Market | Stay Out of Market |
| Stay in Market | BE (−10) <br> CB (−10) | BE (0) <br> CB (25) |
| Leave Market | BE (25) <br> CB (0) | BE (0) <br> CB (0) |

The dominant strategy is for Embraer to stay out of the market and for Bombardier to stay in.
The outcome is the payoff in the upper-right corner

Embraer enters the market. Under these conditions, the payoffs will be those detailed in Table 5.4.

With the subsidy (Table 5.4), the dominant strategy is for Brazil's Embraer to enter the market. If it stays out, it earns 0, but if it enters, it earns either 5 or 40, depending on the reaction of Canada's Bombardier. The latter, however, knows for certain that Embraer will enter the market and that consequently, its own choice is between −10 if it stays in the market, or 0 if it leaves. The rational decision for Bombardier is to leave, ensuring that the Brazilian firm captures the above normal profits that were accruing to the Canadian firm.

Is this scenario feasible? Something like this has already happened in the aircraft industry, both in the large-scale, transcontinental commercial aircraft market and in the smaller, regional aircraft market. The WTO's rules for international competition make it difficult to offer direct subsidies, but in both market segments of this industry, every firm has tried to establish that its competitor is subsidized. For example, Canada and Brazil each have brought the other into the dispute settlement process at the WTO, and tensions have run high over allegations of unfair competition.

While these examples illustrate how subsidies may permit a country to capture, for itself or its firms, the profits of a foreign company, there are at least two practical problems that have been ignored so far. These are in addition to the fact that subsidies violate the WTO's rules for fair competition, and that using them can lead to a trade war. First, we assumed that governments have far more detailed information about costs and profits than is likely. Second, we assumed that there are no counter subsidies offered by the government of the company that loses out.

## Industrial Policy Tools

Although there are a variety of techniques used to carry out industrial policies, they all share the same objective of channeling resources to the targeted industry. This can be accomplished in various ways, but the most obvious is to offer

**TABLE 5.4 ● The Payoff Matrix after a Subsidy of 15**

| Canada's Bombardier (CB) | Brazil's Embraer (BE) | |
|---|---|---|
| | Enter Market | Stay Out of Market |
| Stay in Market | BE (5) CB (−10) | BE (0) CB (25) |
| Leave Market | BE (40) CB (0) | BE (0) CB (0) |

The dominant strategy is for Embraer to enter the market and for Bombardier to leave it. The outcome is the payoff in the lower-left corner.

direct subsidies to firms in the targeted industry. As noted, this runs into the practical difficulty that Uruguay Round rules of the WTO prohibit subsidies for competitive products. Nevertheless, the rules do allow governments to subsidize "precompetitive" activities such as research, and the distinction between the two can be blurry at times. It is not necessary, however, to provide direct subsidies to targeted industries in order to support them. Governments have a wide range of options, ranging from providing information about conditions in foreign markets (many countries do this through their embassies and consulates), helping negotiate contracts, lobbying foreign governments to adopt home country technical standards, or tying foreign aid to purchases from home country firms.

One common practice used by governments in some newly industrializing countries is to sell foreign exchange to targeted firms at below-market prices, thereby enabling them to buy capital goods from abroad at below-market prices. A second common technique is to provide government loans to private firms at below-market interest rates or, alternatively, to provide government guarantees on loans obtained from the private sector, thereby enabling borrowers to obtain favorable interest rates. Similarly, governments may provide special tax treatment to targeted industries. Governments also use their own purchases as a way to develop an industry. This can affect a wide range of activities, including medical equipment for state-owned hospitals, power generating equipment for state-owned utilities, telecommunications equipment for state-owned phone and broadcast media, military hardware, and so on. In some cases—for example suppliers of military hardware in the United States—firms are guaranteed a profit on the development of new products, which essentially removes all risk to the firm and shifts it to taxpayers.

Governments often support industries by encouraging firms to work together, either through the direct funding of the research done by consortia and/or through the relaxation of antitrust laws. This decreases the probability that competing firms will spend resources duplicating each other's research and development, but it increases their market power. Finally, governments may directly own firms, although this is less common after several recent waves of privatization in capitalist countries and the collapse of communism. In countries where government ownership is not unusual (France for example), the firms are run more or less like private firms.

Proponents of industrial policies stress that no matter which technique is used to target an industry, it is critical for governments to refrain from coercion. Firms should be allowed to refuse assistance (with the inevitable strings attached), and governments should recognize that any action they take to penalize noncooperation is likely to weaken the industry and lower the probability of a successful program.

## Problems with Industrial Policies

While every economist recognizes that markets do not always produce the optimal outcome, many are skeptical about the practicality of using industrial policies to solve problems of market failure. One basic problem is that it is difficult to obtain the information necessary to measure the extent of market failure. For example, an efficient industrial policy requires governments to provide precisely the right amount of additional resources to the targeted industry. This implies that governments should keep adding resources as long as the external benefits are greater than the cost of the resources, but in most cases no one is capable of precisely measuring the benefits, particularly if they are spread throughout the economy and if they are only realized over a long period of time. Without the advantage of hard numbers, it is easy to imagine a situation where a government program spends $100 million to capture $50 million of external benefits. Similarly, the implementation of a successful strategic trade policy requires governments to know the costs of production for foreign firms and to be able to anticipate their reaction correctly when they face subsidized competition. While it is conceivable that the production costs may be known, it is impossible to know their reactions.

Even if these objections could somehow be met, there remains the problem of determining which industry to target. If everyone acknowledges that a particular industry has a bright future, then entrepreneurs and investors will jump on it and government support is unnecessary. On the other hand, we know that external benefits lead markets to underinvest. Consequently, one possibility for choosing industries to target is to pick the ones that have the largest external benefits. The problem with this strategy is that the positive externalities that develop out of new technologies and inventions are usually a surprise to everyone involved and it is impossible to know beforehand that they will occur. In 1990, for example, almost no one foresaw the advent of the Internet.

Another strategy that has been advocated for selecting the industries to target is to target high value-added industries, where **value added** is the difference between the cost of materials and the value of the output. Value added is partly determined by the contribution of labor to production, and high value-added industries are usually ones where wages are high. Value added is also determined by the contribution of capital, and therefore it may be high because an industry uses a lot of capital or a lot of highly skilled labor, or both. High value-added industries are often selected as desirable ones to target because they tend to pay high wages or use new technologies that are viewed as important for future prosperity. The problem with this strategy for selecting an industry to target is that it often makes no sense in practice. For example, two of the highest value-added industries in the United States are petroleum refining and tobacco products. No one, to my knowledge, has argued that these industries should be targeted for future development. In any case, it is not clear why high value-added industries will not develop more efficiently through market processes. That is, there is nothing inherent in their nature that creates more external benefits than in other industries.

Another problem with industrial policies is that they encourage rent seeking, which is any activity by firms, individuals, or special interests that is designed to alter the distribution of income in their favor without adding to the amount of total income in the economy. When lobbyists persuade Congress to impose a tax on steel imports, for example, it raises the income of the U.S. steel industry, but lowers the income of steel users. (More steel will be produced, but as a consequence, fewer other things are.) If firms know that governments are willing to use industrial policies, they will spend resources to obtain some of the subsidies. This may require the hiring of lobbyists, economists, or engineers whose jobs are to persuade the legislature or some other rule makers. The downside is that it uses resources but does not add to total output.

The extent to which industrial policies encourage resources to be wasted in lobbying and other non-economically productive activities partly depends on the administrative process through which targeted industries are chosen, and the political culture of the country enacting the industrial policy. Countries that have a greater degree of corruption in their political system are likely to have a much harder time choosing between industries on the basis of scientific, technological, or economic criteria. Even in relatively corruption-free environments, however, the problem of industrial policies encouraging rent seeking is real.

Another problem with industrial policies is that it is impossible to contain the external benefits of R&D spending within national boundaries. New technologies soon spread to every nation that has the technological sophistication to take advantage of them. One set of estimates puts the benefits to foreigners of R&D spending by the home country at around one-fourth of the total benefits. The fact that many U.S. firms have separate joint ventures in research and production with European and Japanese firms increases the chances that a new breakthrough will spread to firms in other countries. Despite these obstacles, industrial policies remain an intensely debated topic, particularly in the arena of economic development. Japan and South Korea used them extensively and are frequently cited as models for developing countries. Opponents of industrial policies continue to argue that sound macroeconomic policies, high rates of saving and investment, and high levels of schooling were the keys to success in those two countries, and that industrial policies were a distraction at best. Proponents view this line of reasoning as an ideological opposition to state-directed economic policy. Given the difficulties of determining cause and effect in economic development, an active debate between opponents and proponents will probably continue for some time. We will examine the East Asian case in greater detail in Chapter 16.

##  U.S. Industrial Policies

Throughout U.S. history and until World War II, a policy of high tariffs was a regular component of U.S. support for specific industries, but the use of direct subsidies was infrequent. Not counting the extensive involvement of state and federal governments in the development of transportation infrastructure (roads, canals, railroads, seaports, highways, and airports), the two main examples of direct subsidies were agriculture and defense industries.

Agriculture experiences externalities from the ability of neighboring farms to copy each other's innovations. Since a farmer who innovates cannot capture all the rewards of his or her innovation, we know that the private market economy will underproduce agricultural research. This principle was intuitively understood by U.S. farmers and legislators and in 1862, the U.S. Congress passed the Morrill Act, giving federally owned lands to states for the purpose of establishing agricultural research colleges. The Morrill Act was followed in 1887 by the Hatch Act setting up agricultural research stations, and in 1914 by the Smith-Lever Act establishing a system of cooperative education for farmers.

It is difficult to disentangle the effects of these policies from several other factors that worked to create a strong agricultural sector in the United States. The climate, the availability of land, soil fertility, the high level of farmer literacy, the ability to overcome labor shortages with innovations in farm machinery, and the development of a transportation infrastructure all worked to create a comparative advantage in agriculture. In all likelihood, the United States would have emerged as a world supplier of grains and other commodities with or without the support of the universities, research stations, and extension service. These institutions undoubtedly made agriculture more productive, but it seems unlikely that they created a comparative advantage in agriculture that would not have been there otherwise.

The theoretical justification for industrial policies in the defense industry is fairly clear. Defense is a public good (if one person gets it, everyone does, whether they pay for it or not) and public goods often create market failures since the economic incentive is for everyone to free ride and let others pay. For this reason, most economists agree that it is impossible for markets to provide defense and that it must be done by governments. This does not mean, however, that governments necessarily have to be directly involved in the production of war goods. In the post–World War II era, the weapons and tools of the U.S. defense forces have been produced by private firms, although the U.S. government has provided substantial resources to keep these firms in business, under the assumption that it would be detrimental to U.S. defense capability if the nation had to rely on foreign producers for major weapon systems.

Few people would disagree in general with this view, although there are disagreements about the optimal level of defense spending and the types of military equipment that are necessary. The main issue about defense spending in the context of industrial policies is that some economists argue that the United States has used the rhetoric of building a strong defense to hide a wide variety of industrial policies that are targeted at commercial developments. The research consortium Sematech is a case in point. Sematech was founded in 1987 by the Department of Defense in response to the growing use of Japanese semiconductors in U.S. jet aircraft. It is an R&D consortium open to any U.S.-based firm and is funded by its members and the federal government. Its initial goal was to regain technological superiority in the manufacture of semiconductors, and it seems to have largely succeeded. Many people, however, view Sematech as simply a subsidy to IBM, Motorola, Texas Instruments, and other U.S. corporations—one given to help restore their international competitiveness, although it was justified on the basis of a military need.

At two specific points in American history, the debate over commercial, non-military, industrial policies has heated up. In both periods, the country felt threatened by outside economic forces. The first period was in the 1790s when the United States feared domination by Great Britain and the second period was in the 1970s and 1980s when fears of Japanese technological and manufacturing superiority began to surface. The first episode gave rise to the classic *Report on Manufactures* by Secretary of the Treasury Alexander Hamilton. Hamilton's report called for a national effort to develop greater manufacturing competitiveness and to lessen U.S. dependence on Britain for manufactured items. The second period of debate began in the late 1970s when U.S. steel production, then consumer electronics, autos, and semiconductors seemed either to vanish or to be on the verge of collapse as waves of Japanese imports captured increasing market shares.

From the vantage point of the twenty-first century, we can see two trends that prompted the questions about using industrial policy. The first occurred in the 1980s when world trade and foreign investment began to reach levels of competitive intensity that were new to the United States. Since the end of World War II, U.S. cars and other products had been relatively insulated from foreign competition, but by the 1980s, American businesses could no longer be complacent about foreign competition. Suddenly, it seemed, a number of highly competitive foreign products were taking away domestic sales from U.S. producers. A second trend was the painful loss of comparative advantage in a number of traditional, labor-intensive, industries. This did not happen overnight, but with the rise of foreign competition, industries such as steel, consumer electronics, and a number of others were shown to be less competitive.

## CASE STUDY

# Subsidizing Commercial Aircraft

The manufacture of commercial aircraft is closely tied to the defense industry, both in its origins and in its current corporate relations. Given the importance of airpower in modern warfare, that fact alone makes the commercial aircraft industry an important strategic asset. But commercial aircraft also combine leading technologies in materials science, power systems, electronics, communication technology, and other key areas at the frontier of industrial performance. Hence, once most countries reach a certain level of industrial development, they try to develop aircraft manufacturing, repair, parts supply, or other related activities that tie them into the world's production system.

The market for multi-passenger commercial aircraft is dominated by the four companies previously mentioned: Airbus (France, Germany, Spain, and the United Kingdom), Boeing (United States), Bombardier (Canada), and Embraer

(Brazil). Other countries, such as India, China, Italy, Taiwan, and Japan have their own aircraft industries, but they are confined strictly to military planes and/or they work as suppliers to the big four or to smaller companies making light aircraft. Airbus, for example, has 1,500 suppliers in 30 countries. There are significant barriers to entering the markets dominated by the big four because it takes many billions of dollars to develop a new generation of airplanes. Once in, however, there are large but intangible benefits in the form of the strategic military advantages, national prestige, and experience working with cutting edge technologies.

Whether it makes more sense for a nation to buy its planes or produce them is a complicated question with no clear answer. What is clear, however, is that all four of the dominant companies have received substantial direct and indirect subsidies from their national governments and other public entities. This has raised a number of complaints within the world trading system. Brazil has challenged Canada and vice versa, while the United States has challenged the governments in Europe that support Airbus and those governments have challenged the U.S. support for Boeing.

In general, subsidies are considered an unfair advantage, although in some cases (agriculture for example) there are few international rules, and in other cases, the subsidy does not damage the economic interests of another country. Subsidies are a common source of friction, however, and therefore it is useful to have agreements as to when they can and cannot be used. In 1979, the Tokyo Round of the GATT prohibited all export subsidies on manufactured items, but left production subsidies alone. (Export subsidies are payments that go to a producer if and only if they export the product, while production subsidies support production regardless of whether the good is sold domestically or exported.) This was amended and extended by the Uruguay Round agreement, which defined prohibited subsidies (including export subsidies) and "actionable" subsidies, which are not prohibited outright but can be challenged under the dispute resolution mechanism in the WTO if they cause "adverse effects" to a third party.

According to the WTO, a subsidy is a financial contribution by a government or public agency that confers a benefit. Specific examples include grants, loans, loan guarantees, provision of goods or services, and fiscal incentives. The WTO left the door open for subsidies that do not hurt third parties, and for financial contributions that go to support basic research and development or what it calls pre-competitive technologies.

Since 1994, there have been two complaints leveled by Canada against Brazil based on a Brazilian program that helped foreign companies finance the purchase of Embraer planes. Similarly, there have been two complaints filed by Brazil against Canada for the support it gave Bombardier which Brazil claimed was equivalent to export subsidies. Both Canada and Brazil won partial judgments against the other and were required to dismantle some of their financial support. Needless to say, their support continues but in somewhat subtler forms. Meanwhile, the United States filed a complaint against the European Community alleging that its support for Airbus constituted export subsidies, and simultaneously, the European Community filed against the United States alleging the same concerns. The U.S.-E.C. dispute is complicated and promises to be a lengthy one, with billions of dollars hanging in the balance. In the interim, Airbus and Boeing continue to integrate their design and production systems into the world economy, and both look less and less like nationally based companies.

## Summary

- Comparative advantage cannot account for a significant part of world trade. A large share, probably over 40 percent at the world level, and more than 50 percent of the trade of industrial countries is intraindustry trade.

- Intraindustry trade is not based on comparative advantage since it consists of the export and import of similar products and occurs mostly between countries that have similar productivity, technology, and factor endowments. Intraindustry trade is based on economies of scale and product differentiation.

- Economies of scale occur whenever average costs decrease as production increases. Economies of scale are an important determinant of trade patterns because they form a separate basis for trade that is in addition to comparative advantage-based trade.

- Economies of scale can be either internal, external, or both. With internal economies of scale, the gains from trade include a wider selection of consumer choices and lower prices. With external economies of scale, the gains from trade are less certain since, in theory, they can lock in production in a less efficient country and prevent the development of production in a more efficient country.

- External economies of scale lead to regional agglomerations of firms. Firms are attracted by several positive factors derived from operating in close geographical proximity to each other. The three main factors are large pools of skilled labor, specialized suppliers of inputs, and knowledge spillovers.

- Industrial policies are premised on the idea that markets may fail to develop an industry that is essential for future prosperity, or that there will be less development than is optimal if many of the benefits of an industry are external to the firms in the industry.

- Historically, governments have used a number of tools to foster the development of industries they thought were essential to future prosperity. These tools included a number of different types of direct and indirect subsidies. The Uruguay Round of the GATT agreement has made it illegal to subsidize a commercial product.

- Problems with industrial policies include the absence of a reliable method for selecting the industry to target; rent seeking; international spillovers, and the difficulty of correctly estimating the optimal amount of support to provide.

# Vocabulary

| | |
|---|---|
| agglomerations | market failure |
| external economies of scale | monopolistic competition |
| externality | oligopoly |
| Grubel-Lloyd index | private returns |
| industrial policy | product differentiation |
| interindustry trade | social returns |
| internal economies of scale | strategic trade policy |
| intraindustry trade | value added |

# Study Questions

1. What is intraindustry trade, how is it measured, and how does it differ from interindustry trade? Are the gains from trade similar?

2. Comparing U.S. trade with Germany and Brazil, is trade with Germany more likely to be based on comparative advantage or economies of scale? Why?

3. What are the differences between external and internal economies of scale with respect to the size of firms, market structure, and gains from trade?

4. What are three key incentives for firms in a particular industry to cluster together in a geographical region?

5. How might trade hurt a country if it imports goods that are produced under conditions of external economies of scale?

6. When the United States signed a free-trade agreement with Canada (1989), no one thought twice about it. When the agreement with Mexico was signed (1994), there was significant opposition. Use the concepts of interindustry and intraindustry trade to explain the differences in opposition to the two trade agreements.

7. What are the theoretical justifications for targeting the development of specific industries?

8. What are some common problems in implementing industrial policies?

9. Figure 5.1 illustrates the case of an industry that generates external social benefits with its production. Draw a supply and demand graph for an industry that creates external costs with its production. Compare and contrast the market determined price and output level with the socially optimal price and output levels.

# A Graphical Illustration of Prices and Costs with Monopolistic Competition

Figure 5.2 illustrates the relationship among the number of firms in the industry, average costs, and output prices. The horizontal axis measures the number of firms in the industry, while the vertical axis measures average costs and prices. Line segment P shows the relationship between the number of firms and prices. It slopes downward to the right because as more firms enter the market, it puts downward pressure on prices. Line segment AC shows the relationship between average cost for each individual firm and the total number of firms in the market. It slopes upward because as more firms enter the market, the quantity each existing firm sells is reduced and their average cost of production increases. At prices above $P_1$, new firms have an incentive to enter the market since price exceeds average costs. At prices below $P_1$, just the opposite occurs and some firms will leave the market because their costs are greater than the market price.

Figure 5.2 also makes obvious the reason why firms want to export. Any firm that exports will be at a competitive advantage since it will have the greater sales it needs to drive down its costs. This idea is illustrated in Figure 5.3, where the alternative cost curve, AC*, is identical to AC except that it belongs to a larger market. For any given number of firms, AC* shows that average costs are lower

## FIGURE 5.2

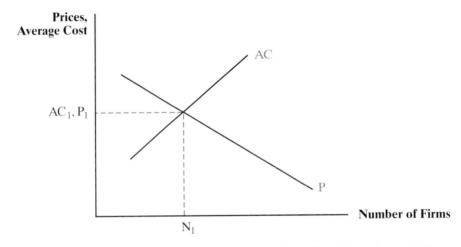

In monopolistic competition, an increase in the number of firms drives down prices and drives up each firm's average costs. Equilibrium occurs when price equals average cost.

**FIGURE 5.3**

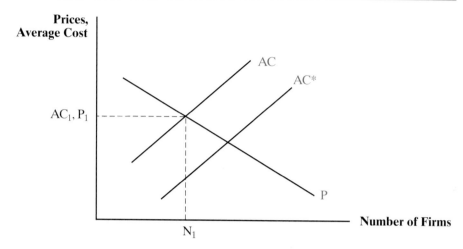

For any given number of firms, an increase in the size of the market through the creation of foreign sales allows economies of scale to be realized and pushes down average costs.

in a larger market. This follows from the economies of scale that each firm experiences and the fact that if the number of firms is held constant, each firm sells more when the size of the market expands.

Export markets enable firms to expand production and to realize their scale economies. Scale economies, together with competition among firms, leads directly to the gains from trade. Increased production causes average costs to fall, while competition forces firms to pass the cost savings on to consumers in the form of lower prices.

# 6 The Theory of Tariffs and Quotas

## Introduction: The Impact of Tariffs

Chapters 6 and 7 are an introduction to the theory and policy of tariffs and quotas. In the economics literature, this analysis is called *commercial policy*. Chapter 6 is an introduction to tariff theory and Chapter 7 focuses on an empirical estimate of the direct costs of protectionism and the arguments used by proponents of restricted trade. The inefficiency and expense of tariffs and quotas as a means to protect industries and jobs will be apparent after measuring their direct costs.

In general, tariffs have been negotiated down to very low levels in the industrial world, with the partial exception of agriculture, textiles, and apparel. These sectors were excluded from the GATT until the Uruguay Round and continue to have relatively high trade barriers. This is an issue for developing countries that often have a comparative advantage in precisely those areas.

### Analysis of a Tariff

Barriers to trade come in all shapes and sizes. Some are obvious or **transparent** whereas others are hidden or **nontransparent**. Quotas directly limit the quantity of imports, while tariffs indirectly limit imports by taxing them. Tariffs and quotas cause consumers to switch to relatively cheaper domestic goods or to drop out of the market altogether. They also encourage domestic producers to increase their output because demand switches from foreign to domestic goods.

In the analysis that follows we will look only at the effects of tariffs and quotas on the industry in which they are imposed. For example, the economy-wide effect of a tariff in, say, the steel industry will not be analyzed. In the language of economics, the analysis in Chapter 6 is known as *partial equilibrium analysis* because it considers the effects of tariffs and quotas on only a part of the economy—the market in which the trade barrier is erected. Before we turn to tariff analysis, however, we must introduce two important concepts: consumer and producer surplus.

## Consumer and Producer Surplus

What is the maximum price you would be willing to pay for a gallon of milk? The answer is likely to be different for each consumer, depending on income, how much they like milk, whether they have kids who need it, whether they can tolerate lactose or not, and a number of other factors, many of which are subjective. The subjective value that consumers place on milk is contained in the market demand curve for milk, which describes the total quantity of a good that consumers are willing and able to buy at each and every price. As the market price falls, a greater quantity is purchased because more consumers will feel that the lower price is equal to or below the value they place on the milk.

Suppose, for example, that you are willing to pay $3.50 for a gallon of milk, but the price is only $3.20. In essence, each gallon of milk provides $0.30 of value that is "free" in the sense that it is over and above what you must pay. This excess value, called **consumer surplus**, is the value received by consumers that is in excess of the price they pay. It occurs because everyone values each good differently, yet for most goods, there is only one price. Consumer surplus can be measured if the demand curve is known. Since the demand curve is a summary of the value that each consumer places on a particular good, the area between the demand curve and the price line is a measurement of consumer surplus.

Figure 6.1 shows hypothetical market demand and supply curves for milk. At the market equilibrium price of $3.20 per gallon, 10,000 gallons will be supplied and demanded. Many people value milk at a higher price, however, and the value

**FIGURE 6.1** ● **Consumer and Producer Surplus**

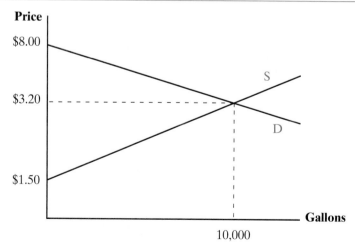

Consumer surplus is the area below the demand curve and above the price line. Producer surplus is the area above the supply curve and below the price line.

they receive in consuming milk is greater than $3.20. In Figure 6.1, consumer surplus is the area below the demand curve and above the price line of $3.20. The size or value of consumer surplus is the area of the triangle given by the formula $(\frac{1}{2}) \times$ (height) $\times$ (width), or $(\frac{1}{2}) \times (\$4.80) \times (10,000)$, which is equal to $24,000. This equals the difference between the value of the milk consumed and the total amount consumers spent for it.

Consumer surplus is a real savings to consumers. If firms had a way to determine the maximum price that each consumer was willing to pay, then theoretically they could charge every individual a different price and thus reduce consumer surplus to zero. Luckily for those of us not in the milk business, firms usually cannot get this information without going through a long and costly interview procedure. As a result, it is usually impractical (and in some cases, illegal) for firms to charge different customers different prices. Nevertheless, some firms such as car dealers manage to charge different prices for the same goods. The easiest strategy for most firms is simply to charge everyone the same price, so consumer surplus is a real savings for most consumers in most markets.

On the production side, the analogous concept is called **producer surplus**. In our hypothetical milk example, if you owned a dairy farm and were willing and able to produce milk at $3.00 per gallon, you would receive producer surplus of $0.20 per gallon if you sold milk at $3.20. Recall that the supply curve for a market is the sum of supply curves for the firms in the market and that it reflects the minimum price firms will accept to produce a given amount. In Figure 6.1, some firms are willing to produce at $2.00 per gallon, and at every price above $1.50 at least some firms will have output to sell. Every firm that is willing to sell for less than the equilibrium price of $3.20 earns revenue that is above the minimum they need. This excess or surplus revenue is their producer surplus.

As in the case of consumer surplus, we can measure producer surplus. Measurement in this case depends on knowing the parameters of the supply curve (where it crosses the price axis and its slope) because producer surplus is the area above the supply curve and below the price line. In our example, it is equal in value to the triangle given by the formula $(\frac{1}{2}) \times (\$1.70) \times (10,000)$, which equals $8,500. This is the revenue received by producers that is in excess of the minimum amount of revenue that would be required to get them to produce 10,000 gallons of milk.

## The Effect of a Tariff on Prices, Output, and Consumption

We will use the concepts of producer and consumer surplus when we discuss the income distribution effects of tariffs and quotas. Before we analyze those effects, however, we must begin with a description of the effects of tariffs on prices, domestic output, and domestic consumption.

Figure 6.2 shows the domestic or national supply and demand for an imported good. We are assuming that there is one price for the good, which we will call the

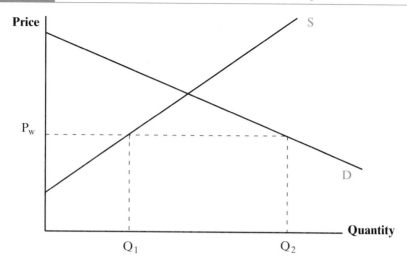

FIGURE 6.2 ● **Domestic Supply and Demand for an Imported Good**

The difference between domestic demand and domestic supply, $Q_2 - Q_1$, is the quantity of imports at price $P_w$.

world price, or $P_w$, and that foreign producers are willing to supply us with all of the units of the good that we want at that price. This is equivalent to assuming that foreign supply is perfectly elastic, or that the United States does not consume a large enough quantity to affect the price. We will drop this assumption when we discuss the case of a large country. Note that the world price is below the domestic equilibrium price. This means that domestic producers are not able to satisfy all of domestic demand at the market price of $P_w$ and that consumers depend on foreign producers for some of their consumption. Specifically, at price $P_w$, consumers demand $Q_2$, but domestic producers supply only $Q_1$. The difference, $Q_2 - Q_1$, or line segment $Q_1 Q_2$, is made up by imports.

Now suppose that the government imposes a tariff of amount "t." Importers will still be able to buy the good from foreign producers for amount $P_w$, but they will have to pay the import tax of "t," which they tack onto the price to domestic consumers. In other words, the price to consumers rises to $P_w + t = P_t$, as shown in Figure 6.3. The price increase in the domestic market has effects on domestic consumption, domestic production, and imports. First, the price increase squeezes some people out of the market, and domestic consumption falls from $Q_2$ to $Q_2^*$. Next, on the production side, the higher price encourages domestic production to increase from $Q_1$ to $Q_1^*$. The increase in domestic production occurs because domestic firms are able to charge a slightly higher price ($P_w + t$) in order to cover their increasing costs while remaining competitive with foreign

**FIGURE 6.3** • **The Effects of a Tariff**

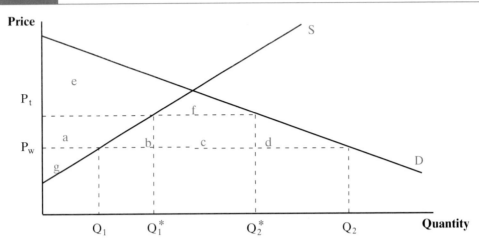

Tariffs cause an increase in domestic prices and domestic production, and a fall in domestic consumption. They increase producer surplus and government revenue, but decrease consumer surplus.

firms. Finally, imports decrease from $Q_1Q_2$ to $Q_1^*Q_2^*$. To summarize, tariffs cause the domestic price to rise by the amount of the tariff, domestic consumption falls, domestic production rises, and imports fall.

## The Effect of a Tariff on Resource Allocation and Income Distribution

Tariffs have more subtle effects than just a rise in prices and a fall in imports. The increase in domestic production requires additional resources of land, labor, and capital to be reallocated from their prior uses into the industry receiving protection under the tariff. Also, when the price changes, consumer and producer surplus do too.

First, let's consider the effect on consumer surplus. Figure 6.3 shows both the pre- and post-tariff price and output levels. Remember that consumer surplus is the entire area above the price line and below the demand curve. When consumers pay price $P_w$, it is areas a + b + c + d + e + f. After the tariff is imposed and the price rises to $P_t$, consumer surplus shrinks to e + f. The difference, area a + b + c + d, represents a loss to consumers.

Unlike consumer surplus, producer surplus grows. Pre-tariff producer surplus is area g, and post-tariff is g + a. The difference, area a, is the additional revenue that is above the minimum necessary to encourage domestic firms to increase their output from $Q_1$ to $Q_1^*$. On net, producers are better off, and consumers are worse off, but what about the nation as a whole?

If we consider the whole loss to consumers, areas a +b + c + d, we see that it can be subdivided into several different areas. Part of the loss, area a, is a transfer from consumer surplus to producer surplus. Although the loss makes consumers worse off, it makes producers better off by the same amount. Therefore, the nation as a whole is neither better nor worse off unless it can be established that giving the resources to producers somehow benefits or harms national welfare. This part of the lost consumer surplus is an income distribution effect of the tariff, since it rearranges national income by transferring resources from one group (consumers) to another group (producers).

Another income distribution effect of the tariff is represented by area c. Note that the height of this area is equal to the tariff, and the width is the amount of imports after the tariff is imposed. Therefore, this part of lost consumer surplus is equal to (tariff) × (imports), which is the amount of revenue collected by the government when it enacts the tariff. In this case, the income distribution effect is a transfer from consumers to the government. Again, it is assumed that there is no net effect on national welfare since the loss by consumers is exactly matched by the gain of government. As long as this transfer does not change national welfare, there is no net effect.

The two remaining areas of lost consumer surplus are b and d. Both represent net national losses, and both involve a misallocation of resources. Consider area d first. Along the demand curve between $Q_2^*$ and $Q_2$, there are consumers that value the good above the cost of purchasing it at the world price. As a result of the tariff, however, they have been squeezed out of the market and are not willing or able to pay price $P_t$. The fact that consumers value the good above the cost of obtaining it in the world market but cannot purchase it is a net loss to the nation. Economists refer to the destruction of value that is not compensated by a gain somewhere else as a **deadweight loss**. Area d is this type of loss.

The final area to consider is b. Along the domestic supply curve between $Q_1$ and $Q_1^*$, output is increased at existing plants. Given that the supply curve slopes upward, firms can only increase their output if the price is allowed to rise. In other words, in order to obtain the additional output, domestic producers must be able to charge a higher price that will cover their rising costs for each additional unit. At the pre-tariff price of $P_w$, the total cost of imports $Q_1Q_1^*$ would have been the price times the quantity, or $(P_w) \times (Q_1Q_1^*)$. The cost of producing the same goods at home is equal to the cost of the imports plus area b. In other words, the triangle b is the additional cost to the nation when it tries to make the extra output Q1Q1* instead of buying it in the world market at price $P_w$. Area b is a resource misallocation and a net loss to the nation because the same goods $(Q_1Q_1^*)$ could have been acquired without giving up this amount. Area b is another deadweight loss, sometimes referred to as an **efficiency loss** because it occurs on the production side.

We can summarize the net effect of the tariff on the nation's welfare by subtracting the gains of producers and government from the losses of consumers: $(a + b + c + d - a - c) = b + d$. The two triangular areas are losses for which there are no compensating gains; therefore, they represent real losses to the nation as a whole. Table 6.1 summarizes the effects of tariffs that we have noted.

## Other Potential Costs

These effects of tariffs are the ones that are most predictable and quantifiable. In Chapter 7 there are some actual estimates of the production and income distribution effects of tariffs and quotas for a number of industries in the United States and Japan. These are not the only effects of tariffs, however—three others should be noted: the effects if trading partners retaliate, the impact of protection on domestic innovation and productivity, and the incentive for firms to engage in rent-seeking behavior. Each of these effects broadens our focus to a consideration of more than the directly affected industry.

**Retaliation.** Retaliation can add to the net loss of a tariff by hurting the export markets of other industries. For example, in 1995 the United States imposed a tariff on European (mainly Italian) pasta because of some trade practices that the United States felt discriminated against its pasta manufacturers. In return, the European Community retaliated by imposing tariffs on U.S. manufacturers of vegetable oils—corn, soybean, safflower, and other cooking oils. The cost of the U.S.-imposed tariff not only affected U.S. consumers of Italian pasta who were forced to pay higher prices, but also affected workers and owners of capital in the U.S. vegetable oil industry. In essence, in addition to the deadweight losses brought on by the tariff, the vegetable oil industry lost export markets. A further problem is that retaliation can quickly escalate. For example, in the 1930s, many depressed nations reduced imports through tariffs. The result was that they

| TABLE 6.1 ● Economic Effects of the Tariff in Figure 6.3 | | |
|---|---|---|
| Variable | Pre-tariff | Post-tariff |
| Price to consumers | $P_w$ | $P_t$ |
| Domestic consumption | $Q_2$ | $Q_2^*$ |
| Domestic production | $Q_1$ | $Q_1^*$ |
| Imports | $Q_1Q_2$ | $Q_1Q_2^*$ |
| Consumer surplus | $a + b + c + d + e + f$ | $e + f$ |
| Producer surplus | $g$ | $g + a$ |
| Government revenue | $0$ | $c$ |
| Deadweight consumption loss | $0$ | $d$ |
| Deadweight production (efficiency) loss | $0$ | $b$ |

Tariffs reallocate income from consumers to producers and government. They also create deadweight losses, one on the consumption side and one on the production side.

gained jobs in industries that competed with imports but lost jobs in industries that produced exports. In the end, no jobs were gained, trade declined, and everyone had a lower standard of living.

**Innovation.** A costly effect of tariffs is that they isolate domestic firms from foreign competition and reduce the incentive to introduce new products or upgrade the quality and features of existing ones. It is difficult to measure this effect, but as Chapter 1 described, there are several types of evidence showing that open economies grow faster than closed ones.

**Rent Seeking.** Hypothetically, tariffs could stimulate product improvement if domestic producers know that the tariffs are temporary and if they believe they will be removed. The problem is that firms with tariff protection can hire lobbyists and work to keep the protection in place. Economists use the term **rent seeking** to describe this type of behavior. Rent seeking is any activity that uses resources to try to capture more income without actually producing a good or service. If it is easier to lobby a government for protection than it is to become more competitive, then firms will use rent seeking tactics. If, on the contrary, lobbying is not likely to succeed in gaining protection, then firms are less likely to engage in that particular form of rent seeking. For this reason, political systems that do not easily provide protective tariffs are much more likely to avoid one source of wasted resources.

## The Large Country Case

Economists distinguish between large and small countries when it comes to tariff analysis. As a practical matter there may not be much difference between the two, but in theory it is possible for large countries to actually improve their national welfare with a tariff as long as their trading partners do not retaliate. In economic terms, a large country is one that imports enough of a particular product so that if it imposes a tariff, the exporting country will reduce its price in order to keep some of the market it might otherwise lose.

An example of the **large country case** tariff is shown in Figure 6.4. Suppose that the United States, a large country, imposes a tariff of size t on its imports of oil. The fall in U.S. demand brought on by the tariff causes $P_w$, the world price, to fall to $P_w{}^*$, offsetting some or all of the deadweight loss from the tariff.

Looking more closely at Figure 6.4, we can compare the large and small country cases. The situation before the tariff is the same as the one shown in Figure 6.3. The main difference between the two cases stems from the fact that foreign suppliers cut the price to $P_w{}^*$ after the tariff is levied. Consequently, less additional domestic production occurs, and fewer consumers are squeezed out of the market. In other words, areas b and d in Figure 6.4 are smaller than they would be in the small country case where there is no price drop. A smaller deadweight loss is not the only effect, however. In Figure 6.4, area g represents tariff revenue, which together with area c is the total tariff revenue collected. However, compared to the pre-tariff situation, area g is a net gain to the importing nation. Pre-

FIGURE 6.4 ● **Tariffs in the Large Country Case**

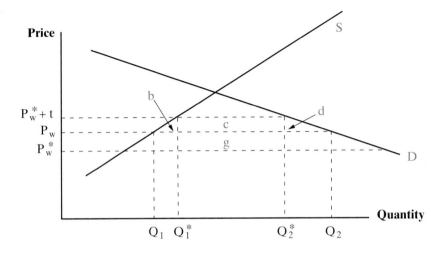

A tariff in a large country reduces demand so much that foreign producers cut their prices.

tariff, area g was part of the money paid for imports. After the tariff, and due to the price decline, it is part of the revenue collected by the government and, hence, stays within the nation.

As long as g > b + d, a large country can improve its welfare by imposing a tariff. This outcome, however, assumes that there is no retaliation, rent seeking, or harmful effects on innovation.

## Effective versus Nominal Rates of Protection

One of the ironies of tariff protection is that often it is not what it seems. In fact, the amount of protection given to any one product depends not only on the tariff rate but also on whether there are tariffs on the inputs used to produce it. Suppose, for example, that the United States decided to impose a tariff on imports of laptop computers. If American-made laptops have foreign parts in them, then the amount of protection they receive from a U.S. tariff depends also on whether there are tariffs on their imported inputs. It is conceivable, in other words, that the protection given by a tariff on laptops could be completely undone by forcing laptop manufacturers to pay tariffs on their imported inputs.

Economists distinguish between the **effective rate of protection** and the **nominal rate of protection**. The nominal rate is what we have discussed so far in this chapter—the rate that is levied on a given product. The effective rate of protection takes into account the nominal rate and any tariffs on intermediate inputs. Consequently, it gives a clearer picture of the overall amount of protection that any given product receives. The effective rate of protection is related to the concept of value added. Value added is the price of a good minus the costs of the intermediate goods used to produce it. **Value added** measures the contributions of capital and labor at a given stage of production. The effective rate of protection is defined as follows:

$$(VA^* - VA) / VA$$

where VA is the amount of domestic value added under free trade, and $VA^*$ is the amount of domestic value added after taking into account all tariffs, both on final goods and intermediate inputs.

Consider the example shown in Table 6.2. Suppose that laptop computers sell for $1,000, and foreign producers are willing to sell to the United States all it wants at that price. In order to make a laptop, American manufacturers must import $600 worth of parts, so that a domestic laptop actually has $400 of value added in the United States ($1,000 − $600 = $400). If the United States imposes a 20 percent tariff, then the price rises to $1,200. Value added in the United States is now $600 ($1,200 − $600), and the effective rate of protection is 50 percent (($600 − $400) / $400). That is, a 20 percent tariff provides 50 percent protection! This happens because a large share of the value of the final product is produced elsewhere, so all of the domestic protection falls on the share produced in the United States.

Now consider what happens if the United States decides also to protect domestic component manufacturers and levies a large tariff on intermediate inputs. If the tariff on foreign parts is 50 percent, then the cost of intermediate inputs rises from $600 to $900. With a 20 percent tariff on the value of the final product, the price of imports stays at $1,200, which is the price American laptop makers must meet. Value added with the tariff on intermediate inputs is $300 ($1,200−$900), and the effective rate of protection is now −25 percent (($300 − $400) / $400). That is, even with a 20 percent tariff on foreign laptops, American

**TABLE 6.2 ● Nominal and Effective Rates of Protection**

| Variable | No Tariff | A 20% Tariff on the Final Product | A 20% Tariff Plus a 50% Tariff on Imported Inputs |
|---|---|---|---|
| Price of a laptop computer | $1,000 | $1,200 | $1,200 |
| Value of foreign inputs | $600 | $600 | $900 |
| Domestic value added | $400 | $600 | $300 |
| **Effective rate of protection** | 0 | 50% | −25% |

Effective rates of protection are higher than nominal rates if intermediate inputs are imported tariff free. If intermediate inputs are subject to tariffs, it reduces the effective rate of protection and can even turn it negative.

laptop makers receive *negative* protection. The tariff on the final product is more than offset by the tariffs on the intermediate products, so that the overall situation leaves producers more exposed to foreign competition than if there were no tariffs levied at all.

Negative rates of effective protection are not uncommon. Part of the reason stems from the fact that tariffs are enacted in a piecemeal fashion over long periods and are not constructed in a planned and coherent way. Pressures from domestic lobbyists, considerations of strategic interests, and numerous other forces go into the shaping of national tariff systems. Consequently, it is not surprising to find contradictory tariff policies where newer tariffs undo the effects of older ones.

This discussion should add a note of caution to attempts to determine exactly which industries are protected. Clearly, the notion of effective rates of protection is more relevant than nominal rates. With tariff rates, what you see may not always be what you get.

## CASE STUDY

# A Comparison of Tariff Rates

The WTO's Doha Development Agenda is focused on the trade problems of developing countries. One impetus for the start of the Doha negotiations, and a factor behind the emphasis on economic development issues, is the complaint by many developing countries that they did not derive sufficient benefits from the Uruguay Round of trade negotiations that concluded in 1993. At issue for many developing countries are the levels of tariffs and other industrial country barriers that block access to agriculture, clothing, and textile markets. These product lines tend to be areas where developing countries have comparative advantage, particularly in cases where climate is a factor or where production uses abundant labor but requires little capital.

For their part, many industrial countries, the World Bank, and the WTO have argued that a major part of the problem faced by developing countries is the relatively high level of protection among developing countries themselves. High tariffs limit their ability to sell into each other's markets—and consequently their ability to follow their comparative advantage.

Figure 6.5 shows trends and levels of tariff rates in three groups of countries that are arranged according to their income levels. In 2005 U.S. dollars, low-income countries have per capita income levels below $875, middle income ranges from $876 to $10,725, and high income is anything above the middle group.

Because it is difficult to gather information on tariff rates for a large number of countries, we must interpret the data in Figure 6.5 with caution. The year-to-year data in each group of countries varies in the number of countries included

## FIGURE 6.5 ● Average Tariff Rates, 1986–2003

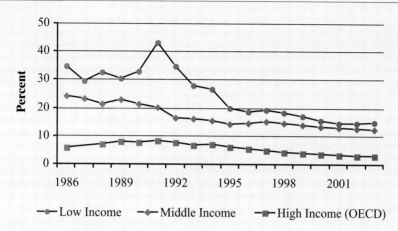

—●—Low Income    —◆—Middle Income    —■—High Income (OECD)

Since the mid-1980s, tariff rates in most countries have fallen. In general, the higher a country's income, the lower the tariff rate.

*Source*: World Bank, http://siteresources.worldbank.org/INTRANETTRADE/Resources/tar2002.xls

in the group average. Furthermore, tariffs are only one form of protection, as we will see later in this chapter.

Despite the data limitations, two notable patterns are visible in Figure 6.5 and are widely accepted as qualitatively accurate. First, the higher a country's income, the lower its tariffs are likely to be. There are exceptions, of course, and one can point to low- and middle-income countries with low tariffs (for example, Indonesia, Madagascar, Estonia, and Latvia) and high-income countries with relatively high tariffs (Barbados and Slovenia), but in general, low income implies relatively higher tariffs and high income implies the opposite. Second, tariffs have come down over time. In each of the three groups mentioned, the average tariff fell by about 50 percent between 1986 and 2003.

Why then, if trade is beneficial for growth, do low-income countries tend to have higher tariff rates? Although the complete answer varies by country circumstances, one of the most important reasons is that tariffs are a relatively easy tax to administer and often form an important part of government revenue. Taxes on income, sales, and property require more complex accounting systems and also organized markets through which a large share of economic activity passes. In countries with large informal markets, where sales of goods and services are not recorded, it is difficult to apply many kinds of taxes. In addition, taxes on income and property run into powerful interest groups that have the power to prevent the creation or payment of taxes. Consequently, tariff revenue is an important source of operating revenue for governments in many developing countries.

# Analysis of Quotas

The economic analysis of quotas is nearly identical to that of tariffs. Quotas are quantitative restrictions that specify a limit on the quantity of imports rather than a tax. The net result is much the same: tariffs and quotas lead to a reduction in imports, a fall in total domestic consumption, and an increase in domestic production. The main difference between quotas and tariffs is that quotas that are not followed up with additional policy actions do not generate tariff revenue for the government. The lost tariff revenue can end up in the hands of foreign producers as they raise their prices to match demand to supply. Hence, the net loss from quotas can exceed that from tariffs.

In terms of Figure 6.3, consumers still lose area a + b + c + d, but the government does not collect area c as a tax. (We will examine what happens to area c, but try to reason it out for yourself first.)

## Types of Quotas

The most transparent type of quota is an outright limitation on the quantity of imports. Limitations are sometimes specified in terms of the quantity of a product coming from a particular country, and at other times there is an overall limit set without regard to which country supplies the product. For example, in the apparel sector, until 2005 the United States set quotas for imports of each type of garment (men's suits, boys' shirts, socks, and so on). The quota for each good was further divided by country, so, for example, Hong Kong and Haiti had different limits on each type of apparel that they could export to the United States.

Another type of quota is an import licensing requirement. The United States uses this form infrequently, but a number of other nations have relied on these quotas for the bulk of their protection. For example, until 1989 they were the main form of protection in Mexico. As the name implies, import licensing requirements force importers to obtain government licenses for their imports. By regulating the number of licenses granted and the quantity permitted under each license, import licenses are essentially the same as quotas. They are less transparent than a quota because governments usually do not publish information on the total allowable quantity of imports, and foreign firms are left in the dark about the specific limits to their exports.

A third form of quota, and the one that has been common in U.S. commercial policy, is the **voluntary export restraint (VER)**, also known as the *voluntary restraint agreement* (VRA). Under a VER, the exporting country "voluntarily" agrees to limit its exports for some period. The agreement usually occurs after a series of negotiations in which the exporter may be threatened with much more severe restrictions if they do not agree to limit exports in a specific market. Given that there is usually more than a hint of coercion, it may be a misnomer to call these restrictions "voluntary."

VERS were popular forms of protection in the 1970s and 1980s, but new limits on their use were implemented under the Uruguay Round agreement. In

2005, however, both the United States and the European Union negotiated export restraints in textiles and apparel with China.

## The Effect on the Profits of Foreign Producers

The main difference between tariffs and quotas is that there is no government revenue from quotas. In place of tariff revenue, there are greater profits for foreign producers, called **quota rents**.

In Figure 6.6, the world price is set at $P_w$, domestic production is $Q_1$, and imports are $Q_1Q_2$. Suppose that the government decides to set a quota on imports of quantity $Q_1Q_2{}^*$. At price $P_w$, demand exceeds supply, which is equal to $Q_1$ domestic plus $Q_1Q_2{}^*$ imports. Consequently, the price rises until supply equals demand when the gap between the domestic supply curve and the domestic demand curve is equal to $Q_1Q_2{}^*$. This is illustrated in Figure 6.7, where domestic supply is shown as having grown to $Q_1{}^*$, and the domestic price is $P_q$, which is above $P_w$. $Q_1{}^*Q_2{}^*$ is equal to $Q_1Q_2{}^*$ in Figure 6.6.

Figure 6.7 looks the same as Figure 6.3, which shows a tariff in a small country case, because they have nearly identical effects on production, consumption, and prices paid by consumers. Indeed, for any given quota there is some tariff that will accomplish the identical import restriction. One difference stands out, however. In the tariff case, the government earned revenue from imports—area c in Figures 6.3 and 6.7. In the quota case, no revenue is earned. Instead, area c represents the extra profits of foreign producers due to the higher prices.

## FIGURE 6.6 ● Analysis of Quota: 1

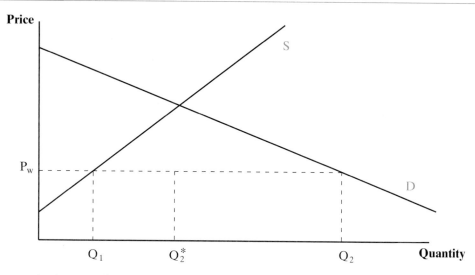

A quota restricts imports to line segment $Q_1Q_2{}^*$ and creates excess demand equal to $Q^*Q_2$.

FIGURE 6.7 ● **Analysis of a Quota: 2**

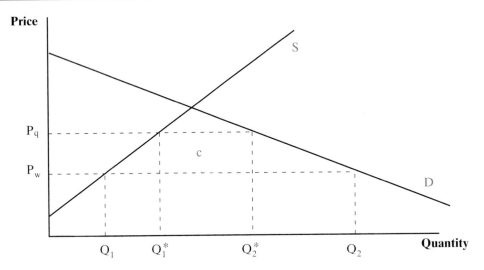

The quota generates extra revenue for foreign producers in area c.

A second important difference between tariffs and quotas relates to their effect on producer surplus over time, as demand for the good increases. If a quota remains fixed, an increase in consumer demand also increases the price paid by consumers and the quantity of producer surplus garnered by domestic firms. In contrast, an increase in consumer demand for an item that has an import tariff increases the quantity of imports and leaves the price intact. This assumes that the country is relatively small and the increase in its demand does not alter the world (pre-tariff) price. Given this difference, it is not surprising that domestic firms prefer quotas over tariffs as a form of protection for their industry.

Two circumstances can mitigate or limit the ability of foreign suppliers to earn extra profits. First, if there is a large number of foreign suppliers, then competitive conditions may prevent them from raising their prices. And second, a clever government can extract the extra profits from foreign producers through the implementation of an auction for import licenses.

Suppose that the country imposing the quota decides to auction off the right to import. How much would a domestic importer be willing to pay? In Figures 6.6 and 6.7, foreign suppliers are willing to sell the amount of the quota ($Q_1Q_2^*$ in Figure 6.6, or $Q_1^*Q_2^*$ in Figure 6.7) at price $P_w$. A domestic importer, recognizing that she can sell the good at price $P_q$, should be willing to pay an amount equal to something slightly less than the difference $P_q$ minus $P_w$. In other words, she pays $P_w$ for the good that she sells for $P_q$. If she pays anything less than $P_q - P_w$ for the right to sell in the market with the quota, she makes a profit. In equilibrium, an auction market should lead to bids for the right to sell that are more or less equal to the projected price increase. With an auction market, then, the government can potentially collect the same revenue with a quota that it would with a tariff. Of course, administrative costs of a quota may be higher, since the government must implement its auction market.

## Hidden Forms of Protection

While outright quantitative restrictions, import licensing requirements, and VERs are all forms of quotas, there are numerous other forms of protection that function the same as quotas. Any kind of trade barrier that reduces imports without imposing a tax functions more or less like a quota. Therefore, economists divide the different forms of protection into two main categories: tariffs and **nontariff barriers (NTBs)**. Nontariff barriers can be subdivided into quotas and **nontariff measures**. Nontariff measures are often nontransparent, or hidden, in that they are not presented as trade barriers or forms of protection even though they serve that purpose.

It is difficult to define all types of nontariff measures because they are often the result of red tape or cumbersome and unevenly applied rules. In general, nontariff measures refer to any regulatory or policy rules other than tariffs and quotas that reduce the physical quantity of imports or exports. Specific examples include special fees imposed on importers, burdensome and unnecessary customs procedures, unreasonable technical standards, phony health and safety standards, state trading companies or other anticompetitive practices, restrictive government procurement rules, and corruption. Nontariff measures may be justified, as when a country imposes technical standards or certification criteria in order to protect its crops from foreign pests or its citizens from unproven drug treatments. What makes this an interesting topic, however, is that it is sometimes impossible to say for certain if a particular nontariff measure is protectionism dressed up as a public benefit, or if it really is in the public interest.

While there is no consensus about the dollar value of economic losses due to nontariff measures, there is a consensus among economists that the world economy would be better off if they were reduced. Research indicates that benefits would accrue through the lowering of prices for many goods, increases in export and import volumes, increases in production levels, and overall economic welfare. In this respect, they are not much different from tariffs or quotas. They are generally much more difficult to eliminate, however, as they are embedded more deeply in national economic policies.

## CASE STUDY

# Intellectual Property Rights and Trade

Intellectual property is usually divided into copyrights and related rights for literary and artistic work, and industrial property rights for trademarks, patents, industrial designs, geographical indications, and the layout of integrated circuits.

The rules for respecting **intellectual property rights** as they relate to trade were negotiated during the Uruguay Round (1986–1994), and culminated in the **Trade Related Aspects Intellectual Property Rights (TRIPS)** agreement.

The growth of world trade over the last half of the twentieth century led to a greater awareness of the importance of intellectual property. More and more, traded goods and services incorporated specialized knowledge and unique ideas. Pharmaceuticals, computer hardware, telecommunications equipment, and other high technology products are valuable because of the innovation and research they incorporate, while software, movies, music, and other artistic expressions are valued for their creativity. The protection given to creators and innovators varied greatly until standardization began with the signing of the TRIPS agreement.

The lack of intellectual property protection is viewed as a nontariff measure since the failure or inability to protect intellectual property restricts trade flows. Exporters are reluctant to sell products into a market if they know that their ideas or brands will be stolen and copied by local producers. Hence, there were strong pressures by developed countries to reach an agreement on enforcement of protections for intellectual property. Since the implementation of the Uruguay Round in 1995, there have been 24 intellectual property complaints settled by the WTO, most having to do with patents, and a large share of those related to pharmaceuticals.

It is probably impossible to prevent copyright infringements that happen through informal networks of families and friends. For example, friends copying each other's music on their iPods or sharing their copy of Microsoft Office cannot easily be stopped when it is done outside a formal market. On the other hand, many countries have very large and very visible markets where fake goods with counterfeit trademarks and illegal copies of DVDs and software are sold. Beijing's famous Silk Market is an example that attracted a lot of attention. In 2005, as part of its commitment to fulfill its WTO obligations, Chinese courts imposed fines on the landlord of the market and began the process of eliminating fake goods, many of which had counterfeit labels from European luxury brands. Furthermore, intellectual property violations in the industrial arena (for example, through copying patented technologies) involves billions of dollars in losses.

The fundamental economic rationale for the TRIPS agreement is that by protecting innovation it gives a financial incentive to firms and individuals to do research and to continue to innovate. Nevertheless, the TRIPS agreement is not uniformly seen as a positive step for world prosperity. Among others, Nobel Laureate Joseph Stiglitz has criticized it for the costs it has imposed on China, Mexico, and other developing countries that must devote scarce resources to its implementation. Mexico, he argues, has spent over $50 million in its implementation. Also, it is not empirically well established that the benefits of innovation outweigh the costs of access, particularly for developing countries. This is particularly true for developing countries that find their access to new technologies curtailed when they must pay royalties and other fees.

Pharmaceuticals are a case in point. With the AIDS crisis in full force in a number of countries, access to anti-AIDS drugs is critical. If patent enforcement under the TRIPS agreement prevents the production of inexpensive copies, then it is harmful to world prosperity. Although a number of exceptions were written into the agreement in order to allow access to life saving medicines and other critical technologies, it is difficult for many developing countries to take advantage of the exceptions because they lack the technical know-how to make generic varieties of expensive and sophisticated drugs.

In the end, many countries simply lack the resources to fully implement the TRIPS agreement. Nevertheless, it remains an area of active interest, particularly by rich developed country markets with large numbers of patents, copyrights, and trademarks to protect.

## Summary

- Tariffs increase domestic production and employment at the cost of greater inefficiency and higher prices. Production and distribution effects are measured by estimating the changes in producer surplus and consumer surplus.

- In addition to short-run welfare and efficiency effects, tariffs have long-run costs of increased rent seeking, slower innovation, and the loss of export markets through the retaliation of trading partners.

- In theory, a large country can improve its welfare with tariffs. In general, welfare-improving tariffs tend to be small, and they only improve welfare if there is no retaliation by supplying nations and no external costs such as increased rent seeking.

- Economists distinguish between nominal and effective rates of protection. The effective rate is the difference in domestic value added with and without tariffs, expressed in percentage terms.

- Quotas have similar effects as tariffs, although the overall national losses are greater due to the transfer of quota rents to foreign producers. Auction markets, in which governments auction the right to import an item under a quota, can reduce the amount of quota rents and, in the limit, provide the same revenue as an equivalent tariff.

- Administratively, quotas take many forms. They can be well-specified quantitative restrictions on imports, negotiated limits on a trading partner's exports, or requirements to obtain a license to import.

- Nontariff measures include a wide variety of regulations and policies that effectively reduce the volume of international trade. They often act as hidden forms of protection, and are commonly embedded deeply in a country's rules and institutions. Together with quotas, they make up nontariff barriers to trade.

**Vocabulary**

consumer surplus

deadweight loss

effective rate of protection

efficiency loss

intellectual property rights

large country case

nominal rate of protection

nontariff barrier (NTB)

nontariff measure

nontransparent

producer surplus

quota rents

rent seeking

transparent

Trade Related Aspects Intellectual Property Rights (TRIPS)

value added

voluntary export restraint (VER)

 **Study Questions**

1. Graph the supply and demand of a good that is produced domestically and imported. Assume that the country is not large enough to affect the world price. Illustrate the effects that a tariff on imports has. Discuss the following:

   a. Income distribution effects

   b. Resource allocation effects

   c. Domestic production and consumption effects

   d. Government revenue effects

   e. Price of the good effects

2. Suppose the world price for a good is 40 and the domestic demand-and-supply curves are given by the following equations:

   Demand: $P = 80 - 2Q$
   Supply: $P = 5 + 3Q$

   a. How much is consumed?

   b. How much is produced at home?

   c. What are the values of consumer and producer surplus?

   d. If a tariff of 10 percent is imposed, by how much do consumption and domestic production change?

   e. What is the change in consumer and producer surplus?

   f. How much revenue does the government earn from the tariff?

   g. What is the net national cost of the tariff?

3. Under what conditions may a tariff actually make a country better off?

4. In addition to the production and consumption side deadweight losses, what are some of the other potential costs of tariffs?

5. The Uruguay Round of the GATT began a process of phasing out the use of voluntary export restraints. Why did they come into widespread use in the 1980s? For example, given that VERs are a form of quotas, and that they create quota rents and a larger reduction in national welfare than a tariff, why did nations use them instead of tariffs?

6. The GATT strongly favors tariffs as a protective measure over quotas or other nontariff measures. It encourages new members to convert quotas to their tariff equivalents. One of the main reasons tariffs are preferred is because they are more transparent, particularly by comparison to nontariff measures. Explain the idea of transparency, and how nontariff measures may be nontransparent.

7. Suppose that in the United States bikes are built from a combination of domestic and foreign parts.
   a.  If a bike sells for $500 but requires $300 of imported parts, what is the domestic value added?
   b.  If a 20 percent tariff is levied on bikes of the same quality and with the same features, how do the price and the domestic value added change? (Assume that the United States cannot cause the world price to change.)
   c.  What is the effective rate of protection?
   d.  If, in addition to the 20 percent tariff on the final good, a 20 percent tariff on imported parts is levied, what is the effective rate of protection for U.S. bike manufacturers?

# 7

# Commercial Policy

 ## Introduction: Commercial Policy and Jobs

An argument was made in Chapter 6 that tariffs and quotas lower national welfare by creating deadweight losses. In this chapter, we examine the dollar value of the effects of tariffs and quotas in the EU, Japan, and the United States. The overall level of tariffs and quotas in these three economic regions are about average for industrial economies. They are also fairly low, implying that the total deadweight loss imposed on each region is relatively minor. The purpose of this exercise, however, is to compare the costs and benefits of trade barriers. As we will see, even low trade barriers have a high ratio of costs to benefits, and should make us question the strategy of trying to gain jobs in this way.

After a look at the dollar costs of protection in three sectors of the European Union, Japan, and the United States, we examine the most common reasons given for protecting specific industries. Again, the purpose is not to question the goals that nations set for themselves, but to look at the efficiency of tariffs and quotas in reaching them. Finally, the chapter ends with a discussion of the mechanisms used to provide protection.

 ## Protection in the European Union, Japan, and the United States

Between the end of World War II and the early 1990s, tariffs around the world fell substantially. With the signing of the GATT's Uruguay Round agreement in 1994, the 123 founding members of the WTO agreed to cut their rates by another 40 percent, and by 2002, average nominal rates were 3.9 percent in the United States, 3.3 percent in Japan, and 3.9 percent in the European Union. A few industries have seen much smaller decreases in protection, however, and in nearly all the leading industrial countries and regions, agriculture, clothing, and textiles remain heavily protected. As we saw in the last chapter, developing countries tend to have higher rates in general, and all countries have high levels of protection in particular industries they deem "sensitive."

In addition to tariffs and quotas, many countries provide generous subsidies to some of their agricultural producers. Among high-income countries, this benefit is particularly prevalent in the European Union, Japan, and the United States. Although these subsidies are not explicitly trade barriers, in effect they have the same import reducing effect as tariffs and quotas.

## Direct Costs and Jobs Saved in Agriculture, Clothing, and Textiles

Very few countries apply tariffs uniformly across all industries. For example, prior to the complete adoption of the Uruguay Round's 40 percent reduction in tariffs, 22 protected sectors in the European Union accounted for about one-half of the total costs to consumers of EU tariffs and quotas. Similarly, 21 sectors in the United States accounted for one-half of the lost consumer surplus, and in Japan, 47 sectors accounted for nearly all the loss of consumer surplus.

Since the phase-in of the Uruguay Round tariff reductions, average tariffs have fallen 40 percent, but few sectors are average. In particular, three sectors have had much smaller changes in tariffs and quotas: agriculture, clothing, and textiles. In the United States, for example, World Bank data shows that while average tariffs fell by 40 percent, tariffs on agricultural goods fell by 12 percent and clothing and textiles by 14 percent each. In addition, all three sectors in the European Union, Japan, and the United States have significant nontariff barriers applied to them, and agriculture is given large subsidies by all of the national governments.

Table 7.1 itemizes the impact of EU, Japanese, and U.S. tariffs and quotas in the three areas discussed. These are not the only products with trade barriers, but all three geographical areas have stiff protection for these sectors. Furthermore, Table 7.1 is based on the largest tariffs and quotas and does not include the cumulative effects of many smaller tariffs and nontariff barriers. Because a significant part of EU, Japanese, and U.S. production in these sectors exists only because of protective measures, trade in these goods has become the focus of an intense debate between developing countries and high-income countries. These tend to be lines of production where developing countries have significant comparative advantages but encounter high trade barriers when they attempt to enter industrial country markets.

Column A of Table 7.1 shows the producer surplus gained at the expense of consumers, column B is tariff revenue, column C shows the quota rents that occur due to the increase in prices charged by foreign suppliers, and column D is the consumption and production side deadweight loss. Because many product lines in these three sectors have tariffs and quotas, all the items show both tariff revenue generated (B) and quota rents (C) that mostly accrue to foreign producers. The final column, C + D, measures the net reduction in national welfare from the direct effects of the tariffs and quotas.

| TABLE 7.1 | EU, Japanese, and U.S. Protection in Three Sectors (Mid-1990s, Millions of US$) | | | | |
|---|---|---|---|---|---|
| | Producer Surplus Gained | Tariff Revenue | Quota Rents | Deadweight Losses | National Welfare Loss |
| **European Union** | **A** | **B** | **C** | **D** | **C+D** |
| Agriculture | 4,717 | 3,001 | 341 | 4,879 | 5,219 |
| Clothing | 1,464 | 1,450 | 2,239 | 1,461 | 3,161 |
| Textiles | 2,290 | 1,490 | 1,716 | 571 | 2,288 |
| **Japan** | | | | | |
| Agriculture | 43,192 | 1,085 | 6,906 | 7,186 | 14,093 |
| Clothing | 1,605 | 386 | 2,673 | 1,701 | 4,375 |
| Textiles | 772 | 275 | 142 | 14 | 156 |
| **United States** | | | | | |
| Agriculture | 1,775 | 176 | 646 | 350 | 996 |
| Clothing | 9,901 | 3,545 | 5,411 | 2,301 | 7,712 |
| Textiles | 1,749 | 632 | 713 | 181 | 894 |

Three sectors account for a large share of protectionism in the three countries and regions. These sectors support the proposition that older sectors tend to be the most protected, particularly in cases where a country has lost a substantial part of its comparative advantage.

*Sources*: Messerlin: *Measuring the Costs of Protection in Europe* 2001; Sazanami, Urata, and Kawai, *Measuring the Costs of Protection in Japan* 1995; Hufbauer and Elliott, *Measuring the Costs of Protection in the United States* 1994. Published in Washington, DC by Institute for International Economics.

Table 7.1 also shows that in the European Union and Japan, the largest national losses occur in agriculture, while in the United States, national losses in agriculture are relatively smaller, but in clothing they are much higher. European losses in agriculture are mostly efficiency losses that result from keeping relatively less efficient producers in operation, whereas in Japan they are efficiency losses plus large quota rents paid to foreign suppliers. That is, despite its protection for its farm sector, Japan is still one of the world's largest food importers. Similarly, the United States imports large quantities of clothing, and its commercial policy creates large net national losses from quotas.

Table 7.2 carries the analysis one step further. The first column of Table 7.2 is the total cost to consumers in the form of lost consumer surplus. It is equal to the sum of columns A, B, C, and D in Table 7.1. The second column shows estimates of the direct number of jobs saved by the tariffs and quotas, and the third column

| TABLE 7.2 | Jobs Saved through Tariffs and Quotas | | |
|---|---|---|---|
| | Cost to Consumers (Millions of US$) | Jobs Saved | Cost per Job Saved (US$) |
| **European Union** | | | |
| Agriculture | 15,130 | 121,192 | 106,751 |
| Clothing | 7,735 | 39,383 | 167,928 |
| Textiles | 7,096 | 33,160 | 182,968 |
| **Japan** | | | |
| Agriculture | 58,058 | 76,600 | 762,000 |
| Clothing | 879 | 13,800 | 461,313 |
| Textiles | 166 | 2,700 | 445,864 |
| **United States** | | | |
| Agriculture | 2,947 | 6,053 | 486,866 |
| Clothing | 21,158 | 152,583 | 138,666 |
| Textiles | 3,275 | 16,203 | 202,123 |

Saving jobs with tariffs and quotas is grossly inefficient and has costs per job saved that are far greater than the average annual income of workers in the protected industry.

*Sources*: Messerlin: *Measuring the Costs of Protection in Europe* 2001; Sazanami, Urata, and Kawai, *Measuring the Costs of Protection in Japan* 1995; Hufbauer and Elliott, *Measuring the Costs of Protection in the United States* 1994. Published in Washington, DC by Institute for International Economics.

is the cost to consumers per job saved (column 1 divided by column 2). In each of the sectors and in all three countries, the cost per job saved exceeds $100,000 per year, often by a large amount. The least expensive jobs to save are in European agriculture, but given that average wages were around $17,000 per year in the mid-1990s, even those jobs look expensive to preserve by this means. In Japan and the United States agriculture is the most expensive, while in the European Union jobs in textiles are most costly.

The purpose of this exercise is to illuminate the hidden costs of using tariffs and quotas to achieve employment objectives. It does not analyze whether societies are better off if they preserve employment in these sectors. That is, this analysis is not useful for understanding the role of agriculture in national culture, or the desirability of preserving garment manufacturing. Rather, it only tells us about the costs of preserving employment when it is accomplished with tariffs and quotas. From this perspective, it shows how grossly inefficient commercial policy is at achieving the objective of job preservation. The analysis also points to the issues of concern in the Doha negotiations. Namely, it raises the question of whether trade barriers to protect these industries in high-income countries have the unintended consequence of increasing poverty in low-income countries.

Agriculture, clothing, and textiles were singled out because they tend to be the most highly protected sectors of industrial countries and because the problem of access to those markets has harmful effects on developing countries. The results shown in Table 7.1 and Table 7.2 are not unique in terms of the cost per job saved, however, and other sectors in all three regions have similar or worse performance when evaluated in those terms. For example, voluntary export restraints imposed by the United States on Japanese automobiles in the 1980s cost U.S. consumers well over $100,000 per job saved, and in the European Union, the cost per job of their trade barriers was estimated at over €550,000 in the 1990s. Even when tariffs are relatively low, the cost per job saved tends to be high.

## The Logic of Collective Action

Given that the costs to consumers are so high for each job saved, why do people tolerate tariffs and quotas? Ignorance is certainly the case for some goods, but for some tariffs and quotas, the costs have been relatively well publicized. For example, many people are aware that quotas on sugar imports cost each man, woman, and child in the United States between $5 and $10 per year. The costs are in the form of higher prices on candy bars, soft drinks, and other products containing sugar. Few of us work in the sugar industry, so the argument that our jobs depend on it is weak at best.

In a surprising way, however, we probably permit our tariffs and quotas because of a version of the jobs argument. The economist Mancur Olson studied this problem and similar ones and noticed two important points about tariffs and quotas. First, the costs of the policy are spread over a great many people. Second, the benefits are concentrated. For example, we all pay a little more for candy bars and soft drinks, but a few sugar producers reap large benefits from our restrictions on sugar imports. Olson found that in cases such as this, there is an asymmetry in the incentives to support and to oppose the policy. With trade protection, the benefits are concentrated in a single industry and consequently, it pays for the industry to commit resources to obtaining or maintaining its protection. The industry will hire lobbyists and perhaps participate directly in the political process through running candidates or supporting friendly candidates. If people in the industry think their entire livelihood depends on their ability to limit foreign competition, they have a very large incentive to become involved in setting policy.

The costs of protection are nowhere near as concentrated as the benefits because they are spread over all consumers of a product. The $5 to $10 per year that sugar quotas cost each of us is hardly worth hiring a lobbyist or protesting in Washington. Thus, one side pushes hard to obtain or keep protection, and the other side is silent on the matter. Given this imbalance, an interesting question asks why there are not more trade barriers.

# CASE STUDY

## The Uruguay and Doha Rounds

The Uruguay Round negotiations concluded in 1993 after seven years of negotiations. They took three years longer than planned, and included one complete breakdown in the talks. The agreement was signed in 1993, ratified by most of its 123 participating countries in 1994, and implemented in 1995.

Table 7.3 summarizes the four main categories of negotiations. Trade barriers were reduced through several mechanisms, including tariff reductions, clarification of the rules on subsidies, a number of new areas of agreement, and institutional reforms within the framework of the existing General Agreement on Tariffs and Trade (GATT). Most notably, the Uruguay Round created the World Trade Organization (WTO) as a body to oversee the implementation and further refinement of the various agreements.

One of the biggest potential changes in world trade patterns coming out of the Uruguay Round was the negotiation of a separate Agreement on Textiles and Clothing (ATC). Until 1994, textiles and clothing had a separate international agreement, called the Multi-Fiber Arrangement, which was a system of quotas and tariffs. Under the ATC, textiles and clothing were integrated into the WTO system, with a complete phase-out of all quotas by 2005, and with allowance for the application of temporary rates of protection in the event of a sudden surge in imports. Subsequently, however, the European Union and the United States have both negotiated side agreements with China to limit the volume of Chinese textile and clothing exports.

| TABLE 7.3  The Uruguay Round | |
|---|---|
| **Category** | **Results** |
| Tariffs | • Most industrial product tariffs cut by 40 percent<br>• Conversion of some agricultural quotas to tariffs |
| Subsidies | • Subsidies defined<br>• Classifies prohibited and actionable subsidies |
| New agreements | • Agreement on Textiles and Clothing<br>• Trade Related Aspects of Intellectual Property Rights<br>• Trade Related Investment Measures<br>• General Agreement on Services |
| Institutional reorganization | • Creates the World Trade Organization<br>• Refines the dispute settlement process<br>• Implements periodic trade policy reviews |

The Uruguay Round included far more than tariff cuts.

Other notable accomplishments of the Uruguay Round were separate agreements on trade in services—General Agreement on Trade in Services (GATS); an agreement on intellectual property enforcement—Trade Related Aspects of Intellectual Property Rights (TRIPS); and an agreement on investment—Trade Related Investment Measures (TRIMS). The Uruguay Round also reorganized the General Agreement on Tariffs and Trade (GATT) into an organization called the World Trade Organization (WTO). The WTO takes the lead in multilateral trade negotiations, administers all the agreements (ATC, GATS, TRIPS, TRIMS, GATT), and provides a more efficient dispute settlement process. In addition, the WTO conducts periodic reviews of individual country trade policies, which it makes available (with much more information) on its Web site at http://www.wto.org.

The Doha Round was launched in 2001 in Doha, Qatar. The goal was to reach an agreement by the end of 2005, but that proved impossible, and in July 2006, the talks were suspended. Not surprisingly, the areas where talks broke down were trade barriers and subsidies in agriculture and textiles and apparel.

The initial Doha Declaration included 21 subjects for negotiation, several of which were dropped along the way. Doha is called the Doha Development Round because the needs of developing countries were given greater visibility. For example, a key issue is the problem of many developing countries in implementing Uruguay Round commitments. In addition, access to life-saving medicines under the terms of the TRIPS agreement has been a problem, and the important developing country sectors of agriculture and textiles and apparel continue to face significant barriers to entering developed country markets.

In the preparations for beginning the Doha Round, during the Round itself, and finally in the suspension of the trade talks, agriculture and textiles and apparel have been the biggest obstacles, with the European Union and the United States being the two main protagonists. Europe fears elimination or substantial reduction of its agricultural trade barriers and subsidies, and the United States fears the removal of barriers to textile and apparel imports, particularly after the surge in imports from China after the full implementation of the Agreement on Textiles and Clothing in 2005.

The Uruguay Round talks were also suspended for a time, and with 135 nations involved in the Doha negotiations, the talks move slowly. Given time and private consultations, it is likely that the main difficulties between the United States and the European Union will be addressed, compromises will be reached, and at some point, the talks will resume.

##  Why Nations Protect Their Industries

Countries use tariffs for a variety of reasons, not the least of which is the revenue they generate. In a developing country's economy, a large percentage of economic activity is unrecorded. Subsistence farmers sell their surplus in the town market, and repairmen and craftsmen take on jobs without leaving a paper trail of work orders or receipts. In this environment, income taxes and sales taxes are difficult if not impossible to impose. Tariffs, on the other hand, can be relatively easily collected by inspectors at the ports and border crossings. They simply have to value the goods coming in and levy a fee (the tariff) on the person transporting the goods. The United States is a case in point, as tariff revenues were the single greatest source of income for the U.S. government until well into the twentieth century.

In addition to the need for revenue, there are four broad categories of reasons that nations give for imposing trade barriers.

## The Labor Argument

The labor argument is a perennial justification for trade barriers. It was used throughout the nineteenth century, and most recently, has been resurrected by many opponents of expanded trade agreements. The argument states that nations must protect their markets against imports from countries where wages are much lower because otherwise, the advantage of lower wages will either wreck the domestic industry or force it to match the lower wages. For example, in the debate leading up to the ratification of NAFTA, opponents argued that Mexico would have an unfair advantage in trade with the United States because Mexican firms pay their workers a fraction (on average, about one-eighth) of the wages paid to American workers.

The labor argument fails to consider productivity differences. Mexican workers, for example, earn about one-eighth of the salary of U.S. workers because their productivity, on average, is about one-eighth of the level of U.S. workers. Mexico has lower productivity because the education and skill levels of its workforce are less than in the United States, Mexican workers have less capital at work than U.S. workers, and the infrastructure of the Mexican economy is not as developed as the infrastructure of the United States. As Mexican workers gain more skills and education, and as the capital available on the job and in the surrounding economy increases, their productivity will rise, and so will their wages.

The labor argument also fails to consider the issues raised at the beginning of this chapter, where we saw that tariffs and quotas are an expensive way to protect jobs. If the goal is an adequate number of jobs to reach full employment, then appropriate macroeconomic and labor market policies are better instruments. Monetary and fiscal policies (see Chapter 11) that maintain economic growth, and labor market policies that provide adjustment assistance to dislocated workers and incentives for employers to hire them are far less expensive than trade policy for this purpose. If the goal is to keep a particular sector alive, then direct subsidies to the producers are preferable because they do not have the distortions that result from forcing consumers out of the market.

## The Infant Industry Argument

A much more sophisticated argument for protection is the **infant industry** argument. The argument is mainly associated with the tariff policies of developing nations that protect their "infant" industries against the competition of more mature firms in industrial countries. Nevertheless, industrial countries use this argument on occasion to justify protection in some high-technology cases (for example, Japanese skis). Two beliefs lie at the root of the infant industry argument. The first is that market forces will not support the development of a particular industry, usually because foreign competition is too well established, but also possibly because the industry is too risky. The second belief is that the industry in question has some spillover benefits, or positive externalities, that make the industry more valuable to the national economy than simply the wages and profits it might generate. Whenever there are spillover benefits, the market may not support the development of an industry to the optimum level. With positive **externalities**, many of the benefits of production are captured by other firms or individuals outside of the producing firm. Since the producers do not get the full benefit of their own production, they produce less than the amount that is most beneficial for society.

Positive externalities are usually argued to be in the form of linkages to other industries or of a technological nature. As an example of the linkage case, many nations have attempted to start their own steel industries because they assumed it would create a cheaper source of steel for other industries, such as cars. The problem with this argument is that it does not demonstrate that there is some inherent advantage in making something as opposed to buying it, or in other words, that the car industry will have a special advantage if it can buy steel from local producers. If the car industry is forced to buy locally at prices above world levels, protection on the domestic steel industry may actually harm the car industry. This is what happened to firms in Brazil when the government tried to start a domestic computer industry by keeping out foreign producers. The policy actually had negative linkage effects on Brazilian businesses because they had to pay higher prices for computers and got lower-quality machines in the bargain. Brazil would have been better off importing its computers, as it does now.

Technological externalities can happen when workers change jobs and take the skills they have learned to their new employment, or whenever an industry creates information or technology that is useful somewhere else in the economy. As a practical matter, however, it is difficult to know in advance when there will be technological spillovers, and, accordingly, it is difficult to judge which industries should be protected.

Even if technological externalities are present, it is not enough to establish the validity of the infant industry argument. Two more conditions must hold. First, the protection that is offered must be limited in time, and second, the protected industry must experience falling costs. The time limits on protection ensure that the industry does not become a permanent recipient of transfers from consumers, while the presence of falling costs ensures that the policy will eventually pay for itself and that the industry will become competitive.

## The National Security Argument

Every nation protects some industries as a way to guard its national security. In trade terms, national security can be interpreted in the narrow sense of military capability or in a broader sense of cultural identity. The most obvious examples of national security in a narrow sense include weapons industries, and somewhat more broadly, strategic technologies. Some nations also include strategic minerals such as the exotic ores used in jet aircraft, but protection for the sake of making available specific resources is not an optimal policy. A better policy is to build stockpiles of the mineral by buying large quantities in peacetime when it is cheap.

A broader definition of national security includes the cultural industries — movies, television programming, music, print media, and theater. Some nations worry that if they allow completely free trade in the cultural industries, then the most commercially viable firms will dominate, and the cultural values of the home country will be obscured and forgotten. Since the United States has the strongest presence in much of the entertainment industry, the goal of protecting national cultural values is usually an argument in favor of protecting a nation's filmmaking, television programming, and music production against complete domination by its U.S. counterparts. For example, the precursor to the North American Free Trade Agreement, called the Canadian-United States Free Trade Agreement (signed in 1988), established the right of Canada to require its TV and radio stations to broadcast a certain proportion of Canadian produced programs. There are similar requirements in music, theater, and the print media. U.S. television and movie producers naturally opposed this limitation on free trade and demanded the right to sell an unlimited amount of U.S.-produced entertainment. They lost this argument, however, and they lost again when the Uruguay Round of the GATT was signed. It allows all nations to place similar restrictions on their film, television, and other cultural industries.

The issue of free trade in military and cultural industries inevitably involves noneconomic values and issues. How, for example, can we begin to assess the effects on Canadian culture and society of limitations on U.S. television programming? Given that many industries argue that their products are absolutely essential to maintaining military capability, how can we assess the strategic value of particular products or technologies? Economists tend to defer to the judgment of scientific and engineering experts on questions of strategic importance, pointing out that a less costly option is stockpiling the needed materials when possible. In the case of protection for cultural industries, economists can point out some of the trade-offs, but they cannot estimate the cultural benefits of, say, a nationally based film industry.

## The Retaliation Argument

A final category of reasons given by nations to justify trade barriers is retaliation for unfair trade practices. When a country decides that another country's trade practices unfairly discriminate against them, a common response is to impose a trade barrier. Retaliatory tariffs and quotas can provide an incentive for negotiations, but they can also lead to escalating trade wars.

Economic analysis is of limited utility in understanding this situation, since the outcome depends on political processes that determine how nations respond to pressure, their willingness to negotiate, and the outcome of negotiations. There are three camps of economists on this issue. One camp argues that free trade is beneficial regardless of the actions of a country's trading partners. If other countries choose to protect their markets, this argument goes, then it lowers their standard of living, and we would be foolish to do the same by imposing trade barriers in retaliation. Another camp argues that since free trade is beneficial, it is in everyone's interest to see it followed as widely as possible. Therefore, if a tariff today will cause other nations to open their markets tomorrow, the world economy will benefit in the long run.

A third group argues that countries that have a closed market or that restrict market access by imposing barriers to trade have an unfair advantage, particularly in high-technology products. They have a domestic market all to themselves, and they can compete freely in other markets that are more open than their own. In cases where the size of the market is important, the ability to sell to a market larger (home plus foreign) than their competitor's may give the firms in the protected market a competitive advantage. If firms in the open market are forced out of business, then the technology, skills, and expertise that go with it will exist only in the firms from the country that adopted the strategy of protecting its market. To ensure that this scenario does not play out, and so that we do not lose critical technologies, some would argue that we should use the threat of retaliation to force open markets that are presently closed.

## CASE STUDY

# Economic Sanctions

Economic sanctions are a form of trade restriction. Unlike tariffs and quotas, which affect imports alone, often sanctions are on exports as well as imports and may include financial components as well. Access to international credit through privately owned banks or international lending agencies may be limited or blocked, as may investment by domestic firms in the country singled out for sanctions. Examples of export prohibitions included the U.S. rule during the Cold War prohibiting computer sales by domestic firms to the Soviet Union, and current prohibitions on selling goods or services to Cuba and North Korea. The world community's boycott of investment in South Africa before the ending of apartheid is an example of an investment and trade sanction.

Economic sanctions go beyond simple trade or investment measures. In most cases they are used as one of several tactics aimed at achieving a broader policy objective—the ending of Soviet expansion or Iranian terrorism or South African apartheid. Another feature of sanctions is that they are often accompanied by additional measures, ranging from diplomatic pressure to military invasion.

The logical question to ask about sanctions is "Do they work?" In an important two-volume study of this question, three economists analyzed 120 episodes of economic sanctions throughout the world since World War I. Table 7.4 summarizes their findings. The economists found it useful to categorize the goals of sanctions into five separate groups: those designed to create a relatively modest policy change (for example, to free a political prisoner or to limit nuclear proliferation); those intended to destabilize a government; those aimed at disrupting a military adventure of another nation (for example, stopping Iraq's invasion of Kuwait); those designed to impair another nation's military potential; and a fifth category of other goals, such as stopping apartheid, or the Arab League's boycott of oil sales to the United States in retaliation for support for Israel.

In order to be classified as a success, the policy outcome must have been the one desired by the country imposing the sanctions, and the sanctions must have been a contributor to the policy outcome. Hufbauer, Schott, and Elliott find 41 successes in the 120 cases they examined, but they report a drop in the number of successes after about 1973. They determined that sanctions are more effective when the target country is small, economically weak, and politically unstable; the target country is an ally; sanctions are imposed quickly and decisively; the costs to the sending country are small; and the goal is a relatively small change.

The more difficult the goal, the more likely is the need for military force to back up the sanctions. The U.S. invasion of Iraq in 2003 is a case in point. United Nations sanctions against Iraq undoubtedly helped to cripple its economy, even though the sanctions were never successfully enforced completely. In that sense, they contributed to the success of U.S. policy in replacing Iraq's government. Still, without a military invasion, it seems unlikely that the sanctions alone would have led to a change of government.

| TABLE 7.4 ● Economic Sanctions since World War I | | |
|---|---|---|
| Goal | Number of Cases | Successes |
| Modest policy change | 51 | 17 |
| Destabilize a government | 21 | 11 |
| Disrupt a military adventure | 18 | 6 |
| Impair military potential | 10 | 2 |
| Other | 20 | 5 |

Sanctions imposed between World War I and 1990 had about a 38 percent success rate.

*Source*: Gary Clyde Hufbauer, Jeffrey J. Schott, and Kimberly Ann Elliott. *Economic Sanctions Reconsidered*. Washington, DC: Institute for International Economics. 1990; "Executive Summary," 1998. http://www.iie.com/FOCUS/SANCTION/execsum.htm#start.

# The Politics of Protection in the United States

Although U.S. trade with the rest of the world has grown, political pressures to protect domestic industries have frequently been intense. Part of the reason stems from the fact that Congressional reforms removed some of the insulation from industry lobbyists that Congress enjoyed in the 1950s and 1960s. Another reason stems from the end of the Cold War and the lessening of U.S. willingness to sacrifice trade issues for the sake of maintaining close geopolitical alliances. A third reason is the rise of the export-oriented East Asian newly industrializing countries (NICs), including China, and the pressure they have put on a number of domestic U.S. industries. Finally, the growth of the U.S. trade deficit and the widespread fear in the 1980s that the United States had lost its competitive edge also contributed to a greater reluctance to open U.S. markets without reciprocity by other countries. More recently, the rapid increase of the U.S. trade deficit and the loss of manufacturing jobs since 2000 are conditions that are likely to bring back the competition fears of the 1980s. For each of these reasons, trade conflicts have intensified.

Protection in the United States is usually obtained through direct action by the president (for example, the VERs on Japanese autos in the 1980s) or through one of the following different legal procedures:

- Countervailing duties
- Antidumping duties
- Escape clause relief
- Section 301 retaliation

In each case, a firm, an industry trade association, or a government agency may petition the federal government to initiate an investigation into foreign country or foreign firm practices.

## Countervailing Duties

A **countervailing duty (CVD)** is a tariff that is granted to an industry that has been hurt by foreign country **subsidies** of its national firms. Since subsidies permit a firm to sell its goods at a lower price and still make a profit, an effect of subsidies is to make firms more competitive. The goal of a countervailing duty is to raise the price of the foreign good to a level high enough to countervail the effect of the subsidy. The idea is to level the playing field between domestic firms that receive no subsidies and foreign ones that do.

Countervailing duties are used less often than other forms of protection, such as antidumping duties. In the United States, there has been an average of 4 to 5 cases per year since 1985. Countervailing duties require a clear definition of a subsidy since they are intended to counteract the effects of subsidies. One of the benefits of the Uruguay Round is that it standardized the definition as a financial contribution by a government (national or local) or public agency that confers a benefit. Subsidies take on a variety of forms, including grants, low interest loans, preferential tax treatments, provision of goods or services for free or below cost, or any of a number of other financial benefits.

## Antidumping Duties

An **antidumping duty (ADD)** is a tariff levied on an import that is selling at a price below the product's **fair value**. The determination of fair value introduces an element of subjectivity into the process of justifying an antidumping duty, as does the fact that the legal analysis and the economic analysis of dumping are not in agreement. Consequently, antidumping duties have become a source of significant trade tension between countries; it is not surprising that a number of countries would like to strengthen the WTO's rules regarding antidumping duties by making them harder to apply.

According to the rules of the WTO, **dumping** occurs when an exporter sells a product at a price below what it charges in its home market. It is not always possible to compare the home market and foreign market prices, however, and wholesalers, transportation costs, and other add-ons to the price may limit the usefulness of the comparison. Therefore, two other methods may be used to determine if a good is being dumped. Comparisons can be made with the price charged in third country markets, or to an estimate of the cost of production. Comparison to prices in another country is similar to the comparison between prices in the exporter's home market and the complaining country's market, and may be uninformative for the same reasons. Therefore, the WTO allows the third method whereby a country estimates the foreign firm's production costs and uses that measure to determine if dumping is occurring. In this case, an exporter does not need to sell below the cost of production to be found guilty of dumping. Dumping charges are supported if the foreign firm is not selling at a price that provides a normal rate of return on invested capital.

One final criterion must be met before antidumping duties are allowed. The country claiming dumping must also be able to show that the dumping has caused material injury to its firms. If dumping occurs, but there are no harmful effects on domestic firms, then antidumping duties are not allowed. This would happen if the dumping margin is too small to matter.

At their most basic level, antidumping duties are a tool of commercial policy that protects against predatory pricing by foreign firms. Selling below cost as a strategy to drive the competition out of business is widely perceived as unfair, and allowing it to happen can harm the economic interest of a country. This is particularly likely if it results in higher prices after the domestic producers have been driven out of the market. Since 1985, the United States has imposed an average of 21 new antidumping duties per year.

Problems arise, however, because the economic theory and the legal definition are not completely in agreement. First, in order for a firm to sell in a foreign market at a price that is below its cost of production, it must have market power at home that allows it to earn higher than normal profits so it can subsidize its foreign sales. If a firm is not earning above average profits somewhere, it cannot maintain a price somewhere else that is below its cost. Yet, when countries investigate a dumping complaint, market structure is rarely considered. This problem is compounded by the use of estimated production costs to determine dumping, since estimated values require some guesswork about technology and other inputs, and this creates a significant margin of error.

Second, within the scope of normal commercial operations, firms often sell below cost. The most obvious case is that of goods that are likely to spoil. A fresh fish exporter, with a load sitting on a dock somewhere, is likely to lower her price progressively as time passes. In this case, the cost of producing the shipment of fish represents sunk costs that have already been incurred, and the only option is to sell the goods for whatever is possible. Firms also sell selected items below cost as a technique for penetrating markets. This is similar to the behavior of large retail chains that offer some goods at an extremely low price in order to create a reputation as a value-oriented retailer. And finally, firms will go for extended periods selling at prices that do not cover the cost of their capital and other fixed costs as long as the costs of their variable inputs such as labor and materials are covered. Since capital costs such as interest on their loans have to be paid no matter what is produced, in the short run, the chief consideration is whether the price is high enough to cover labor costs and material input costs. In the long run, a firm that cannot sell at a high enough price to meet its capital costs will have to shut down, but in the short run, it continues to produce.

The increasing use of antidumping duties has generated a great deal of interest in defining their usage more carefully. As things now stand, there is a wide variation among countries in their application and their willingness to negotiate their usage. Some countries rarely apply them, and some trade agreements, such as the one between Canada and Chile, ban their usage except under exceptional circumstances. Other countries use them frequently—often it seems, as a politically expedient way to satisfy an important industry lobbying group.

In the United States, the procedure for firms to obtain protection requires that a petition be filed with the International Trade Administration in the Department of Commerce. The ITA investigates whether dumping (or subsidization in the case of a petition for countervailing duties) has occurred. If their finding is positive (dumping has occurred), the case is turned over to the United States International Trade Commission (USITC), an independent regulatory commission. The USITC conducts an additional investigation to determine if substantial harm has been done to the domestic industry and if an antidumping or countervailing duty is warranted. The relative success of U.S. firms in proving that foreign companies are dumping has encouraged a growing number of antidumping petitions in recent years.

## Escape Clause Relief

**Escape clause relief** is so named because it refers to a clause in the U.S. and GATT trade rules that permits an industry to escape the pressure of imports by temporarily imposing a tariff. Escape clause relief is a temporary tariff on imports in order to provide a period of adjustment to a domestic industry. It is initiated when an industry or firm petitions the USITC directly for relief from a sudden surge of imports. The burden of escape clause relief is on the firm; it must establish that it is been harmed by imports and not by some other factor, such as bad management decisions. In practice, it has become so difficult to obtain relief from import competition under this procedure that few cases are filed.

## Section 301 and Special 301

**Section 301** of the U.S. Trade Act of 1974 requires the president's chief trade negotiator, the United States Trade Representative (USTR), to take action against any nation that persistently engages in unfair trade practices. The action usually begins with a request for negotiations with the targeted country. The goal of the negotiations is to change the policies of countries that restrict U.S. commerce unreasonably or unjustifiably. Note that it is left to the United States to define unreasonable and unjustifiable restrictions on U.S. commerce.

The types of trade practices that the USTR is required to investigate are quite broad. Recent cases have included an investigation of China's management of its exchange rate, Ukraine's actions to enforce intellectual property rights, and the European Union's lack of compliance with a WTO ruling against its blockage of imports of hormone-fed beef.

A similar program to Section 301 is known as **Special 301**. This part of U.S. trade law requires the USTR to monitor property rights enforcement around the globe. In 2005, the USTR surveyed 90 countries and identified 52 as lacking adequate enforcement or as denying market access to U.S. artists and industries that rely on intellectual property enforcement. Inclusion on this list means that the USTR has some concerns and will continue to monitor the situation.

## CASE STUDY

# Agricultural Subsidies

Agricultural issues have long sparked conflict among the members of the WTO. Some cases have pitted high-income countries against each other, among them disputes between the United States and Japan over apples and EU-U.S. disputes over bananas. More recently, the WTO's Doha Development Agenda has tried to address agricultural issues that are central to relations between developing and industrial countries. In particular, three issues are on the table: tariffs and quotas (market access), export subsidies given by countries to encourage farm exports, and production subsidies granted directly to farmers.

Direct subsidies are viewed as harmful because they lead to overproduction, squeeze out imports, and in some cases result in the dumping of the surplus product in foreign markets. The original GATT agreement included language on agriculture, but there were so many loopholes that it had little impact. Not until the Uruguay Round was finalized in 1993, nearly 50 years after the signing of the original GATT agreement, were significant changes made in the rules for agricultural trade. Many quotas were converted to tariffs, and industrial countries agreed to reduce their direct support for the farm sector by 20 percent. Indirect supports such as research and development and infrastructure construction were recognized as necessary, desirable, and permissible.

While direct-support payments were curtailed, the Uruguay Round left intact direct payments to farmers that theoretically do not increase production, are part of a country's environmental or regional development plan, or are intended to limit production. If you think these are a lot of loopholes, you are right. Consequently, the current round of trade negotiations, the Doha Development Agenda, has taken up the issue of agriculture again, and developing countries in particular are pushing to limit government practices that block their access to markets in high-income countries or that subsidize production by industrial countries.

Table 7.5 shows the range of direct-support payments to agricultural producers in many industrial nations. The fifteen members of the European Union are grouped together because their trade and agricultural policies are formulated at the EU level, not at the national level. In terms of both absolute support and the percentage of their GDP they transfer to farmers, the European Union is the biggest subsidizer. Japan is close in percentage terms but is at about one-half the level in absolute dollar amounts. The United States is also a large subsidizer, and Canada is similar. Not all countries subsidize agriculture, however. Australia's supports are less than one-half the level of the United States, and New Zealand is about one-fifth. Despite the lower support levels and their relatively small economies, both New Zealand and Australia use their comparative advantages to be among the top 15 agricultural exporting countries in the world.

| TABLE 7.5 • **Agricultural Subsidies, 2000** | | |
|---|---|---|
| | Agricultural Subsidies (Millions of US$) | As a Percent of GDP |
| **Australia** | 827 | 0.22 |
| **Canada** | 3,928 | 0.57 |
| **European Union** | 93,083 | 1.17 |
| **Japan** | 47,242 | 1.13 |
| **New Zealand** | 52 | 0.10 |
| **United States** | 49,001 | 0.49 |

The European Union gives the largest subsidies to farmers. Japan and the United States are similar to each other in dollar amounts, but Japan's percentage is more like the European Union's.

*Source*: World Bank, http://siteresources.worldbank.org/INTRANETTRADE/Resources/PSE2001.xls.

# Summary

- Regardless of their cost or their ability to achieve a desired objective, every nation uses trade barriers. In most industrial nations, they are not used to develop comparative advantage in new industries, but rather to protect old industries that can no longer compete or to temporarily protect industries that are under pressure from new competitors. Agriculture, clothing, and textiles are the most protected sectors in many industrial countries.

- Tariffs and quotas are inefficient mechanisms for creating (or keeping) jobs. Because the costs are hidden in the prices consumers pay for foreign and domestic goods, few people realize how inefficient they are.

- The primary beneficiaries of trade barriers are producers who receive protection and governments that receive tariff revenue. The losers are consumers. Because the gains are concentrated among a relatively few people, and the losses are dispersed across many, there is usually a small economic incentive to oppose trade barriers but a large incentive to seek them.

- The valid arguments in favor of protection involve economic returns to society that are undervalued or not counted by markets. That is, it must be the case that the market does not take into consideration the gains that spill over from production. The total value of producing a good, including any spillovers, is extremely difficult to measure, however, and it is often impossible to know the future value of the skills or technology an industry will create.

- In addition to presidential action, there are several forms of protection in the United States: countervailing duties to counter a foreign subsidy, antidumping duties to counter dumping of foreign goods, escape clause relief to counter an import surge, and Section 301 actions to retaliate against foreign trade practices that have been labeled as unfair. Except for escape clause relief, each type of tariff requires a demonstration that foreign products are competing unfairly in the U.S. market and that they have harmed domestic producers. The most common form of tariff imposition is an antidumping duty.

# Vocabulary

| | |
|---|---|
| antidumping duty (ADD) | fair value |
| countervailing duty (CVD) | infant industry |
| dumping | Section 301 |
| escape clause relief | Special 301 |
| externalities | subsidies |

**Study Questions**

1. Which industries are more heavily protected in the United States and Japan? Are high-income or low-income nations more affected by American and Japanese trade barriers? Explain.

2. What new areas of trade and investment received coverage under the agreement signed after the Uruguay Round of the General Agreement on Tariffs and Trade?

3. Given that tariffs and quotas cost consumers and that they are grossly inefficient means for creating or preserving jobs, why do citizens allow these policies to exist?

4. What four main groups of arguments do nations use to justify protection for particular industries? Which are economic, and which are noneconomic?

5. Evaluate the labor and infant industry arguments for protection.

6. Are tariffs justified as a retaliatory measure against other nations? Justify your answer.

7. What are the four legal procedures that American firms have at their disposal for seeking protection? What are the conditions that would generate a request for each kind of protection?

# International Trade and Labor and Environmental Standards

**8**

 ## Introduction: Income and Standards

Since the end of World War II, many of the formal barriers to international trade have been removed. This was accomplished through the sustained efforts of the world's trading nations, often working through the negotiating frameworks provided by the General Agreement on Tariffs and Trade, the World Trade Organization, and more recently, the regional trade agreements around the globe.

As trade barriers are removed, however, new obstacles to increased international economic integration begin to appear. These obstacles are driven by two distinct but equally important forces. First, it sometimes happens that national laws and regulations that were adopted for strictly domestic reasons unintentionally limit international commerce in a more integrated economic environment. For example, a law designed to capture economies of scale by giving one company a monopoly in telephone services makes it impossible for foreign telephone companies to enter the market.

A second obstacle to increased international economic integration is the conflict over standards. These extend from disputes over technical product standards, to health and safety standards, to labor and environmental standards. Issues arise in these areas for a variety of reasons. For example, the adoption of a common set of product standards gives a significant commercial advantage to firms that are already producing to the standard, and hence, each country would like to see the wider application of its own standards. Another reason behind many of the conflicts over standards is the wide variation in world income levels. Trade between developed and developing countries is usually based on comparative advantage and it moves countries along their production possibility curves, causing greater specialization in production. Although each nation's gains from trade may be large, greater specialization creates winners and losers inside each country, and raises questions of fairness.

Economic conditions and living standards inside developing countries are vastly different from conditions inside high-income economies such as the United States. In particular, lower wages, longer hours, less safe working conditions, dirtier industries, and less regard for environmental degradation are relatively more common in low-income than in high-income countries. When trade occurs between countries with different living standards, people begin to wonder about the inexpensive goods they import from low-income countries. Does their production exploit children, are working conditions safe and healthy, do workers have political and civil rights, and are the methods employed environmentally friendly? And if not, can trade barriers such as tariffs, quotas, or complete prohibition of imports effectively pressure the exporting country into changing its practices?

 ## Setting Standards: Harmonization, Mutual Recognition, or Separate?

Two or more economies can be deeply integrated even if they have different rules, regulations, and standards governing their individual economies. The United States is an obvious example, since individual states impose different standards on vehicle emissions, minimum wages, teacher training, food safety, construction codes, and product availability, to name just a few. Lesser forms of integration between sovereign nations, such as partial trade agreements, free-trade areas, customs unions, and common markets are likely to vary even more with respect to rules, regulations, and standards.

Harmonization of product and process standards is one option for countries seeking to expand their commercial ties. **Harmonization of standards** refers to the case where two or more countries share a common set of standards in an area of concern, such as product safety, labor, environment, fair competition, and so on. Another option is **mutual recognition of standards**, in which countries keep their own product and process standards, but accept the standards of others as equally valid and sufficient. For example, a medical doctor trained in a foreign country may not receive the same training as medical doctors in the home country, but under a system of mutual recognition, she is qualified to practice in either country. A third option is **separate standards**. In this case, countries keep their own standards and refuse to recognize those of anyone else. For example, if the home country has a more stringent rule for pesticide residue left on vegetables after harvest, then with separate standards they prohibit imports that are considered unsafe. Most regional trade agreements and the WTO agreements practice a combination of harmonization, mutual recognition, and separate standards.

There are no general rules to determine which approach is most efficient or fairest in all cases. Often it is the case that the harmonization of technical standards having to do with product design or performance is useful, since it leads to a larger, more unified market and creates greater efficiency. Simple examples such as the number of threads per centimeter on screws, or the size of electrical plugs on home appliances are illustrations of cases where harmonization unifies a market and creates efficiency gains across the economy. In other cases, harmonization of standards may pose the potential problem of freezing into place a set of inferior standards. New technologies are a case in point, since the evolution of new products and processes is impossible to forecast, and freezing technical standards into legal requirements may have a harmful effect on future developments. In addition, there are many cases such as labor or environmental legislation where it is unclear which country has the "best" rules. Mutual recognition is a superior option under these conditions, as it allows competition between different standards, which may help clarify the costs and benefits of each one.

Harmonization of standards sometimes poses an additional problem in its failure to take into account the differences between countries. Generally speaking, the lower a country's average income, the less administrative, scientific, and technical capacity it has to design and enforce standards. In addition, national priorities change as income levels change, and there is no reason why the priorities of one group of countries should dominate. Differences in income levels are not always an obstacle to the harmonization of standards, however, because many product standards are technical considerations where the adoption of a common set of rules makes a great deal of sense if it widens the market and lowers prices.

When standards across countries vary by the level of development, it is generally better to mutually recognize each other's standards, or if that is not possible for safety or other reasons, to maintain separate standards. While trade theory is clear on this point, many people living in high-income countries find it hard to accept, particularly with respect to labor and environmental standards. Many fear that in the absence of a common set of labor and environmental standards, low standards abroad create competitive pressures for domestic firms to lower their standards, or to move to a foreign location in order to reduce their costs. This possibility has been labeled a **race to the bottom**, where the bottom is the lowest possible level of standards. In the following sections, we examine this issue and others, in the context of labor and environmental standards.

## CASE STUDY

# Income, Environment, and Society

The World Bank has four categories of income that it uses to classify countries: **low**, **lower-middle**, **upper-middle**, and **high-income**. Table 8.1 shows world population and the level of income in each of the categories.

Note that most of the world's population, and a majority of the countries in the world are classified as low-income or lower-middle income. Income differences as large as those in Table 8.1 lead to very large differences in most social,

**TABLE 8.1** ● **Income and Population by World Bank Categories, 2004**

| Income Category | Number of Countries | Population (Millions) | Income Range (US$ per Person) | Average Income per Person, 2004 (US$) |
|---|---|---|---|---|
| Low | 54 | 2,343.0 | ≤ 875 | 507 |
| Lower middle | 59 | 2,441.6 | 876–3,465 | 1,686 |
| Upper middle | 41 | 576.2 | 3,466–10,725 | 4,769 |
| High | 56 | 1,004.2 | ≥ 10,725 | 32,112 |

Most of the world's population lives in countries classified as low- or lower-middle income, below $3,466 per person per year in 2004.

*Source:* World Bank, *World Development Indicators.*

economic, and environmental indicators. Table 8.2 illustrates this with two environmental and two social indicators.

Table 8.2 displays several patterns of change. Child mortality, measured as the number of deaths of children age 5 or younger per 1,000 children in the 5 or younger population, shows a strong and consistent pattern of decrease with income, reflecting the increase in medical care and sanitation that accompanies income growth. Similarly, the percentage of children in the 10–14 age group who

**TABLE 8.2** ● **Income Levels, Society, and Environment**

| Income Category | Under 5 Mortality, per 1000, 2004 | Percent of Children Age 10–14 in the Labor Force, 2001 | $CO_2$ Emissions, Metric Tons per Person, 2002 | Average Annual Deforestation Percent of Forests, 1990–2000 |
|---|---|---|---|---|
| Low | 79.4 | 18 | 0.8 | 0.8 |
| Lower middle | 31.6 | 6 | 2.6 | −0.1 |
| Upper middle | 23.4 | 6 | 6.2 | 0.5 |
| High | 6.1 | 0 | 12.8 | −0.1 |

Some conditions improve with income growth (for example, mortality and labor), some worsen (for example, carbon dioxide emissions) and some vary widely (for example, rates of deforestation).

*Source:* World Bank, *World Development Indicators.*

work also decreases with income. At low levels of income, 18 percent of children age 10–14 are working, but by the time per capita income reaches the range of $876 to $3,465 (lower-middle income), the number drops to 6 percent.

The two environmental indicators show a mixed pattern. Carbon dioxide ($CO_2$) is the major greenhouse gas responsible for global warming. Consumption of energy is the major reason for $CO_2$ emissions, and high-income countries consume far more energy than the other categories of countries. Hence, on a per capita basis, they generate more than 12 times the carbon dioxide of people living in low-income countries. Another environmental indicator that gets consistently worse with rising incomes is the amount of solid waste (garbage). Many environmental indicators improve with income, however, although the pattern can be highly varied. Deforestation, for example (Table 8.2), shows no steady pattern, but high-income countries as a whole are experiencing reforestation. Other environmental indicators such as airborne particulate matter and sulfur dioxide (a leading cause of acid rain) show a steady deterioration with income growth, followed by a steady improvement as incomes continue to grow. Still others, such as water pollution and sanitation, tend to show constant improvement over all income levels.

##  Labor Standards

Recently, the United States and other countries have demanded that labor and environmental standards be included in all future trade negotiations. This is a politically charged issue that is likely to come and go over time, depending in part on the political party in power, but it also reflects rising worldwide interests in issues related to human rights and the environment. To date, the United States' trade agreements with Canada and Mexico (the North American Free Trade Agreement), Jordan, and Chile, contain language on labor and environmental standards, either in the treaty itself, or as a side agreement. In each case, the language specifies that each country must enforce its own standards or face monetary fines. Many labor and environmental activists view this as inadequate and are pushing to include trade sanctions as part of the enforcement mechanism, both in existing agreements and in future agreements, including those reached by the WTO.

The complaints against trade by labor and environmental interests are relatively similar. In both cases, it is alleged that trade with countries that have lower standards creates a race to the bottom in standards, and that countries with high standards are forced to lower their standards or experience a loss of jobs and industry. Furthermore, it is alleged that this type of trade is unfair, since the failure to enact or to enforce standards gives firms in the countries with lower standards a commercial advantage. Before addressing these issues, it is useful to clarify what is meant by standards, particularly in the case of labor standards.

## Defining Labor Standards

The concept of labor standards is multifaceted, since it covers a wide variety of potential rights, stretching from basic rights such as the right to be free from forced labor, to civic rights such as the right to representation in a union. At present, there is no core set of work-related rights that everyone views as universal human rights.

As a starting point we take the following five labor standards proposed as basic rights by the **International Labor Organization (ILO)** (see the ILO Case Study in this chapter) and revised by the Organization for Economic Cooperation and Development (OECD):

- Prohibition of forced labor
- Freedom of association
- The right to organize and bargain collectively
- An end to the exploitation of child labor
- Nondiscrimination in employment

Most people would probably agree to these rights, although there is a fair amount of ambiguity attached to each of them. For example, conditions that are considered exploitative in a high-income country might seem acceptable in a poor one. Or cultural or religious values regarding employment opportunities for men and women may be at odds with the idea of nondiscrimination.

Other potential standards are significantly more contentious. For example, universal standards for minimum wages, limits on the number of hours someone can work in a day, and health and safety issues in the workplace are difficult to define given the wide variation in incomes and living conditions around the world. High-income countries, where unskilled labor is relatively scarce, face an entirely different set of economic constraints compared to those faced by low-income countries where unskilled labor is relatively abundant. For example, if low-income countries are forced to pay a minimum wage high enough to satisfy critics in high-income countries, many people fear that the result would be the closing down of production and a rise in unemployment rather than an increase in living standards. In other words, too high a minimum wage may be well intentioned, but it may reduce living standards in low-income countries. Even this is ambiguous, however, since it is no easy matter to determine how high is too high.

## CASE STUDY

# Child Labor

Child labor is one of the most difficult issues in the labor standards debate. In large part, the difficulty arises because nations cannot reach consensus on the policies that would effectively eliminate the worst forms of exploitation of children.

The International Labor Organization (ILO) (see the ILO Case Study below) estimates that 190.7 children age 5–14 are working, and that approximately 44.9 percent (74,392,000) are engaged in hazardous work, defined as work that is physically dangerous and/or more than 43 hours per week (Figure 8.1). Geographically, approximately 64 percent of children workers are in the Asia-Pacific region, 26 percent in Sub-Saharan Africa, 3 percent in Latin America and the Caribbean, and 7 percent in the Middle East, North Africa, and the developed world. While the bulk of child labor is concentrated in the Asia-Pacific region, Sub-Saharan Africa has the highest percentage, with more than one in four children in its 5–14 age group working more than 14 hours a week (Figure 8.2). Child labor is more common in rural areas than urban, and three-fourths of working children are employed in family run enterprises, often a subsistence farm.

**FIGURE 8.1** ● **Child labor, 5–14 age group, 2004 (millions)**

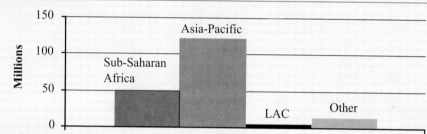

Asia has the most child labor, followed by Sub-Saharan Africa. LAC is Latin America and the Caribbean.

*Source*: F. Hageman, Y. Diallo, A. Etienne, and F. Mehpa (2006). *Global Child Labor Trends, 2000–2004*. Geneva: ILO.

**FIGURE 8.2** ● **Percent of children working, 5–14 age group**

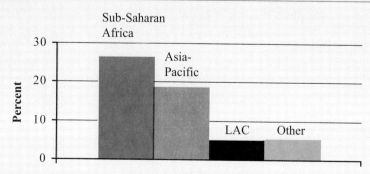

Sub-Saharan Africa has the highest proportion of children working, followed by the Asia-Pacific region.

*Source*: F. Hageman, Y. Diallo, A. Etienne, and F. Mehpa (2006). *Global Child Labor Trends, 2000–2004*. Geneva: ILO.

Worldwide, most children work in activities that are oriented toward production for domestic consumption. The ILO estimates that less than 6 to 7 percent are working in export-oriented industries, such as export manufacturing, mining, or export-oriented agriculture. In general, the use of child labor declines dramatically with GDP, falling from an estimated 30 to 60 percent of children (5–14 age group) in countries with $500 or less of GDP per person (1987 dollars), to 10 to 30 percent in countries with $500 to $1,000 of GDP per person (Table 8.2).

The fact that child labor is tied to poverty and agriculture is precisely what makes it a difficult policy issue. Child labor is a common family survival strategy, and if it were stopped, it would force many families deeper into poverty. We would like to believe that if children did not work, they would attend school, but unfortunately this is often not the case, since many rural areas and poor countries lack enough schools to meet the needs of their children. When countries try to regulate child labor, problems stem from the fact that often children work in family enterprises and in remote areas where it is expensive to send inspectors and to maintain a system of vigilance.

Although the United States officially denies that it has a problem with child labor, it illustrates the difficulties involved in ending the practice. On a world scale, there is little child labor in the United States, but in remote agricultural regions, it is not uncommon. According to U.S. labor law (Fair Labor Standards Act (FLSA)), a child is anyone age 17 or under. The Government Accountability Office (GAO) of the federal government estimates that 300,000 children work in agriculture each year. The GAO also acknowledges that this is an undercount due to methodological problems. The United Farm Workers Union estimates that the true figure is closer to 800,000. Concentrations of child farm workers can be found in Arizona, California, Florida, and Texas, although the group Human Rights Watch states that "virtually no state is without child labor in agriculture."

The FSLA exempts agriculture from many of its standards. For example, employers may legally hire children younger than 12 to work unlimited hours outside of school, and they may legally hire 16- and 17-year-olds to work in hazardous conditions handling toxic chemicals and dangerous machinery. Both of these practices are forbidden in the rest of the economy.

The persistence of child labor in a wealthy country such as the United States underscores the difficulty of the issue. Farm worker families are among the poorest working people in the United States. They live in rural areas where they must migrate as they follow the harvest and they work in a sector of the economy that is partially outside the coverage of the main body of protective standards. For a variety of reasons—history, the seasonal nature of the work, the legislative power of special interests, corruption, official denial of the problem—legislative reform that would effectively curtail the use of child labor has not been achieved.

*Sources*: Human Rights Watch, *Fingers to the Bone: United States Failure to Protect Child Farmworkers.* Human Rights Watch: New York. 2000.
International Labor Office, "Child Labour: Targeting the Intolerable." International Labor Conference. 86th Session. Geneva: 1996.
———, *Child Labour: What Is To Be Done?* Geneva: 1996.
Siddiqi, Faraaz, and Harry Patrinos, "Child Labor: Issues, Causes, and Interventions," Human Capital Development and Operations Policy Working Paper 56. Washington, DC: World Bank.

# Labor Standards and Trade

The major source of disagreements between trade economists and labor activists is over the use of trade barriers to enforce labor standards. That is, should one country use trade barriers to pressure another country into altering its labor standards? Trade economists tend to be more skeptical about the use of trade barriers, partly for the reasons outlined in Chapter 7, where it was shown that they are expensive and grossly inefficient policies for reaching most of the goals for which they are used. In addition to the deadweight losses in consumption and production at home, the use of trade barriers to enforce standards abroad raises several other concerns for economists. These include their effectiveness in creating change in an exporting country, the hazy borderline between protectionism and concern over standards, the lack of agreement over the specific content of standards, and their potential to erupt into a wider trade war. We will examine each of these points next.

**Effectiveness.** In addition to the deadweight losses and income redistribution effects of trade barriers, it is clear that only large countries can hope to use barriers successfully, since a small country cannot have a large enough impact on demand. That is, if a small country such as the Netherlands decides that garment producers in Haiti are exploiting children, then any trade barrier that the Netherlands erects against imports from Haiti are not likely to reduce demand enough to stop the offending Haitian practice. Only countries that constitute a significant share of the Haitian market could erect barriers that would impose costs on Haitian producers, and even then only if there are no alternative markets for Haitian goods. Nor would this necessarily lead to changes, since there are numerous examples (Cuba, Myanmar, and others) where countries have suffered large costs from trade sanctions but have not altered their policies in response. In effect, the general rule is that the effectiveness of the trade barrier increases as more countries join to impose them. For example, the strong unity of the world's industrial economies against South Africa was at least partly responsible for ending the policy of apartheid.

In addition to the problem of creating a coalition of countries, an additional obstacle to the effectiveness of trade barriers is that in some cases they will make conditions worse rather than better. This outcome occurs when sanctions cause producers inside a country to move their facilities into the informal, unregulated economy where it is out of sight of domestic inspectors and regulators. Some share of production in every economy takes place in the **informal economy**. The informal economy does not necessarily produce illegal goods such as drugs, but it is untaxed, unregulated, and uninspected. In developing countries this tends to be a relatively larger share of overall economic activity than in industrial economies, and it is typically composed of small firms operating with little capital. Employees in these enterprises usually earn less and suffer harsher working conditions. If sanctions against a country create incentives for its employers to avoid the scrutiny of labor inspectors, then a larger share of the working population could find themselves laboring under worse conditions.

**Hazy Borderline between Protectionism and Concern.** When does the concern over foreign labor practices become a justification for protectionism? There is no definitive way to answer this question, although it is certain that special interests sometimes use the issue of labor standards as a means to justify their real goal, which is to obtain protection against foreign competition. Indeed, this is the fear of many developing countries, and explains why their governments resist negotiating labor standards. Developing countries tend to have abundant supplies of unskilled labor and they depend on low-wage, low-productivity jobs for a large share of their employment. In these countries, proposals to set labor standards and to use trade barriers as an enforcement mechanism are widely viewed as a new form of protectionism on the part of high-income countries. Given that most high-income countries continue to protect their markets in key areas of developing country production—agriculture, clothing, and textiles— there is a strong suspicion that calls for labor standards are a way to undermine the comparative advantage of low-income countries, and to close the markets of high-income countries in selected areas.

**The Specific Content of Labor Standards.** The problem of reaching agreement on the specific content of standards has yet to be resolved. We have seen how child labor varies by income, and that even the definition of a child varies across countries. For example, disputes over the minimum age at which someone may legally enter the labor force have so far blocked international agreement on child labor, other than vague condemnations of the practice. Other standards are equally contentious, although it is always conceivable that an international consensus may develop in the long run. At the present time, however, the lack of international agreement on the specific content of labor standards, other than the relatively vague proposals from the OECD and ILO, means that trade sanctions are unilateral measures with a large potential for creating conflict and undermining international economic relations.

**The Potential to Set Off a Trade War.** One of the primary obligations of countries in the WTO is to treat other members the same. That is, discrimination by one WTO member against another is not allowed. There are exceptions, as in the case of national security, or in the case of the special benefits given to members of a free-trade area, but in general, discriminatory trade practices are not allowed. Consequently, the use of trade sanctions to enforce labor standards places a country out of compliance with its WTO obligations and opens it to the risk of retaliation by the targeted country. Where this ends is indeterminate.

The purpose of this discussion is to raise questions about the efficacy of trade barriers as a tool for overturning objectionable foreign labor practices. It is not meant to imply that nothing should ever be done. Later in the chapter, a number of alternative approaches are discussed.

## Evidence on Low Standards as a Predatory Practice

One of the concerns expressed by the proponents of trade sanctions is that low standards may reflect a deliberate policy to capture markets and foreign investment. That is, a country may use its coercive power to hold down or repress labor standards, and thereby reduce the costs of producing goods. While theoretically possible, this too has a number of issues that must be examined empirically.

In practice, there is little or no support for the view that countries use low labor standards to attract foreign investment. While there is evidence that a country can reduce production costs by outlawing unions, or by some other repressive practice, there is no evidence that this type of policy has succeeded in giving any country a comparative advantage in lines of production that it did not already have. In other words, low standards can reduce production costs, but they do not change a country's comparative advantage.

This result does not affect the case of competition between countries with the same or similar comparative advantages. Within a particular line of production, such as the clothing industry, countries may compete by lowering labor standards, but then the harmful competitive effects of low standards are on other countries with low standards, not on countries with high standards and with an entirely different comparative advantage.

While low labor standards may help a country compete against another low labor standards country, there is clear evidence that low labor standards are not a successful strategy for attracting foreign investment. The reason is simple. Low labor standards are highly correlated with a labor force that is abundant in illiterate, unskilled labor. Furthermore, it is a sign that the nation's infrastructure of roads, ports, power supply, telecommunications, schools, and sanitation are also undeveloped. Hence, the labor cost savings of low labor standards is more than likely to be offset by higher costs everywhere else in production. Consequently, empirical studies show that countries with low labor standards are less successful at attracting foreign investment.

Finally, there is the case of intolerable practices, such as apartheid in the old South Africa, the gulags of the former Soviet Union, and slavery in Sudan and elsewhere. These types of practices raise a number of moral issues, which make it unreasonable to rely solely on economic analysis. Clearly, however, the more united the world is against a particular inhumane labor practice, the more likely sanctions are to succeed. For example, the United States is isolated in imposing sanctions on Cuba, and although they have imposed significant costs on its economy, the lack of international support for U.S. policies has prevented the sanctions from successfully changing Cuban policies.

## CASE STUDY

# The International Labor Organization (ILO)

The International Labor Organization (ILO) "seeks the promotion of social justice and internationally recognized human and labour rights." The ILO began in 1919 and is the only surviving element of the League of Nations, which was founded after World War I and was the precursor of the United Nations (UN).

In 1946, the ILO was incorporated into the United Nations and since then, most of the world's countries have become members.

The ILO uses several tools to attain its goals. Most prominently, it develops labor standards that are embodied in specific Conventions and Recommendations. Individual countries are encouraged but not required to ratify the ILO Conventions. Currently, there are 183 conventions, about 26 of which have been shelved and are no longer proposed, leaving 157 in force.

On June 18, 1998, the ILO adopted the "Declaration on Fundamental Principles and Rights at Work and its Follow-up." This document specifies the eight **core labor standards** it believes all countries should respect, regardless of which conventions they ratified. The ILO groups the eight core standards into four areas:

- Freedom of association and recognition of the right to collective bargaining
- Elimination of all forms of forced labour
- Effective abolition of child labour
- Elimination of discrimination in employment and occupations

The most serious type of complaint handled by the ILO concerns cases where worker's organizations, firms, or governments file a formal complaint that a member government is not enforcing core labor rights. The process for handling such complaints begins with a consultation with the alleged offender, followed by an official investigation if the consultation does not resolve the issue. The investigating committee may make recommendations, which the target country may appeal to the International Court of Justice. If there is an appeal, afterwards, the ILO can propose actions against the offending country. Economic actions such as trade sanctions are within the legal framework of options available to the ILO. It should be noted, however, that throughout its lengthy history, the ILO has recommended actions against one country only, and it has never proposed trade sanctions.

The ILO's reluctance to use the full extent of its power, along with the failure of some of its members to support it, results in a fairly weak organization. Throughout its lengthy history, the ILO has proposed trade sanctions against only one country, Myanmar. The Southeast Asian nation uses forced labor throughout the country, particularly to fill the ranks of its military. Myanmar came under ILO scrutiny in 1998 and in 2000 the international organization recommended trade sanctions. The sanctions recommendation was withdrawn in 2001 after Myanmar gave assurances that it was addressing the problem. Five years later, in mid-2006, little has changed—Myanmar continues to use forced labor while giving assurances that it is ending the practice and trade sanctions have not been imposed.

In addition to handling complaints and proposing conventions, the ILO also provides technical assistance in all aspects of labor policy, including labor law, worker benefit programs, vocational training, development and administration of cooperatives, and many other areas.

*Sources*: International Labor Organization. http://www.ilo.org. Elliott, Kimberly Ann, "The ILO and Enforcement of Core Labor Standards." Washington, DC: Institute for International Economics. July 2000. http://www.iie.com/NEWSLTR/news00–6.htm. Accessed 10-9-00. "Gathering Mild Rebuke: Myanmar," *The Economist.* September 2, 2006.

#  Trade and the Environment

Over the last 40 years, the realization has grown that our activities profoundly affect the natural environment. Unfortunately, our production and consumption choices do not always reflect the environmental costs of our decisions, and in the short run, our economies too often perform as if environmental costs and limits are irrelevant. When economic agents are allowed to ignore the environmental costs of their actions, then conflict between financial and environmental interests are inevitable. Most high-income countries have a significant amount of such conflict, and trade, along with other economic activities, has received its share of environmental criticism.

## Transboundary and Non-Transboundary Effects

There is a considerable overlap between environmental standards and labor standards. For example, many proponents of putting environmental standards into trade agreements believe that trade sanctions—tariffs, quotas, prohibitions on imports—should be used as enforcement mechanisms, while the critics of trade sanctions have the same concerns raised earlier: they are relatively ineffective, there is a hazy borderline between protectionism and concern for the environment, there is a lack of international agreement, and there is a potential to start trade wars.

There are some differences between labor and environmental standards, however, beginning with the fact that some but not all environmental impacts are transboundary. In other words, low standards in one country can degrade the environment in another country or countries. When it comes to trade policy, the distinction between **transboundary and non-transboundary environmental impacts** is an important one. We will look at non-transboundary, or exclusively national impacts first.

### Trade and Environmental Impacts That Do Not Cross Borders. 
Proponents of trade barriers to enforce environmental standards base their analysis on two types of claims. First, they argue that environmental standards reduce industrial competitiveness. This induces an environmental race to the bottom where countries are forced to rescind standards in order to stay competitive. Second, they argue that standards in rich countries cause them to "export pollution" to developing countries by relocating their dirty industries there. Both effects are harmful to the environment, as they lead to downward pressures on environmental standards and the concentration of dirty industries in a few developing countries.

The first claim, that environmental standards reduce industrial competitiveness, is theoretically valid since standards must raise the costs of production. Essentially, environmental standards prohibit the shifting of environmental costs to the public at large and thereby force firms to take a more complete measure of all their costs of production. If the standards are correctly implemented, they raise national well-being and lead to an economically optimal level of production. This implies that the argument against standards by firms that are subject to them is an argument between their interests and the nation's interests. Clearly, the nation is better off if the production of dirty industries is curtailed somewhat, even though the workers and firms in the shrinking industry may be worse off in the short-to-medium runs. The idea that the sectional interests are so politically strong that they can force environmental deregulation (race to the bottom) or prevent the introduction of new standards altogether may have some merit, but in general, environmental standards in most countries have gotten tougher over time, not more lax.

Countries that compete by offering foreign firms a reduced set of environmental compliance requirements are known as **pollution havens**. Note the essential similarity between the pollution haven concept and the claim that countries compete for foreign investment by lowering their labor standards. Empirically, there is evidence that some dirty industries from high-income industrial economies moved to developing countries in the 1970s when the industrial economies first began cracking down on environmental polluters. Steel and chemical industries fall into this pattern, although it is possible that the developing countries were gaining a comparative advantage in these areas as high-income countries were losing theirs. Regardless, there is strong evidence showing that the idea of pollution havens is invalid. That is, it is impossible to identify any country that successfully competes for new investment on the basis of low environmental standards. The fact that there are no pollution havens is good news, but it does not mean that individual firms cannot move to escape the environmental regulations of a high-standards country. Undoubtedly, there are cases of this, although numbers and overall importance are uncertain.

From a trade perspective, the issue is complicated by the fact that differences in income and preferences make the optimal set of environmental standards variable by country. An optimal set of standards in Europe, for example, might be entirely different from the optimal set in North Africa or Central Asia. The fact that budgets and regulatory abilities are limited implies that countries cannot do everything, and that they must prioritize their efforts. Biodiversity and habitat preservation may receive top priority in one place, while clean water and soil conservation are first in another. When the optimality of standards varies across countries, the introduction of trade barriers as a means of enforcing one country's standards in another country's production system would actually lower global welfare rather than raise it.

**Trade and Transboundary Environmental Problems.** Transboundary environmental impacts happen when one country's pollution spills over into a second country, for example, when a shared watershed is polluted by the upstream user, or industrial production in one country creates acid rain in another country. It can also happen in a mutual way, for example, when heavy truck traffic between two countries creates air pollution in both. And finally, transboundary environmental impacts can occur as the result of similar activities in many countries leading to global impacts such as global warming and ozone depletion.

There are a variety of potential actions that countries may contemplate, from tariffs on the output of the polluting industries, to embargoes, to multicountry or global negotiations.

The analysis of labor standards applies here, as unilateral actions by one country are unlikely to have any effect whatsoever except in the large country case. Even then, the more isolated the sanctions imposing country is, the lower the probability that its actions will successfully alter the policies of the offending countries.

## CASE STUDY

# Trade Barriers and Endangered Species

The connection between trade and endangered species protection is an area where the environmental movement has been critical of the WTO. The original precedent-setting case began with the U.S. ban on imports of tuna that were caught with nets that were particularly harmful to dolphins (see the Case Study in Chapter 6). Under the terms of the Endangered Species Act of 1973, the United States imposed a ban on tuna imports that were not certified as "dolphin-safe." Mexico lodged a complaint, and the outcome of the investigation was a GATT ruling that countries cannot prohibit imports based on the method of production, as long as the goods are legal. Because the United States allowed tuna to be sold in its market, it could not keep out tuna harvested in a way that hurt dolphins.

The U.S. prohibitions on certain shrimp imports was the next important case to draw attention to the conflict between trade and the protection of endangered species. The United States sought to protect endangered sea turtles that are harmed by shrimp trawlers that do not use turtle excluder devices (TED) on their nets. In 1987, it issued guidelines requiring shrimp trawlers to use TEDs and in 1989, it announced that beginning in May of 1991, it would ban shrimp from countries that were not certified. The guidelines applied only to the Caribbean and the Western Atlantic, and countries were given three years to come into compliance. In 1996, a number of additional conditions were placed on shrimp imports, the guidelines were extended worldwide, and countries were given four months to come into compliance.

India, Malaysia, Pakistan, and Thailand immediately protested to the WTO. The primary basis of the protest was that they were given four months to comply with the U.S. rules, while countries in the Caribbean were given three years and technical assistance. In addition, they cited the dolphin–tuna case, and argued that the GATT rules forbid discrimination against imports based on the process of production. After the United States and the Asian nations failed to resolve their dispute through informal consultations, the Asians asked the WTO's Dispute Settlement Body to establish a panel to resolve the issue. The issue wound its way through the dispute resolution process of rulings and appeals and finally culminated in a decision acknowledging the right of countries to impose import barriers in order to protect endangered species. However, the final decision also stated that the United States' failure to negotiate or confer with the affected countries put it in violation of WTO rules. Furthermore, by treating the Asian nations differently, the United States acted in a discriminatory manner. In response, the United States began a series of negotiations with the countries that filed the complaint. In the end, it revised its timetable and procedures for certification, and agreed to provide technical assistance in the use of TEDs.

This case is important because, in the words of the WTO, "We have not decided that the sovereign nations that are Members of the WTO cannot adopt effective measures to protect endangered species, such as sea turtles. Clearly, they can and should." In effect, the WTO forced a multilateral solution by arranging for the United States—which places a relatively high value on sea turtles—to assist a number of developing countries—which place a relatively higher value on their commercial fishing industries—in acquiring the technology they need. This enables the United States to extend its protection of an endangered species worldwide, while the fishing fleets of South Asia remain commercially viable.

The WTO also clarified the controversial issue of products versus processes that first began with the dolphin–tuna dispute. In its ruling, the WTO states that trade measures are permitted to protect endangered species. At the same time, the ruling stressed the need to negotiate a solution and disallowed unilateral action.

*Source*: World Trade Organization, "United States-Import Prohibition of Certain Shrimp and Shrimp Products," AB–1998–4. http://www.wto.org/english/tratop_e/dispu_e/58abr.doc

##  Alternatives to Trade Measures

Currently, it is impossible to predict how, or even if, trade rules might eventually change in order to accommodate labor and environmental standards. These are new issues for the world trading system, and it is possible that they will become a permanent source of tension in international economic relations. As long as there are large income gaps between rich and poor countries, it seems unlikely that differences in standards will disappear. If trade tensions over standards are likely to continue in one form or another, then it is important to look for ways to preserve the benefits created by world trade while simultaneously resolving the conflicts over standards.

In the search for alternatives to trade measures, it is useful to recognize the general economic principle that efficient policies go directly to the root of the problem they are designed to correct. This was illustrated in Chapter 7, where it was demonstrated that trade barriers are an expensive way to solve the problem of job shortages in a particular industry. In the cases of environmental degradation and the exploitation of labor, the root of the problem lies in the production and/or consumption of particular goods, not in their trade. If a steel mill pollutes a river or exploits children, the direct cause of the environmental and human harm is the set of production standards employed by the mill, not the fact that the steel is exported. In some cases of negative environmental effects (for example, air pollution caused by gas burning cars) the root of the problem is consumption, not production. Given that environmental degradation and labor exploitation are by-products of production and consumption decisions, the optimal policies for addressing them is at the level of production and consumption, not at the level of trade measures, since the latter create production and consumption inefficiencies in the country that imposes them. In some cases, such as countries that still allow slavery, trade measures may be the only available option short of military intervention, but in most international conflicts over labor and environmental standards, there are more efficient policies than trade measures.

## Labels for Exports

The idea of labeling is widespread and has been implemented with mixed success. This idea is a certification process producing a label that is attached to the good when it is exported. The label is designed to tell consumers that the good was produced under conditions that are humane or environmentally sustainable. This method is already in place in a few instances, although not always successfully. For example, in 1999, the United States and Cambodia agreed that the United States would increase its quota of Cambodian textiles and garments if the country allowed foreign observers to visit its factories. Cambodia agreed to the intrusion of labor inspectors because it is desperate for the export business. The initial result was a heightening of conflict between Cambodian unions and employers, and a threat by producers to move elsewhere. Coffee is a somewhat more successful example, where retailers have used independent inspection agencies that offer services to firms that import coffee and other tropical products. This allows retailers to advertise that they sell one or more types of coffee that are certified as beneficial to small farmers. Similarly, some cosmetic brands and retailers certify that their products are not tested on animals.

Labeling probably has an important role to play in resolving conflicts, but not in its present form. First, many countries will resist what they consider an infringement of their sovereignty when foreign inspectors are allowed to probe into the details of labor and environmental conditions. A second problem is that consumers will have to be convinced that the label provides reliable information. If a sweater made in Cambodia has a label saying it was made under humane conditions, what degree of confidence should you put on that information? As the procedure of labeling becomes more widespread, it is possible that the true information value of labels will decrease. These problems are not insurmountable, but they have to be addressed before labeling is adopted on a larger scale.

## Requiring Home Country Standards

A second alternative to trade measures is to require home country firms to follow home country standards whenever they open foreign operations. An example was the Sullivan Principles, which asked multinationals operating in South Africa during the apartheid era to practice nondiscrimination. In the case of labor standards, a domestic firm in a high-standards country that wants to open a plant in a developing country would be required by law to adhere to the same labor standards as the ones it must follow at home. This does not mean that wages and benefits must be the same, since the cost of labor varies, but minimum wages might be included, along with some benefits, workplace health and safety standards, child labor standards, hours of work standards, and so on. In the environmental sphere, it is not uncommon for firms to adopt the same standards abroad as they use at home, since environmental control is often built into the technology and a least-cost strategy usually involves the adoption of one set of standards rather than multiple standards.

The advantage of this approach is that it addresses the issue of a race to the bottom by making it impossible for a home-based company to exploit low labor or environmental standards abroad, while, at the same time, preserving access to the low-wage labor of labor abundant countries. Furthermore, this technique shifts the costs of improved standards to firms and consumers in high-income countries—which is where most of the concern originates. It might seem strange to regulate companies operating outside the nation, but it is well within the legal right of nations to impose standards on domestic firms that operate abroad, as long as the standards do not conflict with the laws of the host country. Given that the required standards are meant to be more stringent than those in the host country, this should not be a problem.

One weakness of this approach, however, is that it only addresses the problem of firms in high-standards countries that go abroad, but does not address the problem of foreign-owned and -operated firms that export into the domestic market. In other words, firms based in countries with low standards are untouched by this type of rule. More problematically, a clothing manufacturer based in a high-standards country might outsource its production through contracts with firms based in low-standards countries. This puts part of the production at arm's length and makes it more difficult to ensure that working conditions are satisfactory. Since the firms doing the actual cutting and sewing are foreign-owned, they may lie completely outside the reach of the regulations governing the clothing manufacturer located in the high-standards country.

Nevertheless, regulations placed on domestic firms operating abroad address a significant share of the fears of a race to the bottom. In particular, they remove the threat by domestic firms to relocate abroad if standards are not reduced at home, and ensure that the attraction of foreign-based production is the foreign comparative advantage, not the ability to lower labor standards or ignore the environment. In addition, it avoids the problems created when high-income countries appear to be dictating labor and environmental standards for low- and middle-income countries. Each country sets its own standards, but when firms cross national boundaries, they must conform to whichever standards are higher, either those in the sending country or the receiving country.

## Increasing International Negotiations

A third alternative to trade measures is to increase the level of international negotiations, using either existing international organizations such as the ILO for labor, or creating new agreements and organizations for the environment. In the labor standards arena, proponents of increased negotiations would like to see the ILO publicize examples where countries are out of compliance with core labor rights. It could do this with the information it already gathers on the labor practices of its member countries. An expanded role for the ILO is supported by the growing recognition that it has the technical capability to assess labor policies, whereas the WTO does not.

In the environmental arena, the World Trade Organization reports that there are about two hundred multilateral environmental agreements (for example, the Montreal Protocol regulating the use of chlorofluorocarbons, the Basel Convention regulating the transportation of hazardous waste, and the Convention on International Trade in Endangered Species) and that about twenty of them have the potential to affect trade. In cases where two or more countries have signed an agreement and the agreement allows trade sanctions as part of its enforcement mechanism, the WTO's position is that disputes should be resolved within the environmental agreement and not within the WTO. In cases where there are no environmental agreements, however, as with the United States' shrimp import ban, then WTO rules of nondiscrimination apply.

It is significant that the WTO has staked out a position on the issue of multilateral environmental agreements. The WTO recognizes explicitly that it is not an environmental organization and that it has no expertise in this area. However, it has left room for environmental agreements to develop their own enforcement mechanisms. This does not change the fact that trade sanctions are unlikely to be the optimal (lowest cost) technique for resolving environmental disputes, but it does leave it up to the nations involved to decide on their own methods of enforcement.

## Summary

- The increase in world trade over the last 50 years has reduced tariffs and eliminated quotas, but as a result, many domestic policies have become unintentional barriers to trade. Examples include competition policies, product standards, health and safety standards, and labor and environmental standards.

- Countries do not need to harmonize standards in order to trade. In many cases, harmonization would remove some of the differences between countries and eliminate the gains from trade. Alternative treatment of standards include mutual recognition and maintaining completely separate standards.

- Differing labor and environmental standards have become a point of significant conflict between high-income and low-income countries. Standards differ primarily because of differences in income and factor endowments.
- Core labor standards defined by the OECD and the ILO include prohibitions against forced labor, freedom of association and collective bargaining, the elimination of child labor, and nondiscrimination in employment.
- Child labor is most common in Africa and Asia. Asia has the most children working, but a larger proportion of African children under age fourteen are at work. Child labor is most common in agriculture and in small-scale, family-operated businesses.
- Proponents of using trade barriers to enforce labor and environmental standards abroad argue that differences in standards are an unfair competitive advantage for the low-standards countries. They also fear that trade and foreign investment cause a race to the bottom in standards and that low environmental standards make some countries "pollution havens."
- Evidence is scarce that countries use low standards to attract industry. In practice, low standards are associated with low levels of foreign investment. In addition, there is no evidence of pollution havens.
- Most economists oppose the use of trade measures to enforce standards because they are relatively ineffective, do not go to the root of the problem, are not based on an agreement regarding the content of standards, encourage protectionism in the guise of support for standards, and can lead to wider trade conflict.
- Environmental problems can be transboundary or non-transboundary. International conflicts over both types of problems are similar to conflicts over labor standards. Transboundary problems, in particular, require international negotiations.
- Alternatives to trade measures include labeling, enforcement of home country standards on home country firms operating abroad, and increased international negotiations. Greater support for the ILO and increasing support for international environmental agreements are also more efficient alternatives to trade measures.

## Vocabulary

core labor standards

harmonization of standards

informal economy

International Labor Organization (ILO)

low, lower-middle, upper-middle, and high-income

mutual recognition of standards

pollution havens

race to the bottom

separate standards

transboundary and non-transboundary environmental impacts

# Study Questions

1. What are the three ways for countries to handle different standards abroad? Do standards have to be the same for countries to be integrated?

2. What are the advantages and disadvantages for countries that adopt the same standards?

3. When high-definition television (HDTV) was first considered a possibility in the United States, the U.S. government held a competition to select the technical standards that would be used nationwide. Why would the government see an advantage to setting one standard, and what are the pros and cons for the private businesses that were interested in producing for the U.S. market?

4. Why do standards vary across countries? Illustrate your answer with examples in the area of labor standards.

5. What are labor standards, and why are arguments about labor standards confined primarily to arguments between high-income countries on the one hand, and low- and middle-income countries on the other?

6. Discuss the reasons why using trade barriers to enforce labor or environmental standards may be less efficient than other measures.

7. What are the arguments in favor of using trade barriers to enforce labor and environmental standards? Assess each argument.

8. One common critique of the WTO is that it overturns national environmental protections and forces countries to lower their standards. For example, when the United States tried to protect endangered sea turtles, the WTO prevented it. Assess this claim.

9. What are the alternatives to trade measures for raising labor and environmental standards? What are the strengths and weaknesses of each one?

# International Finance

## PART 3

# 9

# Trade and the Balance of Payments

##  Introduction: The Current Account

The international transactions of a nation are divided into three separate accounts: the *current account*, the *capital account*, and the *financial account*. For most countries, the capital account is relatively minor, and the two most important accounts are the current and financial accounts. The **current account** tracks the flow of goods and services into and out of the country, while the **financial account** is the record of the flow of financial capital. The **capital account** is the record of some specialized types of relatively small capital flows. This chapter examines the accounting system used to keep track of a country's international transactions. One of its primary goals is to understand the accounting relationships among domestic investment, domestic savings, and international flows of goods, services, and financial assets. In addition, we will use the international accounts to examine the meaning of international indebtedness and to discuss its consequences.

### The Trade Balance

In 2005, the United States purchased $1,992 billion in goods and services from foreign suppliers. The composition of the purchases included a wide array of tangibles and intangibles, from Japanese Nintendos to Venezuelan oil and from luxury Mexican vacations to tickets on the European rail system. In the same year, U.S. firms exported $1,275 billion worth of aircraft, software, grains, trips to Disneyworld, and other goods and services. The difference between exports and imports of goods and services is called the **trade balance**. For the United States, the 2005 trade balance was $1,275 billion minus $1,992 billion, or −$717 billion. Because the number is negative, the United States had a trade deficit.

Exports and imports include both goods and services, so the trade balance can be decomposed into the balance on goods and the balance on services. In the case of the United States, the goods balance was in deficit by $783 billion, while the services balance was in surplus by $65 billion. In 2005, services were 30 percent of total exports, and for many years they have been a growing part of U.S. and world trade. The main items in services trade include travel and passenger fares, transportation services, royalties and license fees, and education, financial, business, and technical services. Although the U.S. trade balance for services is in surplus, total trade in services is still too small a share of overall trade to counteract the very large deficit in the merchandise goods trade balance.

## The Current Account Balance

The trade balance is the most commonly cited measurement of a nation's transactions with the rest of the world. The widespread dissemination of the monthly trade balance statistics through press releases and news articles makes it the most familiar concept in international economics as well as the basis of most people's understanding of U.S. international economic relations.

A more comprehensive statistic is the **current account balance**, which measures all current, nonfinancial transactions between a nation and the rest of the world. It has three main items: (1) the value of goods and services exported, minus the value of imports; (2) income received from investments abroad, minus income paid to foreigners on their U.S. investments; and (3) any foreign aid or other transfers received from foreigners, minus that given to foreigners. The simplest framework for conceptualizing these three components is in terms of credits and debits, as portrayed in Table 9.1.

Each of the items—**goods and services**, **investment income**, and **unilateral transfers**—has credit (positive) and debit (negative) components. If the sum of the credits is greater than the sum of the debits, the nation has a current account surplus, otherwise, it has a deficit. The investment income items in Table 9.1 are not movements of investment capital but the income received or income paid on previous flows of financial capital. For example, financial capital sent to Germany to buy a bond would not be included, but the interest received on the bond would be. (The funds that leave the United States are counted in the financial accounts of the United States and Germany.)

### TABLE 9.1 • Components of the Current Account

|  | Credit | Debit |
|---|---|---|
| **1. Goods and services** | Exports | Imports |
| **2. Investment income** | Income received on foreign investments | Income paid to foreigners on their U.S. investments |
| **3. Unilateral transfers** | Transfers received from abroad | Transfers made to foreigners |

There are three main components to the current account. Each component is divided into debit and credit elements.

It is useful to think of investment income flows as payments for the use of another nation's financial capital. If U.S. mutual funds invest in the Mexican stock market, for example, the initial investment will not show up directly in the current account but will be included in the financial account. The subsequent flow of dividends back to the mutual fund in the United States will be counted in the United States as income received and in Mexico as income paid. Conceptually, it is as if U.S. investors are receiving payment for the rental of U.S. capital to Mexican firms, which makes it similar to payments for a service. The third item in the current account balance includes payments made that are not in exchange for a good or service, such as foreign aid, or the remittances (sending home of the wages) of immigrants temporarily residing in another country. In the U.S. case, these payments are usually relatively small, but they can figure very importantly in the current account balances of developing countries receiving either substantial foreign aid or large remittances from their citizens working abroad.

Table 9.2 gives a picture of the U.S. current account in 2002. The $480,861 million deficit is part of the growing trend in U.S. current account deficits, as shown in Figure 9.1. Large deficits in the current account began around 1982, and have been more-or-less a constant feature of the U.S. economy since then. Although the deficit turned into a small surplus of $6.6 billion in 1991 (partly due to large

**TABLE 9.2** ● **The U.S. Current Account Balance, 2005 (Millions of Dollars)**

|  | Credit | Debit |
|---|---|---|
| **1. Goods and services** | | |
| Exports of goods | 894,631 | |
| Exports of services | 380,614 | |
| Imports of goods | | −1,677,371 |
| Imports of services | | −314,604 |
| **2. Investment income** | | |
| Investment income received | 474,647 | |
| Investment income paid | | −463,353 |
| **3. Net unilateral transfers** | | −86,072 |
| **Goods and services balance** | | −716,730 |
| **Current Account Balance** | | −791,508 |

The U.S. current account deficit in 2005 was $791,508 million. The deficit is largely the result of merchandise goods imports exceeding exports. The United States has surpluses in services and investment income.

*Source:* U.S. Department of Commerce, Bureau of Economic Analysis, http://www.bea.gov/.

FIGURE 9.1 • **U.S. Current Account Balance, 1950–2005**

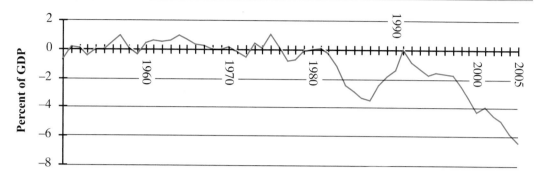

The large U.S. current account deficit began in the 1980s and has persisted since then, with the exception of 1991, during a recession and the Gulf War.

*Source*: U.S. Department of Commerce, Bureau of Economic Analysis, http://www.bea.gov/.

unilateral transfers received by the United States as payment for Operation Desert Storm), since then it has deteriorated significantly.

While the deficit looks ominous and is not sustainable in the long run, economists debate its likely consequences. We will explore this issue later, but here it should be noted that it is not simply a sign of weakness. On the contrary, through much of the 1990s, rapid economic growth raised incomes and created a voracious appetite for imports. Meanwhile, economic growth among the United States' main trading partners ranged between negative and sluggish so that foreign incomes did not rise as rapidly. Consequently, foreign demand for U.S. exports grew less rapidly than the U.S. demand for imports. Therefore, it can be argued that the current account deficit is a sign of relative U.S. economic strength. It would be a mistake to carry this argument too far, however, since everyone agrees that the deficit is not sustainable in the long run and that there is a potential for it to create serious future problems. We will look at this issue later in the chapter after we introduce a few more concepts.

 # Introduction to the Financial and Capital Accounts

The financial and capital accounts are the primary record of the international flow of financial capital and other assets. In most countries, the capital account is of lesser importance and the financial account is the primary statement of international financial flows. The capital account includes transfers of specific types of capital, such as debt forgiveness, the personal assets that migrants take with them when they cross international boundaries, and the transfer of real estate and other fixed assets, such as transfer of ownership of a military base or an embassy. The annual total of these flows is relatively small for most countries.

The financial account is divided into two primary categories: (1) net changes in U.S.-owned assets abroad, and (2) net changes in foreign-owned assets in the United States. Assets can be financial ones such as stocks and bonds, as well as real assets such as factories and businesses. Table 9.3 shows the capital and financial accounts in relation to the current account. Two points about the capital and financial accounts should be kept in mind. First, both accounts present the flow of assets during the year and not the stock of assets that have accumulated over time. Second, all flows are "net" changes rather than "gross" changes. Net changes are the differences between assets sold and assets bought as when, for example, U.S. residents purchase shares in the Mexican stock market while

**TABLE 9.3** ● **The U.S. Balance of Payments, 2005 (Millions of Dollars)**

|  | Credit | Debit |
|---|---|---|
| **Current Account** | | |
| 1. Goods and services | | |
| Exports | 1,275,245 | |
| Imports | | −1,991,975 |
| 2. Investment income | | |
| Investment income received | 474,647 | |
| Investment income paid | | −463,353 |
| 3. Net unilateral transfers | | −86,072 |
| **Capital Account** | | |
| 4. Capital account transactions, net | | -4,351 |
| **Financial Account** | | |
| 5. Net change in U.S. assets abroad (increase/outflow (−)) | | −426,801 |
| 6. Net change in foreign assets in the United States (increase/inflow(+)) | 1,212,250 | |
| **Statistical Discrepancy** | 10,410 | |
| **Memoranda** | | |
| Balance on current account (1 + 2 + 3) | | −791,508 |
| Balance on financial account (5+6) | 785,449 | |

The financial account measures capital inflows and outflows and is nearly the mirror image of the current account.

*Source*: U.S. Department of Commerce, Bureau of Economic Analysis, http://www.bea.gov/.

simultaneously selling Mexican bonds. The net change in U.S.-owned assets is the difference between the value of the shares purchased and the bonds sold. If the stocks and bonds are equal in value, then the net change is zero. Net changes are informative because they measure the monetary value of the change in a country's financial stake in foreign economies.

Under the accounting procedure used to tabulate credits and debits in the financial account, outflows of financial assets are a debit item while inflows are a credit item. This point is most easily understood by considering home country financial outflows as payments for the purchase of foreign-owned assets, and financial inflows as receipts from the sale of home country assets to foreigners. In this manner, the negative and positive signs of asset flows are conceptually similar to imports and exports. In other words, the purchase of foreign assets requires capital outflows and are counted as debit (negative) entries in the financial account. Conversely, when foreigners purchase home country assets, there is a capital inflow and a credit (positive) entry in the financial account.

There is a clear relationship between the current account and financial account balances. As long as the capital account balance is zero, the financial account balance must be the same as the current account balance, but with an opposite sign. If we know that a nation's current account balance is in deficit by $20 billion, its financial account balance must be a $20 billion surplus because every current account transaction (for example, imports or exports) involves a flow of assets that are used to pay for goods and services. For example, suppose that the United States has a $20 billion current account deficit. In order to cover the deficit, the United States must generate net capital inflows of $20 billion. It does this by selling assets, such as stocks, bonds, or factories. In this regard, it is the same for individuals. You may not own factories that you can sell, but if you buy more than your current income allows, then you have to generate financial flows in order to cover the difference. Your credit card company or the department store where you made your purchases might loan you the money, or you might sell some of your wealth that you keep in your bank, or in the stock market, or some other financial institution. Regardless of the source of the financial flows, you must raise enough money to cover the difference between your income and your purchases.

A large share of a nation's financial account transactions, however, is not in response to the current account flows of goods and services. For example, a London-based investment company may buy stock in a Chilean firm, lend money to the government of Thailand, and engage in any number of financial transactions that have nothing to do with the movements of goods and services on the current account. In an accounting sense, these purely financial transactions must have a net value of zero. The reason they add to zero is that the purchase of an asset is simultaneously the sale of an asset of equal value. For example, if you buy a share of stock, you obtain the asset of partial ownership while the person selling the share obtains your cash. It is the same internationally. If a Canadian citizen buys shares in the Mexican stock market (capital outflow), she must sell Canadian dollars or some other asset (capital inflow). (If she pays for her shares by writing a check drawn on a Mexican bank, then it does not enter the financial account since it is a change of one foreign asset for another.) As a result, the financial account is a complete picture of net flows of financial assets during the year.

At the very bottom of Table 9.3, the last item entered is in the row labeled "Statistical discrepancy." Previously, it was stated that the sum of the current account, capital account, and financial account must total zero. In an accounting sense they are zero, but not everything can be measured precisely and the **statistical discrepancy** is the amount of mismeasurement. It is calculated as the sum of the current, capital, and financial accounts, with the sign reversed. In 2000 it was calculated as follows:

$$[(-1) \times (-791,508 - 4,351 + 785,499)] = 10,410$$

The statistical discrepancy exists because our record of all of the transactions in the balance of payments is incomplete. Although the errors could be in any of the three accounts, it is believed that most of the errors are in the financial account since it is the hardest one to measure accurately. Financial flows are intangible, and in certain cases such as money laundering associated with the illegal drug trade, the sending or receiving agents have incentives to hide them.

## Types of Financial Flows

One of the primary concerns of most governments is the form of financial flows entering and leaving their country. Some financial flows are very mobile and represent short-run tendencies. These flows are often vehicles for transmitting a financial crisis from one country to another, or for generating sudden responses to changes in investor expectations about the short-run prospects of an economy. The degree of mobility of financial flows and the potential of some flows to introduce a large element of volatility into an economy have turned the consideration of the type of flows a country receives into a major issue.

As a first approach to a more detailed representation of the financial account, it is useful to subdivide the financial flows in Table 9.3 into categories that reference their origin in the public (governmental) or private sector. In most countries, the bulk of financial flows are private, although in times of crisis this can change. Table 9.4 shows the 2002 financial account for the United States, divided into five subcategories representing the main components of inflows and outflows in terms of public and private assets.

**Official reserve assets** are mainly the currencies of the largest and most stable economies in the world, such as U.S. dollars, German marks (or in 2002, the euro), British pounds, and Japanese yen. Reserve assets also include gold and the IMF's artificial currency, called the SDR (special drawing rights). Reserve assets are used to settle international debts and, consequently, central banks and treasury ministries use them as a store of value. For example, when an importer in a small country such as Chile purchases a shipload of goods from Europe, payment may be in dollars or euros or pounds, but it is unlikely that the supplier would accept Chilean pesos from the purchaser. The importer must convert some pesos

| TABLE 9.4 ● **Components of the U.S. Financial Account, 2005 (Millions of Dollars)** | Credit | Debit |
|---|---|---|
| **1. Net change in U.S. assets abroad (increase/outflow (−))** | | −426,801 |
|   A. U.S. official reserve assets | 14,906 | |
|   B. U.S. government assets, other than official reserve assets | 5,539 | |
|   C. U.S. private assets | | −446,436 |
| **2. Net change in foreign assets in the United States (increase/inflow (+))** | 1,212,250 | |
|   A. Foreign official assets in the United States | 199,495 | |
|   B. Other foreign assets in the United States | 1,012,755 | |

There are five main categories of financial flows. Each of these categories can be further subdivided.

*Source*: U.S. Department of Commerce, Bureau of Economic Analysis, http://www.bea.gov/.

into a reserve currency, such as U.S. dollars, and use them to pay for its imports. If the Chilean central bank is unable to provide dollars or another reserve currency to Chilean banks and importers, then the import business grinds to a halt unless the importer is able to secure some form of credit from the seller.

Since all forms of international debts are settled with reserve assets, especially key currencies, they play a very prominent role in international finance. When they become scarce in a country, it signals that potentially serious problems are arising. For example, as discussed below, when Mexico's economy collapsed in late 1994 and early 1995, it was because Mexicans owed dollars to various international investors, but the sudden outflow of dollars from Mexico during 1994 had severely reduced the supply of dollars and, in the short run, made it impossible for firms and the government to pay their dollar denominated debts. Relief came when Mexico was able to arrange several loans from the IMF, the United States, and Canada, which replenished its supply of official reserve assets.

The fallout from the Mexican crisis of 1994–1995 was a disastrous recession and changes in the government's data reporting system so that everyone could track the inflows and outflows of reserve assets in a more timely manner. Note, however, that since the financial account reports on financial flows, it does not indicate the stock, or total supply, of assets available. Looking at Table 9.4, the United States had a debit of $3,681 million for 2002 in its official reserve assets, representing a purchase of $3,681 million in official reserve assets. There is no indication given of the total stock of reserve assets available, so the financial account gives no idea what the total reserve holdings are. However, Central bank Web sites and numerous other sources, including popular media such as *The Economist*, provide this information.

Row 1.B in Table 9.4 includes other assets acquired by the federal government. These mainly represent loans to foreign governments, the rescheduling of past loans made to foreign governments, payments received on outstanding loans, and changes in nonreserve currency holdings, such as Mexican pesos or Israeli shekels. Line 2.A of Table 9.4 is symmetrical with 1.A. When the federal government needs to borrow money in order to cover its deficit or to refinance its debt, foreign governments usually purchase a share of the Treasury bills or bonds sold, and it shows up in line 2.A. U.S. Treasury securities are equivalent to reserve assets for foreign governments because they are easily sold for dollars and the dollar is universally accepted as payment for international debt. Private foreign interests may also purchase U.S. Treasury or other securities, however, and these purchases show up in line 2.B, along with other private investments in the U.S. economy.

Row 1.C represents the largest value of any of the outflows in the upper part of the table and is conceptually similar to private inflows in row 2.B. Flows of privately owned financial assets are by far the largest element in the account. The main categories of rows 1.C and 2.B are presented in more detail in Table 9.5.

The first subcomponent of financial outflows and inflows (1.A and 2.A) is **foreign direct investment (FDI)**. FDI was discussed in Chapter 4 where Dunning's OLI theory was presented. FDI in the financial account includes tangible items such as real estate, factories, warehouses, transportation facilities, and other physical (real) assets. The second and third subcomponents can be consid-

---

**TABLE 9.5** ● **Private Flows in the U.S. Financial Account, 2005 (Millions of Dollars)**

|  | Credit | Debit |
|---|---|---|
| **1. U.S. private assets abroad, net (increase/outflow(−))** |  | −446,436 |
| *Subcomponents:* |  |  |
| A. Direct investment |  | −9,072 |
| B. Foreign securities |  | −180,125 |
| C. Loans to foreign firms, including banks |  | −257,239 |
| **2. Foreign owned assets in the United States, other than official assets, net (increase/inflow(+))** | 1,012,755 |  |
| *Subcomponents:* |  |  |
| A. Direct investment | 109,754 |  |
| B. U.S. securities and currency | 693,047 |  |
| C. Loans to U.S. firms, including banks | 209,954 |  |

Private assets flows are the largest part of the financial account. These are usefully divided into three symmetrical subcomponents of inflows and outflows.

*Source*: U.S. Department of Commerce, Bureau of Economic Analysis, http://www.bea.gov/.

ered portfolio investment since they represent paper assets such as stocks, bonds, and loans. The similarity between FDI and **foreign portfolio investment** is that they both give their holders a claim on the future output of the foreign economy. They are very different, however, in their time horizons and this can have dramatic effects on the host country, where assets are located. Direct investments usually involve a longer time horizon because they are difficult to liquidate quickly and therefore represent a long-term position in the host country. Portfolio investments in stocks and bonds tend to be more short term. While many investors may decide to hold their foreign securities through all the ups and downs, by their nature, stocks and bonds are much more liquid than real estate or factories. It is common, therefore, for portfolio investors to have a shorter time horizon, and to move quickly if they expect a downturn. Sudden shifts in investor confidence, or sudden increases in uncertainty, can lead to large, destabilizing outflows (1.B and 1.C) as investors sell off their financial assets in the home country and move those assets elsewhere. In most of the financial crises of the last decade (Mexico, 1994; East Asia, 1997; Russia, 1998; Turkey, 2001), there were large and sudden financial outflows as both home country and foreign investors tried to take their assets out of the country before the expected crisis. In late 1994, for example, after Mexico decided to devalue its currency, there was a sudden financial outflow as Mexican stock and bond owners tried to liquidate their holdings and convert the proceeds to dollars before the peso completely collapsed. The sudden sell-off of peso-denominated assets put enormous pressure on the currency. This drained the central bank of most of its reserve assets (dollars) and caused the peso to lose approximately one-half its dollar value. Ultimately, the economy fell into a deep recession.

The growth of stock markets around the world, particularly in the newly industrializing countries of South America and Asia, represents a worldwide expansion of the buying and selling of stocks and related assets. Much of the buying and selling is done by residents of the country, but the banking systems in some developing countries play an important role since they have conduits for acquiring loans from foreign sources. Banks in some countries (it depends on the perception of credit worthiness and economic prospects in the country) borrow abroad in order to acquire funds for lending to domestic residents who use the money to buy stocks, or speculate in real estate, or who expand their businesses. The link from foreign financial capital to domestic borrowers was a key relationship at the root of the East Asian financial crisis in 1997 and the Turkish crisis in 2001, and it highlights the importance of items 1.C and 2.C in Table 9.5. The pattern of borrowing abroad in order to lend at home was particularly damaging in the East Asian case as it created debts that mostly had to be paid in dollars while the domestic lending was in home country currency. Consequently, when the crisis hit and the value of the home country currencies collapsed, the entire banking systems of some countries were thrown into crisis. The payments received by the banks were in their devalued home country currency, which was suddenly inadequate to service their dollar denominated debts.

## Limits on Financial Flows

Until a few years ago, most nations limited the movement of financial flows across their national borders. A typical pattern was to allow financial flows that were related to transactions on the current account, but to limit and regulate financial flows related to financial account transactions severely. In other words, if an importer needed a foreign loan to purchase goods abroad, or if an exporter needed foreign financing in order to buy materials needed to make export goods, then these financial flows were regulated but generally allowed. Conversely, if a bank wanted to borrow abroad in order to make loans at home (for example, to real estate speculators) then the inflow of financial capital to the bank was prohibited or subjected to such onerous terms and conditions that it was undesirable. These types of restrictions on financial flows were a normal part of the international economic landscape, even in industrial economies, until the 1980s and 1990s. For example, the members of the European Union did not completely liberalize financial flows between member countries until 1993.

In the movement toward more open markets over the last decades, there has been a significant lifting of controls on financial flows across international boundaries. This change in international economic policy was seen as desirable because restrictions on financial flows limit the availability of financial capital. Developing countries, in particular, were thought to benefit from liberalization since they have the greatest scarcity of financial capital and their ability to raise incomes and living standards depends greatly on access to adequate financial capital.

In addition, it is difficult to disentangle financial flows related to financing current account transactions from flows that are purely financial account transactions. This makes it difficult to regulate or control international financial flows, and many economists argue that the attempt to do so creates unnecessary red tape and bureaucratic delay and arbitrariness, and reduces economic efficiency. For over a decade, through much of the 1980s and 1990s, the consensus among economists was that it is better to allow financial capital to move freely across international borders.

More recently, the extreme volatility in some financial markets and the severe damage it has caused to a number of countries has revived interest in some form of controls or regulations to limit the damage caused by unexpectedly large financial outflows. It is easy to understand the tensions involved, however. On the one hand, foreign capital inflows are beneficial because they enable countries to increase their investments in factories and ports and other physical assets that help raise living standards and incomes. On the other hand, the sudden outward flight of foreign financial capital can generate a debt crisis and throw a country into deep depression. The key is to capture the benefits of increased investment while minimizing the risks of capital flight. At this point there is not much consensus among economists about the best policies. We will look at this issue in more detail in Chapter 12 after we introduce several more concepts.

## CASE STUDY

# The Mexican Sexenio Crisis

The excitement surrounding the Mexican presidential elections of July 2000 was heightened by two factors, one political and one economic. On the political scorecard, the Institutional Revolutionary Party (PRI) that had been in power for 71 years faced its most serious challenge ever (it lost). On the economic side, the air was filled with the uncertainty of a possible financial collapse after the election. The end-of-term presidential transitions of the previous four presidents—Echeverría (1970–1976), Portillo (1976–1982), de la Madrid (1982–1988), and Salinas (1988–1994)—involved traumatic and destructive economic crises that were triggered by large financial account outflows. Since Mexican presidents serve a single six-year term (a *sexenio*), the financial crises at the end of the terms have come to be called *sexenio* crises. The severity of the *sexenio* crises varied, ranging from the relatively mild crisis at the end of de la Madrid's term in 1988, to the deep and lasting crisis at the end of Portillo's term in 1982, and the even deeper but relatively short recession after Salinas in 1994. Ernesto Zedillo, the outgoing president in 2000, promised to break this pattern.

Each of the four crises shared a set of characteristics: (1) large and sudden outflows of financial capital; (2) rapid outflows of official reserve assets such as U.S. dollars; and (3) a relatively large amount of short-term debt caused by previously large financial inflows to Mexican banks and firms. In addition, with the exception of 1988, there were: (4) a significantly overvalued peso; and (5) a large current account deficit.

These factors are interrelated. For example, an overvalued peso leads to cheaper imports (and makes Mexican exports more expensive to foreigners), resulting in large current account deficits. The expectation that Mexico will have to devalue its currency to eliminate the current account deficit (devaluation makes imports expensive to Mexicans and Mexican goods cheaper to foreigners) causes both Mexicans and foreigners to move financial assets out of the country in an attempt to preserve the value of their investments. Large financial outflows, or *capital flight* as it is called, draw down foreign exchange reserves and make it impossible to service short-term debt. The result is a debt crisis, followed by a falling peso, then inflation and a recession as rising prices reduce real wages and income.

President Zedillo, who has a doctorate in economics from Yale, clearly understood these relationships. He was adamant that Mexico would avoid another sexenio crisis and he took several steps to insulate the economy. First, he reduced the reliance of Mexican investors on foreign financing by putting into place policies that encouraged more domestic savings. This reduced the inflow of bank loans (item 2.C in Table 9.5). He encouraged foreign direct investment in place of portfolio or financial investment (item 2.A instead of 2.B or 2.C) as a means to finance the current account deficit and to avoid short-term borrowing. He balanced the government's budget so there would be no dependence on foreign borrowing by government. In case a crisis began to develop, he arranged $23.7 billion in stand-by lines of emergency credit from the IMF, World Bank, Inter-American Development Bank, Export-Import Bank of the United States, and a funding mechanism under NAFTA called the North American Framework Agreement.

Each step in this reform package helped raise the stock of Mexican official reserve assets while reducing the likelihood of large financial capital outflows that would drain the reserve assets and throw the country into crisis. Finally, and perhaps most important, Zedillo's administration moved the country from a controlled value of the peso to a market-based system in which the peso's value is determined by the supply and demand for the currency. We will examine the effects of this change in Chapter 10. Suffice it to say that the reforms worked and no sexenio crisis occurred in 2000 when Zedillo left office.

*Source*: Heath, Jonathan, and Sidney Weintraub. *Mexico and the Sexenio Curse: Presidential Successions and Economic Crises in Modern Mexico*. Washington, DC: CSIS Press. 1999.

 # The Current Account and the Macroeconomy

There are two important practical reasons for learning about the balance of payments. One is to understand the broader implications of current account imbalances and to analyze the policies that might be used to tame a current account deficit. This is particularly important for small countries that are easily buffeted about by changes in the global economy, but it is also of interest to a big economy such as the United States, where very large current account deficits have been the norm for several years. A second practical reason for studying the balance of payments is to try to understand how countries might avoid a crisis brought on by volatile financial flows, and what policies will minimize the harmful affects of a crisis if it occurs. Economic analysis is still in its infancy when it comes to the problem of volatile financial flows, and there is some distance to travel before there is likely to be a consensus agreement on issues such as free versus restricted capital mobility, or the links from financial flows to economic growth. Nevertheless, there are some basic points of agreement among economists, and we will discuss them in Chapters 10 and 12. Before then, we must examine the relationship of the current account to the macroeconomy, which requires a brief review of basic concepts from the principles of macroeconomics.

## The National Income and Product Accounts

The internal, domestic accounting systems used by countries to keep track of total production and total income are called the **national income** and **product accounts**. These accounts are very detailed presentations of income, output, and other measures of a nation's macroeconomy. We will use the most fundamental concepts from this accounting system, beginning with the concept of **gross domestic product (GDP)**. Recall from the principles of economics that a nation's gross domestic product is the market value of all final goods and services produced inside its borders during some time period, usually a year. GDP is the most common measure of the size of an economy, although it is widely recognized that it ignores some important considerations, such as the value of leisure time and environmental degradation that takes place during the process of producing the nation's output. In addition, GDP only includes goods that pass through organized markets, so household production (cooking, sewing, landscaping, childcare, and so on) and other non–market-oriented production are left out. For these and other reasons, economists caution against using GDP as a sole determinant of the well-being of a society. In spite of these limitations, however, it provides a starting point for understanding different economies.

In order to avoid the problem of double counting, GDP only includes the value of *final* goods and services. This is actually a strength of the measure, since if we added the value of steel sold to a car maker, and the value of the cars, we would be counting the steel twice, once as steel and a second time as part of the value of the car. The final part of the definition states that GDP must be measured over some time period, usually a year. Most countries measure GDP every three months, but for most purposes, including ours, the most useful time period to consider is the span of one year.

An alternative concept for measuring a nation's output is **gross national product (GNP)**. For most countries, the difference between the two concepts is very small, because GNP is the value of all final goods and services produced by the labor, capital, and other resources of a country, regardless of where production occurred. In an accounting sense, GNP is equal to GDP plus investment income and unilateral transfers received from foreigners minus investment income and unilateral transfers paid to foreigners:

$$\text{GDP} + \text{foreign investment income received}$$
$$- \text{ investment income paid to foreigners}$$
$$+ \text{ net unilateral transfers} = \text{GNP}$$

Note that the difference between GNP and GDP is precisely equal to lines 2 and 3 in Tables 9.1, 9.2, and 9.3: the investment income and unilateral transfers components of the current account balance. This fact is useful because GDP includes exports minus imports and it enables us to bring the entire current account concept into the picture.

The usefulness of adding net foreign investment income (investment income received minus investment income paid) plus net unilateral transfers is apparent when we look at the definition of GDP based on its four main components. Table 9.6 defines the necessary variables. GDP is equal to the sum of consumer expenditures plus investment expenditures plus government expenditures on goods and services plus exports of goods and services minus imports of goods and services:

$$\text{GDP} = \text{C} + \text{I} + \text{G} + \text{X} - \text{M}. \tag{9.1}$$

| TABLE 9.6 ● Variable Definitions | |
|---|---|
| Variable | Definition |
| GDP | Gross domestic product |
| GNP | Gross national product |
| C | Consumption expenditures |
| I | Investment expenditures |
| G | Government expenditures on goods and services |
| X | Exports of goods and services |
| M | Imports of goods and services |
| CA | Current account balance |
| S | Private savings (savings of households and firms) |
| T | Net taxes, or taxes paid minus transfer payments received |

Given that GNP is equal to GDP plus net foreign investment income and net unilateral transfers:

$$\text{GNP} = \text{GDP} + (\text{Net foreign investment income} + \text{net transfers}) \quad (9.2)$$

or

$$\text{GNP} = (C + I + G) + (X - M + \text{Net foreign investment income} \quad (9.3)$$
$$+ \text{net transfers})$$

we can write the definition of GNP in terms of the current account balance. Rewriting Equation (9.3) in a simpler form gives us the following:

$$\text{GNP} = C + I + G + CA \quad (9.4)$$

Equation (9.4) explicitly shows the relationship between the current account and the main macroeconomic variables such as consumer spending, investment, and government purchases.

As the total value of goods and services produced by the labor, capital, and other resources of a country, GNP is also the value of income received. This follows from the fact that the production of final goods and services generates incomes that are equal in value to output and is embodied in the basic macroeconomic accounting identity stating that every economy's income must equal its output. From the point of view of the income recipients, there are three choices or obligations: They may consume their income (C), save it (S), or use it to pay taxes (T). In reality, all of us do a combination of the three. This permits us to rewrite the definition of GNP in terms of income and its uses as follows:

$$\text{GNP} = C + S + T \quad (9.5)$$

Since Equations (9.4) and (9.5) are equivalent definitions of GNP, one in terms of the components of output, the other in terms of the uses of income, we can set them equal to each other as follows:

$$C + I + G + CA = C + S + T \qquad (9.6)$$

Subtracting consumption from both sides and rearranging terms gives us the following:

$$I + G + CA = S + T \qquad (9.7)$$

or

$$S + (T - G) = I + CA \qquad (9.8)$$

Equation (9.8) is an accounting identity, or something that is true by definition. It is worth memorizing because it summarizes the important relationship between the current account balance, investment, and public and private savings in the economy. Equation (9.8) does not reveal any of the causal mechanisms through which changes in savings or investment are connected to the current account balance, but it does provide insight into the economy. For example, if total savings remains unchanged while investment increases, then the current account balance must move toward, or deeper into, deficit.

In order to see this, it is necessary to be certain that you understand the term on the left side, $(T - G)$. This is the combined (federal, state, and local) budget balances of all levels of government, or, to say it another way, government savings. It is savings because $(T)$ is government revenue (or income) and $(G)$ is government expenditure. A positive $(T - G)$ states that the combined government budgets are in surplus, which in the governmental sector is equivalent to savings. Conversely, a negative $(T - G)$ is a deficit, or dissavings. By placing governmental budget balances on the left-hand side, we are emphasizing that there are two sources of savings in an economy: the private sector, $(S)$ and the public or governmental sector, $(T - G)$. If governments dissave (run deficits), then they must borrow from the private sector, which reduces total national savings on the left-hand side.

From Equation (9.8) we see that a nation's savings (private plus public) is divided into two uses. First, it is a source of funds for domestic investment $(I)$. This role is crucial because new investments in machinery and equipment are a source of economic growth. Investment is essential as the means to upgrade the skills of the labor force, to provide more capital on the job, and to improve the quality of capital by introducing new technology. According to Equation (9.8), if government budgets are in deficit, the total supply of national savings is reduced, and, all else equal, investment will be less than it might otherwise have been. Conversely, a surplus in government budgets will augment private savings and increase the funds available for investment, all else equal.

The second use for national savings is as a source of funds for foreign investment. If the current account is in surplus, national savings finances the purchase of domestic goods by foreign users of those goods. In return, or as payment, the domestic economy acquires foreign financial assets. Recall from the discussion of the relationship between the current and financial accounts, that the financial account is more or less a mirror image of the current account. In other words, a positive current account is associated with a negative financial account, which is an outflow of financial capital. Equivalence between the outflow's magnitude and the current account surplus ensures that foreigners obtain the financial resources they need to buy more goods and services than they sell in world markets. In a sense, the surplus country provides its savings to the rest of the world, thereby enabling it (the surplus country) to sell more goods abroad than it buys. For a surplus country, a financial capital outflow is an investment because it involves the acquisition of assets that are expected to pay a future return. It is not the same as domestic investment, however, because the assets are outside the country. Hence, another name for the current account balance is *net foreign investment*. A positive balance implies positive foreign investment, while a negative balance implies negative investment (disinvestment), or a reduction in net foreign assets.

With the exception of 1991, when it received large income payments in compensation for the Gulf War, the United States has had a current account deficit every year since 1981 (see Figure 9.1). In 2005, the deficit was 6.2 percent of GNP. Figure 9.2 shows the current account balance since 1991 and the three related macroeconomic variables from Equation 9.8. Since 1991, the general trend in private savings (S) is down while the trend in investment (I) is up. Both of these factors are related to a decline in the current account balance, holding public savings (T − G) constant. (T − G) was not constant, however, and the increase in public savings during the second half of the 1990s could have provided increased funds for domestic and foreign investment, except for the fact that private savings deteriorated as public savings increased. Since 2000, the decline in the government accounts has consumed the slight increase in private savings and the current account has continued to decline.

Table 9.7 shows the same set of variables for six different countries, but at one point in time. The countries represent low, moderate, and high private savings (S). There is an imperfect, but revealing relationship between the level of private savings and domestic investment (I), as low-savings countries tend to have low levels of investment and high-savings countries have high levels of investment. The relationship between (S) and (I) is also mediated by public savings (T − G) and foreign investment (CA). These variables prevent (S) from equaling (I) unless (T − G) equals (CA).

For example, Nicaragua had a very low level of private savings in 2005, yet it managed to invest over one-fourth of its GNP. A relatively high level of domestic investment was possible because it was largely financed by foreign capital inflows, which show up as an enormous (and unsustainable) current account deficit. Tanzania and Italy could invest more at home and/or abroad, but their public savings deficits consume some of their private savings and require foreign finance (CA deficits) in order to maintain their current level of domestic investment. Botswana and Singapore, on the other hand, are able to invest healthy amounts at home and abroad given their high levels of private savings.

**FIGURE 9.2** • **U.S. Savings and Investment, 1991–2005**

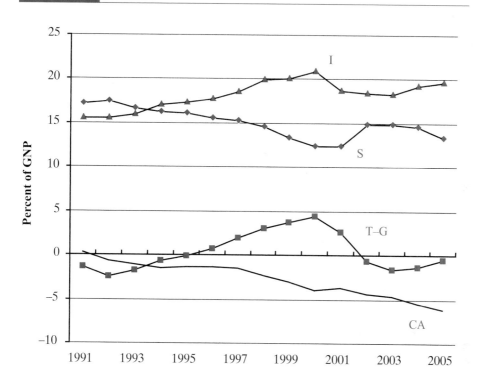

During the 1990s, private saving (S) fell while investment (I) rose. The gap between saving and investment was filled by increased public saving (positive T − G) and capital inflows (negative CA).

*Source*: U.S. Department of Commerce, Bureau of Economic Analysis, http://www.bea.gov.

The pattern across the six countries shown in Table 9.7 makes it abundantly clear that the relationship between government budgets and the current account is not fixed. The only country with a budget balance roughly equivalent to its current account balance is Tanzania, while the rest of the sample have wildly different values for these two variables. This is an important point since public commentary often calls simultaneous budget and current account deficits the "twin deficits." In the 1980s, for example, as the U.S. federal budget and current account balances deteriorated, many observers complained about the twin deficits as if one caused the other. A popular assumption was that federal deficits cause current account deficits. This line of argument is primarily a political argument for reducing deficits, but as we have seen, the relationship between the two variables is not perfect.

| TABLE 9.7 ● Key Macroeconomic Indicators, Percent of GNP, 2004 | | | | |
|---|---|---|---|---|
| | S | T−G | I | CA |
| **Low Saving** | | | | |
| Kyrgyz Republic | 8.6 | −0.5 | 12.9 | −4.8 |
| Nicaragua | 11.7 | −2.3 | 27.1 | −17.7 |
| **Moderate Saving** | | | | |
| Tanzania | 20.0 | −2.9 | 20.9 | −3.9 |
| Italy | 23.1 | −3.2 | 20.7 | −0.8 |
| **High Saving** | | | | |
| Botswana* | 30.8 | −0.3 | 23.9 | 6.5 |
| Singapore | 45.6 | 5.8 | 24.5 | 26.8 |

*2003

The more a country saves (S + T − G), the more it is able to invest at home (I) and abroad (CA).

*Source*: International Monetary Fund, *International Financial Statistics*. July 2006.

## Are Current Account Deficits Harmful?

The relationship between the current account balance, investment, and total national savings is an identity. Consequently, it does not tell us why an economy runs a current account deficit or surplus. In Equation (9.8):

$$S + (T − G) = I + CA$$

the left and right sides are equal by definition. Consequently, we cannot say that the current account is in deficit because saving is too low any more than we can say it is because investment is too high.

There is a general tendency in the media and the public to interpret a current account deficit as a sign of weakness and as harmful to the nation's welfare. Another interpretation is that the deficit enables more investment than would be possible otherwise, and since higher investment is correlated with higher living standards, the current account deficit might be interpreted as beneficial. In addition, the capital inflows that are associated with current account deficits are an implicit vote of confidence by foreigners. For example, between 1980 and 1991, Japan invested more than $25 billion of its trade surplus in U.S. manufacturing. By the start of the 1990s, the Japanese owned 66 steel works, 20 rubber and tire factories, 8 major car assembly plants, and 270 auto parts suppliers, employing more than 100,000 workers. Furthermore, the investment came at a time when the three major U.S.-based auto manufacturers (Chrysler, Ford, and GM) were laying off workers and relocating production abroad. Some of the

Japanese firms were acquisitions (which may have closed if they had not been bought) and many were new plants built from scratch with Japanese savings. During the deficits of the 1990s, foreign investors continued to pour in capital, enabling the United States to raise its level of investment and increase its productivity in spite of its declining savings rate. In this particular case, the current account deficit has been beneficial because, all else equal, it enabled more investment than was possible otherwise, given the savings rate.

Current account deficits can also generate problems, however. The capital inflows that occur with a current account deficit increase the stock of foreign-owned assets inside the home country, raising the possibility that a change in investor expectations about the economy's future can lead to a sudden surge in capital outflows. In the worst case scenario, capital flight is followed by a depletion of international reserves and a financial crisis. This is an experience shared by a number of developing countries since the 1980s, but it should not lead you to believe that the optimal policy for a country is to avoid current account deficits. As we have just seen, they allow countries to invest more than they could otherwise, and this is particularly important for developing countries where investment capital is especially scarce. Furthermore, current account surpluses are no guarantee that a country will be able to avoid a crisis if one develops among its trading partners. International financial crises, like some biological diseases, tend to be contagious. When Mexico slipped into the peso crisis in late 1994 and early 1995, for example, economists and journalists began to write about the "Tequila effect" on Latin America. Similarly, when the currency of Thailand (the baht) lost a large share of its value in July of 1997, the media reported stories of "baht-ulism" spreading across East Asia and the rest of the developing world. In both cases, the size of a country's current account balances was not a good predictor of whether it was drawn into the crisis. (See Chapter 12 for a more detailed discussion of financial crises.)

The experiences of countries in the 1980s and 1990s has taught economists that financial crises are determined by more than the size of the current account deficit, and that there are no absolute thresholds between safe and dangerous levels of a deficit. While deficits of 3 to 4 percent of GDP begin to raise red flags, and deficits of 7 to 9 percent are considered extremely risky, there are too many other factors that must be taken into consideration before the probability of a crisis can be determined.

## CASE STUDY

# Current Account Deficits in the United States

Figures 9.1 and 9.2 illustrate the growing problem of the U.S. current account deficit. In 2005, the deficit was almost $800 billion, over 6 percent of GDP, and required an estimated $8 billion per day in foreign financing in order to finance the current account deficit and the United States' own foreign investments. For most developed countries, current account deficits in the range of 4 to 5 percent of GDP usually trigger adjustments that force a reduction in their size. It seems only natural to ask whether the United States will undergo similar adjustments to reduce its deficit, and if not, then does the size of the deficit constitute a threat to U.S. and/or world prosperity?

To begin, it is useful to point to two features of the deficit that are shown prominently in Figure 9.1. The first is the opening and closing of the deficit in the 1980s and the second is its reopening in the 1990s. It is tempting to see these two episodes as essentially similar, yet they are very different in their origins and their potential consequences. In both episodes, fiscal and monetary policies played a key role, but so did events external to the United States. Beginning around 1981, the budget of the federal government turned the overall (federal-state-local) government balance, $(T - G)$, into a large negative number. Given the lack of private savings to finance both domestic investment (I) and public sector dissaving, foreign finance filled the gap and the current account turned negative. The 1990s story is different in several ways, but perhaps most importantly, in that over the course of the decade, the federal budget moved from a large negative to a positive. If everything had remained the same, this would have reduced the need for foreign savings and pushed the current account in the direction of surplus, but (S) and (I) were not constant. The decade saw sharp increases in investment spending as corporations bought new computer technology and the telecommunications equipment they needed to stay competitive. In addition, a stock market boom followed by a housing market boom made consumers much wealthier, with the result that households rapidly increased their consumption and decreased their personal savings. Therefore, the changes in the government budget were overwhelmed by the increases in investment and by the decline in savings, resulting in a large and growing current account deficit. In 2002, large federal budget deficits returned and put additional pressure on the United States to seek foreign financing for its domestic and foreign investment.

The central concern for many observers is whether the size of the U.S. current account deficit could trigger an economic crisis. One way to eliminate the deficit is to cut U.S. spending (consumption, investment, and government) in order to increase overall savings. This can happen through a "soft landing" in which adjustments occur gradually over time, or a "hard landing" where forced sudden declines in spending lead to a crisis. The most plausible hard landing scenario is triggered by a sudden drop in foreign capital flows to the United States. This would raise interest rates, negatively impact housing and equity markets, reduce consumption and investment spending, and could easily lead to a recession with high unemployment. A fall in the demand for dollars by foreigners who no longer want to buy U.S. assets would also lead to a decline in the value of the dollar and, as a consequence of a weaker dollar, reduce U.S. purchases of foreign products. This could potentially spread the U.S. recession to parts of the world that depend on U.S. demand for their goods as a stimulus to their economies. A soft landing scenario is much less painful, but requires a coordinated set of policies to bring it about. Appropriate policies for a soft landing include tighter fiscal policies in the United States in order to reduce the federal deficit, a gradual depreciation of the dollar, and economic stimulus in Europe and Asia to pick up the slack caused by the loss of U.S. demand for foreign goods and services.

In general, most economists are not forecasting a sudden decline in the flow of foreign capital to the United States. That is, it is thought that governments and businesses outside the United States will continue to view the United States as a secure place to invest, and will continue to send their large capital flows. This does not mean that no crisis will occur, but rather it makes more sense to think of persistent current account deficits as gradually increasing the probability of a crisis, but still not pushing it into the range where it becomes inevitable. Perhaps the most damaging short-run effect is the political pressure generated by the deficit for increased protectionism inside the United States. Complaints that the trade deficit is caused by markets that are too open, or the unfair trade policies of other countries, gain currency when the deficit is large and persistent. Inevitably, this causes pressures to close markets and delay agreements to open new ones. In the long run, the United States is accumulating sizable debts to foreigners, which will be liabilities in the future. This is not a problem if the current account deficit is used to enhance productivity, but if it mainly fuels consumption then the future debts will be burdensome and adversely affect U.S. living standards.

 **International Debt**

Current account deficits must be financed through inflows of financial capital. Recall from Table 9.5 and the previous discussion that capital inflows take different forms, from direct investment to purchases of stocks, bonds, and currency, to loans. Loans from abroad add to a country's stock of **external debt** and generate **debt service** obligations requiring interest payments and repayment of the principal. Theoretically, foreign loans are no more harmful than any other type of debt. That is, as long as the borrowed funds are used to increase skills and production levels, the borrower will be able to service the debt without difficulty. In practice, however, it is not uncommon for borrowed funds to be used in a manner that does not contribute to the expansion of the country's productive capacity, and often debt service becomes an unsustainable burden that holds back economic development.

All countries, rich and poor, have external debt. In the case of high-income countries, debt service is rarely an issue, because the amount of debt is usually relatively small compared to the size of the economy. Low- and middle-income countries are another matter. In a number of cases, the size of the external debt burden is unsustainable, given the economy's ability to make interest payments and to repay the principal.

Unsustainable debt occurs for a number of reasons. In some cases, countries are dependent on exports of one or two basic commodities such as copper and coffee. The shock of a sudden drop in world commodity prices reduces the value of exports and sometimes generates unexpectedly large current account deficits. In other cases, countries experience natural disasters such as hurricanes and earthquakes that create a need for relief and foreign assistance, or civil conflicts that fuel a demand for arms purchases. Corruption too can play a role, as described later in the case of the Democratic Republic of the Congo. Even electoral politics may be a factor, as when officials try to gain support through unsustainable expenditures targeted at important constituents. Finally, the behavior of foreign lenders also plays a role, as described next.

In 2001, 138 developing countries classified as low- and middle-income by the World Bank (see Chapter 8 for definitions) had external debts that totaled US$2,332.1 billion, 62.9 percent of which was owed either directly by developing country governments or by the private sector but guaranteed by the government. One of the primary problems of excessive debt is that it worsens the central government's budget position by adding large debt service payments to the other items in the budget. In addition to potential budgetary problems, excessive debt can severely reduce the quantity of resources available for investing in economic development. Schools, health clinics, roads, ports, and other infrastructure and social needs are less likely to be addressed if debt service is substantial.

Debt is also a problem because it can intensify and spread a crisis. For example, during the 1997–1998 East Asian crisis, the debt problems of Thailand, Indonesia, and a few other countries deepened the crisis and help spread it throughout the region. Because firms and governments could not pay their external debts, the crisis spilled beyond the region and threatened the economic stability of the entire world. We will look at the contagion effects and the transmission of crises in more detail in Chapter 12.

Table 9.8 shows the five largest low- and middle-income country debtors, along with the two indicators used to determine when debt is excessive. The indicators are debt divided by exports of goods and services and debt divided by gross national product. Debt levels are compared to exports, because countries must earn foreign exchange (dollars, euros, pounds, or another internationally acceptable currency) in order to service their debts.

Debt problems of developing countries have received considerable attention. The governments of high-income countries together with multilateral agencies such as the World Bank and the International Monetary Fund have developed a number of strategies for addressing the debt problems of low- and middle-income countries, particularly when the debt level appears to be unsustainable and likely to lead to a crisis. In addition, a number of private organizations, such as Jubilee 2000, Jubilee Plus, Oxfam, and the European Network on Debt and Development (Eurodad), have put forward debt-relief proposals and have applied significant moral pressure for debt relief.

One politically important debt-relief effort is the Highly Indebted Poor Countries (HIPC, or the Expanded HIPC) initiative, which is supported by the World Bank, the IMF, and high-income country governments. Under the HIPC initiative, countries can qualify for debt relief based on their level of poverty, a good track record of economic reform, and a high level of external debt relative to

| TABLE 9.8 The Five Largest Developing Country Debtors, 2004 | | | |
| --- | --- | --- | --- |
| Country | Debt, Billions US$ | Debt/Exports*<br>(Percent) | Debt/GNP*<br>(Percent) |
| China | 248.9 | 46 | 57 |
| Brazil | 220.0 | 258 | 47 |
| Russia | 197.3 | 120 | 46 |
| Argentina | 169.2 | 510 | 159 |
| Turkey | 161.6 | 221 | 69 |

*Debt is the present value of debt.

Some countries, China for example, can handle high levels of debt due to their current account surplus and large holdings of reserves. Others, with smaller debts, are more vulnerable to macroeconomic disturbances.

*Source:* World Bank, *Global Development Finance, 2005.*

exports. Currently, 40 countries are included in the HIPC program, 34 of which are nations in sub-Saharan Africa.

The HIPC initiative has been strongly criticized, particularly by Jubilee Plus and other nongovernmental organizations, for providing an inadequate amount of debt relief and for failing to address the responsibility of the lenders, many of whom tie their loans to purchases from suppliers in the lending country. Even the supporters of the HIPC recognize that part of the problem is that loans are sometimes made in order to fill loan quotas in the lending countries, or for other equally inappropriate reasons. Consequently, solutions to the problem of unsustainable debt must take into account the incentives for lenders to make loans.

## CASE STUDY

# Odious Debt

Thirty-four of the forty-two HIPC countries are in sub-Saharan Africa, where per-capita income averages $300 per year (excluding South Africa), life expectancy at birth is 46 years of age, and only 20 percent of the eligible population is enrolled in secondary school. Given the poverty and the lack of progress in meeting development goals, it is hard to argue against debt relief for these countries. Yet some observers question the value of debt forgiveness.

The primary argument against debt relief is that it is "money down a foreign aid rathole." Opponents say that because countries with large foreign debt may be poorly administered, debt relief can quickly turn into a new round of borrowing that will restore previous debt levels. Furthermore, some people fear that debt relief will encourage other countries to borrow excessively with the hope that their debts may be forgiven in the future. In this case, debt forgiveness today could spawn greater problems tomorrow. Economists do not have a single point of view on this issue, although many favor some sort of debt relief despite the arguments just made. The cost of debt forgiveness for the most severely indebted poor countries is inconsequential compared to the economies of the high-income countries, which are the ones that would be called upon to forgive the debts. In addition, some share of the debt is classified as odious debt and in those cases the arguments in favor of debt relief are impossible to ignore. **Odious debt** is legally defined as debt incurred without the consent of the people and that is not used for their benefit. It is associated with corrupt governments and countries where freedom is severely limited or does not exist.

Many cases of odious debt can be found among the 42 countries that qualify for the HIPC initiative. For example, in sub-Saharan Africa, the Democratic Republic of the Congo (formerly Zaire), Kenya, and Uganda almost certainly fall into this category, while at least part of the debt of many other countries would as well. Between 1972 and 1999, about 60 percent of the loans to HIPC countries went to regimes considered "not free" by Freedom House, an international organization that ranks countries as free, partly free, or not free. And between 1985 and 1995, about 67 percent of the loans made to HIPC countries went to places that were considered corrupt by the *International Country Risk Guide*, a risk analysis service.

The Democratic Republic of the Congo (DRC) is a clear-cut case. From 1965 to 1997, the DRC was ruled by the dictator Joseph Desire Mobutu. During Mobutu's reign, real GDP, measured in the equivalent of U.S. dollars at 2000 prices, fell from $317 per person to $110 per person while the regime amassed billions of dollars in foreign aid and loans. Mobutu's personal fortune was estimated to have reached $4 to $6 billion, most of which was deposited in Swiss bank accounts. In 2004, per capita income was at $88 and international debts were around $12 billion. The latter was equivalent to about 225 percent of GDP and 1,280 percent of a year's exports.

Given the continued decline in incomes and the large number of unfinished projects that were financed by various governments and multilateral agencies, there is little evidence that the borrowed money was successfully used for development purposes. Furthermore, lenders knew the situation when they made their loans, but they went ahead anyway since they wanted to secure access to the DRC's mineral deposits of cobalt and other strategic metals. Cases like the DRC make it difficult to argue that its citizens should be forced to pay off the debt. In 2003, the DRC was admitted to the HIPC program and qualified for up to 80 percent debt forgiveness, depending on its macroeconomic performance.

*Sources*: Birdsall and Williamson, *Delivering on Debt Relief*, 2002, Center for Global Development and Institute for International Economics, Washington, DC; World Bank, *Global Development Finance*, 2003, World Bank, Washington, DC.

**The International Investment Position**

Each year a nation runs a current account deficit, it borrows from abroad and adds to its indebtedness to foreigners. Each year it runs a current account surplus, it lends to foreigners and reduces its overall indebtedness. If the total of all domestic assets owned by foreigners is subtracted from the total of all foreign assets owned by residents of the home country, the result is the **international investment position**. If the international investment position is positive, then the home country could sell all its foreign assets and have more than enough revenue to purchase all the domestic assets owned by foreigners. If it is negative, then selling all foreign assets would not provide enough revenue to buy all the domestic assets owned by foreigners.

As an example of the international investment position, consider the United States at the end of 2005. The market value of all assets outside the United States and owned by governments, businesses, and residents of the United States, was $11,079 billion. Among other things, these assets included factories, shares of stock, bonds, foreign currency, and bank loans. At the same time, the market value of assets located in the United States and owned by governments, businesses, and residents abroad, was $13,625 billion. As a result, the international investment position of the United States at the end of 2005 was −2,546 billion. To summarize:

> International investment position
> = domestically owned foreign assets − foreign owned domestic assets
> = $11,079 billion − $13,625 billion
> = −2,546 billion

The large current account deficits of the 1980s, 1990s, and 2000s have eroded the United States' investment position from a positive $288.6 billion in 1983 to zero in 1989, and negative since then. Each year a country experiences a current account deficit, foreigners acquire more assets inside its boundaries than its residents acquire abroad, and the international investment position shrinks further.

We have considered many of the costs and benefits of capital inflows. They enable countries to invest more than would otherwise be the case, but they also make it possible for governments and consumers to spend more (save less). One of the benefits not discussed so far is the possibility of **technology transfer**. When capital inflows take the form of direct investment, they may bring new technologies, new management techniques, and new ideas to the host country. This transfer is particularly important for developing countries that lack access or information about newer technologies, but it is also important for high-income countries. Technology transfer is by no means an inevitable outcome of foreign direct investment, and much of the current research on this type of capital flow seeks to understand the conditions that encourage or discourage it.

One of the costs of capital inflows that has not been discussed is their potential to provide access to political power. Much depends on the political culture of the host country receiving the capital inflows, but large direct investment flows, as well as portfolio investment flows, are likely to provide access to politically significant people. This is the case in large and small countries, but it is particularly important in low- and middle-income countries, where wealth encounters fewer countervailing powers or contending interests.

 ## Summary

- Every nation's transactions with the rest of the world are summarized in its balance of payments. The balance of payments has three components: the current account, the capital account, and the financial account. The two most important components are the current and financial accounts.

- The current account is a record of a nation's trade, investment income, and transfers between it and the rest of the world.

- The financial account is a record of financial capital flows between a country and the rest of the world. The financial account is equal to the current account plus the capital account, with the sign reversed. This follows from the accounting principle that every purchase or sale of a good or service must generate a payment or a receipt.

- Capital flows in the financial account are grouped together as governmental and private. Private flows are the bulk of international capital flows. They are grouped into categories of direct investment and portfolio investment. In general, direct investment is longer-term and, therefore, less volatile.

- Large, sudden outflows of financial capital have created economic instability in many countries, particularly during the 1990s. This has created an active debate over the merits of restricting foreign capital flows. Economists are divided on this point, with some favoring restrictions and some favoring free capital mobility.

- There is a fundamental economic identity that total private and public saving in an economy must be equal to domestic investment plus net foreign investment. The current account balance is equal to net foreign investment, and a negative balance is equivalent to disinvestment abroad.

- Current account deficits enable a country to invest more than it could otherwise, which has a beneficial effect on national income. If deficits are too large, however, they increase the vulnerability of a country to sudden outflows of financial capital.

- Forty low-income countries are classified as highly indebted poor countries (HIPC). Thirty-four of the countries are in sub-Saharan Africa. All forty have unsustainable debt levels, some of which may be considered odious debt because it is debt incurred without the consent of the country's citizens and is not used for their benefit.

- The international investment position is the difference between foreign-based assets owned by residents in the home country and home-based assets owned by residents of foreign countries.
- Foreign investment has costs and benefits for the host country. While it may lead to technology transfer and higher investment levels, it can also become a mechanism for spreading a crisis and give foreigners a voice in the nation's internal political affairs.

# Vocabulary

| | |
|---|---|
| capital account | international investment position |
| current account | investment income |
| current account balance | national income |
| debt service | odious debt |
| external debt | official reserve assets |
| financial account | product accounts |
| foreign direct investment (FDI) | statistical discrepancy |
| foreign portfolio investment | technology transfer |
| goods and services | trade balance |
| gross domestic product (GDP) | unilateral transfers |
| gross national product (GNP) | |

# Study Questions

1. Use the following information to answer the questions below. Assume that the capital account is equal to 0.

| | |
|---|---|
| Net unilateral transfers | 250 |
| Exports of goods and services | 500 |
| Net increase in U.S. government's nonreserve foreign assets | 30 |
| Net increase in foreign ownership of U.S.-based nonreserve assets | 400 |
| Net increase in U.S. private assets abroad | 250 |
| Invest income received in the United States | 200 |
| Net increase in U.S. ownership of official reserve assets | 20 |
| Imports of goods and services | 600 |
| Net increase in foreign ownership of U.S.-based reserve assets | 100 |
| Investment income paid abroad by the United States | 300 |

    a.  What is the current account balance?

    b.  Does the financial account equal the current account?

    c.  What is the statistical discrepancy?

2.  Look at each of the cases below from the point of view of the balance of payments for the United States. Determine the subcategory of the current account or financial account that each transaction would be classified in, and state whether it would enter as a credit or debit.

    a.  The U.S. government sells gold for dollars.

    b.  A migrant worker in California sends $500 home to his village in Mexico.

    c.  An American mutual fund manager uses the deposits of his fund investors to buy Brazilian telecommunication stocks.

    d.  A Japanese firm in Tennessee buys car parts from a subsidiary in Malaysia.

    e.  An American church donates five tons of rice to the Sudan to help with famine relief.

    f.  An American retired couple flies from Seattle to Tokyo on Japan Airlines.

    g.  The Mexican government sells pesos to the United States Treasury and buys dollars.

3.  Weigh the pros and cons of a large trade deficit.

4.  Is the budget deficit of a country linked to its current account balance? How so? Explain how it is possible for the United States' current account deficit to grow while the budget deficit has disappeared.

5.  Compare and contrast portfolio capital flows with direct investment capital flows.

6.  Why is a current account surplus equivalent to foreign investment?


## APPENDIX A

# Measuring the International Investment Position

It may seem like a straightforward job to add up the value of assets, but nothing could be further from the truth. Consider the following problem: The United States ran trade surpluses in the 1950s and 1960s and accumulated large holdings of foreign assets. In the 1980s and 1990s, the United States ran trade deficits and foreigners accumulated large holdings inside the United States. By 2000, a sizable proportion of U.S.-owned assets had been purchased decades ago when prices were much lower, and foreign-owned assets were purchased recently, after the worldwide inflation of the 1970s and the early 1980s. If asset values are tallied using their historical costs, the price at the time of purchase, then foreign-owned assets appear more valuable, not necessarily because they are but because they were acquired more recently when world prices were higher.

It seems logical to expect that the reporting of asset values would be done on a current cost basis, rather than a historical cost basis, where current cost is the cost of purchasing the asset in the current period. Unfortunately, it does not happen this way. In the United States, firms use historical cost as the basis for valuation of assets in company records, and they use this when they report their foreign holdings to the agency that collects the data, the Bureau of Economic Analysis. The difference between current cost and historical cost does not affect the measurement of portfolio investment, which is relatively short term, but it has significant effects on the measurement of direct investment since it is held for longer time periods.

Until 1991, the United States only calculated the historical cost of U.S.-owned foreign assets. As a result, the U.S. international investment position appeared to become negative very rapidly as large trade deficits in the mid-1980s led to a rapid accumulation of new assets in the United States by foreign interests. More recently, in the 1990s, the United States began to report all assets on a current value basis. The primary deficiency in this data as it now stands is that it cannot be broken down into country-specific or industry-specific data. Therefore, we know the overall international investment position for the United States, but we cannot accurately examine the U.S.-Japan bilateral investment position, since we have U.S. assets in Japan only on a historical cost basis.

## APPENDIX B

# Balance of Payments Data

Current account and international investment data are readily available for most nations of the world.

## International Financial Statistics (IFS)

This is a regular publication of the International Monetary Fund. It appears monthly, with an annual *Yearbook* at the year's end. As the name implies, the IFS focuses on financial data, but it also contains information on current accounts and international capital flows. Coverage is of most of the world's nations, and the most recent *Yearbook* usually contains a decade of data for each country. The IMF publications are one of the sources used by many international agencies and private enterprises. Nearly all university libraries and many city libraries will have the IFS.

## Balance of Payments Statistics (BOPS)

This is a sister publication of the International Monetary Fund that complements the data in the *IFS*. The *BOPS* has the most up-to-date and detailed current account statistics of any international data source. In addition, it contains detailed breakdowns of capital flows.

## United Nations' Statistical Yearbook and Related Volumes

The *Statistical Yearbook* is generally somewhat less current than the IMF data listed earlier. It contains a much greater variety of data, however. The *Statistical Yearbook* is a combination of data from several more specialized UN sources, including the *United Nations' National Account Statistics, Demographic Yearbook, Industrial Statistics Yearbook, Energy Statistics Yearbook*, and *International Trade Statistics Yearbook*. The *Statistical Yearbook* has the advantage of combining in one place a great quantity of data, usually going back one decade. Its major disadvantage is that it lacks the detail that can be found in the more specialized volumes. The most current data can be located in the United Nations' *Monthly Bulletin of Statistics*. Most university libraries are likely to have one or all of these volumes.

# Exchange Rates and Exchange Rate Systems

## Introduction: Fixed, Flexible, or In-Between?

The topics of exchange rates and exchange rate systems are less settled than most issues examined so far. The lack of consensus is partly because countries must decide on the type of exchange rate system that best suits their conditions, and there is a fairly extensive menu of choices for selection. Some of the choices are relatively recent innovations, such as crawling pegs or target rate zones, and their performance characteristics under a wide array of economic conditions have yet to be fully analyzed. In general, the choice of an exchange rate system varies along a continuum from completely flexible rates that are determined by the market forces of supply and demand, to completely fixed rates that are set and maintained by a country's central bank. Between these two poles, there are many intermediate forms combining various degrees of fixity and flexibility in the determination of the exchange rate.

A further complication is that each type of exchange rate requires a different set of policies by government officials and each responds differently to pressures from the world economy. All three of these factors—exchange rate system, government policy, and the world economy—interact in ways that are at times impossible to predict and, as a result, have given rise to an active set of debates over the selection and management of a country's exchange rate system.

## Exchange Rates and Currency Trading

The **exchange rate** is the price of one currency stated in terms of a second currency. An exchange rate can be given in one of two ways, either as units of domestic currency per unit of foreign currency or vice versa. For example, we might give the U.S.-Mexico exchange rate as dollars per peso (0.10 dollars) or pesos per dollar (10 pesos). The custom varies with the currency. For example, the U.S. dollar–British pound exchange rate is usually quoted in terms of dollars per pound, but the U.S. dollar–Mexican peso exchange rate is usually pesos per dollar. In this chapter and the rest of the book, the exchange rate is always given as the number of units of domestic currency per unit of foreign currency. For the United States, this means it is dollars per peso and dollars per pound.

Exchange rates are reported on a daily basis in the financial pages of every major newspaper and in numerous Web sites. Table 10.1 shows a selection of exchange rates taken from the September 1, 2006, daily posting by the Federal

**TABLE 10.1** • **Exchange Rates for Selected Countries, September 1, 2006**

| Country | Currency | Units per U.S. Dollar | U.S. Dollars per Unit |
|---------|----------|----------------------|----------------------|
| Australia | Dollar | 1.3049 | 0.7663 |
| Brazil | Real | 2.1397 | 0.4673 |
| Canada | Dollar | 1.1056 | 0.9045 |
| China, PR | Yuan | 7.9533 | 0.1257 |
| Denmark | Krone | 5.8125 | 0.1720 |
| EMU members | Euro | 0.7792 | 1.2833 |
| Hong Kong | Dollar | 7.7780 | 0.1286 |
| India | Rupee | 46.38 | 0.0216 |
| Japan | Yen | 117.21 | 0.0085 |
| Malaysia | Ringgit | 3.6655 | 0.2728 |
| Mexico | Peso | 10.894 | 0.0918 |
| New Zealand | Dollar | 1.5267 | 0.6550 |
| Norway | Krone | 6.3350 | 0.1578 |
| Singapore | Dollar | 1.5721 | 0.6361 |
| South Africa | Rand | 7.2155 | 0.1386 |
| South Korea | Won | 960.30 | 0.0010 |
| Sri Lanka | Rupee | 102.180 | 0.0098 |
| Sweden | Krona | 7.2666 | 0.1376 |
| Switzerland | Franc | 1.2308 | 0.8125 |
| Taiwan | Dollar | 32.850 | 0.0304 |
| Thailand | Baht | 37.480 | 0.0267 |
| United Kingdom | Pound | 0.5249 | 1.9050 |
| Venezuela | Bolivar | 2144.60 | 0.0005 |

*Source*: U.S. Federal Reserve, http://www.federalreserve.gov/releases/h10/update/.

Reserve. These rates, like all the rates reported by the financial press, are wholesale prices rather than retail. In order to realize the listed exchange rate, a bank or currency trader has to purchase large quantities of the currency, typically one million dollars or more. Although Table 10.1 lists the U.S. dollar price of the Indian rupee as $0.0216 on September 1, 2006, tourists such as you and I could not have bought it at this price. However, banks, currency traders, and corporations that wanted to buy or sell millions of dollars worth of foreign exchange on that date would have found prices fairly close to those listed in the table.

The values in Table 10.1 are in a state of constant change. Most of the countries in the table have flexible exchange rate systems that allow the value or price of its currency to be determined by supply and demand. When a currency becomes more valuable, it buys more units of another currency and is said to have gained **appreciation**. When it loses value, it is described as **depreciation**. Note that since this text will define the exchange rate as the units of domestic currency per unit of foreign currency, an increase or appreciation in the home country's currency is a fall in the exchange rate. For example, if the U.S. dollar appreciates against the British pound, it might move from 1.6654 dollars per pound to 1.60 dollars. This is an appreciation of the dollar because it takes fewer dollars to buy a pound—1.60 instead of 1.6654.

## Reasons for Holding Foreign Currencies

Economists identify three reasons for holding foreign currency. The first is for trade and investment purposes. Traders (importers and exporters) and investors routinely transact in foreign currencies, either receiving or making payments in another country's money. Tourists are included in this category because they hold foreign exchange in order to buy foreign goods and services.

The second reason for holding foreign exchange is to take advantage of interest rate differentials, or **interest rate arbitrage**. Arbitrage conveys the idea of buying something where it is relatively cheap and selling it where it is relatively expensive. Interest rate arbitrage is similar in that arbitrageurs acquire money where interest rates are relatively low and lend it where rates are relatively high. By moving financial capital in this way, interest rate arbitrage keeps interest rates from diverging too far, and also constitutes one of the primary linkages between national economies. Capital inflows to the high interest rate countries puts downward pressure on interest rates, while the outflow from the low interest rate countries dries up the supply and puts upward pressure on rates. This drawing together of interest rates in different countries is one way in which economic conditions are transmitted across national borders. Various other factors intervene in this relationship, such as perceptions of risk, but in general, interest rate arbitrage is a powerful force in the world economy and tends to be one of the main reasons for holding foreign currency.

The third reason for holding foreign exchange is to speculate. Speculators are businesses who buy or sell a currency because they expect its price to rise or fall. They have no need for foreign exchange to buy goods or services or financial assets; rather, they hope to realize profits or avoid losses through correctly anticipating changes in a currency's market value. Speculators are often reviled in the popular press, but in fact they help to bring currencies into equilibrium after they have become over- or undervalued. If speculators view a currency as overvalued, they will sell it and, in the process, drive down its value and thereby realize the result they anticipated. If they guess wrong, however, they tend to lose a lot of money since they place their bets on a result that does not materialize. For this reason, some economists have argued that speculation either serves the useful function of bringing currency values into proper alignment, or its practitioners lose money and go out of business. Not everyone agrees with this view, however, and some economists feel that speculation against a currency can be destabilizing in the sense that it does not always push an exchange rate to its equilibrium value, but instead, will sometimes lead to a grossly over- or undervalued currency, which is a major problem for the country involved. Needless to say, the role of speculation in the market for foreign exchange is an issue that has not reached a consensus.

## Institutions

There are four main participants in foreign currency markets: retail customers, commercial banks, foreign exchange brokers, and central banks. Of these four, commercial banks are the most important. Retail customers include firms and individuals that hold foreign exchange for any of the three reasons given above—to engage in purchases, to adjust their portfolios, or to profit from expected future currency movements. In most cases, they buy and sell through a commercial bank. Commercial banks in many parts of the world hold inventories of foreign currencies as part of the services offered to customers. Not all banks provide this service, but those that do usually have a relationship with several foreign banks where they hold their balances of foreign currencies. When a surplus accumulates, or a shortage develops, the banks trade with each other to adjust their holdings.

In the United States, foreign exchange brokers also play an important role. It is not very common for U.S. banks to trade currency with foreign banks. Instead, U.S. banks tend to go through foreign exchange brokers, who act as middlemen between buyers and sellers since they do not usually hold foreign exchange. Brokers can also serve as agents for central banks. The market, then, works as follows. An individual or firm that needs foreign exchange calls its bank. The bank quotes a price at which it will sell the currency. The price is based on one of two possible sources of supply: The bank may have an account with another bank in the country where the currency is used, or it may call a foreign exchange broker. The broker keeps track of buyers and sellers of currencies and acts as a deal maker by bringing together a seller and a bank that is buying for its customer.

In most cases, currency trades take the form of credits and debits to a firm's bank accounts. For example, a local U.S. importer that must make payment in yen can call and tell its bank to transfer yen to the Japanese bank of the firm that supplies the importer with goods. The importer will have a debit to its local bank account that is equivalent to the cost of the yen. If the U.S. bank has a branch or correspondence bank in Japan, they can electronically notify it to debit the yen from the account of the U.S. bank and credit it to the Japanese bank of the supplier. If the U.S. bank goes through a currency trader instead of dealing directly with a Japanese bank, then first, it buys yen that are in an account with a Japanese bank. Next, it requests that some or all of its yen assets be transferred to the bank of the Japanese supplier of the U.S. importer.

## Exchange Rate Risk

Firms that do business in more than one country are subject to **exchange rate risks**. These risks stem from the fact that currencies are constantly changing in value and, as a result, expected future payments that will be made or received in a foreign currency will be a different domestic currency amount from when the contract was signed.

Suppose, for example, that a U.S. semiconductor manufacturer signs a contract to send a British computer manufacturer a shipment of microprocessors in six months. If the U.S. manufacturer agrees on a price in British pounds, it must know the value of the pound six months from now in order to know the dollar equivalent of its future revenue. If the U.S. manufacturer specifies that the microprocessors be paid for in dollars, then it shifts the exchange rate risk to the British firm. The U.S. company knows the exact dollar amount it will receive in six months, but the British firm is uncertain of the price of the dollar, and therefore the pound price of microprocessors.

Financial markets recognized this problem long ago and, in the nineteenth century they created mechanisms for dealing with it. The mechanisms are the forward exchange rate and the forward market. The **forward exchange rate** is the price of a currency that will be delivered in the future; the **forward market** refers to the market in which the buying and selling of currencies for future delivery takes place. Forward markets for currencies are an everyday tool for international traders, investors, and speculators because they are a way to eliminate the exchange rate risk associated with future payments and receipts. Forward foreign exchange markets allow an exporter or importer to sign a currency contract on the day they sign an agreement to ship or receive goods. The currency contract guarantees a set price for the foreign currency, usually 30, 90, or 180 days into the future. By contrast, the market for buying and selling in the present is called a **spot market**. The prices of foreign currencies quoted in Table 10.1 are "spot prices."

Suppose the U.S. semiconductor manufacturer signs a contract to deliver the microprocessors to the British firm in six months. Suppose also that the price is stated in British pounds. The manufacturer knows precisely how many pounds it will earn six months from now, but it does not know whether the pound will rise or fall in value, so it does not know what it will earn in dollar terms. The solution is to sign a forward contract to sell British pounds six months from now in exchange for U.S. dollars at a price agreed upon today. Using the forward market, the U.S. manufacturer avoids the risk that comes from exchange rate fluctuations.

Forward markets are important to financial investors and speculators as well as exporters and importers. For example, bondholders and other interest rate arbitrageurs often use forward markets to protect themselves against the foreign exchange risk incurred while holding foreign bonds and other financial assets. This is called **hedging** and it is accomplished by buying a forward contract to sell foreign currency at the same time that the bond or other interest earning asset matures. When interest rate arbitrageurs use the forward market to insure against exchange rate risk, it is called **covered interest arbitrage**.

# The Supply and Demand for Foreign Exchange

The value of one nation's money, like most things, can be analyzed by looking at its supply and demand. Under a system of flexible, or floating exchange rates, an increase in the demand for the dollar will raise its price (cause an appreciation in its value), while an increase in its supply will lower its price (cause a depreciation). Under a fixed exchange rate system, the value of the dollar is held constant through the actions of the central bank that counteract the market forces of supply and demand. Consequently, supply and demand analysis is a useful tool for understanding the pressures on a currency regardless of the type of exchange rate system adopted. For this reason, we begin with the assumption that exchange rates are completely flexible. After examining the usefulness of supply and demand analysis, we will turn to alternative systems, including gold standards and other variations on fixed exchange rates.

## Supply and Demand with Flexible Exchange Rates

Figure 10.1 shows the demand for British pounds in the United States. The curve is a normal downward-sloping demand curve, indicating that as the pound depreciates relative to the dollar, the quantity of pounds demanded by Americans increases. Note also that we are measuring the price of the pound—the exchange rate—on the vertical axis. Since it is dollars per pound ($/£), it is the price of a pound in terms of dollars and an increase in the exchange rate (R) is a decline in the value of the dollar. In other words, movements up the vertical axis represent an increase in the price of the pound, which is equivalent to a fall in the price of the dollar. Similarly, movements down the vertical axis represent a decrease in the price of the pound.

For Americans, British goods are less expensive when the pound is cheaper and the dollar is stronger. Hence, at depreciated values for the pound, Americans will switch from U.S. or third-party suppliers of goods and services to British suppliers. However, before they can purchase goods made in Britain, first they must exchange dollars for British pounds. Consequently, the increased demand for British goods is simultaneously an increase in the quantity of British pounds demanded.

**FIGURE 10.1** ● **The Demand Curve for Foreign Exchange**

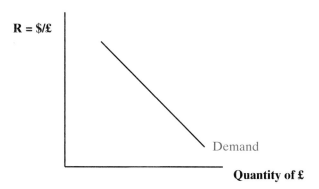

As the exchange rate falls, the dollar appreciates and the dollar price of British goods falls. The quantity of pounds demanded by the U.S. market increases as U.S. consumers and firms purchase more goods and services in Britain.

Figure 10.2 shows the supply side of the picture. The supply curve slopes up because British firms and consumers are willing to buy a greater quantity of American goods as the dollar becomes cheaper. That is, they receive more dollars per pound. However, before British customers can buy American goods, first they must convert pounds into dollars, so the increase in the quantity of American goods demanded is simultaneously an increase in the quantity of foreign currency supplied to the United States.

**FIGURE 10.2** ● **The Supply of Foreign Exchange**

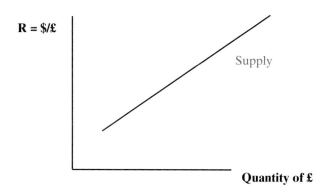

As the exchange rate rises, the dollar depreciates and the pound price of U.S. goods falls. The quantity of pounds supplied to the U.S. market increases as British consumers and firms purchase more goods in the United States.

Figure 10.3 combines the supply and demand curves. The intersection determines the market exchange rate and the quantity of pounds supplied to the United States. At exchange rate $R_1$, the demand and supply of British pounds to the United States is $Q_1$.

## Exchange Rates in the Long Run

We have determined that the supply curve slopes up to the right and the demand curve slopes down. The next step in supply and demand analysis is to consider the factors that determine the intersection of supply and demand and the actual exchange rate. We will continue to assume that the exchange rate is completely flexible. Later in the chapter we look at exchange rates that are fixed, and at intermediate rates between fixed and flexible.

In Figure 10.4, an increase in the U.S. demand for the pound (rightward shift of the demand curve), causes a rise in the exchange rate, an appreciation in the pound, and a depreciation in the dollar. Conversely, a fall in demand would shift the demand curve left and lead to a falling pound and a rising dollar. On the supply side, an increase in the supply of pounds to the U.S. market (supply curve shifts right) is illustrated in Figure 10.5, where a new intersection for supply and demand occurs at a lower exchange rate and an appreciated dollar. A decrease in the supply of pounds shifts the curve leftward, causing the exchange rate to rise and the dollar to depreciate.

The causal factors behind the shifts in the supply and demand are easier to conceptualize if we divide the determinants of exchange rates into three periods: long run, medium run, and short run. This seems to be accurate empirically, as

**FIGURE 10.3** ● **Supply and Demand in the Foreign Exchange Market**

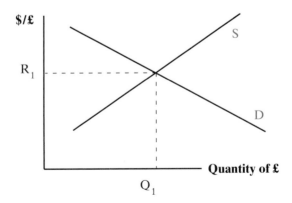

The intersection of the supply of British pounds to the U.S. market, and the U.S. demand for British pounds determines the quantity of pounds available in the United States ($Q_1$), and their dollar price (exchange rate $R_1$).

FIGURE 10.4 ● **An Increase in Demand for British Pounds**

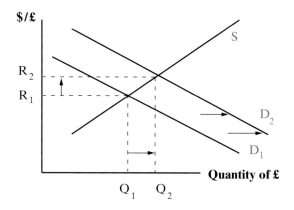

An increase in the U.S. demand for British pounds (rightward shift of the curve) causes the dollar to depreciate.

FIGURE 10.5 ● **An Increase in the Supply of British Pounds**

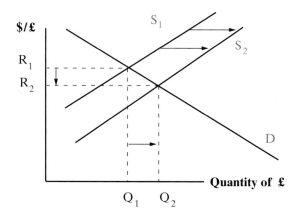

An increase in the supply of British pounds to the U.S. market (rightward shift of the curve) causes the dollar to appreciate.

not all the factors that determine an exchange rate show up instantaneously. In fact, some causal factors take a very long time—a decade or more—to exert their full influence, and in the meantime, a number of short-run or medium-run factors may push in a completely opposite direction.

Looking at the long run first, **purchasing power parity** states that the equilibrium value of an exchange rate is at the level that allows a given amount of money to buy the same quantity of goods abroad that it will buy at home. By this criteria, the equilibrium exchange rate is the point where the dollar buys pounds at a rate that keeps its purchasing power over goods and services constant. That is, $100 buys the right amount of pounds to enable the purchase of the same basket of goods and services in Britain that $100 buys in the United States. Table 10.2 illustrates this idea.

In Table 10.2, a basket of goods costs $1,000 or £500, depending on the country where it is purchased. Accordingly, the long-run tendency is for the exchange rate to move to $2 per £. If it is above that, the pound is overvalued and the dollar is undervalued. An overvalued pound buys more in the United States than in Britain since it would be possible to convert £500 to more than $1,000 and buy a larger basket of goods than can be bought in Britain. Exchange rates less than $2 would imply the opposite—the pound is undervalued and the dollar overvalued.

It should be stressed that this is an underlying tendency and not a description of actual exchange rates at any point in time. Over the long run, purchasing power parity exerts influence over exchange rates, but in the short to medium run, there are significant deviations from this pattern. If you have traveled outside your home country, you are probably aware of cases where your domestic currency buys you so much foreign currency that your standard of living is higher when you travel. You might be able to stay in a better class of hotel, eat in better restaurants, and shop for items that you cannot afford at home. Or, you may be familiar with the opposite, where your standard of living declines because you get so little foreign currency in exchange for your domestic currency that everything seems inordinately expensive.

Purchasing power parity influences currency values indirectly. When a currency is overvalued or undervalued, it creates profit-making opportunities for merchants that can move goods across international borders. Suppose, for example, that the dollar is overvalued and that instead of $2 per pound, the exchange rate is $1.75 per pound. Prices are assumed to be the same as those shown in Table 10.2. In this case, $1,000 buys £571.43 (1,000/1.75). If merchants take the £571.43 and buy British goods and then ship the goods to the United States, they can earn more than $1,000. (They earn $1,142.86 since goods prices are 2 to 1.) In the long run, the demand for British pounds increases and, as shown in Figure 10.4, the exchange rate rises. The process will continue until the exchange rate hits $2 per £, and there are no more profit-making opportunities from shipping goods from Britain to the United States.

The process just described is reinforced by the flow of goods from Britain to the United States. The supply of goods shrinks in Britain, leading to rising prices there. In the United States, supply rises and under normal competitive conditions, prices will fall. These effects will take awhile to exert themselves, but they are another factor reinforcing purchasing power parity. In this case, however, prices are moving in the direction that equalizes the purchasing power of the two currencies, instead of equalization through exchange rate movement as in the

| **TABLE 10.2** ● **A Hypothetical Example of the Exchange Rate in the Long Run** | |
|---|---|
| | Cost of the Same Basket of Goods in Each Country |
| **Price in dollars** | $1,000 |
| **Price in pounds** | £500 |
| **Long-run equilibrium exchange rate** | ($1,000/£500) = $2/£ |

Purchasing power parity states that dollars will tend to exchange for pounds at a rate that maintains a constant purchasing power of a given quantity of currency.

previous example. In theory, it does not matter which changes—prices or exchange rates—but given that prices in many countries tend not to fall easily, while exchange rates are relatively easily moved, most of the equalization probably occurs through exchange rate movements.

The story of goods arbitrage—buying where the goods are cheaper and selling where they are more expensive—which stands behind purchasing power parity, obviously has a few unrealistic assumptions. In particular, it requires that goods flow costlessly across international borders and that all goods and services can be traded. In reality, there are transportation costs involved with moving goods. This means that our merchant who buys £571.43 of goods in Britain and sells them for $1,142.86 in the United States loses some of her $142.86 profit to shipping, insurance, and other transaction costs. In addition, she pays a fee to a bank or a currency broker when she buys the needed pounds.

Nor is this the only obstacle standing in the way of her profits. Few nations have eliminated all their barriers to the entry of foreign goods and services. The merchant may face a tariff, import license fees, inspection fees, or some other barrier at the border that adds to her cost. In the limit, imports of the goods in question may be prohibited and goods arbitrage may be impossible at any price differential. In addition, some goods and many services are not traded. For example, restaurant meals, haircuts, landscape maintenance, and a host of other services that must be consumed on the spot are rarely, if ever, traded.

Once the assumptions of purchasing power parity are examined, it is not surprising that it exerts its influence over exchange rates only in the long run. If there are significant profit-making opportunities through goods arbitrage, then in spite of today's obstacles, entrepreneurs will work to create the conditions that will allow them to take advantage of the price differentials across markets. They will look for ways to lower transport costs, to minimize the costs of compliance with import rules and regulations, and to change the rules where it is feasible. All of these steps take time, but in spite of the real obstacles to its operation, purchasing power parity remains a significant long-run force in the determination of exchange rates.

## Exchange Rates in the Medium Run and Short Run

While purchasing power parity is working slowly in the background, other forces have more immediate impacts on the position of the supply and demand curves for foreign exchange. We turn first to the forces that are correlated with the business cycle, the natural but irregular rhythms of expansion and recession that every country undergoes. Given that the time period from the peak of one expansion to the next is usually several years in duration, the forces that are tied to the business cycle can be considered medium run. That is, they are pressures on an exchange rate that may last for several years, but almost always less than a decade and usually less than five to seven years.

The most important medium-run force is the strength of a country's economic growth. Rapid growth implies rising incomes and increased consumption. When consumers feel secure in their jobs and at the same time experience a rapid growth in their incomes, they spend more, some of which will be on imports and travel abroad. As a result, rapid economic growth at home is translated into increased imports and an outward shift in the demand for foreign currency, as shown in Figure 10.4. Holding constant a host of short-run forces that may be in play at the same time, the effect of rapid economic growth at home is a depreciating currency.

The effect of growth is symmetrical, both with respect to slower growth at home, and with respect to the rate of economic growth abroad. Slower growth, such as a recession during which output declines (negative economic growth), raises consumer uncertainty about jobs and reduces many people's incomes. For the economy as a whole, as consumption expenditures fall, expenditures on imports decline as well, and the demand for foreign exchange falls. A leftward shift of the demand curve reduces the exchange rate and appreciates the currency. In other words, just as more rapid economic growth can cause a depreciation in a country's currency, slower growth sets forces in motion that lead to an appreciation.

Growth abroad does not have a direct effect on the home country's demand for foreign exchange (although it may have an indirect effect through its stimulation of the home economy), but it will directly affect the supply curve. More rapid foreign growth leads to more exports from the home country, and slower foreign growth results in fewer exports. More exports to foreigners increase the supply of foreign currency and shifts the supply curve rightward, as shown in Figure 10.5. Fewer exports have the opposite effect. You should practice drawing the effects of changes in the rates of home and foreign economic growth on the supply and demand curves for foreign exchange.

Turning from the medium run of the business cycle to short-run periods of a year or less, a number of forces are constantly at work shaping currency values. The foremost short-run force is the flow of financial capital. The effects of financial flows range from minor and subtle to dramatic and, at times, catastrophic. They are as capable of creating slight day-to-day variations in the value of a currency as they are of creating complete financial chaos and bringing down governments. The degree of volatility in financial flows varies greatly and is highly responsive to governmental policies and conditions in the world economy. The impact on exchange rates of large-scale, short-run movements in financial capital has become one of the most serious issues in international economics.

Two variables in particular are responsible for a large share of short-run capital flows: interest rates and expectations about future exchange rates. These two forces often influence each other and are capable of creating unpredictable interactions, as when a change in interest rates reshapes investor confidence or catalyzes speculative actions in currency markets.

The role of interest rates in the short-run determination of exchange rates is crucial. The interest rate–exchange rate relationship is summed up in the **interest parity** condition, which states that the difference between any pair of countries' interest rates is approximately equal to the expected change in the exchange rate. The appendix at the end of this chapter develops the algebra of this relationship, but the intuition is not difficult to grasp. Interest rate arbitrageurs have a choice of investing in the home country or investing abroad. For the sake of simplicity, we will compare two alternatives, which are called *Home* and *Foreign*. At Home, investors expect to earn the interest rate i, while in Foreign they can earn i*. The three possibilities are as follows:

$$i = i^*, \tag{10.1}$$

$$i > i^*, \tag{10.2}$$

or

$$i < i^* \tag{10.3}$$

In case (10.1), investors are indifferent between the two options. In case (10.2), home investments are preferred to foreign (home experiences capital inflows) and in case (10.3) foreign investments are preferred (home experiences capital outflows). As long as financial capital moves across international borders, there are exchange rate risks for the sending country's investors. When international investors eventually convert back to their own currency, the exchange rate is likely to be different from the rate they paid when they moved assets out of their country. Admittedly, they might gain or lose in the conversion process, but if their original intention is to take advantage of interest rate differentials, it is unlikely that they are seeking to speculate in currencies. Therefore, interest rate arbitrageurs usually act in a similar way to merchants and sign a forward contract to sell the proceeds of their foreign currency earnings when they mature.

The difference between the forward and spot exchange rates reflects the expected appreciation or depreciation of the home currency. For example, if the forward rate for a given maturity (30 days, 180 days, and so on) is 3 percent less than the spot rate, it signals that currency markets expect the home currency to appreciate by 3 percent over the maturity period of the forward rate. As noted earlier, no one can actually predict an exchange rate 30 or 180 days into the future, but the spread between the forward and spot rates reflects the best available market information at the time the contract is signed. If foreign investors move their financial capital into home, they can expect a 3 percent appreciation in the value of their assets when measured in terms of foreign's prices. In other words, they could earn 3 percent less in interest over the same period and still come out even, given that they will gain 3 percent in the conversion back into their own currency. This relationship is summarized in the following interest parity equation:

$$i - i^* \approx (F - R) / R,$$

where F stands for a forward exchange rate with the same term to maturity as the interest rates i and $i^*$. The right-hand side is the percentage difference in the forward and spot rates. If it is positive, then $F > R$, home currency is expected to depreciate, and home interest rates must exceed foreign rates by an approximately equivalent percentage. If $F < R$, an appreciation is expected in the value of home currency and interest rates will be below foreign rates by an approximately equivalent percentage. The algebra of this relationship is developed in the appendix at the end of this chapter.

The utility of the interest parity condition is that it brings together the reason for a significant share of international capital flows, domestic interest rate policy, and exchange rate expectations. Suppose for example, that case (10.3) is operative, and home interest rates are below foreign: $i < i^*$. This tells us that the forward rate is below the spot rate ($F < R$) and that markets expect an appreciation in the home currency. To see why the interest parity condition is an equilibrium toward which the exchange rate will move, consider what happens if the percentage difference in the forward and spot rates is insufficient to compensate for lower interest rates. In this case, financial capital will flow out of home and into foreign. Suppose for example that $i < i^*$, and $F = R$. As a result, currency markets are signaling that no changes are expected in the exchange rate, and both home and foreign investors can do better if they invest in foreign since the interest rate they earn is higher. Capital would flow out of home, increasing the demand for foreign currency, and perhaps raising the price of financial capital in home, which is i. In addition, the supply of foreign's currency would decline since fewer investors in foreign would invest in home. As a result, R rises (from the increase in the demand and decrease in the supply of foreign's currency) and i rises (due to the decrease in the supply of financial capital to home). Both effects work to restore an equilibrium where the interest rate differential is approximately equal to the percentage difference between forward and spot exchange rates.

Consider another example. Suppose that home interest rates are less than foreign ($i < i^*$) and that forward rates are less than spot rates ($F < R$) by an appropriate amount so that the interest parity condition holds. Beginning at this point, home policymakers decide for some reason to raise their interest rates to the same level as foreign rates: $i = i^*$. Now, investors in both home and foreign will invest more in home because they earn the same rate of interest, and they expect Home's currency to appreciate in value (since $F < R$). Figure 10.6 illustrates these shifts. Note that both the demand curve for foreign's currency and the supply curve of foreign's currency shift, with demand moving in and supply moving out. Taken together, both shifts reinforce a downward movement in the spot rate.

FIGURE 10.6  **The Effects of an Increase in Home's Interest Rate**

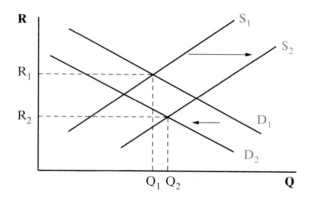

An increase in home's interest rate causes a decrease in demand and an increase in supply of the foreign currency. Both effects cause an appreciation in the exchange rate from $R_1$ to $R_2$.

As R falls, home's currency appreciates and the gap between F and R closes. If $i = i^*$, the process ends when F = R.

In addition to their impact on the forward-spot rate differential, expectations play a crucial role in the determination of exchange rates in another way. A sudden change in the expected future value of an exchange rate can have a dramatic and often self-fulfilling impact on a country's currency. For example, if investors suddenly come to believe that a currency must depreciate more than they had anticipated, it lowers the expected value of assets denominated in that currency. This can create a sudden exodus of financial capital and put enormous pressure on the country's supply of foreign exchange reserves. To a significant extent, episodes of capital flight can be self-fulfilling in their expectations about an exchange rate. If investors expect depreciation, they try to convert their assets to another currency. This raises the demand for foreign exchange and depresses the supply, fulfilling the expectation of a depreciation.

There are numerous potential causes of this type of volatility in financial capital flows and exchange rate shifts. It also seems likely that technological changes in telecommunications have altered the sensitivity of markets toward changes in expectations, although this is yet to be established definitively. Nevertheless, it is certain that a frequent cause of sudden shifts in expectations is the realization that a particular government is practicing economic policies that are internally inconsistent and unsustainable. We will examine this in more detail in Chapters 11 and 12, but it is relatively easy to get a sense of the meaning of inconsistent policies. An example is policies that are designed to stimulate the economy strongly (more growth→more imports→more demand for foreign exchange) when the supply of foreign exchange is severely limited (not enough exports, very low interest rates).

## CASE STUDY

# The Largest Market in the World

In 2004, the world's foreign exchange markets traded an estimated $1,880 billion dollars worth of currency per day. Another way to look at this is that every 6.25 days, currency trades equaled the value of U.S. annual GDP. These estimates come from a survey of 52 central banks that is conducted every three years by the Bank for International Settlements (BIS), a "central bank for central banks." The BIS survey is the *Triennial Central Bank Survey of Foreign Exchange and Derivatives Market Activity in April 2004*, and is available from the BIS at http://www.bis.org.

Between 1989 and 2004, the volume of exchange rate transactions grew from $590 billion per day to $1,880 billion. This is an annual growth rate of over 8 percent per year and far higher than the growth of the world economy. In 2004, 88.7 percent of every currency trade involved the U.S. dollar, and 37.2 percent involved the EU's euro (see Table 10.3). Not surprisingly, the U.S. dollar–euro exchange was the most common with 28 percent of all transactions, followed by the U.S. dollar–yen (17 percent) and the U.S. dollar–UK pound (14 percent).

Note that the total in Table 10.3 is 200 percent rather than 100 percent because every sale is simultaneously a purchase. The dollar is so often traded because it is used as an international medium of exchange and because of the cross-trading that occurs between pairs of currencies. That is, a Chilean importer may pay her Mexican supplier in U.S. dollars, or she may use Chilean pesos to

| TABLE 10.3 ● Composition of World Currency Trades, April 2004 | |
|---|---|
| Currency | Percent of Total Trades |
| U.S. dollar | 88.7 |
| EU euro | 37.2 |
| Japanese yen | 20.3 |
| UK pound | 16.9 |
| Swiss franc | 6.1 |
| Australian dollar | 5.5 |
| Canadian dollar | 4.2 |
| Emerging markets | 5.2 |
| Other | 15.9 |

*Source*: Bank for International Settlements, http://www.bis.org/publ/rpfx04.pdf.

buy dollars and use the dollars to buy Mexican pesos. It is unlikely that the Mexican exporter would accept Chilean pesos, so one way or another, the importer has to come up with dollars.

Currency trading is concentrated in four main centers: London, New York, Tokyo, and Singapore. London is by far the largest center of foreign exchange trading, as is illustrated by the BIS survey's finding that more U.S. dollars are traded in London than in New York (see Table 10.4). Given the preponderance of the U.S. dollar in currency trades and the importance of London as a trading center, it follows that most of the trades in London do not involve the British pound.

| TABLE 10.4 Currency Trading Centers | |
|---|---|
| Location | Percent of World Currency Trading |
| United Kingdom | 31.3 |
| United States | 19.2 |
| Japan | 8.3 |
| Singapore | 5.2 |
| Germany | 4.9 |
| Hong Kong | 4.2 |
| Australia | 3.4 |
| Switzerland | 3.3 |
| Other | 20.2 |

*Source*: Bank for International Settlements, http://www.bis.org/publ/rpfx04.pdf.

The mechanisms from inconsistent policy to exchange rate crisis and collapse are fairly well understood, but this begs the question about the cause of a sudden shift in expectations. Many recent episodes of sudden exchange rate shifts have occurred when investors lost confidence in a particular currency. Yet why the sudden change in investor confidence? Government policies had been in place for years in some cases, yet suddenly they were deemed unsustainable and likely to lead to a severe depreciation. In order to understand this, economists will have to develop a far deeper understanding of the subtle relationships between actual economic conditions and psychological expectations. Reaching this goal is a way off at this point.

Table 10.5 summarizes the long-, medium-, and short-run factors that have been discussed. The list is not exhaustive, but the main elements are included.

| TABLE 10.5 ● Major Determinants of an Appreciation or Depreciation | | |
|---|---|---|
| | R Falls: An Appreciation in the Domestic Currency | R Rises: A Depreciation in the Domestic Currency |
| **Long run:** Purchasing Power Parity | Home goods are less expensive than foreign goods | Home goods are more expensive than foreign goods |
| **Medium run:** The Business Cycle | Home's economy grows more slowly than foreign | Home's economy grows faster than foreign |
| **Short run (1):** Interest Parity | Home interest rates rise, or foreign rates fall | Home interest rates fall, or foreign rates rise |
| **Short run (2):** Speculation | Expectations of a future appreciation | Expectations of a future depreciation |

# The Real Exchange Rate

The concept of the exchange rate that has been used so far and that is exemplified by the values shown in Table 10.1 does not really tell us what a foreign currency is worth. Exchange rates tell us how many units of domestic currency we give up for one unit of foreign currency, but unless we know what foreign prices are, we still do not know the purchasing power of our domestic money when it is converted to a foreign currency. As an illustration of this problem, suppose that the U.S. dollar–Malaysian ringgit exchange rate is $0.25 and that it stays constant over the year. However, suppose also that Malaysian inflation is 4 percent while U.S. inflation is 1 percent. After one year, the four ringgits that cost one dollar will buy 3 percent less in Malaysia than the dollar buys in the United States. The relatively higher inflation in Malaysia erodes the value of a dollar's worth of ringgits more rapidly than the dollar loses value at home. Consequently, when converted to ringgits, the real purchasing power of the dollar has declined even though the exchange rate is still $0.25 per ringgit.

From the point of view of tourists and business people who use foreign exchange, the key item of interest is the purchasing power they get when they convert their dollars, not the number of units of a foreign currency. An American importer trying to decide between Malaysian and Chinese textiles does not really care if she gets four ringgits per dollar or eight Chinese yuan per dollar. The biggest concern is the volume of textiles that can be purchased in Malaysia with four ringgits and in China with eight yuan.

The **real exchange rate** is the market exchange rate (or **nominal exchange rate**) adjusted for price differences. The two are closely connected. By way of illustration, let's consider the case of a wine merchant who is trying to decide whether to stock her shop with American or French wine. Let's say that French wine of a given quality cost 200 euros and American wine of the same quality costs 180 dollars. What the merchant needs to know is the real exchange rate between French and American wine. Suppose that the nominal rate is $1.20 per euro so that $180 is equivalent to 150 euros in the currency market. In this case, French wine costs one-third more than American wine, and the real exchange rate is 1 ⅓ cases of American wine per case of French wine. The algebra is straightforward:

> Real exchange rate
> = [(Nominal exchange rate) × (Foreign price)] / (Domestic price)
> = [($1.20 per euro) × (200 euros per case)] / ($180 per case)
> = ($240 per case of French wine) / ($180 per case of American wine)
> = 1 ⅓ cases of American wine per one case of French wine

Since the real purchasing power of the dollar is much less in France than in the United States, the choice facing the wine merchant is obvious.

In this example, the main lesson is clear. What matters most to exporters and importers is not the nominal exchange rate, but the real exchange rate—in other words, how much purchasing power they have in the countries under comparison. Let $R_r$ symbolize the real exchange rate, $R_n$ the nominal rate. Since we are interested in the whole economy rather than just one market such as the market for wine, we will use a price index to measure overall prices in the two countries. Price indexes are equivalent to the average price of a basket of goods and services in each economy. Let P stand for the home country price index, and $P^*$ represent foreign prices. Then, following the algebra of the wine merchant's calculation:

> Real exchange rate
> = [(Nominal exchange rate) × (Foreign prices)] / (Domestic prices),

or, more compactly,

$$R_r = R_n(P^* / P).$$

Suppose, for example, that the U.S. dollar–EU euro nominal exchange rate is $1.20 per euro and that both price levels are initially set at 100. In this case, the cost of a basket of goods and services is the same in real terms in both countries and

$$R_r = R_n(P^* / P) = R_n(100 / 100) = R_n.$$

The real rate equals the nominal rate when the purchasing power is the same in both countries. Note that purchasing power parity indicates that this is the long-run equilibrium. Over time, however, if inflation is higher at home than in the foreign country, then P rises more than $P^*$, and $R_r$ falls, meaning the domestic currency appreciates in real terms.

By way of illustration, suppose that the United States has 10 percent inflation while the EU has 0 percent. Then, the real U.S.-EU exchange rate (in terms of dollars per euro) would be as follows:

$$R_r = (\$1.20 \text{ per euro}) \times (100 / 110) = \$1.0909 \text{ per euro}$$

Tourists, investors, and business people can still trade dollars and euros at the nominal rate of $1.20 per euro (plus whatever commissions they pay to the seller), but the real purchasing power of the U.S. dollar has risen in the EU compared to what it buys at home. The real exchange rate of $1.0909 per euro tells us that EU goods are now 9 percent cheaper than the U.S. goods that have risen in price. As a result, unless the nominal rate changes, the dollar goes further in the EU than at home. In real terms, the euro has depreciated and the dollar has appreciated.

Changes in the value of real exchange rates play an important role in international macroeconomic relations. When countries control the value of their nominal exchange rate, for example, they must be certain that their prices do not change in relation to the prices of their trading partners. If inflation runs higher at home, then the real value of their currency appreciates. Over a period of time, if uncorrected, this can lead to a build-up in the current account deficit as imports increase and exports decrease. In a number of cases, the end result has been currency crises and the collapse of nominal exchange rates. (For example, Mexico in December 1994 and Thailand in July 1997.)

##  Alternatives to Flexible Exchange Rates

Exchange rate systems are all modifications of two fundamental categories: fixed and floating (flexible) exchange rate systems. The differences are basic. In a **fixed exchange rate system**, the value of a nation's money is defined in terms of a fixed amount of a commodity, such as gold or in terms of a fixed amount of another currency, such as the U.S. dollar. In a **flexible (floating) exchange rate system**, the value of a nation's money is allowed to "float" up and down in response to the market forces described earlier in the chapter. Through the first 70 years of the twentieth century, fixed exchange rates were the norm, often within a framework that defined the value of a country's currency in terms of a fixed amount of gold. After World War II, many nations shifted away from gold and pegged the value of their currencies to the U.S. dollar or to the currency of another country with which they had strong historical ties. For example, a number of former French colonies in sub-Saharan Africa fixed their currencies to the franc. Beginning in the 1970s, the use of fixed exchange rate systems began a swift decline, first in the high-income industrial economies, and then in many developing countries during the 1980s and 1990s. By the end of the twentieth century, flexible exchange rate systems were the norm in every region of the world.

Although the weight of current economic opinion probably favors floating exchange rates, there is widespread recognition that individual country conditions are unique and that there is no single type of exchange rate system appropriate for every country. The analysis of the pros and cons of different systems in the context of individual country conditions is a very active area of research, and no one can say whether the trend toward flexible rates during the last decades is irreversible, or if world economic conditions might not change in ways that encourage countries to return to some form of fixed exchange rate.

 **Fixed Exchange Rate Systems**

**Gold standards** are a form of fixed exchange rates. Under a pure gold standard, nations keep gold as their international reserve. Gold is used to settle most international obligations and nations must be prepared to trade it for their own currency whenever foreigners attempt to "redeem" the home currency they have earned by selling goods and services. In this sense, the nation's money is backed by gold.

There are essentially three rules that countries must follow in order to maintain a gold exchange standard. First, they must fix the value of their currency unit (the dollar, the pound, the yen, and so on) in terms of gold. This fixes the exchange rate. For example, under the modified gold standard of the **Bretton Woods exchange rate system** that was developed at the end of World War II (1947–1971), the U.S. dollar was fixed at $35 per ounce and the British pound was set at £12.5 per ounce. Since both were fixed in terms of gold, they were implicitly set in terms of each other: $35 = one ounce of gold = £12.5, or 2.80 dollars per pound (2.80 = 35 / 12.5).

The second rule of the gold standard is that nations keep the supply of their domestic money fixed in some constant proportion to their supply of gold. This requirement is an informal one, but is necessary in order to ensure that the domestic money supply does not grow beyond the capacity of the gold supply to support it. The third rule of a gold standard is that nations must stand ready and willing to provide gold in exchange for their home country currency.

Consider what would happen if a country decided to print large quantities of money for which there is no gold backing. In the short run, purchases of domestically produced goods would rise, causing domestic prices to rise as well. As domestic prices rise, foreign goods become more attractive, since a fixed exchange rate means that they have not increased in price. As imports in the home country increase, foreigners accumulate an unwanted supply of the home country's currency. This is the point at which the gold standard would begin to become unhinged. If gold supplies are low in relation to the supply of domestic currency, at some point, the gold reserves will begin to run out as the country pays out gold in exchange for its currency. This spells crisis and a possible end to the gold standard.

Under a fixed exchange rate system, the national supply and demand for foreign currencies may vary but the nominal exchange rate does not. It is the responsibility of the monetary authorities (the central bank or treasury department) to keep the exchange rate fixed. Figure 10.7 illustrates the task before a national government when it wishes to keep its currency fixed. Suppose that the United States and United Kingdom are both on the gold standard and the U.S. demand for British pounds increases.

## FIGURE 10.7 ● Fixed Exchange Rates and Changes in Demand

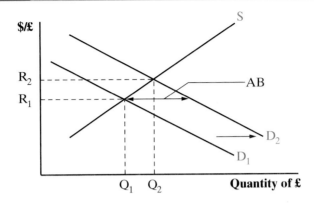

An increase in the demand for British pounds puts pressure on the exchange rate and will cause the dollar to depreciate to $R_2$ unless the increase in demand is countered by an increase in supply equal to line segment AB.

In the short run or medium run, a rise in demand for pounds from $D_1$ to $D_2$ is caused by one of the factors listed in Table 10.5: increased U.S. demand for UK goods, higher UK or lower U.S. interest rates, or speculation that the value of the dollar might not remain fixed for much longer. If $R_1$ is the fixed U.S.–UK exchange rate, then the United States must counter the weakening dollar and prevent the rate from depreciating to $R_2$. One option is to sell the United States' gold reserves in exchange for dollars. This puts gold in the hands of merchants, investors, or speculators, who are trying to obtain British pounds. The quantity of gold that must be sold is equivalent to the value of the pounds represented by line segment AB. In effect, the United States meets the increased demand for British pounds by supplying international money—gold—to the market through a sale of some of its gold stock. Since gold and pounds are interchangeable, an increase in the supply of gold is equivalent to an increase in the supply of pounds, as shown in Figure 10.8, and the exchange rate stays at $R_1$.

Under a pure gold standard, countries hold gold as a reserve instead of foreign currencies and sell their gold reserves in exchange for their own currency. This action increases the supply of gold—which is international money—and offsets the pressure on the home currency to depreciate. Actually, there are two possibilities for the home country as it sells its gold reserves. Either the demand for gold is satisfied and the pressure on its currency eases, or it begins to run out of gold. If the latter happens, the home country may be forced into a devaluation that is accomplished by changing the gold price of its currency. As an illustration, if the dollar is fixed at $35 per ounce of gold, a devaluation would shift the price of gold to something more than $35, say $50, and each ounce of gold sold by the United States buys back a greater quantity of dollars.

FIGURE 10.8 ◦ **Selling Reserves of Pounds to Counter a Weakening Dollar**

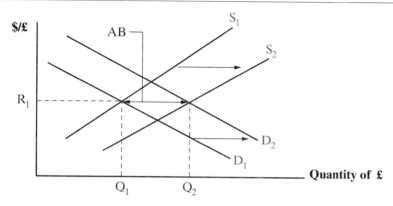

By selling gold equal in value to AB pounds, the United States prevents a depreciation in the dollar-pound exchange rate.

Pure gold standards have been rare since the 1930s. More commonly, countries have adopted modified gold standards, such as the Bretton Woods system (1947–1971) (see the Case Study), or fixed exchange rate systems called **pegged exchange rates**. Pegged exchange rate systems operate similarly to a gold standard except that instead of gold, another currency is used to "anchor" the value of the home currency.

One potential source of problems with a pegged currency is that the home currency's value is synchronized with its peg, so changes between the peg and a third-party currency are identical for the home currency and the third party. An example will clarify. Suppose that Thailand decides to peg its currency to the U.S. dollar at the rate of 25 Thai baht per U.S. dollar. The goal of Thailand's central bank must be to supply dollars whenever it is asked to redeem its own baht. If the dollar appreciates against the Japanese yen, then so does the Thai baht, and at the same rate. Appreciation against the Japanese yen may or may not be a problem for Thailand's producers, depending on the importance of the Japan–Thailand trade relationship. In 1997, it turned out to be very important, and declining Thai competitiveness from its appreciating currency played a prominent role in triggering the Asian financial crisis of 1997–1998.

The simplest way to avoid this type of problem is to peg the currency not to one single currency, but to a group of currencies. This is, in fact, closer to Thailand's actual policy in 1997. While this is slightly more complex arithmetically, it reduces the importance of any single country's currency in the determination of the home country's currency value. Typically, countries that adopt this strategy select the currencies of their most important trading partners as elements of the basket.

Pegged exchange rates can work very well under many circumstances, but another factor that can cause them to unravel is a significant difference in inflation rates between the home country and its peg. We saw previously that real exchange rates play a greater role in determining trade patterns than nominal rates. Using the United States–Thailand example, and looking at the equation that describes the relationship between real and nominal exchange rates from Thailand's point of view (as the home country) we have the following:

$$R_r = (25 \text{ baht per dollar}) \times [(\text{U.S. price level}) / (\text{Thai price level})]$$
$$= R_n(P^* / P)$$

Relatively high inflation in Thailand appears as a faster rate of change in P, and leads to a real appreciation in the baht. Under these circumstances, Thai producers are less competitive and U.S. producers are more so (in Thailand). If the situation persists, speculators will likely step in and begin to sell bahts in the expectation that the pegged nominal rate of 25 baht per dollar will be devalued to offset the appreciation in the real rate. Moving the nominal peg from 25 to 30 or 40 baht per dollar may be necessary to restore balance.

The most common technique for dealing with this problem is through the adoption of a **crawling peg**. Crawling pegs are fixed—that is, pegged—exchange rates that are periodically adjusted. The idea is to offset any differences in inflation (changes in P) through regular adjustments in $R_n$. If correctly handled, the real exchange rate remains constant and the impact of inflation differences never shows up as a change in competitiveness.

There are several other variations on the theme of managed exchange rates. One of the key points to keep in mind is that purely fixed or purely flexible exchange rate arrangements are rare. When a currency is fixed in value, it is still subject to market pressures of supply and demand which, at times, can force governments to alter its value. Similarly, when countries adopt a flexible exchange rate system, there is usually some degree of government intervention in currency markets to try to shape its value. Consequently, many countries that claim to have a flexible exchange rate actually have adopted a **managed float** in which they occasionally sell or buy their currency as they try to nudge the exchange rate up or down.

## CASE STUDY

# Dollarization and Currency Boards

**Dollarization** is the adoption of the U.S. dollar as a country's own currency. In an abstract sense, the term has come to signify the adoption of any currency other than one's own, but for many countries, the universal acceptability of the U.S. dollar makes it the alternative currency of choice. For example, Panama dollarized its economy by pegging its currency, the cordoba, to the dollar and then declaring the dollar to be legal tender. Ecuador went one step further in September 2000 and officially adopted the dollar as its currency, as did El Salvador in November 2000. There is no barrier in international law that prevents countries from adopting the dollar, and about two-thirds of all dollars in circulation are outside the United States. In Latin America, Bolivia, Peru, and Uruguay each have a greater quantity of dollar deposits in their financial systems than they have deposits of the domestic currency.

As you might imagine, there can be a great deal of popular opposition to relinquishing something as symbolic as the national currency. For many people abandoning the nation's currency is akin to giving up the nation's flag. Still, informal dollarization has proceeded in a number of places where formal dollarization has not. Informal dollarization occurs when businesses and consumers use dollars for some or all of their transactions even though the official currency is available. For example, real estate in Mexico is often sold in dollars, not pesos, and many personal service providers along the U.S.-Mexican border prefer to receive dollars as payment. This activity is spontaneous, but in other countries, government policy actively encourages the use of dollars as a means of increasing the foreign exchange reserves of the country.

Argentina's dollarization highlights another possibility for exchange rate policy. Argentina did not dollarize formally, but in 1991 it tied its currency to the dollar at a one-to-one ratio and prevented the creation of new Argentine pesos unless there was a new dollar for every new peso. This exchange-rate arrangement was introduced for the purpose of tackling a severe inflation problem, and it worked very well for a number of years. Unfortunately, when it came apart in late 2001, an enormous depression followed. Economists and economic policy analysts are still learning the lessons of the Argentine experience, and it is probably a case that will be discussed for generations.

Throughout the 1980s, Argentina suffered from extremely high rates of inflation (see Table 10.6). Between 1985 and 1990, the lowest rate was 82 percent in 1986, but in 1989 the inflation rate rose above 3,000 percent. Most of the inflation arose from the government's excessive creation of new pesos to pay its bills.

## TABLE 10.6 • Inflation in Argentina, 1985–1994

| 1985 | 1986 | 1987 | 1988 | 1989 |
|------|------|------|------|------|
| 672 | 90 | 131 | 343 | 3,080 |
| **1990** | **1991** | **1992** | **1993** | **1994** |
| 2,314 | 172 | 25 | 11 | 4 |

*Source*: Inter-American Development Bank, *Overcoming Volatility*, Economic and Social Progress in Latin America, 1995 Report, p. 25.

The tax system provided insufficient revenue, and households and businesses were unwilling to buy enough government bonds to cover the gap between revenues and expenditures. Argentina borrowed in international capital markets, thus adding to its foreign debt, but this borrowing too was insufficient to finance all of the government's deficit. Hence, it resorted to the inflation tax, and printed money.

Argentina tried a number of reforms in the mid-1980s. The most famous, the Austral Plan, included a currency reform in which the Argentine peso was replaced with a new currency called the austral, and a crawling peg system was implemented to try to stabilize the real rate exchange rate. In addition, the government fixed the prices of government services, hoping that they would "anchor" prices elsewhere in the economy and prevent them from rising. When economywide prices rose anyway, the fixed prices for government services resulted in large budget deficits and the printing of lots of new money. The resulting inflation quickly turned into hyperinflation, the condition in which money ceases to have value and barter becomes common. Traffic fines, for example, were denominated in terms of gallons of gasoline rather than australs. An added problem was that despite the regular adjustments of the nominal exchange rate, the rate of inflation made it impossible to keep up with the price increases, and the real exchange rate became seriously overvalued. Predictably, the overvalued exchange rate resulted in a growing trade deficit and a looming balance-of-payments crisis.

In 1991, the government of Carlos Menem passed Argentina's **Convertibility Law**, which fixed the value of the new currency, now called the peso once again, to the U.S. dollar at the rate of one-to-one. In order to ensure that the currency stayed fixed, the Convertibility Law required the government to hold an equivalent quantity of dollars before it printed new pesos. The law created a **currency board** to oversee the exchange rate system and gave it responsibility for enforcing the one-to-one relation between U.S. dollars and Argentine pesos. Although the system was more rigid on paper than in practice, it did severely limit the creation of new money by transferring responsibility from the government to the independent currency board. The problems of inadequate government revenue and a spiraling budget deficit were addressed through several measures to increase government tax revenues (including the firing of a large number of tax collectors suspected of corruption) and to reduce government expenditures.

The currency board worked extremely well through most of the 1990s, until 1998. Before then, Argentina had good growth rates with low inflation and a promising future. Currency boards overseeing fixed exchange rates were cited around the world as one feasible solution to the problems of inflation and exchange rate volatility, and the Argentine case was widely viewed as a successful model for other countries. In the end, the rigid one-to-one ratio, the failure to reduce government expenditures sufficiently, and a lot of bad luck led to a spectacular collapse of the system in late 2001.

Problems began in 1998 when the global fallout of the East Asian crisis led to a recession in Argentina and Chile and other emerging markets. Argentina's main trading partner, Brazil, devalued its currency in early 1999, thus putting pressure on the peso. Argentina's trade with Brazil became lopsided, and the decline of its export industries intensified the recession. In retrospect, this is the point where it becomes uncertain what the government should have done. Some observers argue that Argentina should have sought more flexibility in its policies by severing the one-to-one relationship between the peso and the dollar. Others argue that it should have made deeper cuts in its budgets, because that was the only way to maintain confidence in its currency. The government tried the latter approach at first, but political and institutional obstacles prevented the budget cuts from being large enough, and few people were convinced that the government could avoid returning to its previous policies of printing money to pay for its deficits. In part, the budget cuts were inadequate because it is extremely hard for any government to cut expenditures and raise taxes during a recession.

After a succession of presidents and finance ministers—most of whom tried wildly unpopular and unsuccessful strategies to save the one-to-one exchange rate—the government gave up. In January 2002, the peso was devalued by 29 percent and was allowed to float. By mid-2002, it was trading at 3.4 pesos per dollar, a loss of about 70 percent of its previous value. Analysts are still trying to unravel the relative importance of the various factors, and the case will be written about for years. While the policy lessons are still being learned, the Argentine case appears in many respects to be a new version of the old problem of how to maintain credibility for a fixed exchange rate that must be devalued.

Although Argentina never officially dollarized, during the 1990s businesses and consumers widely accepted the dollar as a medium of exchange. It was a form of semi-official dollarization in which both the dollar and the domestic currency circulate, and a fixed rate of exchange is maintained. Consequently, the lessons for would-be dollarizers include a note of caution. When an outside shock hits the domestic economy, as happened to Argentina when Brazil devalued and the U.S. dollar rose in value worldwide, will the shock make export industries uncompetitive and lead to capital flight? Or can industries respond with price cuts and productivity increases? One thing that is absolutely clear is that countries that adopt the dollar have no ability whatsoever to influence their exchange rate.

## Choosing the Right Exchange Rate System

Given the menu of choices for exchange rate systems, an active area of economic research has focused on the performance characteristics of systems under different economic conditions and institutional arrangements. For many years, economists debated the pros and cons of fixed and flexible rates, but as the variety of exchange rate options has grown, as capital mobility has increased, and as international trade and investment relations have deepened, researchers have become more concerned with understanding how varying degrees of flexibility or fixity might best serve the interests of individual countries. In particular, economists have tried to learn how different exchange rate systems might influence the core elements of a country's macroeconomy such as the rate of economic growth, the rate of inflation, and the frequency of currency crises.

Traditional views held that countries with fixed exchange rate systems were better at controlling inflation, but that they paid a price in the form of slower economic growth. The reasoning behind this view was that in order to maintain a fixed rate, governments have to be very careful about issuing new money. Since most of the episodes of hyperinflation during the second half of the twentieth century resulted from overexpanding the money supply, it seems reasonable that an exchange rate policy that limits the supply of money would also help avoid inflation. However, in the view of some economists, the limits placed on the ability of a country to manipulate its money supply also remove an important tool that governments use to help manage the rate of economic growth. Therefore, the tradeoff was lower growth for lower inflation.

More recent research, particularly with data from the 1990s, has failed to demonstrate a strong relationship between the type of exchange rate system and either inflation or economic growth. Prior to the 1990s, countries with fixed or pegged exchange rates tended to have lower rates of inflation, but during the 1990s their advantages on the inflation front diminished substantially. Similarly, there is evidence that countries with more flexible rates tend to have higher average rates of economic growth, but this result depends on the classification of the fastest growing Asian economies. Technically, many of these countries have flexible exchange rates, but at the same time they manage them very closely. When they are omitted from the analysis, there is no significant difference in the rate of growth between countries with relatively fixed and relatively flexible rates. And finally, neither fixed nor flexible rates seem to offer superior protection against a currency crisis. As a result, no particular system seems to rank above any other in its ability to provide superior macroeconomic performance.

Insofar as economists have been able to devise a set of rules for selecting an exchange rate system, they are very general and very basic. If the goal is to find the system that helps minimize negative shocks to an economy, then the source of the shock determines whether a more flexible or more fixed system should be adopted. When the shocks originate in the monetary sector—for example, a central bank that goes overboard in printing new money—a fixed rate is better, and Argentina is a good example. On the other hand, if the shocks to an economy originate in the external environment—for example, a sudden change in the price of imported oil—then relatively more flexibility in the exchange rate enables the country to adapt to the changes more easily. The general argument here is that individual country characteristics matter a great deal. The problem with these rules, however, is that the source of the shocks to an economy are likely to vary from episode to episode and, as a consequence, the basic rules outlined above provide less practical guidance than desired.

One interpretation of these two rules is that smaller economies that are open to the world economy will do better with more flexible exchange rates. Flexibility will help to minimize the potentially negative effects of shocks that originate in the world economy by allowing changes in the exchange rate to absorb some of the shock and to act as a buffer between the domestic economy and the rest of the world. Given that the actual trend for many small, open, developing economies has been toward greater use of flexible exchange rate systems, theory and practice seem to confirm each other.

On the other hand, exchange rate pegs are still popular, particularly with many developing countries. There are a couple of reasons for this. First, all economists agree that one of the most important elements of an exchange rate system is its credibility. That is, no matter what type of exchange rate is adopted, a successful system must generate confidence and the widespread belief that it is sustainable. Exchange rate systems that lack credibility are guaranteed to fail in their basic job of providing a smooth and reliable conversion between domestic and foreign money. Under some conditions, exchange rate pegs may offer greater credibility. One of the conditions, and the second reason why some countries continue to peg their currencies, is a relatively high degree of trade dependence on a single, major economy. Consider the case of Mexico, with about 80 percent of its trade with the United States. Given its trade dependence on the United States, Mexico pegged its peso to the U.S. dollar for many years. Because Mexican inflation ran higher than the U.S. rate, a crawling peg was favored as the means of keeping the real exchange rate relatively constant. The purpose of the dollar peg was to provide benefits to Mexican businesses and consumers by eliminating some of the price variation in Mexican imports and exports. The rule seems to be that when a country is closely tied to the economy of a large, industrial country such as the United States, pegging to its currency may provide additional stability and help businesses to plan their futures with greater confidence.

This view is shared by many, but at the same time it is widely accepted that, in Mexico's case at least, the use of a flexible exchange rate has served it better than the pegged rates it used before 1994. The reason for the discrepancy between what might work in theory and what has worked in practice highlights the complexity of choosing an exchange rate system when every country has unique economic factors and its own set of institutions shaping its economic outcomes. In Mexico's case, due to a set of agreements between the business sector, organized labor, and government, it was unable to make the periodic adjustments to its nominal exchange rate that are required with a crawling peg. In effect, Mexico's institutional inability to adjust its nominal exchange rate undermined the credibility of the exchange rate system. The lack of credibility led to periodic bouts of speculation against the peso whenever it was perceived to be overvalued and vulnerable. Several of these speculative bouts were followed by a peso collapse and economic recession. The lesson, in the end, seems to be that the first criterion for choosing an exchange rate system is that it must have credibility in currency and financial markets.

## CASE STUDY

# The End of the Bretton Woods System

The Bretton Woods system of exchange rates was enacted at the end of World War II. It included most nations outside the former Soviet Union and its allies. The exchange rate system was a major component of the institutions that were designed to manage international economic conflict and to support international economic cooperation. In addition to the exchange rate system, the other institutions that were created at the same time included the International Monetary Fund (IMF), the International Bank for Reconstruction and Development (IBRD) or World Bank, and the General Agreement on Tariffs and Trade (GATT). (See Chapter 2.)

Each institution had its own role in the management of world economic affairs. The roles of the exchange rate were to provide stability by eliminating excess currency fluctuations, to prevent nations from using exchange rate devaluations as a tactic for gaining markets for their goods, and to ensure that there was an adequate supply of internationally accepted reserves so that nations could meet their international obligations.

In the Bretton Woods exchange rate system, the dollar was fixed to gold at the rate of $1 equalling $1/35$ of an ounce of gold, or $35 per ounce. Every other currency within the system was fixed to the dollar and, therefore, indirectly to gold. Unlike a pure gold standard, however, countries could use U.S. dollars as their international reserve and did not have to accumulate gold or tie their money supply to their gold reserves.

The Bretton Woods exchange rate system had one fatal flaw—the dollar. The United States was in a privileged position since its currency was treated the same as gold. This meant that the United States could simply increase its money supply (the supply of dollars) and gain increased purchasing power over European, Japanese, and other countries' goods. Other nations preferred the United States to maintain a relatively robust supply of dollars, since this insured that there was an adequate supply of international reserves for the world economy.

Problems with this arrangement began when the U.S. economy expanded at a different rate than the economies of its trading partners. In the mid-to-late 1960s, the United States deepened its involvement in the Vietnam War while it simultaneously created the "War on Poverty" at home. Both policies generated large fiscal expenditures that stimulated the economy. While U.S. expansion raced ahead of expansion elsewhere, Europeans found themselves accumulating dollars more rapidly than they desired. The dollars were a by-product of U.S. economic expansion and partially reflected the price increases that were accompanying the expansion.

Under a different type of exchange rate system, it would have been appropriate for the United States to devalue its currency. U.S. prices had risen relative to foreign prices, the real exchange rate had appreciated as a consequence, and trade deficits were beginning to become a permanent feature of the U.S. economy.

One policy would have been to devalue the nominal dollar exchange rate, but this was not an option. Since every currency was tied to the dollar, there was no way for the United States to devalue against a group of other currencies selectively. An alternative was for the United States to devalue against all currencies by changing the gold value of the dollar. By the late 1960s, it was becoming apparent that this would be necessary.

Persistent U.S. deficits had led to an accumulation of dollars outside the United States, which greatly exceeded the United States' supply of gold. In other words, the United States lacked the gold reserves to back all of the dollars that were in circulation. Official recognition of this fact led to the **Smithsonian Agreement** of December 1971, in which the major industrialized countries agreed to devalue the gold content of the dollar by around 8 percent, from $35 per ounce to $38.02. In addition, Japan, Germany, and other trade surplus countries increased the value of their currencies.

Although the Smithsonian Agreement was hailed by President Nixon as a fundamental reorganization of international monetary affairs, it quickly proved to be too little and of only temporary benefit. The gold value of the dollar was realigned again in early 1973, from $38.02 to $42.22. In addition, further devaluation occurred against other European currencies. The end of the system came in March 1973 when the major currencies began to float against each other. A few currencies, such as the British pound, had begun to float earlier.

In each case, the strategy of allowing the exchange rate to float in response to supply and demand conditions was adopted as a means of coping with speculation. When speculators had perceived that the dollar was overvalued at $38 per ounce or $42 per ounce, they sold dollars in anticipation of a future devaluation. Nor was the dollar the only currency speculated against. Other weak currencies such as the pound and the Italian lira had also been correctly perceived as overvalued and had been sold off by speculators. In the end, the central banks of the weak-currency countries found it impossible to support an unrealistically high value of their currency. The costs of buying up the excess supply of their currencies at overvalued prices proved to be too great. The simplest solution was to let the currencies float.

 ## Single Currency Areas

On January 1, 1999, 11 of the 15 members of the European Union adopted the euro as their currency. Shortly thereafter, a 12th member joined the euro group. Initially, the use of the euro was limited to government bonds and other financial instruments, and it served mainly as an accounting unit. By 2002, euro coins and paper money circulated, and shortly thereafter, the francs, marks, and pesetas of the 12 members were withdrawn from circulation. It has taken awhile for the EU-12 to arrive at this point. The adoption of a single currency has been under serious consideration since the 1970s (at least), and the official agreements between the member states have been in place since the early 1990s. Given that one of the strongest symbols of national independence is a nation's money, the 30 years it has taken to arrive at the point where the citizens and policymakers of the European Union are willing to give up their centuries-old forms of money may not seem so long.

The EU's experience with the euro is examined in more detail in Chapter 14, but any discussion of single currency areas has to recognize that it has excited the imagination of people all over the world. Researchers have begun to analyze other regions to see if they are suitable areas for the use of a single currency, and within the EU itself, there has been a huge amount of discussion of the single currency. The starting point for the economic analysis of the pros and cons of adopting a single currency is the work by the Nobel Prize–winning economist Robert Mundell, whose work on the theory of **optimal currency areas** developed the criteria used to determine whether two or more countries would be economically better off sharing a currency rather than maintaining their own national money.

There are at least four potential reasons why a group of countries might want to share a common money. First, a single currency eliminates the need to convert each other's money and thereby reduces transaction costs in a number of ways. It eliminates the fees paid to banks or to the currency brokers that arrange the conversion, it simplifies accounting and bookkeeping, and it enables consumers and investors to compare prices across international boundaries more accurately. Each of these advantages provide some gain in efficiency and a reduction in business costs. Second, a single currency eliminates price fluctuations that are caused by changes in the exchange rate. When speculators move their money into or out of a country, or when temporary interest rate changes in one country alter the supply and demand for foreign exchange, one country may become (temporarily) cheaper or more expensive for business. As a result, business decisions may reflect temporary shifts in currency values rather than underlying issues of economic efficiency. The elimination of misleading price signals that result from exchange rate fluctuations is also a potential gain in efficiency.

Third, the elimination of exchange rates through the adoption of a single currency can help increase political trust between countries seeking to increase their integration. A single currency removes some of the friction between integrating nations by eliminating the problems that are caused by exchange rate misalignments. An example may help clarify this point. On the EU's way to a single currency, it experienced a speculative episode that was directed against the British pound and the French franc, among other currencies. After some initial attempts to fend off the speculation against the pound, Britain let it depreciate. France, on the other hand, raised its interest rates in order to increase the demand for the franc. As a result, the pound was suddenly, significantly depreciated against the franc. European businesses in France and elsewhere noted this development and moved several factories from the continent to England and Scotland. As you can imagine, this did not sit well with politicians in France and Holland (which also lost jobs to Britain). This episode illustrates the benefits of eliminating exchange rate misalignments, or sudden dramatic changes in exchange rates. For most pairs of countries, this is not an important issue, but for members of a regional trade alliance, particularly one that is seeking deeper levels of integration than simply free trade, it can be a very important political benefit from a single currency.

Fourth, and finally, for some developing countries, the adoption of a common currency may give their exchange rate system greater credibility. This is particularly applicable if the common currency is the dollar or the euro or some other widely traded currency. Use of such a currency can reduce exchange rate fluctuations and create greater confidence in the financial system of the adopting country, possibly leading to lower interest rates and an increased availability of credit, although this depends on the overall soundness of the financial system.

Nations that give up their national money do not do so without cost. In addition to its political symbolism, the adoption of a common currency also means that the country no longer has its own money supply as a tool for managing its economic growth. The topic of monetary policy is taken up in more detail in Chapter 11, but the basic point is easy to grasp. Countries with their own currency can influence the rate of growth of the economy in the short run (but not in the long run) through a change in the supply of money. While these policies are somewhat controversial, most countries use changes in the money supply to counteract an economic slowdown. When a country adopts a common currency with one or more other countries, it gives up this tool. After the introduction of the common currency, there is only one money supply and, consequently, one rate of growth of the money supply. New York, for example, shares a common currency with California and, as a consequence, both states experience the same changes in the money supply. If New York is growing fast and California is growing slowly, it would be impossible for the Federal Reserve to alter the money supply in a way that would speed up growth in California and slow it down in New York. With a single currency, there is a "one-size-fits-all" monetary policy.

## Conditions for Adopting a Single Currency

Economic analysis offers four conditions for determining if the gains from a single currency will outweigh the costs of giving up a national money. None of these conditions is absolute, and if one is not met, it may be compensated for in one of the other three. Ultimately, the desirability of a single currency is not subject to hard and fast rules and it is a judgment call for the economists, politicians, and citizens of the affected nations.

The first criterion relates to the cost just noted. If countries have relatively similar economic experiences, then they tend to enter expansions and recessions at more or less similar points in time and one-size-fits-all policy for expanding or contracting the money supply will be appropriate for all members of the currency area. In this case, there is little or no cost associated with the loss of the national money as a tool to expand or contract the national economy. In fact, however, few countries are that well synchronized in their business cycles. Even the states of the United States enter and leave recessions at different points in time, and the national figures on growth only reflect an average across all 50 states.

The second condition is a high degree of labor and capital mobility between the member countries. This allows workers and capital to leave countries or regions where work is scarce and to join the supply of labor and capital in booming regions. In effect, free migration of the factors of production smooths out some of the differences in the business cycle by taking unemployed inputs and moving them to where they are needed. This is how the 50 states of the United States compensate for a lack of complete synchronization in the business cycles of individual states. When conditions are bad in one region, workers and investors move their labor and capital to another region, freeing inputs from areas where they are not needed and providing them to areas where they are.

While capital tends to be relatively mobile, labor is less so, even within countries. Therefore, a third condition is that there are regional policies capable of addressing the imbalances that may develop. Depressed areas may remain depressed if people cannot move or choose not to because the psychological or other costs are too high. Insofar as the economics of regional policies are concerned, they may be determined at any level, from the currency area (multicountry) to individual nation-states, to subnational units (provinces or cities). The key point is not the agency responsible, but that there are effective policies for assisting regions that may not be synchronized with the majority of the currency area's economy.

Finally, the first three conditions point to the fourth: The nations involved must be seeking a level of integration that goes beyond simple free trade. Free trade requires that nations remove their tariffs, quotas, and other border barriers that inhibit the flow of goods. If this is the goal, a common currency is unnecessary. If something much deeper is sought, however, such as a greater harmonization of national economies and much closer economic and political ties, then a single currency can be helpful, provided the other three conditions are observed. This condition is admittedly ambiguous and is part of the reason why policymakers do not always agree in their analysis. It is somewhat circular reasoning, but true nevertheless, that the desirability of a single currency partly depends on the goals of the countries involved.

## CASE STUDY

# Is the NAFTA Region an Optimal Currency Area?

The European Union is one model for the creation of a single currency. In the EU model, an entirely new currency is created and each joining country gives up its national money. The discussion of a single currency in the NAFTA countries has favored a different model. So far, discussion has centered on the adoption of the U.S. dollar by all three countries instead of the creation of an entirely new currency. Either model leads to the same outcome: a single currency area.

Is the discussion realistic? That is, are the proponents of a single currency dreaming or is there something to be gained in such a move? Whether a single currency for the NAFTA region will be created in the near future or not, its proponents are very serious. Even before taking office in 2000, Mexico's President Vicente Fox began talking about the possibility of more integration among Canada, Mexico, and the United States, including the opening of international borders to a freer movement of workers and wider use of the dollar. In 1999, Senator Mack from Florida introduced into the U.S. Senate the International Monetary Stabilization Act to encourage other countries to adopt the U.S. dollar, and corporate heads in Mexico continue to press the Mexican government on the issue. While interest in a single currency for the NAFTA region has waxed and waned, it is likely that over the long term it will continue to increase. Indeed, there is a great deal of interest throughout Latin America in the pros and cons of adopting the dollar.

It is clear that whatever the long-run advantages or disadvantages of a single currency might be, there is a long way to go before the NAFTA countries meet the four conditions necessary for a single currency area to be an optimal policy. First, the business cycles of the three countries have not been synchronized, at least historically. While the macroeconomies of Canada and the United States have often moved together, Mexico has historically had a very different pattern of business cycles. This may be changing, however, since the Mexican cycle appears to be much closer to that of the United States since 1994. Second, given the legal restrictions on labor movement and the political obstacles to opening a North American labor market, labor flows cannot be counted on to help synchronize national business cycles. Third, there are no regional policies within the NAFTA framework as there are within the European Union. In the EU, national governments tax themselves to create a regional fund that is used to provide assistance to areas that lag in economic growth. This is useful for overcoming regional imbalances and removes some of the sting that a region might feel if the EU's other policies are not supportive. And finally, NAFTA was originally conceived as a means to reduce border barriers. While its ultimate goal will surely evolve over time, at present there does not appear to be a consensus that it should be something more than a free-trade area.

As it is presently constituted, the NAFTA region is clearly not an optimal currency area. Nevertheless, it is a safe bet that dollarization will continue to be explored, particularly in Mexico. In part, this is because there are counterarguments to each of the above objections: a single currency will help synchronize the three economies; it is possible to formulate an agreement that allows a guest worker program such as the United States and Mexico had in the 1940s, 1950s, and 1960s; regional policies are simply a matter of political will and financial means, but they would not require huge expenditures; and closer integration of the NAFTA partners is inevitable. The counterarguments are, in turn, debatable, but a second reason why discussion will continue is that there are potentially significant gains for Mexico.

It is inevitable that if Mexico dollarized, its economy would become more tied to the United States. In the view of some economists, this would have a number of positive effects, including a dramatic increase in trade, lower interest rates, more credit for small and medium-sized firms, and less inflation. If this is correct, then dollarization could significantly enhance Mexico's rate of growth. No one can say for certain at this point whether this analysis is correct. It is a tantalizing prospect, however, and is therefore guaranteed to generate further discussion.

## Summary

- People hold foreign currency in order to buy goods and services, to take advantage of interest rate differentials, and to speculate. The primary institutions in the exchange-rate market are commercial banks and foreign exchange brokers.

- Exchange rates can be analyzed with supply and demand analysis, as if they are just another commodity in the economy. Increases (decreases) in the supply of foreign exchange cause the domestic currency to appreciate (depreciate). Increases (decreases) in the demand for foreign exchange cause the domestic currency to depreciate (appreciate).

- Exchange rates are unpredictable, because they are simultaneously influenced by long-run, medium-run, and short-run factors. In the long run, purchasing power parity is important. In the medium run, the business cycle is important, and in the short run, interest-rate differentials and speculation are important.

- The interest parity condition says that the interest rate differential between two countries is approximately equal to the percentage difference between the forward and spot exchange rates.

- Firms use forward exchange rate markets to protect against exchange rate risk.

- Real exchange rates are equal to nominal or market exchange rates adjusted for inflation. They give a better picture of the purchasing power of a nation's currency.

- Fixed exchange rate systems were thought to help limit the growth of inflation, but there is little evidence of this over the last two decades. Fixed exchange rates eliminate the ability of governments to use monetary policies to regulate the macroeconomy.

- Flexible exchange rate systems were thought to help increase growth, but there is little evidence of this over the last two decades. Flexible exchange rates free a nation's macroeconomic policies from the need to maintain a fixed exchange rate.

- All exchange rate systems are on a continuum between fixed and flexible rates. Pegged exchange rates, crawling pegs, and a managed float are examples of intermediary-type systems. The most important rule for countries is that their exchange rate system is credible.

- Optimal currency areas are geographical regions within which it is optimal for countries to adopt the same currency. The criteria for an optimal currency area are a synchronized business cycle, complete factor mobility, regional programs for lagging areas, and a desire to achieve a higher level of economic and political integration.

# Vocabulary

| | |
|---|---|
| appreciation | forward exchange rate |
| Bretton Woods exchange rate system | forward market |
| Convertibility Law | gold standard |
| covered interest arbitrage | hedging |
| crawling peg | interest rate arbitrage |
| currency board | interest parity |
| depreciation | managed float |
| dollarization | nominal exchange rate |
| exchange rate | optimal currency area |
| exchange rate risk | pegged exchange rate |
| fixed exchange rate system | purchasing power parity |
| flexible (floating) exchange rate system | real exchange rate |
| | Smithsonian Agreement |
| | spot market |

# Study Questions

1. Draw a graph of the supply of and demand for the Canadian dollar by the U.S. market. Diagram the effect of each of the following on the exchange rate, state in words whether the effect is long, medium, or short run, and explain your reasoning.
   a. More rapid growth in Canada than in the United States
   b. A rise in U.S. interest rates
   c. Goods are more expensive in Canada than in the United States
   d. A recession in the United States
   e. Expectations of a future depreciation in the Canadian dollar

2. Suppose the U.S. dollar–euro exchange rate is 1.20 dollars per euro, and the U.S. dollar–Mexican peso rate is 0.10 dollars per peso. What is the euro-peso rate?

3. Suppose the U.S. dollar–yen exchange rate is 0.01 dollars per yen. Since the base year, inflation has been 2 percent in Japan and 10 percent in the United States. What is the real exchange rate? In real terms, has the dollar appreciated or depreciated against the yen?

4. Which of the three motives for holding foreign exchange are applicable to each of the following?
   a. A tourist
   b. A bond trader
   c. A portfolio manager
   d. A manufacturer

5. If U.S. visitors to Mexico can buy more goods in Mexico than they can in the United States when they convert their dollars to pesos, is the dollar undervalued or overvalued? Explain.

6. In a fixed exchange rate system, how do countries address the problem of currency market pressures that threaten to lower or raise the value of their currency?

7. In the debate on fixed versus floating exchange rates, the strongest argument for a floating rate is that it frees macroeconomic policy from taking care of the exchange rate. This is also the weakest argument. Explain.

8. Brazil, Argentina, Paraguay, and Uruguay are members of MERCOSUR, a regional trade area that is trying to become a common market. What issues should they consider before they accept or reject a common currency?

9. Suppose that U.S. interest rates are 4 percent more than rates in the European Union.
   a. Would you expect the dollar to appreciate or depreciate against the euro, and by how much?
   b. If, contrary to your expectations, the forward and spot rates are the same, in which direction would you expect financial capital to flow? Why?

10. Why do some economists claim that the most important feature of any exchange rate system is its credibility?

# The Interest Rate Parity Condition

The following variables are defined as in the chapter:

$i$ = home country interest rate

$i^*$ = foreign interest rate

$R$ = the nominal exchange rate in units of home country currency per unit of foreign currency

$F$ = the forward exchange rate

and the forward rate and the interest rates have the same term to maturity.

An investor has a choice between $i$ and $i^*$. Letting the dollar be the home currency, \$1 invested today will return \$1$(1 + i)$ next period if invested at home. To make the comparison with a foreign investment, the dollar first has to be converted into the foreign currency, then invested, and the earnings must be converted back into dollars. The equivalent of \$1 in foreign currency is $1 / R$. If $1 / R$ is invested abroad, at the end of next period it returns $(1 / R)(1 + i^*)$, which is in units of foreign currency. The reconversion to dollars can be done in the forward market where the exchange rate for a forward contract is $F$. Therefore, in dollars, \$1 invested abroad will return $(1 / R)(1 + i^*)F$ next period.

The interest parity condition states that investors will be indifferent between home and foreign investments (of similar risk), implying that they will move their funds around and cause interest rates and exchange rates to change until the returns are the same in the two cases:

$$1 + i = (1 / R) (1 + i^*) F = (1 + i^*) (F / R)$$

Divide by $(1 + i^*)$:

$$(1 + i) / (1 + i^*) = F / R$$

Subtract 1 from both sides:

$$[(1 + i) / (1 + i^*)] - [(1 + i^*) / (1 + i^*)] = F / R - R / R$$
$$[(1 + i) - (1 + i^*)] / [(1 + i^*)] = (F - R) / R$$
$$(i - i^*) / (1 + i^*) = (F - R) / R$$

The left-hand side denominator is close to 1 for small values of $i^*$ (this is why we state the interest parity condition as an approximation). The right-hand side is the percentage difference between the forward and spot rates. If it is negative, markets expect an appreciation in the home currency. Rewriting the last equation:

$$i - i^* \approx (F - R) / R$$

which says that the difference between home country and foreign interest rates is approximately equal to the expected depreciation in the home country currency.

# 11 An Introduction to Open Economy Macroeconomics

## Introduction: The Macroeconomy in a Global Setting

Chapters 9 and 10 introduced the concepts of the balance of payments and the exchange rate. In this chapter we look more closely at their relationship to each other and to the overall national economy. After a brief review of a few key macroeconomic concepts, the chapter focuses on the interactions among the current account, exchange rates, and key components of the macroeconomy—consumption, investment, and government spending. National governments are important to this chapter since they rarely take a passive role in the economy. Indeed, since the worldwide Great Depression of the 1930s, and especially since the end of World War II, national governments have shouldered a significant share of the responsibility for keeping the growth of the economy on track, the unemployment rate low, and prices stable. Whether this government role is desirable or not, and whether governments are successful or not, most people expect their governments to do something during a recession. Therefore, a major focus of this chapter is the impact of macroeconomic policies on the exchange rate and current account.

The impacts of activist macroeconomic policies are one focus of this chapter, but it is also important to recognize that these are not the only links between a nation's macroeconomy and the rest of the world. Usually governments control a significant share of the national product and as a consequence, their normal, day-to-day operating decisions affect exchange rates and the current account. In addition, the same is true for consumers and businesses. In most economies, expenditures on consumption goods and services comprise the largest single component of the macroeconomy, and as we have already seen, an increase in economic growth causes consumers to draw in a greater quantity of imports, increasing the demand for foreign exchange and pushing the current account toward the deficit side.

# Aggregate Demand and Aggregate Supply

Table 11.1 shows the four main economic agents in the macroeconomy: households, businesses, government, and foreigners. In our simplified model of the macroeconomy, households supply all the factors of production (land, labor, and capital) that businesses need to produce the nation's output. In return, the revenue that businesses earn when they sell their goods is used to pay for the factors supplied by households. Accordingly, all of the income generated in the economy accrues to households since they supply all of the factor inputs. This is a fundamental identity in the macroeconomy: The income for the economy as a whole equals the value of its output.

When we track income and output, it is important to understand the position of **intermediate inputs**—goods purchased by one business from another to use in production. For example, a car manufacturer hires not only labor, land, and capital (for which it pays wages and salaries, rents, interest, and dividends) but it also purchases glass, tires, steel, and so on. The payment for auto glass is not directly income to households because it is paid to another business, but if we trace it back, it ultimately becomes income. For example, the glass manufacturer

| TABLE 11.1 • The Main Economic Agents in the Macroeconomy | |
|---|---|
| Agent | Function |
| Households | • Supply factors (land, labor, capital) to business <br> • Purchase consumer goods and services (C) <br> • Save <br> • Pay taxes |
| Businesses | • Use the factors supplied by households to produce the nation's output <br> • Purchase investment goods (I) |
| Government | • Purchase government goods and services (G) <br> • Collect taxes (T) |
| Foreigners | • Purchase exports (EX) <br> • Supply imports (IM) |

There are four main agents in the macroeconomy. Each one is a different source of demand for goods and services.

receives payment from the car company and it uses the payment to pay wages, rent, interest, and dividends, as well as its suppliers. We can keep following the flow of payments, through the suppliers to the glass firms, or more simply, we can recognize that all of the payments are incorporated into the value of the car. That is, the purchase price of the car ultimately generates an equivalent amount of income. As a result, the fundamental identity holds between income and output.

The identity between total expenditures on final goods and services and the value of total output in an economy can be looked at in another way. Figure 11.1 is similar to a graph of supply and demand in a single market, except that the demand curve is total demand for all final goods and services and the supply curve is total output. In other words, the curve with a negative slope is **aggregate demand (AD)**, and the curve with a positive slope is **aggregate supply (AS)**. In a simple supply and demand graph, the horizontal axis measures quantity and the vertical axis measures price, but in the AD/AS graph shown in Figure 11.1, all final goods (GDP) are included on the horizontal axis and the price level, (P) is shown on the vertical axis. The price level is somewhat more abstract than the price of a single good, but it is equivalent to the consumer price index or another measure of economywide prices. Points along the AD curve show the equilib-

**FIGURE 11.1** ● **Aggregate Demand (AD) and Aggregate Supply (AS)**

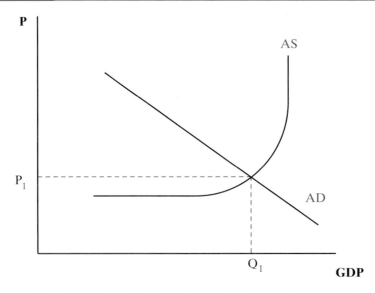

The aggregate demand (AD) curve shows the levels of output (GDP) and price (P) where expenditure decisions and production decisions match; aggregate supply (AS) shows the levels of output and prices where decisions to supply inputs and production decisions match. Together they show the levels of equilibrium output ($Q_1$) and prices ($P_1$).

rium levels of output and prices that are consistent on the demand side of the economy, while the AS curve shows the points that are consistent from a supply-side point of view. Together, they show the levels of equilibrium output (Q1) and prices ($P_1$) at a given point in time.

The shape of the aggregate supply curve is designed to call attention to three regions of GDP. On the horizontal part of the AS curve, the economy is operating below full employment. Theoretically, the availability of unemployed workers and other idle resources allows an increase in output to occur without putting upward pressure on prices. Workers and the owners of other factors cannot demand higher wages or other payments in return for more inputs of labor and capital because there are plenty of idle workers and other resources willing and able to contribute at the going rate. Hence, an increase in production can be relatively easily achieved without causing shortages of inputs or increases in prices. The middle, upward-sloping part of the AS curve symbolizes the range of GDP where inputs begin to become scarce. Some wage increases or other factor price increases are necessary in order to obtain more inputs and to produce more output. In the vertical region of the AS curve, the economy is at full employment and no more output is possible until new workers enter the labor force or new factories and machines are built. Figure 11.1 portrays this region as an absolute limit to production. In fact, it is possible to exceed this level for short periods of time; for example, during wars or other extraordinary events that cause people to work longer hours or at a faster pace than they are willing to maintain over the long run. Given that output levels beyond the vertical region can be sustained only for a short period, it is useful to think of the vertical portion of the AS curve as signifying the full-employment level of GDP.

In the short run and medium run, the focus is on changes in aggregate demand that are initiated by one or more of the economic agents listed in Table 11.1. Significant changes in expenditures are not at all uncommon over the course of a year or more. For example, as an economy goes into recession, consumers and businesses may quickly alter their expectations and their spending (C and I) as they reassess their economic circumstances. Similarly, recessions, wars, natural disasters, and other factors can cause large shifts in government tax (T) and expenditure (G) policies, as well as changes in other policies that directly affect consumer and business spending. And finally, economic booms or depressions abroad sometimes cause a rapid change in foreign purchases of products exported (EX) from the home country.

Figure 11.2 illustrates the case of an increase in aggregate demand. The source of the change could be an increase in expenditures by any one of the economic agents listed in Table 11.1. That is, it could be due to an increase in consumption expenditures (C), business investment (I), government purchases of final goods and services (G), government tax cuts that stimulate consumer or business spending, or exports (EX) purchased by foreigners. The net result of any of the changes is qualitatively the same. Prices rise slightly from $P_1$ to $P_2$ as factor inputs become scarcer, and GDP rises from $Q_1$ to $Q_2$. If the economy initially happened to be on the horizontal part of the AS curve, then prices would not have risen,

**FIGURE 11.2** ● **A Shift in the AD Curve**

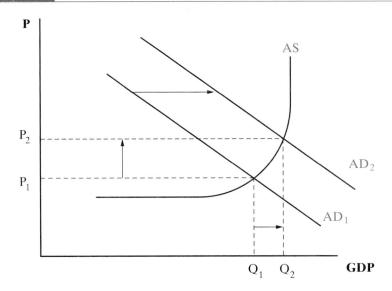

An increase in aggregate demand will cause an increase in GDP and a rise in the price level.

but output would still have gone up. If the changes commenced from a position of full employment on the vertical part of the AS curve, then all of the change would have been in the price level, and no increase in output would occur. If AD falls instead of rising, the effects are symmetrical and in the opposite direction of the changes caused by an increase in AD.

Although the simple relationships between AD, AS, P, and GDP portrayed in Figures 11.1 and 11.2 are a useful way to conceptualize the interactions of a number of key macroeconomic variables, the graphs and the description hide a great deal of complexity. For example, the graphs illustrate only one point in time, and they do not show what happens as the economy grows over time. If an economy grows, it must have more labor or more physical capital or natural resources and be capable of producing more output. Hence, economic growth could be added by shifting the whole AS curve rightward. Consequently, the changes in Figure 11.2 must be viewed as short-run or medium-run changes that take effect separately from economic growth.

Another factor that is hiding behind Figure 11.2 is the actual mechanism that moves the economy from one level of GDP ($Q_1$) to a higher level ($Q_2$). Suppose, for example, that AD begins to shift rightward due to rising business optimism that prompts many firms to increase their investment spending. Firms order new machines or start new construction projects, and total spending in the economy goes up. This is not the end of the story, however, as the firms that supply the machines or do the construction will have to increase their output levels, and that will put additional income in the hands of their owners and workers. Those suppliers and their workers are likely to spend at least part of their additional income. Statistical analysis over long periods of time has shown that there is a very close quantitative relationship between income received by households and household consumption patterns. That is, as income rises, so do expenditures. Consequently, the workers and business owners who supply goods and services to the investing firms increase their own expenditures as well. They buy houses, furniture, cars, college education, medical care, and all the other things that households spend money on, thus creating another round of income increases and expenditures.

In effect, the original increase in investment spending causes an increase in production. Because output equals income in the macroeconomy, incomes go up by an amount that is equal to the value of the increased production. In turn, higher incomes lead to another set of expenditures and production increases, and another round of income increases. And so on. When a new equilibrium is eventually reached and the effect of the original change in spending has completely worked its way through the economy, the total increase in GDP is greater than the original increase in spending. This is the **multiplier effect** of an increase in aggregate demand. For any given increase in spending that is not directly caused by an increase in income, the impact on equilibrium GDP is greater than the initial spending increase. There is no consensus among economists about the size of the multiplier effect, although most empirical estimates have put it between 1.0 and 2.0, with a majority in the middle of that range. If the multiplier is 1.5, it would mean that a sudden increase in spending of, say, $100 million would raise equilibrium GDP by $150 million. The multiplier undoubtedly varies in different countries and even in the same country at different times, and the source of the initial increase in aggregate demand is important so that an increase in consumption spending may not have the same ultimate impact as an increase in government spending.

The multiplier process of spending-production-income-spending and so on might seem as if it could go on forever, but in fact, the impact of the original expenditure gets smaller and smaller, rather like the waves that radiate out from a rock thrown into a pond. There are several forces that dampen the impact over time and that bring GDP to a new equilibrium level. Three of the dampening forces are taxes, saving, and imports. In most countries, each successive increase in income will lead to additional taxes and saving, as well as additional spending. On average, when incomes rise, people spend part of the increase, pay taxes with part of the increase, and save part of the increase. Taxes vary by country, and as we saw in Chapter 9, the amount saved varies as well. The larger the part that is taken by government or that is saved by households, the faster the impact of the original expenditure dissipates.

Each successive increase in income in the spending-production-income-spending cycle will also trigger an increase in imports. We can be certain of this effect because part of what households buy is imported, so that if they increase their purchases, they will also be buying more imported goods. All three of the variables—taxes, savings, and imports—cause the next round of spending on goods that are domestically produced to be less than the first round; therefore, they ensure that the income and spending effects moving through the economy are becoming smaller and smaller in each successive round. In addition, the three variables also show why the multiplier varies from country to country. The greater imports are as a share of spending, or savings, or taxes, the more each successive round of spending is reduced from the previous. That is, countries with larger propensities to import, higher saving rates, or higher tax rates will have smaller multipliers.

#  Fiscal and Monetary Policies

The discussion of aggregate demand, aggregate supply, and the multiplier is background for the analysis of the effects of fiscal and monetary policies on GDP and prices. **Fiscal policy** includes government taxation and expenditures, while **monetary policy** covers the money supply and interest rates. The institutions that enact fiscal and monetary policy vary across countries, but generally, the legislative and executive branches are responsible for tax policy and for determining spending priorities, and the central bank and the finance ministry set monetary policy, sometimes with direct input from the executive branch of government. Recently, there is a trend toward granting central banks complete independence in setting monetary policy, as has historically been the case in a number of countries, including the United States.

## Fiscal Policy

Government's fiscal policies of expenditure and taxation are an important element of every country's macroeconomy, because they are a major determinant of the total demand for goods and services. All else equal, when a government increases its spending, the increase ripples through the economy as a series of production-income-spending increases that lead to higher levels of equilibrium GDP. Similarly, when governments cut their expenditures, the same effect occurs, but in the opposite direction as production, income, and spending all decrease.

Changes in tax levels are similar in their analysis. A decrease in taxes will raise household income—what is available to save or spend—because fewer taxes are withdrawn from paychecks. The increase in after-tax income will in turn lead to increases in spending, production, and income again. Figure 11.2 can be interpreted as either an increase in government spending or a cut in taxes. In both cases, the AD curve shifts rightward, and both GDP and the price level rise.

For obvious reasons, cuts in taxes and increases in government spending are referred to as **expansionary fiscal policy**. The opposite, **contractionary fiscal policy**, is a tax increase or a cut in government spending, both of which reduce the level of equilibrium GDP by shifting the AD curve to the left. Contractionary policy is symmetrical with expansionary policy, so that tax increases and government spending cuts have a negative multiplier effect on total output, while tax cuts and government spending increases have a positive multiplier effect. It is important to note that we are assuming that nothing else changes other than the single change in fiscal policy. For example, there is no assumption that government budgets are balanced, and an increase in government spending does not imply a simultaneous increase in taxes. Similarly, cuts in taxes are not countered by cuts in spending, nor are tax increases balanced by government spending increases.

For many macroeconomists of the 1940s and 1950s, the discovery of the multiplier effect of fiscal policy was like finding the holy grail of macroeconomics. It seemed to offer a technique for managing the economy and, most importantly, for avoiding disasters such as the Great Depression of the 1930s. Needless to say, most economists today are much more cautious about the use of fiscal policy. The reasons are not hard to understand. First, expansionary policies tend to cause inflation, which offsets some of the increased consumer spending by absorbing it into higher prices instead of higher output. Second, there is a substantial margin of error in the estimation of the size of the multiplier. Does a $50 billion tax cut lead to a $50 billion, $75 billion, or $100 billion increase in income? Third, the use of fiscal policy is complicated by its variation in effects stemming from the different possibilities for financing an expansionary policy. If governments accommodate the expansionary fiscal policy with an expansion of the money supply, the multiplier is larger than if there is no accommodation. Taken together, the three technical problems of inflation, the margin for error in measuring the multiplier, and variation in the multiplier's size depending on the means of paying for the expansion make it difficult to use fiscal policy precisely.

But this is not all. The politics of turning government spending off and on, or turning taxes off and on, is a long, drawn-out, and complicated process. By the time the legislation is passed, the purpose for which it was originally intended may have disappeared entirely. In other words, fiscal policy as a tool for managing the economy to avoid recessions and curtail inflation is politically cumbersome. Taken together, the political problem plus the technical problem of measuring its precise effects make fiscal policy a less used tool for managing the economy. Nevertheless, it is still important to study, since government spending and taxation policies have significant impacts on the macroeconomy and the current account, regardless of whether they are implemented to achieve a particular macroeconomic objective.

## Monetary Policy

Monetary policy is the other main category of policies that national governments use to influence the macroeconomy. As noted, in the United States, the European Union, and a growing number of other nations, monetary policy is determined by an independent central bank. Therefore, it reflects the views of the central bank and its responses to economic conditions rather than the views of a particular political party or the executive branch of government.

Monetary policy works through a combination of changes to the supply of money and changes to interest rates. When the central bank changes the supply of money, it does so by changing the quantity of funds in financial institutions that are available for lending. The most frequently used technique for accomplishing this is called **open market operations**. Open market operations are simply the buying and selling of bonds in the open market. When a central bank sells bonds, banks and other financial institutions give up some of their cash. Consequently, cash reserves shrink throughout the financial system. Buying bonds has the opposite effect on the financial system's reserves of cash and is the primary technique for expanding the money supply.

As cash reserves in the financial system increase, there is likely to be more investment. That is, financial institutions such as banks need to generate revenue by making loans. Money sitting in the vaults earns the bank no revenue, so an increase in bank reserves leads banks to make more loans. In order to encourage businesses to borrow additional funds, however, interest rates must fall.

Figure 11.3 illustrates the process of a fall in interest rates with a simple supply and demand diagram showing an increase in the supply of money. The horizontal axis measures the quantity of money in the system, where money is defined to be cash, checking accounts, and other easily spendable assets such as money market accounts that allow check writing. The easier it is to spend an asset, the more *liquid* it is considered to be. Cash is the most liquid asset, while checking accounts are slightly less so, but still highly liquid compared to, say, stocks or bonds.

**FIGURE 11.3** ● **Money Supply and Demand**

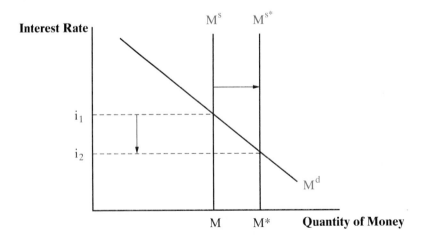

An increase in the supply of money reduces the rate of interest.

The supply curve is represented with a vertical line instead of the more common upward sloping supply curve because we are assuming that the central bank fixes the quantity of money at a given level, and that the quantity does not vary with the level of interest rates, measured on the vertical axis. The interest rate can be considered similar to the price of money. There are two reasons for this: It is the price you pay to borrow money and it is the opportunity cost of holding your assets in the form of money instead of some other, interest-earning, form. This is admittedly a simplification, since borrowing costs and the return on savings are always different, and since some types of money earn interest (for example, money market accounts). Still, it is a simplification that is useful and one that captures the essential relationship between interest rates and the quantity of money in the economy.

The fall in interest rates shown in Figure 11.3 is the key to the increase in investment that comes about as a result of an expansionary monetary policy. Once investment increases, the expenditure multiplier takes over and the production-income-spending cycle is set in motion. Hence, an increase in the money supply will expand the economy and increase incomes. Not surprisingly, monetary policy is also symmetrical with respect to its contractionary and expansionary impacts, so a decrease in the money supply will result in a decline in production and incomes.

**Expansionary monetary policy** involves an increase in the money supply and a fall in interest rates, leading to a positive expansion in income. **Contractionary monetary policy** is exactly the reverse, and involves a decrease in the money supply and a rise in interest rates, leading to a contraction in income. As with fiscal policies, both expansionary and contractionary monetary policies work through the multiplier process to raise or lower income, depending on whether the policy is expansionary or contractionary.

## CASE STUDY

# Fiscal and Monetary Policy during the Great Depression

The Great Depression is the name Americans give to the worst economic period in modern American history. It was a worldwide phenomenon, however, and most countries felt hard times. The onset of the crisis varied from country to country, but in the United States, it started in July 1929, with an unnoticed modest decline in economic activity. Stock prices continued to rise through the summer of 1929, in spite of the overall decline in output and income. September and October were bad months for the market, culminating in the panic of Black Thursday, on October 24, when the market fell by more than one-third. Most people thought that the worst was over and many argued that the stock market collapse was good for the economy since it squeezed out excess speculation.

The small recession that began during the summer of 1929 grew into one of the worst decades in American history. By 1933, over 25 percent of the labor force was unemployed and real GDP had fallen by nearly 26 percent. Out of the cauldron of the Great Depression came Social Security, the Fair Labor Standards Act to regulate working conditions and wages, the Securities and Exchange Commission to oversee stock trading, the Federal Deposit Insurance Corporation to protect bank deposits, the Tennessee Valley Authority, and a host of other programs that inserted the federal government much deeper into American economic life.

Most Americans probably think of the 1930s and the Great Depression as synonymous, but there were two separate recessions in the United States during the decade. The first and most severe, is the one that began in 1929 and lasted until 1933. The second began in 1937 and lasted into 1938. Between these two downturns in economic activity, there was a strong recovery, and by 1936, real GDP was above where it had been in 1929, the last year of overall positive growth until 1934. Figure 11.4 illustrates the annual rate of growth, 1930–1941.

In hindsight, it is easy to see the policy mistakes that prolonged the recession and made it far more severe than it needed to be. Based on what we know today about expansionary fiscal and monetary policy, the federal government should have done one or more of the following: raise government spending for goods and services, cut taxes, increase the money supply to lower interest rates. The problem in the 1930s was that no one was aware of the relations discussed in this chapter. In a very real sense, if you read the first part of this chapter, then you know more about fiscal policy than Presidents Roosevelt and Hoover and all of their advisers knew.

Instead of using increases in government spending and cuts in taxes to stimulate the economy, Presidents Hoover (1929–1933) and Roosevelt (1933–1945)

**FIGURE 11.4** ● **Real GDP Growth, United States**

*Source:* Bureau of Economic Analysis.

worried about the federal budget deficits that emerged during the 1930s. Both Roosevelt and Hoover thought that budget deficits undermined business confidence and were a major reason for the recession. Consequently, the budget deficit became a major issue of the 1932 presidential election, in which Roosevelt successfully campaigned on the platform of a balanced federal budget. As it turned out, however, the federal budget was in deficit during every year of Roosevelt's presidency.

Hoover and Roosevelt tried to balance the budget. Both presidents unsuccessfully opposed legislation to offer war veterans early payment of the retirement money they were owed, and both presidents supported tax increases when deficits began to appear after 1929. Hoover introduced a dramatic tax increase in 1932, while Roosevelt increased taxes at several points in time, most dramatically with the beginning of social security taxes in 1937. Given the contractionary impact of tax increases, it is not surprising that 1932 was the worst year of the depression, nor that the economy slipped back into recession in 1938 after the implementation of the new social security tax.

If fiscal policy was not helpful during the 1930s, monetary policy was a disaster. Between 1929 and 1933, the money supply (currency, checking accounts, and savings deposits) fell by nearly 31 percent. Credit became scarce and investment disappeared. In other words, if fiscal policy could be considered more or less neutral during most years of the Great Depression (neither expansionary nor contractionary), then monetary policy was contractionary.

In retrospect, it is easy to understand the failure to use expansionary fiscal policy. No one in the 1930s understood the macroeconomy well enough to discern how to use fiscal policy to fight the recession. It is more difficult to justify the misuse of monetary policy, however, because more was known about the relationships between the money supply, bank reserves, and investment. For many years, prominent economists such as Nobel Prize winner Milton Friedman argued that the Federal Reserve was simply incompetent. This view cannot be ruled out, but more recent scholarship has shed new light on this historic episode. Rather than incompetence, the Fed's actions reflected a different set of priorities. In particular, it may have been acting responsibly if its first priority was to protect the gold standard.

Under the rules of the gold standard, central banks are required to use interest rates and monetary policy to attract gold whenever gold reserves run low. This usually means an interest rate hike in order to increase the demand for the domestic currency and to reduce the demand for foreign currencies.

In 1928, U.S. monetary policy turned contractionary as the Fed was worried about speculation in the stock market and wanted to make it more difficult for brokers to borrow from banks. The Fed raised interest rates and, unintentionally, created an inflow of gold to the United States. U.S. policy put pressure on European countries, which began to lose their gold reserves. Consequently, the contractionary policy in the United States spread across the Atlantic as countries began to raise their interest rates and slow their rate of money growth in order to stop the outflow of gold. The irony is that each country was acting responsibly according to the dictates of the gold standard, but they were following polices that resulted in a worldwide economic catastrophe.

At several points during the years that followed, U.S. and foreign policies turned even more contractionary. In 1931, it was widely expected that the United Kingdom would leave the gold standard altogether, and speculation turned against the pound. In September 1931, Britain left the gold standard and speculators immediately shifted their attention to the dollar. Expecting a similar decline in the value of the dollar, they began to sell dollars and dollar-denominated assets, all of which resulted in gold outflows. Once again, the Fed responded by raising interest rates in September and October 1931, and the U.S. economy continued its downward spiral.

It is no coincidence that the first countries to leave the gold standard (the United Kingdom and the countries that followed it out of the gold standard in September 1931) were the first to experience recovery. Once their policies were freed from the constraint of supporting a fixed rate of exchange, they could turn them toward economic expansion. In the United States, Roosevelt's first act after taking office in March 1933 was to suspend the gold standard. It seems unlikely that he completely understood the relationship of gold to the depression, but it was a good move, as the economy began its recovery from the worst economic crisis of the twentieth century.

##  Current Account Balances Revisited

Chapter 9 described the identity between private savings, government budget balances, investment, and the current account as follows:

$$S + (T - G) = I + CA$$

Now we are ready to look more closely at this identity and to incorporate the links between monetary and fiscal policy, income, and the current account. The goal is to analyze how a change in income caused by a change in monetary or fiscal policy influences the country's current account. We will do this in two steps. In the first step we will explore the links between changes in monetary and fiscal policies, interest rates, and exchange rates. The link from monetary policy to interest rates has already been described, but as we will see, fiscal policies have interest rate effects as well. In the second step we will put together policy changes, interest rates, exchange rates, and the current account balance. Once we have done this we will have a much clearer understanding of the policies a country must follow if it needs to eliminate a trade imbalance in its current account.

It is important to emphasize that we are looking at changes in income and other macroeconomic variables that are likely to take place over the span of a few years or less, while ignoring long-run impacts that may take many years, perhaps even a decade or longer, to materialize. We will return to this point later in the chapter when we try to distinguish long-run, permanent changes from short-run changes.

## Fiscal and Monetary Policies, Interest Rates, and Exchange Rates

From Chapter 10 and the interest parity condition, we know that interest rate increases lead to an appreciation of the domestic currency (the exchange rate, (R), falls) and interest rate decreases lead to a depreciation (the exchange rate rises). Recall that this occurs through changes in the demand and supply of foreign currency. As interest rates rise, it increases the supply of foreign currency since interest arbitrageurs are constantly searching for the highest possible rate of interest. Similarly, a decline in interest rates reduces the inflow of foreign financial capital, decreasing the supply of foreign currency. Demand side effects are present in both cases as well, since home country interest arbitrageurs have the same motivation to move their capital in and out of the country.

The exchange rate effects of monetary policy are easily identified. We have already seen how an expansion of the money supply increases bank reserves and pushes down interest rates. Consequently, in addition to increasing income, expansionary monetary policy must also cause a depreciation of the exchange rate. Given the symmetry between expansionary and contractionary policies, monetary contraction reduces bank reserves and drives up interest rates, leading to an appreciation of the exchange rate.

Since a rapidly depreciating currency is a feature of most international financial crises, contractionary monetary policy is a very commonly adopted technique to stop a depreciation. This technique is discussed more fully in Chapter 12, but it should be noted that the downside of using monetary policy this way is a contraction in income and possibly even the cause of a recession. This illustrates once again that it is not unusual for a tradeoff to exist between a country's exchange rate goal and its goals for income growth and employment. The Fed's action to raise interest rates to protect the dollar in 1931 is a classic example of a conflict between the needs of the domestic economy and the desire to protect the exchange rate.

The interest rate effects of fiscal policy are less easily identified, but they are present nonetheless. The key to understanding these links lies in the behavior of households and the changes they make when their incomes rise or fall. Looking first at the case of a rise in household income, we know that consumption expenditures will also rise. Furthermore—and this is key—rising incomes cause households to reevaluate the division of their assets between liquid forms such as money, and relatively less liquid forms such as stocks and bonds. When income rises, the average household will hold more money. In economic terms, the demand for money increases, as shown in Figure 11.5.

Why do households increase their demand for money when their incomes increase? The reasons are straightforward. First, at higher levels of income, they consume more. That is, they need a higher level of money holdings to pay for their purchases. Second, the opportunity cost of the interest they lose on holding money instead of an interest-paying asset becomes less burdensome. In other words, when households have more income, they can "afford" to hold more money.

FIGURE 11.5 ● **An Increase in the Demand for Money**

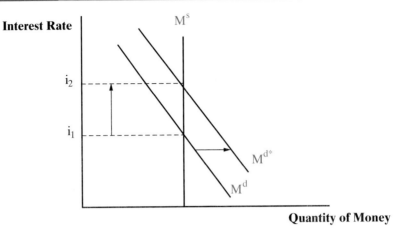

An increase in income causes households to increase their money holdings. As a consequence, interest rates rise.

Lest this seem too abstract and immaterial to your personal situation, think about what you might do if your income doubled. Most likely, you would increase the amount of money in your wallet and checking account. You would also probably put aside some of your increased income into long-term savings. The point is that if you are more or less average in your spending behavior, an increase in income would cause you to spend more and you would facilitate your increased spending by carrying around more cash and larger balances in your checking account.

Now we have all of the pieces to analyze the exchange rate effects of fiscal policy. Expansionary fiscal policy will raise incomes and consumption. One outcome of these effects is an increase in the demand for money which, as shown in Figure 11.5, leads to higher interest rates. Given the relationship between interest rates and exchange rates, we know that higher interest rates, all else equal, lead to an inflow of foreign capital and a fall in the exchange rate (an appreciation). As usual, the effects of contractionary policy are symmetrical. A cut in government spending or an increase in taxes will cause income and money demand to fall, followed by a drop in interest rates and a rise in the exchange rate (depreciation).

## Fiscal and Monetary Policy and the Current Account

Once the exchange rate effects of monetary and fiscal policy have been identified, it is relatively easy to describe their effects on the current account. As we will see, the effect of fiscal policy on the current account is definite, while the effect of monetary policy is ambiguous. We turn now to the analysis of these impacts.

Taking the case of expansionary monetary policy first, we have seen that an increase in the money supply reduces interest rates and causes a depreciation in the domestic currency. Exchange rate depreciation switches some consumer spending from foreign goods (imports) to domestic goods, because foreign goods become relatively expensive. The effect of **expenditure switching** is to offset the increase in imports caused by rising income partially or completely. As a result, there is a more robust expansion of the domestic economy because less of the expansion of demand leaks out of the economy as an increase in imports. In other words, expansionary monetary policy is reinforced by the changes in the exchange rate.

Contractionary monetary policy has an opposite effect. Interest rates rise, causing an appreciation of the domestic currency, which makes imports relatively cheaper. As a consequence, consumers switch some of their expenditures away from domestic goods toward foreign ones. The reduction in demand for domestic goods reinforces the impact of contractionary monetary policy on income, consumption, and investment, and leads to a more vigorous decline in economic activity than would occur in a closed economy.

To summarize, the impact of monetary policy on income is magnified by its exchange rate effects. We cannot definitely say, however, what the effects are on the current account balance since the income effect of monetary policy on the current account is the opposite of the exchange rate effect. The current account balance could rise or fall with either expansionary or contractionary policy. However, a key idea in the chain of causation is the notion of expenditure switching. This refers to switching back and forth between domestic and foreign goods which, in this case, is in response to a change in the exchange rate. Expenditure switching magnifies the effects of monetary policy. Note, however, that this result depends on exchange rate flexibility. In an economy with a fixed exchange rate, changes in the money supply will not cause expenditure switching.

The effect of fiscal policy on the current account is more certain. As shown, expansionary fiscal policy increases interest rates, causing an exchange rate appreciation. Appreciation switches expenditures toward foreign goods since it makes them relatively cheaper, thereby increasing imports and reducing the current account balance. The expansionary fiscal policy leads to more imports, both from the rise in income and from exchange rate appreciation, which creates a feedback effect on domestic income. The shift in expenditures toward foreign goods offsets some of the increase in the demand for domestic goods and diminishes the impact of expansionary fiscal policy. Similarly, the exchange rate effect of contractionary fiscal policy switches expenditures away from foreign goods and toward domestic goods, diluting some of the contractionary effects of the policy.

The major short-run to medium-run effects of fiscal and monetary policy are summarized in Table 11.2. The differences between the two begin with their interest rate effects and carry over to exchange rates and current accounts. In the case of monetary policy, changes in the exchange rate and income have offsetting effects on the current account, but with fiscal policy, changes in the exchange rate and income have reinforcing effects on the current account. As a result, the

| TABLE 11.2 | The Main Effects of Fiscal and Monetary Policies | | | | |
|---|---|---|---|---|---|
| | **Monetary Policy** | | **Fiscal Policy** | | |
| | Contractionary | Expansionary | Contractionary | Expansionary |
| **Y and C** | ⇓ | ⇑ | ⇓ | ⇑ |
| **i** | ⇑ | ⇓ | ⇓ | ⇑ |
| **R\*** | ⇓ | ⇑ | ⇑ | ⇓ |
| **CA** | ⇑ or ⇓ | ⇑ or ⇓ | ⇑ | ⇓ |

Monetary and fiscal policies have different impacts on interest rates, exchange rates, and the current account. Monetary policy's impact on exchange rates and income partially offset each other's impact on the current account.

\*A fall in R is an appreciation, while a rise is a depreciation.

impact of monetary policy on the current account is indeterminate, while the impact of fiscal policy is definite.

## The Long Run

How permanent are the effects? Economists more or less agree that in the long run, the level of output in an economy tends to fluctuate around a level that is consistent with full employment. Note that full employment does not mean that everyone has a job. No matter how strong the economy is, there is always some unemployment from the entry of new workers into the labor force, or the return of workers after an absence from work. While searching for their jobs, both groups are considered unemployed. In addition, there are always a number of people who have voluntarily quit their jobs to look for better ones, and people who lack the job skills they need to find a job.

In a strong economy, unemployment may temporarily fall to a very low level, but this tends to resolve itself. Initially, employers may grab whoever is available to fill their job vacancies, but as the pool of the unemployed dries up, they raise wages and look for ways to get by with fewer workers. Ultimately, this returns the unemployment rate to its normal level. Conversely, in a weak economy, unemployed workers put downward pressure on wages, which ultimately resolves the problem of unemployment, since employers hire more workers when wages fall. The most controversial issue is how long these changes might take. Some observers believe they happen fast, while others are skeptical, particularly about the speed at which wages fall. In one sense, the debate over the amount of time it takes an economy to reach its long-run equilibrium at full employment is a debate over the meaning of the long run. Is it two years, five years, or ten?

In Chapter 10, we saw that in the long run, purchasing power parity determines exchange rates. Fiscal and monetary policy may cause deviations from purchasing power parity, but in the long run, a combination of exchange rate changes and changes in domestic prices will restore balance to the purchasing power of national currencies.

The current account must also tend toward balance in the long run. No nation can run deficits forever, nor can it run surpluses forever. Since deficits are equivalent to foreign borrowing and surpluses equivalent to foreign lending, there are limits in each direction. The limits are not well defined, however, and countries such as the United States have been able to run enormous deficits for long periods, while countries such as Japan have run surpluses.

 # Macro Policies for Current Account Imbalances

Fiscal, monetary, and exchange rate policies are essential tools for eliminating a current account imbalance. While any persistent imbalance can be portrayed as a problem, in practice the most dangerous imbalances are large current account deficits. Persistently large surpluses may bother a country's trading partners, but they rarely threaten a national economy the way that large deficits sometimes do. The macro policies for addressing a current account deficit are a combination of fiscal, monetary, and exchange rate policies, often collectively called **expenditure switching policies** and **expenditure reducing policies**. Both are essential.

We have already seen one type of expenditure switching policy when we talked about the exchange rate effects of fiscal and monetary policy. In general, an appropriate expenditure switching policy for eliminating a current account deficit is one that turns domestic expenditures away from foreign-produced goods and toward domestic goods. As discussed, an exchange rate depreciation is one way to do this. Recall that a depreciation raises the domestic price of foreign goods. An alternative type of expenditure switching policy is a trade barrier such as a temporary tariff to make foreign goods more expensive.

Expenditure reducing policies are simply contractionary fiscal or monetary policies that cut the overall level of demand in the economy. In most cases, they are necessary along with expenditure switching policies because without overall expenditure reductions, inflation ensues as home country domestic expenditures switch away from foreign producers and toward domestic producers. For this reason, expenditure switching policies must be accompanied by reductions in overall expenditures.

While expenditure shifts without expenditure reductions are inflationary, expenditure reductions without shifts toward domestic producers are recessionary. This makes the expenditure shifts necessary, since a shift in spending toward domestic producers offsets the decline in demand and leaves the economy with the same level of output but without a current account deficit. Given the need to use both types of policies simultaneously, expenditure reductions and expenditure shifts are not viewed as alternatives to each other but rather as two equally essential components of a macroeconomic policy designed to address a current account deficit.

## The Adjustment Process

The term **adjustment process** is used to describe changes in the trade deficit that are caused by a change in the exchange rate. We have already seen that a depreciation raises the real price of foreign goods, making domestic substitutes relatively more attractive. While this is an accurate description of the general pattern, depreciations often have delayed effects. In the United States, for example, there is a median average lag of about nine and a half months between a change in the exchange rate and an impact on U.S. exports. The median average lag for import responses is slightly less, but still more than seven months. Consequently, it is a mistake to think that exchange rate changes will affect trade flows overnight.

In addition to the lag effects, the first impact of a depreciation on the current account may be a further deterioration rather than an improvement. This deterioration is known as the **J-curve**, and is shown in Figure 11.6.

After a depreciation, there is usually a short period of no noticeable impact on the flow of goods and services. When imports and exports begin to respond, the immediate change is an increase in the value of imports, pushing the current account balance deeper into deficit. The size of the deterioration and the length of time before there is an actual improvement varies from country to country. In the United States, a depreciation results in an improvement in the trade balance

### FIGURE 11.6 ● The J-Curve

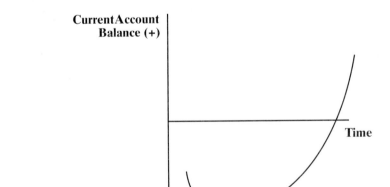

Initially, depreciations often cause the current account balance to deteriorate further. With time, substitutions of domestic goods for foreign goods leads to an improvement in the balance.

only after a year or more. The reasons are straightforward. A depreciation makes foreign goods immediately more expensive, but it takes time for households and businesses to find substitutes. In the short run they lack information, and it takes time to find new suppliers in the domestic economy, to check the quality of their products, and to negotiate contracts. Meanwhile, until the alternative suppliers are found, foreign goods continue to be used even though they cost more.

## CASE STUDY

# The Adjustment Process in the United States

From the third quarter of 1980 to mid-1987, the U.S. trade deficit widened from 0.48 percent of GDP to over 3.5 percent of GDP. In 1985, the Plaza Accord among the G5 (France, Germany, Japan, the United States, and the United Kingdom) created a cooperative effort to bring down the value of the dollar. The dollar began to fall in early 1985 with the introduction of a new team of officials at the Treasury Department; from January 1985, to January 1987, it fell from an index of 152.83 to 101.13, or nearly 34 percent.

While the dollar was falling, the trade deficit continued to widen. This was unsettling to a number of politicians, economists, and others, who had predicted a significant decline in the U.S. trade deficit as a result of the depreciation. Some journalists and politicians began to argue that the trade deficit would never respond to a change in the value of the dollar, that foreign trade barriers would make it impossible for the United States to substantially expand exports, and that our own open market would ensure a growing volume of imports regardless of the dollar's value.

Nevertheless, after a little more than two years, the trade balance began to respond to the fall in the dollar. Figure 11.7 shows the change in the value of the dollar and the trade balance from 1980 to 1988. Note that the time scale for the trade deficit is offset two years to reflect the long lag in the adjustment process. This offset pairs the exchange rate with the value of the trade balance two years later. It is apparent that there is a striking similarity in their movement, once adjustment is made for the two-year lag.

The question economists have debated since this episode is why it took so long for trade balances to respond to the decline in the value of the dollar. There are several possible explanations. One is that the prior increase in the dollar's value had padded the profit margins of foreign producers. From 1980 to 1985, their exports to the United States rose in terms of their domestic prices even though they sold in the United States for the same dollar prices. Consequently, when the dollar began to fall, foreign producers were initially able to keep dollar prices constant and absorb the decline in its value by realizing lower profits in terms of their domestic currency.

Another possible reason for the long lag is that there were still impacts from earlier appreciations working through the system. A third reason for the long lag

**FIGURE 11.7** ● **The U.S. Trade Balance and the Exchange Rate, 1980–1988**

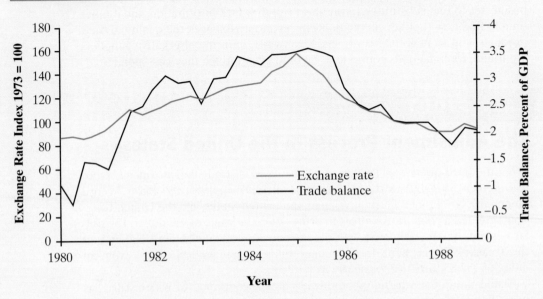

In the 1980s, changes in the U.S. trade balance mirrored changes in the exchange rate with a lag of two years.

*Source:* Business Cycles Indicators, BCI DataManager, Gary F. Langer; *Economic Report of the President.*

is that exports began to increase from a much lower base than imports, and needed to increase much more rapidly in percentage terms in order for the trade deficit to begin to close.

## Macroeconomic Policy Coordination in Developed Countries

Coordination of macroeconomic policies is a frequent issue for the leading industrial economies. The annual meetings of the G8 (Canada, France, Germany, Italy, Japan, Russia, United Kingdom, and the United States) are often an extended discussion of shared macroeconomic issues, international economic relations, and relations with developing countries. When global economic imbalances arise, for example large U.S. current account deficits and growing Chinese surpluses, macroeconomic coordination becomes a topic of discussion. Actual coordination of macroeconomic policies is fairly rare, but not impossible. For example, the previous case study describes the agreement between five leading industrial economies to arrange a coordinated depreciation of the dollar, known as the Plaza Accord.

There are a variety of objectives sought with macroeconomic policy coordination, from achieving a desirable level of world economic growth to avoiding a global economic crisis. The purpose of coordination is to avoid imposing a disproportionate burden on one of the major world economies. Unequal burdens result when one country pays a large share of the costs of economic adjustment. As an illustration, suppose that the world economy is in a period of relatively slow growth. Not every economy will experience this, but it may be the case that enough economies are in recession or growing slowly so that the average rate of growth throughout the world is too slow to raise living standards or to pull people out of poverty. If a group of industrial economies decide jointly to expand their economies with fiscal and monetary policies, then growth in their incomes raises incomes around the world as their demand for imports stimulates production in other countries. If all economies expand simultaneously, then no one country is burdened by a sudden excess of imports over exports—their exports grow along with their imports and with the growth in demand in their trading partner's economies. For a variety of reasons, such as existing large budget deficits, or fear of the inflationary effects of expansionary policy, some countries may choose not to expand their economies. In this case, the effectiveness of the expanding economies as engines of growth across the globe is reduced. Furthermore, the country or countries using expansionary policy will probably experience a deterioration in their current accounts since their trading partners are not growing at the same rate. If expansionary fiscal policies cause interest rates to rise, then a further deterioration in the current account is likely due to the appreciation of the currency as a result of the inflow of foreign capital.

The way out of this dilemma is for a coordinated effort at macroeconomic expansion. There are both political and economic problems with coordination, however. The political problem is that there is no international organization capable of arranging a multilateral agreement among nations, nor is one possible without a significant sacrifice of national sovereignty. The economic problem is that there is rarely a period in which nations find it in their own interest to pursue the same policies as their trading partners. Countries enter and leave slow growth periods and recessions at different points in time and it is rare that one policy is suitable for everyone. Coordination remains a topic of discussion among the world's leading economies, however, since it is always in one or more countries' interest.

## Summary

- Households supply all the factors of production (land, labor, and capital) that businesses need to produce the nation's output. In return, they receive all the income, or factor payments, which are payments for the use of their land (rents), labor (wages and salaries), and capital (dividends, profits, and interest). The income received by households is equivalent to the value of the output produced by businesses.

- Businesses use financial institutions to borrow household savings. They use the savings to invest. Businesses also produce the nation's output. Governments spend on goods and services, using tax revenues from the income flow going to households. The foreign sector supplies imports and demands exports.

- Fiscal policies are government tax and expenditure policies. Monetary policies are for interest rates and the money supply. Expansionary policies raise GDP and national income, while contractionary policies do the opposite.

- Fiscal and monetary policies work by changing total demand. Fiscal policies either change government spending on goods and services, which is a direct change in demand, or they change household income through a change in taxes. This is an indirect change in total demand. Monetary policies work through a change in interest rates, which changes investment.

- The multiplier explains how an initial change in spending (demand) is multiplied through the economy into a larger change in spending.

- Fiscal policy is considered more difficult to implement than monetary policy because it requires Congress to pass legislation that must be signed by the president. Monetary policy is easier because it is conducted by the Federal Reserve.

- Both fiscal and monetary policy influence exchange rates and the current account balance. In each case, the effect is through a change in interest rates brought on by the fiscal or monetary policy. Neither policy is likely to have long-run effects on income.

- In order to reduce or eliminate a current account deficit, countries must practice expenditure switching and expenditure reducing policies. Expenditure switching policies turn demand away from the foreign sector and toward domestic production. Expenditure reducing policies cut back on the overall level of demand.

- The J-curve describes how a policy designed to eliminate a current account deficit may initially make it larger before reducing it. The lag between a depreciation and a reduction in the size of a current account deficit is one to two years in the United States.

## Vocabulary

adjustment process

aggregate demand (AD)

aggregate supply (AS)

contractionary fiscal policy

contractionary monetary policy

expansionary fiscal policy

expansionary monetary policy

expenditure reducing policy

expenditure switching

expenditure switching policy

fiscal policy

intermediate inputs

J-curve

monetary policy

multiplier effect

open market operations

# Study Questions

1. Using aggregate demand and aggregate supply, graph the effects on the price level and GDP of each of the following.

   a. A cut in income taxes

   b. An increase in military spending

   c. A drop in export demand by foreign purchasers

   d. An increase in imports

   e. A decline in business investment spending

2. Explain the concepts of fiscal and monetary policy. Who conducts them and how do they work their way through the economy?

3. What are some of the problems in trying to use fiscal and monetary policies? Why can't economists and politicians make precise predictions about the effects of a policy change on income and output?

4. Describe the mechanism that leads from a change in fiscal policy to changes in interest rates, the exchange rate, and the current account balance. Do the same for monetary policy.

5. Some countries have fixed exchange rate systems instead of flexible systems. How does the exchange rate system limit their ability to use monetary policy?

6. The United States is currently running a large current account deficit. If Congress and the White House decide to enact policies to reduce or eliminate the deficit, what actions should they take? Describe the set of policy options available to them.

7. Describe the larger economic effects of the policies in the previous question. That is, what would be the effects on income, consumption, employment, interest rates, and real exchange rates of policies designed to reduce or eliminate a current account deficit.

8. During the second half of the 1980s, the United States depreciated the dollar in hopes that it would reduce the current account deficit. After a year, the deficit was actually larger and newspaper editorialists were writing columns claiming that there is no link between the exchange rate and the current account. Explain why they got this wrong.

9. Suppose the United States, Japan, and many other places around the world go into recession, but growth remains strong in Europe. Why would macro-economic policy coordination help, who should coordinate, and what are some of the obstacles to coordination?

## International Financial Crises

### Introduction: The Challenge to Financial Integration

Increasing international economic integration has created opportunities for growth and development, but it has also made it easier for crises to spread from one country to another. In 1992, currency speculation against the British pound and a few other European currencies nearly caused the collapse of monetary arrangements in Europe, and inflicted high costs on a number of countries in the European Union. In late 1994, speculation against the Mexican peso led to its collapse, and spread a "Tequila effect" through South America. In 1997, several East Asian economies were thrown into steep recession by a wave of sudden capital outflows, and in 1998, Russia's default on its international debt sent shockwaves as far as Latin America.

Financial crises are not new, but the way they develop and spread continues to evolve with the world's financial and economic integration. In some instances, they are an almost predictable result of inconsistent or unrealistic macroeconomic policies, but in other cases, countries with fundamentally sound macroeconomic policies have been pulled into a currency or **financial crisis** for no obvious reason. This makes financial crises difficult to predict, but it also increases the value of a set of early warning indicators. The **contagion effects** of a crisis do not conform to a single pattern and they reinforce the idea that there are different types of crises with their own rules of behavior.

Financial crises have brought down governments, ruined economies, and destroyed individual lives. Their enormous costs have created an intense amount of research into causes, prevention, and treatment. This chapter reviews some of the basic themes of this literature. It begins by describing two types of crises that have been observed during the last 20 years. Then it turns to a discussion of several key issues, including the steps a country might take to avoid or minimize a crisis, and the policy choices it faces once one begins.

Much of the research in this area is designed to formulate sound principles for international financial reforms. The many reform proposals that have appeared in recent years are usually referred to as proposals for reform of the **international financial architecture**. Often their contents revolve around a set of proposed changes to the International Monetary Fund (IMF) and other multilateral institutions with a role in international financial relations. The final section of this chapter looks at two of the main questions in that discussion: Does the world economy need a **lender of last resort**, and what type of conditions should a lender impose on the recipients of its assistance?

##  Definition of a Financial Crisis

Financial crises have a variety of potential characteristics, but the term usually refers to an exchange rate crisis, a banking crisis, or some combination of the two. Exchange rates and banking systems are not the only components, but in recent crises they have been points of vulnerability, partly because they are often the variables through which the contagion effects of a crisis are spread from one country to another, and between the financial system and the rest of the economy.

A **banking crisis** occurs when the banking system becomes unable to perform its normal lending functions, and some or all of a nation's banks are threatened with insolvency. A bank, like any other business, is considered insolvent or bankrupt if its assets are less than its liabilities, or, to put it another way, if its net worth is negative.

The primary role of banks is **intermediation** between savers and borrowers. Simply put, banks and other financial institutions pool the savings of households and make them available to businesses that want to invest. If the businesses that borrow from a bank go under, then the bank cannot repay its depositors, and the bank may go out of business as well. **Disintermediation** occurs when banks are unable to act as intermediaries between savers and investors—it is a serious problem with negative economic consequences.

When a bank fails, everyone that deposited money in the bank loses all or a portion of their money, unless the country has a functioning deposit insurance system. The loss of savings causes households to cut back on consumption and spreads the recessionary effect wider and wider through the economy. This is one way a crisis gets transmitted within an economy. Unaffected banks may stop making new loans as they take a cautious approach, new investment slows or stops altogether, layoffs occur, and the economy falls deeper into the vicious circle of a downward spiraling recession.

An **exchange rate crisis** is caused by a sudden and unexpected collapse in the value of a nation's currency. This can happen under a fixed, flexible, or intermediate type of exchange rate. If the exchange rate system is some form of a fixed exchange rate, the crisis entails a loss of international reserves, followed by a sudden devaluation once it appears that the reserves will run out. Devaluation is intended to accumulate reserves or to conserve existing reserves by making the rate of exchange less favorable to people trying to convert their domestic currency to dollars or another international reserve currency. If a country uses some form of flexible exchange rate, an exchange rate crisis involves a rapid and uncontrolled depreciation of the currency. While no type of exchange rate system guarantees safety, current research favors the idea that countries that adopt a pegged exchange rate may be more vulnerable to an exchange rate crisis.

Similar to the effects of a banking crisis, an exchange rate crisis often results in a steep recession. There are several channels through which recessionary effects may be transmitted, but one of the most common channels is the banking system. For example, prior to the Asian crisis of 1997 and 1998, banks borrowed dollars in international capital markets. When their home country currencies collapsed, the dollar value of their debt increased enormously. Consequently, many banks failed, disintermediation took place, new investment stopped, and the economies slid into a deep recession.

#  Two Types of International Financial Crises

It is safe to say that every international financial crisis is unique in its origins and in the way it causes domestic economies to unravel. Nevertheless, it is helpful to consider two separate origins of crises. The first type is a result of definite and identifiable macroeconomic imbalances. For this type, the moment of crisis onset is difficult to predict, but unless the underlying conditions are corrected, it is almost certain to occur eventually. The second type is brought on by volatile flows of financial capital that move into and out of a country quickly. A sudden change in investor expectations may be a triggering factor, and underlying fragility in the banking and financial sector may be present. Still, this type of crisis can be puzzling because in several recent cases, it has affected countries with particularly strong international positions and stable macroeconomic policies.

## Crises Caused by Macroeconomic Imbalances

During the last few decades, a number of crises have been triggered by severe macroeconomic imbalances, usually accompanied by an exchange rate system that intensifies the country's vulnerability. The best example of this type of crisis is the Third World debt crisis of the 1980s. The most common type of macroeconomic imbalances are overly expansionary fiscal policies that create large government budget deficits, often financed by a high growth rate of the money supply. When expansionary fiscal and monetary policies are joined with a crawling peg exchange rate system, the various components of economic policy often interact in ways that lead to a crisis followed by a severe recession.

Taking the budget deficit first, in Chapter 11 it was argued that expansionary monetary and fiscal policies are intended to stimulate the economy and raise the level of output. After World War II, most developing countries experimented with industrial development strategies that used the government and its budget as a primary engine of economic development. That is, in addition to using the government budget as a way to stimulate demand and cure a recession, many developing countries made the government budget one of the primary tools of long-run, industrial development. Governments operated steel mills, airlines, phone companies, and many of the other pieces of a modern industrial economy. Furthermore, they were (and are) involved in providing social services, income support, and subsidies for groups of businesses and consumers.

In many cases, the potential problems of government spending are compounded by inefficient and unreliable tax systems, which means that government tax revenues may be insufficient for its expenditure programs. Under these circumstances, governments have resorted to selling bonds to finance expenditures. This has its own problems, however, as capital markets in many low- and middle-income countries are underdeveloped, and few people have the resources or the willingness to take on the risk of buying a bond (lending money to the government), particularly if they have safer places to put their savings. Consequently, sometimes governments require the central bank to buy the bonds. In effect, then, the money supply increases by the amount borrowed, leading to inflationary pressures.

At this point, there is a deficit that is being financed by borrowed money, which has an inflationary impact through two possible channels. One is the increase in purchasing power from the added government spending and the other is the expansion of the money supply from the purchase of the bonds by the central bank. With either a fixed or crawling peg exchange rate system, higher inflation can have serious repercussions on the real value of the exchange rate. Recall from Chapter 10 on exchange rates, that if the nominal rate adjusts more slowly than the inflation differential between the home country and its trading partners, the real rate becomes overvalued.

In particular, capital flight starts if people begin to suspect that the exchange rate is overvalued and that a correction is likely in the near future. The economic incentive is to sell domestic assets and convert them to foreign exchange, which people believe will be more valuable in the future after the domestic currency falls in value. As more people try to convert their domestic currency to a foreign one, the government begins to run out of international reserves and, in order to conserve its remaining supply, it devalues the currency.

With some exchange rate systems—a crawling peg, for example—it is sometimes difficult to arrange a smooth devaluation. Devaluations can undermine faith in the government's ability to manage the economy and they inevitably lead to political complications. Crawling pegs are designed to minimize currency fluctuations while keeping the real exchange rate relatively constant. Sudden devaluations can be politically difficult since they erode the purchasing power of the domestic currency and hurt some groups that depend on foreign goods. A delay in devaluing the currency, however, sometimes causes a deeper crisis when it eventually takes place, since a small devaluation may no longer be viewed as sufficient, and speculators may continue to expect further declines in the currency. In other words, a small devaluation may be insufficient to stem the outflow of capital since it does not change people's view of the currency, and can be viewed as a signal that policymakers do not understand the depth of the crisis. If exchange rate policies are not seen as credible, a crisis will continue to deepen.

In addition to large budget deficits, inflationary pressures, and an overvalued currency, the most common indicator of a potential crisis is a large and growing current account deficit. All of these symptoms share the same prescription for their treatment: austerity. In economic policy terms, **austerity** is composed of the same expenditure reduction and expenditure switching policies that were described in Chapter 11 as appropriate for curing a current account deficit. Recall that expenditure reducing policies address the budget deficits through tax increases and expenditure cuts, while the expenditure switching policies address the current account deficit and the run on reserves through devaluation and, if necessary, temporary measures against imports. This policy is relatively straightforward, but painful, as it easily results in a recession.

## Crises Caused by Volatile Capital Flows

Not all crises are the result of unsustainable expansions in fiscal and monetary policies. National economies are increasingly vulnerable to the effects of technology that instantaneously shift vast sums of financial capital from one market to another. Together with the high degree of financial openness achieved in the last few decades, the contagion effects of crisis can spill across oceans and national borders. The best example of this kind of crisis is the one that hit some of the economies of East Asia in 1997 and 1998. While several economies had underlying weaknesses in their financial sectors, others such as Singapore, Hong Kong, and Taiwan were adversely affected even without the same weaknesses.

The fundamental cause of this type of crisis is that financial capital is highly volatile and technological advances have reinforced this volatility. The discovery of large emerging markets and the drive by financial investors in high-income countries to diversify their portfolios caused hundreds of billions of dollars to be invested throughout the world. Most savings in a nation never leaves, but an increasingly large volume of savings has entered international capital markets, where it moves relatively freely in response to interest rates, exchange rate expectations, and economic activity. This creates opportunities as well as problems. For example, one of the main problems in financial markets is that portfolio managers look at the actions of each other for information about the direction of the market. This creates a kind of herd behavior that takes over at critical moments and intensifies a small problem, turning it into a major crisis as large numbers of investors simultaneously lose confidence in a country. What begins as a trickle of funds out of a country can be interpreted as bad news about underlying conditions and lead to an avalanche of capital flight. When that happens, international reserves disappear, exchange rates tumble, and the financial sector can suddenly look very weak.

A weak financial sector can also intensify the problems. A case in point is a banking sector that borrows internationally and lends locally. If the funds obtained in the international market are short term and are used to fund long-term loans such as real estate, problems arise when the international loans must be repaid. As long as international lenders are willing to roll over the debt and extend new loans, everything moves along smoothly. As soon as the lenders believe that there is a problem with a borrowing bank, they refuse to roll over the debt, creating a liquidity problem if the bank's assets are tied up in real estate loans. In the short run, real estate is relatively illiquid and cannot be used to make a payment. When a number of banks are confronted with similar problems, their attempt to unload real estate depresses prices even further and undermines the solvency of the banking system since every bank with real estate investments is suddenly holding a portfolio of declining value.

This type of scenario is particularly troubling because it can go either way. That is, it may resolve itself without a crisis if international lenders are willing to extend additional credit while banks sell their long-term assets. Alternatively, if international investors expect a crisis and as a result are unwilling to give domestic banks the time they need to convert illiquid assets into liquid ones, then the crisis becomes a self-fulfilling prophecy. The belief in a crisis causes lenders to refuse to rollover the banking debts, and the banks, which are illiquid, become insolvent.

Several parts of this scenario are unsettling to economists and policymakers. First, there are multiple possible outcomes, or in economic terms, there are *multiple equilibria*, depending on the responses of international lenders. Second, one of the possible outcomes is a crisis, but the crisis is self-fulfilling. It is not predetermined, nor is it necessary. Third, the crisis affects banks that are fundamentally sound, but that have mismatches between the maturities of their debts and their assets. In other words, they are illiquid, but not insolvent.

These factors seem to imply that it should be possible to avoid this type of crisis. In part, it requires that banks pay closer attention to the maturity match between their debts and assets. In some cases, this requires a higher degree of supervision and regulation on the part of the banking authorities. For their part, international lenders must be more informed about the activities of their borrowers. This requires greater information flows, the use of standard accounting practices, and overall greater transparency in domestic and international financial systems. And, as a final point, once a crisis occurs, international agencies such as the IMF that are called in to make emergency loans need to be able to distinguish between insolvency and illiquidity. The distinction is more complex than it seems, but it is crucial, since the appropriate response will vary depending on the short- to medium-run prospects of the borrowing country.

## CASE STUDY

# The Mexican Peso Crisis of 1994 and 1995

The collapse of the Mexican peso and the ensuing crisis that began at the end of 1994 has elements of a crisis caused by macroeconomic imbalances and one caused by volatile capital flows and financial sector weakness. On the one hand, there were definite signs of macroeconomic imbalances, including an overvalued real exchange rate and a large current account deficit. On the other hand, the Mexican government operated a relatively austere fiscal policy, and not counting foreign interest payments on its debt, the government budget was in surplus, not deficit. Similarly, inflation came down during the early 1990s and reached 7 percent overall in 1994, down from 22.7 percent in 1991. Between 1990 and 1993, Mexico experienced capital inflows of $91 billion, or an average of about $23 billion per year, the most of any developing country. The capital inflow was in the form of private portfolio investments ($61 billion), direct investments ($16.6 billion), and bank loans ($13.4 billion).

The administration of President Salinas (1988–1994) actively encouraged large inflows of foreign capital as a way to maintain investment rates far above the level that domestic Mexican savings could support. Recall from Chapter 9 the macroeconomic identity that private savings plus the government budget balance must equal domestic investment plus the current account balance:

$$S_p + (T - G) = I + CA.$$

In 1994, Mexican savings of around 14 percent of GDP could not support investment of more than 20 percent of GDP unless there was an inflow of savings from the rest of the world. Mexico ran large current account deficits, equal to 5 percent of GDP in 1991 and 6.5 percent in 1992 and 1993. The enormous inflow of foreign goods and services permitted more investment by providing capital goods that Mexico could not make itself, and by satisfying consumption through foreign goods and thereby allowing domestic factories to produce investment goods. This was the strategy of the Salinas government, and it seemed to be working. The North American Free Trade Agreement (NAFTA) between Canada, the United States, and Mexico took effect on January 1, 1994, and throughout the year, U.S.-Mexican trade expanded by almost one-fourth (23.7 percent). NAFTA inspired confidence in Mexico's institutional stability and guaranteed access to the wealthy U.S. market for any goods made in Mexico.

During 1994, the world capital market began to shift toward a more conservative, risk-averse stance. In February 1994, interest rate movements in the United States and exchange rate movements around the world led to large losses for a number of banks and other investors. Portfolio managers began to reassess their investments and to look for ways to reduce their exposure to risk. Political events also prompted investors to reassess their financial positions in Mexico. First, on January 1, 1994, at the moment NAFTA began implementation, subsistence farmers in the poorest Mexican state of Chiapas revolted against the federal government. Second, in March, the leading presidential candidate was assassinated while campaigning for office. While the lead-up to the signing and implementation of NAFTA had encouraged the view that Mexico was a safe, stable, and modernizing country, these events shocked investors into taking a closer look. Financial prudence seemed to call for reducing the level of exposure to Mexico, and many investors inside and outside the country sold their peso-denominated assets.

Less than three weeks after taking office in early December 1994, President Ernesto Zedillo finally agreed that the peso was overvalued and announced a 15 percent devaluation. Ordinarily this measure might have been interpreted as a cautious and responsible move to address the problem of an overvalued currency. Unfortunately, currency traders and economists had expected a 20 to 30 percent devaluation, and President Zedillo's actions made it appear as if his administration did not understand the severity of the crisis. Consequently, rather than the calming effect he had hoped for, Zedillo's announcement of a 15 percent devaluation sent currency and financial markets into even greater turmoil. More capital fled the country, dollar reserves shrank, and the credibility of Mexico's exchange rate policies came under severe questioning.

Two days after announcing the devaluation, the government of Mexico announced that it would move to a floating exchange rate system. Although this was the right move, the damage had been done, and both foreign and domestic capital continued to leave the country. By March 1995, the peso had fallen to more than seven per dollar, a loss of more than 50 percent of its value compared to early December 1994 (see Figure 12.1).

Zedillo addressed the short-run problems of the crisis by seeking financial support from the NAFTA partners and the IMF. Relief came in late January 1995, in the form of a line of credit and loans. Within weeks, currency markets were calmed down and the rate of capital flight slowed as the holders of peso-denominated assets began to relax in the knowledge that the government would be able to convert any amount of pesos to dollars. The peso regained some of its lost value, and by the end of April 1995, it was trading at six per dollar.

The medium- and long-run problems were addressed with a package of austerity measures that cut government spending, increased taxes (T up, G down), and reduced consumption. The large current account deficit at the end of 1994 increased the vulnerability of Mexico's financial system to capital flight and had

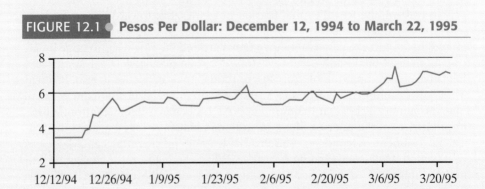

**FIGURE 12.1** ● **Pesos Per Dollar: December 12, 1994 to March 22, 1995**

The peso lost over half its value between December 20, 1994 and March 9, 1995.

*Source:* Federal Reserve Board, http://www.federalreserve.gov/releases/H10/hist/.

been partly responsible for the draining of dollar reserves. Expenditure reduction policies were therefore an appropriate step taken to address the crisis, because tax increases and government expenditure cuts would help reduce the current account deficit. Electricity prices and gasoline prices were raised (both were supplied through government-owned enterprises), and credit was restricted through steep increases in interest rates and new limits on bank lending. These measures reduced consumption and boosted saving, provided a greater pool of domestic funds for investment purposes, and decreased the country's dependence on foreign capital inflows. The fall in consumption and government expenditures brought a recession, however; Mexico's GDP fell by 6.2 percent in 1995, and more than 500,000 people lost their jobs.

Analysts are still digesting the lessons of the peso collapse, but a few things stand out. For Mexico, the policy of relying on large foreign inflows of world savings through a large financial account surplus (current account deficit) proved to be unstable. Too much of the foreign capital was invested in short-term portfolios rather than longer-term direct investment. This distribution is not inherently unsafe, but once the peso became overvalued, both foreign and domestic investors feared that a surprise devaluation would destroy the value of their assets, and they began to convert large numbers of pesos into dollars. In addition, the peso crisis demonstrated how hard it is to arrange an orderly devaluation in a crawling peg system. Mexico's 15 percent devaluation was a cautious step in the right direction, but instead of calming market fears, it undermined credibility in the exchange rate system. Since then, many economists have argued in favor of completely fixed exchange rates with no discretionary monetary policy, or a floating exchange rate such as Mexico has followed since the crisis.

 ## Domestic Issues in Crisis Avoidance

Not all crises are avoidable. Nevertheless, there are steps countries can take to try to minimize the likelihood of crises and the damage they cause when they happen. In addition to the need to maintain credible and sustainable fiscal and monetary policies, governments must engage in active supervision and regulation of the financial system and provide timely information about key economic variables such as the central bank's holding of international reserves.

In these areas, the design of effective policies is relatively straightforward, but in other areas, there is a wide array of expert opinion, and consensus remains elusive. Should countries bail out their banks if they fail, and what type of penalties should they impose if they do? Should they try to limit foreign capital inflows and outflows? Which type of exchange rate system is most stable? It is possible that in some areas, there is no single optimal policy for avoiding a crisis and countries have a variety of equally viable options. In those cases, it is also possible that there are choices that are better for some countries, but not others, depending on the conditions inside the country.

## Moral Hazard and Financial Sector Regulation

When a country's financial sector becomes dysfunctional, problems spread to the rest of the economy. Credit dries up, investment disappears, households worry about their lost savings, consumption falls, and the economy falls into recession. Hence, there is a big incentive to keep the financial sector operational, even if it means that governments have to spend revenues in order to keep the sector in working order.

This creates a dilemma for policymakers, since the knowledge that you will be bailed out if you fail usually leads people, including bankers, to take greater risks than are prudent. That is, if the costs of failure are removed, the incentive for the decision makers inside financial institutions to take normal precautions and to behave responsibly are also removed.

In economic terms, this is the problem of **moral hazard**. Moral hazards occur when there is an incentive to withold essential information or to act in a manner that creates personal benefits at the expense of the common goal. For example, when selling a used car, the seller has a financial incentive not to divulge negative information about the car, and people seeking life insurance have an incentive not to divulge negative information about their health. Similarly, in the financial sector, banks and other institutions have an incentive to make riskier investments that pay a higher return if they know they will be bailed out.

Moral hazard problems are particularly acute when the government of a country uses the credit system to make loans for specific economic development goals, or even worse, for satisfying important political constituencies. For example, a government may determine that the development of a particular steel plant is in the interests of the country, or that the economic enterprises of politically well-connected elites should be supported with easy credit. Many governments use state-owned banks to make such loans, or they provide financial incentives or threats to private banks to get them to make the loans. The result in either case is that the loans may not meet market criteria for lending, and there are either implicit or explicit guarantees to the banking sector that they will be bailed out if something bad happens. In the Asian crisis of 1997 and 1998, these types of loans gave rise to the term **crony capitalism**. In several countries, a significant reform component is to remove politics from lending considerations.

The problem of moral hazard is inescapable if there is a general policy of protecting the financial system from collapse. In effect, no matter how it is administered, the policy of protecting the sector is a form of insurance, and all insurance systems have moral hazard elements. There is no way to eliminate the problem of moral hazard completely, but it can be minimized through various actions.

To this end, bank regulators from the industrial countries met in Basel, Switzerland, under the auspices of the Bank for International Settlements (BIS) to agree on a set of operational standards, including supervision and regulation, for internationally active banks (see Chapter 10 for a brief description of BIS). This led to the 1989 **Basel Capital Accord**, which was eventually adopted by more than 100 countries. In 2001, a New Basel Capital Accord was issued, updating the previous standards.

The New Basel Capital Accord is a set of recommended best practices that emphasize the three areas of capital requirements, supervisory review, and information disclosure. **Capital requirements** help to reduce moral hazard elements in the banking sector by requiring the owners of banking institutions to invest a percentage of their own capital in their bank so that bank losses are personal losses to shareholders and other bank owners, as well as losses to the bank's depositors. Bank **supervisory review** and regulations are designed to act as oversight to assist with risk management and to provide standards for daily business practices. Inadequate bank supervision and the inexperience of local bank managers actively involved in international financial markets were key weaknesses in the economies of East Asia and were partly responsible for the onset of the crisis in 1997. Hence, supervision and oversight of financial markets, including banks, has become a central component of recommendations for avoiding crises. The final area, **information disclosure**, is designed to encourage market discipline by requiring banks to disclose all the relevant information that lenders, investors, and depositors need to understand the full scope of a particular bank's operations.

All three of the elements are key to reducing the problem of moral hazard, and to ensuring that if a crisis strikes, the financial system will return to economic health as soon as possible. The Accord is a set of recommended practices without an enforcement component; therefore, countries are under no obligation to follow them. In addition, in many developing countries, the technical expertise required to implement some of the more complex supervisory functions may be in short supply. In other words, there is no guarantee that a country that adopts the standards set forth in the Accord is actually adhering to them, or even that it is capable of implementing them.

## Exchange Rate Policy

Through the 1970s and 1980s, many countries adopted a crawling peg exchange rate system, often as part of an anti-inflation strategy. Recall from Chapter 10 that the "pegged" part of a crawling peg involves fixing the exchange rate to a major world currency such as the dollar or the euro, or to a basket of currencies that include the home country's major trading partners. The "crawling" part of the exchange rate involves regular—often daily—devaluations of a fixed amount. Theoretically, a crawling peg allows a country to increase or decrease the value of its currency periodically, but since pegs are usually intended to stabilize the real exchange rate in a country with higher inflation than its trading partners, most crawling pegs are set to a constant rate of devaluation rather than revaluation. That is, if domestic inflation is higher than foreign inflation, nominal devaluation keeps the real exchange rate constant. Given the definition of the real rate as

$$R_r = R_n \, (P^* / P),$$

then if the change in P (domestic prices) is greater than the change in P* (foreign prices), the nominal rate, $R_n$, must rise (devalue) in order to keep the real rate constant. Maintaining the peg requires the monetary authority to exercise discipline in the creation of new money, and is anti-inflationary in that sense. In addition, many countries tried to reinforce the anti-inflation tendency of the crawling peg by intentionally devaluing at a slower pace than the difference between home and foreign inflation. This created real appreciation in the exchange rate, and was intended to act as a brake on domestic inflation. Foreign goods steadily became cheaper in real terms, limiting the price increases that domestic producers were able to impose. The use of the exchange rate in this manner had mixed success in helping to control inflation, but in a number of cases it led to severe overvaluation of the real exchange rate and increased the country's vulnerability to a crisis.

Another way in which a crawling peg exchange rate system increases a country's vulnerability to crisis is that it is politically difficult to find a way to exit from the system if it becomes overvalued. When a government announces a change in the system, it runs the risk of losing its credibility. Both domestic and foreign economic agents accommodate the existing system, and a sudden large devaluation leads to economic losses and a loss of confidence in the country's policymakers. Consequently, it is common for countries to delay addressing the problem of overvaluation, and when the correction comes, it has to be larger. The end of Mexico's crawling peg in 1994 is a good example.

Currently, many economists believe that countries should adopt either a "hard peg," which is akin to a fixed exchange rate, or they should use a floating exchange rate, which is managed by the central bank. Hard pegs include fixed rates, dollarization, and the use of currency boards. In any of its possible forms, the monetary authority must exercise discipline in the creation of new money. Credibility of the peg is of the utmost importance to its survival, and it is only assured if there is a tight control on the money supply. Floating exchange rates allow more flexibility in the conduct of monetary policy, but they raise the specter of a lack of monetary discipline and a return to deficit financing through the printing of money. They also lead to greater volatility as the domestic currency swings up and down. For these reasons, many countries are reluctant to adopt flexible exchange rates.

## Capital Controls

Many economists hold that the free movement of capital is a desirable objective because it allows investors to send their financial capital wherever the return is highest, which raises world welfare by putting financial capital to its most valuable use. At the same time, capital mobility allows countries to invest more than is possible with their domestic savings alone, which again raises world welfare when there are valuable investment projects and insufficient savings to realize them. Others, however, claim that the benefits of complete capital mobility are based on theory, but are never fully demonstrated empirically. In addition, capital mobility generates very high costs in the form of macroeconomic crises, and these costs must be offset against any economic gain.

This issue is unsettled, and although economists agree that trade in goods and services raises a country's welfare, there is less agreement about the benefits of free capital movements. The sources of the disagreement cover not only the potential benefits of capital inflows versus the potential costs of sudden capital outflows, but also include debates over the actual ability of **capital controls** to prevent capital movements, whether controls on the movement of capital can stop a crisis once it begins, and whether it is better to limit inflows, outflows, or both.

Through much of the twentieth century, countries guarded against the problems of capital mobility by restricting its movement. This seems to imply that countries are able to prevent capital from crossing their borders, but what may have been true in 1970 is much more doubtful today. The growth of emerging stock markets and the implementation of technology to facilitate capital transfers have created both the incentive and the means for investors to send their capital abroad.

Ordinarily, capital flow restrictions are imposed by limiting transactions that are part of the financial account of the balance of payments. (See Chapter 9 for a discussion of the components of the balance of payments.) Capital movements to support transactions on the current account are usually permitted since they are necessary for trade. Consequently, one of the primary ways in which firms can get around capital account restrictions is to overinvoice imports. This allows them to make payments abroad that are larger than necessary for the purchase of imports. Alternatively, they can underinvoice exports, so that the reported payments received are smaller than the actual payments, and the difference can be invested outside the country without reporting to authorities. While these techniques are common, and perhaps fraudulent, outright corruption in the form of bribes is also a possibility for getting money out of the country.

Whether these types of practices make controls on capital outflows completely ineffective is open to debate, but they clearly reduce the effectiveness of capital controls. For this reason, as a general rule, restrictions on inflows are seen as more workable than restrictions on outflows. Inflow restrictions can take a variety of forms, but they share the common goal of trying to reduce the inflow of volatile, short-run capital, which may add to the stock of liquid assets ready to flee the country.

Restrictions on capital inflows cannot stop a crisis once it begins, however. Consequently, there is an ongoing debate over the utility of imposing restrictions on capital outflows once a crisis starts. Since many crises include a speculative attack against the home country currency, some argue that a temporary limitation on capital outflows could help to stop a crisis by artificially reducing the demand for foreign exchange. In theory, this would prop up the value of the domestic currency and eliminate expectations of a large decline in its value.

In the midst of the Asian crisis, Malaysia followed this policy in spite of a number of warnings that it would undermine investor confidence in Malaysian policies, cut them off from international capital markets, and do long-term damage to the economy. None of the dire predictions materialized and Malaysia recovered from the crisis at about the same speed as Korea, which went the other way and eliminated some of its controls on capital flows. The fact that two different policies led to more or less similar outcomes is a measure of how much we do not know.

## CASE STUDY

# Chilean Taxes on Capital Inflows

One of the most discussed examples of a successful implementation of restrictions on capital inflows is Chile. Chile is not the only country to adopt this type of policy, but it has often been cited as a case in which controls on inflows successfully insulated the economy from the contagion effects of crises elsewhere in the world.

Chile experienced two periods of restrictions on capital inflows, the first lasting from 1978 through 1982, and the second from June 1991 through September 1998. In both periods policy was oriented toward limiting short-term, portfolio investment, without causing a loss in longer-term, foreign direct investment. Regulations varied between the two periods, but the main component was a rule forcing portfolio investors to deposit reserves into a noninterest-bearing account at the central bank. In 1991, foreign investors were required to deposit 20 percent of the value of their investment in the noninterest-bearing account, and in 1992, the reserve requirement was raised to 30 percent. In 1998, in the wake of the Asian crisis, as the government sought to protect the economy from a sudden loss of foreign investment due to the contagion effects of the crisis, they dropped the requirement to 10 percent, and then eliminated it altogether.

The forgone interest on the reserves is one way to measure the cost of investing in short-term, Chilean portfolios. For most of the period, 1991 to 1998, the reserves were required to remain on deposit for one year. Consequently, the implicit cost of investing declined as the maturity of the investment increased. For example, investments with a maturity of 180 days faced an implicit tax of 2 to 5 percent over the period from 1991 to 1998, while investments with a maturity of three years were taxed at a rate between .5 and 1 percent.

Chile's objective of limiting short-term capital flows was relatively successful by most measures. The percentage of inflows with a maturity of one year or less declined steeply, while the overall inflow of foreign capital seems not to have suffered at all. Nevertheless, several other countries, Mexico and Argentina, for example, also experienced a lengthening of the term structure of foreign-held assets without resorting to capital controls.

In the longer run, the capital controls imposed in Chile seem to have isolated the country from some external shocks, such as the 1994–1995 Mexican crisis, but not from others. One hypothesis is that Chile's policies are adequate for a moderate disturbance in the international economy, but provide little or no protection against the turbulence of a major crisis, such as the one that occurred in Asia in 1997 and 1998.

*Source:* Edwards, Sebastian, "How Effective Are Capital Controls," *The Journal of Economic Perspectives.* Fall 1999.

# Domestic Policies for Crisis Management

It is relatively easy to prescribe a cure for financial crises that result from inconsistent macroeconomic policies. For example, if a crisis is triggered by a collapsing currency, which, in turn is the result of large government budget deficits financed by money expansion with a fixed or crawling peg exchange rate, then the prescription is relatively straightforward in economic terms: Cut the deficit, raise interest rates to help defend the currency, and, perhaps, let the currency float. In other words, the solution to a fiscal crisis brought on by macroeconomic imbalances is to correct the imbalances.

The problem is that the economic austerity of budget cuts and higher interest rates may not be politically feasible. In addition, several economic problems are often present. Tax systems in many countries are unenforceable, meaning that tax increases may not generate more revenue. The adoption of a floating exchange rate system may undermine the credibility of the government's commitment to fighting inflation, since financial sector interests often fear that it will remove the last bit of restraint over money creation and lead to hyperinflation. Governments may not be able to cut expenditures easily, since government employees may be unionized with multiyear contracts, or provide essential domestic services, or other elements of the budget may support powerful domestic interests.

The case of a crisis brought on by sudden capital flight in the context of relatively stable and credible macroeconomic policies is even more difficult to resolve. Given that this type of crisis may have multiple equilibria outcomes, depending on the direction taken by expectations, there is a powerful argument for addressing the problem of a collapsing currency through interest rates hikes, sales of reserves, and other actions that might help convince investors that the currency is strong. On the other hand, high interest rates and other actions to defend the currency are likely to intensify bankruptcies and other contractionary forces that develop during a crisis. Hence, defending a currency may push a small downturn into a full-blown depression.

In crises caused by either macroeconomic imbalances or sudden capital flows, there is a strong desire to avoid a recession. In the first type, however, both fiscal and monetary policies are usually overextended and the crisis is partly a result of policies that are unsustainable and overly expansionary. In effect, this forecloses fiscal and monetary policies as tools to avoid the recessionary aspects of the crisis and the only way out is usually through some sort of recession.

In the second case, however, fiscal and monetary imbalances may not be part of the initial problem, so that the use of fiscal and monetary policies is not entirely ruled out. However, the dilemma faced by governments in this position is that expansionary policies include a reduction in interest rates, which can cause a further depreciation in the domestic currency. If domestic firms have debts that are denominated in dollars or another foreign currency, a depreciation implies a sudden increase in the size of their debts and spreads additional bankruptcies through the economy.

In effect, this implies that fiscal and monetary policies are limited if there is an international component to the crisis. It also creates a stark set of choices for handling the crisis. Either defend the currency with high interest rates and spread the recessionary effects of the crisis, or defend the domestic economy against the recessionary effects of a crisis and intensify the problems of a collapsing currency. Much of the debate over the policies recommended by the IMF during the Asian Crisis of 1997 and 1998 (raise interest rates to try to stabilize the collapsing currencies) turned on precisely this point. Clearly, if there was an easy, nonrecessionary, way to end a crisis, policymakers would use it.

## CASE STUDY

# The Asian Crisis of 1997 and 1998

The Asian financial crisis began in Thailand in July 1997. From there, it spread to a number of other countries, including Malaysia, the Philippines, Indonesia, and South Korea. The outward symptoms of the crisis were fairly similar across countries: currency speculation and steep depreciations, capital flight, and financial and industrial sector bankruptcies. It is tempting to interpret these symptoms as signs of the region's weaknesses, but ironically, the causes are at least in part due to the region's great strengths.

## Current Account Deficits and Financial Account Surpluses

The most severely affected countries all had large trade deficits. Table 12.1 shows current account deficits in 1996, the year before the crisis. For the five countries in the top panel, deficits averaged 5.2 percent of GDP in 1996. In Thailand, where the crisis began, the current account deficit was nearly 8 percent of GDP. The three countries in the bottom panel of Table 12.1 all felt reverberations from the crisis in spite of their small deficits (Hong Kong) or large surpluses (Singapore and Taiwan).

Large current account deficits necessarily imply large financial account surpluses, and the countries listed in the top half of Table 12.1 all experienced large capital inflows. Foreign investors were more than willing to send their capital to East Asia as the region had averaged about 5 percent growth per year in real GDP for the last 30 years, and there was no reason to believe that would change anytime soon. Furthermore, slow growth in Japan and Europe during much of the 1990s caused many international investors to scour the globe looking for higher returns, and the stable and dynamic economies of southeast Asia stood out prominently. Low inflation, small budget deficits or consistent government surpluses, and the high rates of economic growth made them highly desirable places to invest and to loan funds.

**TABLE 12.1 • Current Account Balances and Currency Depreciations**

|  | Current Account Balance, 1996, Percent of GDP | Currency Depreciation in Dollars, 7/1/97 to 12/31/97 |
|---|---|---|
| **Countries with large deficits** | | |
| Indonesia | −3.4 | −44.4 |
| Malaysia | −4.9 | −35.0 |
| Philippines | −4.7 | −33.9 |
| South Korea | −4.9 | −47.7 |
| Thailand | −7.9 | −48.7 |
| **Countries with small deficits or surpluses** | | |
| Hong Kong | −1.3 | 0.0 |
| Singapore | +15.7 | −15.0 |
| Taiwan | +4.0 | −14.8 |

Large current account deficits led to large depreciations. Nevertheless, some countries were hit with depreciations even when they had large surpluses.

*Source*: Goldstein, Morris, *The Asian Financial Crisis: Causes, Cures, and Systemic Implications*, Washington, DC: Institute for International Economics, June 1998.

## Exchange Rate Policies

Exchange rate policies in the region usually involved pegging to the dollar, so that as the dollar appreciated in the mid-1990s, it caused many exchange rates to appreciate along with it, resulting in a number of significant currency misalignments. The pegged exchange rates became harder and harder to sustain, partly because they made it more difficult for the pegged countries to export. According to some observers, this problem was exacerbated by China's devaluation of its fixed exchange rate in 1994 and the significant depreciation of the Japanese yen throughout the period of dollar appreciation. The movements in these two currencies made the exports of Thailand and several others less competitive.

## Financial Sector Problems

The downturn in export revenues exposed several other weaknesses, including those in regulatory systems, corporate structures, and financial systems. Many countries in East Asia rely on corporate structures built around family ties and personal networks. This can have significant advantages for small and medium-size enterprises, but as firms grow, the lack of disclosure and transparency make it difficult for outside lenders to assess the microeconomic risks of lending. In addition, the lack of hard data and information make it difficult to implement the kinds of regulatory controls that all economies need for stability, especially in the financial sector. For example, many banks experienced the kind of mismatches between the maturities of their assets and liabilities that is described as a serious vulnerability earlier in the chapter. These firms took out short-term loans in international capital markets and used the money to finance real estate developments with long and risky payoffs.

Another major weakness in the financial sector stemmed from the politicization of the financial systems of many countries. Banks in many nations were forced to make loans to politically well-connected firms and favored industries. These loans were often at below-market interest rates and, in many cases, were a component of the industrial support policies implemented by the national government. In Indonesia, for example, industries that were favored with cheap bank credit were owned by family members of President Suharto and individuals with personal political connections.

As long as growth remained robust, the weaknesses in the economy stemming from a lack of regulatory oversight and financial sector misallocations were invisible. In a growing economy, there are always new opportunities to make profits, and banks with bad loans on their books made up for it by charging their other customers higher interest rates. As exchange rate misalignments accumulated, however, export revenues slipped, and current account deficits widened. The IMF and a number of private economists warned of the building instabilities and advised Thailand (and others) to reduce their trade deficits. The IMF is obliged to keep quiet about its warnings to a country in order to avoid setting off a crisis, and so most people were unaware of its concerns.

## Crisis and Contagion

The event that triggers a crisis is often relatively unimportant. For example, some analysts blame the decline in Thailand's export earnings that stemmed from the downturn in prices for computer chips. In any case, the huge trade imbalance and the disappointment on export revenues undermined investor confidence in Thailand's ability to keep its exchange rate pegged to the dollar. People began to expect a devaluation and did not want to be holding the Thai baht when it came. Furthermore, many of the loans to the Thai financial sector were short-term loans obtained in international capital markets, and required repayment in dollars. This raised the cost of a devaluation because Thai financial institutions earned revenue in baht, but owed a fixed amount of dollars. Any change in investor confidence could undermine the entire economy.

How the Thai crisis spread internationally is one of the less certain components of the overall crisis. One hypothesis is that Thailand served as a "wake up call" for investors to examine more closely their holdings in other countries. Another hypothesis is that the Thai devaluation made exports from several neighboring countries less competitive and forced them to engage in competitive devaluations. Regardless, there was a contagion element in the Thai crisis and it soon spread to countries as far away as Brazil and Russia.

Some of the consequences of the Asian crisis are easily visible in Table 12.2, which shows the growth rate of real GDP in 1998 and 1999. With the exceptions of Singapore and Taiwan, every country affected by the crisis experienced a recession in 1998. Given their large trade surpluses and their ample international reserves, Singapore and Taiwan were able to focus on their domestic economies rather than trying to defend their currencies, thereby avoiding recessions. By the second quarter of 1999, every country had returned to positive growth.

The rapid recoveries in Table 12.2 caught most analysts by surprise, yet the flexibility and fundamental soundness of macroeconomic policies throughout East Asia facilitated swift recovery. Still, Table 12.2 does not tell the whole story since poverty rose significantly throughout the region and will take many years to return to its pre-crisis level. In addition, without fundamental financial sector reform, the chances of a repeat episode remain fairly high.

## Crisis Management

Three issues in crisis management remain unresolved after this episode. First, did the IMF make a mistake in advising the borrowing countries to defend their currencies with interest rate hikes? Second, were there moral hazard elements present, perhaps as a result of the Mexican bailout in 1995? Third, are capital controls helpful as a temporary measure to stem a crisis?

### TABLE 12.2 ● Real GDP Growth

|  | 1998 | 1999 |
|---|---|---|
| **Real GDP growth in countries with large current account deficits** | | |
| Indonesia | −13.2 | +0.2 |
| Malaysia | −7.5 | +5.4 |
| Philippines | −0.6 | +3.3 |
| South Korea | −6.7 | +10.7 |
| Thailand | −10.2 | +4.2 |
| **Real GDP growth in countries with small current account deficits, or surpluses** | | |
| Hong Kong | −5.1 | +3.0 |
| Singapore | +0.4 | +5.4 |
| Taiwan | +4.6 | +5.7 |

Many countries experienced deep depressions in 1998, but by the second quarter of 1999, virtually every crisis country had returned to positive growth.

*Source*: Asian Development Bank, "Economic and Statistics, Regional Data," available at http://www.adb.org/Statistics/regdata.asp [February 24, 2001].

The first issue is a specific instance of the dilemma referred to earlier. Should countries try to protect their domestic economies or must they defend their currencies? For countries with large trade surpluses and ample international reserves, defense of the domestic economy through lower interest rates seems feasible. The real question applies to the five countries with large current account deficits. Some critics of the IMF blame it for turning a financial panic in those countries into full blown depressions by counseling them to raise their interest rates. The critics charge that the IMF treated the crisis as if it were the same as the Latin American debt crisis of the 1980s, in which governments had large budget deficits and high rates of inflation. In East Asia, governments were running surpluses or small deficits, so there was no need to temporarily contract the economy with interest rate increases. Defenders of the IMF argue that interest rate hikes were necessary as a means to stop the slide in currency values. The temporary, but harmful effects on economic activity caused by interest rate hikes were much smaller than the harm that would have been done if the currency depreciations were not stopped.

A second issue relates to the moral hazard of bailing out a bank or corporation. If banks know they will be bailed out if they make bad lending decisions, then they have less reason to exercise prudence and caution, and more reason to take greater risks that offer higher returns. Some critics allege that the IMF loans to Mexico set a precedent that taught lenders their mistakes would be covered by loans from the IMF, and consequently, the Asian crisis became more likely. The counterargument is that "bailouts" are not really bailouts in the full sense of the word because they do not protect investors from losses. Most investors in East Asia saw sizable reductions in the values of their portfolios, so they have plenty of reason to exercise caution when lending.

A final unresolved issue is the problem of capital flight. Can it be stopped, at least in the short term, with controls on capital outflows? Malaysia thought so, and implemented capital controls that appeared to have some success in removing pressures on the Malaysian ringgit to depreciate. Malaysia acted in spite of a number of warnings that it would lose its access to international capital markets, yet its recovery from the crisis was as rapid as in any of the other affected countries On the other hand, Korea went the other way and removed some of the controls it had on capital flows, and it also recovered quickly. Did capital controls make a difference? As with the previous two issues, an answer awaits further research.

##  Reform of the International Financial Architecture

The frequency of international financial crises coupled with their high costs has generated a great deal of interest in finding the right policies for avoiding a crisis and for handling one if it begins. Taken as a whole, the discussion of new international policies for crisis avoidance and management is referred to as reforming the international financial architecture. In particular, a lot of attention is focused on the role of the IMF and the conditions it imposes as part of its loan packages.

A number of ideas for reforming the international financial architecture have been advanced in recent years. Private think tanks such as the Council on Foreign Relations, the Overseas Development Council, and the Centre for Economic Policy and Research in London have each published proposals, as have multilateral agencies such as the United Nations Conference on Trade and Development (UNCTAD) and government appointed bodies such as the International Financial Institutions Advisory Commission of the U.S. Congress.

The proposals for international financial reform express a variety of conflicting viewpoints, but they agree that two issues are at the center of the discussion. The first is the role of an international lender of last resort, and the rules governing its lending practices. A second issue is the type of conditions such a lender might impose on its borrowers. In effect, both these issues are questions about the role of the IMF and its current practices.

## A Lender of Last Resort

Recall from Chapter 2 that a lender of last resort is a source of loanable funds after all commercial sources of lending have disappeared. In a national economy, this role is usually filled by the central bank. In the international economy, it is filled by the IMF, often with the support of high-income, industrial economies such as Canada, France, Germany, Japan, and others. As a lender of last resort, the IMF is often asked to intervene when countries reach a crisis point in their finances and cannot make payment on their international loans, or cannot convert their domestic currency into dollars or another foreign currency due to an insufficiency of international reserves.

Not everyone agrees that there should be a lender of last resort, and some observers worry about the moral hazard problems of such lending. This is particularly problematic as a crisis begins to develop and some firms are on the verge of collapse. The moral hazard problem can intensify since managers of failing firms have a large incentive to gamble on high-stakes, high-risk, ventures, that, if they pay off, will cover all their losses. In response, those who favor maintaining the IMF in its current role as an international lender of last resort stress the importance of financial sector regulation, including the elements outlined in the Basel Capital Accord. If the owners of financial firms risk a substantial loss in the event of financial meltdown, they are less likely to take on excessive risk.

Three other issues that are central to the discussion of the IMF's role as a lender of last resort are the question of how high an interest rate it should charge when it makes loans, the length of the payback period, and the size of its loans. Taking the interest rate issue first, the traditional prescription for a lender of last resort is that it lends at a relatively high, or penalty level, interest rate. Most IMF loans are at a rate of interest that is equivalent to a weighted average of short-term government borrowing rates in leading industrial economies, plus a slight surcharge. In practice, these tend to be fairly low-interest loans and definitely not a penalty rate.

Some fear that this encourages countries to borrow, while others argue that the interest rate does not affect the incentive to borrow in a crisis. It may affect the length of time countries take to pay back the loan, however, and in this sense, a higher rate may encourage countries to get out from under their IMF debt. Some proponents of higher interest rates on IMF loans also believe it is necessary to shorten the loan period, while others point out that higher interest rates will encourage countries to pay off their loans faster. The length of IMF loans varies by type of loan, with some as short as one year, and others as long as ten years, depending on whether the loan is for immediate relief or long-term structural adjustment.

The final issue about the rules for IMF loans is the size of the loan. Countries pay a subscription, called a *quota*, to join the IMF. The size of the quota mainly depends on the size of the economy and its strength. The quota determines how much a country can borrow in a "normal" crisis, as well as how many votes the country has in setting IMF policy. Generally, countries can borrow up to 300 percent of their quota, but in extraordinary circumstances such as the Mexican peso crisis, the Asian crisis, or other crises with the potential to spread, the limits on country borrowing are determined more or less by the needs at the time, as well as the amounts available directly from other governments.

Although some countries have borrowed enormous sums that are well above 300 percent of their quota, the limits on borrowing have not kept up with the growth in the size of national economies. Some argue that borrowing limits should be greatly expanded, while others propose differentiating between crises that have a high probability of spreading and those that are contained within a single country. In many cases, it may not be possible to determine the difference, but systemwide crises definitely have the potential to impose greater costs. Hence, there is a clear rationale for intervening with larger sums if they will stop a crisis faster.

## Conditionality

The second set of issues surrounding the role of a lender of last resort such as the IMF is the issue of conditionality. IMF **conditionality** refers to the changes in economic policy that borrowing nations are required to make in order to receive IMF loans. Conditionality typically covers monetary and fiscal policies, exchange rate policies, and structural policies affecting the financial sector, international trade, and public enterprises. The IMF makes its loans in **tranches**, or installments on the total loan, with each additional tranche of the loan dependent on the completion of a set of reform targets. For example, a loan recipient may have to promise to develop a plan for privatization in order to receive the first tranche, have a workable plan in order to receive the second tranche, begin implementation for the third tranche, and so on.

Often these types of reforms generate significant opposition since they seem to override national sovereignty and generally impose contractionary macroeconomic policies. Some economists argue that conditionality requirements intensify the recessionary tendencies of a crisis, although there is a debate whether countries recover faster with IMF assistance than without it. Until the early 1990s, the IMF focused its efforts on economic policy reforms in a way that more or less ignored their social consequences. Public outcry against the effects of conditionality on the vulnerable members of societies forced a closer look at the social impacts of policies, and the IMF has tried to make adjustments. Even so, there are still widespread complaints that IMF conditionality is too punitive and too contractionary, and a few countries in crisis have refused IMF assistance. The most notable example is Malaysia during the Asian crisis of 1997 and 1998. Apparently, refusing to work with the IMF did not hurt, since it recovered from the crisis as fast as any other country.

Prior to the 1970s, IMF conditionality focused primarily on correcting the immediate source of the problem that led to a crisis, and avoided involvement with underlying economic issues, such as trade policy and privatization. This was criticized as too short-sighted, and it was agreed that the Fund should involve itself beyond short-run economic policy. New loan programs were developed to provide money and technical assistance to countries that needed help in restructuring their economies. This shift involved the IMF in far more than crisis resolution, as it took on an active role in assisting in privatization, the design of social policies, trade policy reform, agricultural policies, environmental policies, and a number of other areas.

By the late 1990s, there was growing recognition that "mission creep" had become a problem and that the Fund had taken on responsibilities that were better left to the World Bank, regional development banks, or some other agency designed to address the long-run issues of economic development. Several of the proposals for reforming the international financial architecture envision a reduced role for the IMF in this area.

In addition to dealing with the problem of mission creep, several of the reform proposals argue in favor of a set of requirements that countries must pass before they will be allowed to borrow. These proposals favor a prequalifying examination of country policies as a means to avoid crises in the first place. Proponents argue that in order to receive assistance, countries should first demonstrate that they meet a number of requirements such as open financial markets, adequate bank capital, transparent reporting of financial sector data, and others. Those who propose this type of prequalification for IMF assistance argue that it will force countries to adopt fundamentally sound financial sector policies that will minimize the probability of a crisis.

Critics of the prequalification idea point out that prequalification will not avoid crises since they do not deter speculative attacks on a country's currency. They may even promote instability if they induce complacency about a country that prequalifies. In addition, it would be impossible for the IMF to ignore the needs of member countries that fail to prequalify, and this would lead to other, less open ways to handle a crisis. Finally, the IMF has already implemented a pre-qualification procedure for one type of loan, but to date no country has tried to prequalify since it might be interpreted as a signal to the rest of the world that problems are developing.

Two additional issues are worth mentioning as part of the reforms of the inter-national financial architecture. First is the issue of a set of standards for transparency and data reporting in the financial sector. The purpose of greater transparency is to make a country's financial standing clearer to potential lenders. The issue of transparency and data reporting is moving forward with the Basel Capital Accord and the IMF's own development of standards for data reporting, called the **data dissemination standards**.

The second issue is the need to find ways to coordinate private sector involvement in times of crisis. Less progress has been made on this issue than on the data dissemination issue, and it continues to be a serious concern. When a country reaches a crisis, the insistence by numerous private creditors that they be paid first can make it more difficult to resolve a crisis. Hence, proposals have been put forward for **standstills**, in which the IMF officially recognizes the need for a country in crisis to stop interest and principal repayments on its debt temporarily. This would also impose a burden on the country's creditors, and reduce the moral hazard element in their lending practices.

Conflict between private creditors over who deserves first repayment has often been an obstacle to resolving a crisis. Consequently, many analysts see the need for **collective action clauses** in all international bond loans. A collective action clause would require each lender to agree to a collective mediation between all lenders and the debtor in the event of a crisis. This avoids the problem that an uncooperative creditor may be able to block a solution that is agreed to by a majority of the lenders. It would also promote a quicker resolution to a crisis caused by a borrowing country's insolvency.

## Reform Urgency

In the aftermath of the Asian crisis, a wide number of reform proposals were circulated among academics, government officials, and the staff of multilateral organizations. The crisis drove home the points that international financial flows had grown dramatically over the previous decades, that many developing countries are now active participants in world finance, and that contagion effects can instantaneously spread a crisis from one country or region to another. Reform, beginning with a reconsideration of the role of the IMF, was at the top of everyone's agenda.

A decade later, not much has happened and reform of the world's financial system is much less urgent. While many individual countries have redoubled their efforts to provide better oversight of financial institutions and more transparency to their data systems, reaching an international consensus on issues such as IMF conditionality has proven difficult. At the same time, a relatively stable period of world economic growth since 2001 has diverted attention to other issues, such as security, terrorism, energy, and climate change. Small steps have been taken; for example, the decision in 2006 to increase the IMF quotas, and votes, for Mexico, Turkey, South Korea, and China, in order to reflect more accurately the relative size of their economies. This is a very marginal change in the system, however, and without the urgency of a major crisis it may be all that is possible.

It is pure speculation to guess the source of the next crisis and the next likely trigger of reform talk. It might be a bumpy correction to the large imbalances in world savings and investment caused by U.S. deficits and large surpluses in China and Japan. Or it might be the growth and expansion of exotic new financial services and instruments, such as hedge funds and derivatives, that are often beyond the reach of national regulators and for which there is little historical experience for regulators to draw on. Or it might be something relatively trivial, such as was the case in 1997 when a decline in Thailand's export competitiveness set off the Asian crisis. More likely than not, the next crisis could be triggered by something that no one is thinking about today and that lies beyond our ability to anticipate.

International financial relations are a constantly moving target. The financial sector is constantly innovating, new countries continue to enter world markets for savings and investment, and the task for national regulators is constantly changing as financial instruments and relations change. As international financial linkages change, international systems embodied in the IMF, the Bank for International Settlements, and other entities must respond. Consequently, it is very unlikely that the world will ever reach a point where international financial arrangements are set and no longer require further change.

## Summary

- International financial crises are generally characterized by financial disintermediation in the crisis country, a collapsing currency value, and a steep recession.

- One type of crisis is caused by severe macroeconomic imbalances, such as large budget deficits, hyperinflation, overvalued real exchange rates, and large current account deficits.

- Another type of crisis is the result of a speculative attack on a currency that prompts large outflows of financial capital and a run on the country's international reserves. This type of crisis can be self-fulfilling because economic agents that believe an attack on the currency is imminent will abandon the currency, which is equivalent to an attack on the currency.

- The Mexican peso crisis of 1994–1995 had elements of both types of crises, as did the Asian crisis of 1997–1998. However, several countries in East Asia were subjected to speculative attacks on their currencies even though their underlying macroeconomic fundamentals were very strong.

- Responding to a crisis is complicated by the problem of moral hazard. If the government or the IMF bail out the banks and other firms hit by crisis, it may encourage future risky behavior. The problem of moral hazard is particularly acute if the government has directed credit to specific enterprises for political or developmental purposes because directed credit either explicitly or implicitly includes a government guarantee.

- The Basel Capital Accord and the New Basel Capital Accord are a set of recommendations for internationally active banks and financial enterprises. They cover the supervision and regulation of enterprises, minimum capital requirements, and standards for information disclosure.

- Many economists believe that a crawling peg exchange rate makes countries more vulnerable to a crisis because they become overvalued more easily and there is no smooth way to abandon them when a crisis begins to brew.

- Capital controls on capital outflows are generally viewed as ineffective in the long run, although there is some debate about their temporary efficacy in times of crisis. Capital controls on the inflow of short-term financial capital have more supporters, but there is no consensus on their efficacy in avoiding crisis. Some research shows that they can help a country avoid a small crisis, but are less effective at avoiding a large crisis.

- The optimal response to a crisis depends on its causes. If it is caused by macroeconomic imbalances, then changes in macroeconomic policies are essential. If it is caused by sudden, unexplained capital flight, then the optimal response is less certain. Some economists, particularly those at the IMF, argue that stabilizing the currency with high interest rates will lead to a quicker recovery, even though this intensifies the contractionary elements of the crisis in the short run. Others favor expansionary fiscal and monetary policies to minimize the short-run effects of a recession.

- Reform of the international financial architecture includes a revaluation of the role of the IMF and other international agencies. A few favor abolishing the IMF as a lender of last resort, while most favor keeping it but reconsidering some of its policies. In particular, questions have been raised about the interest rates it charges on its loans, the length of the loan period, and the limits on the size of loans.

- The most contentious element of IMF lending policies is conditionality. In particular, there is widespread agreement that the IMF tries to support too many different types of reform and that it should refocus on its core competencies, which include financial sector reform, balance of payments assistance, and exchange rate policies. There is some discussion about whether it should require countries to prequalify before they are eligible for its lending programs.

- Other issues in the international financial reform discussion include standards for data dissemination and policies to create greater involvement of private creditors in working out the solutions to international financial crises when they occur.

# Vocabulary

austerity

banking crisis

Basel Capital Accord

capital controls

capital requirements

collective action clauses

conditionality

contagion effects

crony capitalism

data dissemination standards

disintermediation

exchange rate crisis

financial crisis

information disclosure

intermediation

international financial architecture

lender of last resort

moral hazard

standstills

supervisory review

tranches

# Study Questions

1. What is an international financial crisis, and what are the two main causes?

2. In the text, the point is made that the expectation of a crisis from volatile capital flows is sometimes a self-fulfilling crisis. How can a crisis develop as the self-fulfillment of the expectation of a crisis?

3. What are three things countries can do to minimize the probability of being hit by a severe international financial crisis?

4. Why are crises associated with severe recessions? Specifically, what happens during an international financial crisis to create a recession in the affected country or countries?

5. What type of exchange rate is associated with a higher probability of experiencing a crisis? Why?

6. In a crisis not caused by macroeconomic imbalances, economists are uncertain whether a country should try to guard against recession or try to defend its currency. Why are these mutually exclusive, and what are the pros and cons of each alternative?

7. Explain the moral hazard problems inherent in responding to a crisis.

8. Some people argue that U.S. loans to Mexico in 1995 led to the Asian crisis. Explain the logic of this argument.

9. Some countries impose capital controls as a means of preventing a crisis. Evaluate the pros and cons of this policy.

10. How has the role of the IMF come under scrutiny in the recent discussion of reforms in the international financial architecture?

# Regional Issues in the Global Economy

# 13

# Economic Integration in North America

## Introduction: Expanding Economic Relations

After several years of negotiations, the North American Free Trade Agreement (NAFTA) came into effect on January 1, 1994. In Mexico NAFTA was greeted by a group of armed rebels that seized several towns in the southern state of Chiapas. In the United States NAFTA was ratified by Congress after a close and bitter debate in which both the proponents and opponents had exaggerated—and misread—the likely impacts. The debate in Canada was not nearly as dramatic, however. Canadians had just gone through a similarly divisive struggle over the **Canadian-U.S. Trade Agreement (CUSTA)** that began in 1989, and Canadian commerce with Mexico is relatively small.

For many U.S. economists, it seemed odd that a relatively dry and straightforward agreement would turn into one of the most contentious economic issues of the 1990s. After all, U.S. barriers to Mexican imports were already low; if Mexico decided to lower its barriers to U.S. and Canadian products, what could be so controversial? Plenty, as it turns out. This chapter explores the initial controversy surrounding NAFTA.

## Economic and Demographic Characteristics of North America

Before we turn to the history and controversy over NAFTA, it is useful to have an idea of the size of the combined North American market. Table 13.1 shows population and GNP comparisons measured in two different ways. By any measure, the combined market is enormous. With more than 430 million residents in 2005, the NAFTA region continues to be one of the largest trade agreement areas in the world today.

International income comparisons are more complicated than population comparisons. The third column in the table is a typical way to make compar-

| Country | Population (Millions) | GDP (US$, Billions) | GDP per Capita (US$) | GDP per Capita (US$, PPP*) |
|---|---|---|---|---|
| **TABLE 13.1** • **Population and GDP for Canada, Mexico, and the United States, 2005** | | | | |
| Canada | 32.3 | 1,115 | 34,520 | 32,886 |
| Mexico | 103.1 | 768 | 7,449 | 10,209 |
| United States | 296.5 | 12,455 | 42,006 | 42,006 |
| **Total** | 431.9 | 14,338 | 33,197 | 33,734 |

The NAFTA market is over 430 million people and $14.3 trillion.

*Purchasing power parity.

*Source*: The World Bank, *World Development Indicators*, online version, 2006. http://publications.worldbank.org/WDI.

isons. Mexican and Canadian incomes are converted to U.S. dollars using the average exchange rate over the entire year. This method shows that the average Canadian income is about 82 percent of the United States' average income, and the average Mexican income is around 18 percent. The first problem with this comparison is that regardless of changes in either nation's output, fluctuations in the exchange rate can lead to dramatically different values for Mexican or Canadian GDP when measured in U.S. dollars. A second problem is that real prices vary across countries. Haircuts, restaurant meals, and maid services, for instance, cost far less in real terms in Mexico than in the United States. These goods and services are not traded, and Mexico's relative abundance of labor makes production of labor-intensive goods cheaper. As a consequence, the average annual income in Mexico of $7,449 buys more goods and services than a similar income in the United States.

The fourth column shows income comparisons in **purchasing power parity** terms. Purchasing power parity comparisons use an artificial exhange rate to make adjustments for differences in prices. It can be interpreted as the U.S. dollar value of the real quantity of goods and services that a typical Mexican income buys. In other words, GDP per person in Mexico is enough income to buy goods and services that would cost $10,209 in the United States. However, if a Mexican citizen took that amount of pesos, converted them to dollars, and brought them to the United States, they would only get $7,449 worth of goods and services.

Measurements of GDP per capita at market exchange rates and at purchasing power parity prices both convey important information. Market exchange rates tell what a nation can buy externally (outside the nation), while purchasing power parity prices tell what it can buy internally (inside the nation). As an exporter, one would be more interested in the former, but as someone interested in knowing how Mexico's living standards compare to those of the United States, one would want to know the latter.

# North American Free Trade Agreement Members

Map by Dr. Chris Lukinbeal
Revised by Harry D. Johnson

Lambert Equal Area Projection

| TABLE 13.2 • Trade within the NAFTA Region, 2005 (Millions of U.S. dollars) | | | | |
|---|---|---|---|---|
| | Exports by: | | | |
| Imports by: | Canada | Mexico | United States | World |
| Canada | — | 4,234 | 244,964 | 385,388 |
| Mexico | 6,169 | — | 140,893 | 221,819 |
| United States | 315,863 | 186,972 | — | 1,991,975 |
| World | 427,952 | 214,233 | 1,275,245 | — |

Seventy-four percent of Canada's exports and 87 percent of Mexico's exports go to the United States.

*Sources*: Statistics Canada; Instituto Nacional de Estadística, Geografía, e Informática; U.S. Department of Commerce.

Two more points about Table 13.1 are worth considering. First, even though Mexico is a developing country, the NAFTA market is very rich. Few countries have a higher GDP per capita than the weighted average of Canada, Mexico, and the United States, and total GDP at market exchange rates is over $14 *trillion*.

Second, NAFTA combines nations that are at very different levels of economic development. Even though Mexico is one of the wealthiest nations in Latin America, the gap between its per capita income and that of the United States adds a layer of political and social tension to NAFTA. Issues such as immigration and environmental and labor standards are more contentious than in other trade blocs.

Table 13.2 shows the importance of trade between each pair of countries. Note that the trade between each pair of countries is an important share of each nation's overall trade, with the exception of Canada–Mexico. Both Canada's and Mexico's trade with the United States is far greater than their trade with any other country. In 2005 Canada was the United States' number one trading partner, and Mexico was number two.

Mexico and Canada depend on trade more than the United States does. Recall that one way to measure how much a country depends on trade is to calculate its openness ratio ((Exports + Imports) / GDP). Using this measure, 2005 trade was equal to nearly 72 percent of Canada's GDP, 60 percent of Mexico's GDP, and 26 percent of the United States' GDP. These numbers reflect the general proposition that the smaller a nation, the more it must trade in order to achieve a given level of prosperity.

 ## The Canada-U.S. Trade Relationship

The United States and Canada trade more than any pair of countries in the world. In 2005 total trade between the two was valued at $560 billion. Figure 13.1 illustrates the nearly constant upward trend in bilateral trade. On average, from

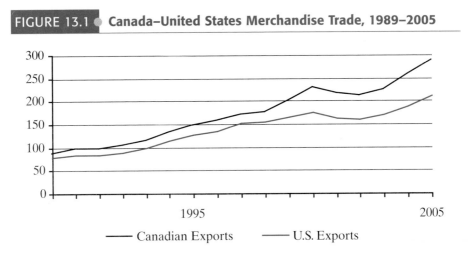

FIGURE 13.1 ● **Canada–United States Merchandise Trade, 1989–2005**

— Canadian Exports        — U.S. Exports

Canadian-U.S. trade has grown 7 percent per year since the implementation of the Canadian-U.S. Free Trade Agreement; at that rate it doubles nearly every 10 years.

1989 to 2005 Canada-U.S. trade grew at 7 percent per year and doubles approximately every decade.

Given the history of close ties and the importance of trade, it is not surprising that the United States and Canada would join together to form a free-trade area and that they would do so before NAFTA was created. The Canadian-U.S. Trade Agreement, or CUSTA, was signed in 1988 and implemented on January 1, 1989, exactly five years before NAFTA. CUSTA, however, was not the first important trade agreement between Canada and the United States. In 1965 24 years before the implementation of CUSTA, Canada and the United States signed an agreement on trade and investment in automotive products, the single largest component of U.S.-Canadian trade.

## The Auto Pact of 1965

Although the **Auto Pact** agreement was limited to trade in automotive products, it is a very successful example of gains from trade. By removing barriers to trade, the Pact permitted the big three Detroit automakers (General Motors, Ford, and Chrysler) to produce for a single, combined market. Prior to the agreement, Canadian content laws required that cars sold in Canada had to be mostly produced there as well. The relatively small market size caused factories in Canada to lose some of the economies of scale of their American counterparts, and not surprisingly, Canada's productivity in automotive products was around 30 percent below the U.S. level.

With the coming of free trade in cars and car parts, Detroit automakers (who were also Canadian automakers) were able to reorganize production in Canada and the United States, and both locations began to produce for both markets. The impact on trade was stunning. Between 1963 and 1969, when firms began to anticipate an opening of Canada-U.S. auto trade, Canadian exports to the United States grew 169 percent, while U.S. exports to Canada grew 114 percent. Most of the trade growth was in automotive products, and even today, they remain the single largest component of trade between the United States and Canada.

## The Canadian-U.S. Trade Agreement (CUSTA) of 1989

From the Canadian viewpoint, the 1980s brought to the foreground two trends that had to be addressed. First, the United States began to be a less reliable trade partner. The problem was the United States' expanded use of countervailing and antidumping duties, and "voluntary" export restrictions (VERs) that were imposed on a number of U.S. imports. In addition, U.S. rhetoric indicated a greater willingness to use these measures as a means of gaining political support from declining U.S. industries. Although VERs and antidumping and counter-vailing duties did not directly affect an important share of U.S.-Canadian trade, the specter of the United States turning increasingly protectionist was a problem for Canada. Their dependence on international trade means that protectionism in the United States is a direct threat to their standard of living.

The second problem facing Canada in the 1980s was the need to restructure many of its firms and industries in order to keep them competitive in a more global environment. Many observers inside Canada felt that Asian manufacturing was beginning to exert strong competitive pressures on Canadian firms and without significant modernization and rebuilding, Canadian firms were likely to lose markets at home and abroad.

Creating a free-trade agreement with the United States was one solution to the problem of growing U.S. protectionism and increasing Asian competitiveness in manufacturing industries. This solution locks the United States into an international agreement requiring it to keep its market open and, at the same time, puts pressure on Canadian manufacturers to make the necessary changes.

The impacts of CUSTA were more or less as expected. Between 1989 and 1994, Canadian exports to the United States grew 55 percent ($47 billion increase), while U.S. exports to Canada grew 46.6 percent ($36.5 billion increase). In percentage terms this growth is not quite as rapid as the period before and after the implementation of the Auto Pact, but given that trade was already at a high level in 1987, a 50 percent increase represents an enormous volume of trade.

The debate over U.S.-Canadian free trade was low key and dispassionate in the United States. In Canada, however, a heated public discussion erupted when it was announced that the United States and Canada were negotiating an agreement. The opponents of the trade agreement feared that (1) Canada might not be able to compete with U.S. firms, which had the advantages of economies of scale; (2) expanded trade might force Canada to jettison many of its social programs; and (3) Canadian culture might come to be dominated by the U.S. news, information, arts, and entertainment industries.

The issue of Canadian competitiveness was largely one about the need to gain economies of scale and to increase productivity through organizational or technological changes within firms. For the most part, the real issue for a high-income, industrialized country such as Canada is the length of time over which the changes can be expected to occur, and not whether firms are capable of competing.

The Canadian opponents of CUSTA also argued that it would erode Canada's social programs. For many citizens, Canada's more extensive social programs, such as universal health care and income maintenance, are part of a national identity that make Canada unlike the United States. The opponents of CUSTA argued that the intensification of competition with the United States would undermine these social programs. They reasoned that social programs would be cut in order to reduce business taxes and make Canadian firms more competitive. Given that taxes are but one component of business costs, and that in some cases there are offsetting reductions in cost elsewhere, it was not at all certain what the final impact of free trade would be on Canadian social programs. In the case of health care, for example, it makes more sense to argue that the United States' system is a competitive disadvantage, since it raises the cost of hiring workers when they must be provided with health care benefits by their employer. In Canada, by contrast, health care coverage is universal and is paid for out of general government revenues and individual taxes. A complicating factor for examining the impact of free trade on social spending is that by the mid-1990s, Canada's federal and provincial deficits had grown to the point where governments were forced to scale back some social programs. The cuts were a result of large and unsustainable deficits at both the provincial and federal levels, however, and were not caused by increased trade.

The final and most contentious issue from the Canadian point of view was the possibility of U.S. cultural domination. A very wide spectrum of opinion, including both opponents and proponents of expanded free trade, argue that the combination of Canada's smaller population and its proximity to the United States will destroy its national identity if it allows completely free trade in the cultural industries. These industries include music in all of its venues, as well as radio, television, newspapers, book publishing, magazines, drama, cinema, and painting. Under the rules of CUSTA, Canada is allowed to protect its national identity by imposing quantitative restrictions on imports of "cultural products." In most cases the rules allow Canada to impose domestic content requirements on television, radio, and theater. The content requirements make it illegal for a radio or TV station to program content originating in the United States 24 hours a day. Cable TV companies give preferences to Canadian-based TV networks, and there are national rules that favor Canadian theater companies, artists, and writers.

# Canadian Provinces

Newfoundland

Quebec

Ontario

Prince Edward Island

Nova Scotia

New Brunswick

Montreal

Ottawa

Toronto

Manitoba

Winnipeg

Saskatchewan

Nunavut

Alberta

Edmonton

British Columbia

Vancouver

Northwest Territories

Yukon Territory

60°

60°

60°

90°

90°

90°

120°

120°

150°

150°

60°

Map by Dr. Chris Lukinbeal
Revised by Harry D. Johnson

Lambert Equal Area Projection

0          500          1000 Miles

# Recent Mexican Economic History

Canada's interests in CUSTA were relatively straightforward, but Mexico's interests in signing NAFTA were more complex. Like Canada, Mexico wanted to guarantee its access to the U.S. market; unlike Canada, however, Mexico needed to alter its economic strategy fundamentally. The decision to seek closer economic ties to the United States was one of many major policy changes that Mexico made between the late 1980s and early 1990s. By the time the agreement was ratified in 1993, Mexico had completely abandoned the economic policies it had followed since the end of World War II.

## The Slowdown in Economic Growth

Mexico's shift from a closed and inward economic orientation to an open and outward set of policies began in the mid-1980s after a long period of crisis caused by international trends and a series of domestic policy mistakes. The most important international trend was the slowdown in world economic growth that began in the early 1970s, more than a decade before the shift in policies. Economists disagree about the causes of the growth slowdown, but it affected all of Latin America, Africa, Europe, North America, and the Soviet Union. A few areas in Asia escaped the trend, but most countries around the world found that it was impossible to maintain the same rates of growth they had achieved in the 1950s and 1960s.

In the 1970s national governments across Latin America, including Mexico, began to borrow heavily in order to obtain the financial resources needed to keep their economies expanding. Capital markets were relatively open to international lending, and banks in New York, London, and other financial centers were driven to make large loans by the huge deposits they had received from oil producing countries. Mexico and a number of other countries moved away from the cautious fiscal and monetary policies they had followed in the 1950s and 1960s, and accepted large budget deficits and expansionary monetary policies as the price of economic growth in a slowing world economy.

Budget deficits and expansionary monetary policies seemed to work at first, but they came at a high cost. Recall from Chapters 10, 11, and 12, that monetary expansion can lead to higher and accelerating rates of inflation which, in turn, cause a real appreciation of a currency. The demand stimulus from deficit spending plus the real appreciation of the Mexican peso resulted in growing current account deficits. This pattern was not confined to Mexico, nor to Latin America, but was repeated in many parts of the world.

The first crisis hit Mexico in 1976, and was followed by an IMF bailout and cuts in government spending. The restraints were temporary, however; in 1978, Mexico's large oil reserves began to reach the world market. According to international lenders, this made the country a good credit risk as Mexico's reserves were large and it was widely believed that the price of oil would continue to rise. Unfortunately for the lenders and for Mexico, oil prices began to fall in 1981. By

1982 the country was no longer able to pay interest or repay principal on its foreign loans. In relatively rapid succession, a number of countries were also exposed as lacking sufficient international reserves to service their debt. This began the **debt crisis** of the 1980s.

## The Lost Decade of the 1980s

Once it was revealed that many developing country borrowers were no longer able to service their debts, international lending stopped. In Mexico the crisis brought on a series of devaluations in the peso which fueled inflation by making imported goods more expensive and eroded the purchasing power of wages. The devaluations resulted in some expenditure switching, as consumers shifted from imported goods to domestic goods, however, it was not sufficient to counteract the large expenditure reduction caused by the cuts to government spending. Furthermore, many private firms had become dependent on international borrowing, and the sudden cessation in foreign loans led to a steep decline in private spending by businesses. The culmination of these forces was a deep economic depression many refer to as the **"Lost Decade."**

Ordinarily, the solution for a country in this situation would be to export their way out. Ideally, by exporting goods and services that other countries want to buy, they could accumulate dollars that could be used to pay debts and to revive the economy. This is essentially how the East Asian economies escaped from their financial crises of 1997–98. In Mexico's case, however, the ability to export was undermined by four decades of **import substitution industrialization (ISI)** policies.

ISI policies target the development of manufacturing through various kinds of support for the production of goods that substitute for imports. ISI was the dominant development strategy in Latin America and most of the developing world from approximately the end of World War II until the middle of the 1980s. This will be discussed in more detail in Chapter 15. ISI theorists believed that industrial development could be accomplished through a series of stages beginning with a focus on simple consumer goods (foodstuffs, beverages, furniture, apparel). In the second stage, ISI policies prescribed support for more complex consumer goods and intermediate industrial goods (appliances, autos, pumps, generators), and finally, in the last stage, support for the development of complex industrial goods production (chemicals, electronics, machine tools). By the time a country reached the last stage, it would be among the industrial economies of the world.

Various tools were used to support ISI policies, including subsidies and high levels of protection against competition from imports. By raising the private benefits of investment in the production of goods intended for the domestic market, Mexico and other ISI countries pulled land, labor, and capital into those favored industries, but unintentionally made exports relatively less profitable, since they were not as favored with subsidies, tax breaks, and protection from imports. Several decades of protection from foreign competition meant that Mexico's manufacturing sector was not very competitive in the early 1980s, precisely the time it needed exports in order to earn dollars. Ironically, ISI policies that had tried to strengthen industrial development and increase self-sufficiency caused the opposite to occur.

## Economic Policy Reforms in the Mexican Economy

The debt crisis of the 1980s led to a steep fall in real incomes and wages. Between 1983 and 1988, real wages fell by 40 to 50 percent, and real per capita GDP fell by 15 percent between 1982 and 1986. As a result, health care, education, and income support programs were all hit hard.

There were three main lessons that Mexico's policymakers learned from the crisis. First, management of the macroeconomy had to improve. Lack of concern for budget and trade deficits led to severe crises in 1976 and 1982, and in the future, economic policymakers could not ignore macroeconomic imbalances. In effect this meant that government could no longer use public expenditures as the main support for economic growth. Second, it was seen that markets needed to play a larger role in resource allocation decisions, in part, to increase the competitiveness of Mexican firms and to attract the capital Mexico needed for investment and growth. Third, ISI policies were no longer viewed as the best policy for industrial development, and more traditional ideas of comparative advantage began to take center stage. This point was driven home by other trends in the world economy, including a number of multicountry academic studies that were critical of ISI, and the tremendous success of several export-oriented Asian economies that abandoned ISI in the late 1960s and early 1970s. (See the Case Study of the Republic of Korea in Chapter 3.)

President Salinas entered office in December 1988. He faced an economy that was weakened by several years of negative or sub-par growth, a private sector that was unwilling to risk new investments, and large foreign debts that took all or nearly all of the country's export earnings. Salinas' primary goal was to raise capital for investment, but in order to do that he needed to change the expectations of potential investors, both domestic and international. This required a stronger market orientation so that investors would know that their success was dependent on market forces and not government rules that seemed to change arbitrarily.

Salinas continued many of the reforms that began under his predecessor, de la Madrid (1982–1988), including progress on bringing the federal budget under control. He also increased the rate of privatization of businesses that began under de la Madrid, and Mexico saw a decline in state-owned firms from 1,155 in 1982 to 217 by 1992. In May 1990 Salinas announced that Mexico would re-privatize its banking sector, and early in his presidency, he began to tackle the debt crisis.

In 1989 when the United States announced the start of the **Brady Plan** for international debt relief, Salinas quickly put Mexico first in line to qualify for the partial debt forgiveness proposed under the terms of the plan. Named after U.S.

Secretary of Treasury Brady, the plan offered modest amounts of debt relief in return for domestic policy reforms, most of which Mexico had accomplished by 1989 (see Chapter 15 for a more detailed discussion of the Brady Plan). More important than the small amount of debt relief, the plan significantly altered international perceptions about Mexico and its economic stability and future.

On the trade front, Salinas continued to reduce tariffs and eliminate import licensing requirements. These reforms, along with privatization, curbs on inflation, and a fiscally prudent budget, were not necessarily permanent. Until the electoral reforms of the 1990s, Mexican presidents concentrated a great deal of power in their office, and all of the reforms could be overturned by a future president. In order to confront this problem, in 1989 Salinas took the very bold and unexpected step of proposing a free trade agreement with the United States. He had two central goals he wanted to achieve. First, he wanted to tie up the reforms in an international treaty, making a return to inward oriented and protectionist policies all but impossible. Second, he wanted to add to the low level of domestic savings by attracting foreign capital for development of the Mexican economy.

Closer economic ties with the United States seemed to offer Mexico the guarantees that international investors wanted. Not only would it make future policy reversals more difficult, it offered full access to the wealthy American market for anyone that produced their goods in Mexico. The proposal seemed to accomplish its goals; capital began to pour into Mexico, from both foreign investors and from Mexican nationals who had sent their savings out of the country during the turmoil of the 1980s. Between 1990 and 1993, Mexico attracted over $90 billion in outside capital, or about one in every five dollars that went to developing countries from private sources.

## CASE STUDY

# Mexico's Export Processing Industry

A large share of the trade between the United States and Mexico is intrafirm (25 to 35 percent) and occurs in the context of Mexico's special export processing sector. Mexico began its program in 1965, when the government initiated the Border Industrialization Program (BIP) with its Decree for the Development and Operation of the Maquiladora Export Industry. The primary purpose of the plan was to generate employment along its northern border, where large numbers of workers had suddenly become unemployed due to the termination of the agricultural guest worker program (called the *bracero* program) in the United States.

The BIP created an **export processing zone (EPZ)**, in which foreign firms could set up an assembly-type operation and escape Mexican tariffs on the parts and materials they imported, as long as they exported the assembled goods. In addition, U.S. tariffs on imports from the EPZ were usually limited to the share of the value of the product created in Mexico. In other words, American firms such as General Motors or 3M could set up assembly operations in Mexico and pay no Mexican tariffs on the inputs the assemblers brought into Mexico, as long as they exported the output. When the output was shipped back to the United States, it qualified for special U.S. tariff treatment, which allowed them to avoid tariffs on the share of the value that was created outside Mexico.

The firms that located in the export processing zone became known as *maquila* (mah-keé-lah), and the industry as a whole is referred to as the **maquiladora** (mah-kee-lah-dor´-ah) industry. Although any region in the country can host maquilas, about two-thirds of all firms are located in border states, and especially in the larger cities such as Tijuana and Ciudad Juarez that lie on the border with the United States.

The *maquiladora* industry grew steadily during the 1970s, and by 1980, there were 620 plants employing 120,000 workers. After the crisis of 1982, a decision was made in Mexico City to diversify exports away from oil, and greater encouragement was given to *maquiladora* operations. In addition, the depreciation of the peso and the proximity to the U.S. market made these operations more attractive to foreign investment. As a result, the period of most rapid growth began after 1983.

By the middle of 2003, the *maquiladora* industry employed more than one million workers in more than 3,100 firms and was responsible for more than half of the total Mexican exports. The industry runs a large trade surplus that generated more than $18 billion in U.S. dollar reserves in 2002. That amount is more than all other sources combined, including the remittances sent home by Mexican migrants working in the United States, oil exports, and tourism revenues.

Non-Mexican firms were motivated to locate a branch of their production in the *maquiladora* industry by several factors in addition to tariffs. Labor costs are a primary consideration. In 2002 total compensation costs averaged $2.38 versus $21.33 for production workers in U.S. manufacturing. The differences in labor costs indicate that much of the intrafirm trade between U.S. firms and their subsidiaries or affiliates in the *maquiladora* industry is an example of trade based on comparative advantage and factor cost differences.

In many low-wage countries low labor costs are more than offset by the lack of nearby suppliers and the poor condition of roads, sewer hookups, and other critical pieces of infrastructure. In the case of the *maquiladora*, most firms are close to the U.S. market, where suppliers are also located and poor road conditions are less of an aggravation. In addition, Mexico has built many full-service industrial parks that provide good infrastructure to the firms that locate in them.

The *maquiladora* industry is responsive to conditions inside the United States more than macroeconomic conditions in Mexico. For example, during the recession of 1995, Mexico's GDP fell by 6.2 percent, but employment in the *maquiladora* industry grew by 9.4 percent. Given that about 80 percent of the industry is located in the northern Mexican states adjacent to the border, the business cycle in northern Mexico is more synchronized with the United States than are those in the interior and southern parts of the nation.

One of the greatest challenges facing the industry today is competition from very low-wage countries in Central America and Asia. China's entrance into the WTO has had an important impact on a number of production lines in Mexico, and changes in the industry are ongoing. Mexico, however, has very strong locational advantages due to its proximity to the United States. The *maquiladora* industry also remains very competitive for product lines that need a quick turn-around time from order to delivery, that need to manage a just-in-time inventory system, or that are heavy and bulky relative to their value.

Since its beginning in the mid-1960s, the industry has undergone a profound technological evolution. The earliest plants were labor-intensive assembly operations that used unskilled, low-wage labor and very limited technology. Textile, apparel, and furniture-manufacturing factories are examples. Firms like these are still in operation, but over the course of the 1980s, a second generation of plants gradually emerged. These were oriented toward manufacturing using automated and semiautomated processes along with a higher proportion of technicians and engineers. Examples include manufacturers of wiring harnesses for automobiles, television sets, and all sorts of electrical appliances. In the 1990s a third generation began to appear alongside the first and second generations. These newer and more modern plants incorporate advanced production techniques, perform research and development, and are at the technological frontier of their production lines. Examples include medical devices, measuring and control instruments, auto parts, and even a handful of defense contractors. While first-generation firms appear to be very vulnerable to low-wage competition from nations such as China, third-generation firms are well integrated into the international competitive strategies of multinational firms and are an important avenue to the future economic success of Mexico.

# The North American Free Trade Agreement (NAFTA)

Trade flows between the United States and its NAFTA partners increased significantly in the 1990s. Given that trade flows were growing before the implementation of NAFTA, and that they have continued to grow afterward, it is impossible to say how much of the increase in trade is directly due to the trade agreement. Some of the increase before NAFTA's implementation may have been in anticipation of freer trade, while much of the growth since then may have occurred without the agreement. Given that tariffs on about half of the goods traded between the United States and Mexico were eliminated immediately in 1994, it makes sense to think that NAFTA caused at least some of the growth in trade. U.S.-Canadian trade also expanded, even though there was little change in trade barriers. In part, the growth in trade among NAFTA partners was a reflection of the overall growth of the three economies. NAFTA, however, facilitated the trade growth.

The first important feature of NAFTA is that most forms of trade barriers came down. Since the United States and Canada were relatively open economies with few trade barriers before NAFTA, most of the change came on the Mexican side. For example, between 1993 and 1996, average U.S. tariffs on Mexican goods fell from 2.07 to 0.65 percent. By contrast, Mexican tariffs on U.S. goods fell from 10 to 2.9 percent. These reductions in tariffs under NAFTA were a continuation of the reduction in trade barriers that began in the mid-1980s. Between 1982 and 1992, the percentage of Mexico's imports that required import licenses from the government declined from 100 to 11 percent and tariffs fell from an average level of 27 to 13.1 percent. By 1994, Mexico's economy was substantially open to the world.

The phase-out period for the remaining tariffs and investment restrictions varied from sector to sector. In cases where there was expected to be significant new competition, industries were given a longer grace period to prepare themselves. Although each country wants the gains from trade, they also want to avoid a sudden disruption of their economies.

A second feature of NAFTA is that it specifies North American content requirements for goods that are subject to free trade. That is, in order to qualify for free trade or the reduced tariff provisions of the agreement, a specified percentage (usually 50 percent) of the value of the good must be made in North America. The purpose of local content requirements is to prevent non-NAFTA countries from using low tariffs in one NAFTA country to gain access to all three. Most trade economists dislike these provisions because they increase the likelihood of trade diversion. Production of inputs in lower-cost, non-member countries could be reduced if firms move their operations to NAFTA countries in order to meet the content requirements. Trade diversion occurred in the apparel industry, for example. Firms moved from the Caribbean to Mexico even though Mexico was not the lowest-cost producer. Mexico's exports to the United States paid zero tariffs, so goods produced there could sell for less than goods produced in lower-cost countries facing high tariffs when entering the United States. Nevertheless, content requirements were politically necessary in order to pass the agreement in Canada and the United States.

A third feature of the agreement is that it establishes a system of dispute resolution. When a disagreement arises, any country may request an investigation. This will set in motion a bi-national panel that investigates the issue and makes a report. Both countries are bound by the results of their analysis. It is hoped that this will lead to greater consultation and cooperation between countries and prevent trade disputes from escalating.

 ## The NAFTA Debate in the United States

The proposal for a trade agreement with Mexico reignited the debate over free trade in the United States. In particular, organized labor and environmental groups opposed the agreement, along with a handful of specific industrial and agricultural interests that feared stiffer competition with Mexico. Non-economic opposition to NAFTA came from a number of politicians and citizens who expressed doubts about signing a trade agreement with a country that lacked strong democratic institutions.

## Labor Issues

Blue-collar industrial labor unions were the most vocal opponents of NAFTA. Their reasons parallel the dicussion of trade, jobs, and labor standards in Chapters 7 and 8. Recall that the labor argument rejects free trade because of the fear that competition with low-wage countries will drive down wages at home, cause jobs to migrate overseas, and create a race to the bottom in labor standards. The relevant ideas have been discussed in the earlier chapters, but it is worth repeating that the core mistake of this view is the failure to take into account the productivity differences between U.S. and foreign workers. Labor in Mexico, for example, earns less for three reasons: (1) average Mexican education and skill levels are lower than in the United States; (2) the average Mexican worker has less capital at work; and (3) the public infrastructure of roads, ports, water systems, communication systems, and power and waste disposal systems is less reliable and less developed than in the United States. The net outcome of these three fundamental differences in human and physical capital is that productivity levels are lower in Mexico, and, as a consequence, wages are lower.

Recall, however, that the Stolper-Samuelson theorem predicts that U.S. workers with skills that are in abundance in Mexico may be hurt by the agreement. In the model of Chapter 4, trade favors the abundant factors that are used intensively to make the export good and trade hurts the scarce factors that are used intensively in the production of the import good. Given that Mexico is relatively well endowed with low-skilled labor and that the United States is relatively well endowed with skilled labor, trade between the United States and Mexico is likely to exert downward pressure on the wages of low-skilled U.S. labor. Garment workers, low-skilled and semiskilled autoworkers, and low-skilled assembly line workers may find their wages held down or their jobs moved out of the country. As always, the key question is how big an effect there will be, particularly in comparison to the macroeconomic policies of the Federal Reserve, which, in the short run, exert far more influence over wages and jobs than trade. In addition, since Mexico's GDP is only about 5 percent as large as that of the United States, its ability to absorb capital investment is limited.

Organized labor in the United States is still a significant political force, even though a relatively small share of the workforce belongs to industrial unions. During the NAFTA debate, labor unions formed the core of a pressure group that pushed the Clinton administration to seek a separate agreement that paralleled NAFTA but focused solely on labor issues. The agreement came to be known as the side agreement on labor, or, more formally, the **North American Agreement on Labor Cooperation**. It was one of two such agreements, the other dealing with environmental issues. The labor side agreement requires both the United States and Mexico to enforce their own labor laws, especially laws pertaining to child labor, minimum wages, and workplace safety. Countries are required to permit investigators to examine alleged infringements of these protections, and fines may be levied. The agreement does not permit investigations into the rights of workers to organize, nor does it cover this aspect of labor law.

In the United States labor interests sought the side agreement in order to prevent U.S. companies from fleeing to Mexico in order to take advantage of lax enforcement of labor laws. In addition, they wanted to be certain that Mexico did not gain a competitive advantage over U.S. firms and workers by using child labor, by paying less than minimum wage, or by cost cutting that allowed unsafe and unhealthy working conditions. Ironically, the first instance in which the international panel was called to investigate the nonenforcement of workplace health and safety rules was in the United States. In 1996 Mexican unions protested that a U.S. firm was abusing Hispanic telemarketers in San Francisco and that the U.S. government had failed to enforce U.S. workplace health and safety laws.

Most labor groups continue to express dissatisfaction with the labor side agreement and to oppose ratification of new agreements. They remain unconvinced that U.S. workers can compete with Mexican or other developing-country workers without lowering their own wages. In their view, much, if not all, of U.S. trade with developing countries is unfair to U.S. workers and is responsible for a significant erosion in living standards in the United States.

Recall from the discussion in Chapter 4 about trade and income inequality that the bulk of the increase in inequality in the 1970s, 1980s, and 1990s is attributable to technological changes that reduced the demand for low-skilled workers. NAFTA has little to do with this trend. Nevertheless, it is fair to say that while the NAFTA countries benefited from increased trade, the agreement has caused some economic restructuring, and not every individual has benefited.

In another sense, however, trade unionists may be correct. The labor side agreement works by shining an international light on unacceptable labor practices. But because it does not give anyone significant power to compel the release of information, investigators often have a hard time obtaining evidence. Critics argue that this is by design; that the labor side agreement is only for show and that its real purpose was to win votes in the U.S. Congress during the ratification process in 1993.

## Environmental Issues

The second major side agreement is called the **North American Agreement on Environmental Cooperation**. This agreement was motivated by two main concerns. One was the desire to prevent U.S. and Canadian firms from relocating to Mexico where they might take advantage of less stringent environmental enforcement. The second concern was the growth of environmental pollution along the U.S.-Mexico border. Mexico's environmental laws are quite good in general, but enforcement has often been lacking, due to a lack of resources, a lack of administrative capacity, or corruption. The high visibility of this issue in North America required Mexico to get tougher in its enforcement, and in this way, NAFTA has helped generate some desirable environmental outcomes.

Recall from the discussion in Chapter 8 about trade and the environment the distinction between transboundary and non-transboundary environmental problems. In the context of NAFTA, transboundary pollution along the U.S.-Mexico border is an issue of considerable importance to both countries. Since the 1980s, rapid population growth on both sides of the border has created a number of environmental challenges that are compounded by the rapid growth of manufacturing in northern Mexico. A significant share of the *maquiladora* manufacturing is located in cities on the border, as close as possible to the U.S. market and the U.S. transportation network. In many cases, U.S. and Mexican cities share watersheds, air basins, and ecological habitats, making whatever happens on one side of the border of concern to the other side.

The rapid influx of people to the border region, coming from elsewhere in the United States to take advantage of the warm climate and sunny weather, and coming from the interior of Mexico to find jobs and a decent income, has put a heavy burden on roads, sewers, water systems, and other public infrastructure. Unfortunately, a large increase in population and manufacturing growth on the Mexican side of the border occurred in the 1980s, during the debt crisis in Mexico, when there were few resources for urban development. Consequently, sewage and water capacity have been strained beyond capacity and there is a backlog of projects needing attention and resources.

As noted in Chapter 8, it is unrealistic to expect environmental standards, clean-up preferences, or resource commitments to be identical in countries with different income levels. Nevertheless, NAFTA provides an excellent opportunity to address the issue of transboundary environmental problems. Most notably, the agreement provides a formal, institutional framework in which issues and problems can be discussed and resolved. Specifically, the side agreement on the environment creates a mechanism for investigating environmental disputes, such as cases where it is alleged that Mexico (or the United States or Canada) is gaining competitive advantages by not enforcing environmental laws. Investigation of these cases is followed by a resolution of the dispute through binding arbitration if both sides cannot agree.

The side agreement also established the **North American Development Bank (NADBank)** to help finance border cleanup costs. NADBank has several hundred million dollars of initial funds provided by the United States and Mexico, but the majority of funds are expected to come from either international agencies or private sources. Estimates of border cleanup costs vary widely, from $2 billion to $8 billion. In addition to the NADBank, the environmental side agreement created the Border Environmental Cooperation Commission (BECC) to analyze and certify the technical and scientific components of border cleanup proposals for NADBank funding. The NADBank, the BECC, and other binational, cooperative, border environmental programs (Border XXI, for example), are targeted at issues such as increasing the availability of clean drinking water, wastewater treatment, air quality monitoring and improvement, solid and hazardous waste disposal, and other issues of mutual concern.

Like the labor side agreement, the environmental side agreement has a mixed record. This fact, coupled with the fact that the NADBank has been slow in distributing funds for projects, has led many to complain that the positive institutional features of the side agreements are little more than window dressing and that they do not confront the real problems of trade between industrial United States and developing Mexico.

## Immigration

Immigration is probably the most contentious issue in U.S.-Mexico relations. No one knows how many Mexicans enter the United States each year without authorization, but the 2000 U.S. census counted over 9 million people born in Mexico and living in the United States. This number is a mixture of citizens, legal residents, and Mexicans without authorization to be in the United States. Most estimates find that the number of unauthorized or illegal immigrants total about one-half the total number of U.S. residents born in Mexico, or 4 to 5 million. The yearly flow of Mexican migrants that enter the United States is estimated to be 300,000 to 400,000. Most settle in states on the U.S.-Mexico border, with California (42.8 percent), Texas (20.5 percent), and Arizona (4.8) accounting for over 68 percent of the total. Increasingly, migrants are finding work outside of border states, and over time, the share living in the border region will decline.

Chapter 4 discussed the basic economic factors behind migration, including **demand-pull**, **supply-push**, and **social networks**. All of these factors are relevant to U.S.-Mexico migration. For example, once in the United States, migrants are easily able to find jobs in agriculture, construction, restaurants and hotels, building and landscape maintenance, meat packing, and other sectors, while penalties for hiring undocumented workers are infrequently enforced. These jobs are very attractive to ambitious Mexicans who often face economic uncertainties in their home communities. For example, the average manufacturing wage in the U.S. border state, Arizona was $48,000 per year in 2001; across the border in the Mexican border state of Sonora, manufacturing production workers earned the annual equivalent of $5,220 at market exchange rates, about one-ninth the U.S. level.

The United States is conflicted by the issue of illegal immigration from Mexico. On the one hand, migrants who entered without authorization are breaking the law and that bothers many Americans. On the other hand, they often settle in the United States, raise families, and contribute to community life. Majority opinion does not support the idea of mass deportations and it is rare that the federal government attempts to enforce laws against hiring undocumented immigrants; when they do, there is an outcry from the businesses and communities that have come to depend on immigrant labor. Under these circumstances, the politically expedient policy is to try to close the border, except at legal points of entry and exit. In effect this is what the United States has done by increasing the level of vigilance along the border and by building fences and other barriers. Most research shows that this strategy is not effective, however, and that the annual number of unauthorized immigrants has increased since the implementation of stricter border enforcement policies.

There are three reasons why increased border enforcement has not worked. First, the border is 2,000 miles long, spans two major North American deserts and several mountain ranges, and is impossible to patrol effectively. Second, the economic incentive to enter the United States is high. Wages are higher, jobs are plentiful, and the probability of being caught and deported is low once a migrant finds work in the United States. Third, nearly one-half of all illegal immigrants in the United States enter legally, but overstay the duration of their visas. These individuals come through legal ports of entry and are not hindered by fences.

The strategy of fencing out immigrants pushes those without visas into the deserts and mountains where their physical safety is compromised; every year since 1994, between 200 and 400 migrants have died from exposure in the wilderness regions along the border. Migrants have reacted rationally to this human tragedy by hiring border crossing guides and increasing their length-of-stay once they make it into the United States. In addition, more women and children are migrating as a result of the fencing and increased border enforcement. This seems contradictory, but it has a simple explanation. Prior to the stepped up enforcement, many undocumented migrants moved back and forth between Mexico and the United States, returning home, for example during holiday seasons. Once it became more difficult and expensive to move back and forth, many decided to bring family members with them as a way to avoid a prolonged separation and to maintain family integrity.

For political reasons, many proponents of NAFTA chose to emphasize the claim that it would reduce immigration. President Salinas, for example, picked up this theme. When addressing U.S. audiences, he often rallied support by stating, "Mexico wants to export goods, not people." His point was that NAFTA would give Mexico greater access to the U.S. market and would create faster growth in Mexico. As a result, the nation would experience a greater capacity to absorb labor into the national economy. Most simulations of the effects of NAFTA found a similar effect. The faster the Mexican economy grows, the weaker the supply-push factors will be. Nevertheless, in the short and medium runs, the immigration-increasing supply-push factors are probably stronger than the long-run immigration-reducing supply-push factors. That is, in the short run, agricultural reorganization and market opening probably have a bigger impact in the determination of the number of Mexican migrants than does overall economic growth and the spread of jobs and opportunities across Mexico. The net effect is that NAFTA probably causes less migration from Mexico to the United States than if there was no agreement, however, changes in the Mexican economy cause migration to increase.

Migration remains a topic of serious debate both inside the United States and between the United States and Mexico. Before September 11, 2001, it appeared that the two countries might reach an accord that would permit Mexican nationals to work in the United States for a limited period each year as "guest workers," but the terrorist attack on the United States halted the political momentum toward agreement. Pressures for an agreement, however, will not go away completely for two essential reasons. First, economic changes in Mexico generally guarantee that a large share of its labor force will continue to be mobile. Older industries are disappearing and new ones are developing, but during the lifespan of an average worker, there are a limited number of opportunities for significant economic advancement. Most Mexican workers can increase their real wages by at least five or six times if they migrate to the United States. This is a powerful driver, particularly when future economic conditions in Mexico are uncertain. Second, while some Americans are bothered by the social and cultural changes that occur with increased migration, many powerful economic interests in the United States want access to Mexican labor. Consequently, Mexico continues to push for an agreement to open the border for at least a proportion of its labor force, and many U.S. interests continue to propose guest-worker and temporary visa programs. Meanwhile, the humanitarian crisis of migrant deaths remains an open wound in U.S.-Mexico relations.

##  Jobs, Politics, and the Future

The most common issue in the internal U.S. debate over NAFTA was its effects on U.S. jobs. Many trade economists were discouraged by this, because the key effect of any trade agreement is the increased productive efficiency that comes with a reallocation of resources, not job gains or losses. Placing the focus of the debate on workers who might be dislocated was politically inevitable, but it ignored the real economic advantages of expanded trade.

Many people also lost sight of the fact that Mexico's economy is less than 5 percent as large as the U.S. economy. This makes it roughly the same size as Illinois, Pennsylvania, or Florida in terms of gross output. Consequently, it is unlikely that expanded trade can have a large economic impact on the United States. This point is well illustrated by an examination of the predicted effects of NAFTA on the U.S. economy. Before its implementation, a number of forecasts were made by academic economists and various interest groups. In each category (employment effects, wage effects, impact on overall U.S. current account balance), a majority of forecasts predicted either no effect on the national economy or effects too small to be measured. Note that this does not imply that there are no local effects, particularly along the border or in states that have a relatively large share of their overall trade with Mexico—for example, Texas. In more general terms, however, U.S.-Mexico trade under NAFTA was predicted to grow but not in a way that had a significant impact on the overall U.S. trade balance.

As shown in Figure 13.2, U.S.-Mexico trade has grown significantly for more than a decade. U.S. exports have grown from $25 billion in 1989 to $120 billion in 2005, while Mexican exports expanded from $27 billion to $170 over the same period. Figure 13.2 also shows a slight decline in U.S. exports and relative stagnation in Mexican exports from 2001–2003. The downturn was caused by a mild recession in the United States, which hit the manufacturing sector particularly hard.

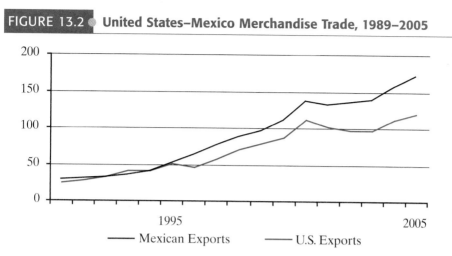

**FIGURE 13.2** **United States–Mexico Merchandise Trade, 1989–2005**

——— Mexican Exports    ——— U.S. Exports

U.S.-Mexican merchandise trade has grown 11 percent per year since the beginning of NAFTA negotiations in 1989; at that rate trade doubles approximately every seven years.

Some aspects of Mexico's recent economic history are a clear illustration of trade and growth driven by economies of scale (see Chapter 5). The inward orientation of Mexican economic policy up until the mid-1980s meant that production for the internal market was favored over exports. Consequently, firms with high fixed costs and high transport costs tried to locate near the internal Mexican market, leading to the rapid growth of Mexico City and its environs. In the 1980s, as policy changes made it more profitable to export, firms began to locate as close as possible to foreign markets, in this case, the United States. The result is the extremely rapid growth of population and manufacturing production in northern Mexican states along the U.S.-Mexico border. In the medium to long run, this rapid northern growth is perhaps the most dramatic effect of the opening of the Mexican market through trade liberalization and NAFTA. The rapidly industrializing northern states of Mexico now have per capita regional incomes (regional GDP) that are three to five times greater than some of the poorest states in Mexico, most of which are located in the south. Such regional disparity within the country is a source of great concern, as the parts of the country that are not well connected to the world economy are falling further behind the more prosperous areas.

Turning to analyses of the impact of NAFTA on U.S. jobs, recent analysis has concluded that most estimates have exaggerated both the number of job displacements due to imports and the number of jobs created due to exports. Measurement is difficult because Mexican imports usually do not displace U.S. goods one-to-one. Imported goods are often complementary to domestic goods, not substitutes. They may enter distinct market niches that complement the demand for domestically produced goods, or they may satisfy a part of the increase in overall domestic demand. As the U.S. and Mexican economies become more integrated, we should expect to see increased complementarities in production. For example, Detroit automakers find it profitable to maintain product lines in Mexico that they would otherwise abandon if their production was entirely conducted in the United States and Canada. Maintenance of these product lines increases the demand for related U.S. parts and components. In addition, imports from Mexico may, in many cases, displace imports from other Latin American or Asian countries. In those cases, an increase in imports from Mexico is offset by a reduction in imports from another country. Similarly, job creation due to exports has probably been exaggerated by the pro-NAFTA side of the debate. A good deal of U.S. "export" business consists of intermediate inputs that are incorporated into final products shipped back to the United States. Consequently, as production of a final good moves to Mexico, shipments of intermediate inputs from the United States to Mexico are often misinterpreted as an increase in the number of jobs supported by exports.

In-depth analysis has concluded that the impact of NAFTA on net creation of jobs in the United States has been very small but positive; a few tens of thousands of jobs were created in the first few years of the agreement. To put this into perspective, it should be noted that the United States generates about two million new jobs (net) a year. In other words, NAFTA's effect on jobs in three years was probably less than the equivalent of two months of job creation in an average year.

The politics of trade make discussion of job impacts necessary even though the ability of an economy to generate jobs is determined by labor market policies and fiscal and monetary policies, not by trade policies. Furthermore, there is widespread agreement among economists that the real test of success or failure for a trade agreement is whether it leads to a more efficient allocation of resources. By this criterion, the growth in trade between all three NAFTA partners is a positive indicator of increasing specialization, economies of scale, and efficiency. It is interesting that this tendency predates NAFTA and has simply continued since its implementation.

It is tempting to downplay the importance of the NAFTA agreement, especially in the United States and Canada. From the Canadian perspective, trade with Mexico is growing, but it is still a relatively small share of Canadian trade. Additionally, the 1989 CUSTA locked in most of the gains from trade with the United States. From the United States' perspective, Mexico's relatively small economy, about 5 percent of the U.S. economy, means that it is unlikely that trade can have a major impact on the national economy, even if there are pockets of the United States that feel the effects, both positive and negative. In Mexico, however, NAFTA has solidified the openness of the Mexican economy and acted as an impetus for a broad set of economic reforms in trade, agriculture, industrial policy, and increasingly, the legal system. From a purely economic perspective, the conclusion seems to be that NAFTA is important to Mexico, and relatively unimportant to the United States and Canada. It is a mistake, however, to limit our view in this way.

Mexico is the most populous Spanish-speaking country in the world, and as the country with the second largest GDP in Latin America, it is viewed as a leader throughout the hemisphere. It is at the forefront of economic and political change in Latin America, and has a young population that migrates in large numbers; however, it has also become a destination for increasing numbers of U.S. and Canadian retirees. Along the Mexican border with the United States, an urban population is rapidly growing around clusters of manufacturing industries in electronics, autos, medical devices, and others. Cultural and linguistic integration in the border regions is very advanced, and family and social networks knit together many communities spanning the international boundary. NAFTA has facilitated the creation of new bi-national and tri-national organizations for managing specific issues, such as labor and environmental concerns. It has also indirectly supported the development of numerous civic and business organizations, and helped to widen the channels of communication between the member countries. There is still a long way to go before there is a North American Community, but NAFTA has played a key role in moving all three nations toward greater awareness and understanding of each other's interests and concerns. In the long run, the direction of historical change in key indicators such as population movements, language, investment patterns, civic engagement, and regional planning, all point toward deeper and more permanent forms of integration.

## The Expansion of NAFTA

In July 2005 the United States ratified the Dominican Republic–Central American Free Trade Agreement (DR-CAFTA), with the Dominican Republic and five Central American countries: Guatemala, Honduras, El Salvador, Nicaragua, and Costa Rica. Canada and Mexico were not part of the agreement, however, Mexico has individual free trade agreements with each of the countries except the Dominican Republic, and Canada has a free trade agreement with Costa Rica, but not with the others.

The extension southward is a natural development, particularly since the United States provided expanded access to its markets for Caribbean and Central American countries beginning in the 1980s with various unilateral cuts in trade barriers. As shown in Table 13.3, the nations in DR-CAFTA add over 45 million people to the North American market, although problems of poverty and inequality are enormous. Other than Costa Rica and the Dominican Republic, most of the countries are relatively poor, and the six nations combined have a regional GDP less than many metropolitan areas in the United States. For example, the Los Angeles metropolitan area (Los Angeles and Long Beach) has a regional personal income that is more than four times the GDP of the six countries listed in Table 13.3.

The countries shown in Table 13.3 are small and not likely to register a strong impact in the United States. Nevertheless, they have been able to capture some of Mexico's apparel trade with the United States and pose a challenge to some producers in Mexico, particularly those that use large amounts of unskilled and

| TABLE 13.3 • Population and GDP for the DR-CAFTA Countries, 2005 | | | |
|---|---|---|---|
| Country | Population (Millions) | GDP (US$, Billions) | GDP per Capita (US$) | GDP per Capita (International $, PPP*) |
| Costa Rica | 4.3 | 19.4 | 4,512 | 9,985 |
| Dominican Republic | 8.9 | 28.3 | 3,180 | 7,579 |
| El Salvador | 6.9 | 17.0 | 2,464 | 5,301 |
| Guatemala | 12.6 | 31.7 | 2,516 | 4,468 |
| Honduras | 7.2 | 8.0 | 1,111 | 2,789 |
| Nicaragua | 5.5 | 4.9 | 890 | 3,680 |
| **Total** | 45.4 | 109.3 | 2,407 | 5,365 |

Population in the DR-CAFTA countries is slightly more than 10 percent of the NAFTA region, but their combined GDP is less than 1 percent (0.7%).

*Purchasing power parity.

Source: The World Bank, *World Development Indicators*, online version, 2006. http://publications.worldbank.org/WDI.

semiskilled labor. Given that labor costs are generally higher in Mexico than in Central America, the biggest impact in the NAFTA region will be on Mexico. More importantly, however, the agreement is likely to be felt strongly in Central America, particularly as U.S. agricultural products gain greater access and challenge traditional and small scale producers of corn (maize) and other basic grains. Other major effects are likely to be felt as U.S. service companies gain greater access to insurance, banking, and telecommunications markets.

## The Future of NAFTA: A North American Community?

By comparison to the European Union (see Chapter 14), Canada, Mexico, and the United States are in an early stage of economic integration. A free trade agreement is in place and capital flows freely as it would in a common market. But restrictions on the movement of labor are very strong and there are no permanent NAFTA organizations comparable to the governing bodies of the European Union. Additionally, almost all policies are made independently by each of the three members, including market access rules for non-members, environmental standards, telecommunications, transportation, and most business laws.

The timing and speed of further integration is dependent on politics, however, there are a number of next steps that follow systematically from what has already been accomplished. One option is to do nothing, or even to begin the dismantling of the agreement, although it is hard to imagine either case over the long run. Slowly, market forces are knitting together the three national economies, and already the costs of trying to undo the agreement would be very high. Three issues top the agenda of those who would like to see NAFTA evolve into a North American Community:

- A customs union
- Improved trilateral organizations for managing a more integrated community
- A focus on development and closing the economic gap between Mexico and the other members

One of the inefficiencies of free trade areas is that they require **rules of origin**. Rules of origin define which goods qualify for free trade, and which are imports from outside the region. The problem is that many goods are a combination of North American and non-North American inputs, so it is far from straightforward to determine which goods qualify for free movement within the NAFTA countries. For example, a car may be assembled in Mexico out of parts that are made in Mexico and 10 or 15 other countries, including the United States and Canada. For the assembled car to be classified as Mexican or North American in origin, there has to be a rule about the percent of the value that is created in North America. Given that autos are assembled from tens of thousands of parts, this is a complicated accounting process that ties up significant resources without actually contributing to the production of a single car. Verification of the origin of shipments slows the flow of trade at the borders, and adds significantly to transaction costs.

In a customs union, member countries have the same tariffs toward non-members. Consequently, any goods entering the NAFTA region would pay the tariff owed and then move freely within the NAFTA region. This reduces transaction costs, speeds up trade flows, and simplifies accounting. The cost to each country is partly political in that it must give up its ability to set its own tariffs independently of the other members of the customs union. In addition, there may be a revenue loss to a member government if it is required to reduce its taiffs in order to comply with the customs union. In the case of the NAFTA countries, Mexico has the overall highest tariffs toward non-members and would likely lose some of its revenue if the three countries formed a customs union.

A second item on the agenda of a North American Community is the creation of additional permanent organizations for managing economic relations. Some fear that this would duplicate the many large bureaucracies of the European Union, while others argue that the lack of organizational structure in NAFTA creates chaos and disorganization. One of the key benefits of the NAFTA agreement is that it began the development of trilateral organizations, but these are limited in scope and do not address many of the issues that have emerged since the agreement was signed. For example, there are potential benefits from organizations that can manage a North American security perimeter, that develop new infrastructure for a more efficient North American transportation system, that address regional disparities, and begin to propose solutions to the development gap.

Third, a North American Community must develop mechanisms for managing migration in an amicable and less contentious way. Some argue that the migration debate in the United States must be broadened to a discussion of development in Mexico since, in the long run, migration will end when the high level of economic uncertainty facing Mexican families and communities is reduced. This will not happen suddenly, and as long as a Mexican worker can increase his income by a factor of five or six simply by crossing the border, migration will continue. However, it is possible to think about migration in terms of development, and to manage the entire process in a more humane way.

## CASE STUDY

# Doing Business in Canada, Mexico, and the United States

In 1989 Peruvian economist Hernando de Soto published *The Other Path*, a brilliant work that argued against cumbersome, complex, and unnecessary business regulations in developing countries. De Soto made his case with a simple yet powerful experiment; he hired a small team of researchers in Lima, Peru, to work full time at obtaining a business license for a small textile firm. The researchers spent 289 days, or nearly 10 months and paid an amount equal to 32 times a monthly minimum wage to obtain the signatures and permits required to register their business officially. Then they duplicated this experiment in a number of other developing countries to show that Peru is not atypical. Ultimately, these barriers constrain the economic growth of national economies by limiting the growth of small business.

De Soto's work found its way onto a larger stage at the World Bank where his ideas were built into an ongoing research project and an online database comparing the ease of doing business in 175 countries. Using a standardized methodology, the Doing Business Web site (http://www.doingbusiness.org) issues an annual report on the degree of regulation, regulatory outcomes, legal protections for investors, and employment flexibility. Table 13.4 shows comparisons for Mexico, Canada, and the United States for 2006.

Looking at the categories in Table 13.4, Mexico's biggest obstacles for business people are the regulatory outcomes, including contract enforcement, compliance with the import and export processes, and hiring and laying off workers. The tax system also imposes a burden, which is ironic given that Mexico has a very low rate of tax collection. The United States and Canada rank high overall, but Canadians have a relatively lower ranking in the area of licensing of busi-

## TABLE 13.4 Doing Business in the NAFTA Countries

| Process | Rank among 175 Countries | | |
|---|---|---|---|
| | Mexico | Canada | United States |
| **Overall: Doing Business** | 43 | 4 | 3 |
| **Degree of regulation** | | | |
| Starting a business | 61 | 1 | 3 |
| Dealing with licenses | 30 | 32 | 22 |
| Registering property | 79 | 22 | 10 |
| Closing a business | 25 | 5 | 16 |
| **Regulatory outcomes** | | | |
| Enforcing contracts | 87 | 16 | 6 |
| Trading across borders | 86 | 8 | 11 |
| Ease of employing workers | 108 | 13 | 1 |
| **Legal protections** | | | |
| Paying taxes | 126 | 22 | 62 |
| Protecting investors | 33 | 5 | 5 |
| Getting credit | 65 | 7 | 7 |

Mexico ranks 43 out of 175 countries for the overall ease of doing business; Canada is fourth and the United States is third.

*Source*: World Bank, http//:www.doingbusiness.org; Accessed October 2006.

nesses, and the U.S. tax system is relatively more burdensome than in many other countries. For a complete description of the methods and meanings of the rankings, visit the World Bank's Doing Business Web site.

## Summary

- Canada is the United States' closest ally. In addition, it is mostly English-speaking, has a similar standard of living, and a long democratic tradition. Mexico, on the other hand, is a vastly different society with historical reasons for wariness toward the United States. Furthermore, economic integration with Mexico is much more contentious than with Canada. Labor and environmental standards, worker displacement, poorly developed infrastructure, corruption in the political and judicial systems, immigration, and the drug trade are all areas of existing or potential conflict.

- The United States and Canada have had a free-trade agreement since 1989 (CUSTA). It was preceded by an agreement in 1965 (the Auto Pact) to allow free trade in autos and automobile parts between the two countries.

- Mexico's long process of opening its economy began in the mid-1980s and was a result of the collapse of its traditional economic policy of import substitution industrialization (ISI). ISI stresses self-sufficiency and independence from world markets. The collapse of the Mexican economy in 1982 was due to its inability to repay its international loans; that episode began the Third-World debt crisis. The recessions that followed came to be known throughout Latin America as the "Lost Decade."

- The most contentious issues in the United States related to the signing of the NAFTA agreement were issues of labor policy, environmental policy and enforcement, and migration.

- To date, the main impact of NAFTA has been to continue an ongoing trend toward increased trade. It is impossible to accurately measure the effects of NAFTA on jobs and wages, but most economists estimate a small, positive effect on job creation.

- U.S. benefits from NAFTA are political as well as economic. It offers the opportunity to develop institutions that provide formal mechanisms for discussion, consultation, and resolution of issues.

## Vocabulary

Auto Pact

Brady Plan

Canadian-U.S. Trade Agreement (CUSTA)

debt crisis

demand-pull

export processing zone (EPZ)

import substitution industrialization (ISI)

"Lost Decade"

*maquiladora*

North American Development Bank (NADBank)

North American Agreement on Environmental Cooperation

North American Agreement on Labor Cooperation

purchasing power parity

rules of origin

social networks

supply-push

# Study Questions

1. How does Mexico's GDP per person compare to that of the United States? Discuss the different approaches economists can use to make this calculation.

2. Why is the openness indicator for Canada greater than that for the United States?

3. Explain how an increase in U.S. and Canadian intraindustry trade altered the level of productivity in the affected Canadian sector.

4. What were Canada's motives for proposing and signing the Canadian-U.S. Free Trade Agreement?

5. What were the forces at work in the Mexican economy that led to the market reforms and market opening of the mid-1980s?

6. What were Mexico's motives for proposing and signing the North American Free Trade Agreement?

7. In what areas are there NAFTA side agreements? Discuss the pros and cons of these agreements.

8. What are the three main categories of factors that determine the number of immigrants to the United States from Mexico? Give specific examples of each.

9. Explain why claims about job creation and job destruction due to NAFTA are likely to be misleading and inaccurate.

# 14 The European Union: Many Markets into One

 **Introduction: The European Union**

The European Union is an economic union of 27 nations with over 488 million citizens and more than $13,410 billion in output. It is the largest, oldest, and most integrated of regional agreements. It helped put an end to over a century of wars on the European continent, and its incorporation of new members from Central Europe has reintegrated several countries that had been cut off from their historical and cultural ties to Western Europe. There are a number of lessons to be learned from the struggle of the European Union to expand and deepen the economic ties of its member nations.

Since 2004 12 new members have joined, including three independent nations that were part of the former Soviet Union and seven ex-socialist countries in Central Europe. The rapid accession of many new members is not the first expansion of the European Union. Since its inception in 1957 it has undergone several periods of growth in its numbers and its responsibilities. In 1979 the nine members of what was then called the **European Community (EC)** linked their exchange rates in a system designed to eliminate wide fluctuations among currencies. By 1986 the EC had grown to 12 members, and in 1987, they signed the **Single European Act**, with the intention of creating a single European identity that would form an umbrella over the various national cultures, economies, and political systems. In effect, the Single European Act turned the EC into a common market by allowing for the free movement of labor and capital as complements to the already free movement of goods and services. In 1992 the members signed the **Treaty on European Union**, which led directly to the creation of the common currency, the euro, in 1999.

None of these changes has been easy, or carried out according to a preconceived master plan. Instead, the member states have been forced to act pragmatically as world events called for changes. The shift from fixed to floating exchange rates in the 1970s and 1980s, the fall of the Berlin Wall in 1989, the collapse of communism, the integration of world capital markets and increasing international capital flows, the rise of environmental awareness, and many other forces have shaped the European Union's development. As changes in the world economy have led to new arrangements and new responsibilities for EU institutions, the goal of peaceful political, social, and economic integration has stayed on track. In this regard, the European Union is a truly remarkable achievement, particularly when one considers the bloody history of twentieth-century Europe and the low expectations of most observers when the original documents were signed in 1957.

The European Union is the most ambitious integration agreement in the world today. It has its own revenue and budget, a set of institutions for making laws and regulating areas of common interest, a common currency, and freedom of movement for people, money, goods, and services. Despite this profound integration, it has managed to protect the sovereignty of its member states and to avoid homogenization of cultures and linguistic regions. Indeed, integration in the larger sphere of nation-states has enabled a number of historical national identities to re-emerge and to claim greater autonomy in their political systems. Examples include the Catalans of Spain and the Welsh and Scots of the United Kingdom.

Due to its history and its increasing importance on the world stage, the European Union holds many lessons for other integration areas. Before we move on, however, it is useful to clarify the use of the name **European Union (EU)** The European Union was formerly called the European Community (EC), and before that, the **European Economic Community (EEC)**. When the agreement was implemented in 1958, the six member countries were called the European Economic Community, but as they took on more responsibilities of a social and political nature, they were no longer solely an *economic* community and usage changed to the European Community. In 1993, with the implementation of the Treaty on European Union, also called the **Maastricht Treaty**, the EC became the European Union. This chapter refers to the EC when talking about events before 1993, and to the EU, or European Union for events thereafter.

## The Size of the European Market

Before discussing the history or economics of economic integration in Western Europe, let us define the nations and groups that are important to get an idea of the size of the market. In terms of population, the European Union is the largest integrated market in the world. By implication, the European Union is likely to have a major role in determining future international political arrangements, trade patterns and rules, and international economic relations in general. Few countries will be able to grow and prosper without selling their goods in the European market, which is a powerful incentive to accept European leadership on international issues.

Table 14.1 lists the members of the European Union and their population and incomes in 2005. As shown in Table 13.1, income is measured in absolute and per

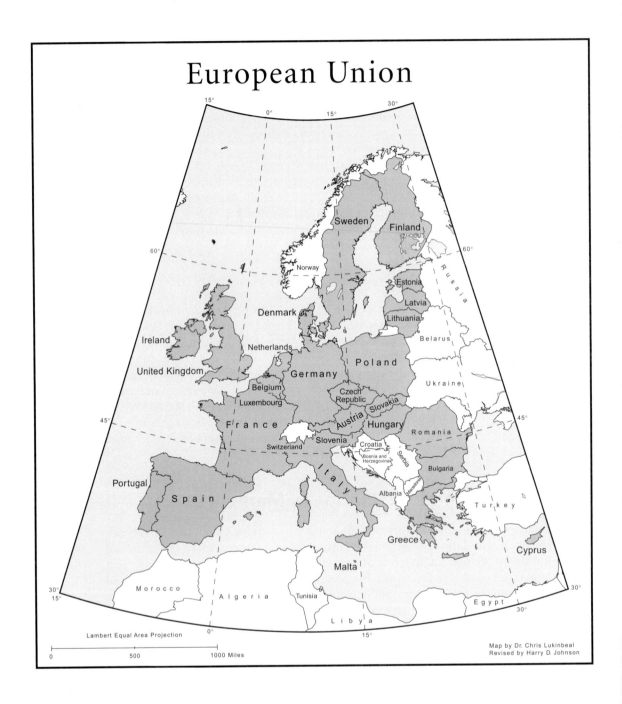

European Union

| TABLE 14.1 • Population and Income in the European Union, 2005 | | | | |
|---|---|---|---|---|
| | Population (Millions) | GDP (US$, Billions) | GDP per Capita (US$) | GDP per Capita (US$, PPP) |
| **Original members** | | | | |
| Belgium | 10.5 | 365 | 34,834 | 32,195 |
| France | 60.7 | 2,110 | 34,740 | 30,120 |
| Germany | 82.5 | 2,782 | 33,726 | 29,309 |
| Italy | 57.5 | 1,723 | 29,981 | 29,019 |
| Luxembourg | 0.5 | 34 | 73,961 | 74,573 |
| Netherlands | 16.3 | 595 | 36,423 | 32,927 |
| **Members, 1973–1995** | | | | |
| Austria | 8.2 | 305 | 37,086 | 33,662 |
| Denmark | 5.4 | 254 | 46,952 | 33,722 |
| Finland | 5.2 | 193 | 36,830 | 31,245 |
| Greece | 11.1 | 214 | 19,271 | 23,591 |
| Ireland | 4.2 | 196 | 47,316 | 40,942 |
| Portugal | 10.6 | 173 | 16,396 | 20,124 |
| Spain | 43.4 | 1,124 | 25,898 | 26,125 |
| Sweden | 9.0 | 354 | 39,241 | 31,062 |
| United Kingdom | 60.2 | 2,193 | 36,420 | 32,005 |
| **Members, 2004–2007** | | | | |
| Bulgaria | 7.7 | 27 | 3,442 | 8,794 |
| Cyprus | 0.8 | NA | NA | NA |
| Czech Republic | 10.2 | 122 | 11,999 | 21,317 |
| Estonia | 1.3 | 13 | 9,745 | 16,228 |
| Hungary | 10.1 | 109 | 10,820 | 18,086 |
| Latvia | 2.3 | 16 | 6,857 | 13,631 |
| Lithuania | 3.4 | 25 | 7,466 | 14,382 |
| Malta | 0.4 | 6 | 13,783 | 19,541 |
| Poland | 38.2 | 299 | 7,838 | 13,980 |
| Romania | 21.6 | 99 | 4,556 | 9,208 |
| Slovak Republic | 5.4 | 46 | 8,615 | 16,459 |
| Slovenia | 2.0 | 34 | 17,030 | 22,292 |
| **EU-27** | 488.7 | 13,410 | 27,441 | 26,346 |

The 27 members of the European Union have income and population totals that are comparable to those for the NAFTA region.

capita terms, and at market exchange rates and purchasing power parity rates. Comparisons at market exchange rates are a less accurate indicator of living standards than comparisons at purchasing power parity rates, but they are a more accurate indicator of the size of each market in terms of its ability to buy goods and services that are imported. Several features of Table 14.1 are worth highlighting. First, not all West European nations are members. Norway, which voted against joining in 1970 and in 1995, and Switzerland are noticeably absent. In addition, a number of the smaller nations, including Iceland, Liechtenstein, San Marino, and Monaco are not members. Second, the majority of nations in the European Union are relatively small. The unification of Germany in the early 1990s created the largest country in the European Union, but only six of the 27 nations (France, Germany, Italy, Spain, Poland, and the United Kingdom) can be considered large, and none are as populous as the United States or Mexico. Third, the combined EU market is very similar to the size of the NAFTA market, in terms of population and GDP. In 2005 the European Union counted 488.7 million people while the NAFTA nations counted 431.9 million; GDP comparisons were $13,410 billion in the European Union and $14,338 billion in NAFTA.

#  Before the European Union

The European Economic Community was born on March 25, 1957, with the signing of the **Treaty of Rome** by the original six members. The Treaty went into effect about nine months later, on January 1, 1958. The Treaty remains the fundamental agreement while more recent agreements, such as the Single European Act and the Maastricht Agreement were passed as amendments to the original treaty. The six founding members include the Benelux countries (Belgium, Netherlands, and Luxembourg), France, West Germany, and Italy.

## The Treaty of Rome

The European Economic Community grew out of the reconstruction of Europe at the end of World War II. The goals of the founders of the EEC were to rebuild their destroyed economies and to prevent the destruction from happening again. The original vision of the founders of the EEC was for a political union that they hoped to create through economic integration. In 1950 the first step was a proposal by Robert Schuman, the foreign minister of France, to pool the European coal and steel industries. Coal and steel were chosen because they were large industrial activities that served as the backbone of military strength. Schuman's plan was to pool the industries of Germany and France, the two largest West European antagonists, but Luxembourg, Belgium, the Netherlands, and Italy signed on as well. The **European Coal and Steel Community (ECSC)** Treaty was signed in 1951 and included provisions for the establishment of the ECSC High Authority, an international agency with regulatory powers. Coal and steel trade between the six members grew by 129 percent in the first five years of the treaty.

The success of the ECSC led to early attempts at integration in political and military areas (the European Defense Community and the European Political Community), but these efforts failed when they were rejected by the French Parliament in 1954. At that point, European leaders decided to focus their efforts on economic integration. In 1955 the six foreign ministers of the ECSC countries launched a round of talks in Messina, Italy, to discuss the creation of the European Economic Community and **European Atomic Energy Community (EAEC or Euratom)**. The goal of the former was to create a single, integrated market for goods, services, labor, and capital. The latter sought jointly to develop nuclear energy for peaceful purposes. Two separate treaties were signed in 1957 in Rome, creating the EEC and Euratom.

## Institutional Structure of the EEC

The founders of the EEC envisioned a federation in which local, regional, national, and European authorities cooperate and complement each other. The model was similar to the interaction between the cities, counties, states, and federal government in the United States, or local, provincial, and federal governments in Canada.

In EU jargon, **subsidiarity** describes the relationship between national and EU areas of authority, and between national and EU institutions. Subsidiarity is defined as the principle that the Union will only have authority to tackle issues that are more effectively handled through international action than by individual nations acting alone. In some cases, these issues are easily defined, but in others they are not. Current thinking places the responsibility for environmental and regional policy, research and technology development, and economic and monetary union under EU control.

Areas that are less clear-cut and where there continues to be some degree of controversy include the issues of labor market policies, social policies, and competition policies. The presence of controversy, however, has not prevented the European Union from agreeing to a common competition policy and a common set of labor market policies, called the Social Charter. Both areas continue to be sources of significant disagreement and political maneuvering, as national policies reflect fundamental philosophical differences in values and choices. The conflict between policies that reflect national values and the desire to obtain greater gains from trade through economic integration is a pervasive problem in every instance of economic integration. Given that nations rarely speak with a single voice, but are themselves composed of factions and special interests, the struggle over the transfer of sovereignty is all the more contentious.

The European Union is governed by five main institutions and a number of lesser ones. The five most prominent are the **European Commission**, the **Council of the European Union**, the **European Parliament**, the **Court of Justice**, and the **Court of Auditors**. The first three are representative bodies composed of members from each country. Their roles are to initiate and implement laws and regulations for the European Union. Table 14.2 displays the number of votes in each institution, as well as the range of votes granted to each country.

**TABLE 14.2** • **Votes in the Main EU Institutions**

|  | Total Votes* | Votes per Country | |
|---|---|---|---|
|  |  | Minimum | Maximum |
| **European Commission** | 25 | 1 | 1 |
| **Council of the European Union** | 321 | 3 | 29 |
| **European Parliament** | 732 | 5 | 99 |

*Prior to accession of Bulgaria and Romania in 2007.

**The European Commission.** The executive body of the European Union is the European Commission. Each country has one vote in the commission. Future members will also be given one vote. Commissioners serve five-year terms that are renewable, and they are appointed by national governments with the mutual approval of the member states. The Commission elects one of its own members to serve as its president. Work is divided in a way that gives each commissioner responsibility for one or more policy areas, but all decisions are a collective responsibility.

The Commission's primary responsibility is to act as the guardian of the treaties, ensuring that they are faithfully and legally enforced. This role includes responsibility for creating the rules for implementing treaty articles and for EU budget appropriations. As the executive branch, the Commission has the sole right to initiate EU laws and the same right as the national governments to submit proposals.

**The Council of the European Union.** The Council is the primary legislative branch of the European Union, a responsibility it shares with the European Parliament. Each country has between 3 (Malta) and 29 (France, Germany, Italy, United Kingdom) votes. The Council is the primary body for enacting laws proposed by the Commission and has more control over the budget than the Parliament or the Commission. Its membership consists of ministers from each nation, with participation varying according to the topic under discussion. For example, labor ministers convene to discuss labor issues, and environmental ministers to discuss environmental legislation. Most legislative decisions require either unanimity among all countries or a **qualified majority**, which is a majority of countries and 232 of 321 votes (72.3 percent).

The Council's presidency rotates among the member states in six-month terms. The chance to serve as President of the Council for six months is an important mechanism for individual member states to bring up their own legislative agendas and has been instrumental in the adoption of key EU regulations.

**The European Parliament.** The European Parliament has 732 members, directly elected by the people for five-year terms and apportioned among the member states according to population. Members associate by political affiliation rather than national origin. The Parliament has three main responsibilities as follows:

- Passing laws
- Supervising other institutions within the European Union
- Passing the final EU budget

EU laws are usually a co-decision of the Council and Parliament, although the Council alone may make laws in certain areas. The Parliament also provides oversight of the work of the other main bodies, such as the Commission. And finally, passage of the annual budget of the European Union requires approval of the Parliament. Over time, the role of the Parliament has probably changed more than any other institution. In its early years it was primarily an advisory body with little real authority, but as the European Union has grown it has taken on more authority, in part because it provides democratic legitimacy as the only institution directly elected by the citizens of the European Union.

**Other Institutions.** The final two main institutions are the Court of Justice and the Court of Auditors. The Court of Justice acts as the European Union's Supreme Court, with responsibility for interpreting laws and treaties. The Court's rulings are binding and take precedence over the 27 national courts. The Court of Auditors monitors the finances of the institutions and reports on the use and misuse of funds.

While these five institutions are the main ones, a number of other institutions have had important roles in EU governance. For example, the European Economic and Social Committee offers an institutional voice to civil society, and the Committee of the Regions represents the interests of specific regions, many of which make up areas in more than one country.

**The European Constitution.** On October 29, 2004, heads of state from the member countries signed the Constitution for Europe. This document will not take effect until it is ratified by each member and a few countries, such as, France and the Netherlands have voted no, leaving its future in doubt. Nevertheless, political and administrative pressures will continue to push for simplification of the many existing treaties by combining them into one main document. A main goal of the constitution was to simplify decision making within the European Union after ten new members joined in 2004 and two more in 2007. The Constitution for Europe is also intended to guarantee civil and human rights, clarify the functions of EU institutions, and define the separation of powers and responsibilities between national governments and the European Union. It would create an EU Foreign Minister, and provide for greater cooperation in the areas of defense, police and judicial affairs, and economic coordination.

**Financing the European Union.** The total budget of the European Union for 2006 was €111.9 billion ($140 billion). This amounts to slightly more than 1 percent of the gross national income of the member states, and is a relatively small amount of revenue by comparison to that of national governments, which often have total revenue equivalent to 30 to 50 percent or more of the nation's gross national income. The budget is financed through three main sources:

- Tariffs on goods entering the European Union
- An EU share of national value added taxes
- A payment from each member country based on the size of its economy

The latter category is by far the largest, accounting for about 68 percent of the total revenue collected by the European Union.

The two largest expenditure categories of the European Union are for agricultural support, both direct payments in the form of subsidies and indirect payments in the form of rural development, and **cohesion funds**. Agricultural support programs take nearly 40 percent of the budget directly, with another uncertain amount, which is counted as rural development or cohesion expenditures. Cohesion funds take almost 30 percent of the budget and are used to support the less developed regions within the European Union, particularly the new members from Central Europe that have incomes below the EU average. This is accomplished through infrastructure development, particularly environmental projects such as water treatment and transportation projects.

#  Deepening and Widening the Community in the 1970s and 1980s

When Europeans speak of increasing the level of cooperation between member countries, they use the term *deepening*. Deepening refers to economic and noneconomic activities that cause increased levels of integration of the national economies. For example, the movement from a free market to a customs union, the harmonization of technical standards in industry, or agreements to develop a common security and defense policy are deepening activities that increase interactions between the member states. On the other hand, when Europeans speak about extending the boundaries of the European Union to include new members, they use the term *widening*. Between 1957, when the agreement was signed to create the European Economic Community, and 1995, nine new members were added, bringing the total from six original members to 15. In 2004 10 more members were added and in 2007 Bulgaria and Romania joined. In the next section of this chapter we will look at the various stages of deepening.

## Before the Euro

In 1979 the members of the European Economic Community began to link their currencies in an effort to prevent radical fluctuation in currency values. The EC wanted to prevent competitive devaluations, in which one country devalues in order to capture the export markets of another country. **Competitive devaluations** inevitably generate conflict and lead to a breakdown in cooperation, since the devaluing country is viewed as gaining exports and jobs at the expense of others. Nations sometimes find it difficult to resist devaluation, especially during recessions. This tactic is viewed as unfair, however, and in the medium to long term, it is usually ineffective since the nondevaluing countries are obliged to follow suit and retaliate with their own devaluations.

In addition to looking for a mechanism that might discourage competitive devaluations, the EC sought to remove some of the uncertainty and risk from trading and investing across national boundaries. While forward markets can be used to protect against exchange rate risk, they only work about six months into the future.

The goal was to create an environment in which trade and investment throughout the EC was determined by considerations of comparative advantage and efficient resource allocation, rather than by changes in exchange rates. The result was the **European Monetary System (EMS)** and the **exchange rate mechanism (ERM)**. The formation of the EMS in 1979 was a significant deepening of the EC and served to prepare the way for the eventual introduction of a single currency. It was designed to prevent extreme currency fluctuations by tying each currency's value to the weighted average of the others. The group average, the **European currency unit (ECU)**, was used as a unit of account, but not as a means of payment.

The ERM system was an example of an exchange rate band. Each currency in the band was fixed to the ECU, but was allowed to fluctuate several percentage points up or down. If a currency began to move out of the bandwidth of several percentage points around the fixed rate, the central bank of the country was obligated to intervene, by either buying its currency in order to prop it up, or by selling currency in order to push it down in value. In September 1992, for example, the United Kingdom spent an estimated $30 billion in just a few days, in an attempt to protect the British pound from market speculators who had become convinced that it was going to fall in value. In the end, the speculators were right, and the Bank of England lost a lot of money trying to move against the market.

Given the ineffectiveness of market intervention in the face of a strong and determined market movement, most analysts predicted that the ERM would fail as a mechanism for maintaining stable European currency values. An ERM-type arrangement was attempted in 1973, but it soon collapsed as a result of the first oil shortage and its effects on national inflation rates. When the EC proposed a similar arrangement in 1979, many were skeptical that it would survive for very long or that it would effectively stabilize currencies. To most economists' surprise, the ERM effectively linked EC exchange rates for two decades.

The ERM experienced several adjustments, but none of them threatened the functioning of the system until 1992. Oddly enough, it was the reunification of Germany that caused the system to nearly collapse and led to a much weaker linkage between exchange rates. Because German reunification had a profound effect on the ERM, and because it is an interesting lesson in the costs of tying currencies together, it is useful to look at this episode in more detail.

Problems began in 1990 with Germany's decision to speed up its reunification with the German Democratic Republic (East Germany) after the fall of the Berlin Wall in November 1989. Economic conditions in East Germany were worse than expected, and it was soon apparent that the costs of building a productive economy would be enormous. The infrastructure (roads, bridges, ports, utilities, schools, hospitals) was in worse shape than most people realized, and environmental pollution was significant. In order to build a prosperous economy in its eastern region, Germany had to raise the productivity levels of the people living there, which required huge investments in infrastructure and the environment. The unexpectedly large expenditures to raise the productivity of East Germany resulted in a very large fiscal stimulus to the German economy. Such large expenditures by both the government and private sector were also expected to have an inflationary impact, and the Bundesbank (Germany's central bank) acted to counteract the increased probability of future inflation by raising interest rates. An increase in interest rates is expected to slow the economy by increasing the costs of using borrowed capital. Germany, therefore, had an expansionary fiscal policy that was partially offset by a contractionary monetary policy.

High interest rates in Germany made German financial instruments more attractive and caused capital to flow into Germany from the other EC countries. This resulted in the selling of British pounds, French francs, and other currencies in order to buy German marks (and then German bonds) and caused the pound, the franc, and other currencies to fall in value. At first, the movement was within the 2.25 percent bandwidth, and most of the EC hoped that they would somehow muddle through without making any drastic changes in the ERM or the EMS.

One solution would have been for the countries with falling currencies to raise their interest rates to match Germany's. This would have stemmed the outflow of financial capital looking for better rates of return in Germany. Some of the countries—the United Kingdom, for example—were entering recessions in 1990 and 1991 and did not want to raise interest rates just as a recession was taking hold. The likely effect would have been to hasten and deepen the recession, something no policymaker wants to be accused of doing. Other countries, France for example, were not yet entering the recessionary phase of their business cycle, but they had very high unemployment rates, and contractionary monetary policy was not desirable.

The dilemma faced by the EC countries is a good example of a recurring theme in the history of exchange rate systems. By tying their exchange rates to each other, the EC countries gave up a large measure of independence in their monetary policies. Because Germany was the largest country and the one with the most influential central bank, its monetary policy set the tone for the rest of the EC, and, at a time when many of the members wanted expansionary monetary policy, they were forced to adopt contractionary policies. The 1992 episode illustrates the recurrent tension that occurs between the appropriate external policies (exchange rate management) and the appropriate internal policies (full employment, reasonable growth, low inflation) when nations tie their exchange rates together. Since the "right" policy choice for meeting the exchange rate problem was diametrically opposite to meeting the needs of the internal economy, EC members were left with a tough decision. They would have to honor their commitments to the ERM and make their unemployment and growth rates worse, or do the right thing for internal growth and watch the ERM fall apart. In the French case, an interest rate increase threw the country into recession, but France remained within the ERM. In Italy and the United Kingdom, the ERM was abandoned, and their currencies were allowed to freely float against other EC currencies. A third option was chosen by Spain, where the parity, or center of the band, was shifted. In order to lessen the probability of future repeats of this problem, the bandwidth was widened in 1993 from ±2.25 percent to ±15 percent.

## The Second Wave of Deepening: The Single European Act

Other than the creation of the European Monetary System in 1979, the changes in the EC were minor through the 1970s and the first half of the 1980s. In the early 1980s most West European countries suffered through a recession that left their unemployment rates high, even as their economic growth recovered in 1984 and 1985. The European economies seemed stale and incapable of new dynamism and many in the United States began to refer to the European situation as "Eurosclerosis," signifying a permanent hardening of the arteries of commerce and industry.

By the late 1980s, people in North America and Europe had stopped using "Eurosclerosis" and begun to speak of "Europhoria." While both terms were exaggerations, dramatic events had reshaped the EC in the intervening years. What was previously dismissed in the early 1980s as a hopeless case of bureaucratic inefficiency was now regarded as a dynamic, forward-looking, integrated regional economy. Europe seemed to be "on the move."

## CASE STUDY

## The Schengen Agreement

The Schengen Agreement was signed by five countries (Belgium, France, Germany, Luxembourg, and the Netherlands) in the town of Schengen, Luxembourg, in 1985. The purpose of the agreement is to eliminate all passport and customs controls at the common borders of the five nations. Given that they enjoyed free trade, and given the flow of people between the countries, the purpose of examining passports or checking customs paperwork seemed inefficient and unnecessary. Over the next few years, more members of the European Union joined the agreement. When the Single European Act was completely implemented, the idea of a common market allowing free movement of people gave it added logic. By 1995, the agreement was extended to more countries and more areas of activity, including cooperation among police forces, drug enforcement agencies, and the sharing of criminal justice information. Originally, the Schengen Agreement and its subsequent extension were outside the legal framework of the European Union; but in 1999, it was incorporated into EU law. Eventually non-EU countries, among them Iceland and Norway, were allowed to participate.

The dismantling of border-control stations, including passport and customs inspections, undoubtedly has had a positive effect on EU efficiency, because it reduces travel time for both goods and people. It also demonstrates a high degree of social trust among the member nations and contributes to goodwill and better relations. In effect, it shifts customs and passport controls to the perimeter of the European Union, where non-EU citizens and goods first enter the region. While this is beneficial, two main problems have arisen from the shifting of control to the perimeter.

First, Ireland and the United Kingdom have not accepted the dismantling of passport controls at the border because they fear the freedom of movement this will give terrorists. However, as members of the European Union, they must extend the rights of all other EU citizens to travel freely and reside inside their borders, even as they maintain passport checks at the border. Second, the eventual extension of the Schengen Agreement to the 12 new members since 2004 depends on those members' ability to demonstrate control over their own borders to the east, and on the development of a new EU data system for sharing information about individuals and lost or stolen objects. The timetable for extending Schengen beyond its current membership (13 EU members, plus Norway and Iceland) is not set.

## The Delors Report

Reshaping the EC got under way with the selection of the former French finance minister, Jacques Delors, to serve a five-year term as president of the European Commission. Delors was a compromise candidate, and no one expected unusual or dramatic changes in the EC under his stewardship. Delors's vision of the EC, however, was of a fully integrated union, and as president of the EC's executive branch, he had a platform from which he could initiate significant change. His vision was shaped in part by the belief that the institutions of the EC could help return individual national economies to economic prosperity and by the desire to complete the task of building an economic and political union.

Delors' first step, and perhaps his most significant one, was to issue a report called "Completing the Internal Market," which detailed 300 specific changes necessary for the EC to move from a quasi-customs union to an economic union. It laid out a timetable for completing the changes and removed the need for unanimous voting in the Council of Ministers. Delors proposed that most measures be allowed to pass with a "qualified majority" and that unanimity be reserved for only the most momentous issues, such as taxes. Although the qualified majority still allowed a minority of countries to block a measure, it prevented any single country from blocking a proposed change.

After some relatively minor changes in the **Delors Report**, it was adopted in its entirety in 1987, as the Single European Act (SEA). Of the 300 steps, or "directives," 279 were included in the SEA. Many of the 21 not included were considered too difficult to accomplish in the time period the EC gave itself, but were taken up as goals of the next round of deepening. For example, monetary union under a single currency was moved forward to the next round of deepening.

The date for implementation of the SEA was January 1, 1993. By the end of 1992, it was expected that the "four freedoms" (freedom of movement for goods, services, capital, and labor) spelled out in the SEA would be instituted and, as a result, the EC would be at the common market level of economic integration. In order to accomplish these goals it was necessary to determine the method of implementation of each of the 279 directives and for each of the 12 member nations to make the necessary changes in their internal laws, standards, and customary practices. While some areas remain incomplete, the vast majority of the directives were put into practice by the end of 1992, and the EC achieved common market status.

The steps taken to implement the SEA can be broadly divided into three areas: (1) the elimination of physical barriers, such as passport and customs controls at the borders between member countries; (2) the elimination of technical barriers, such as differences in product and safety standards; and (3) the elimination of fiscal barriers, such as differences in taxes, subsidies, and public procurement. Each of these poses its own benefits and challenges and will be discussed in more detail. First, we will consider the gains that the EC hoped to reap from the elimination of these barriers.

## Forecasts of the Gains from the Single European Act

One of the central reasons for supporting the SEA was to achieve gains in economic efficiency. One set of gains was anticipated to come from the freeing of the movement of goods and services. While the SEA did not mandate the elimination of border inspections, it did grant freedom of movement to people and goods. In many cases, border controls were dismantled, also with support from the Schengen Agreement, but in some cases "tax inspections" replaced customs inspections due to the European Union's inability to establish a common system of value-added taxation. Nevertheless, substantial progress has been made in eliminating long border waits and in speeding up the distribution of goods throughout the EC.

Integration also created economic benefits from greater economies of scale and increased competitiveness. Economies of scale are possible because EC firms are able to produce at one site, or in a fewer number of sites for the entire European market and will not have to duplicate production facilities across national boundaries. This enables some companies to consolidate their operations and to avoid duplication in their production and support services, such as accounting. The increase in competitiveness comes from several sources. For example, the increased pressure of competition will force some firms to make productive investments that they would not otherwise have made. In addition, the openness of the competitive environment will generate a larger, more mobile pool of labor that carries skills from one firm to another. Finally, the free flow of goods and services will generate a greater flow of information and ideas so that firms have easier access to the best new ideas.

## Problems in the Implementation of the SEA

One of the most interesting lessons of the Single European Act is that it is still difficult to reduce barriers to trade and investment even when the citizens, businesses, and governments of the involved countries are united in their desire to do so. According to all the polls, the SEA enjoyed very broad support throughout the EC. Still, from the time when it was first proposed in 1985 until its final implementation in 1993, there were very difficult negotiations among the member countries.

**The Effects of Restructuring.** As we saw in Chapter 3, when a national economy goes from a relatively closed position to a relatively open one, economic restructuring takes place. The less efficient firms are squeezed out, and the more efficient ones grow; overall economic welfare expands as countries concentrate on what they do best, which inevitably means abandoning some industries and expanding others. In the case of the EC, it was forecast that almost all manufacturing industries would see shrinkage in the number of firms. The most extreme case was the footwear industry, which was predicted to lose 207 of its 739 firms. In some cases, the majority of the disappearing firms were concentrated in one or two countries, such as the UK carpet industry, where it was predicted that 31 of 52 manufacturers would go out of business.

The firms that go out of business are part of the economy-wide shift to a more efficient use of labor and capital resources, but it is obvious that there are immediate human costs. In the long run, it is easy to show that the gains in efficiency and the improvement in living standards outweigh the costs of restructuring, but in the short run, individuals and communities can feel acute pain. Due to the inevitable costs from restructuring, many people predicted that adversely affected firms and labor unions, along with the communities and regions that depend on the firms, would fight to prevent the full implementation of the SEA.

The auto industry is the best example of an economic interest that fought to prevent the full realization of the goals of the SEA. Car prices vary throughout the European Union due to a lack of harmonization of national technical standards, documentation requirements, and rates of taxation. Ordinarily, such large price differences would present an opportunity for consumers and distributors to move cars from the low-price countries to the high-price ones and, in the process, bring about a reduction in price differences. The auto industry is covered by a separate set of tax laws, however, that require buyers to pay the tax rate of the country where they register the car, not where they buy the car. This effectively discourages buyers from crossing national borders in order to search out the best deal on car prices and helps maintain the status quo in automobile production.

One significant reason why there have not been more exceptions to the dropping of trade barriers is that the European Union has a broad array of programs to address the problems of structural change. Some of these programs are funded out of the EU budget, and others are national in origin. Programs include the European Union's Regional Development Funds, which can be used to address problems of structural unemployment, and the member nations' income maintenance, education, and retraining funds. The latter vary across the member countries, but, in general, they reduce the costs to individuals and communities of unemployment and structural change by providing a generous social safety net for laid-off workers. The programs can also have positive effects in reducing political opposition to economic change because workers in a factory that is shut down may not fight the closing as much given the economic support system provided for laid-off employees. At the same time, the society-wide perception that workers who have been hurt by restructuring will be taken care of may effectively reduce opposition to change on the grounds of "fairness."

It should be noted that although the generosity of the social safety net in the European Union may be politically instrumental in reducing opposition to economic restructuring, many economists and politicians argue that the generosity created by the social safety net can cause additional problems as well. In particular, many see it as a primary reason for the relatively high unemployment rates since the late 1980s. By providing generous benefits to the unemployed, the European Union has reduced the cost of unemployment and removed some of the incentives to look for work. In addition, taxes for these social programs often fall on employers; therefore, many firms are reluctant to hire new employees during an economic expansion. This is an ongoing debate within the European Union.

**Harmonization of Technical Standards.** A second major obstacle to the creation of the four freedoms was the problem of harmonizing standards. These include everything from building codes, industrial equipment, consumer safety, and health standards, to university degrees and worker qualifications. The European Union estimated that there were more than 100,000 technical standards that required harmonization in order to realize the benefits of a completely integrated market. Many of the technical standards involved rules that directly touch upon cultural identities. Nowhere was this more true than in the case of food processing. For example, there were discussions around the allowable level of bacteria in French cheese, the type of wheat required to make Italian pasta, the ingredients of German beer, and the oatmeal content of English bangers (breakfast sausages). In the end, the European Union recognized that complete harmonization of standards would generate significant hostility and that the work required to agree on a set of common standards was beyond its capacity. Consequently, a combination of harmonization and mutual recognition of standards was adopted. In particularly sensitive cases, mutual recognition is the rule, but individual nations are allowed to keep their own national production requirements. For example, German beer must be certified as having been made according to the German standards, but Germany must allow all brands of beers to be sold within its borders.

As the discussion in Chapter 8 noted, standards do not have to be the same in order to create a single market, but the gains in economic efficiency that come from sharing the same standard can be significant. Shared standards permit manufacturers to produce to one standard, rather than many, and to capture important economies of scale in the process. These economies also pass outside the European Union, since U.S. or Japanese manufacturers share the benefits of being able to produce to one set of standards as well. Additionally, non-EU-based firms only have to get their product certified once in order to sell in all 27 countries. For this reason, the United States has had a keen interest in the standards-setting process and has looked to create joint U.S.-EU agreements on standards and the procedures by which they are set. The preference of the United States has been to use the procedures of the International Standards Organization (ISO) to streamline the process of harmonization. The ISO is an international organization that provides technical standards and whose ISO-9000 is a set of certifications applying to nearly all types of economic activity.

**Value-Added Taxes.** A third difficulty standing in the way of completely realizing the four freedoms is the issue of value-added taxes (VAT). These taxes function essentially like sales taxes and are levied by each of the EU members but at a wide variety of rates and coverage. When the SEA was first proposed in 1987, there were significant differences in the dependence of the member governments of the European Union on value-added taxes, ranging from 19 to 35 percent of total government revenue. The European Commission studied the United States to determine the effects of different rates of sales taxation on states sharing common borders and found that once the difference in sales taxes exceeded 5 percent, the higher-tax state lost revenues, sales, and jobs to the neighboring lower-tax state. In other words, a 5 percent difference was enough to cause consumers to cross state boundaries to make purchases. The standard VAT rate in the European Union before the SEA varied from 12 percent at the low end (Luxembourg and Spain) to 20 percent in the Netherlands, 22 percent in

Denmark, and 25 percent in Ireland. In addition, there were special rates for sensitive goods, which varied a great deal more than the standard rates.

VAT rates proved impossible to completely harmonize because they go to the heart of national political philosophy. High-tax countries expect the state to play a relatively greater role in national economic life, while low-tax countries are closer to the laissez-faire end of the political economy spectrum. The level of value-added taxes, and the degree to which the national government depends on them are in large part determined by the political philosophy of the nation. In turn, these philosophical attitudes are shaped by economics, as well as complex historical, cultural, and social factors..

The attempt to harmonize value-added taxes created an inability to agree on a single rate. What was accomplished, however, was the creation of minimum and maximum rates that were set at 15 and 25 percent. Since the difference still exceeds the 5 percent differential that is the threshold at which high-tax countries lose revenue and sales, a number of controls were established to prevent revenue loss, even though these controls prevent the complete realization of the four freedoms.

Despite these obstacles, however, there are still significant incentives for cross-border shopping. Although the SEA has not brought a 100 percent free flow of goods and services, it is important to keep the exceptions in perspective. For most goods and services, in most border regions, consumers are free to cross national boundaries to bring back unlimited quantities of goods, and will not be stopped at a border inspection station.

**Public Procurement.** Public procurement is the purchase of goods and services by governments or government-owned enterprises, such as state-run television companies, utilities, or hospitals. Most nations of the world tend to use procurement processes that discriminate in favor of nationally owned suppliers, although there are limits on their ability to do so if they belong to the WTO.

Since 1970, the European Union has attempted to eliminate discrimination in public procurement but this has proved difficult. It is a problem particularly in the areas of telecommunications, pharmaceuticals, railway equipment, and electrical equipment. In many instances national governments have attempted to create firms that would serve as "national champions" in world competition. One method was to favor those firms in the government procurement process so that they would have a guaranteed market for their output while they were still learning the most efficient methods of production. Needless to say, firms and industries that receive favorable treatment often develop effective lobbying efforts, particularly if there are a large number of jobs in the industry, or if it can make a credible argument that it is essential to the nation's future development or its national security.

Discrimination in public procurement, however, limits the benefits of restructuring and the gains from trade. If the EU countries are able to successfully develop a common security and foreign policy, the national security argument for discrimination in public procurement begins to lose a great deal of its justification.

# The Third Wave of Deepening: The Maastricht Treaty

By 1989, planning for the implementation of the Single European Act in January 1993 was well under way. Europe had seen several years of economic expansion, and the excitement of the SEA seemed to signal that the time was right to consider some of the directives proposed in the Delors Report that had been set aside because they were seen as too complex to accomplish by 1993. In 1990 the European Commission convened an Intergovernmental Conference on Economic and Monetary Union. The purpose of the conference was to bring together the leaders of the 12 nations to discuss the steps necessary to create a monetary union under a single currency. There were other issues on the agenda, but this was the one that attracted the most interest inside and outside the European Union.

The Intergovernmental Conference continued through most of 1991. The final draft of the proposed agreement was completed in December in the Dutch town of Maastricht and, ever since, has been known as the Maastricht Treaty. Many of the provisions in the agreement are technical and cover such arcane issues as the tax treatment of holiday homes in Denmark, or the status of the pope in trade disputes with the Vatican. Other issues dealing with basic EU social policy are much more fundamental. For example, the Maastricht Treaty calls for the creation of a "Social Charter" defining a uniform set of labor laws and worker rights. It defines the right of all residents in a community to vote and stand for election in local contests, regardless of the resident's nationality; it puts more control over health, education, cultural, and consumer safety issues in the hands of the European Commission; it calls for a common defense and security policy along with a common military force; and it defines the steps for achieving a common currency under the control of a European Central Bank by 1999, at the latest.

It is the last goal that has attracted the most attention. Achieving a single currency requires each country to give up its ability to set its own monetary policy and to accept whatever contractionary or expansionary policy the European Central Bank chooses. This is the most controversial feature of the Maastricht Treaty, inside and outside of the European Union. The controversy stems from the fact that no group of countries has ever given up their monetary system to create a single currency, there is significant political opposition to its realization, and there are economic risks associated with voluntarily giving up one of the few tools that governments have to counteract recessions. If, for example, Germany is booming, but Spain is in an economic slump, there is no common monetary policy that will be suitable to both countries. Germany would need a contractionary policy to cool off the economy and to prevent the ignition of inflation, while Spain would need an expansionary policy to create employment and growth. These controversies led to a very different public reception for the Maastricht Treaty than that received by the Single European Act. Whereas citizens, businesses, and governments were solidly behind the SEA, support for the Maastricht Treaty has been much more tentative.

# Monetary Union and the Euro

The timetable for monetary union under a single currency is scheduled to occur in three separate stages. Stage one began in 1990 with the lifting of controls on the movement of financial capital within the European Union. Stage two began in 1994 with the creation of the European Monetary Institute, based in Frankfurt, Germany. The Institute was charged with the responsibility for coordinating the move to monetary union and gradually took on elements of a supranational central bank. The third stage began in 1999 with the phased-in introduction of the **euro** and the European Central Bank.

During stage one and two, nations were expected to bring their monetary and fiscal policies into harmony so that the introduction of the euro would not happen under wildly different sets of monetary and fiscal policies. In order to judge when individual national policies were in agreement, the European Union developed a set of **convergence criteria**. These were objective measures that signaled whether the national policies were in conflict or in agreement, and whether individual nations were ready for monetary union. Table 14.3 lists the specific monetary and fiscal variables that are required to be coordinated and the target ranges for each.

Initially, nations were expected to meet all five goals for monetary union. The experience of the first half of the 1990s, however, indicated that no nation, except perhaps Luxembourg, could consistently maintain each of these targets and that some countries would never meet them. For example, Italian and Belgian central government debts were well over 100 percent of their annual GDP, and there was no way to change this in the span of a few years. Some economists questioned why these particular criteria were chosen in the first place, since a country that can maintain its interest rates, debts, deficits, inflation, and exchange rates in the target range is already doing what the European Union hopes to

| TABLE 14.3 ● Convergence Criteria for Monetary Union | |
|---|---|
| Goals | Targets |
| 1. Stabilize exchange rates | Maintain currency within the ERM band |
| 2. Control inflation | Reduce it to less than 1.5 percent above the average of the three lowest rates |
| 3. Harmonize long-term interest rates | Bring to within 2 percent of the average of the three lowest rates |
| 4. Government deficits | Reduce to less than 3 percent of national GDP |
| 5. Government debt | Reduce to less than 60 percent of national GDP |

These five goals were designed to harmonize fiscal and monetary policies in preparation for the single currency.

achieve with monetary union. In other words, meeting the convergence criteria was an indicator that the nation can do what monetary union does but without actually giving up its currency. Why, then, should countries surrender control over monetary policy, and why should they give up their national currency, particularly since there are hidden costs?

## Costs and Benefits of Monetary Union

There is no doubt that there are benefits to having one currency in a market as large as the European Union's. For example, the average cost of currency conversion for travelers is 2.5 percent of the amount converted. A trip from Portugal to Sweden, with stops along the way, can quickly eat up a sizable portion of one's vacation money. Businesses fare much better, however, and if they buy in quantities greater than the equivalent of $U.S. 5 million, then the costs are a much smaller 0.05 percent, or $5,000 to convert $10 million. One estimate combining tourists and businesses puts the total costs of currency conversion at 0.4 percent of the European Union's GDP. This is not a trivial sum, but it is not huge, either. The 0.4 percent figure could be higher, however, given the costs of maintaining separate accounting systems and separate money management processes for the different currencies.

A second reason for desiring monetary union is to reduce the effects of exchange-rate uncertainty on trade and investment. Since orders for goods are often placed long before delivery occurs, traders face a good deal of uncertainty about their earnings (if they export) and their payments (if they import). A single currency eliminates this uncertainty, in the same way, for example, that California manufacturers can always be certain of the value of payments they will receive when they ship goods to New York. Recall from Chapter 10 that traders and investors can protect themselves from currency fluctuations with forward markets. Therefore, it should not be surprising that there is not much evidence that the elimination of currency fluctuations through a monetary union will increase cross-border trade and investment. On the other hand, tests of this idea are difficult because there are few examples of monetary unions. Recently, however, some evidence has emerged that shows large positive effects on trade and investment flows from the creation of a single currency. Ultimately, the European Union's experience will prove to be a valuable case study.

Given these considerations, the benefits of a single currency appear to be uncertain. The same cannot be said for the potential costs. A single currency does not allow individual nations to pursue an independent monetary policy, in the same way that the state of New York cannot have a monetary policy that differs from California's or the rest of the United States. In a single-currency area, there is a "one size fits all" monetary policy. It is optimal to have a single currency, and to eliminate the costs of currency conversion and other transaction costs, as long as the regions in the single currency area have synchronized business cycles and mobile labor forces. Synchronization of business cycles means that there is a single monetary policy—expansionary, neutral, or contractionary—that is appropriate for everybody. A mobile labor force guarantees that if some regions are not well synchronized, labor will move from the shrinking region to the expanding one, making the business cycles move together. If, however, the business cycles are not synchronized and labor is relatively immobile, then the single monetary policy will be right for some areas but wrong for others.

Business cycles in Europe have never been synchronized, although the convergence criteria were partly designed with this goal in mind. In addition, the Single European Act's guarantee of freedom for labor mobility does not seem to have created significantly more continent-wide labor mobility, and Europeans are far less mobile than Americans. Given that most conventional measures show that the European Union fails both criteria for being an optimal currency area, it seems natural to ask why they are taking this momentous step.

## The Political Economy of a Single Currency

Most policies that offer uncertain benefits and potentially large costs should be rejected. Why, then, did monetary union push ahead? This is the question that many economists have asked, and the answers are less than clear. The easiest answers are that the leaders of the European Union believe that monetary union will create substantial trade and investment flows, or that the leaders of the European Union are simply swept up in a euphoric rush to greater political and economic unity. The latter explanation suffers from the defect that the European Union has been unable to forge a consensus around a common defense and security policy, as evidenced by the divisions over the conflict in the former Yugoslavia.

The best explanation for the push to monetary union seems to be that it is politically necessary in the wake of the capital market liberalization required under the Single European Act. Prior to 1990, many countries had controls on the movement of foreign exchange into their country. Regulatory measures were common, such as taxes on foreign currency holdings, or on assets denominated in foreign currencies, and limitations on the uses of foreign currencies were widespread. The removal of these controls made it easier to speculate in foreign currency markets. One outcome of the removal of capital controls was the turmoil of 1992, when speculators became convinced that a number of currencies in the ERM would ultimately have to be devalued, prompting them to sell off large quantities of the currencies. During the sell-off, Portugal, Ireland, and Spain all devalued; Italy temporarily suspended participation in the ERM; and the United Kingdom dropped out permanently. Ultimately, the British pound fell by 25 percent from its peak before the speculative attacks. Soon after it left the ERM, there were several cases of firms that announced their intentions to close plants inside EU countries and move to the United Kingdom. Philips Electronics, the giant Dutch firm, for example, closed plants in Holland, and SC Johnson and the Hoover Company closed French plants, all in order to open new plants in the United Kingdom where French and Dutch currencies bought more land, labor, buildings, and machinery.

Political friction increases and cooperation decreases when one country loses jobs to another as a result of currency depreciations. The desire to reduce these types of frictions is the reason why the European Monetary System, with its Exchange Rate Mechanism, was created in 1979. Consequently, it is the reason why a flexible exchange rate system is not an option. Although floating exchange rates have the advantage of permitting the greatest amount of flexibility in a nation's monetary policies, the European Union's economic integration plans have closed the door on the use of flexible exchange rate systems.

Given that flexible rates are ruled out, it seems logical to ask why the European Union did not choose to institute a system of fixed exchange rates. In fact, the ERM acted somewhat like a fixed exchange rate system because it tied each country's currency to a weighted average of the other currencies. Exchange rates were not completely fixed, however, and there were bands that the currencies tried to stay within. The European Union's problem with a fixed exchange rate system is that it lacked the ability to keep the currencies within their bands, let alone to completely fix them. International currency markets know that there are definite limits to the resolve and the resources of member countries trying to defend their currencies. The European Union partially solved this by changing the bandwidths from ±2.25 percent to ±15 percent, which removed the minor short-term speculative pressures against particular currencies by letting them float down more before intervention became required. This, however, did nothing about the serious pressure against a currency that the United Kingdom and Italy experienced in 1992. In other words, the European Union is not willing to defend their fixed rates if the costs grow too high, which means that fixed rates are not really "fixed."

## Implementation of the Single Currency

The inability of the European Union to maintain a set of fixed rates, coupled with the political undesirability of floating rates, made the single-currency option an attractive choice. Membership in the monetary union, however, is a subset of the European Union. The United Kingdom has left the ERM and, along with Denmark and Sweden, did not join the move to a single currency. Few, if any, of the countries met the convergence criteria for compliance by the 1998 deadline. Nevertheless, in May of 1998, it was announced that 11 countries (the 15 members of the European Union, minus the United Kingdom, Sweden, Denmark, and Greece) would adopt the single currency on January 1, 1999. Greece adopted the euro one year later.

In the first stage of the implementation process, countries kept their national currencies, but fixed their exchange rates to each other. Until euro coins and notes began to circulate in 2002, each of the euro area countries continued to use its own national money, which was fixed in value to the euro and, therefore, to the money of the other member countries. During the transition period before the introduction of euro coins and notes, national currencies were managed as separate, national manifestations of the euro. The German mark, for example,

**FIGURE 14.1** ● **Dollars per Euro**

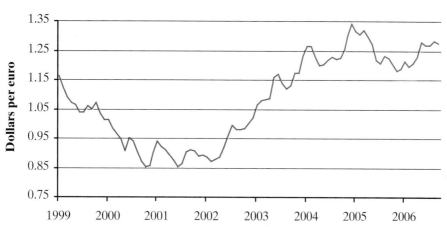

was worth about one-half a euro, just as two quarters are worth one-half a U.S. dollar. Consequently, speculation against any one currency was equivalent to speculating against all of them. The euro itself is on a flexible exchange rate system, so it is free to move up or down against the dollar, the yen, and other currencies. The euro is managed by the European Central Bank (ECB), which also conducts monetary policy in the euro region.

Since its introduction in 1999 at $U.S. 1.18, the euro value has varied significantly (see Figure 14.1). Or, one might say that the dollar's value has fluctuated significantly; either way, the same meaning is implied. The euro lost about one-fourth of its value within the first 18 months and since then has rapidly gained it all back. The decline and the subsequent rise were larger than expected. The decline in 1999 and 2000 was attributed to high—and rising—U.S. interest rates, the high rate of growth in the United States, and the soaring U.S. stock market. The rise in the euro that began in 2002 is perhaps related to the ballooning U.S. trade deficit and the expectation of future declines in the dollar that will be necessary to restore balance, along with the historically low level of U.S. interest rates.

 # Widening the European Union

After the achievement of monetary union, one of the most pressing problems facing the European Union was the timetable and conditions under which new members would be added to the European Union.

## Central and Eastern Europe

Ten countries joined the European Union in 2004 and two more joined in 2007. Ten of the twelve new members are from Central Europe and have undergone profound economic and political transformations as they abandoned relatively closed socialist economies in favor of democratic and capitalist systems.

There are three criteria for membership. First, each of the countries must be stable, functioning democracies. Second, they must have market-based economies, and third, they must formally adopt the EU-wide rules, called the ***acquis communautaire***. These include technical standards, environmental and technical inspections, banking supervision, public accounts, statistical reporting requirements, and other elements of EU law. The *acquis* is sovereign over national laws and must be completely adopted by each new member before it is granted full membership.

In the years leading up to membership, the European Union consults and provides technical assistance to candidate nations. To qualify for admission to the European Union, prospective members must develop the administrative capacity for implementing and enforcing EU rules. Building this capacity requires training legions of professional and technical workers, including judges, lawyers, environmental health and safety inspectors, financial institution supervisors, accountants, and a number of other skilled occupations. The professionals in these areas must become versed in EU law, technical standards, and administrative processes. Failure to demonstrate an ability to enforce the rules can lead to a denial of admission into the European Union.

There are four major problems with the planned expansion. The first is agriculture and agricultural policies. Several of the new members in Central Europe have large agricultural sectors. Poland, for example, is a large country, with a population of 38 million and about 18 percent of its labor force in agriculture. Agriculture is important to several other new members as well, because it generates exports and earns much needed foreign exchange. Large agricultural sectors are a problem for the European Union, however, because of the European Union's agricultural policies, known collectively as the **Common Agricultural Policy (CAP)**. The CAP is the world's most extensive set of farm price supports and farm income maintenance programs. One indicator of the importance of the CAP is that it continues to be the largest item in the EU budget at 40 percent in spite of a number of ongoing reforms to the agricultural support system. In addition, a significant share of expenditures on regional development is agricultural supports that have been reclassified for administrative reasons and to avoid complaints filed through the WTO system.

The CAP sets farm prices, guarantees a market for farm products, and provides direct income payments to farmers. Under a set of reforms passed in 2005, direct payments to farmers will be phased out gradually and decoupled from production. While desirable on their own account, the reforms are necessary in part due to the accession of the new members with large agricultural sectors and low incomes. Agricultural support payments on the same scale as those given to the EU-15 are impossible, given the budget of the European Union. The 12 new members will receive some payments that are phased in gradually over a 10-year period.

The second major issue of expansion is migration. The Single European Act created the right for all EU citizens to move freely and reside wherever they choose. Furthermore, it attempts to create a single labor market that allows workers to search for employment in any member country. Nevertheless, in 2004, when 10 countries joined, only the United Kingdom offered an open labor market, and no countries have shown signs of opening their doors to Romanian and Bulgarian workers when they joined in 2007. Under the rules of accession, countries that were members before 2004 have up to seven years before they must open their labor markets to the new members. New members must also wait for the dismantling of passport controls on their movement (see the Case Study on the Schengen Agreement).

A third issue with expansion is governance. As the original six members of the EEC grew into the 15 members of the European Union, and then added 12 more members, the institutions and governing bodies of the European Union became too complex and cumbersome. The proposed solution, the Constitution for Europe, was intended to simplify decision making processes, among other things, but the proposed document has not been well received by the citizens of the European Union and it is unlikely that it will pass.

Fourth, income difference between the new and existing members is much larger than any previous differences. This creates a variety of tensions, from potential migration pressures, to differences in institutional capacity, and demands on the EU budget for agricultural support payments, cohesion funds, and regional development funds. In the short-to-medium term, the European Union has addressed the migration issue by allowing countries to delay the opening of their labor markets for seven years. It has addressed the institutional gap with a lengthy accession period in which it provided technical assistance and financial support to the new members in order to assist the development of their legal, administrative, and regulatory institutions and to ensure that the new members were capable of enforcing the European Union's body of rules and regulations, or the *aquis communitaire*.

The most serious potential problems associated with the accession of relatively poor members from Central Europe can be ameliorated, if not eliminated completely, by a closing of the income differences between the new and old members. In this regard, the recent experiences of Ireland, Spain, Portugal, and Greece are instructive. Their accession in the 1970s and 1980s led to a similar gap between the richest and poorest members, although not quite as large as the current gap. Recognizing the tensions created by large disparities, the European Union created the Cohesion Fund and expanded its Regional Development Fund. These, and other sources of financing, are now being used to build infrastructure and to connect the new regions to the Western Europe and the global economies.

## Turkey

Turkey officially submitted its application for membership in 1987, and in 2004 the European Commission recommended to start negotiations in 2005. Turkey's population of 72.6 million in 2005 would make it the second largest member, although its GDP per capita was only $8,400 at purchasing power parity rates of exchange and $5,004 at market exchange rates. The market rate is less than 20 percent of the EU average, but more than some of the current members, such as Romania and Bulgaria.

The political challenges posed by Turkey's accession are significant. In order to begin negotiations, potential members must demonstrate that they are a stable democracy with respect for human rights, including protections for ethnic minorities, have a functioning market economy, and can implement and enforce the rules and laws of the European Union. Turkey fulfilled these criteria as a precondition for opening negotiations over accession, but it must continue its reforms. In particular, EU officials have warned that the country continues to stifle freedom of speech, that it has not curbed the use of torture in its prisons, and that it has not established civilian control over its military. In addition, Turkey's accession is hampered by the problem of Cyprus, a member of the European Union that is geographically divided into two ethnic regions, a northern half that is Turkish and a southern territory that is ethnically mixed, but largely Greek. Turkey's reluctance to open its ports to Cypriot ships is another barrier to its accession, in part due to the fact that Cyprus can block Turkey's accession under EU rules that grant member countries veto rights over the accession of new members.

It is not certain that Turkey will join the European Union eventually. If it does, the situation will be reminiscent of the situation of Mexico in the NAFTA region. Both are large developing countries with similar per capita income levels. EU pre-accession support programs in financial and technical assistance, and post-accession supports with Cohesion Funds and Regional Development Funds will be critical.

## CASE STUDY

# Spain's Switch from Emigration to Immigration

Spain's period of highest emigration was from 1881 to 1930, when approximately 4.3 million people left. In 1910 its population was just under 20 million, so a loss of 4.3 million people was significant. The decade with the highest out-migration was 1910 to 1920, when 1.3 million people or well over 5 percent of the population left.

Emigration was slowed by the world depression of the 1930s and World War II, but began again in earnest after 1950. Unlike the earlier migrations, when the majority of migrants went to the Americas, increasing numbers headed for other countries in Central and Western Europe. In particular, France, Germany, and Switzerland were major recipients of Spanish citizens.

By the time Spain joined the European Union in 1986, changes were occurring in the Spanish economy that were reducing the supply-push forces that cause emigration. In 1950 Spain's work force was nearly 50 percent agricultural, but by 1970 agriculture's share of the labor force had fallen to less than 25 percent. With more industry came higher productivity and a shrinking wage gap with France, Germany, and even Switzerland. By the early 1990s, Spain's economic success was turning it into a net attractor of migrants, rather than a net sender. As a result, in the second half of the 1990s, immigration to Spain was accelerating, particularly from North Africa, South America, and western Europe. Well-off Europeans discovered Spain's Mediterranean coast, while Colombians, Ecuadorians, Moroccans, and Mauritanians came for jobs and wages that were significantly higher than what they could earn at home. In 2004 42 percent of the foreign population residing in Spain was from the Americas; they were predominantly Colombians who wished to escape the ongoing violence at home and Ecuadorians looking for work and higher wages. Another 33 percent were Europeans, mostly from western Europe and relatively wealthy and 19 percent were Africans, predominantly from Morocco.

Immigration creates a reaction in most countries where the numbers of immigrants are large. The U.S.–Mexican case is famous but there are numerous others. Mexico itself resists immigration from Guatemalans on its southern border, while Costa Ricans appreciate the hard work of Nicaraguans who come to pick the coffee crop, but they complain about their behavior and use of social services. Germans have a long love-hate relationship with Turks, the French with Algerian immigrants, and so on around the globe. Spain's policy has been relatively accommodating toward immigrants, including six amnesties for undocumented workers since 1990. Its last amnesty occurred in 2005 and offered legal status to more than 700,000 foreigners. At the same time, Spain increased its program of border enforcement, which is primarily aimed at deterring Africans. It also built walls around Ceuta and Melilla, two Spanish territories located inside Morocco, and stepped-up its coastal patrols.

Migration policies are fraught with uncertain side-effects, but one of the most frequent consequences of increased enforcement at the border is a displacement of immigrants to alternative points of entry. In the Spanish case, the walls around Ceuta and Melilla, together with increased vigilance along the coast, resulted in migrants moving their point of departure from Morocco to Western Sahara, a disputed territory on Morocco's southern border. From there, migrants could reach the Canary Islands, which is Spanish territory. When Spain increased its patrols off the coast of Western Sahara, migrants moved their departure points south to Mauritania, and then farther south to Senegal when Spain began to target Mauritania.

It is difficult to name a country that has not gone through a period of high rates of out-migration at some point in its development. Europeans went to the Americas, U.S. citizens went west into what was Mexico and the frontier,

Koreans spread around the globe, and the Japanese went to North and South America. Spain's period of high emigration is over, and it is now one of the desirable target countries where emigrants prefer to settle.

 # The Demographic Challenge of the Future

As the European Union looks toward the future, a number of challenges are visible. In the short-to-medium run, it must continue to create convergence in income and living standards between its poorest and its most well-off members. Over the medium run, it must also prepare for further widening, in particular for the possible accession of Turkey, a large nation with per capita income levels about one-fifth of the EU average. And finally, in the long run, it must adapt its economies and social support systems to prepare for a much older population.

One of the primary determinants of social spending in virtually all countries is the age structure of the population. As populations age, they need more health care, more pensions, and more long term care. Each of these entails increases in public spending, and given that older citizens regularly vote, democracies usually respond to their demands. A small part of increased spending on services for the elderly will be offset by decreases in educational spending and unemployment benefits, as a smaller share of the total population will need schooling or experience involuntary unemployment. However, these savings will not begin to offset the increases in social spending associated with an aging population. According to estimates carried out by the European Commission, if current policies are left in place, the average EU government will have to increase the public sector by 10 percent simply to maintain its existing programs at their current levels.

Table 14.4 shows a projection of EU population (27 countries) through 2040. By 2040 the percent of the population 65 and over is expected to reach nearly 28 percent of the total, up from below an estimated 18 percent in 2010. The ability of governments to manage a much larger population of retired people will be constrained by the fact that after 2011, the working age population is forecast to begin declining, and after 2018, the total number of people working is projected to start declining as well. Corresponding to the increase in the population over 65, is a nearly equal drop in the working age population, as shown in Table 14.4. Fewer workers means that the rate of economic growth will fall, and that new resources for supporting an aging population will be harder to acquire. At the same time, the number of available workers to support the production of social services needed by the aging population will be both relatively and absolutely smaller.

Migration can play a role at the margin to ameliorate the changes, but it is unlikely that migration alone will have a major impact. Simply to return the estimated 2040 working age population (15–64) to its 2010 estimates would require the immigration of more than 54 million people, or 11 percent of the predicted 2040 population. And this still would not compensate for the absolute increase

| TABLE 14.4 | **Population Forecast, 2010–2040: 27 Members of the European Union** | | | |
|---|---|---|---|---|
| | Population, 2010 (Millions) | Percent, 2010 | Population, 2040 (Millions) | Percent, 2040 |
| **Total** | 489.0 | 100.0 | 468.6 | 100.0 |
| **By age category** | | | | |
| Ages 0–15 | 74.6 | 15.3 | 63.2 | 13.5 |
| Ages 15–64 | 328.7 | 67.2 | 274.5 | 58.6 |
| Ages 65+ | 85.7 | 17.5 | 130.9 | 27.9 |

Population in the European Union will stop growing and begin to age rapidly after 2010.

*Source*: U.S. Census Bureau.

in the number of people 65 and over. Nevertheless, given the potential for EU expansion beyond its current members along with the migration pressures emanating from North Africa and elsewhere, any assumption about the capacity of the European Union to absorb migrants may turn out to be false.

The Commission of the European Union has begun to analyze trends and to recommend changes to pension and health care systems. Several countries have begun to experiment, for example linking pensions to changes in life expectancy, and to encourage workers to postpone retirement. Demographic changes are clearly visible and well understood; whether or not the European Union and the national governments respond will depend on the flexibility and adaptability of their electorates.

# Summary

- The 27-member European Union was created in several stages. The earliest stage involved agreements over open trade for coal and steel (ECSC), followed by cooperation over the peaceful development of nuclear energy (Euratom) and a free trade agreement.

- The main institutions of the European Union are the Commission, the Council, the Court of Justice, the Court of Auditors, and the European Parliament. The roles of these institutions have evolved.

- The Treaty of Rome was signed in 1957 and was put into effect in 1958, creating a six-country, free-trade area that was phased in gradually over the next 10 years.

- The next wave of deepening was the creation of the European Monetary System in 1979, linking exchange rates.

- Following the EMS, the Single European Act was passed, creating a common market by 1993. While preparations were taking place for the implementation of the SEA, the Maastricht Treaty, or Treaty on European Union, was signed in 1991 and approved by the national governments in late 1993.

- The Maastricht Treaty created a common currency. In preparation, a set of convergence criteria was developed with targets for interest rates, inflation, government spending, and government debt.

- While the European Union was undergoing its several rounds of deepening integration, it was also widening membership to nearly all of Western Europe. Between 1958 and 1995, it expanded from the original six members to 15. In 2004 10 more countries joined, followed by two more in 2007.

- Eastward expansion of the European Union created problems in the areas of agricultural policy, governance, income differences, and migration.

 **Vocabulary**

| | |
|---|---|
| *acquis communautaire* | European Community (EC) |
| cohesion funds | European Currency Unit (ECU) |
| Common Agricultural Policy (CAP) | European Economic Community (EEC) |
| competitive devaluation | |
| convergence criteria | Monetary System (EMS) |
| Council of the European Union | European Parliament |
| Court of Auditors | European Union (EU) |
| Court of Justice | exchange rate mechanism (ERM) |
| Delors Report | Maastricht Treaty |
| euro | qualified majority |
| European Atomic Energy Community (EAEC or Euratom) | Single European Act (SEA) |
| | subsidiarity |
| European Coal and Steel Community (ECSC) | Treaty of Rome |
| | Treaty on European Union |
| European Commission | |

## Study Questions

1. What were the three main stages of deepening that occurred in the European Community after the Treaty of Rome was passed?

2. What are the five main institutions of the European Union, and what are their responsibilities?

3. The Single European Act is a case in which it was difficult to create an agreement, despite the fact that there was near unanimity in support of an agreement. If everyone wanted the agreement, why was it hard to negotiate?

4. How did the European Union expect to create gains from trade with the implementation of the Single European Act?

5. A sudden sharp increase in the demand for the German mark almost destroyed the Exchange Rate Mechanism in 1992. Explain how a rise in the demand for a currency can jeopardize a target zone or exchange rate band.

6. Discuss the pros and cons of the single currency.

7. What are the pressures on the European Union to admit new members?

8. What problems arose from the admission of 12 new members between 2004 and 2007?

9. How does the European Union compare and contrast to the NAFTA region in size, institutional structure, and depth of integration?

# 15 Trade and Policy Reform in Latin America

## Introduction: Defining a "Latin American" Economy

Latin America stretches from Tijuana on the U.S.-Mexico border to Cape Horn at the southern tip of South America. Within this vast geographic area lies such a diversity of languages and cultures that any definition of Latin America must have exceptions and contradictions. For example, *Merriam-Webster's Collegiate Dictionary* defines the region as Spanish America and Brazil, a standard view that must leave out a few small countries in Central and South America (Belize, Suriname, Guyana, and French Guiana) and the island nations of the Caribbean that were outside the region of Spanish and Portuguese settlement. *Webster's* second definition "All of the Americas south of the United States," is more inclusive, but it is perhaps less important to give a precise definition than it is to recognize the variety of physical geography, cultures, and income levels that coexist within any definition. In fact, the variety is so great that it is worth asking whether these nations can truly constitute a single world region. In other words, what is the "Latin American" experience, and how does it allow us to group together nations as different as Argentina, with its European culture and relative prosperity, and Guatemala, with its indigenous culture and great poverty?

The diversity within Latin America should make us careful not to overgeneralize. Nevertheless, there are several common themes shared by all, or nearly all, the nations in the region. First, there are common historical threads, beginning with the fact that a great many nations share a heritage of Spanish and Portuguese colonization, and a common linguistic base. In some countries, however, the languages of indigenous people are important as well. A second part of their shared histories is that many Latin American countries gained their national independence from Spain and Portugal during the nationalist revolutions of the early and middle nineteenth century. This differentiates them from the colonial experiences of Africa and Asia, and implies that the national identities of Latin Americans are perhaps deeper than in many parts of the developing world.

During the twentieth century, Latin American nations had much in common. The Great Depression of the 1930s, for example, caused most nations to shift their policies away from an outward, export orientation toward an inward, targeted industrial strategy. The new strategy eventually developed its own theoreticians and came to be known as "import substitution industrialization." More recently, most nations were borrowers in the 1970s, and severely indebted in the 1980s. Finally, beginning in the 1980s and continuing through to the twenty-first century, the region began a wide-ranging set of economic policy reforms, similar in scope to the transformation of Central and Eastern Europe after the collapse of communism.

In this chapter, we examine the origins and extent of the economic crisis that hit Latin America in the 1980s and analyze the responses. Before we examine the crisis of the 1980s and the economic reforms of the late 1980s and 1990s, first we must step back and look at the long-run performance of the economies of Latin America. When seen in the light of history, we understand why the miserable economic growth record of the 1980s gave rise to a dramatic shift in policies.

#  Population, Income, and Economic Growth

Table 15.1 is a snapshot of the current levels of income and population. The nations of Latin America are home to more than 550 million, or 120 million more people than the three nations of NAFTA, and 62 million more than the 27 nations of the European Union.

Table 15.1 shows the extent to which four countries account for the bulk of the population and production in Latin America. These are, in order by size of population: Brazil, Mexico, Colombia, and Argentina. Together, they add up to about 67 percent of the population of Latin America and over 75 percent of the GDP.

For long stretches of the twentieth century, Latin America was one of the fastest-growing regions of the world. In particular, from 1900 to 1960, the region's real GDP per capita grew as fast or faster than that of Europe, the United States, or Asia. Individual experiences varied, but most countries saw adequate to excellent growth along with rising living standards. As shown in Table 15.2, growth continued from 1960 to 1980, but as world economic growth slowed after 1973, the experiences of the main Latin American economies became more varied. Some grew faster or nearly as fast, while some experienced a dramatic slowdown.

The slowdown in world economic growth after 1973 caused many Latin American politicians to rely more heavily on government expenditures as a major growth stimulus. In the 1970s, world financial markets were ready and willing to extend bank loans to sovereign governments, and countries throughout Latin America and elsewhere borrowed and spent heavily to keep the demand

**TABLE 15.1** • **Population and GDP for Latin America and the Caribbean, 2005**

| | Population (Millions) | GDP (US$, Billions) | GDP per Capita (US$) | GDP per Capita (US$, PPP*) |
|---|---|---|---|---|
| **Andean Community** | | | | |
| Bolivia | 9.2 | 9.3 | 1,011 | 2,856 |
| Colombia | 45.6 | 122.3 | 2,682 | 7,769 |
| Ecuador | 13.2 | 36.2 | 2,742 | 4,272 |
| Peru | 28 | 78.4 | 2,800 | 6,226 |
| **Central American Common Market** | | | | |
| Costa Rica | 4.3 | 19.4 | 4,512 | 9,985 |
| El Salvador | 6.9 | 17 | 2,464 | 5,301 |
| Guatemala | 12.6 | 31.7 | 2,516 | 4,468 |
| Honduras | 7.2 | 8 | 1,111 | 2,789 |
| Nicaragua | 5.5 | 4.9 | 890 | 3,680 |
| **MERCOSUR** | | | | |
| Argentina | 38.7 | 183.3 | 4,736 | 14,421 |
| Brazil | 186.4 | 794.1 | 4,260 | 8,730 |
| Paraguay | 6.2 | 8.2 | 1,323 | 4,960 |
| Uruguay | 3.5 | 16.8 | 4,800 | 10,160 |
| Venezuela | 26.6 | 138.9 | 5,222 | 6,531 |
| **Other Countries** | | | | |
| Chile | 16.3 | 115.2 | 7,067 | 12,635 |
| Dominican Republic | 8.9 | 28.3 | 3,180 | 7,579 |
| Haiti | 8.5 | 4.2 | 494 | 1,836 |
| Mexico | 103.1 | 768.4 | 7,453 | 10,209 |
| Panama | 3.2 | 15.5 | 4,844 | 7,884 |
| **Latin America and the Caribbean** | 551.4 | 2,455.6 | 4,453 | 8,469 |

Latin America has more than one-half a billion people and over $2,400 billion in output. Two-thirds of the population and more than three-fourths of the output are concentrated in Argentina, Brazil, Colombia, and Mexico.

*Purchasing Power Parity

*Source*: World Bank, *World Development Indicators*.

| TABLE 15.2 Average Annual Growth in Real GDP, 1960–2000 | | | |
|---|---|---|---|
| | **Annual Growth in Real GDP per Capita** | | |
| Country/Region | 1960–1980 | 1980–1990 | 1990–2000 |
| Argentina | 1.9 | –2.2 | 3.2 |
| Brazil | 4.5 | 0.7 | 1.3 |
| Chile | 1.5 | 2.6 | 4.9 |
| Colombia | 2.8 | 1.5 | 0.8 |
| Mexico | 3.9 | –1.0 | 1.8 |
| Peru | 1.8 | –2.5 | 2.1 |
| Venezuela | 0.7 | –1.5 | –0.1 |
| Latin America | | –0.3 | 2.0 |

Growth slowed in the 1980s but picked up again in the 1990s.

*Source*: Penn World Tables (Mark 5.6); World Bank *World Development Indicators, 2003*; author's calculations.

side of the economy growing. In August 1982, Mexico revealed that it lacked the reserves to continue payment on the interest and principal it owed, and soon thereafter a number of other heavy borrowers were also shown to be indebted beyond their capacity to repay. International lending ceased and most of Latin America entered a period of negative per capita growth that lasted more or less until the end of the 1980s.

A few countries, notably Chile and Colombia, emerged from the crisis by the mid-1980s, but the majority of countries, including the largest economies, had negative growth or very low positive growth rates over the entire decade. The impact of the crisis on living standards and well-being were profoundly negative, as policymakers searched for several years for a set of policies that would address the crisis. In the end, nearly 50 years of economic strategies came to an end, as Latin America abandoned its inward oriented and interventionist policies in favor of more openness and greater reliance on market mechanisms. The degree and timing of the reforms varied, but every country in Latin America moved away from the previous 50 years of policy.

# Import Substitution Industrialization

Economic policy reform in Latin America brought the demise of the economic development strategy known as **import substitution industrialization (ISI)**. Every Latin American country—and many developing countries outside the

# Latin America

Robinson Projection

0   500   1000 Miles

Map by Dr. Chris Lukinbeal
Revised by Harry D. Johnson

region—had used the ISI strategy since at least the 1950s, when it became the consensus theory of economic development. In Latin America, ISI policies were brought to an end by their inability to resolve the crisis of the 1980s, together with the growing perception that they were creating long-term economic inefficiencies. Because these policies were so central, and because they illustrate an attempt to foster economic development through an inward orientation, they are worth learning about in greater detail.

## Origins and Goals of ISI

From the second half of the nineteenth century until the middle of the twentieth century, most of Latin America relied on exports of agricultural commodities (tropical fruits, coffee, cotton, and grains) and minerals (petroleum, copper, and tin) to earn foreign revenue. These export sectors were often developed or controlled by foreign capital and had few economic linkages to the domestic economy, functioning instead as foreign enclaves within the nation. In cases where the export sector was domestically owned, it usually brought wealth to a relatively small number of people and added greatly to the inequality of power and money that is pervasive in Latin American society. As a result of this history, powerful proindustrial interests have often viewed the traditional export sector with suspicion and hostility despite the fact that the exports produced in these sectors were important sources of foreign revenue.

The disruption of world trade caused by World War I and the Great Depression was particularly hard on countries that depended on primary commodity exports as a major source of income. In particular, the Depression was harmful because it caused a large reduction in demand and falling prices for the agricultural and mineral commodities that Latin America exported. In the 1940s, however, primary commodity producers in Latin America found that many of the effects of the Depression were reversed by World War II. While it created new risks for shipping, many nations earned large reserves of foreign currency from the materials they sold during the war. This trend ended after the war with a sudden decrease in the demand for primary commodities from Latin America. The United States no longer needed as many raw materials, and Europe was unable to buy.

As export earnings dried up, it became apparent that declining foreign exchange earnings would impede further economic development. Latin American countries would no longer be earning the dollars they needed in order to buy imports of machinery and other items required for their industrial development. In addition to slumping foreign exchange, another obstacle began to loom large. The decline in world demand for the exports of Latin American agricultural and mineral products led investigators to examine the long-run trend in export prices. At the newly formed United Nations, a young Argentine economist named Raul Prebisch and a German exile named Hans Singer offered evidence of a long-run decline in the prices of raw materials relative to the prices of manufactured goods. Singer and Prebisch argued that coffee, tin, copper, bananas, and other items exported by Latin American countries would exchange for a smaller and smaller quantity of imported manufactured goods.

In trade analysis, the ratio of average export prices to average import prices is called the **terms of trade (TOT)**:

$$TOT = \text{(Index of export prices)} / \text{(Index of import prices)}.$$

Latin America exported raw materials and imported finished goods, so the Prebisch–Singer prediction was that the terms of trade for the region would decline. For obvious reasons, this view was given the label **export pessimism**.

The reasoning behind export pessimism included both statistical studies and economic theory. Statistical analysis showed raw material prices falling over periods as long as several decades. More recent analysis shows that while prices may fall for extended periods of time, there is no long-run trend up or down. Economic theory holds that as incomes rise, people spend a smaller share of their overall income on foodstuffs and other raw material-based goods such as textiles and apparel, and they spend more on manufactured items. Consequently, the demand for raw materials declines in relation to the demand for manufactured goods. Note, however, that this effect does not necessarily lead to a decline in the terms of trade for raw material producers. In particular, productivity increases in manufacturing can overwhelm increases in demand and push down the real prices of manufactured goods.

Export pessimism formed the basis of orthodox economic policy from roughly the 1950s through the 1970s. As the head of the United Nations' **Economic Commission on Latin America** (**ECLA** in English; **CEPAL** in Spanish), Prebisch guided economic policies throughout Latin America and reinforced a shift that had begun with the destruction of trade in the 1930s. The loss of markets during the Great Depression temporarily forced Latin America away from dependence on raw material exports and toward industrial development through the replacement of imported manufactured goods with domestically produced ones—hence the name "import substitution industrialization." Ironically, domestic production of manufactured import substitutes required the importation of large quantities of capital goods (machinery and parts), and in order to earn the revenues needed to buy these imports, most nations continued to depend on raw material exports in the decades after World War II. Primary commodities still make up a significant share of today's exports from Latin America.

ISI is a form of industrial policy that focuses on those industries that produce substitutes for imported goods. According to Prebisch and Singer, the inevitable decline in the terms of trade for primary commodities means that the biggest constraint on industrial development is the shortage of foreign exchange. Lower export prices mean that countries find it harder and harder to earn the foreign exchange they need in order to buy the machinery and other capital goods they cannot produce themselves. One of the most important roles of import substitution is to reduce the need for foreign exchange that is used to buy goods that could be made at home.

ISI theorists argued that a country should begin by producing inexpensive and relatively simple consumer items, such as toys, clothing, food products (e.g., beverages and canned goods), and furniture. Gradually, the focus of industrial tar-geting should move on to more complex consumer goods (e.g., appliances and autos) and intermediate industrial goods (e.g., pumps, generators, basic metals). In the third stage, complex industrial goods would be produced (e.g., chemicals, electronic equipment, machine tools).

## Criticisms of ISI

The economic tools for implementing ISI are the same as those for industrial policies discussed in Chapter 5. These include a variety of different types of gov-ernment support, from subsidies of all kinds to trade protection and monopoly power in the domestic market. In retrospect, import substitution industrializa-tion generated a number of unintended consequences that caused inefficiencies and wasted resources. Among the many criticisms that have been leveled at ISI are the following: (1) governments misallocated resources when they became too involved in production decisions; (2) exchange rates were often overvalued; (3) policy was overly biased in favor of urban areas; (4) income inequality worsened; and (5) ISI fostered widespread rent seeking.

Foremost among the problems of ISI are those related to an overconfident and naive belief in the ability of the state to direct resources efficiently into their best uses. In the 1950s and 1960s, it was often assumed that **market failures** were far more common in developing nations than in industrial ones, and that one of the main goals of any state should be to correct these through selective and care-ful state intervention in the economy. In this context, ISI can be interpreted as a set of policies in which government uses its economic and political power to improve on the market. Recall from Chapter 5 how difficult it is to measure mar-ket failures and to know the required corrective action.

This model is not totally wrong but it overestimates the technical ability of government officials to identify market failures and their solutions. It also assumes that government bureaucrats are selfless individuals who ignore politi-cal considerations and focus only on economic efficiency and what is best for the nation as a whole. This naive model of political reality caused an underemphasis on problems related to the implementation of economic policies, such as cor-ruption and the lobbying power of economic elites. It also failed to take into account the slow accumulation of special provisions, favors, and economic inef-ficiencies that built up over time when policies were heavily influenced by poli-tics. Naturally, this problem was magnified by the inequality in wealth and income throughout Latin America. Powerful interest groups were able to use ISI policies to their own benefit, rather than in the national interest.

A second problem of ISI was the development and persistence of overvalued exchange rates. Overvaluation was a deliberate policy in some countries, while in others it was a chronic problem stemming from the maintenance of a fixed exchange rate under conditions of higher inflation than among the countries' trading partners. As a deliberate policy, overvaluation of the exchange rate accomplished several goals. In particular, it made it easier for the targeted industries to obtain the imported capital goods they needed. It also helped to maintain political alliances between the urban working classes and the political parties in power. It did this by providing access to relatively less expensive foreign goods, which kept living standards higher than they would have been otherwise. As evidence of this point, when governments were forced to depreciate in the 1980s and 1990s, they often lost the political support of the urban classes.

Although overvalued exchange rates had some benefits, they also had costs. Most importantly, they made it difficult to export because they raised the foreign price of domestic goods. This hurt the agricultural and traditional export sectors because it made exports less profitable. In turn, capital was directed away from agriculture, causing productivity and income in rural areas to remain low and stagnant.

Overvalued exchange rates also stung the parts of industry that did not produce substitutes for imports because it was less profitable to export. In addition, the overvalued exchange rate made foreign machinery less expensive and caused industrial investment to be too capital intensive and insufficiently labor intensive. Consequently, industry did not create enough new jobs to absorb the growing labor force and the labor that left agriculture for the cities. Furthermore, since most industry is located in urban areas, government investment in infrastructure improvements—such as transportation, communication, and water—were heavily targeted toward cities and their environs. As a result, subsistence farmers and their families did not benefit from, or contribute to, national economic development, and Latin America continued to have the highest levels of inequality of any region in the world.

In addition to a persistent tendency toward overvalued exchange rates, ISI trade and competition policies were heavily protectionist and often favored the creation of domestic monopolies. The lack of foreign and domestic competition meant that manufacturing remained inefficient, uncompetitive, and inwardly focused. With profits from a protected domestic market, many producers saw no reason to invest in modern equipment, further reinforcing the uncompetitiveness of their products. It is ironic that as a consequence of ISI, many countries became more vulnerable to economic shocks that originated outside of Latin America, which was precisely the opposite effect from the one that motivated ISI in the first place.

A final problem of ISI is the development of widespread rent seeking behavior. When governments intervene in the planning and directing of industrial development, they give government officials and bureaucrats a wide range of valuable commodities to distribute. These include the many subsidies and licenses that are a part of ISI policies. For example, in order to protect the domestic market and to ensure access to needed imports, governments often required import licenses and at the same time, provided foreign exchange at subsidized prices to the importer. When government policy creates something of value, such as the license to import or a subsidy to buy foreign exchange, the private sector will spend resources to obtain it. In the absence of strong institutions to ensure the independence of the bureaucracy—and, often, even when they are present— bribes and corruption become a part of the decision making. Ultimately, some decisions are made for the wrong reasons, and economic waste is the result.

## CASE STUDY

# ISI in Mexico

The Mexican constitution of 1917 established the power and the responsibility of the federal government to intervene in the economy in order to act as the leading agent of economic growth and as the referee of social conflict. This role was not institutionalized inside the Mexican government until the Mexican revolution was consolidated in the 1930s under the presidency of Cárdenas, whose son was a leading opponent of the dismantling of ISI during the reforms of the 1980s and 1990s.

In order to lead and direct economic growth, government could legitimately claim the need to be powerful—otherwise, powerful social classes could resist the government's directives and initiatives, particularly those with distributional goals or consequences. Therefore, economic policy served not only to meet the needs of the country for economic growth and a fairer distribution, but also to increase the political power of government. Mexico nationalized its oil industries in 1938, and throughout the twentieth century, a number of sectors were nationalized and turned into state-run monopolies (telephones, airlines, banks, railroads, and mineral development companies). The use of the government budget in this manner guaranteed access to investment funds, while monopoly markets ensured that the favored firms would succeed, at least within the nation.

The government also offered loans and loan guarantees to many firms in targeted industries. Loans and loan guarantees helped firms obtain capital at interest rates that were below what they would have normally paid. Similarly, the government sold foreign exchange at artificially low prices to targeted firms who needed to buy imports. Mexican exporters were required to convert their foreign exchange earnings into pesos at an overvalued peso rate—too few pesos per dollar—which made exporting relatively less profitable; the government then sold the cheaply acquired foreign exchange to targeted industries. In effect, exporters were subsidizing the development of the targeted industries.

Unlike many ISI nations, Mexico limited foreign investment. Like most ISI nations, however, when investment was permitted (e.g., autos), performance requirements were placed on the foreign firms. A common requirement was that the foreign firm balance its foreign exchange requirements so that each peso of imports was matched by a peso of export earnings. Further interventions occurred in the area of commercial policy where import licenses limited many types of imports. Recall that import licenses are essentially quotas. By the 1970s about 60 percent of all imports were subject to licensing.

From 1950 to 1973, Mexico's real GDP per capita grew at the rate of 3.1 percent per year. By comparison, the United States grew 2.2 percent per year; the fourteen largest OECD nations grew 3.5 percent per year; and growth in the six largest Latin American economies was 2.5 percent. At the same time that the economy was undergoing relatively rapid economic growth, industrialization was changing the structure of the economy. Mexico's manufacturing sector expanded from 21.5 percent of GDP to 29.4 percent. Growth began to slow in the 1970s, as it did in many parts of the world.

One widely shared view is that Mexico's growth began to stall because the country was running out of easy targets for industrial development. Light manufacturing and simple consumer goods industries are relatively easy to start up, and the conversion of a part of the nation's economy from subsistence agriculture to simple manufacturing makes growth rates look good. The next stages require more sophisticated manufacturing, however, and are relatively harder to start up. According to this view, Mexico had run out of simple industries to start and was inevitably having a harder time producing more sophisticated goods that were further from its comparative advantage.

In spite of rapid economic growth during the 1950s and 1960s, poverty and income inequality continued. Large numbers of Mexicans, many of them indigenous people living in rural areas, did not participate in the growth of the economy. This is evidenced by the fact that in the 1980s much of the agricultural industry was still at a subsistence level, using 26 percent of the nation's labor force to produce just 9 percent of the nation's GDP. The urban bias in Mexico's development strategy turned Mexico City into one of the largest metropolises in the world, with more than 15,000,000 people in the greater metropolitan area by the late 1980s. The sensational growth and crowding of people and industry into the basin that holds Mexico City resulted in serious pollution problems.

There is no consensus among economists as to the role played by ISI in Mexico's debt crisis of the 1980s. Certainly, ISI policies expanded the role of the federal government in economic activity and increased government expenditures and borrowing during the 1970s. Nevertheless, overall economic growth remained fairly robust until the mid-1970s. One widespread view is that the easy gains of ISI were gone by the 1970s, and in order to keep growth on track, Mexican presidents used their power over public finances to increase expenditures dramatically. At first the government argued that it could easily afford to borrow in foreign capital markets because the nation had recently, in 1978, become a major oil exporter. Ultimately, the government's fiscal policies generated enormous public sector deficits, fears of devaluation, and capital flight. By 1982, a year after the price of oil fell, the nation had run out of international reserves and could no longer service its international debt. If the government had not resorted to unsustainable macroeconomic policies, would it have fallen into the debt crisis and rejected ISI policies in the mid-1980s?

# Macroeconomic Instability and Economic Populism

Many economists are convinced that while ISI policies are suboptimal, they had less of a direct effect in creating the economic crisis of the 1980s than did misguided macroeconomic policies. The reasons are relatively straightforward. ISI policies involve trade barriers and government support for selected industries. Collectively, these policies may lower a nation's income by a few percentage points, but they rarely lead to a full-blown economic crisis. Faulty macroeconomic policies, on the other hand, often lead to hyperinflation, depression, and balance of payments crises. In addition, while most of Latin America used ISI policies from the 1950s through the 1980s, economic growth remained at fairly high levels for most countries until the early 1980s when growth turned negative in nearly all countries. While it is entirely possible that the 1980s crisis was the culmination of several decades of ISI policies, it is certain that the crisis was directly linked to the faulty macroeconomic policies of the late 1970s and early 1980s.

## Populism in Latin America

Many Latin America specialists blame the faulty macroeconomic policies of the region on populist or economic populist political movements that use economic tools to reach specific goals, such as obtaining support from labor and domestically oriented business, or isolating rural elites and foreign interests. Examples of populist leaders abound: in Argentina, Juan Perón (1946–1955 and 1973–1976) and Raúl Alfonsín (early 1980s); in Brazil, Getúlio Vargas (1951–1954), João Goulart (1961–1964), and José Sarney (1985–1990); in Chile, Carlos Ibáñez (1952–1958) and Salvador Allende (1970–1973); in Peru, Fernando Belaúnde Terry (1963–1968), Juan Velasco Alvarado (1968–1975), and Alan García (1985–1990); in Mexico, Luis Echeverría (1970–1976) and José Lopez Portillo (1976–1982); in Venezuela, Hugo Chavez (1998–). Populist movements in Latin America share nationalistic ideologies and a focus on economic growth and income redistribution. The central economic problem generated by these movements is the use of expansionary fiscal and monetary policies without regard for the importance of inflation risks, budget deficits, and foreign exchange constraints.

   **Economic populism** is usually triggered by three initial conditions. First, there is a deep dissatisfaction with the status quo, usually as a result of slow growth or recession. Second, policymakers reject the traditional constraints on macro policy. Budget deficits financed through printing money are justified by the existence of high unemployment and idle factories, which offer room for expansion without inflation. Third, policymakers promise to raise wages while freezing prices and to restructure the economy by expanding the domestic production of imported goods, thereby lessening the need for foreign exchange. In the words of one analyst, the policies call for "reactivating, redistributing, and restructuring" the economy.

Early in the populist regime, there is a vindication of the policies. The economic stimulus of government expenditures and newly created money leads to rising growth rates and rising wages. Soon, however, bottlenecks begin to set in. For example, construction firms run out of particular inputs, such as cement or specialized steel products, and manufacturing firms cannot find the parts they need to repair their machinery. Prices begin to rise, and the budget deficit grows. In the next stage, inflation begins an extreme acceleration, and shortages become pervasive throughout the economy. The budget falls into serious deficit as policies become unsustainable, and wage increases cease keeping up with inflation. In the final stage, countries experience massive capital flight as fears of a devaluation develop. The flight of capital out of the country depresses investment and further depresses real wages.

In the end, real wages are often lower than before the cycle began, and there is an international intervention under the sponsorship of the IMF, which is designed to stop the high inflation and end a balance of payments crisis. Typically, the IMF oversees the implementation of stabilization and structural reform policies that call for serious budget cuts, a slowdown in the growth of the money supply, a reduction in trade barriers, and in general, greater reliance on market mechanisms and less government intervention. While these stages of the populist cycle are an idealization, they capture the essence of the populist experience as it has occurred in many Latin nations.

 # The Debt Crisis of the 1980s

In August 1982 Mexico announced that it lacked the international reserves it needed to pay the interest and principal due on its foreign debt. Mexico was not the first country to declare its inability to service its debt, but it was the biggest up to that point. Its announcement soon led to the realization that a number of other countries, including most of Latin America, were in similar circumstances. Thus began the Lost Decade.

## Proximate Causes of the Debt Crisis

In Mexico's case, the collapse of oil prices in 1981 undermined its ability to earn the revenue it needed to service its debt. The problem was compounded by the fact that a significant portion of its debt was owed in dollars at variable interest rates and that efforts to combat inflation in the United States and elsewhere had resulted in a higher level of world interest rates. Consequently, interest payments on Mexico's debt rose at the same time that the nation's ability to earn dollars shrank.

The collapse of oil prices in 1981 and the rise in world interest rates were not the only external shocks to the economies of Latin America. In 1981–1982, the world's industrial economies entered a deep recession that reduced world demand and prices for many of the raw materials produced in Latin America and elsewhere. In Mexico's case, oil was the critical commodity, but a number of other primary commodity exports experienced a similar decline in their world price.

The price decline for Latin America's exports and the rise in interest rates were significant parts of the mix of events that led up to the debt crisis. These external economic shocks probably would not have caused a generalized debt crisis without some additional factors, however. Historically, debt crises not only require a set of external shocks to the indebted countries but also an acceleration of international lending, which occurred between 1974–1982. Added to these two factors was the complicating problem of mismanagement of national macroeconomic policies in the late 1970s and early 1980s.

During the 1970s, financial institutions throughout the developed world were awash in money that they were anxious to lend. The rise in oil prices in 1973 and 1974, and again in 1979, led to an enormous expansion of bank deposits by the oil-rich nations of the world. Banks in New York, London, Paris, and Frankfurt were anxious to lend these deposits and aggressively sought new borrowers beginning in 1974. For Latin America and the Caribbean, long-term, publicly guaranteed debt rose from slightly over $37 billion in 1973 to more than $261 billion in 1983. The sudden acceleration in commercial bank lending and the rise in the amount of debt made the economies vulnerable to a sudden and unforeseen economic shock.

Table 15.3 shows the size of the debt for some of the most heavily indebted countries after the first year of the crisis. The second column of numbers expresses the debt in net terms (gross debt minus debt owed by foreigners) as a percentage of GDP. The third column shows the net interest payments owed as a percentage of exports of goods and services. This is a useful indicator because nations ultimately have to pay the interest on their international debts out of the revenues they earn from their exports. What we see is that between 10 and 63 percent of the revenue earned by exports went to pay interest and, consequently, was unavailable for purchasing imports or for investing domestically.

## Responses to the Debt Crisis

Initially, most analysts in the United States and in the international financial institutions such as the IMF perceived the debt crisis to be a temporary, short-run liquidity problem. Under this assumption, the reasonable response is to increase capital flows to Latin America and other indebted regions so that they would have the financial resources to service their debts. If additional capital flows can stimulate higher rates of economic growth, then it is a reasonable policy because an adequate growth rate would allow the countries to outgrow their debt.

From the standpoint of U.S. policy, the key to growth was viewed as increased investment, which was only possible if capital flows into the region were restored. The first policy proposal along these lines was that of U.S. Treasury Secretary, James Baker, in 1985. The **Baker Plan** tried to organize a renewed lending program by commercial banks. The problem was that most banks that had

| | Gross External Debt (Millions of US$) | Net External Debt as a Percentage of GDP | Net Interest Payments as a Percentage of Exports |
|---|---|---|---|
| **TABLE 15.3** | **Debt Indicators at the Onset of the Debt Crisis, 1983** | | |
| Country | | | |
| Argentina | 43,634 | 75.3 | 62.8 |
| Bolivia | 3,328 | 141.9 | 38.5 |
| Brazil | 92,961 | 48.3 | 38.7 |
| Chile | 17,315 | 87.6 | 32.9 |
| Colombia | 10,306 | 25.1 | 18.8 |
| Costa Rica | 3,646 | 137.8 | 45.4 |
| Mexico | 86,081 | 63.8 | 32.1 |
| Peru | 10,712 | 52.4 | 20.1 |
| Venezuela | 32,158 | 38.8 | 9.6 |

A large percentage of the exports of indebted countries went to pay interest on their debts.

*Source*: Cline, William, *International Debt Reexamined*, 1995; World Bank, *World Debt Tables*, 1987.

Latin American loans in their portfolios were trying to reduce their exposure to the region, not increase it. Consequently, few resources were forthcoming under this plan.

Without capital flows from developed country banks, the choices were not attractive. Outright default and disavowal of the debt would cut off most of a nation's trade and investment linkages. The consequences for investment and growth would be risky and potentially disastrous, depending on the reaction of the United States and other governments. On the other hand, if they continued to make interest payments, and, potentially principal repayment, it would require huge trade surpluses in order to earn the revenue they needed to pay for imports plus interest on the debt.

Interest payment on the debt owed to foreigners enters the current account as a debit in the category of income paid abroad, as discussed in Chapter 9. Consequently, interest payments severely increased the current account deficits of many countries. Recall the fundamental accounting balance of an open economy:

$$S_p + T - G = I + CA,$$

where $S_p$ is private savings, $T - G$ is government (public) savings, $I$ is investment, and $CA$ is the current account balance. Without financial capital inflows to finance their current account deficits, countries must eliminate the deficit through a combination of increased exports and reduced imports. The policies that accomplish this are expenditure-switching and expenditure-reducing policies. Recall from Chapter 11 that expenditure-switching policies such as devaluations of the currency turn the demand for foreign goods into a demand for domestic goods and raise CA directly. Expenditure-reducing policies, such as tax increases and cuts in government spending, raise T – G and, indirectly, reduce consumption, investment, and imports. The net effect of expenditure-reducing policies is often a recession in which the demand for domestic and imported goods falls due to a fall in domestic income.

In other words, in order to accumulate the resources they needed for their interest payments, governments were forced to follow contractionary policies that caused deep recessions throughout the region. Between 1982–1986, the average rate of growth of real per capita GDP was –1.8 percent per year in Latin America and the Caribbean.

By 1987 it was apparent to analysts throughout the world that restoring capital flows was not enough. There was a need for deep reform in the economies of Latin America. First, it was observed that the faulty macroeconomic policies of the region consistently left aggregate national expenditure above national income and that the likelihood of a return to growth was small as long as the gap between the two remained. Second, in their attempt to keep government expenditures higher than warranted, many countries had resorted to printing money, which resulted in high and increasing rates of inflation. Third, the burden of the debt itself was becoming apparent to everyone inside and outside Latin America. After the interest and principal payments were made, insufficient export earnings remained for domestic investment and consumption, and growth was stunted. By 1988–1989, both creditors and the multilateral lending agencies such as the IMF were in agreement that debt relief was in everyone's interest.

The growing consensus on the need for debt relief led to the **Brady Plan** in 1989, named after the secretary of the treasury during the Bush administration, Nicholas Brady. Essentially, the Brady Plan gave something to everyone. Creditors were expected to restructure some of the old debt into longer-term debt with a lower interest rate and to make some additional new loans. The multilateral lending agencies, such as the IMF, were expected to provide additional loans on concessional terms; that is, below market interest rates, and borrowers were required to provide evidence of their willingness to begin serious economic reform before any new loans would be forthcoming. The Brady Plan did not end the debt crisis, but it was a significant step toward greater stability in the region. Countries that renegotiated their debt with the Brady Plan package were perceived to have greater credibility and sounder finances by the international financial community. Consequently, after 1989, capital flows began to return to Latin America but this time not in the form of bank loans. Rather, savers and investors in the United States, Europe, and Asia began to increase their direct investment in Latin America, as well as their holdings of various financial assets, such as stocks and bonds issued by private companies doing business there. While large inflows of capital can present problems, particularly if they reverse and flow out, they are the additional savings and investment that are needed if the region is to return to its historical levels of growth. To a large degree, the new capital that has been flowing into the region since 1989 is a vote of confidence by investors around the world.

From the vantage point of the first decade of the twenty-first century, the most lasting effects of the debt crisis—other than the forgone output due to the recessions of the 1980s—are the deep economic reforms that have taken place in country after country. These reforms are key to explaining the return of capital flows to Latin America. Reforms vary by country, both in kind and degree, but they mark a historical shift away from the protectionist and interventionist policies of ISI and economic populism and toward more open and market-oriented policies.

# Economic Policy Reform and the "Washington Consensus"

By the late 1980s most countries in Latin America had started a series of economic policy reforms that began to alter the fundamental relationships between business and government and between their national economy and the world. After 1989 the reforms intensified and became more general. In most cases, the reforms consisted of three separate but interrelated features. First, and with varying degrees of success, governments implemented stabilization plans to stop inflation and to control their budget deficits. Second, most countries began privatizing the government-owned parts of their economies, such as manufacturing enterprises, financial and other services, mining operations, tourism, and utility companies. Third, trade policies became more open and less discriminatory against exports.

Throughout Latin America, this package of reforms has come to be known as the "**neoliberal model**" or **neoliberalism**, because it represents a partial return to classic nineteenth-century European liberalism that favored free markets and minimal government intervention in the economy. By 1992 growth had returned to most countries.

In spite of the benefits of policy reform, however, many problems persist. Poverty and inequality continued to increase in many countries, since growth did not filter down into all sectors. The problem of poverty was compounded by the lack of adequate infrastructure, which made it harder for all segments of society to benefit from economic growth. The absence of schools, health clinics, roads, clean water, and other infrastructure elements, particularly in rural areas where poverty is greatest, limits the reach of restored economic growth.

## Stabilization Policies to Control Inflation

Many countries sought to avoid the recessionary consequences of the onset of the debt crisis by increasing government spending. The only way to finance government spending, however, was through the printing of more money, because tax systems were inadequate and government borrowing abilities were limited by the debt crisis. The reckless printing of money to finance government spending drove a number of nations into periods of hyperinflation, as detailed in Table 15.4.

The solution to the hyperinflation experienced by Argentina, Bolivia, Brazil, and Peru is simple to prescribe: cut government spending and stop printing money. The implementation of this prescription was difficult, however. In the short run, if price increases outstrip wage increases, as is often the case in a period of disinflation, then the burden of bringing down the rate of inflation falls mainly on wage earners who experience a fall in their real wages. Consequently, anti-inflation policies create economic hardship and alienate the political support of many wage earners, making governments unpopular with a large share of the population.

A further complication was the lack of agreement over the causes of inflation. Some argued that it was caused by inertia since everyone expected future inflation to be high. This caused producers to raise prices in anticipation of higher future input costs. The problem of inflation developing a momentum of its own, and a lack of empirical information about the depth of this problem led to two different policy prescriptions for controlling inflation: the orthodox model and the heterodox model.

The **orthodox** model minimizes government involvement in the economy. Consequently, its anti-inflation prescription is straightforward—cut government spending, reform the tax system to increase compliance and revenues, and limit the creation of new money. The heterodox model calls for the same actions plus the freezing of wages and prices. In the **heterodox** view, inflationary expectations

**TABLE 15.4** ● **Inflation Rates, 1982–1992**

| | Inflation (in Percents) | | |
|---|---|---|---|
| Country | Average 1982–1987 | Average 1987–1992 | Highest 1982–1992 |
| Argentina | 316 | 447 | 4924 (1989) |
| Bolivia | 776 | 16 | 8170 (1985) |
| Brazil | 158 | 851 | 1862 (1989) |
| Chile | 21 | 19 | 27 (1990) |
| Colombia | 21 | 27 | 32 (1990) |
| Mexico | 73 | 48 | 159 (1987) |
| Peru | 103 | 733 | 7650 (1990) |
| Venezuela | 10 | 40 | 81 (1989) |

High rates of inflation were a common problem of the 1980s.

*Source:* Edwards, Sebastian, *Crisis and Reform in Latin America,* 1995.

are so embedded in economic decision making that price increases will continue even if government spending and new money creation cease. In practice, heterodox plans often ignored the budget deficits that were part of the problem.

Between 1986 and 1992, Brazil implemented five separate heterodox stabilization plans to end inflation, and not one of them worked. Similarly, heterodox plans in Argentina and Peru in 1985, succeeded for approximately a year but then failed, as inflation returned with a vengeance. Nevertheless, Brazil and Mexico each ultimately controlled inflation using heterodox methods.

One issue that neither the heterodox nor orthodox models address directly is institutional reform. In Mexico's case, the freezing of wages and prices was an outcome of a formal agreement between labor interests, business interests, and the government, known as the *Social Solidarity Pact* (Pacto de Solidaridad Social, or "El Pacto"), which was passed in 1987. Brazil's successful plan under President Cardoso (the Real Plan, 1994) was widely discussed in Congress before it was implemented, and Argentina's plan (the Convertibility Plan, 1991) was part of a set of institutional reforms that limited the ability of the central bank to print new money. Bolivia was able to control its hyperinflation without the extensive use of price and wage freezes, but it depended on a series of financial reforms that significantly lessened direct government control over the financial services sector and reformed the tax system to make revenue collection more reliable.

An issue that continued to plague many nations was the problem of inconsistency between inflation stabilization and exchange rate policy. Mexico's experience is a good example of the problem and stems from the fact that the exchange rate is a powerful weapon in the fight against inflation. Mexico fixed its peso to the dollar in the mid-1980s as part of its anti-inflation strategy. Argentina and Brazil did the same under their stabilization plans of 1991 and 1994, respectively. Domestic producers that compete with U.S. goods were forced to avoid price increases so they would remain competitive. Furthermore, prices did not increase on imports of U.S.-made capital goods, which were essential to Mexican industry, thereby helping to hold down Mexican prices for finished manufactured goods. Since Mexico's inflation was still slightly higher than U.S. inflation, the peso became overvalued over a period of time. Ultimately, this contributed to a serious trade imbalance and the collapse of the peso in December 1994, followed by a deep recession in 1995. Since 1994, Mexico has let the peso float against the dollar and has stopped trying to use the exchange rate as an anchor against the current of inflation.

In Argentina's case, the peso remained fixed against the dollar, but when turmoil in international financial markets spread to Latin America in the fall of 1998, Brazil devalued. In effect, this made Brazil's currency cheaper and its industries more competitive against Argentine industries. Brazil is Argentina's main trading partner, and the two countries are linked together in a free-trade area (MERCOSUR) that is moving toward becoming a customs union. Hence, the Brazilian devaluation had a decidedly negative impact on Argentina's trade balance and industrial production. Given that the government had tied the peso to the U.S. dollar in order to achieve credibility for its anti-inflation policy, Argentina was extremely reluctant to follow Brazil's lead and devalue its currency. Its failure to act, however, led to greater imbalances in its trade accounts, and when the peso was finally uncoupled from the dollar, it collapsed in a severe financial and banking crisis. By late 2002, the peso had fallen from 1:1 against the U.S. dollar to only 28 cents, and Argentina's real GDP fell by 4 percent in 2001 and 11 percent in 2002.

## Structural Reform and Open Trade

Stabilization policies to control inflation and curtail large budget deficits are usually one part of a package that also includes **structural reform policies**. One way to keep the two types of policies separate is to recognize that stabilization generally focuses on macroeconomic policies, for example, inflation and government budgets, while structural reform tends to be more microeconomic, dealing with issues of resource allocation. Structural reform policies include the privatization of government-owned enterprises, deregulation and redesign of the regulatory environment of overregulated industries such as financial services, and the reform of trade policy.

The many initiatives to privatize and reform the regulatory environments of the economies of Latin America are quite remarkable, but this section will focus on the most impressive area of structural reform to date: the economic integration of the region with the world economy. Prior to the onset of the debt crisis, the economies of Latin America had the most restricted trade systems of all the nations in the noncommunist world. In many countries, the debt crisis reinforced the belief that isolation from the world economy was the only way to protect a nation from shocks that originated in the external environment.

In the 1970s, Chile broke with this tradition and began to reform its trade policies. Mexico and Bolivia followed in 1985 and 1986, and by 1987–1988, it was apparent throughout Latin America that trade had to be more open if economic growth was to be restored. In the late 1980s and early 1990s, nearly all the countries of Latin America began reducing both the level of tariffs and nontariff barriers (NTBs) and the variability of tariff rates across industries and goods. Table 15.5 shows the changes in tariffs that occurred between the mid-1980s, when the reforms began, and the early 1990s. As large as the tariff reductions were, the effect of the elimination of nontariff barriers such as quotas and import licensing requirements was even more dramatic, as many countries eliminated all or nearly all these barriers. By the early 1990s, most of the tariff and nontariff changes had been implemented, and countries began to turn to alternative forms of market opening.

The three main goals of trade reform were to reduce the anti-export bias of trade policies that favored production for domestic markets over production for foreign markets, to raise the growth rate of productivity, and to make consumers better off by lowering the real cost of traded goods. In response to the changes in trade policy, the growth rate of exports picked up in most countries, while non-

**TABLE 15.5** • **Average Tariff Rates in Latin America**

| Country | Average Tariff Rate | | |
|---|---|---|---|
| | 1985 | 1992 | 2004 |
| Argentina | 28.0 | 14.8 | 12.7 |
| Bolivia | 20.0 | 9.8 | 9.4 |
| Brazil | 80.0 | 17.6 | 12.4 |
| Chile | 36.0 | 11.0 | 6.0 |
| Colombia | 83.0 | 11.6 | 12.2 |
| Costa Rica | 92.0 | 16.0 | 5.9 |
| Mexico | 34.0 | 13.1 | 18.0 |
| Peru | 64.0 | 17.6 | 10.2 |
| Uruguay | 32.0 | 18.3 | 13.3 |
| Venezuela | 30.0 | 11.8 | 12.7 |

Latin America dramatically reduced trade barriers in the latter part of the 1980s.

*Source*: Inter-American Development Bank.

traditional exports increased dramatically. Furthermore, productivity rose in a majority of countries for which there is data. The productivity increase is at least partly the result of trade opening due to the impact of technology transfers, the improved investment climate, and the pressures on local firms to remain competitive.

Table 15.6 shows the openness indexes for 19 countries. Since 1985, the average percentage change in openness was 54 percent for the countries listed. The pattern of openness conforms to the usual one, in which trade has a greater weight in the GDP of smaller countries than it does in larger ones, but the pattern of increase across nearly all countries, both big and small, is remarkable. Table 15.6 does not distinguish between intraregional trade that occurs within the framework of a regional trade agreement, and interregional trade with nonmembers. Regardless, there were significant increases in the relative importance of trade to Latin American economies.

It is difficult to judge whether more open trade has, as yet, contributed to an increase in the standard of living of consumers throughout Latin America. As long as productivity is rising, living standards will follow, although often with a lag. It may also be the case that the benefits of rising productivity are limited to specific sectors, however, where productivity growth occurs or where unions have more bargaining power over wages. Overall, economic growth in the 1990s surpassed the experience of the 1980s, but in many countries, growth has not reached into all sectors of society.

# Latin America: Trade Blocs

TRADE BLOCS

MERCOSÜR

Andean Community

Central American Common Market

Robinson Projection

0        500        1000 Miles

Map by Dr. Chris Lukinbeal
Revised by Harry D. Johnson

| TABLE 15.6 ● Openness Indexes, 1985 and 2004 | | | |
|---|---|---|---|
| | 1985 | 2004 | % Change |
| **Andean Community** | | | |
| Bolivia | 0.42 | 0.58 | 38.8 |
| Colombia | 0.26 | 0.43 | 64.7 |
| Ecuador | 0.52 | 0.51 | −2.0 |
| Peru | 0.39 | 0.39 | −0.6 |
| **Central America Common Market** | | | |
| Costa Rica | 0.63 | 0.96 | 51.6 |
| El Salvador | 0.52 | 0.71 | 36.8 |
| Guatemala | 0.25 | 0.48 | 92.9 |
| Honduras | 0.54 | 0.85 | 56.9 |
| Nicaragua | 0.37 | 0.81 | 121.9 |
| **MERCOSUR** | | | |
| Argentina | 0.18 | 0.43 | 141.1 |
| Brazil | 0.19 | 0.31 | 62.2 |
| Paraguay | 0.48 | 0.73 | 51.2 |
| Uruguay | 0.48 | 0.58 | 20.3 |
| Venezuela | 0.42 | 0.56 | 33.6 |
| **Other Countries** | | | |
| Chile | 0.54 | 0.73 | 34.8 |
| Dominican Republic | 0.65 | 0.98 | 50.5 |
| Mexico | 0.26 | 0.61 | 137.6 |
| Panama | 1.28 | 1.23 | −3.8 |

Openness indexes have increased significantly over the last 20 years.

*Source*: World Bank, *World Development Indicators.*

## CASE STUDY

# Regional Trade Blocs in Latin America

Latin America has more regional trade agreements than any other world region, and it has some of the oldest agreements as well. The first wave of agreements were signed in the 1960s as Prebisch and others began to recognize that ISI strategies eliminated the possibility for economies of scale and productivity increases that come with it. As long as production was limited to the home market, firms in many sectors would not be large enough to invest in research and development and to compete internationally. The solution was to encourage regional trade agreements such as the Central American Common Market (1961), the Caribbean Free Trade Association (1966, now called the Caribbean Community and Common Market) and the Andean Pact (1969, now called the Andean Community). The goals of these agreements are shown in Table 15-7. While the agreements conferred commercial advantages on firms located in member countries, they did not significantly alter trade patterns nor did they increase the flow of trade within the regions. Countries resisted pressures to lower their tariffs and momentum toward freer trade within trade blocs quickly dissipated. By the 1980s, the agreements were on paper only and were having scant effects on member countries.

With the onset of trade reforms in the mid-to-late 1980s, regional trade agreements once again became popular. Mexico took the lead with its announcement in 1989 that it was pursuing a free trade agreement with the United States. In addition to economies of scale, trade agreements seemed to hold the promise of attracting foreign investment as well as increasing market access and possibly

**TABLE 15.7 ● Regional Trade Blocs**

| Regional Trade Bloc | Year | Members | Goals |
|---|---|---|---|
| Andean Community | 1969 | Bolivia, Colombia, Ecuador, Peru | Common market |
| Caribbean Community and Common Market | 1973 | Antigua and Barbuda, The Bahamas, Barbados, Belize, Dominica, Grenada, Guyana, Jamaica, Montserrat, St. Kitts and Nevis, Saint Lucia, St. Vincent and the Grenadines, Suriname, Trinidad and Tobago | Common market |
| Central American Common Market | 1961 | Costa Rica, El Salvador, Guatemala, Honduras, Nicaragua | Customs union |
| Dominican Republic–Central America Free Trade Agreement | 2005 | Costa Rica, Dominican Republic, El Salvador, Guatemala, Honduras, Nicaragua, United States | Free trade area |
| Latin American Integration Area | 1980 | Argentina, Bolivia, Brazil, Chile, Colombia, Cuba, Ecuador, Mexico, Paraguay, Peru, Uruguay, Venezuela | Economic cooperation |
| MERCOSUR | 1991 | Argentina, Brazil, Paraguay, Uruguay, Venezuela | Common market |
| NAFTA | 1994 | Canada, Mexico, United States | Free trade area |

diversifying trade partners. Two years after the NAFTA negotiations began, Brazil, Argentina, Paraguay, and Uruguay signed the Treaty of Asunción, establishing the Common Market of the South, or MERCOSUR. In 2006, Venezuela dropped out of the Andean Community and joined with Brazil and its partners. While MERCOSUR was in its infancy, Mexico, Canada, and the United States signed NAFTA (1994) and the Andean Pact was reborn as the Andean Community (1996).

The NAFTA agreement was implemented on January 1, 1994. In December of that year, leaders from 34 countries in the Western Hemisphere met at the First Summit of the Americas where they committed their countries to negotiate a **Free Trade Agreement of the Americas (FTAA)**, and to conclude all negotiations no later than 2005. By 2002, political obstacles were beginning to undermine movement toward the FTAA, and it now appears that it is unlikely negotiations will be successful. Nevertheless, a number of countries in South and Central America have continued to sign new agreements, including the Dominican Republic-Central American Free Trade Agreement discussed in Chapter 13 and numerous bilateral agreements. Chile, for example, has signed free trade agreements with Canada, China, the European Union, Korea, Mexico, Panama, Peru, Singapore, and the United States, among others. It has also joined MERCOSUR as an associate member, freeing it from the requirement that it adopt the common external tariff, and is negotiating to rejoin the Andean Community that it left 30 years ago. Similarly, Mexico has signed agreements with the European Union, Israel, Japan, and a number of South American nations in addition to its membership in NAFTA.

## The Washington Consensus

The term **Washington Consensus** was coined by the economist John Williamson as a short hand for a set of economic policies that constitute a broad consensus among conservative and liberal economists. Williamson developed the list while thinking about Latin America and its elements provide a clear picture of the first generation of reforms that were implemented beginning in the mid-1980s. The "Washington" part of the name refers not only to the central site of the U.S. government, but also the site of the leading institutions in the international financial community (IMF and World Bank) and the unofficial community of think tanks which is centered there. The "Consensus" part of the name refers to the fact that these were thought to be uncontroversial elements that a majority of economists in the U.S. government, IMF, World Bank, and Washington think tanks believe to be good economic policy.

The Washington Consensus, as proposed by Williamson, has 10 elements and can be divided into five macroeconomic components and five microeconomic ones.

Macroeconomic reforms:

**1.** Avoid large budget deficits

2. Spend public money on health, education, and basic services rather than special interests or huge projects

3. Cut taxes, but tax a wider range of activities and make the collection system effective

4. Make certain that real interest rates are positive, limiting the use of preferential rates

5. Make the exchange rate competitive and credible

Microeconomic reforms:

6. Use tariffs instead of quotas, and gradually reduce them

7. Encourage foreign direct investment

8. Privatize state enterprises in activities where the market works

9. Remove the barriers to firm entry and eliminate restrictions on competition

10. Guarantee the security of property rights

Williamson suggested these 10 points for policymakers as a lowest common denominator of ideas that he believed were shared by analysts on both the political right and the political left. He did not think that he had designed a blueprint for development and he willingly acknowledged that the consensus did not address a significant number of important issues for which there is no consensus. Among the most important omissions were the appropriate government response to market failures, the priority to be given environmental concerns, how best to address problems of inequality and poverty, and the need to make economies better able to withstand international financial crises.

The subsequent history of the Washington Consensus is a lesson in how ideas take on a life of their own. It was quickly interpreted on the political right as further support for free-market policies and as a complete list of the all things governments should do in order to return to growth and prosperity. On the political left, observers agreed with the meaning of the Consensus, but were in complete disagreement over its validity. While Williamson tried to argue with both sides in favor of a more sophisticated view of the Consensus as a starting point and not as an ending point for policymakers, common usage of the term usually means something closer to the conservative, free-market interpretation, rather than Williamson's own idea.

## The Next Generation of Reforms

The Washington Consensus overlaps with stabilization policies and structural reforms, and they are commonly mixed together under the label neoliberalism. Neoliberalism is a negative term throughout most of Latin America, primarily because the reforms of the last two decades have created uncertainty and change, but they have not begun to fulfill expectations of growth and prosperity. That is, the narrowly defined Washington Consensus may have helped some countries to end hyperinflation or runaway budget deficits, but it has not solved some of the region's most pressing and fundamental long-term problems. Inadequate growth rates, dramatic inequality, and vulnerability to macroeconomic crises and volatility continue to plague most of the countries of the region. After the reforms of the 1980s and 1990s, economic growth rates increased, but were still too low to offer much encouragement, and poverty and inequality either stayed the same or, in some cases, worsened. Analysts in the mid-1990s began to talk about "reforming the reforms" and a "second generation of reforms," while popular frustration over the lack of growth spilled over into violence and political instability in some countries. Venezuela, for example, elected a populist president who immediately returned to the days of large budget deficits, state ownership, and growing trade deficits.

Reform-minded observers and policymakers have begun to specify a second generation of reforms that are more cognizant of the role of political and administrative institutions, and that take into account the problems created by Latin America's hugely unequal income distribution. The reformers' goals are to develop a more inclusionary economic system by creating opportunities for excluded groups, to make countries less prone to macroeconomic crises, and to create greater flexibility by addressing some of the legal and institutional rigidities. For example, many small firms and individual-owned businesses or homes are located on property for which owners do not have a formal title. This situation makes it impossible for them to use their assets as collateral for loans, or to participate in the formal financial system. In effect, it limits growth by disallowing the full economic participation of a large share of small-scale entrepreneurs. To address this problem, bureaucratic processes must be redesigned and simplified, while legal and judicial structures must be reorganized to meet the needs of small businesses and individuals, rather than large companies and powerful political interests. Similarly, bankruptcy laws that encourage risk-taking, competition policies that break up monopolies, and financial sector supervision that limits unnecessary or unwanted risk are all areas that need work.

Mechanisms for addressing Latin America's highly unequal distribution of income are also on the agenda. In many countries, a long history of exclusion has blocked economic opportunity for particular groups including, indigenous people, African Americans, and isolated subsistence farmers. Although conditions vary greatly, most countries share an income distribution that is among the least equal of any region of the world. The mechanisms for addressing inequality are politically difficult because inevitably they involve an increase in tax collections and the redirecting of expenditures toward groups and regions that tend to be among the least powerful and the least influential. Nevertheless, an increase in expenditures for rural infrastructure to connect isolated groups to the national economy, along with education, health care, and microcredit lending programs, will all play a role in solving the long-standing problem of inequality.

Over the last 20 years, a few countries, including Mexico and Chile, have become among the most open and outward-oriented countries anywhere. Others, such as Brazil and Argentina, continue to expand their linkages to the global economy while becoming more integrated with each other. In a relatively short period, Latin America has undergone a historical shift from a closed, inwardly oriented region of the world to one of the most open and outwardly oriented. This shift has required fundamental changes in economic policy and in the thinking of politicians and citizens. In many respects, the region had no choice, because the previous strategy of ISI was floundering and unable to ease the debt crisis of the 1980s. So far, the results of these reforms are disappointing, but they highlight the need for reformers to consider more than economics alone, as they struggle to find the sources of economic development in a more integrated world environment.

# Summary

- Latin America has been one of the fastest-growing regions of the world throughout most of the twentieth century. Growth came crashing to a halt in the 1980s, however, and only began to return in the late 1980s and early 1990s.

- Until the recent reforms, Latin American economic growth has focused on inward development rather than outward orientation. Productivity in subsistence agriculture has lagged behind overall growth, leading to much higher rates of poverty in rural areas than in urban ones.

- The primary development strategy of Latin America was adopted in the 1930s, 1940s, and 1950s. It came to be called import substitution industrialization and focused on the inwardly oriented development of industries that could produce goods that would substitute for imports. This model of development was favored because it was thought that Latin America would suffer ever-declining terms of trade for its primary commodity exports, and that ISI would reduce the need for foreign exchange and imports, thereby making the region less vulnerable to economic shocks from outside.

- Economic growth under ISI was adequate, but ultimately it led to an inefficient manufacturing sector, excessive rent seeking, a persistent tendency toward overvalued exchange rates, and too great a concentration of resources on the urban sector.

- ISI policies were often made worse by the tendencies of many countries to elect or support economic populists. Populists favored economic growth and redistribution while, in the extreme, they ignored economic constraints such as government budgets and foreign exchange shortages.

- Populist policies generated macroeconomic instability, which often led to hyperinflation and falling real wages.

- The debt crisis that began in 1982 affected every country of the region, even those without high levels of debt or debt problems. As a result of the crisis, it became extremely difficult to borrow internationally.

- The main causes of the debt crisis were the increases in lending during the 1970s and the external shocks of interest rate hikes and primary commodity price decreases, especially oil. The faulty macroeconomic policies of many Latin American governments during the late 1970s and early 1980s made them more vulnerable to the shocks.

- The debt crisis resulted in negative growth throughout the region for most of the period from 1982 through 1987. By 1987–1988, the need for significant reforms in economic policy was apparent to almost all governments.

- From the mid-1980s through the present, the governments of Latin America have engaged in serious reforms of economic policy. The reforms have first tried to create macroeconomic stability through controlling inflation and reducing budget deficits. Stabilization policies have been followed by structural reforms that have opened trade, privatized, and reduced and redesigned the regulatory environment.

- Growth has returned to most of Latin America, but dissatisfaction with the economic reforms is widespread. Job creation is less than desired, inequality persists, and economic growth is below the rate necessary to significantly reduce poverty.

# Vocabulary

Baker Plan

Brady Plan

Economic Commission on Latin America (ECLA, or CEPAL in Spanish)

economic populism

export pessimism

Free Trade Agreement of the Americas (FTAA)

heterodox stabilization policies

import substitution industrialization (ISI)

market failure

"neoliberal model" or neoliberalism

orthodox stabilization policies

structural reform policies

terms of trade (TOT)

Washington Consensus

# Study Questions

1. What were the main characteristics of economic growth in Latin America from the end of World War II until the debt crisis of the 1980s?

2. What is import substitution industrialization? Explain its goals and methods.

3. What are the main criticisms of import substitution industrialization? Did ISI fail?

4. Describe a typical cycle of economic populism. Why does it often leave its supporters worse off than before the cycle begins?

5. Explain how economic populist policies usually lead to overvalued exchange rates and large trade deficits.

6. What were the proximate causes of the debt crisis? How did the United States and other industrial countries respond?

7. Why did the Latin American debt crisis of the 1980s cause recessions in each country?

8. What is the difference between stabilization policies and structural adjustment policies? Give examples of each.

9. What is neoliberalism? Why do some people consider it a negative term?

10. What was the content of Latin American trade reforms of the late 1980s and 1990s? How do the actions taken relate to the desired goals?

# 16 Export-Oriented Growth in East Asia

## Introduction: The High-Performance Asian Economies

One of the most interesting economic stories of the last 50 years is how high-growth economies of East Asia have taken off. The World Bank coined the term **high-performance Asian economies**, or **HPAEs**, to refer to the eight countries of Hong Kong, Indonesia, Japan, Malaysia, Singapore, South Korea, Taiwan, and Thailand. They vary in their income levels and living standards, but they share a number economic policies, including an outward orientation and extremely rapid growth by world standards. These eight countries form the core of what has also been called the *East Asian miracle*, and their success continues to have a profound impact on the formation of economic policy around the world, particularly in Latin America and other developing regions.

After the severe economic and financial crisis that hit the HPAE region in the summer of 1997, it is reasonable to ask whether their success is a long-run trend, or a temporary economic bubble. The worst hit countries were Indonesia, Malaysia, South Korea, and Thailand. While problems continued to linger for several years, in many respects the crisis highlights the robust strength of these economies. By 2000, they were all on positive growth paths in the range of 5 to 10 percent per year in real terms. The crisis of 1997–1998 was severe and exposed the need for change, but it did not put an end to the story of their remarkable economic growth and development. Understanding their experiences continues to be well worth the effort, particularly because they illustrate a case where developing countries use international trade and the international economy to achieve high rates of economic growth.

Before proceeding, it is useful to explain some of the terms used to describe this part of the world. A common name for one group of countries that began its rapid economic growth period shortly after Japan took off in the 1950s is the **Four Tigers**. This group includes the two city-states of Hong Kong and Singapore, and Korea and Taiwan. They are also sometimes referred to as the *Four Dragons*, or the *Little Dragons*, and all four are classified by the World

Bank as high income. Another group, which is broader and not confined to East Asia, is the **newly industrializing economies**, or **NIEs**. There are a number of these economies in Latin America (Argentina, Brazil, Chile, and Mexico), as well as East Asia. NIEs in the HPAEs are Indonesia, Malaysia, and Thailand. China may also be considered an NIE, but it is usually placed in its own category due to its size and the legacy of communism. All of the NIEs began their high rates of economic growth after the economies of the Four Tigers took off.

Economists agree on several of the keys to the growth of the HPAE. For example, unlike the experience of Latin America, and in spite of their own recent financial chaos, macroeconomic stability has been a high priority of their economic policies. A second fact that stands in contrast to other regions is that there is a strong and credible commitment to sharing economic growth with all layers of society, in part through access to education, health care, and land reform. This proved to have numerous benefits, including the rapid creation of a skilled workforce. A third difference is that the HPAE nations promoted their export sectors while remaining more open to imports than most developing countries. This, too, had numerous advantages, including access to technology, high export earnings, and an implicit incentive to foreign investment.

Several questions about the HPAE experience remain unanswered. For example, the importance of industrial policies, or industrial targeting is unclear. Were these policies incidental, or were they instrumental in creating growth? Another series of questions revolves around the use of interventionist government policies and the avoidance of rent seeking. Specifically, in the various government interventions in economic activity, how did HPAE nations avoid the problem of rent seeking that has been so costly to Latin America? On the other hand, some have argued that they did not avoid it, and that it is one of the reasons for the collapse of the financial sector in several countries during the summer and fall of 1997. This is a big unknown, particularly in light of the crisis. Finally, does the "East Asian Miracle" represent a new model for economic growth or are the HPAEs doing fundamentally the same thing that the United States and other industrialized nations did to achieve high incomes?

This chapter examines these and several other questions as it explains the issues surrounding the successes of the East Asian high-growth economies. In particular, the contrast with Latin America is emphasized, along with East Asian trade and international economic relations.

#  Population, Income, and Economic Growth

Table 16.1 illustrates the size and income levels of the HPAEs along with several other large Asian economies. In contrast to Latin America, income levels are high in the HPAEs. Measured in either market exchange rates or purchasing power parity terms, GNP per person is high in Singapore, Japan, Hong Kong, Tai-

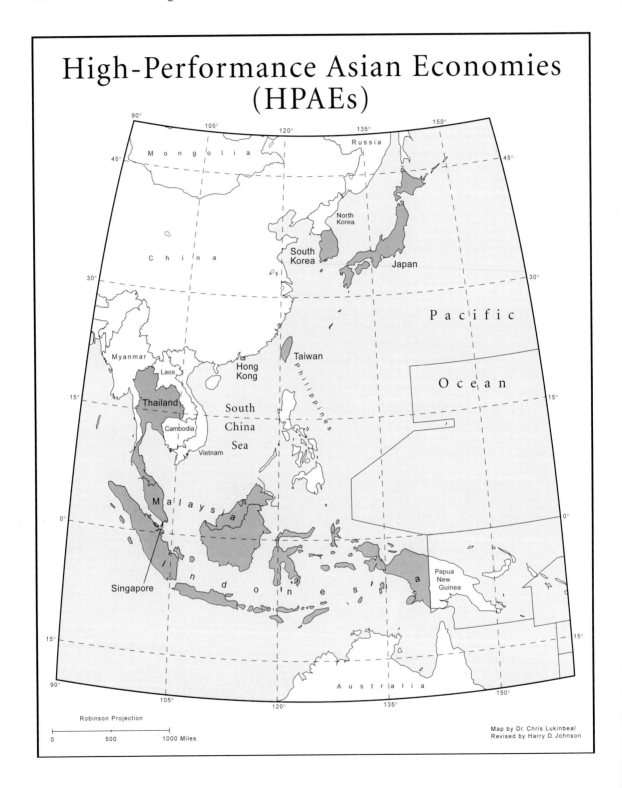

# High-Performance Asian Economies (HPAEs)

Robinson Projection

0  500  1000 Miles

Map by Dr. Chris Lukinbeal
Revised by Harry D. Johnson

| TABLE 16.1 ● Population and GDP for the High Growth Asian Economies, 2005 | | | | |
|---|---|---|---|---|
| | Population (Millions) | GDP (US$, Billions) | GDP per Capita (US$) | GDP per Capita (US$, PPP*) |
| **HPAEs** | | | | |
| Hong Kong, China | 6.9 | 177.7 | 25,595 | 31,165 |
| Indonesia | 220.6 | 287.2 | 1,302 | 3,842 |
| Japan | 128.0 | 4,505.9 | 35,215 | 30,821 |
| Korea, Republic | 48.3 | 787.6 | 16,309 | 21,868 |
| Malaysia | 25.3 | 130.1 | 5,134 | 10,843 |
| Singapore | 4.4 | 116.8 | 26,834 | 29,921 |
| Taiwan, Republic of China | 22.7 | 346.4 | 15,291 | |
| Thailand | 64.2 | 176.6 | 2,749 | 8,551 |
| **Other** | | | | |
| China | 1,304.5 | 2,228.9 | 1,709 | 6,572 |
| Philippines | 83.1 | 98.3 | 1,184 | 4,920 |
| Vietnam | 83.0 | 52.4 | 632 | 3,062 |

Countries in the World Bank category of "High Performance Asian Economies" have attained a high degree of economic success.

*Source*: World Bank, *World Development Indicators*; Taiwan, Republic of China, Director General of Budgeting, Accounting, and Statistics.

wan, and South Korea. The three remaining countries, Thailand, Malaysia, and Indonesia, began their period of rapid growth later and are considerably behind the other five.

Table 16.2 is arranged so that it is directly comparable to Table 15.2 in Chapter 15 for the decade of the 1980s. Several of the HPAEs, as well as a number of other Asian economies, experienced accelerated growth through the decade and much higher growth rates than Latin American economies. It is one of the most important contrasts between the regions and it is also a primary reason why East

**A Note on Hong Kong.** On July 1, 1997, Great Britain officially returned the colony of Hong Kong to China after more than 150 years of British rule. China has pledged itself to follow the policy of "one country, two systems" in its relations with Hong Kong. In practical terms, this means that China will allow Hong Kong to keep its own currency, will limit migration between Hong Kong and the mainland, and will generally try to preserve Hong Kong's current system. Statistics for Hong Kong and China are treated separately.

**TABLE 16.2 ● Average Annual Growth in Real GDP per Person, 1980–2005**

| | Annual Growth in Real GDP per Capita | |
|---|---|---|
| | 1980–1990 | 1990–2005 |
| **HPAEs** | | |
| Hong Kong, China | 5.7 | 3.1 |
| Indonesia | 4.3 | 2.9 |
| Japan | 3.4 | 1.1 |
| Korea, Republic | 8.2 | 4.7 |
| Malaysia | 2.5 | 3.8 |
| Singapore | 5.0 | 3.8 |
| Taiwan, Republic of China | 6.7 | 5.8* |
| Thailand | 5.9 | 3.5 |
| **Other** | | |
| China | 8.5 | 9.1 |
| Philippines | −1.6 | 1.4 |
| Vetnam | 0.9+ | 5.9 |
| **Low-income countries** | 2.0 | 2.9 |
| **Middle-income countries** | 1.1 | 3.0 |
| **High-income countries** | 1.7 | 2.4 |

*1990–2004; +1984–1990.

Growth rates in the HPAE have exceeded rates in most other parts of the world for several decades.

*Source*: World Bank, *World Development Indicators*; Heston, Summers, and Aten, *Penn World Table Version 6.2*; author's calculations.

Asia attracted attention in Latin America. China's growth record might also qualify it as a member of the "high-performance" club, but the differences in its policies and institutions make it unlike any other Asian economy in Tables 16.1 and 16.2.

According to the "Rule of 72," if a variable (income, for example) grows at the rate $X$, then it doubles in approximately $72/X$ years. In other words, Korea's 8.2 percent annual rate of growth between 1980 and 1990 implies that its per capita real GDP doubled in 8.8 years (72/8.2), and over the decade, its income more than doubled. While the majority of developing countries have not begun to close the gap with high income countries, income differences between the HPAE and the world's richest countries have been shrinking for several decades. Table

16.2 also shows the rate of growth of GDP per person for the high income countries. As shown in the table, growth rates for every HPAE exceed the high income average, except in the case of Japan, which is already a high income country and suffered a long period of low growth through the 1990s.

# General Characteristics of Growth in the HPAEs

Recall from Chapter 15 that from the end of World War II until the mid- to late 1980s, economic growth in Latin America was characterized by high levels of inequality, periods of macroeconomic instability, and an inward orientation. The contrast with the HPAEs could not be more striking, since their growth was built around falling inequality, generally sound macroeconomic fundamentals, and the promotion of exports. It is worth looking at each of the elements in more detail.

## Shared Growth

One of the most remarkable features of growth in the HPAEs is that it was accompanied by rising economic equality. This feature is even more remarkable when it is realized that inequality in income and wealth was already relatively low at the start of the period of high growth. Since the 1950s pioneering work of the economist Simon Kuznets, it was thought that growth in developing countries would first result in falling economic equality, followed later by rising equality. While Kuznets' work was based on measurements from a large number of countries, the East Asian experience has called into question the idea that economic growth in developing countries follows a "Kuznets' curve," in which equality first declines and then rises.

Table 16.3 compares income distribution in the HPAEs with Latin America. The columns show the percent of the nation's income received by the poorest 20 percent of households, the percent received by the richest 20 percent, and the ratio of the two. The poorest households in the five Latin American nations receive an average of 3.2 percent of society's income, while in the HPAEs, the poorest receive 6.8 percent, or twice as large a share of national income. The richest 20 percent receive 57.4 percent in the Latin American sample and 46 percent of total income in the HPAEs. Among the HPAEs, the top 20 percent of the most well-off households have income levels that are on average 6.7 times greater than the poorest households. Meanwhile, in the largest Latin American countries, the same group of well-off households have incomes that average almost 18 times greater than the poorest households. Given the extreme concentration of wealth in Latin America, if we were to focus on the top 5 percent or the top 1 percent, the difference between Latin America and the HPAE would be even more striking.

The conditions that led to greater income equality were rooted in the unique historical experiences of each country. Nevertheless, each of the HPAEs had a

**TABLE 16.3** • **Measures of Income Distribution, East Asia and Latin America**

|  | Year* | Income Share of Bottom 20% | Income Share of Top 20% | Ratio |
|---|---|---|---|---|
| **HPAEs** | | | | |
| Hong Kong | 1996 | 5.3 | 50.7 | 9.6 |
| Indonesia | 2002 | 8.4 | 43.3 | 5.2 |
| Japan | 1993 | 10.6 | 35.7 | 3.4 |
| Korea, Republic | 1998 | 7.9 | 37.5 | 4.7 |
| Malaysia | 1997 | 4.4 | 54.3 | 12.3 |
| Singapore | 1998 | 5.0 | 49.0 | 9.8 |
| Taiwan | 1999 | 7.1 | 39.2 | 5.5 |
| Thailand | 2000 | 6.1 | 50.0 | 6.7 |
| *Average* | | 6.8 | 46.0 | 6.7 |
| **Latin America** | | | | |
| Brazil | 1998 | 2.2 | 64.1 | 29.1 |
| Colombia | 1996 | 3.0 | 60.9 | 20.3 |
| Mexico | 1998 | 3.4 | 57.6 | 16.9 |
| Peru | 1996 | 4.4 | 51.2 | 11.6 |
| Venezuela | 1998 | 3.0 | 53.2 | 17.7 |
| *Average* | | 3.2 | 57.4 | 17.9 |

Income is distributed much more equally in the HPAEs than in Latin America.

*Comparisons of income distribution must rely on country studies that are done in different years.

*Source*: World Bank, *World Development Indicators, 2003*; Republic of China (Taiwan), Director General of Budget, Accounting, and Statistics.

similar set of highly visible wealth-sharing mechanisms. Specifically, these included land reform, free public education, free basic health care, and significant investments in rural infrastructure, such as clean water systems, transportation, and communication systems. These policies did not equalize incomes, but they provided people with the tools they needed to raise their individual incomes and gave hope for the future. This had several positive effects. For example, when purchasing power is spread more widely through a society, it increases the opportunities for small- and medium-scale entrepreneurs that produce for the local market. The experiences gained in meeting local demand helps small firms develop into larger enterprises and may carry over into numerous other activities. In addition, rising incomes across a broad spectrum of socioeconomic groups raise hopes in general for future improvements and encourage coopera-tion among the different classes of society while conferring legitimacy on the rul-ing governments. Both factors contribute to political stability as well as the willingness by the business elites to commit to long-term investments.

## Rapid Accumulation of Physical and Human Capital

Rising levels of equality were closely tied to very rapid rates of accumulation of physical and human capital. Rapid accumulation of physical capital is synony-mous with high levels of investment. Investment, in turn, depended on high sav-ings rates. The level of savings in the HPAEs is considerably higher than in many other parts of the world. The explanations for high savings are varied. In part, it is a result of the rapid **demographic transition** experienced by those nations after World War II. The demographic transition is the shift from high birth rates and high death rates to low birth and death rates that accompanies modernization. Countries that have completed a demographic transition have fewer children below working age and a larger percentage of the population engaged in economically productive work. Hence, they tend to have higher sav-ings rates.

Another factor that increased both the level of savings and the level of invest-ment was the absence of high inflation and the presence of stable financial insti-tutions. The crisis of 1997 calls into question whether people will continue to have confidence in their financial institutions and whether this will affect savings rates. Until the crisis, most investors acted as if they believed their financial sav-ings were protected against loss of value through high inflation and against a col-lapse in the banking system.

While the rapid demographic transition, low inflation rates, and stable finan-cial institutions appear to have caused savings rates to be high, probably the most important factor was simply the rapid rate of income growth. That is, sav-ings and income growth are interdependent, and the HPAEs seemed to have cre-ated a "virtuous cycle" in which rapid income growth caused high savings. Savings led to high rates of investment, which fed back into a second round of income growth and high savings.

Investment in people was as important as the accumulation of physical capi-tal. One of the key features of the HPAEs' educational policy is that public investment in education was focused on the primary and secondary levels. Edu-cational dollars go farther at this level, and the social impact is much greater per dollar spent than at the university level. These investments raised literacy rates dramatically and laid the foundation for a highly skilled workforce that was capable of tackling increasingly sophisticated forms of production. In effect, the continuous rise in human capital endowments of the HPAEs constituted an ongoing shift in the comparative advantages of those nations, so that new invest-ments could continually push into new product lines.

## Rapid Growth of Manufactured Exports

Each of the eight HPAEs actively and successfully promoted exports, although each began its development pushes with import substitution policies. ISI policies, however, were quickly replaced with an emphasis on export promotion. The timing of the switch from ISI to export promotion varied by country. Japan began promoting exports in the late 1950s and early 1960s, the Four Tigers (Hong Kong, Korea, Singapore, Taiwan) started in the late 1960s, and the newly industrializing economies, NIEs (Indonesia, Malaysia, and Thailand) began in the early 1980s.

Table 16.4 shows the results of the export push. Between 1965 and 2000 the HPAEs more than doubled their share of total world exports and total world manufactured exports. In part, the success of the export promotion drives was the result of education policies that favored primary and secondary schooling. These policies created widespread literacy and an adaptable and easily trained labor force. In addition, each of the HPAEs pursued various export promotion policies. For example, Japan and the Four Tigers made export financing credit readily available; they required export targets for firms that wished to receive favorable credit terms or tax benefits; and they provided tariff-free access to imports of capital equipment used to manufacture exports. Policies in the NIEs were somewhat less interventionist and relied to a greater extent on attracting direct foreign investment in export activities.

The connection between export promotion and high rates of growth is an area of some controversy in economics. There are several possible connections that are explored in greater detail later in the chapter. A second controversy is the possibility of other nations using similar export promotion strategies. In many cases, these policies generate trade conflicts and may be at odds with the rules for fair trade agreed to by the members of the WTO.

## Stable Macroeconomic Environments

A fourth and final characteristic of the HPAE economies is the maintenance of stable macroeconomic environments. Chapter 15 argued that one of the persistent problems of Latin America has been the frequent reoccurrence of macro-

**TABLE 16.4** ● **The Share of HPAEs in World Exports, 1965–2000**

|  | HPAEs' Share of World Exports | | |
|---|---|---|---|
|  | 1965 | 1980 | 2000 |
| **Total Exports** | 7.9 | 13.1 | 19.9 |
| **Exports of Manufactures** | 9.4 | 17.3 | 21.3 |

HPAEs' exports have significantly increased their share of world exports.

*Source*: World Bank, *The East Asian Miracle*; and World Bank, *World Development Indicators, 2003*.

economic crises. Even before the crisis of 1997, the high-performance economies of East Asia were not completely free of macroeconomic crises, but when they occurred, policy responses were usually quick and appropriate. Responses to the 1997 crisis were no different in this regard. Macroeconomic stability can have several components, and the factors that are usually emphasized in this context are a commitment to keeping inflation under control, good management of both internal government debt and externally owed foreign debt, and the quick resolution of crises when they occurred. In general, macroeconomic policy has been characterized as "pragmatic and flexible."

On average, budget deficits and foreign debt were not dramatically smaller than in other regions of the world although there was a significant amount of variation across countries. The difference in the HPAEs, however, is that with the exception of the recent crisis, deficits and debts remained manageable. High growth rates helped ease the constraints imposed by a given level of debt, partly because the high levels of exports earned the foreign assets necessary for debt servicing. The crisis of 1997 is the exception that proves this rule, since one of the key triggers of the crisis was a significant reduction of export earnings in a couple of countries and the growth of large current account deficits. To many foreign investors, these deficits began to seem larger than was warranted, and this triggered significant capital flight.

The commitment to low inflation helped keep real interest rates stable and enabled firms to take a longer-run view of their investments. In addition, low inflation helped avoid severe real appreciations in the exchange rate. Low inflation also meant that variations in the real exchange rate, the real interest rate, and the inflation rate were relatively low. In turn, this helped to foster a greater security in the minds of investors.

##  The Institutional Environment

Economic success stems from an ability to mobilize and allocate resources. In the HPAEs, large flows of savings were generated, they were channeled into the financial system, and they were lent to business enterprises that used them productively. Simultaneously, governments emphasized education and universal literacy. Ultimately, an efficient mobilization and allocation of resources is based on the decisions of individuals and businesses that own resources. In order to ensure that individuals and businesses use their resources in the most productive manner, governments must create rules that foster efficient outcomes. In this regard, the institutional environments of the HPAEs are essential to their success.

Several components of the institutional environment are critical insofar as they help to make government policy credible. In particular, property rights are relatively secure and free from the threat of nationalization. Bureaucracies are generally competent; individuals and businesses are free to make contracts that will be enforced; access to information is widespread; and regulations tend to be clear and well publicized. Of course, there are exceptions to each of the above, depending on the time and place, but, in general, these features characterize the institutional environments of the HPAEs.

These characteristics should not be confused with the characteristics of open, democratic societies. The fact that several of the HPAEs do not support political and civil liberties raises a question about the relationship between authoritarian rule and economic growth. Specifically, do the lack of political and civil liberties, and the concentration of power in the executive branch of government confer advantages for economic development?

The answer to this question is complex and beyond the scope of this book. Nevertheless, it should be noted that many dictatorships have failed in their bid to mobilize and allocate resources. Dictatorships or authoritarian regimes may be as likely to prey upon society as they are to foster its economic development. However authoritarian they are, the HPAEs fostered growth rather than the enrichment of a small elite at the expense of the majority.

A second issue that arises from the general lack of traditionally defined democratic rights is the relevancy of the HPAE experience to other regions of the world, such as Latin America. Some social scientists argue that the context of authoritarian rule makes the HPAE experience irrelevant to nations such as Bolivia and Argentina, where policy reform is taking place within an institutional setting that allows far more dissent.

The relationship between authoritarian rule and economic growth and the applicability of the HPAE experience to the rest of the developing world, are contentious and lack consensus. Generally speaking, there does not seem to be a correlation between the type of government (democratic or authoritarian) and the ability to put good policies into place.

## Fiscal Discipline

Democratic or not, governments must create a stable macroeconomic environment in order for economic growth to succeed. The characteristic of macroeconomic stability has already been discussed, but it is worth revisiting because of its central importance and its contrast with the experiences of other regions such as Latin America.

The maintenance of a stable macroeconomic environment requires fiscal discipline and an acceptance of the resource constraints that limit government actions. Budget deficits and foreign debt must be kept manageable, and the real exchange rate must be relatively stable. The benefits of accepting these limitations are that it increases the credibility of government policy and builds the private sector's confidence. The result is more investment and less capital flight.

## Business-Government Relations

Stable macroeconomic policies are necessary for growth, but they are no guarantee. For example, macroeconomic stability does not address the very significant problem in all developing countries of the coordination of interdependent investment projects. The coordination problem results from the fact that many private sector investments are interdependent. That is, their profitability depends on the simultaneous or prior creation of a complementary investment. The same often holds true for private sector/public sector investments. For example, profitable investment in warehousing facilities at a seaport depends on the prior investment in sufficient port infrastructure to provide an adequate flow of goods through the warehouses. Yet, the port and related transportation linkages may not be worthwhile unless there is a simultaneous investment or a guarantee of future investment in the warehouses.

## CASE STUDY

# Deliberation Councils in the Ministry of International Trade and Industry (MITI)

Japan's use of deliberation councils has been more extensive than any other country's. In Japan, the councils are attached to a particular ministry, or bureaucracy, such as the Ministry of International Trade and Industry (MITI). Since MITI is one of the largest bureaucracies in Japan, and because it has more control over Japanese economic policy than any other bureaucracy—with the exception of the Ministry of Finance—it has numerous deliberation councils. According to one account, in 1990, there were 17 major regular deliberative councils attached to MITI.

Councils in MITI are of two basic types. They are industry specific, such as the Textile Industry Council, or they are thematic, such as the Industrial Structure Council. Thematic councils deal with a broad range of issues and, consequently, are composed of numerous committees. For example, the Industrial Structure Council had 18 committees in 1990, ranging from the Industrial Finance Committee and the Industrial Labor Committee, to the Industrial Location Committee.

The method for using deliberation councils involves a feedback process in which the first step is for MITI officials to call a hearing and invite comments from various interested parties. Based on the information it collects, MITI officials issue a draft report that is then forwarded for discussion to a deliberative council. The council may include affected industry representatives, academics, journalists, consumer and labor representatives, former bureaucrats, financial representatives, and politicians. Representation is not proportional in any sense, nor are representatives elected. Based on the feedback that MITI gets from the council, it makes changes in its draft plan and issues a final document that details the steps that will be taken, such as policy changes or new policy initiatives. The final action taken by MITI is essentially a public relations campaign to sell the plan to the wider public.

*Source*: Campos and Root, *The Key to the East Asian Miracle.*

The coordination of interdependent investment activities is difficult in a purely free-market framework. The difficulty stems from the fact that the flow of information is not sufficient to let all investors know of the intentions of each other. Six of the eight HPAEs surmounted this problem through the creation of **deliberation councils**, a set of quasi-legislative bodies that bring together representatives from the private and the public sectors. In effect, deliberation councils coordinate the information flow between businesses and policymakers.

Individual councils are usually created to deal with a limited set of issues involving one industry or a particular set of policy issues, such as the government budget. By bringing together government officials and affected business groups, the councils reduce the cost of acquiring information about new policies, provide a forum for bargaining over policies, instill greater investor confidence, and raise the level of credibility of the government's policies. More than perhaps any other function, however, deliberation councils serve as a vehicle for the business elites to have a strong voice in the setting of government policy and thereby ensure their cooperation in the overall economic strategy.

## Avoiding Rent Seeking

Economic policy in the HPAEs has been relatively interventionist. That is, the laissez-faire ideology of letting markets determine outcomes has not been followed. Hong Kong is somewhat of an exception, but even in Hong Kong, government has directed and actively participated in the creation of extensive public housing. In the next section, we examine some of the issues related to the effectiveness and extent of government intervention in the economy. Whether extensive or not, however, one of the biggest puzzles surrounding HPAE economic policy was the degree to which most countries were able to avoid the costs and inefficiencies associated with private sector rent seeking.

When governments intervene to help specific industries or to channel resources in a particular direction, they create benefits that are of value to someone. Generally speaking, when private interests perceive the possibility of obtaining something of value from government, for instance, credit subsidies, import protection, and business licenses, they will devote scarce resources to obtaining those benefits. The result, as discussed in several earlier chapters, is wasteful rent seeking.

Government policies in the HPAEs created numerous benefits of value to specific industries, yet in spite of this, there was relatively little rent seeking by those interests. To be sure, rent seeking still occurs, and there is significant variation by HPAE nations. Nevertheless, there is less overall rent seeking than in many other societies.

It is unlikely that there is a single, simple explanation for this lack of rent-seeking behavior, but the deliberation councils probably played a key role. By providing a policy forum in which various interests can make their views known and have a chance to argue in favor of policies that are particularly beneficial, the need to hire lobbyists is reduced. Furthermore, given that industrial and business interests meet with government officials as a group, rather than single interests by themselves, there is greater transparency and less worry about what competing interests may be doing behind the scenes.

In addition to the role played by deliberation councils, some analysts point to the fact that whenever governments offer something of value, they usually attach performance requirements. For example, firms receiving credit subsidies or import protection are usually required to meet specific targets—often export targets—or else the subsidies are taken away. What is remarkable, and not clearly understood, is how HPAE governments are able to enforce the performance requirements they lay down. Many nations outside East Asia, including many Latin American governments, have used performance requirements as incentive mechanisms, but often they have proven to be unenforceable. That is, when firms have not met their production or export targets, governments outside the HPAEs have often been unable to withdraw the special considerations they are providing to the noncompliant firms.

Two key elements that have played a role in enforceability are the presence of a well-educated bureaucracy along with its insulation from the political process. In most of the HPAEs, civil service careers are highly respected and well paid. Consequently, bureaucrats are well educated and competent. In addition to ability, their insulation from the political process gives them the room to make decisions based on merit rather than on the basis of special interests.

A final explanation for the relative lack of rent seeking is the commitment to shared growth that we saw at the beginning of the chapter. The fact that business elites are convinced that they will share the benefits of economic growth reduces the pressure for them to seek added benefits through the manipulation of the political process. In effect, greater equality in the HPAEs reduces the number of individuals and groups that feel left out of the growth process and eliminates the underlying cause of much rent seeking.

## CASE STUDY

# Were East Asian Economies Open?

High growth Asian economies relied on their export sectors for a substantial part of their growth. They actively promoted exports in various ways and to varying degrees, and there is a consensus among economists that manufactured exports played a key role in their economic development. Export promotion is not the same thing as an open economy, however, and there is disagreement about their trade policies and the extent of their openness.

It would seem that it should be easy to settle the debate simply by looking at tariff rates and quotas. Unfortunately, these are inadequate measures of trade policy, particularly if a country has significant non-tariff measures that it uses to block imports. For example, the U.S. auto industry argued for years that red tape and unnecessary safety inspections made their cars uncompetitive in Japanese markets. This may or may not have been the case; U.S. cars were not designed for Japan and the marketing and distribution systems are fundamentally different from those in the United States. Did U.S. cars fare poorly because the playing field was tilted to favor Japanese brands, or was the playing field level and U.S. automakers had products that were less competitive?

It is possible that high growth Asian economies promoted their exports and severely restricted imports in order to protect domestic markets. In that case, their policies were not market-oriented, but instead reflected a high degree of government intervention with the purpose of determining outcomes selected by planners and bureaucrats. In this view, some East Asian economies followed the policies of mercantilism and viewed exports as the path to wealth creation and imports as destructive to their wealth and prosperity (see Chapter 3). Alternatively, East Asian economies did not set tough constraints on imports, but followed relatively open export promotion policies that contributed to rapid economic growth, more-or-less in line with market-based incentives.

This is an important debate. The HPAEs were the first group of countries since World War II to go from developing to developed, or low and middle income to high income. If mercantilism is the key to their success, it would be an important empirical case against the paradigm of comparative advantage and the gains from trade.

Table 16.5 contrasts imports and exports for high growth East Asian countries with the main Latin American economies. Imports and exports include goods and services and are measured relative to the size of each country's GDP. In addition, larger countries tend to export and import less, all else equal. Data is provided for two years. In 1980, most of the East Asian economies were practicing export promotion policies, and Latin America had weak export sectors and relatively closed economies. By 2004, Latin American policies had changed toward much greater open policies.

China and Brazil are the two largest countries in each region, and imports and export shares of GDP were very similar in 1980. In 1980, however, China had just begun to open its economy. Over the subsequent 24 years, as Latin American economies, including Brazil, became more open, Brazilian imports grew to become 13.4 percent of GDP. Meanwhile, Chinese imports reached almost one-third of GDP (31.4 percent) in 2004. Setting aside Hong Kong, which is a city-state and a special case, nearly all the East Asian economies had larger import sectors in 1980 than the relatively closed Latin American economies. By 2004, Latin American economies were much more open; they had signed many free trade agreements, joined the GATT, if not already members, and reduced tariffs and quotas dramatically. Yet, most of the East Asian economies still imported relatively more. The exception is Japan, a large country in economic terms, and to a lesser extent, Indonesia, which is also a large country.

## TABLE 16.5 • Imports and Exports as a Share of GDP

| | Imports | | Exports | |
|---|---|---|---|---|
| | 1980 | 2004 | 1980 | 2004 |
| **East Asia** | | | | |
| China | 11.1 | 31.4 | 10.7 | 34.0 |
| Hong Kong, China | 89.4 | 181.3 | 88.9 | 190.2 |
| Indonesia | 20.2 | 27.3 | 34.2 | 31.3 |
| Japan | 14.5 | 10.2 | 13.6 | 11.8 |
| Korea, Republic | 40.0 | 39.7 | 32.1 | 44.1 |
| Malaysia | 54.3 | 99.9 | 56.7 | 121.2 |
| Thailand | 30.4 | 65.8 | 24.1 | 70.5 |
| Taiwan | 52.6 | 61.3 | 51.4 | 64.8 |
| **Latin America** | | | | |
| Argentina | 6.5 | 18.1 | 5.1 | 25.3 |
| Brazil | 11.3 | 13.4 | 9.0 | 18.0 |
| Chile | 27.0 | 31.9 | 22.8 | 40.8 |
| Colombia | 15.6 | 21.5 | 16.2 | 21.9 |
| Mexico | 13.0 | 31.6 | 10.7 | 29.6 |
| Peru | 19.4 | 18.3 | 22.4 | 20.9 |
| Venezuela | 21.8 | 20.1 | 28.8 | 36.2 |

East Asian economies promoted exports but also absorbed large quantities of imports.

*Source*: World Bank, *World Development Indicators.*

East Asian economies apparently did not close their import sectors, but rather imported quite a large amount of goods and services. They still may have used selective protection for targeted industries, but in general the data do not support the idea that they were relatively closed to imports. This is entirely consistent with theoretical models showing that protectionism often hurts exports by causing the currency to appreciate as a result of a lack of demand for foreign goods, and due to the higher returns protectionism creates for the production of import substitutes. In other words, just as Latin America's depressed imports went hand-in-hand with its depressed exports in 1980, East Asia's high level of exports went hand-in-hand with a relatively high level of imports.

#  The Role of Industrial Policies

The most influential study to date of the high-performance Asian economies is the World Bank's policy research report entitled *The East Asian Miracle: Economic Growth and Public Policy*. The World Bank's research team concluded that government interventions were common in three areas: (1) targeting of specific industries, that is, industrial policies narrowly defined; (2) directed credit; and (3) export promotion. In this section, we examine the debate over the effectiveness of industrial policies and offer a word of caution about the use of directed credit.

## Targeting Specific Industries in the HPAEs

Recall from Chapter 5 that industrial policies can be defined in broad or narrow terms. The broad definition is policies that alter a nation's endowment in a way that does not favor particular industries. For example, we have already seen that the East Asian success story involves high rates of primary and secondary schooling that altered the characteristics of the labor force and the high rates of savings and investment that created the infrastructure and capital goods necessary to enter more sophisticated lines of manufacturing.

The narrow definition of industrial policies is the targeted development of specific industries. In effect, targeted industrial policies attempt to change the comparative advantage of a nation through the alteration of its industrial structure. These policies channel resources to favored industries and are often criticized as being "government bureaucrats picking winners and losers."

With the exception of Hong Kong, every HPAE has had or still has some form of targeted industrial policy. They were strongest in Japan, Korea, and Taiwan (the "northern tier" of HPAEs), but were significant in the other countries as well. In Japan, the focus has been on steel, autos, textiles, shipbuilding, aluminum, electronics, and semiconductors, among others. The height of Korean policies was between 1973–1979 with the Heavy and Chemical Industries (HCI) program, which targeted steel, shipbuilding, petrochemicals, and other heavy industries. While lacking the same clear focus as Japan and Korea, Taiwan's programs have provided research institutes, science parks, and basic infrastructure for a variety of industries and seem to have targeted the development of import substitutes.

Malaysian policies took off in the early 1980s with the Look East policy, which emulated Korea's and Japan's industrial development. Malaysia created the Heavy Industries Corporation of Malaysia (HICOM) to develop steel, nonferrous metals, machinery, paper and paper products, and petrochemicals, but it ran into financial constraints in the late 1980s when a number of the firms under HICOM proved to be unprofitable and required government bailouts. Since then, Malaysia has privatized many firms and reduced the degree of state control in others. Indonesia and Thailand did not make systematic efforts such as Japan and Korea did, but the Thai Board of Investment has promoted industries that it deemed to have the potential for technological learning. Indonesia has attempted to use large state-run enterprises to advance from labor-intensive to high-technology industries. Singapore's policies have focused largely on encouraging technology transfer from firms in industrial nations through the promotion of foreign direct investment.

The tools that nations use to promote specific industries include the instruments of trade policies. Restrictions on imports, through licensing, quotas, or tariffs, and export subsidies were all used. In many cases, protection from foreign competition enabled firms to earn high profits in domestic markets, which compensated for the losses they suffered in foreign markets. In addition to trade policy, the HPAEs used numerous other mechanisms to channel resources to targeted industries. Directed credit was one of the most important tools, because even when it was small in size, it signaled the private sector that government policy favored the industry receiving the funds. This official stamp of approval was an important device for encouraging private lending to new and potentially risky industries. Other tools included subsidies, market information—especially with respect to foreign markets, infrastructure construction, and research—and development funds.

There are two essential elements to these policies that make them different from most other national attempts to promote specific industries. First, resources were usually only provided as long as the companies receiving them met specific export targets. If the targets were not met, the resources (protection, credit, and so on) were withdrawn. Export targets are argued to be a better criterion than profits because many firms had monopolies or significant market power in their domestic markets; hence, profitability may be unrelated to efficiency. Second, governments placed macroeconomic stability above industrial policies. If they began to experience fiscal problems that were caused by the industrial promotion programs, they scaled back or abandoned them.

The World Bank view of these programs is that they were insulated from purely political influences so that industrial targeting decisions were based on technical analysis rather than politics. The collapse of the financial sectors in many countries in 1997 and 1998 has called this assumption into question. For example, government use of directed credit programs appears to be one of the main causes of the financial crisis. Government involvement in credit allocation forced financial institutions to make unsound loans. In turn, the failure to apply business criteria led to a mountain of bad debt, which ultimately sank many banks and whole financial sectors. In the future, conventional economic wisdom will undoubtedly be much more cautious about the benefits of directed credit programs to target industrial development.

## Did Industrial Policies Work?

The role of industrial policies in the story of HPAE growth is controversial. Ideally, we would like to know the answers to two simple questions. First, did they work? A successful policy would be one that increases the overall rate of GDP growth or the rate of productivity growth. Second, if they worked, were they important? That is, was their contribution to economic growth significant enough to be considered one of the reasons for East Asian success?

With respect to the question of whether they made a positive contribution to growth, opinion ranges from "no effect" to "positive effect." The reason for the lack of consensus on this important issue is that, in general, it is difficult to measure the effects of policy interventions on growth rates. There are conceptual disagreements about the measurements that should be made, and few countries have data of sufficient quality. In the World Bank's view, "reasoned judgments" must be used to settle the issue. Unfortunately, the paucity of data, together with disagreements over measurement techniques, results in the use of qualitative judgments of the sort that inevitably lead researchers to confirm the opinions that they began with.

In spite of these obstacles to assessing industrial policies, the variety of opinions among researchers can be characterized as falling into two camps. One camp is represented by the World Bank's research. In their view, some government interventions fostered economic growth (export promotion and directed credit), but, in general, industrial policies did not. They assert that industrial policies usually targeted the same industries that market forces were developing and, therefore, were unnecessary. In the cases where the "wrong" industries were targeted, pragmatic and flexible policymakers of the HPAEs managed to quickly change policies before any damage was done to the rest of the economy.

The World Bank's analysis rests on two pieces of evidence. First, they compare the growth rates of productivity in the targeted and nontargeted sectors in the three countries with sufficient data (Japan, Korea, and Taiwan). In general, they find that productivity change in the promoted sectors was high but no higher than in the rest of the economy. Possible exceptions to their general finding are Japan's chemical and metalworking industries and Korea's chemical industry. One problem for the advocates of industrial policies is that the unpromoted textile sector did as well as any of the promoted sectors. Second, they examine the change over time in the industrial structure of the HPAEs. If industrial policies worked, they should have led to a different pattern of industrial growth than the pattern that is caused by a change in factor endowments. They conclude that industrial policies were at most marginally effective, since the sector-by-sector growth pattern is as expected, given the national endowments of labor and the high savings and investment rates.

Critiques of the World Bank's findings usually rest on two points. First, the fact that productivity growth was generally no faster in promoted sectors is irrelevant, according to the critics. The important issue is what the growth rates would have been without promotion. It is conceivable that without industrial policies, growth in the targeted industries would have been much slower than with the policies. Second, the critics point out that the World Bank analysis is overly general. In their view, it is based on industry groupings that are too broad to uncover the details of selective targeting. For example, some components of the textile industry were heavily promoted in both Japan and Korea in the early period of their industrial policies. Therefore, it is not surprising that textiles overall have experienced a rapid increase in productivity and that they remain a larger than expected component of Japanese and Korean industry.

At present, there is no way to resolve this debate. Consequently, there are a variety of opinions about the relevance of industrial policies for developing countries outside the HPAE group. To the extent that there is agreement, most analysts share the view that if industrial policies are to be successful, they should have three key characteristics. Countries must have (1) clear performance criteria such as export targets; (2) institutional mechanisms to monitor compliance and enforce compliance; and (3) low costs so that nontargeted sectors do not suffer.

## CASE STUDY

# HCI in Korea

Most observers agree that Korean industrial policies have at least partially succeeded. The most enthusiastic observers argue that they have accelerated the rate of overall growth without creating offsetting inefficiencies elsewhere in the economy. Less optimistic observers concede success in generating exports and in changing the industrial structure of the country, but they offset many of those gains with the huge financial costs of the Heavy and Chemical Industries (HCI) promotion in the 1970s.

Korea's industrial promotion drive began a few years after the Korean War in the early 1960s. Early efforts at industrial targeting focused on key industrial materials such as cement, fertilizer, and petroleum refining. The government typically supported large-scale conglomerates, called *chaebol*, which were given monopolies in the domestic market. Trade policy in the form of an aggressive promotion of exports along with high levels of protection was the main tool for targeting industries, but directed credit and tax breaks were important as well.

Industrial targeting evolved into the Heavy and Chemical Industries program, which was at its most active from 1973–1979. HCI targeted six specific industrial groups: steel, petrochemicals, nonferrous metals for enhanced self-sufficiency, shipbuilding, electronics, and machinery (especially earth-moving equipment and autos) for export. The tools used to promote these industries were the same as previously described but with a different emphasis. By the mid-1970s, trade policy had become somewhat more liberal, although most industries still received significant protection. Greater emphasis was placed on subsidies, directed credit through loans at below-market interest rates, and special tax exemptions.

The cost of promotion during the HCI period was significant. Direct funds provided to targeted industries were around 5 percent of the overall budget, and tax exemptions amounted to about 3 percent of total tax revenues. In 1977, around 45 percent of the banking system's total provision of domestic credit went to the targeted industries. Gradually, bottlenecks and large debts began to accumulate.

By 1979, when the second oil crisis hit, inflation was high, the exchange rate had appreciated, causing exports to falter, and the targeted industries had significant idle capacity. In addition, the labor-intensive sectors, which had not been targeted, were starved for credits, and bad debts and financial insolvencies were growing in the HCI sector.

Policymakers quickly switched course. HCI promotion was curtailed, the currency was devalued, and financial market and import liberalization were hastened. One of the main efforts of policymakers in the 1980s was to restructure a number of the distressed industries that were overpromoted in the 1970s. The cost to the government budget has been significant, as it has been forced to bail out bankrupt firms and dispose of nonperforming loans.

Was HCI promotion worth it? It is impossible to answer this question definitively because we can never know what would have happened under an alternative set of policies. During the height of the HCI program and its immediate aftermath, Korea's growth rate dipped slightly (from the mid-1970s through the mid-1980s), but the change was slight and growth overall remained extremely high, even by HPAE standards. Korea achieved classification as a high-income nation, a feat that only Japan and the city-states of Singapore and Hong Kong have accomplished in the twentieth century.

*Source*: World Bank, *The East Asian Miracle*; and Westphal, "Industrial Policy in an Export-Propelled Economy: Lessons from South Korea's Experience," in *The Journal of Economic Perspectives*, Summer 1990.

#  The Role of Manufactured Exports

The promotion of manufactured exports played a significant role in the industrial strategies of each of the HPAEs. These policies were largely successful, and the exports of each country grew even faster than their GDP. Given these facts, it is reasonable to assume that there might be a connection between the two. That is, a number of studies of the HPAEs and other regions have shown that higher rates of growth of exports are correlated with higher rates of growth of GDP. What is the mechanism that causes this?

## The Connections between Growth and Exports

It is true by definition that exports are part of the GDP, so it would seem that growth in exports is simply a part of overall GDP growth. Export growth may not add to GDP growth, however, if it crowds out growth in the output of goods for domestic consumption, such as consumer goods or investment. In effect, the idea that export growth causes faster GDP growth is an assertion that export growth causes the overall capacity of the economy to grow faster than it would have if production was focused on goods for the domestic market.

If production focused on exports results in greater overall growth, then there must be something in the production process or its links to the rest of the economy that is absent from domestically focused production. One possibility is that because exports are produced for the world market, economies of scale come into play in a way that is absent when firms produce for a small domestic market. Larger firms often have lower average costs because they can spread their fixed costs for capital and machinery over a larger volume of output. Another possible reason why exports might foster growth is that as firms produce for a world market, there are added incentives to increase R&D. Economies of scale may make it more worthwhile, and the need to keep up with foreign competition may make it more necessary.

Other connections between export growth and GDP growth are possible as well. Exports may speed up the adoption and mastery of international best practices. Firms that operate in global markets are not protected from competition. In fact, they are going up against the world's best, and the competitive pressures may force firms to stay abreast of the latest developments in their product area and production process. Measurement of this possible effect is complicated by the presence of some form of export promotion in the HPAEs. An exporter does not have to be among the world's best if it receives subsidies (for example, direct payment or access to low-interest loans or tax breaks). Firms can be competitive due to subsidies received at home, which may reduce the pressures to compete based on efficiency or quality. Successful export promotion programs, such as those in Korea, are well aware of this problem, and since their goal is to develop firms that are capable of head-to-head international competition without special breaks, they carefully monitor the programs to ensure that the subsidies granted to the exporters do not become the reason for competitive success abroad. In addition, subsidies are gradually reduced. Note, however, that since 1995, the international rules for subsidies have tightened considerably, and it is much harder for countries to provide them within the WTO framework.

Production of exports has several other potential advantages. Exports make possible the purchase of imports. Developing countries are not usually on the technology frontier, and the creation of an efficient manufacturing enterprise is often dependent on imports of machinery and other capital goods. A scarcity of exports impairs a country's ability to purchase imports, with the result that firms are unable to obtain the imported inputs they need in order to raise their efficiency. A related advantage of exports is that the need to meet export targets tied the HPAEs to policies that openly encouraged inward foreign direct investment (FDI) and the acquisition of new technology. One way to overcome the backwardness of domestic manufacturing is to encourage foreign firms to invest. Most of the HPAEs welcomed FDI; Singapore went so far as to build its industrial policies around it. At the same time that FDI was encouraged, several countries also sought to provide incentives for the foreign firm to license its technology to potential domestic rivals. This was a particularly common strategy in Japan, where the incentive of access to the large Japanese market was sufficient to encourage many firms to sign technology licensing agreements.

The ability to import capital and modern technology is seen by some as the most critical ingredient in policies that successfully close the gap between developing and developed countries. Export promotion can encourage the acquisition of new technologies because in order to succeed, governments must allow access to whatever imports firms need to become efficient. Most of the HPAEs selectively protected their domestic markets, but they also adjusted their policies so that exporters were given access to needed imports. In general, they used less protection than other developing areas.

## Is Export Promotion a Good Model for Other Regions?

The export promotion model has succeeded so well in East Asia that, inevitably, it is being prescribed for other developing areas. In Latin America, for example, the economic crisis of the 1980s, together with the very visible counterexample of East Asia, has propelled many nations into similar types of policies. A serious question is whether other areas can duplicate the export successes of the HPAEs.

If developing countries around the world begin to emphasize export promotion policies, an issue arises whether the world's industrial nations can absorb the exports of a series of newly industrializing countries. One possibility is that these exports will undermine industries in industrial nations and lead to renewed trade conflicts and calls for protection. Developing countries (low and middle income) were responsible for nearly 26 percent of world merchandise exports in 2002. This figure has been relatively stable over a long period of time, even though there has been a long-run increase in exports from Asia, as well as strong growth in the export ability of a number of non-Asian developing countries such as Mexico. In 1980, low- and middle-income countries produced nearly the same share, or 27 percent of the world's merchandise exports. Consequently, high-income countries have kept pace with the growth of exports from developing countries, and the overall expansion of world trade has provided opportunities for all regions.

Perhaps the greatest obstacle for countries that wish to replicate the export promotion policies of the HPAEs is the Uruguay Round of the GATT. Under the rules that went into effect in 1994, developing countries must eliminate any subsidies that are contingent on export performance. The phase-out period is eight years, and no new subsidies may be provided in the intervening years. Extremely poor countries with per capita GDP less than $1,000 are exempted. Essentially, the new GATT rules eliminate the possibility that developing countries can use the same tools—credit subsidies, tax breaks, direct payments—that the HPAEs used. The only exceptions are the poorest countries, who do not export manufactured goods in any quantity. In all countries, subsidies for non-commercial R&D, regional development, and promoting compliance with environmental regulations are allowed.

## CASE STUDY

# Asian Trade Blocs

The first edition of this text (1994) began this case study as follows: "Asia is the one region of the world without significant trade blocs." Since then, and more particularly since 2000, that has changed dramatically. Table 16.6 shows the progression in Asia of the signing of trade agreements.

Prior to the growth of trade agreements in the 1990s, the **Association of South East Asian Nations (ASEAN)** was the most notable example of an Asian cooperation agreement. Founded in 1967 with five members (Indonesia, Malaysia, Philippines, Singapore, and Thailand), it added five more countries (Brunei Darussalam, Vietnam, Lao PDR, Myanmar, and Cambodia) between 1984 and 1999. ASEAN's initial mission was political and security cooperation, but it has expanded into trade and economic arenas. In 1992 it created the ASEAN Free Trade Area (AFTA) which was implemented over a 15-year span.

Other trade agreements began to take shape in the 1990s. After the Asian crisis of 1997–1998, the number increased dramatically. The crisis shifted the focus from multilateral to regional agreements, as leaders in many countries recognized that their economies and regulatory agencies were not prepared for the rise of international trade and investment flows. The advice of the IMF during the crisis was controversial and some countries questioned whether it was in their interest to follow it; some, such as Malaysia, rejected it altogether. Stronger bilateral linkages on the other hand, were thought to offer greater stability through enhanced regional cooperation. New regional agreements were signed, such as the Japan-Singapore Economic Partnership Agreement, and the **ASEAN+3** which created bilateral agreements between ASEAN and China, Korea, and Japan. In addition, there seemed to be a waning of confidence in multilateral agreements through the WTO and a greater recognition of the advan-

TABLE 16.6 **Free Trade Areas in Asia and Oceania**

| Year | Under Negotiation | Concluded | Proposed |
|------|-------------------|-----------|----------|
| 1989 | 0 | 3 | 1 |
| 1995 | 0 | 22 | 1 |
| 2000 | 1 | 39 | 3 |
| 2006 | 54 | 93 | 46 |

The number of trade blocs in Asia increased dramatically after the Asian Crisis of 1997–1998.

*Source*: Asian Development Bank, Asia Regional Integration Center. http://aric.adb.org. Accessed October 20, 2006.

tages of bilateral agreements. Hence, many of the new bilateral agreements are with non-Asian countries. For example, Japan negotiated an agreement with Mexico; Korea and Chile signed an agreement; and Singapore and the United States signed an FTA.

Trade agreements were not the only type of regional cooperation pursued after the crisis. The **Chiang Mai Initiative (CMI)** is an ASEAN+3 agreement to loan currency between central banks. **Swap agreements,** or **swaps**, are a useful tool for short term borrowing when a central bank encounters a shortage in international reserves. For example, in an emergency the CMI would allow Thailand to borrow dollar reserves from China. China, or another lending country, would play a role similar to the IMF, but with greater flexibility and a faster response. If this agreement had existed prior to the Asian crisis, it is possible that it would have limited its spread. There are other initiatives in development, one of which is a proposal to create an alternative to the IMF that would focus on the Asian region only.

ASEAN+3 nations are also a part of a trade region known as **Asia Pacific Economic Cooperation (APEC)**. APEC has 21 members, the 13 ASEAN+3 countries, Australia, New Zealand, Russia, the United States, Canada, Mexico, Peru, and Chile. The goal of APEC, as set forth in the 1994 Declaration of Common Resolve, is "free and open trade and investment in the region no later than 2010 for the industrialized economies and 2020 for the developing economies." APEC is not a trade bloc in the normal sense since its goal is not only a free trade area among its members, but also the goal that each member will practice free trade with all other countries and not only other APEC members. It is uncertain if this will be achieved, but meanwhile APEC serves as a forum for regional discussion and coordination.

*Sources*: Asian Development Bank, http://www.adb.org; Asian Regional Integration Center, http://aric.adb.org; Asia-Pacific Regional Cooperation, http://www.apec.org.

 # Is There an Asian Model of Economic Growth?

The East Asian "miracle" has given rise to a large number of studies that seek to explain rapid growth in the HPAEs and China. While the issue may superficially appear academic, it has become one of the more interesting and heated debates in recent popular economics. Proponents of laissez-faire economics have used the relative openness of the East Asian economies, their use of private markets, and their strong macroeconomic fundamentals to argue for government policies that are less activist. Proponents of a more activist government have pointed to selective interventions, such as export promotion, industrial policies, and deliberation councils, to argue in favor of a larger government role in the economy. Some Asian politicians have pointed to their restrictions on civil and political liberties as laying a foundation for order and the avoidance of chaos.

Is there an Asian model of the economy? That is, have the HPAEs managed to achieve their extraordinary growth rates through policies that are fundamentally different from the policy advice dispensed by proponents of the Washington Consensus (see Chapter 15)? At stake are the paths followed by today's developing economies and the future role of government policy in the industrial countries. Naturally, with a question so controversial, there are a variety of answers and opinions. Recent work, however, seems to be pointing toward a robust set of conclusions.

In order to describe some interesting recent studies, we must briefly review the idea of growth accounting. Recall that labor productivity is a measurement that is defined as output per worker. The growth in labor productivity is highly correlated with the growth in income (or output) per member of the population, but they are not the same thing. East Asian growth is remarkable for its growth in per capita income and its growth in labor productivity.

Any given rate of growth of labor productivity can be broken down into the share that is due to more capital and the share that is due to more skills or education. In the economics literature, such an exercise is called a *growth accounting*. When growth accounts are constructed for a country or a region, there is always some share of the growth in labor productivity that cannot be explained by the amount of additional capital or education. This share is a measure of the effects of using the available inputs more efficiently. That is, if more growth occurs than can be explained by the growth of capital or education, it must be due to a more productive use of the available inputs. For example, the organization of production may have changed so that people are working more efficiently, or the quality of technology may have changed so that each unit of capital and labor input produces more units of output.

Another name for the share of labor productivity that is not explained by capital or education is **total factor productivity**, or **TFP**. TFP growth reflects changes in output that are unrelated to changes in capital or labor inputs but that are related to new technologies, innovation, and organizational improvements. According to most estimates, over the long run, a majority of per capita income growth in high-income countries has resulted from increases in total factor productivity.

Growth accounting may seem a long way from the debate on East Asia, but it is actually very relevant. As it turns out, the vast bulk of Asian growth since 1960 can be accounted for by increases in capital and education, while TFP plays a much smaller role. Table 16.7 provides the details and some comparisons over the same period.

What we observe in Table 16.7 is that in the sample of six HPAEs, TFP growth accounts for between 24 and 36 percent of overall growth. In the slower-growing United States, it accounts for 27 percent, and in the other industrial nations, the figure is 37 percent. The fact that TFP growth accounts for about the same overall share of growth in the HPAEs was surprising to many observers for two reasons: First, the HPAEs are not on the frontier of new technologies like the United States and the rest of the industrial world. Consequently, they should be

**TABLE 16.7** • **Sources of Growth, 1960–1994 (Percent)**

| Country/Region | Growth of Output per Worker | Contribution of | | |
| | | Capital per Worker | Education per Worker | Total Factor Productivity |
| --- | --- | --- | --- | --- |
| Indonesia | 3.4 | 2.1 | 0.5 | 0.8 |
| Korea, Republic | 5.7 | 3.3 | 0.8 | 1.5 |
| Malaysia | 3.8 | 2.3 | 0.5 | 0.9 |
| Singapore | 5.4 | 3.4 | 0.4 | 1.5 |
| Thailand | 5.0 | 2.7 | 0.4 | 1.8 |
| Taiwan | 5.8 | 3.1 | 0.6 | 2.0 |
| Latin America | 1.5 | 0.9 | 0.4 | 0.2 |
| United States | 1.1 | 0.4 | 0.4 | 0.3 |
| Industrial Nations* | 2.9 | 1.5 | 0.4 | 1.1 |

Economic growth in East Asia is mainly a result of capital accumulation.

*Including Japan, excluding the United States.

*Source*: Collins and Bosworth, "Economic Growth in East Asia: Accumulation Versus Assimilation," in *Brooking Papers on Economic Activity*, 2: 1996.

able to more easily borrow techniques that increase their TFP. Second, the proponents of a new Asian model of economic growth have argued that the selective interventions such as industrial policies and export promotion have increased productivity. In fact, what they appear to have done, if anything, is to increase the quantity of capital per worker.

The last point is key to understanding this debate. When growth is decomposed into its various causes, what appears to account for the bulk of HPAE growth is capital accumulation and not increased total factor productivity. These results appear to be fairly strong, since several other researchers have done similar growth accounting exercises and have reached the same conclusions. The growth accounts for East Asia are important because they paint a consistent, if surprising, picture of the East Asian "miracle." They tell us that there may be no miracle at all, just the hard work and sacrifice that comes from forgoing today's consumption in order to raise savings and investment rates. For example, between 1966 and 1985, Singapore raised investment from 11 percent of GDP to 40 percent. It is no surprise then, that capital accumulation accounts for the bulk of its growth.

If these measures are accurate, the argument for a distinct Asian model looks weak. Rather than selective interventions that target specific industries, the keys were high savings and high investment, together with the other factors outlined in this chapter.

# Summary

- The major characteristics of economic growth in the high-performance Asian economies are (1) increasing equality, (2) rapid accumulation of savings and high rates of investment, (3) rapid increases in levels of schooling, (4) rapid growth of manufactured exports, and (5) stable macroeconomic environments.

- The institutional environment is instrumental in creating confidence in policymakers. The policymaking bureaucracy tends to be insulated from the push and pull of the political system. This leads some to decry the lack of representation of the population in policy decisions, but it allows decisions to be made on technical merit rather than political expediency. The voice of business and industry, and to a lesser extent other groups such as consumers, is often heard through consultative bodies known as *deliberation councils*. Deliberation councils are a mechanism for the private sector and government policymakers to exchange information and discuss policies.

- One of the key elements of policy is fiscal control over inflation, the budget, foreign debt, and exchange rates. While inflation, budgets, and foreign debt all vary country by country, inflation is kept under control, and budget deficits and foreign debt are kept within the boundaries defined by the government's and the economy's ability to finance them.

- With the exception of Hong Kong, each of the HPAEs followed industrial policies that targeted the development of particular industries. These policies were most focused in the "northern tier" of Japan, Korea, and Taiwan. The effects of these policies are difficult to measure, and there is a long and contentious debate about their efficacy.

- Each of the HPAEs promoted manufactured exports. These policies largely succeeded, although the mechanisms that link export growth to faster GDP growth are still uncertain.

- Recent empirical work shows that the main contributor to economic growth in the HPAEs is the extremely rapid accumulation of physical capital. Consequently, the argument that the HPAEs have pioneered a model that leads to more rapid total factor productivity growth appears false, and the keys to growth should be looked for in the policies that raise savings and investment.

# Vocabulary

Asia Pacific Economic Cooperation (APEC)

Association of South-East Asian Nations (ASEAN)

ASEAN+3

Chiang Mai Initiative (CMI)

deliberation councils

demographic transition

Four Tigers

high-performance Asian economies (HPAEs)

newly industrializing economies (NIEs)

Swap agreements

total factor productivity (TFP)

 ## Study Questions

1. Contrast the characteristics of economic growth in the HPAEs with those characteristics of Latin America.

2. How can passage through a demographic transition lead to high savings and investment rates?

3. What are the characteristics of East Asian institutional environments that contributed to rapid economic growth?

4. Economists are divided over the effectiveness of East Asian industrial policies. Provide a balanced assessment of the issues relevant to understanding the role of industrial policies in fostering growth. Do you think one point of view is better than another? Why?

5. How might manufactured exports contribute to economic growth?

6. Is there a uniquely Asian model of economic growth? What are the issues, and how might we go about answering that question?

# China and India in the World Economy

## Introduction: The Challenges of Openness

The emergence of China and India from their relative economic isolation is one of the most important contemporary trends in the international economy. Their increased openness and growing interdependence with the outside world have generated positive and negative effects, opportunities, and challenges. Openness and a change in their economic models enabled hundreds of millions of people to escape poverty, caused many manufactured goods and services to become less expensive, and helped hold world interest rates down, due in part to China's enormous pool of savings. The later tendency helped make real estate more affordable, spurred construction in developed countries, and is partly responsible for a boom in housing prices. Simultaneously, producers of manufactured goods in both developed and developing countries experienced intense competitive pressures that forced some of them to downsize, outsource, and change their business practices. For the first time in history, the service sector has begun to move jobs overseas and growing trade imbalances increase the chances of future crises and protectionist reactions.

China and India have a lot in common and a lot that is different. Both are nuclear powers, sites of ancient civilizations, and the two largest populations in the world. Both have transformed their economic systems by moving away from relative isolation and emphasizing markets over state control. Although China's reforms began earlier than India's, both countries succeeded in creating higher economic growth rates that have been sustained through a variety of conditions at home and abroad.

Among the most important differences is that India is the world's largest democracy while China remains in the grip of the Communist Party. In India decision making is sometimes contentious and must take into account opposing views, while Chinese decision making is highly centralized within a leadership that is never subjected to popular vote. India's manufacturing sector is much smaller than China's, even after adjusting for the overall size of the economy. As a consequence, trade plays a smaller role in India's economy than in China's, and India's impact on world trade has much less. India's command of information technology industries and services has drawn a great deal of attention, while China's ability to export manufactured goods, from apparel to automobiles to sophisticated electronics, has altered trade patterns and challenges the manufacturing sectors of countries around the world.

India and China are potentially great powers and both are beginning to assume positions in the world economy that are consistent with their sizes and histories. When great powers emerge, history tells us that it usually creates a difficult period filled with transitions and tensions. This chapter surveys the major economic issues associated with the emergence in the world economy of China and India.

 # Demographic and Economic Characteristics

Table 17.1 shows the size of the Chinese and Indian economies. In 2005 their combined population was three-eighths (37.5 percent) of world population, and over $3 trillion at market exchange rates. At current economic growth rates, China's economy will become the world's largest around 2040. It currently has the world's third largest GDP, behind the United States and Japan, and is about three times larger than India. On a per capita basis, China will lag the world's leaders for many decades even at present growth rates.

The growth of GDP has been remarkable in both countries. Since 1980 real GDP growth has averaged 5.9 percent per year in India and an astonishing 9.8 percent per year in China. The precise number of people who have been pulled from extreme poverty in each country is unknown, but it is in the hundreds of millions and accounts for the majority of the decline in poverty worldwide. One estimate puts the figure at 727 million in China (1980–2000) and 207 million in India (see Surjit Bhalla, *Imagine There's No Country*, page 143). Improvements in living standards that are only slightly above extreme poverty still represent deprivation and hardship, and both countries still have large numbers of people

**TABLE 17.1 ● Population and Income in China and India, 2005**

|  | Population (Millions) | GDP (US$, Billions) | GDP per Capita (US$) | GDP per Capita (US$, PPP) |
|---|---|---|---|---|
| **China** | 1,304 | 2,230 | 1,709 | 6,572 |
| **India** | 1,095 | 785 | 718 | 3,485 |

India and China are the two most populous countries in the world.

*Source*: World Bank, *World Development Indicators*.

without access to adequate nutrition, health care, and other necessities. Never-theless, a reduction in extreme poverty is highly desirable as well as a useful marker of societal improvement.

While poverty has fallen, a middle class has grown in size. The populations of both countries are so large that even a small middle class represents enormous purchasing power. The size of the middle class in both countries is unknown, but consider the following hypothetical situation. Suppose that 10 percent of both populations is middle class with purchasing power parity incomes of $12,000 or more. That would be a total of 240 million people, or nearly equivalent to the combined populations of France, Germany, Italy, and the United Kingdom. In both countries, but particularly in the case of China, it is this potential future market that has elicited so much international interest and foreign investment. The history of western pursuit of the Chinese market is long and mostly unhappy, but many western firms believe that they cannot afford not to have a presence in China.

Population totals in India and China have more than doubled since 1950, as shown in Figure 17.1. China's limits on family size sharply curtailed its popula-tion growth rate, and between 2020 and 2030, India is predicted to pass it in absolute size. China's restrictive population policies mean fewer children and an older population, but a slowing population growth rate. If current trends hold, between 2030 and 2040 it will fall below replacement levels and its population will actually begin to decline. Given China's lack of health care, pension systems, and democracy, an aging population will not exert the same pressures on the gov-ernment budget as it will in the European Union (see Chapter 14).

**FIGURE 17.1 ● Population and Projections, 1950–2050**

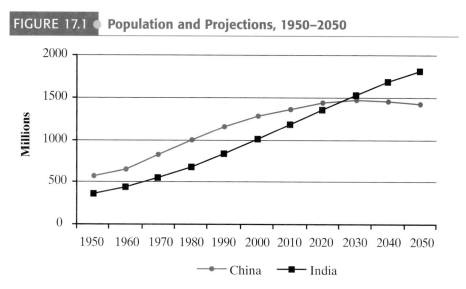

*Source*: U.S. Census Bureau.

## Economic Reforms in China and India

Economic reform of China's communist system began in 1978. Under communism, every aspect of China's economy was controlled by the state. Private enterprise did not exist, and the basic decisions that every economy makes about what to produce, how to produce it, and who should receive it, were made from the top-down by government planners and Communist Party politicians. China had limited contact with outsiders, and the emphasis of its economic policy was self-sufficiency in all goods and services.

India's reforms began in the 1980s, and then gathered momentum in 1991 when the government was forced to respond to a balance of payments crisis. India's economic system was best characterized as socialist, with a mix of state ownership and control, together with private enterprise. Most large industrial enterprises were state-owned, however, and the Indian system of regulation meant that all firms had to obtain permits for even minor changes. If a firm wanted to expand, if it wanted to change its product lines, or even if it wanted to change its board of directors, first it had to obtain a permit from the government.

After their transitions, both countries are much more market oriented and far more outward looking. The remarkable degree of opening is apparent in their openness indexes, 1975–2005, shown in Figure 17.2. The index for China rises over the entire period, as major changes began in 1978. India's index is more or less flat until 1990–1995, and then begins a surge upward. The usual negative relationship between country size and openness is weak, as Chinese reforms in particular have emphasized international economic integration through both trade and investment, and have led to an unusually large openness index given its population. China's index is an indication of its dependence on world trade (and by implication, investment) for its continued success.

## The Reform Process in China

A country's decision to undertake large scale economic reform can come from many directions. As we saw in Chapter 15, reforms in a number of Latin American countries were a result of the debt crisis of the 1980s together with the failure of traditional policies to resolve the crisis. Other countries, New Zealand for example, began large scale economic reforms without the urgency created by an economic crisis. In China's case there was no immediate crisis, but rather a long period of instability and disappointment with the results achieved under communism. The leader of Chinese economic reforms, **Deng Xiaoping**, put it in terms of a choice between distributing poverty under the old system, and distributing wealth under a new system.

There was no master plan for Chinese reforms, but rather a gradual, steady dismantling of the controls exercised by the state and the Communist Party. Deng Xiaoping is famously reported to have described the reforms as analogous to "feeling the stones to cross the river." You advance one foot, see if it holds, then advance another. The slow and steady pace of reform was dictated in part

**FIGURE 17.2** • **Openness Index, 1975–2004**

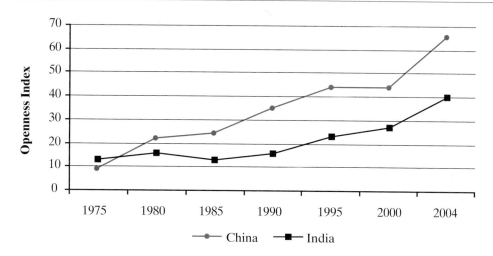

Chinese trade began to grow in the late 1970s; India's in the early 1990s.

*Source:* World Bank, *World Development Indicators.*

by a lack of experience and information about how to proceed but also by the fear of a reaction from the hard-line, conservative, anti-reformers.

The first changes were confined to agriculture and involved loosening the constraints on peasant producers by allowing them more control and ownership of individual plots of land. Peasants were allowed to sell their product in markets and were soon increasing the quantity of foodstuff available. Foreign trade under the old system was controlled by 12 **foreign trading corporations (FTC)**, which were attached to the various branches of government. All exports and imports went through the FTC and were strictly regulated with no consideration given to comparative advantage. The reforms gradually opened trade, first through the creation of additional FTC and then through a series of steps that removed price controls and ended export subsidies. In order to limit the initial impact of reforms on the domestic economy and to prevent a political backlash, China created a number of **Special Economic Zones (SEZ)** which were modeled on the concept of export processing zones. SEZ went further by giving provincial and local authorities wide latitude to experiment with radically different economic and trade policies. Incentives were given to form joint ventures with foreign producers who came to the SEZ to set up production facilities. Between 1979 and 1988, China created five SEZ, all of which successfully attracted foreign investment (particularly from Taiwan, Hong Kong, and the overseas Chinese business communities), generated a large flow of exports, and helped raised the rate of economic growth. The SEZ created a demonstration effect for the rest of China and other regions began to push for similar policies.

China also applied to join the WTO in 1986. Membership requires a country to describe all trade and economic policies that may affect WTO agreements, and to open bilateral negotiations with individual members over any issues of concern. Negotiations were difficult and lasted until China joined the WTO in 2001. The protracted period of negotiations probably kept the reform process moving forward, and ultimately resulted in a strong Chinese commitment to an open economy, both for trade and investment.

## Indian Economic Reforms

Indian reforms began gradually in the 1980s and speeded up considerably after the 1991 crisis. Three forces played significant roles in preparing Indian policy-makers for the necessary changes. First, India's primary trade partner, the USSR, suffered a number of setbacks through the 1980s and finally dissolved itself in 1991. India had partially modeled its economic policies on the USSR, and its demise laid bare the failure of its economy to produce prosperity. Second, the success of several East Asian countries was important. In 1960, South Korean and Indian income per capita were about the same, but by 1990, Korea was entering the ranks of the developed world, while India remained stuck at low levels of income. When **Manmohan Singh**, the finance minister who carried out many of the reforms, visited Korea in 1987, he was shocked to see how far behind India had fallen. Third in the list of forces was a financial crisis that developed as a result of heavy borrowing by the government. When the Gulf War drove up oil prices and cut off the flow of remittances back home from Indian workers in the Gulf States, the country was left with inadequate foreign reserves and an inability to finance its debt.

The changes in economic policy that followed touched on a number of areas, including the permitting process. India's regulation of its economy was based on a system of permits that stifled innovation and creativity with their extensive, complicated, and inefficient rules. Permits were intended to be a means for preventing the creation of powerful interests that might undermine democracy and promote inequality. Yet their unintended consequence was that they fostered inefficiency and by protecting Indian businesses from competition, both domestic and foreign, they thereby allowed them to operate without regard for product quality or firm efficiency. Many of the larger firms were state-owned, under the belief that the state planners could better select product lines and operating procedures than could markets, and as in the Chinese and Russian cases, the state-owned sector of the economy operated without the imperative of profitability. Firms could lose money for years and still continue in business since they had no hard budget constraints. Losses were covered by the government budget, even as it meant an enormous drain on government revenue and fewer resources for important public projects such as safe drinking water, highways and ports, rural education, and other needs. De-nationalization was the second set of reforms begun after the crisis of 1991.

A final critical area that began to receive attention from the reformers was international trade and investment. Indian trade policy was based on the idea of import substitution industrialization (see Chapter 15), as in Latin America and other developing countries after World War II. Domestic firms received high levels of protection, exports were implicitly discouraged, and self sufficiency was the goal. India's famous Ambassador car is an example. Protected from foreign imports, it remained essentially the same for nearly 40 years. Why go through the expense of changing the product line if there is a captive market? In addition to dismantling many of the restrictions on trade, India also began to dismantle the restrictions on inward foreign investment.

## Remaining Issues

In both the Chinese and Indian cases, profound changes have taken place. The depth and breadth of the reforms represent a break in each country's historical path, and a shift from low growth, isolationist policies toward high growth and integration with the world economy. The domestic reforms are not over, however, and a number of changes are still in the works.

In the case of China, the legacy of communism and state ownership of productive resources remains in the form of 150,000 state owned enterprises. This is down from 300,000 since 1990, but they continue to be a burden on local governments that support them, and a drain on the productive use of savings and investments. These enterprises operate regardless of their profitability and are sometimes the main source of employment in villages and towns, a characteristic that makes it even harder to shut them down. In addition, they are often the only source of pensions and health care and when they close, the workers lose access to both of those social benefits. Hence, closing them has an effect on political and social stability.

An indicator of the reform progress in both China and India is the World Bank's Doing Business index discussed in Chapter 13 (http://www.doingbusiness.org). Recall that the index ranks 175 countries on 10 dimensions of business regulations. These range from the ease of starting or closing a business, to employing workers, dealing with licenses, paying taxes, and enforcing contracts, among others. The rankings are based on the number of steps, the amount of time, and the cost, to comply with business regulations in each of the 10 areas. In 2006 China ranked 93 out of 175, while India did much worse at 134. In other words, neither country is a world leader in the ease of doing business.

China did particularly poor in the ease of paying taxes (168th out of 175) and dealing with licenses (153rd). India's weakest areas were enforcing contracts (173rd) and paying taxes (158th). It was particularly good at protecting investors (33rd), however, while China did well at registering property (21st). Perhaps most notably, China's score for trading across borders was 38th, and India's was 139th. Much of the difference appears to be related to the lack of transportation infrastructure and port facilities in India, which means that goods are held up at the dock for longer periods. Ultimately, this results in costs that are 2.5 times higher in India than China to export a standardized cargo and 3 times higher to import.

## CASE STUDY

# Why Did the USSR Collapse and China Succeed?

Before the collapse of the Soviet Union, college bookstores and academic presses carried a significant number of works describing the transition from capitalism to socialism, as if it was an inevitable future for some portion of humankind. Almost nothing was published about the reverse process, the transition from socialism to capitalism. Such a book would have seemed strange; no one was writing anything along those lines, and probably few publishers would have given it a second look. When China began its gradual transition in 1978, its meaning was unclear to most observers and it took years to understand that it was abandoning communism. In 1989 when the Berlin Wall fell and Central Europeans began to migrate west, no one knew if the USSR or the socialist governments would permit people to leave. And when the USSR announced that it was dissolving into 15 separate nations, nearly everyone was taken by surprise. It is no wonder then, that the academic and policymaking worlds were unprepared for the transition from socialism to capitalism.

The economies that abandoned socialism or communism in favor of market-based systems came to be known as the **transition economies.** One of the first controversies was over the speed of the transition. "You cannot cross a chasm in two leaps" (go fast) was one view. The other view was that of Deng Xiaoping, the Chinese leader who likened reform to "feeling the stones to cross the river." The IMF and the U.S. government favored quick transitions, while a number of academics sounded a more cautious note. In many respects, the fortunes of Russia (fast) and China (slow) came to symbolize the two approaches.

Russian reformers quickly moved to create a private economy where none had existed before. This involved an enormous amount of work, not just in the economic realm, but in politics and institution building as well. To begin, the economy had to be stabilized to avoid unsustainable budget deficits and hyperinflation. This was not entirely successful for a variety of reasons, not the least of which was the turmoil caused by the transition and the breakup of the USSR. Throughout the new economy, administrative controls were replaced with market-based mechanisms so that prices could be freed from bureaucratic control. The barriers to firms that prevent them from entering and leaving markets were dismantled, and important new markets were created. New labor markets required unemployment insurance, pension systems, and safety nets, while financial markets needed the regulatory apparatus of banking oversight, security laws, and tax rules. The transfer of property rights was begun, and government officials began the creation of the legal infrastructure for settling disputes and enforcing contracts. One of the most complicated and difficult tasks was the privatization of firms and factories that had been state owned. In Russia, that was nearly the entire productive apparatus of the economy. The end result was an enormous concentration of wealth and a general understanding that the process of privatization favored a small group of insiders. In sum, a wide variety of new institutional structures had to be created.

The outcome was tragic for a large segment of the population. By 1996, Russia's economy was about 64 percent of its size in 1990. Infant mortality increased dramatically, birth rates fell below replacement levels, and wealth became highly concentrated. Russia was not unique in this way, as all but one of the 15 countries that the USSR split into saw income declines of 25 percent or more. Six countries watched as their incomes fell by more than 50 percent and civil wars broke out in a couple of cases.

By contrast, the Chinese economy did not decline at all during its transition from communism to capitalism. Although its reforms were begun in 1978, until the mid-1980s, they mainly affected the agricultural sector. Since China had such a large share of its population in rural areas, the positive effects on food output and rural incomes were significant. Primarily, the agricultural reforms let families and villages take individual responsibility for meeting their production quotas, and allowed them to consume or sell whatever amount they produced above the quota. Villages and communes were allowed to disband the collectivist system of production and individual incentives began to rule the efforts and decision making of producers.

In the mid-1980s, China extended its market based reforms to a number of Special Economic Zones (SEZ), Economic and Technology Development Zones (ETDZ), High Technology Development Zones (HTDZ), and other special developmental areas, mostly located along the coast. The rules of each type of zone varied, but in general, they allowed far more independent, profit oriented, market-based, decision making. The SEZ in particular, were encouraged to experiment with new forms of economic organization, and to develop joint ventures by attracting foreign investment. These areas began to account for the bulk of Chinese growth, exports, and foreign investment.

China's transition strategy is considered a gradualist strategy because it did not attempt to reform the entire economic structure all at once. Rather, it used a **dual track strategy**, which localized reforms to certain areas or sectors (e.g., agriculture) while maintaining traditional, central planning structures in the remainder of the economy. Slowly, subsidized prices were raised to the market level and the mandatory production targets were reduced to a small share of the total output or zero. By the early to mid-1990s, more than 90 percent of retail prices and 80 to 90 percent of agricultural and intermediate goods prices were decontrolled. China has been much slower to privatize its state owned sector.

Many observers argue that the gradual implementation of reforms in a slow but steady sequence removed the pressure to instantaneously develop new institutions and economic relations. By adopting a dual track approach, China allowed the market economy to develop alongside the centrally planned economy, and to gradually take over more and more of its functions. Perhaps even more importantly than avoiding an economic downturn, it gave the Chinese people time to adjust their expectations to fit a market-based system and reduced the shock of change.

The proponents of rapid reform see China as a special case. First, central planning was less extensive in China, with the result that its economy was less distorted and less over-concentrated on heavy industry. Second, and most importantly, China's economy is much more agricultural. In 1978, when China began its reforms, 71 percent of the labor force was in agriculture. The figure for Russia in 1990 at the beginning of its transition was 13 percent. China's heavier concentration in agriculture gives it a large rural labor force with very low productivity. If these workers leave the countryside, the resulting loss of output is small, while the offsetting productivity gains from employment in urban and village industrial enterprises are significant. Hence, China can move labor from agriculture into the new enterprises but Russia had to take labor out of heavy industry to staff the new enterprises.

Janos Kornai, the eminent Hungarian economist and perceptive observer of the transition summarized the debate in the following terms:

> *Some developments are rapid, others slow. Some call for a one-stroke intervention while many others come about through incremental changes... The emphasis has to be on consolidation, stability, and sustainability, not on breaking speed records* (Finance and Development, September 2000).

#  China and India in the World Economy

China's accession to the WTO was notable. Accession ended 15 years of negotiations and established beyond all doubt that China would not turn away from its march toward capitalism. WTO accession also meant that foreign concerns about property rights and market access would be resolved and that investment in China would not be subject to arbitrary rules by the Chinese government or by foreign governments that might try to discriminate against manufacture imports from China.

India was a member of the WTO from the beginning, but its reforms of the 1990s caused exports and imports to take off. With a much smaller manufacturing sector than China, the absolute value of its trade is far less. Nevertheless, its growth rate is high and recent concerns about the outsourcing of services and India's high technology sector are important reasons for a closer look at its trade patterns.

## Chinese and Indian Trade Patterns

Figure 17.3 shows the average annual growth of trade, both exports and imports, in constant dollar terms and five-year increments, from 1980 to 2005. In China's case, every five-year period except one (1985–1990) experienced growth in both exports and their rate of growth. India's exports and export growth rate also increased in every period but one (1995–2000), when the growth rate fell slightly but still was above 10 percent. Imports also show strong growth with no periods of absolute decline except 1985–1990 in China.

Figure 17.3 illustrates an important point regarding trade: exports and imports are tied together. In the case of China this is particularly important to note given the large volume of its exports and the disruption they are causing in trade networks. Chinese exports depend on imported inputs and technology since a large share its trade consists of commoditized goods that China assembles into a final form and exports. For example, Chapter 4, Table 4.3, lists the top 10 Chinese exports to the United States. These are either low technology goods such as footwear, bedding accessories, and briefcases, or high technology goods such as automatic data processing machines. The high technology products, however, are often only assembled in China from parts produced elsewhere. An example is the laptop computer. Taiwan was the leading producer of laptops, but shifted all of its production to China. The processing chips come from Intel, software is supplied by Microsoft, the display panel and memory chips are produced in Korea and Taiwan, and the hard drives are supplied by Japan. China assembles the parts and exports laptop computers (automatic data processing machines).

**FIGURE 17.3** • **Average Annual Growth of Imports and Exports, 1980–2005**

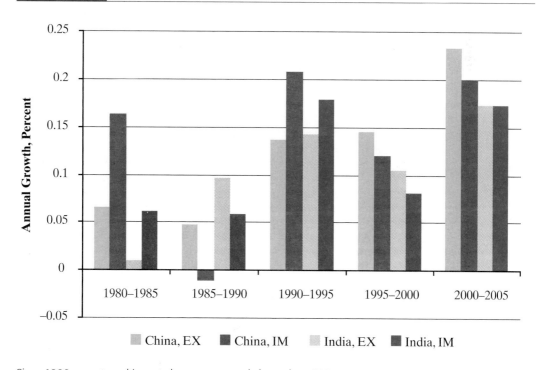

Since 1990, exports and imports have grown much faster than GDP.

*Source:* World Bank, *World Development Indicators.*

If China is not presently a high technology producer, it is certainly moving in that direction, in part through its rapid expansion of its science, engineering, research, and development capacity. The number of patents granted by its national patent office was nearly 50,000 in 2005 (versus 164,000 in the United States), and it is spending large amounts on infrastructure that will make the entire society more productive. Nevertheless, at this point it still has limited collaboration with universities and its absorption and diffusion of imported technology is weak. In the present, much of its domestic technology sector depends on its ability to copy (often illegally) foreign products, and it continues to depend on foreign direct investment for technology, management, and access to international networks. This is likely to change in the future, however.

Table 17.2 compares Indian and Chinese trade in goods and services. Note first that Chinese exports are about six times larger than India's, and its imports are about four times greater. Even in the area of services, where Indian exports are on the rise and have been much noted, China's total is still about a third larger. Table 17.2 illustrates clearly how much more of an impact China's growth is having on the world economy. Its goods exports account for 7.3 percent of the world's total, and it ranks number three in the world in both goods exports and goods imports.

| TABLE 17.2 • Chinese and Indian Export and Import Totals, 2005 | | | |
|---|---|---|---|
| | US$, Millions | Share in World Trade | Rank among Countries |
| **India: Exports** | | | |
| Goods | 95.1 | 0.91 | 29 |
| Services | 56.1 | 2.32 | 11 |
| **India: Imports** | | | |
| Goods | 134.8 | 1.25 | 17 |
| Services | 52.2 | 2.22 | 13 |
| **China: Exports** | | | |
| Goods | 762.0 | 7.30 | 3 |
| Services | 73.9 | 3.06 | 9 |
| **China: Imports** | | | |
| Goods | 660.0 | 6.12 | 3 |
| Services | 83.2 | 3.54 | 7 |

China's trade sector is much larger than India's, even in services.

*Source:* World Trade Organization, *Trade Profiles.*

In recent years, Indian trade has captured the world's attention though its ability to participate in the growing area of services trade. Several factors account for this, not the least of which is the fact that English is spoken by educated Indians. In addition, India's leadership has consistently emphasized higher education and technology, and although it has a severe shortage of places in its universities, its leading institutions such as the India Institute of Technology (IIT) are among the world's best. There is possibly no greater example of a sector or a country that has benefited from the advent of the telecommunications revolution than India's high tech sector.

A closer examination of Chinese and Indian service exports highlights this fact and points to an important difference in the two economies. As shown in Table 17.2, China's service exports are larger than India's, although not by as much as its goods exports. More important is the composition of each country's service exports, which is not shown in Table 17.2. China has a $10 billion deficit in services, which primarily comprise transportation and travel services (shipping costs and business and personal travel). India has a $4 billion surplus in services, which primarily comprise information services and other business services. According to the IMF's *Balance of Payments Statistics,* these two items grew a remarkable 30 percent per year between 1997 and 2003, the most recent year of available data.

Computer and information services and other business services include the call centers that Thomas Friedman (*The World Is Flat*) and others have written about, along with the outsourcing of medical consultations, data entry, legal briefs, and the myriad other activities that are now sometimes performed at a distance and then sent over to the Internet to the final user of the information. As described in Chapter 4, the outsourcing of services depends on the telecommunications revolution, with the Internet, video conferencing, satellite communications, and the software to use them. In the past, most services were consumed at the point of production, but as technology allows a separation of production from consumption or use, services have begun to be outsourced in the same way that manufacturing has been for decades.

##  The Challenges of India and China in the World Economy

There are numerous challenges to existing trade patterns and trade relations posed by the entrance of the world's two most populous countries in the world trading system. We will look at three such challenges: Indian services, Chinese manufacturing, and the demand for resources.

**Services.** Services such as shipping have been traded for decades as shipping companies hire crews around the world and register their vessels in the most convenient location, selling their services to firms wherever they are in need. Business services and information services, however, are a relatively new to international trade since they can only be traded if technology and infrastructure can pass large amounts of information across long distances at low costs. Since the mid-1990s, this has been possible and trade in information and computer services has taken off. The outsourcing of services from high income industrial economies to India is a new arena for the application of comparative advantage.

As with all economic changes, some people benefit and some are hurt. It is clear, however, that there are net benefits overall for national economies. Consider the case of the United States. As the hardware for computer and information technology (IT) has become less expensive, IT services and software are taking the majority share of total IT spending by U.S. businesses. Outsourcing reduces the price of IT services and software, makes business-specific applications cheaper to purchase, and allows businesses to achieve higher levels of productivity at a lower cost. Higher productivity, in turn, raises living standards overall, although not necessarily for every individual. It is another case of comparative advantage based trade, the same as described in Chapters 3 and 4. In this case, India's comparative advantage allows it to trade with the United States and to contribute to the increase in U.S. productivity while at the same time it creates good paying jobs and advances its own economy.

Those who oppose this form of trade fear that all computer and IT work will end up in developing countries. This seems highly unlikely. For example, the U.S. Bureau of Labor Statistics projects job growth in the United States in IT related occupations to be three times faster than in the rest of the economy until at least 2010. These new workers and many already in the IT services sector will not continue to do the same thing, however, as the comparative advantage of the United States is shifting within the IT field. The danger is not that jobs will disappear, but that the United States will fail to produce enough qualified people, or that the mix of skills and qualifications will not match the demand by businesses, or that new limits on trade in services will put businesses at a competitive disadvantage.

**Manufacturing.** China's emergence as an export platform and as a high volume manufacturer of consumer goods challenges existing trade patterns and manufacturing trends. The challenge to emerging markets such as Mexico, Brazil, Malaysia, and Thailand is that they cannot depend on low wages as the primary source of their comparative advantage. The challenge appears in the form of intense competitive pressures from low-cost goods produced in China. Chinese manufacturing wages are estimated to be about one-fourth of the amount paid in Brazil and Mexico, and given China's other advantages, competition on the basis of labor cost alone is increasingly less likely to succeed. For example, Mexico's export processing zone (the *maquiladora* industry, see Chapter 13) lost a large share of its apparel sector when China entered the WTO. Mexico's geographic advantage next to the U.S. market was nullified for products that do not need a rapid turn-around between order and delivery. The effect on some of the manufacturing in high income countries is similar, such as apparel in the United States and Italy. Furthermore, as China begins to expand its exports of more sophisticated products such as cars, the competitive pressure is likely to spread into other sectors of manufacturing.

China has several sources of comparative advantage in manufacturing. Its abundance of low wage, low skilled labor has already been mentioned, and its large domestic market has been alluded to. One way to look at China is as a large free trade area where firms can take advantage of scale economies when producing for the domestic market. Coupled with overall growth and expansion of its middle class, the demand for manufactured goods is increasing rapidly and will continue to absorb a larger share of Chinese output. A third advantage is China's coastal areas, which have potentially convenient logistics for trading internationally. China continues to invest heavily in its port facilities and coastal infrastructure in an effort to develop its geographic advantages.

There are also a few institutional disadvantages that reduce its competitiveness. One is the overall business climate. While China ranks well ahead of India is the World Bank's Doing Business Index, its position at 93 out of 175 hardly qualifies as world leading. Taxes, the availability of credit, licensing, steps to start a business, investor protections, and closing a business are all in the bottom half of the world rankings. The World Bank does not quantify corruption, but Transparency International puts China at number 70 out of 163, not in the bottom half, but not far.

A related disadvantage of the business climate is China's inability to enforce intellectual property rights. This was the main point of contention between the United States and China in its accession to the WTO, and continues to be a major issue in China's relations with its trading partners. Some firms routinely resist making investments in China for fear that their products will be copied, and firms that do invest often limit themselves to product lines that do not contain trade secrets. China meets WTO standards but its enforcement is ineffective. Chinese firms frequently reverse engineer products, produce a knock-off at a fraction of the price of the imported good since no royalties are paid, and expand across the domestic market. This has generated a reaction in Europe and the United States, but the problems associated with enforcement of property rights are significant. Many observers believe that China's enforcement will not become effective until China itself has significant intellectual property to protect.

**Resources.** China's rapid growth has increased its appetite for natural resources. For resource producers in Latin America and Africa, this has been a boon since China is below the world per capita average in all major natural resources except coal. Copper, oil, iron ore, and other minerals have experienced spikes in their world prices, which are in part related to Chinese demand. Simultaneously, a number of developing countries have been able to sign long-term agreements that will provide them with investment for exploration and supply contracts for the delivery of their resources. China's substantial export earnings are available for purchasing the resources it will need as it continues its development.

The fact that China buys its resources from other developing countries does not guarantee that the countries selling the resources will spend the money well. Furthermore, in some cases these purchases pose a direct challenge to the geopolitical strategies of the United States, as China has signed agreements with a number of countries the United States has tried to isolate (e.g., Iran, Sudan, and Venezuela, all of which have signed oil delivery contracts). At this point, Chinese oil purchases have not grown faster than the expansion of known reserves, so it is unlikely that Chinese demand is responsible for much of the increase in world prices.

## Unresolved Issues

China's large manufacturing sector and the remarkable growth of its exports has generated a number of concerns. Some concerns are based on misconceptions, others are a projection onto China of problems that originate elsewhere, and some are valid. This part of the chapter looks at three such issues: trade balances, the environment, and the call for political reform in the midst of China's increasing level of unrest.

**Unbalanced Trade.** Competition created by the rapid growth of China's exports has generated pressures for protectionism in a number of countries. In the United States, for example, a $200 billion trade deficit with China in 2005 fueled protectionist sentiments and calls for Chinese currency reform. Since the mid-1990s, China has run a significant surplus in both its current account and its trade in goods and services. While large by world standards, neither comes close to being as large as the United States' current account deficit. Figure 17.4 shows the trends in current account balances for China, the 12 countries of the European Monetary Union (EMU), Japan, and the United States. To the extent that world trade is vulnerable from its imbalances, it appears that U.S. deficits and not Chinese surpluses are the source of vulnerability.

EMU is the European Monetary Union, the 12 countries that used the euro in 2006. Global imbalances are primarily the result of U.S. deficits, not Chinese surpluses.

A few observers argue that a significant portion of China's manufacturing competitiveness is due to its fixed exchange rate system. Before July 21, 2005, China pegged its currency, the renminbi, to the U.S. dollar. Consequently, when the dollar weakened beginning in 2002, the renminbi weakened with it. In many quarters this was seen as an unfair trade advantage for China. In 2005, China announced that it was adopting a narrow exchange rate band and that it would use a trade weighted index instead of a dollar peg. In other words, the People's Bank of China (PBOC) has adopted an exchange rate that is permitted to fluctuate in a narrow band and that is pegged to a weighted average of its major trading partners. Moving the peg off the dollar and setting it on a basket of currencies resulted in a slight appreciation of China renminbi against the U.S. dollar as the latter lost value in world markets. In all likelihood, as Chinese export strength continues to grow, calls for more significant appreciations of its currency will also continue.

A related issue is the effect of China's savings on U.S. government finances. China's trade surplus is related to its relatively high savings rate, as discussed in

**FIGURE 17.4** ◉ **Current Account Balance in Three Countries and the EMU**

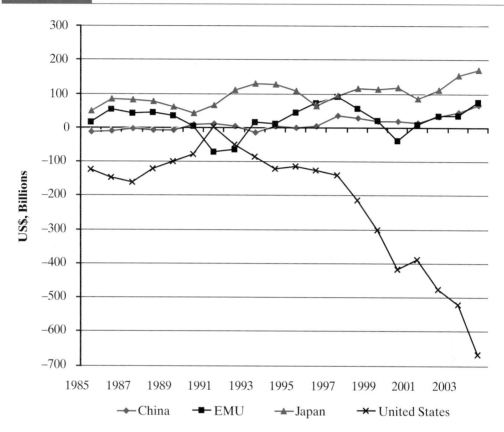

*Source*: World Bank, *World Development Indicators*.

Chapter 9. The export surplus and the large inflow of FDI have caused it to accumulate the largest foreign reserves holdings of any country in the world, valued at over $1 trillion in late 2006. The inflow of dollars through trade and FDI leads to an expansion of the Chinese money supply as firms convert their export earnings into renminbi and the People's Bank of China supplies whatever level of domestic currency is needed to mop up the dollars. If they did not do this, the price of the renminbi would rise, or in other words, China's currency would appreciate. China then takes a large portion of the newly created renminbi off the market by selling bonds. This is known as **sterilization** because it counteracts the effect on the local currency of the dollar inflow. The local bonds pay low interest rates, and China turns around and buys higher interest foreign assets such as U.S. government bonds with its dollar holdings. In effect, Chinese savings finance U.S. government deficits.

This relationship naturally leads to the fear that if China stopped buying U.S. bonds, it might touch off a crisis in the United States. To the extent this is true, the solution is for the United States to reduce its budget deficits and its trade deficits, which require a large inflow of foreign capital for their financing. In all likelihood, however, the effect of a cessation of Chinese purchases of U.S. bonds is not great enough to trigger a crisis. According to the U.S. Federal Reserve Bank, China accounts for about 15 percent of the net purchases of U.S. government bonds, and a cessation of all purchases could be countered by a 0.2 to 0.25 percent rise in long-term U.S. interest rates. In other words, the argument that the United States is dependent on China to finance its deficits is highly misleading.

**Environmental Pressures.** Growth has come at a high environmental cost. Currently China has 16 of the 20 most polluted cities in the world and 90 percent of its urban groundwater is contaminated. In the last decade, 200 million people have moved from the country to the city, and most live without connection to sewage treatment plants. China's per capita energy consumption is well below the level of the United States, but it is moving up rapidly. Given its large coal deposits (its one abundant natural resource), over the next 20 years it will probably become one of the top contributors to the production of carbon dioxide, a major cause of global warming. If the costs of China's environmental destruction are subtracted from its GDP, its growth rate falls from 9 to 10 percent per year to around 2 percent per year.

China's future economic success is likely to depend significantly on its ability to respond to the negative effects of the environmental destruction created by its growth. Unfortunately, the centralization of control and decision making in the Communist Party works against the creation of flexible and rapid responses to environmental problems. Local areas that are the first to perceive changes in environmental conditions lack a voice in China's highly centralized system and by the time information filters up to the authorities, conditions have deteriorated to the point where far more expensive and disruptive remediation becomes necessary.

**Political Reform and Protest.** In general, China's leaders recognize their country's environmental problems but their grip on power and their fear of the consequences if they were to loosen it somewhat, prevent them from decentralizing authority and control. Nevertheless, environmental pressures are only one of several forces pressing for greater decentralization of the authority and power of the ruling Communist Party. Some economists have long argued that free markets inevitably lead to political freedoms, but as yet, this has not been the case in China.

In 1993 official Chinese sources reported 8,700 incidents of unrest and/or protest. In 2005 the number was 10 times greater, around 87,000. The momentous and rapid changes running through Chinese society are generating increasing levels of unease, discomfort, and anger. China has over 140 million internal migrants who are on the move in search of work and opportunities. Villagers frequently complain about local officials who forcibly take land for the construction of factories, and workers laid off from state-owned factories protest the loss of health care and pension benefits when their unproductive enterprises close without compensation for the workforce. And local citizens complain about provincial authorities that refuse to respond to environmental problems such as toxic spills in local waterways or noxious fumes from manufacturing plants.

China has well over 100 million Internet users, nearly 300,000 nongovernmental organizations (NGOs) and 120,000 newly minted lawyers. The economic changes that it is undergoing are profoundly reshaping society beyond its economy, and while the political system is slow to respond, it is uncertain if the Communist Party will be able to maintain its control.

## The Choices Ahead

As China and India succeed, the pressures will mount to limit their participation in world markets. Negotiations for China's accession to the WTO led to a series of bilateral agreements between China and its trading partners that allow voluntary export restraints and other measures to block Chinese exports if they threaten firms in importing countries. The U.S. Congress introduced, and then retracted under political pressure, a measure that would label China's exchange rate management system as an unfair trade advantage. If passed, it would legitimize blocking some Chinese exports from entering the United States. Similar measures have not been proposed for India, although the outsourcing by firms of their IT work has led to calls for the re-examination of policies that may be encouraging firms to go abroad. In the end, however, measures against China and India become difficult to enforce because for every firm hurt by Chinese or Indian imports, others are helped by the low prices and availability of their goods and services. Hence, trade measures to stem trade flows will hurt businesses and consumers that depend on the imports.

If Chinese success in particular is frightening to some politicians, businesses, and workers, Chinese failure should be seen as an even greater threat. For example, the country is unlikely to begin to make serious headway in addressing its environmental problems unless it has political stability and some degree of economic prosperity. It has enormous reserves of coal, which is one of the greatest contributors to global warming when it is burned to generate energy. A switch to cleaner fuels is highly unlikely if the country is struggling against economic failure or political instability. The same holds for its ability to address the problems of water and air pollution, missing urban infrastructure, and other remediation needed in order to counter the effects of rapid economic growth.

A financial crisis in either China or India could radiate out in ways that are impossible to predict. As the world's two most populous nations, there are literally hundreds of millions of people who might be affected domestically and the consequences outside of either country could be dramatic. Crises work against stability and peace, and the growth of social protest in China in recent years reduces the likelihood that an economic crisis would be resolved without significant social conflict.

Furthermore, China and India have large parts of their populations that are living in poverty or not far above. While conditions have significantly improved for many, not everyone has benefited from growth and many who have are falling farther and farther behind the new economic elites in both countries. In China this has led to growing dissatisfaction and rising protest. India's democratic system creates more legitimate means for changing leaders who do not deliver, whereas China's growing inequality is seen by many as a potential threat to the current system. A failure of its economic project would undoubtedly worsen economic inequality and lead to greater social unrest.

When governments are undemocratic, social unrest can be a good thing. When they also have nuclear weapons and the world's largest army, too much social unrest can be a threat to the rest of the world. The consequences of a breakdown in order, an economic collapse, or even economic stagnation, are impossible to predict, but any of them would probably pose a serious challenge to prosperity and stability outside China.

## Summary

- China and India are the two most populous countries in the world. Taken together, they account for about three-eighths (37.5 percent) of the world's population in 2005.

- Both countries have undertaken extensive economic reforms and both have achieved high rates of economic growth since 1980. China's economy is about 3 times larger than India's and its growth rate is about 1.5 times higher.

- Economic reforms began in 1978 in China and in the 1980s in India. Indian reforms became much more serious and intense after a financial crisis in 1991. China is one of the few formerly communist countries that did not suffer a loss of output during its transition to the market economy. In part this is probably due to the more cautious nature and slower speed of its reforms, but also because of its large agricultural sector. When it began its reforms, about 70 percent of its labor force was in agriculture, much of it very low productivity. A loss of workers to that sector did not result in a decline in output.

- The state owned sector in China continues to be a problem, often generating large economic losses but difficult to privatize for political and social reasons. Both China and India score low on the Doing Business index of the World Bank, indicating that there are a number of institutional changes yet to be made.

- Both countries have seen a very rapid growth of imports and exports. China's manufacturing sector is extremely competitive but relies heavily on technology imports. Its exports are mostly either low technology goods or high technology goods that are assembled in China from imported parts.

Exports of Indian business services and computer and information services have taken off since the middle of the 1990s. This type of trade in services represents a new area of trade but is another application of the theory of comparative advantage.

- Trade and growth in China and India pose several challenges for other countries. China's manufacturing sector has a strong comparative advantage in the production of goods that need abundant supplies of low wage labor, while India's production of business services and computer and information services is supported by abundant supplies of English speaking engineers and technicians.

- Large U.S. budget and current account deficits do not depend on China for their financing, but raise the probability of a reaction against China's success in world markets.

- China's inability to enforce intellectual property rights is a constant source of tension between it and its trading partners.

- China's growth has posed an enormous toll on both society and the environment. Its water and air resources are degrading rapidly, and its ability to contain the outbreak and spread of new diseases is under question. The escalation of social protests this has generated has become a major issue for the ruling Communist Party, which seeks to contain the protest.

## Vocabulary

| | |
|---|---|
| Deng Xiaoping | Special Economic Zone (SEZ) |
| dual track strategy | sterilization |
| foreign trading corporation (FTC) | transition economies |
| Manmohan Singh | |

## Study Questions

**1.** How are the economies of China and India alike? How are they different?

**2.** Describe the process of Chinese reforms, from their beginning in 1978 up until China's accession to the WTO.

**3.** What were the factors that led to economic reform in India, and what were the main elements of the reforms?

**4.** Why did economic reform in Russia and most other transition economies lead to large declines in their GDP but not in China?

**5.** What are the sources of China's comparative advantage and how does that show up in the goods it trades?

6. What are the factors that make India competitive in business services and computer and information services? Do these factors give it a comparative advantage or do they reflect some other source of competitiveness?

7. What challenges to the world economy do India and China pose?

8. Chinese policies have created a great deal of controversy and discussion. For each of the following topics, describe the issues raised by China's trading partners and evaluate their concerns.

   a. China's trade surplus

   b. China's exchange rate system

   c. Intellectual property

# Suggested Readings

## Chapter 1: The United States in a Global Economy

Baldwin, Richard, and Phillippe Martin, "Two Waves Globalization: Superficial Similarities, Fundamental Differences." *NBER Working Paper No. 6904.* Boston: National Bureau of Economic Research. January 1999.

Bordo, Michael, Barry Eichengreen, and Douglas Irwin, "Is Globalization Today Really Different than Globalization a Hundred Years Ago?" National Bureau of Economic Research Working Paper. WP7195. June 1999.

Dollar, David, and Aart Kraay, "Growth *Is* Good for the Poor." World Bank Working Paper, Development Research Group. March 2000.

Edwards, Sebastian, "Openness, Trade Liberalization, and Growth in Developing Countries," *Journal of Economic Literature.* September 1993.

Feenstra, Robert C., "Integration of Trade and Disintegration of Production in the Global Economy," *Journal of Economic Perspectives.* Fall 1998.

Frankel, Jeffrey, and David Romer, "Does Trade Cause Growth?" *American Economic Review.* June 1999.

Friedman, Thomas, *The Lexus and the Olive Tree: Understanding Globalization.* New York: Farrar, Straus, Giroux. 1999.

Irwin, Douglas, "The United States in a New Global Economy? A Century's Perspective." *The American Economic Review.* May 1996.

Krugman, Paul, "The Localization of the World Economy," *Pop Internationalism.* Cambridge, MA: MIT Press. 1997.

Lindert, Peter H., and Jeffrey G. Williamson, "Does Globalization Make the World More Unequal?" *Globalization in Historical Perspective*, Michael D. Bordo, Alan M. Taylor, and Jeffrey G. Williamson, editors. Chicago: University of Chicago Press. 2002.

Maddison, Angus, *The World Economy in the 20th Century.* Paris: OECD. 1989.

——, *Monitoring the World Economy, 1820–1992.* Paris: OECD. 1995.

## Chapter 2: International Economic Institutions since World War II

Bhagwati, Jagdish N., *In Defense of Globalization*, New York: Oxford University Press. 2004.

Bhagwati, Jagdish, and Anne O. Krueger, *The Dangerous Drift to Preferential Trade Agreements*. Washington, DC: The American Enterprise Institute. 1995.

Fischer, Stanley, "On the Need for a Lender of Last Resort," *Journal of Economic Perspectives*. Fall 1999.

Helliwell, John, *How Much Do National Borders Matter?* Washington, DC: The Brookings Institute. 1998.

Kenen, Peter B., editor, *Managing the World Economy: Fifty Years after Bretton Woods*. Washington, DC: Institute for International Economics. 1994.

Kindleberger, Charles, *The International Economic Order: Essays on Financial Crisis and International Public Goods*. Hertfordshire, England: Harvester-Wheatsheaf. 1988.

Krueger, Anne O., "Are Preferential Trading Arrangements Trade-Liberalizing or Protectionist?" *Journal of Economic Perspectives*. Fall 1999.

Lindert, Peter H., and Jeffrey G. Williamson, "Does Globalization Make the World More Unequal?" *Globalization in Historical Perspective*, Michael D. Bordo, Alan M. Taylor, and Jeffrey G. Williamson, editors. Chicago: University of Chicago Press. 2002.

Robinson, Joan, "Beggar-My-Neighbour Remedies for Unemployment," in *Readings in the Theory of International Trade*, H.S. Ellis and L.M. Metzler, editors. Homewood, IL: Irwin. 1950.

Schott, Jeffrey, *The Uruguay Round: An Assessment*. Washington, DC: Institute for International Economics. 1994.

Stiglitz, Joseph, *Globalization and Its Discontents*. New York: W.W. Norton & Company. 2003.

———, *Making Globalization Work*. New York: W.W. Norton & Company. 2006.

Williamson, Jeffrey, "Globalization, Labor Markets, and Policy Backlash in the Past," *Journal of Economic Perspectives*. Fall 1998.

Wolf, Martin, *Why Globalization Works*. New Haven: Yale University Press. 2004.

## Chapter 3: Comparative Advantage and the Gains from Trade

Balassa, Bela, "An Empirical Demonstration of Classical Comparative Cost Theory," *Review of Economics and Statistics*. August 1963.

Blaug, Mark, "Adam Smith" and "David Ricardo," *Economic Theory in Retrospect*. New York: Cambridge University Press. 1978.

Chipman, J.S., "A Survey of the Theory of International Trade," *Econometrica*. July 1965.

Greenaway, David, editor, *Current Issues in International Trade*. New York: St. Martin's Press. 1996.

Grossman, Gene M., and Rogoff, Kenneth (editors), *Handbook of International Economics, V.3*. New York: North Holland. 1995.

Irwin, Douglas, *Against the Tide: An Intellectual History of Free Trade*. Princeton, New Jersey: Princeton University Press. 1996.

Jones, Ronald W., and Kenen, Peter B. (editors), *Handbook of International Economics, V.1*. New York: North Holland. 1984.

Krugman, Paul, "Competitiveness: A Dangerous Obsession," *Pop Internationalism*. Cambridge, MA: MIT Press. 1996.

——, "What Do Undergrads Need to Know about Trade?" *op. cit.*

MacDougall, G.D.A., "British and American Exports: A Study Suggested by the Theory of Comparative Costs," *Economic Journal*. December 1951 (Part 1), and September 1952 (Part 2).

Ricardo, David, *Principles of Political Economy and Taxation*. New York: Dutton. 1911.

Smith, Adam, *An Inquiry into the Nature and Causes of the Wealth of Nations*. New York: Modern Library. 1965.

Viner, Jacob, *Studies in the Theory of International Trade*. London: Allen & Unwin. 1964.

Yergin, Daniel, *The Prize: The Epic Quest for Oil, Money, and Power*. New York: Simon and Schuster. 1991.

## Chapter 4: Comparative Advantage and Factor Endowments

Baldwin, Robert, "The Effects of Trade and Foreign Direct Investment on Employment and Relative Wages," *OECD Economic Studies*, No. 23. Winter 1994.

Belassa, Bela, "The Changing Pattern of Comparative Advantage in Manufactured Goods," *Review of Economics and Statistics*. May 1979.

Cline, William, *Trade and Income Distribution*. Washington, DC: Institute for International Economics. 1997.

Deardorff, Alan, "Testing Trade Theories and Predicting Trade Flows," in *Handbook of International Economics*, Ronald Jones and Peter Kenen, editors. New York: North Holland. 1984.

Freeman, Richard, "Are Your Wages Set in Beijing?" *Journal of Economic Perspectives*. Summer 1995.

Friedman, Thomas L., *The World Is Flat: A Brief History of the Twenty-First Century*. New York: Farrar, Straus and Giroux. 2005.

Heckscher, Eli, "The Effect of Foreign Trade on the Distribution of Income," in *Readings in the Theory of International Trade*, H.S. Ellis and L.M. Metzler, editors. Homewood, IL: Irwin. 1950.

Kletzer, Lori G., *Job Loss from Imports: Measuring the Costs*. Washington, DC: Institute for International Economics. 2001.

Samuelson, Paul, "The Gains from International Trade," *Canadian Journal of Economics and Political Science*. May 1939. Reprinted in *Readings in the Theory of International Trade*, H.S. Ellis and L.M. Metzler, editors. Homewood, IL: Irwin. 1950.

Stolper, Wolfgang, and Paul Samuelson, "Protection and Real Wages," *Review of Economic Studies*. November 1941.

Vernon, Raymond, "International Investment and International Trade in the Product Cycle," *Quarterly Journal of Economics*. May 1966.

## Chapter 5: Beyond Comparative Advantage

Grubel, H.G., and P.G. Lloyd, *Intra-Industry Trade: The Theory and Measurement of International Trade in Differentiated Products*. New York: Halstead. 1975.

Krueger, Anne O., "Government Failures in Development," *The Journal of Economic Perspectives*. Summer 1990.

Krugman, Paul, "Is Free Trade Passé?" *Journal of Economic Perspectives*. Fall 1987.

——, "Increasing Returns and Economic Geography." *Journal of Political Economy*. June 1991.

——, "What's New about the New Economic Geography." *Oxford Review of Economic Policy*. 1999.

——, "Scale Economies, Product Differentiation and the Pattern of Trade." *American Economic Review*. 1980.

Noland, Marcus, and Howard Pack, *Industrial Policy in an Era of Globalization: Lessons from Asia*. Washington, DC: Institute for International Economics. 2003.

Norton, R.D., "Industrial Policy and American Renewal," *Journal of Economic Literature*. 24:1. 1986.

Ostroy, Sylvia, and Richard Nelson, *Techno-Nationalism and Techno-Globalism: Conflict and Cooperation*. Brookings Institute. 1995.

Ottaviano, Gianmarco, and Diego Puga, "Agglomeration in the Global Economy," *The World Economy*. 21:6, 707–731. 1998.

Tyson, Laura D'Andrea, *Who's Bashing Whom?: Trade Conflict in High-Technology Industries*. Institute for International Economics. 1992.

Venables, Anthony, "The Assessment: Trade and Location," *Oxford Review of Economic Policy*. 14:2, 1–6. 1999.

## Chapter 6: The Theory of Tariffs and Quotas

Baldwin, Robert, "Trade Policies in Developing Countries," in *Handbook of International Economics*, Ronald Jones and Peter Kenen, editors. New York: North Holland. 1984.

Bhagwati, Jagdish, "On the Equivalence of Tariffs and Quotas," in *Trade, Growth, and the Balance of Payments: Essays in Honor of Gottfried Haberler*, Robert Baldwin, et al., editors. Chicago: Rand McNally. 1965.

Bhagwati, Jagdish, and Marvin Kosters, *Trade and Wages: Leveling Wages Down?* Washington, DC: American Enterprise Institute. 1994.

Corden, W.M., *Trade Policy and Economic Welfare.* Oxford: Oxford University Press. 1974.

Crandall, Robert, *Regulating the Automobile.* Washington, DC: The Brookings Institute. 1986.

Destler, I.M., *American Trade Politics.* Washington, DC: Institute for International Economics. 1995.

Dornbusch, Rudiger, "The Case for Trade Liberalization in Developing Countries," *Journal of Economic Perspectives.* Winter 1992.

Martin, L., and L. Alan Winters, *The Uruguay Round.* Washington, DC: The World Bank. 1995.

Rodrik, Dani, "The Limits of Trade Policy Reform in Developing Countries," *Journal of Economic Perspectives.* Winter 1992.

## Chapter 7: Commercial Policy

Bhagwati, Jagdish, *Protectionism.* Cambridge, MA: MIT Press. 1988.

Edwards, Sebastian, "Openness, Trade Liberalization and Growth in Developing Countries." *Journal of Economic Literature*, 31, 1358–1393, September 1993.

Elliott, Kimberly Ann, *Delivering on Doha: Farm Trade and the Poor.* Washington, DC: Institute for International Economics. 2006.

Feenstra, Robert, "How Costly Is Protectionism?" *Journal of Economic Perspectives.* Summer 1992.

——, "Estimating the Effects of Trade Policy," in *Handbook of International Economics, V.III.* Gene Grossman and Kenneth Rogoff, editors. Amsterdam: Elsevier. 1995.

Hufbauer, Gary Clyde, and Kimberly Ann Elliott. *Measuring the Costs of Protection in the United States.* Washington, DC: Institute for International Economics. 1994.

Krugman, Paul, "Free Trade and Protection," in *The Age of Diminished Expectations.* Cambridge, MA: The MIT Press. 1994.

Laird, S, and A. Yeats, *Quantitative Methods for Trade-Barrier Analysis.* New York: NYU Press. 1990.

Rodrik, Dani, "Political Economy of Trade Policy," in *Handbook of International Economics, V.III.* Gene Grossman and Kenneth Rogoff, editors. Amsterdam: Elsevier. 1995.

Salvatore, Dominick, *National Trade Policies.* New York: Greenwood Press. 1992.

Sazanami, Yoko, Shujiro Urata, and Hiroki Kawai, *Measuring the Costs of Protection in Japan.* Washington, DC: Institute for International Economics. 1995.

Shugang, Zhang, Zhang Yansheng, and Wan Zhongxin, *Measuring the Costs of Protection in China.* Washington, DC: Institute for International Economics. 1998.

## Chapter 8: International Trade and Labor and Environmental Standards

Bhagwati, Jagdish, "Trade Liberalisation and 'Fair Trade' Demands: Addressing the Environmental and Labour Standards Issues," in *A Steam of Windows: Unsettling Reflections on Trade, Immigration, and Democracy.* Cambridge, MA: MIT Press. 1998.

Bhagwati, Jagdish, and Robert Hudec, editors, *Fair Trade and Harmonization: Prerequisites for Free Trade?* 2 Vols. Cambridge, MA: MIT Press. 1996.

Elliott, Kimberly Ann, "The ILO and Enforcement of Core Labor Standards." Washington, DC: Institute for International Economics. July 2000. http://www.iie.com/NEWSLTR/ news00-6.htm. Accessed 10-9-00.

Esty, Daniel C., *Greening the GATT: Trade, Environment and the Future.* Washington, DC: Institute for International Economics. 1994.

Graham, Edward M., *Fighting the Wrong Enemy: Antiglobal Activists and Multinational Enterprises.* Washington, DC: Institute for International Economics. 2000.

Human Rights Watch, *Fingers to the Bone: United States Failure to Protect Child Farmworkers.* New York: Human Rights Watch. 2000.

International Labor Office, "Child Labour: Targeting the Intolerable." International Labor Conference. 86th Session. Geneva. 1996.

——, *Child Labour: What Is to Be Done?* ILO: Geneva. 1996.

Krugman, Paul, "What Should Trade Negotiators Negotiate About?" *Journal of Economic Literature*, 35:1, 113–120. March 1997.

Siddiqi, Faraaz, and Harry Patrinos, "Child Labor: Issues, Causes, and Interventions," Human Capital Development and Operations Policy Working Paper 56. Washington, DC: World Bank. No date.

Stern, Robert, "Labor Standards and International Trade," *Integration and Trade.* 3:7/8. January–August 1999.

## Chapter 9: Trade and the Balance of Payments

Dunning, J. H., *Multinational Enterprises and the Global Economy.* Reading, MA: Addison Wesley. 1993.

Graham, Edward, and Paul Krugman, *Foreign Direct Investment in the United States.* 3rd Edition. Washington, DC: Institute for International Economics. 1995.

Grunwald, Joseph, and Kenneth Flamm, *The Global Factory.* Washington, DC: Brookings Institute. 1985.

Heath, Jonathan, and Sidney Weintraub, *Mexico and the Sexenio Curse: Presidential Successions and Economic Crises in Modern Mexico.* Washington, DC: CSIS Press. 1999.

International Monetary Fund, *Balance of Payments Statistics.* Washington, DC: IMF. Quarterly.

Krugman, Paul, "The Trade Deficit" and "Global Finance," *The Age of Diminished Expectations.* 3rd Edition. Cambridge, MA: MIT Press. 1997.

Lancaster, Carol, *Transforming Foreign Aid: United States Assistance in the 21st Century.* Washington, DC: Institute for International Economics. 2000.

Mann, Catherine, *Is the U.S. Trade Deficit Sustainable?* Washington, DC: Institute for International Economics. 1999.

Meade, James, *The Balance of Payments.* London: Oxford University Press. 1951.

United States Department of Commerce, *Survey of Current Business.* Washington, DC: Government Printing Office. Monthly.

## Chapter 10: Exchange Rates and Exchange Rate Systems

Calvo, Guillermo, and Carmen Reinhart, "Fear of Floating." *Quarterly Journal of Economics*, 117, 379–408. May 2002.

Dominguez, Kathryn, and Jeffrey Frankel, *Does Foreign Exchange Intervention Work?* Washington, DC: Institute for International Economics. 1993.

Dornbusch, Rudiger, "Expectations and Exchange Rate Dynamics," *Journal of Political Economy.* December 1976.

Eichengreen, Barry, editor, *The Gold Standard in Theory and History.* New York: Methuen, Inc. 1985.

——, "The Origins and Nature of the Great Slump Revisited," *Economic History Review.* May 1992.

Feldstein, Martin, "Does One Market Require One Money?" *Policy Implications of Trade and Currency Zones.* A Symposium Sponsored by the Federal Reserve Bank of Kansas City. 1991.

Frankel, Jeffrey, and Andrew Rose, "Empirical Research on Nominal Exchange Rates," in *Handbook of International Economics, V.III.* Gene Grossman and Kenneth Rogoff, editors. Amsterdam: Elsevier. 1995.

Jennings, Thomas, "Dollarization: A Primer." *International Economic Review.* USITC Publication 3298. April/May 2000. Available at http://www.usitc.gov/ier.htm.

Jennings, Thomas, and Souphala Chomsisengpet, "Nafta: An Optimum Currency Area? *International Economic Review.* USITC Publication 3331. June/July 2000. Available at http://www.usitc.gov/ier.htm.

Krugman, Paul, *Has the Adjustment Process Worked?* Washington, DC: Institute for International Economics. 1991.

Mundell, Robert, "A Theory of Optimum Currency Areas." *American Economic Review*, 51, 509–517. November 1961.

Rogoff, Kenneth, "The Purchasing Power Parity Puzzle," *Journal of Economic Literature.* June 1996.

## Chapter 11: An Introduction to Open Economy Macroeconomics

Friedman, Milton, and Anna Jacobson Schwarz, *The Great Contraction: 1929–1933.* Princeton, NJ: Princeton University Press.

Grossman, Gene M., and Rogoff, Kenneth (editors), *Handbook of International Economics, V.3.* New York: North Holland. 1995.

Jones, Ronald W., and Kenen, Peter B. (editors), *Handbook of International Economics, V.2.* New York: North Holland. 1988.

Kindleberger, Charles, *The World in Depression: 1929–1933.* Berkeley, CA: University of California Press. 1986.

Krugman, Paul, *The Age of Diminished Expectations.* Cambridge, MA: MIT Press. 1997.

——, *Peddling Prosperity: Sense and Nonsense in the Age of Diminished Expectations.* New York: W.W. Norton & Company. 1994.

Stein, Herbert, *The Fiscal Revolution in America: Policy in Pursuit of Reality.* Washington, DC: American Enterprise Institute. 1996.

——, *Presidential Economics: The Making of Economic Policy from Roosevelt to Clinton.* Washington, DC: American Enterprise Institute. 1994.

Temin, Peter, *Did Monetary Forces Cause the Great Depression?* New York: W.W. Norton & Company. 1976.

——, *Lessons from the Great Depression.* Cambridge, MA: MIT Press. 1989.

## Chapter 12: International Financial Crises

Bordo, Michael, and Barry Eichengreen, "Crises Now and Then: What Lessons from the Last Era of Financial Globalization?" *NBER Working Paper No. 8716.* Boston: National Bureau of Economic Research. January 2002.

Calvo, Guillermo, "Capital Flows and Capital-Market Crises: The Simple Economics of Sudden Stops." *Journal of Applied Economics*, 1, 35–54. November 1998.

Eichengreen, Barry J., *Financial Crises and What to Do about Them.* Oxford: Oxford University Press. 2002.

——, *Globalizing Capital: A History of the International Monetary System.* Princeton, NJ: Princeton University Press. 1996.

——, *Toward a New International Financial Architecture: A Practical Post-Asia Agenda.* Washington, DC: Institute for International Economics. 1999.

Federal Reserve Bank of Kansas City, *Policy Implications of Trade and Currency Zones: A Symposium Sponsored by The Federal Reserve Bank of Kansas City.* Kansas City: FRB. 1991.

Goldstein, Morris, *The Asian Financial Crisis: Causes, Cures, and Systemic Implications.* Washington, DC: Institute for International Economics. 1998.

Isard, Peter, *Globalization and the International Financial System: What's Wrong and What Can Be Done?* New York: Cambridge University Press. 2005.

Kindleberger, Charles, *Manias, Panics, and Crashes.* New York: John Wiley and Sons. 2000.

Krugman, Paul, *The Return of Depression Economics.* New York: W.W. Norton & Company. 2000.

Mann, Catherine, "Market Mechanisms to Reduce the Need for IMF Bailouts." Institute for International Economics, Policy Brief, 99-4. 1999.

Mishkin, Frederic, *The Next Great Globalization: How Disadvantaged Nations Can Harness Their Financial Systems to Get Rich.* Princeton, NJ: Princeton University Press. 2006.

Radalet, Stephen, and Jeffrey Sachs, "The East Asia Financial Crisis: Diagnosis, Remedies, Prospects." *Brookings Papers on Economic Activity.* 1998.

Rogoff, Kenneth, "International Institutions for Reducing Global Financial Instability." *The Journal of Economic Perspectives.* Fall 1999.

Woo, Wing Thye, Jeffrey D. Sachs, and Klaus Schwab, editors, *The Asian Financial Crisis: Lessons for a Resilient Asia.* Cambridge, MA: MIT Press. 2000.

## Chapter 13: Economic Integration in North America

Freeman, Alan, and Patrick Grady, *Dividing the House: Planning for a Canada without Quebec.* Toronto: Harper Collins. 1995.

Gallagher, Kevin, *Free Trade and the Environment: Mexico, NAFTA and Beyond.* Palo Alto, CA: Stanford University Press. 2004.

Hufbauer, Gary Clyde, Jeffrey J. Schott, Paul L.E. Grieco, and Yee Wong, *NAFTA Revisited: Achievements and Challenges.* Washington, DC: Institute for International Economics. 2005.

Hufbauer, Gary Clyde, and Jeffrey J. Schott, *NAFTA: An Assessment.* Washington, DC: The Institute for International Economics. 1993.

Lustig, Nora, *Mexico: The Remaking of an Economy.* Washington, DC: The Brookings Institute. 1992.

Lustig, Nora, Barry Bosworth, and Robert Lawrence, editors, *North American Free Trade: Assessing the Impact.* Washington, DC: The Brookings Institute. 1992.

Martin, Philip, *Trade and Migration: NAFTA and Agriculture.* Washington, DC: The Institute for International Economics. 1993.

Massey, Douglas S., Jorge Durand, and Nolan J. Malone, *Beyond Smoke and Mirrors: Mexican Immigration in an Era of Economic Integration.* New York: Russell Sage Foundation. 2002.

McDougall, John N., *Drifting Together: The Political Economy of Canada–U.S. Integration.* Peterborough, Ontario: Broadview Press. 2006.

Pastor, Robert, *Towards a North American Community: Lessons from the Old World for the New.* Washington, DC: Institute for International Economics. 2001.

Weintraub, Sidney, *NAFTA at Three: A Progress Report.* Washington, DC: CSIS. 1997.

Wonnacott, Paul, *The United States and Canada: The Quest for Free Trade.* Washington, DC: Institute for International Economics. 1987.

## Chapter 14: The European Union: Many Markets into One

Bakker, A.F.P., *International Financial Institutions*, Chapters 9–11. New York: Longman. 1996.

Baun, Michael J., *A Wider Europe: The Process and Politics of European Union Enlargement.* Lanham, MD: Rowman & Littlefield Publishers. 2000.

Crouch, Colin, *After the Euro: Shaping Institutions for Governance in the Wake of European Monetary Union.* New York: Oxford University Press. 2000.

Dinan, Desmond, editor, *Encyclopedia of the European Union*. Boulder, CO: Lynne Rienner Publishers. 2000.

Eichengreen, Barry, and Jeffry Frieden, editors, *The Political Economy of European Monetary Unification*. Boulder, CO: Westview Press. 2001.

Henning, C. Randall, "Cooperating with Europe's Monetary Union." Washington, DC: Institute for International Economics. 1997.

Henning, C. Randall, and Pier Carlo Padoan, *Transatlantic Perspectives on the Euro*. Pittsburgh, PA: European Community Studies Association; Washington, DC: Brookings Institution Press. 2000.

Hirtis, T., *European Community Economics*. New York: St. Martin's Press. 1991.

United States Congress, House Committee on Ways and Means, Subcommittee on Trade, "Trade relations with Europe and the new transatlantic economic partnership: hearing before the Subcommittee on Trade of the Committee on Ways and Means, House of Representatives, One Hundred Fifth Congress, second session, July 28, 1998." Washington, DC: U.S. G.P.O. 2000.

Wallace, William, *Regional Integration: The West European Experience*. Washington, DC: Brookings Institute. 1994.

## Chapter 15: Trade and Policy Reform in Latin America

Barber, William J., "Chile con Chicago: A Review Essay." *Journal of Economic Literature*. December 1995.

Birdsall, Nancy, Carol Graham, and Richard Sabot, editors, *Beyond Tradeoffs: Market Reform and Equitable Growth in Latin America*. Washington, DC: Inter-American Development Bank and Brookings Institute Press. 1998.

Birdsall, Nancy, and Frederick Jaspersen, editors, *Pathways to Growth: Comparing East Asia and Latin America*. Washington, DC: Inter-American Development Bank. 1997.

de Janvry, Alain, and Elisabeth Sadoulet, " Growth, Poverty, and Inequality in Latin America: A Causal Analysis, 1970–1994." *Review of Income and Wealth*, 46, September 2000.

Ffrench-Davis, Ricardo, Oscar Muñoz, and Ricardo Palma, "The Latin American Economies, 1950–1990," in *Latin America: Economy and Society since 1930*, Leslie Bethell, editor. New York: Cambridge University Press. 1998.

Ffrench-Davis, Ricardo, *Reforming Latin America's Economies after Market Fundamentalism*. New York: Palgrave. 2005.

Franko, Patrice, *The Puzzle of Latin American Development*. Lanham, MD: Rowman and Littlefield. 1999.

Kuczynski, Pedro-Pablo, and John Williamson, *After the Washington Consensus: Restarting Growth and Reform in Latin America*. Washington, DC: Institute for International Economics. 2003.

Sokoloff, Kenneth, and Stanley Engerman, "Institutions, Factor Endowments, and Paths of Development in the New World," *Journal of Economic Perspectives*. Summer 2000.

Stallings, Barbara, and Wilson Peres, *Growth, Employment and Equity: The Impact of the Economic Reforms in Latin America and the Caribbean.* Washington, DC: The Brookings Institute and the United Nations. 2000.

World Bank, *Economic Growth in the 1990s: Learning from a Decade of Reform.* Washington, DC: 2005.

## Chapter 16: Export-Oriented Growth in East Asia

Campos, Jose Edgardo, and Hilton L. Root, *The Key to the East Asian Miracle: Making Shared Growth Credible.* Washington, DC: The Brookings Institution. 1996.

Choi, Inbom, and Jeffrey J. Schott, *Free Trade between Korea and the United States?* Washington, DC: Institute for International Economics. 2001.

Collins, Susan, and Barry Bosworth, "Economic Growth in East Asia: Accumulation versus Assimilation," in *Brooking Papers on Economic Activity*, 2. 1996.

Fishlow, Albert, Catherine Gwin, Stephan Haggard, Dani Rodrik, and Robert Wade, *Miracle or Design: Lessons from the East Asian Experience.* Washington, DC: Overseas Development Council. 1994.

Frankel, Jeffrey, "Is Japan Creating a Yen Bloc in East Asia and the Pacific?" in *Regionalism and Rivalry: Japan and the United States in Pacific Asia*, Jeffrey Frankel and Miles Kahler, editors. Chicago: University of Chicago Press. 1993.

Posen, Adam, "Japan 2001—Decisive Action or Financial Panic?" Institute for International Economics Policy Brief 01-4. March 2001.

Rodrik, Dani, "Getting Interventions Right: How South Korea and Taiwan Grew Rich." *Economic Policy*, 20, 55–107. 1995.

Stiglitz, Joseph, "Some Lessons from the East Asian Miracle," in *The World Bank Research Observer.* August 1996.

Westphal, Larry, "Industrial Policy in an Export-Propelled Economy: Lessons from South Korea's Experience," in *The Journal of Economic Perspectives.* Summer 1990.

World Bank, *The East Asian Miracle: Economic Growth and Public Policy.* New York: Oxford University Press. 1993.

## Chapter 17: China and India in the World Economy

Bannister, Judith, "Manufacturing Employment in China," *Monthly Labor Review.* 2005. Available: http://www.bls.gov/opub/mlr/2005/07/art2full.pdf.

——, "Manufacturing Earnings and Compensation in China," *Monthly Labor Review.* 2005. Available: http://www.bls.gov/opub/mlr/2005/08/art3full.pdf.

Bergsten, C. Fred, Bates Gill, Nicholas Lardy, and Derek Mitchell. *China: The Balance Sheet.* New York: Public Affairs. 2006.

Bhagwati, Jagdish N., *India in Transition: Freeing the Economy.* New York: Oxford University Press. 1993.

Gilboy, George J., "The Myth Behind China's Miracle," *Foreign Affairs*, 83:4, 33–48. 2004.

Huang, Yasheng, *Selling China: Foreign Direct Investment during the Reform Era*. New York: Cambridge University Press. 2003.

Kynge, James, *China Shakes the World: A Titan's Rise and Troubled Future—and the Challenge for America*. New York: Houghton Mifflin. 2006.

Lardy, Nicholas R., *Integrating China into the Global Economy*. Washington, DC: Brookings. 2002.

Quinlan, J.P. "Ties That Bind," *Foreign Affairs*, 81, 116–126. 2002.

Sen, Amartya, *The Argumentative Indian: Writings on Indian History, Culture and Identity*. New York: Farrar, Straus and Giroux. 2005.

Srinivasan, T.N., and Suresh D. Tendulkar, *Reintegrating India with the World Economy*. Washington, DC: Institute for International Economics. 2003.

Yergin, Daniel, and Joseph Stanislaw, *The Commanding Heights: The Battle for the World Economy*. New York: Free Press. 2002.

# Glossary

**Absolute productivity advantage,** or **absolute advantage.** A country has an absolute productivity advantage in a good if its labor productivity is higher; that is, it is able to produce more output with an hour of labor than its trading partner can.

**Accession protocol.** The rules and procedures that countries must follow in order to qualify for membership in the European Union. The term may also refer to the rules and procedures for joining any grouping of nations, such as the World Trade Organization.

**Acquis communautaire.** The European Union rules governing technical standards, environmental and technical inspections, banking supervision, public accounts, statistical reporting requirements, and other elements of EU law.

**Adjustable peg exchange rate.** An exchange rate that is fixed in value to a foreign currency, but that is periodically devalued or revalued as conditions warrant.

**Adjustment process.** Usually refers to the changes in a country's current account that occur as a result of a fall in the value of its currency.

**Agglomeration.** Regional or local concentrations of firms that are in the same or a related industry.

**Aggregate demand (AD).** The sum of household consumption, business investment, government spending on final goods and services, and net exports.

**Aggregate supply (AS).** The total output of an economy.

**Antidumping duty (ADD).** A tariff levied on imports in retaliation for selling below fair value. *See also* Fair value.

**Appreciation.** An increase in a currency's value under a floating exchange rate system. *See also* Revaluation.

**ASEAN + 3.** ASEAN + 3 refers to bilateral agreements between ASEAN and China, Korea, and Japan.

**Asia Pacific Economic Cooperation (APEC).** A group of Pacific-region nations founded in 1989 for the purpose of creating free trade among all its members by 2020. APEC includes the United States, Japan, and China, among others. APEC's goal is not a free trade area; instead, it is to get all members to commit to free trade and open investment flows as a part of their trade policies toward all nations.

**Association of Southeast Asian Nations (ASEAN).** Mainly a political and security group of seven nations in Southeast Asia. ASEAN was founded in 1967 and has recently begun a slow movement toward creating a free trade zone.

**Austerity.** Usually refers to the cuts in government spending and increases in taxes that are implemented to reduce or eliminate a government budget deficit.

**Autarky.** The complete absence of foreign trade; total self sufficiency of a national economy.

**Auto Pact.** The 1965 agreement between the United States and Canada that created free trade in the automotive sector.

**Autonomy.** Self-governing, or independent. As used in the book, it also means free from outside influence.

**Baker Plan.** The first U.S. plan (1985) to assist indebted nations during the debt crisis of the 1980s.

**Baltic Republics.** Latvia, Lithuania, and Estonia.

**Banking crisis.** A common feature of international financial crises; a banking crisis occurs when banks fail and disintermediation spreads.

**Basel Capital Accords.** A set of recommended "best practices" designed to help countries avoid banking and financial crises. The accords emphasize capital requirements, supervisory review, and information disclosure.

**Brady Plan.** A 1989 plan of U.S. Treasury Secretary Nicholas Brady intended to help indebted developing countries. Unlike previous plans, the Brady Plan offered a modest amount of debt relief.

**Bretton Woods.** A small town in New Hampshire that was, in July 1944, the site of talks establishing the international financial and economic order after World War II. The International Monetary Fund and the World Bank emerged from the Bretton Woods Conference.

**Bretton Woods exchange rate system.** The exchange rate system that emerged from the Bretton Woods Conference at the end of World War II. *See also* Smithsonian Agreement.

**Canada–United States Trade Agreement (CUSTA).** A 1989 free trade agreement between the United States and Canada, and a precursor of NAFTA.

**Capital account.** A record of the transactions in highly specialized financial assets and liabilities between the residents of a nation and the rest of the world.

**Capital controls.** National controls on the inflow and/or outflow of funds.

**Capital requirements.** Requirements that owners of financial institutions invest a percentage of their own capital so that all losses are personal losses to shareholders and other bank owners, as well as to depositors.

**Chiang Mai Initiative.** The Chiang Mai Initiative is an ASEAN+3 agreement to lend currency between central banks.

**Cohesion funds.** Cohesion funds are a type of EU funding used to support regional development. They are directed toward less developed regions, particularly new members with incomes below the EU average. The funds pay for infrastructure development and environmental projects such as water treatment and transportation projects.

**Collective action clauses.** A requirement that each international lender agrees to collective mediation between all lenders and the debtor in the event of an international crisis.

**Common Agricultural Policy (CAP).** The system of support payments and other forms of assistance that is the main agricultural program of the European Union.

**Common external tariff.** The policy of customs unions in which the members adopt the same tariffs toward non-members.

**Common market.** A regional trade agreement whose member nations allow the free movement of inputs as well as outputs, and who share a common external tariff toward non-members.

**Comparative productivity advantage,** or **comparative advantage**. Achieved in a good when a country has lower opportunity costs of producing the good than those of its trading partners.

**Competition policy.** A rule within a nation that governs economic competition. Competition policies are primarily concerned with the limits to cooperation between firms, especially mergers, acquisitions, collusion, and joint ventures.

**Competitive advantage.** The ability to sell a good at the lowest price. Competitive advantage may be the result of high productivity and a comparative advantage. Alternatively, it may be the result of government subsidies for inefficient industries.

**Competitive devaluation.** A devaluation or depreciation in a currency with the intent to gain export markets.

**Conditionality.** *See* IMF conditionality.

**Consumer surplus.** The difference between the value of a good to consumers and the price they have to pay. Graphically it is the area under the demand curve and above the price line. *See also* Producer surplus.

**Contagion effects.** The spread of a crisis from one country to another. This may happen through trade flows, through currency and exchange rate movements, or through a change in the perceptions of foreign investors.

**Contractionary fiscal policy.** Tax increases and/or cuts in government spending.

**Contractionary monetary policy.** A cut in the money supply and a rise in interest rates.

**Convergence criteria.** The five indicators of readiness to begin the single currency in the European Union: stable exchange rates, low inflation, harmonization of long-term interest rates, reduction of government deficits, and reduction of government debt.

**Convertibility law.** A 1991 law passed by Argentina that required the central bank to hold one U.S. dollar in reserve for each new peso it issued. This law was overturned in 2000 when Argentina left the 1:1 exchange rate with the dollar.

**Core labor standards.** Eight core labor rights developed and advocated by the ILO, and embodied in eight ILO conventions. They cover areas such as freedom from coercion, minimum work age, freedom to bargain collectively, and others.

**Council of the European Union.** The chief executive body of the European Union.

**Council of Ministers.** The legislative body of the EU.

**Countervailing duty (CVD).** A tariff on imports that is levied in retaliation against foreign subsidies. *See also* Subsidy.

**Court of Auditors.** The European Union agency responsible for maintaining propriety in financial EU accounts.

**Court of Justice.** The judicial body of the European Union.

**Covered interest arbitrage.** Interest rate arbitrage that includes the signing of a forward currency contract to sell the foreign currency when the foreign assets mature. *See also* Interest rate arbitrage.

**Crawling peg exchange rate system.** A system in which a country fixes its currency to another currency (or a basket of currencies) and makes regular periodic adjustments in the nominal exchange rate in order to offset or control movement in the real exchange rate.

**Crony capitalism.** A term used to describe conditions in which resources such as bank loans are allocated for political and personal reasons rather than on the basis of market-oriented criteria.

**Currency board.** A government board that strictly regulates the creation of new money.

**Currency convertibility.** A currency that is freely exchangeable for another.

**Current account.** A record of transactions in goods, services, investment income, and unilateral transfers between the residents of a country and the rest of the world.

**Current account balance.** The broadest measure of a nation's commerce with the rest of the world.

**Customs union.** An agreement among two or more member countries to engage in free trade with each other and to share a common external tariff toward non-members.

**Data dissemination standards.** The IMF's standards for reporting macroeconomic data.

**Deadweight loss.** A pure economic loss with no corresponding gains elsewhere in the economy. *See also* Efficiency loss.

**Debt crisis.** Usually refers to the period between 1982 and 1989 when many indebted developing countries were unable to make interest or principal amortization payments.

**Debt service.** Principal repayment and interest payments that are made in order to pay off a debt.

**Deep integration.** Economic integration beyond removal of barriers at each country's border. Deep integration requires changes in domestic laws and regulations that sometimes inadvertently restrict trade.

**Deliberation councils.** Quasi-legislative bodies that combine representatives from industry with government and that have the purpose of discussing government policy and private sector investment. Japan, Korea, Malaysia, Singapore, and Thailand use deliberation councils.

**Delors Report.** Named after the President of the European Commission during the 1980s, the report contained 300 steps that the European Union needed to follow in order to become a common market. The report was adopted in 1987 and led to the creation of a common market under the Single European Act.

**Demand-pull factors in migration.** Economic conditions in the receiving country that "pull" in migrants. *See also* Supply push factors in migration.

**Demographic transition.** The shift from high birth rates and high death rates (characteristic of nearly all pre-industrial societies) to low birth rates and low death rates, characteristic of high-income, industrial societies.

**Depreciation.** A decrease in a currency's value under a floating exchange rate system. *See also* Devaluation.

**Derived demand.** Demand for a good or service that is derived from the demand for something else. For example, the demand for labor is derived from the demand for goods and services.

**Devaluation.** Equivalent to a depreciation, except that it refers to a decline in a currency's value under a fixed exchange rate system. *See also* Depreciation.

**Disintermediation.** A failure on the part of the banking system that prevents savings from being channeled into investment.

**Doha Development Agenda.** The name for the trade negotiations that began in 2000 under the auspices of the World Trade Organization.

**Dollarization.** The use of the dollar in place of a country's domestic currency. Technically, dollarization can refer to the use of any currency that is not the country's own.

**Dual track strategy.** China's strategy for transitioning from communism to capitalism is known as a dual track strategy because it localized market reforms to certain geographical areas or economic sectors (e.g., agriculture) while maintaining government planning for the remainder of the economy.

**Dumping.** Selling in a foreign market at less than fair value. *See also* Fair value.

**Economic Commission on Latin America (ECLA, CEPAL).** The United Nation's agency that oversees UN activity and information gathering in Latin America.

**Economic nationalism.** The modern form of mercantilism. Economic nationalists discount the benefits of trade. They share the fallacious belief that national welfare can be improved by limiting imports and curtailing foreign investment.

**Economic populism.** Economic policies emphasizing growth and redistribution that simultaneously de-emphasize (or deny the importance of) inflation risks, deficit finance, external constraints (i.e., trade and exchange rate issues), and the reactions of economic agents.

**Economic restructuring.** A movement from one point to another along a country's production possibility curve.

**Economic union.** The most complete form of economic integration, these unions are common markets that also harmonize many standards while having the same or substantially similar fiscal and monetary policies. Economic unions may include a common currency.

**Economies of scale.** A decline in average cost while the number of units produced increases.

**Effective rates of protection.** Effective rates of protection consider levels of protection on intermediate inputs as well as the nominal tariff levied on the protected good. Effective rates are measured as the percentage change in the domestic value added after tariffs on the intermediate and final goods are levied. *See also* Nominal rates of protection.

**Efficiency loss.** A form of deadweight loss that refers to the loss of income or output that occurs when a nation produces a good at a cost higher than the world price.

**Escape clause relief.** Temporary tariff protection granted to an industry that experiences a sudden and harmful surge in imports.

**Euratom.** An agreement concurrent with the Treaty of Rome that committed the six countries to the peaceful and cooperative development of nuclear energy.

**Euro.** The new currency of the European Union. Formally introduced as the unit of account in 1999, the euro appeared in January 2002.

**European Coal and Steel Community (ECSC).** A 1951 agreement among the six countries that eventually formed the EEC, creating free trade in the coal and steel industries.

**European Commission.** The executive branch of the European Union.

**European Community (EC).** The name for the European Union prior to the signing of the Maastricht Treaty and the creation of the economic union.

**European Council.** The EU body consisting of the leaders of each country. The Council has taken some power from the Commission in recent years.

**European Economic Community (EEC).** The original name for the community founded by the Treaty of Rome. The EEC eventually became the EC, and then the EU.

**European Monetary System (EMS).** An exchange rate system started in 1979 that linked the currencies of each of the members of the EC. The EMS was replaced in 1999 by the euro.

**European Parliament.** A quasi-advisory body of the European Union. The Parliament is the only directly elected government body in the European Union, and it has been moving toward becoming a true legislature.

**European Union.** Twenty-seven Western European nations that are an economic union.

**Exchange rate.** The price of one currency expressed in terms of a second currency. Exchange rates may be measured in real or nominal terms.

**Exchange rate crisis.** A collapse of a country's currency.

**Exchange rate mechanism (ERM).** The system adopted by the EC when it used the EMS. The ERM was a target zone exchange rate that allowed some limited flexibility in an otherwise fixed set of exchange rates.

**Exchange rate risk.** Risk that occurs when an individual or firm holds assets that are denominated in a foreign currency. The risk is the potential for unexpected losses (or gains) due to unforeseen fluctuations in the value of the foreign currency.

**Expansionary fiscal policy.** Tax cuts and/or increases in government spending.

**Expansionary monetary policy.** Increases in the money supply and cuts in interest rates.

**Expenditure reducing policies.** Policies that reduce the overall level of domestic expenditure. These are appropriate for addressing the problem of a trade deficit, and they include cuts in government expenditures and/or increases in taxes.

**Expenditure switching policies.** Policies designed to shift the expenditures of domestic residents. If the problem is a trade deficit, they should shift toward domestically produced goods; if the problem is a trade surplus, they should shift toward foreign goods. Examples of these policies are changes in the exchange rate and changes in tariffs and quotas.

**Export pessimism.** The views of Argentine economist Raul Prebisch and his followers, who believed real prices received by Latin American countries for their exports would fall over time.

**Export processing zone (EPZ).** A geographical region in which firms are free from tariffs as long as they export the goods that are made from imports. Rules and regulations governing EPZs vary by country but all of them are aimed at encouraging exports, often through encouragement given to investment.

**External debt.** Debt that is owed to agents outside a country's national boundaries.

**External economies of scale.** Scale economies that are external to a firm, but internal to an industry. Consequently, all the firms in an industry experience declining average costs as the size of the industry increases.

**Externality.** A divergence between social and private returns.

**Factor abundance, factor scarcity.** These are relative terms because, strictly speaking, all factors are scarce. Relative factor abundance implies that an economy has more of a particular factor, in relation to some other factor, and by comparison to another economy. Relative factor scarcity implies the opposite.

**Fair value.** A standard for determining if dumping is occurring. Generally, in the United States, fair value is the average price in the exporter's home market or the average price in third country markets. Definitions vary by country, making fair value a source of disagreement.

**Financial account.** The part of the balance of payments that tracks capital flows between a national economy and the rest of the world.

**Financial crisis.** Usually involves a banking crisis and may also entail an exchange rate crisis. A financial crisis results in disintermediation and a slowdown in economic activity that may be severe.

**Fiscal policy.** Policies related to government expenditures and taxation.

**Fixed exchange rate.** An exchange rate that is fixed and unchanging, relative to some other currency or group of currencies.

**Flexible (floating) exchange rate.** When supply and demand for foreign exchange determine the value of a nation's money.

**Foreign direct investment (FDI).** The purchase of physical assets such as real estate or businesses by a foreign company or individual. It can be outward (citizens or businesses in the home country purchase assets in a foreign country) or inward (foreigners purchase assets in the home country). *See also* Foreign portfolio investment.

**Foreign exchange reserves.** Assets held by the national monetary authority that can be used to settle international payments. Dollars, euros, yen, and monetary gold are examples of reserves.

**Foreign portfolio investment.** The purchase of financial assets such as stocks, bonds, bank accounts, or related financial instruments. As with FDI, it can be inward or outward.

**Foreign trade corporation (FTC).** Prior to reform, all foreign trade in China was controlled by 12 enterprises that were attached to various branches of government. These enterprises were called foreign trade corporations.

**Forward exchange rate.** The exchange rate in a forward market.

**Forward markets.** Markets in which buyers and sellers agree on a quantity and a price for a foreign exchange or other transaction that takes place in (usually) 30, 90, or 180 days from the time the contract is signed. *See also* Spot markets.

**Four Tigers.** Hong Kong, Korea, Singapore, and Taiwan. Their economic growth began shortly after Japan's post-World War II development. They are classified by the World Bank as either high-income or upper-middle-income economies. (The Four Tigers are sometimes called the Four Dragons or the Little Dragons.) *See also* High-performance Asian economies and Newly industrializing economies.

**Free riding.** Occurs when a person lets others pay for a good or service, or lets them do the work when they know they cannot be excluded from consumption of the good or from the benefits of the work.

**Free Trade Agreement of the Americas (FTAA).** An agreement currently under negotiation to create a free trade area among thirty-four countries in the Western Hemisphere.

**Free trade area.** A preferential trade agreement in which countries permit the free movement of outputs (goods and services) across their borders as long as they originate in one of the member countries.

**Gains from trade.** The increase in consumption made possible by specialization and trade.

**General Agreement on Tariffs and Trade (GATT).** The main international agreement covering the rules of trade in most, but not all goods. The GATT's origins can be traced to negotiations that took place in 1946, after World War II.

**General Agreement on Trade in Services (GATS).** An attempt to extend the rules and principles of the GATT to trade in services. GATS was one of the outcomes of the Uruguay Round.

**Gold standard.** A fixed exchange rate system that uses gold as its standard of value.

**Gross domestic product (GDP).** The market value of all final goods and services produced in a year inside a nation.

**Gross national product (GNP).** The market value of all final goods and services produced by the residents of a nation, regardless of where the production takes place. GNP equals GDP minus income paid to foreigners plus income received from abroad.

**Grubel-Lloyd index.** A measure used to determine the importance of intraindustry trade.

**Harmonization of standards.** Harmonization of standards occurs when two or more countries negotiate a common standard or policy. Harmonization can occur with respect to safety standards, technical standards, environmental standards, legal standards, certification, or with respect to any requirement set forth by national policies. *See also* Mutual recognition of standards.

**Heckscher-Ohlin Theorem.** A trade theorem that predicts the goods and services countries export and import. The theorem states that countries will export goods the production of which intensively uses its relatively abundant factors, and import goods that require its relatively scarce factors to produce.

**Hedging.** Eliminating risk (e.g., exchange rate risk can be eliminated, or hedged, by signing a forward contract).

**Heterodox stabilization policies.** A heterodox stabilization policy is designed to cure inflation by the following: cutting government spending, limiting the creation of new money, reforming the tax system, and freezing wages and prices. *See also* Orthodox stabilization policies.

**High-performance Asian economies (HPAE).** The eight high-performance Asian economies of Hong Kong, Japan, Indonesia, Korea, Malaysia, Singapore, Taiwan, and Thailand. *See also* Four Tigers and Newly industrializing economies.

**IMF conditionality.** The changes in economic policy that borrowing nations are required to make in order to receive International Monetary Fund loans. The changes usually involve policies that reduce or eliminate a severe trade deficit and/or a central government budget deficit. In practical terms, they involve reduced expenditures by the government and by the private sector (to reduce imports) and increased taxes. *See also* International Monetary Fund.

**Import substitution industrialization (ISI).** An economic development strategy that emphasizes the domestic production of goods that substitute for imports. ISI policies decrease imports and exports.

**Index of openness.** A measure of the importance of trade to a national economy, consisting of exports plus imports divided by GDP.

**Industrial policy.** A policy designed to create new industries or to provide support for existing ones.

**Infant industry argument.** An argument for tariff protection based on the belief that a particular industry is incapable of competing at present but that it will soon grow into a mature and competitive industry that no longer needs protection.

**Informal economy.** The part of a national or local economy that is unmeasured, untaxed, and unregulated.

**Information disclosure.** One of the three areas emphasized by the Basel Accord in its list of recommended practices. Information disclosure is intended to encourage market discipline by requiring banks to disclose the relevant information that lenders, investors, and depositors need to understand the full scope of a particular bank's operations.

**Institution.** A set of rules of behavior. Institutions set limits, or constraints, on social, political, and economic interaction. An institution may be informal (e.g., manners, taboos, or customs) or formal (e.g., constitutions or laws).

**Intellectual property rights.** Intellectual property is divided into copyrights and related rights for literary and artistic work, and industrial property rights for trademarks, patents, industrial designs, geographical indications, and the layout of integrated circuits.

**Interest parity.** The notion that the interest rate differential between two countries is approximately equal to the percentage difference between the forward and spot exchange rates.

**Interest rate arbitrage.** The transfer of funds from one financial asset and currency to another to take advantage of higher interest rates. *See also* Covered interest arbitrage.

**Interindustry trade.** Trade that involves exports and imports of goods that are produced in different industries, for example, when the United States exports cars and imports sugar cane.

**Intermediate inputs.** Parts and materials that are incorporated into a final good such as a consumer good or investment good.

**Intermediation.** The role of banks as institutions that concentrate savings from many sources and lend the money to investors.

**Internal economies of scale.** The idea that an individual firm experiences a decline in its average cost of production as it increases the number of units produced.

**International financial architecture.** The complex of institutions, international organizations, governments, and private economic agents that make up the international financial system.

**International investment position.** The value of all foreign assets owned by a nation's residents, businesses, and government, minus the value of all domestic assets owned by foreigners.

**International Labor Organization (ILO).** The international organization charged with responsibilities for researching international labor conditions and providing technical assistance in the area of labor conditions and standards.

**International Monetary Fund (IMF).** One of the original Bretton Woods institutions, IMF responsibilities include helping member countries that suffer from instability or problems with their balance of payments. It also provides technical expertise in international financial relations.

**Intra-firm trade.** International trade between two or more divisions of the same company that are located in different countries.

**Intraindustry trade.** Exports and imports of the same category of goods and/or services.

**Investment income.** A subcomponent of the current account; income received or paid abroad.

**J-curve.** A currency depreciation often results in a worsening of the trade deficit in the short run and an improvement in the long run.

**Labor argument.** The argument for trade protection based on the false belief that high-wage countries will be harmed by imports from low-wage countries.

**Labor productivity.** The amount of output per unit of labor input.

**Large country case for a tariff.** A country that purchases a significant share of the world's output of a particular good may improve its welfare by imposing a tariff that causes import prices to fall.

**Lender of last resort.** In international economics, a place where nations can borrow after all sources of commercial lending have dried up. Today, the IMF (International Monetary Fund) fills this role.

**Lost Decade.** The period of recession in Latin America brought on by the region-wide debt crisis beginning in August 1982. There is no official date ending the Lost Decade, but 1989 is a useful benchmark, since it coincided with a new strategy for handling the crisis.

**Low-, lower-middle, upper-middle, and high-income countries.** Categories used by the World Bank to classify countries by their level of per capita income. The criteria for categories change over time. Currently, low income is less than $876 per year, lower-middle income is $876 to $3,465 per year, upper-middle income is $3,466 to $10,725 per year, and high income is above $10,725 per year.

**Maastricht Treaty.** Sometimes called the Treaty on Economic and Monetary Union. Ratified in 1991 by the members of the European Union, its most visible provision includes the single currency program that began in 1999. It creates an economic union among the members of the European Union.

**Magnification effect.** The idea that a rise or decline in goods prices has a larger effect in the same direction on the income of the factor used intensively in its production.

**Managed float.** A floating exchange rate in which the monetary authority occasionally intervenes to cause a rise or fall in the value of the country's currency.

**Maquiladora.** Mexican manufacturing firms, mostly along the U.S.-Mexico border that receive special tax breaks.

**Market failure.** A situation in which markets do not produce the most beneficial economic outcome. Market failure has numerous causes, including externalities and monopolistic or oligopolistic market structures.

**Mercantilism.** The economic system that arose in Western Europe in the 1500s, during the period in which modern nation states were emerging from feudal monarchies. Mercantilism has been called the politics and economics of nation building because it stressed the need for nations to run trade surpluses to obtain revenues for armies and national construction projects. Mercantilists favored granting monopoly rights to individuals and companies, they shunned competition, and they viewed exports as positive and imports as negative. Today, the term *mercantilism* is sometimes used to describe the policies of nations that promote their exports while keeping their markets relatively closed to imports.

**Merchandise trade balance.** Exports of goods minus imports of goods.

**MERCOSUR.** The Mercado Común del Sur, or Common Market of the South, is the largest regional trade grouping in South America. It includes four countries: Brazil, Argentina, Uruguay, Paraguay, and Venezuela.

**Monetary policy.** National macroeconomic policies related to the money supply and interest.

**Monopolistic competition.** Competition between differentiated products, combining elements of perfect competition and monopoly.

**Moral hazard.** A financial incentive to withhold information, take on excessive risk, or behave in a manner that generates significant social costs.

**Most-favored nation (MFN).** The idea that every member of the World Trade Organization (WTO) is required to treat each of its trading partners as well as it treats its most favored trading partner. In effect, MFN prohibits one country from discriminating against another.

**Multilateralism.** An approach to trade and investment issues that involves large numbers of countries. Multilateralism stands for the belief that market openings should benefit all nations. Multilateral institutions include the World Trade Organization, the World Bank, and the International Monetary Fund.

**Multiplier effect.** The macroeconomic concept that a change in spending has an impact on the national product, which is ultimately larger than the original spending change.

**Mutual recognition of standards.** An alternative to the harmonization of standards. Under a mutual recognition system, countries keep different standards while agreeing to recognize and accept each other's standards within their national jurisdictions.

**National income and product accounts.** A nation's accounts measuring macroeconomic activity.

**National treatment.** The idea that foreign firms operating inside a nation should not be treated differently than domestic firms.

**Neoliberalism.** Market fundamentalism that became common throughout Latin America in the late 1980s and 1990s.

**Newly industrializing economies (NIEs).** The most recent wave of rapidly growing and industrializ-

ing developing nations. There are a number of these economies in Latin America (e.g., Argentina, Brazil, Chile, and Mexico) as well as in East Asia (the HPAE, Indonesia, Malaysia, and Thailand fall into this category).

**Nominal exchange rate.** The price of a unit of foreign exchange. *See also* Real exchange rate.

**Nominal rates of protection.** The amount of a tariff (or the tariff equivalent of a quota) expressed as a percentage of the good's price. *See also* Effective rates of protection.

**Nominal tariff.** The tax on imports of a particular good, expressed in either percentages or absolute amounts. *See also* Effective rates of protection.

**Nondiminishable.** A good or service that is not reduced by consumption. For example, listening to a radio broadcast does not reduce its availability to others.

**Nondiscrimination.** The notion that national laws should not treat foreign firms differently than domestic firms.

**Nonexcludable.** When people who do not pay for a good or service cannot be excluded from its consumption. National defense is an example.

**Nonrival.** *See* Nondiminishable.

**Nontariff barrier (NTB).** Any trade barrier that is not a tariff. Most important are quotas, which are physical limits on the quantity of permitted imports. Nontariff barriers include red tape and regulations, rules requiring governments to purchase from domestic producers, and a large number of other practices that indirectly limit imports.

**Nontariff measure (NTM).** Nontariff measures are nontariff barriers that are not quotas. They include red tape or cumbersome and unevenly applied rules. In general, the term refers to any regulatory or policy rules other than tariffs and quotas that reduce the physical quantity of imports or exports.

**Nontransparent.** Not easily interpreted or understood. For example, some countries use red tape and bureaucratic rules to block imports.

**North American Agreement on Environmental Cooperation.** The environmental "side agreement" to the NAFTA.

**North American Agreement on Labor Cooperation.** The labor "side agreement" to the NAFTA.

**North American Development Bank (NADBank).** A financial institution responsible for raising private funds and providing its financing for development projects along the U.S.-Mexico border.

**North American Free Trade Agreement (NAFTA).** The free trade area formed by Canada, Mexico, and the United States. NAFTA began in 1994.

**Odious debt.** Debt that is contracted by a country with an unrepresentative government and that is used in ways that do not benefit the people of the nation.

**Official reserve assets.** Assets held by governments for use in settling international debts. Official resource assets consist primarily of key foreign currencies.

**OLI theory.** A model of the determinants of foreign direct investment that is based on the key variables Ownership-Location-Internalization.

**Oligopoly.** A market with so few producers that each firm can influence the market price.

**Open market operations.** The main tool of monetary policy, consisting of the buying and selling of government debt (bills, notes, and bonds) in order to influence bank reserves and interest rates.

**Openness.** *See* Index of openness.

**Opportunity cost.** The value of the best forgone alternative to the activity actually chosen.

**Optimal currency area.** A region of fixed exchange rates or a single currency. A currency area is optimal in the sense that it is precisely the right geographical size to capture the benefits of fixed rates without incurring the costs.

**Orthodox stabilization policies.** An orthodox stabilization policy is designed to cure inflation by the following: cutting government spending, limiting the creation of new money, and reforming the tax system. *See also* Heterodox stabilization policies.

**Outsourcing.** Outsourcing is the shifting of procurement from within a firm to outside a firm. It is often used to refer to services that are purchased abroad, such as the procurement of business services in India by a firm based in Europe or the United States.

**Partial trade agreement.** An agreement that covers only some goods and/or services and is less than a free trade agreement.

**Pegged exchange rate.** A form of fixed exchange rate. *See* Crawling peg exchange rate system.

**Permanent normal trade relations (PNTR).** The U.S. term for most favored nation (MFN).

**Pollution havens.** Countries that compete for investment by advertising their low environmental standards.

**Populism.** A political movement that is based on direct popular appeal, often by a charismatic leader. Latin American populists often incorporated elements of democratic inclusion, social justice, and economic nationalism.

**Price line.** The rate at which one good trades for another in a two-good model; the slope of the price line is the relative price. The same as a trade line.

**Private returns.** The value of all private benefits minus all private costs, properly adjusted to take into account that some costs and benefits are in the future and must be discounted to show their value in today's dollars. *See also* Social returns.

**Producer surplus.** The difference between the minimum price a producer would accept to produce a given quantity and the price they actually receive. Graphically it is the area under the price line and above the supply curve. *See also* Consumer surplus.

**Product cycle.** The idea that manufactured goods go through a cycle of heavy research and development requiring experimentation in the product and the manufacturing process, followed by stabilization of design and production, and a final stage of complete standardization.

**Product differentiation.** Two products that serve similar purposes but that are different in one or more dimension. Most consumer goods are differentiated products.

**Production possibilities curve (PPC).** This curve shows the maximum amount of output possible, given the available supply of inputs. It also shows the trade-off that a country must make if it wishes to increase the output of one of its goods.

**Public goods.** Goods that share two characteristics: nonexcludability and nonrivalry or nondiminishability. If they are excludable but nondiminishable goods, they are sometimes called collective goods.

**Purchasing power parity.** An adjustment to exchange rates or incomes designed to keep constant the real purchasing power of money when converted from one currency to another.

**Qualified majority.** Most EU legislation passed by the European Union Council of Ministers requires a qualified majority, equivalent to about 72 percent of the total votes cast.

**Quota.** A numerical limit on the volume of imports.

**Quota rents.** The excess profits earned by foreign producers (and sometimes domestic distributors of foreign products) in an export market. Quota rents occur whenever a quota causes a price increase in the market receiving the exports.

**Race to the bottom.** Downward pressure on labor, environmental, or other standards, that comes about through price competition.

**Real exchange rate.** The inflation-adjusted nominal rate. The real rate is useful for examining changes in the relative purchasing power of foreign currencies over time.

**Regional trade agreement (RTA).** Agreements between two or more countries, each offering the others preferential access to their markets. RTAs provide varying degrees of access and variable amounts of deep integration.

**Relative price.** The price of one good in terms of another good. It is similar to a money price, which expresses the price in terms of dollars and cents; but relative price is in terms of the quantity of the first good that must be given up in order to buy a second good.

**Rent seeking.** Any activity by firms, individuals, or special interests that is designed to alter the distribution of income to their favor. Political lobbying, legal challenges, and bribery are common forms of rent-seeking behaviors, which use resources (labor and capital) but do not add to national output. For this reason, rent seeking is a net loss to the nation.

**Retained earnings.** Profits that a firm keeps as a source of financial capital for future investment.

**Revaluation.** An increase in the value of a currency under a fixed exchange rate system. *See also* Appreciation.

**Section 301.** A clause in U.S. trade legislation that requires the United States Trade Representative to take action against any nation that persistently engages in what the United States considers unfair trade practices. *See also* Special 301.

**Separate standards.** Environmental, labor, or other standards that are unique to each country.

**Shallow integration.** The elimination or reduction of tariffs, quotas, and other border-related barriers (such as customs procedures) that restrict the flow of goods across borders. *See also* Deep integration.

**Single European Act (SEA).** The act that created a common market among the members of the European Community. The SEA was implemented in 1993.

**Smithsonian Agreement.** This 1971 agreement by major industrialized countries to devalue the gold content of the dollar was the beginning of the end for the Bretton Woods exchange rate system.

**Social networks.** Members of a migrant's family or village that provide support in the migrant's new location.

**Social returns.** Social returns include private returns, but they add costs and benefits to the elements of society that are not taken into consideration in the private returns. For example, a firm that generates pollution that it does not have to clean up imposes costs on society, which causes social returns to be lower than private returns.

**Sovereign.** Free from outside intervention, or self-determining.

**Special 301.** A part of U.S. trade law requiring the United States Trade Representative to monitor property rights enforcement around the globe.

**Special drawing right (SDR).** The unit of account and artificial currency used by the International Monetary Fund (IMF). The SDR is a weighted average of several currencies and serves as an official reserve asset.

**Special economic zone (SEZ).** A special region in China, in which local officials are encouraged to experiment with new economic policies. SEZs are designed to encourage foreign investment and exports.

**Specific factors model.** A trade model that allows for mobile and immobile factors of production.

**Spot markets.** Market transactions that are concluded at the same time the price is agreed upon. In the currency spot market there is usually a day's lag before the currency is actually delivered. *See also* Forward markets.

**Stabilization policies.** National macroeconomic policies designed to cure inflation and reduce a government deficit. Stabilization policies are usually a first step in compliance with IMF conditionality during a macroeconomic crisis. *See also* Structural adjustment policies, Orthodox stabilization policies, and Heterodox stabilization policies.

**Standstills.** An agreement between international creditors and debtors to allow a temporary halt to the payment of interest and principal on previous loans.

**Statistical discrepancy.** The sum of the current, capital, and financial accounts (multiplied by minus one).

**Sterilization.** Sterilization refers to the actions by a central bank to counteract the money supply effects of an inflow of foreign currency. Without sterilization, foreign currency inflows will expand the domestic money supply as recipients of foreign funds convert them to domestic money. With sterilization, the central bank removes excess money from the economy with open market operations.

**Stolper-Samuelson theorem.** A corollary of the Heckscher-Ohlin Theorem stating that changes in import or export prices lead to a change in the same direction of the income of factors used intensively in its production.

**Strategic trade policy.** The use of trade barriers, subsidies, or other industrial support policies designed to capture the profits of foreign firms for domestic firms.

**Structural adjustment policies.** Policies that are designed to increase the role of market forces in a national economy. Structural adjustment policies are mainly microeconomic in nature and include privatization, deregulation, and trade reform. *See also* Stabilization policies.

**Structural reform policies.** A set of reform policies designed to make economies more efficient. These usually include the freeing of prices (ending of price subsidies), liberalization of trade, privatization, and the removal of interest rate controls, among others.

**Subsidiarity.** The principle that the authority of the European Union to involve itself in individual national affairs is limited to those issues that are transnational in scope. In current practice, this includes environmental policies, regional policies, research and technology development, and economic and monetary union.

**Subsidy.** Government assistance for industry. The Uruguay Round of the GATT defined subsidies as direct loans or transfers, preferential tax treatments, a direct supply of goods, or income and price supports.

**Supervisory review.** One of the areas of reform emphasized by the Basel Accord, dealing with the supervision of risk management and standards for daily business practices for banks engaged in international borrowing.

**Supply push factors in migration.** The factors that "push" migrants out of their home country. *See also* Demand-pull factors in migration.

**Swap agreements.** Also called swaps, useful tools for short-term borrowing when a central bank encounters a shortage in international reserves. For example, Chiang Mai Initiative among the ASEAN + 3 countries allows Thailand to borrow dollar reserves from China. China, or another lending country, plays a role similar to the IMF, but with greater flexibility and a faster response.

**Target zone exchange rate.** An exchange rate system in which currencies are allowed to float against another currency or group of currencies, as long as it stays within a predefined band. Once the currency begins to move out of the band, the nation must intervene to pull it back.

**Tariffs.** Taxes imposed on imports. Tarrifs raise the price to the domestic consumer and reduce the quantity demanded.

**Technology transfer.** The spread of technological information and capacity from one country to another.

**Terms of trade (TOT).** The average price of a country's exports divided by the average price of imports: TOT = (index of export prices)/(index of import prices). A decline in the terms of trade means that each unit of exports buys a smaller amount of imports.

**Total factor productivity (TFP).** A measurement of the quantity of output per unit of input. Increases in TFP mean that overall productivity has improved and that a given level of inputs will create more output; hence, technology or enterprise organization must have improved.

**Trade adjustment assistance (TAA).** Government programs that offer temporary assistance to workers who lose jobs because of foreign trade or their firms moving abroad.

**Trade balance.** Net exports; that is, the difference between exports of goods and services and imports of goods and services.

**Trade bloc.** A preferential trade area; a group of nations that reduces or eliminates barriers between themselves while maintaining higher tariffs and other barriers to trade against non-member, third party countries.

**Trade creation.** The opposite of trade diversion. Trade creation occurs when trade policies cause a shift in production from a higher cost producer (often a domestic one) to a lower cost producer.

**Trade deficit.** A negative merchandise trade balance; the deficit may or may not include measurement of services trade.

**Trade diversion.** The opposite of trade creation. Trade diversion occurs when trade policies cause a shift in production and imports from a lower cost producer to a higher cost producer.

**Trade line.** *See* Price line.

**Trade Related Aspects of Intellectual Property Rights (TRIPS).** An agreement that emerged from the Uruguay Round of the GATT. It requires increased enforcement of intellectual property.

**Trade rounds.** Multilateral negotiating rounds under the auspices of the GATT or the WTO.

**Tranches.** Parts of an IMF loan that are made in several installments.

**Transaction costs.** The costs of gathering market information, arranging a market agreement, and enforcing the agreement. Transaction costs include legal, marketing, and insurance costs, as well as quality checks, advertising, distribution, and after-sales service costs.

**Transboundary and non-transboundary environmental problems.** Environmental externalities that do or do not cross international borders.

**Transition economies.** Countries that are in the process of moving from bureaucratically controlled economies to market-based economies. Transition economies include most of the countries that adopted socialist or communist ideologies during the twentieth century.

**Transparency.** Any trade barrier that is clearly defined as a barrier. Tariffs have the most transparency (are the most transparent) because they are usually clearly specified and published in each country's tariff code. Any disguised or hidden trade barriers cause a country's trade policy to be nontransparent.

**Treaty of Rome.** The funding document of the European Economic Community (EEC), the Treaty of Rome was signed by six nations in 1957 and went into force in 1958. The EEC has since become the European Union and includes fifteen members, but the Treaty of Rome remains its core legal document.

**Treaty on European Union.** Also known as the Maastricht Treaty, it is the agreement that deepened EU integration from a common market to an economic union.

**Unilateral transfers.** A component of the current account that measures the grants from one country to another.

**Uruguay Round.** The latest round of tariff negotiations within the GATT framework, the Uruguay Round began in 1986 in Punta del Este, Uruguay, concluded in 1993, and was ratified in 1994. Among other accomplishments, it created the World Trade Organization.

**Value added.** The price of a good minus the value of intermediate inputs used to produce it. Value added measures the contribution of capital and labor at a given stage of production.

**Voluntary export restraint (VER).** An agreement between nations in which the exporting nation voluntarily agrees to limit its exports in order to reduce competition in the importing country.

**Washington Consensus.** A set of policies prescribed for developing countries by the U.S. government, the International Monetary Fund and World Bank, and the unofficial community of think tanks centered in Washington, D.C. In general, the policies favor the use of market forces over government direction as allocative mechanism.

**World Bank.** A Bretton Woods institution, originally charged with the responsibility for providing financial and technical assistance to the war-torn economies of Europe. In the 1950s, the World Bank began to shift its focus to developing countries.

**World Trade Organization (WTO).** An umbrella organization created by the Uruguay Round of the GATT talks, the WTO houses the GATT and many other agreements. It is the main international body through which multilateral trade talks take place.

**Zero sum.** The costs and benefits of an activity cancel each other (equal zero).

# Index

**Absolute productivity advantage**, 40–42, 50
*Acquis communautaire*, 356
**AD (aggregate demand)**, 250–254
**ADDs (antidumping duties)**, 149–150
**Adjustment process**, 266–268
Africa
  child labor in, 161
  debt-relief effort for, 200–201
  Highly Indebted Poor Countries program in, 14
  odious debt, case study, 201–202
  prominent regional trade blocs of, 25
AFTA (ASEAN Free Trade Area), 417
**Agglomerations**, 97–98
**Aggregate demand (AD)**, 250–254
**Aggregate supply (AS)**, 250–254
Agreement on Textiles and Clothing (ATC), 141
Agriculture
  child labor in, 162
  China's reform process in, 427
  European Union issues on, 356
  European Union subsidizing, 137–140, 340
  Japanese subsidizing, 137–140
  under NAFTA, 71
  subsidies, case study, 151–152
  U.S. subsidizing, 108–109, 137–140
  U.S. using immigrant labor for, 81–82
Airbus, 100, 110–112
Aircraft industry
  industrial policies for, 100–101
  national security and, 144–145
  strategic trade policy in, 104–105
  subsidizing commercial aircraft, case study, 110–112
  U.S. competitive advantage in, 99–100
Ambassador car, 429
Andean Pact (Andean Community), 387
Antidumping, Canadian-U.S. Trade Agreement, 307
**Antidumping duties (ADDs)**, 149–150

**APEC (Asia Pacific Economic Cooperation)**, 9, 418
**Appreciation**, 211, 226
**Arbitrage**, 211, 214
Argentina
  dollarization and currency board in, 233–235
  inflation control measures of, 382–383
  openness and outwardness of, 390
**AS (aggregate supply)**, 250–254
ASEAN Free Trade Area (AFTA), 97
**ASEAN+3**, 417–418
**Asia Pacific Economic Cooperation (APEC)**, 9, 418
Asian crisis of 1997 and 1998, 288–292
  capital controls during, 285–286
  crisis and contagion, 290–291
  crisis management, 291–292
  current account deficits, 288–289
  defining, 288
  exchange rate policies, 289
  financial account surpluses, 288–289
  financial sector problems, 289–290
Asia-Pacific region, child labor in, 161
**Association of South East Asian Nations (ASEAN)**, 417
ATC (Agreement on Textiles and Clothing), 141
**Austerity**, 277, 280–281
Australia
  agricultural subsidies of, 152
  as currency trading center, 225
  world currency trades in 2004, 224
**Autarky**, 46
Authoritarian rule, 404
Auto industry
  economic restructuring and, 53–54
  geography and trade in, 97
  under NAFTA, 71
  against Single European Act, 347
  U.S.-Canada trade agreement in, 95–96, 306–307
Auto Pact agreement, 95–96, 306–307

Baker, James, 377–379
**Baker Plan**, 377–379
Balance of payments, and trade, 178–208
   capital account. *See* Capital account
   current account. *See* Current account
   data on, 207–208
   financial account. *See* Financial account
   international debt, 199–201
   international debt, case study, 201–202
   international investment position, 203–204,
     206–207
   Mexican sexenio crisis, case study, 189–190
   study questions, 205–206
   summary, 204–205
   trade balance and, 178–179
   vocabulary, 205
Balance of Payments Statistics (BOPS), 208
Bank for International Settlements (BIS), 224–226,
   283–284
**Banking crisis**, 274
Banks
   acquiring loans from foreign sources, 187–188
   in foreign currency markets, 212–213
   monetary policy and, 255–257
   reducing moral hazard elements in, 283–284
   volatile capital flows and, 277–278
**Basel Capital Accord**, 282–283
BECC (Border Environmental Cooperation
   Commission), 319–320
BENELUX Union, 26
Berlin Wall, 430
BIP (Border Industrialization Program), 313
BIS (Bank for International Settlements), 224–226,
   283–284
Black Thursday, 1929, 257–260
Boeing, 110–112
Bolivia, 382
Bombardier, 104–105, 110–112
Bonds
   effect of China's savings on U.S. government,
     438–440
   indicators of potential financial crises, 276–277
   open market operations with, 256
BOPS (Balance of Payments Statistics), 208
Border enforcement
   dismantling in EU, 343–344
   at U.S.-Mexican border, 320–321
Border Environmental Cooperation Commission
   (BECC), 319–320
Border Industrialization Program (BIP), 313
*Bracero* program, 313
Brady, Nicholas, 379–380

**Brady Plan**, 312–313
   response to debt crisis of 1980s in Latin
     America, 379–380
Brazil
   aircraft industry in, 100
   inflation control measures of, 382–383
   openness and outwardness of, 390
   subsidizing commercial aircraft, case study,
     110–112
**Bretton Woods conference**, 19, 29–31
**Bretton Woods exchange rate system**
   countries modifying, 231
   defined, 229
   end of, 238–239
Business people
   ease in NAFTA countries, 328–329
   vs. economists, on trade issues, 51–53
   in macroeconomy, 249

Canada. *See also* NAFTA (North American Free
   Trade Agreement)
   Auto Pact with U.S., 95–96, 306–307
   CUSTA, 307–309
   ease of doing business in, 328–329
   as economic union, 26
   economics/demographics of, 302–305
   subsidizing agriculture, 152
   subsidizing commercial aircraft, 110–112
   U.S. environmental and labor standards and, 159
   world currency trades in 2004, 224
Canadian-United States Trade Agreement
   (CUSTA), 70, 145, 307–309
**CAP (Common Agricultural Policy)**, 356–357
Capital
   adopting single currencies and, 242
   gains from trade in HO model, 62–63
   growth in HPAEs, 401
   under NAFTA, 70–72
**Capital account**
   defined, 178
   limits on financial flows, 188
   overview of, 181–184
   in U.S. balance of payments, 182
**Capital controls**, 284–286
Capital flight
   Asian crisis of 1997 and 1998, 292
   current account deficits and, 197
   effect on foreign exchange reserves, 189
   indicators of potential financial crises, 276
Capital flows
   across international boundaries, 5–7
   crisis management and, 287

in Debt Crisis of 1980s in Latin America, 377–379
debt of developing countries and, 13–14
increasing at this time, 7
restricting with capital controls, 284–286
volatile, causing financial crises, 277–281
**Capital requirements**, 283
Carbon dioxide ($CO_2$), income growth and, 159
Caribbean Community and Common Market, 387
Caribbean Free Trade Association, 387
Central American Common Market, 387
Central banks, 212–213, 255–257
Central Europe, joining EU, 356
**CEPAL (Economic Commission on Latin America)**, 370
*Chaebol*, 413
Child labor
  agreeing to definition of, 164
  case study, 160–162
Child mortality, 158
Chile
  openness and outwardness of, 390
  taxes on capital inflows, 286
  U.S. environmental and labor standards for, 159
China, 423–444
  comparing India with, 423–424
  demographics, 424–425
  economic reforms, 425–428
  environmental pressures, 440
  future choices, 441–442
  Hong Kong's separation from, 397
  intellectual property rights in, 132
  manufacturing challenges of, 436–437
  political reform and protest issues, 440–441
  resource challenges of, 437–438
  state-owned enterprise issues in, 429
  study questions, 443–444
  summary, 442–443
  trade patterns, 432–435
  trade with United States, case study, 77–78
  transition to capitalism, case study, 430–432
  unbalanced trade issues of, 438–440
  vocabulary, 443
  in world economy, 432
Clothing manufacturing
  EU, Japan, and U.S. protection of, 137–140
  immigrant labor used in U.S., 81
  under NAFTA, 70–71
**CMI (Chiang Mai Initiative)**, 418
Coffee industry, labels for exports in, 171
**Cohesion funds**, 340, 357
Cold War, 146

**Collective action clauses**, international bond loans, 296
Commercial advantage, 51–53, 159
Commercial banks, 212–213, 377–379
Commercial policy, 136–154. *See also* Quotas; Subsidies; Tariffs
  agricultural subsidies, case study, 151–152
  economic sanctions, case study, 146–147
  EU protection of, 136–140
  Japanese protection of, 136–140
  study questions, 154
  summary, 153
  Uruguay and Doha Rounds, case study, 141–142
  U.S. politics of protection, 148–151
  U.S. protection of, 136–140
  vocabulary, 153
  why nations protect industries, 142–146
**Common Agricultural Policy (CAP)**, 356–357
**Common external tariff**, 26
**Common market**, 26
Communism, 429, 430
**Comparative advantage**, 60–89
  empirical tests of, 72–73
  finding trade data, 87–89
  foreign trade vs. foreign investment, 75–77
  Heckscher-Ohlin trade model, 61–65
  impact of trade on wages and jobs, 82–84
  income distribution effects of trade, 65–70
  intra-firm trade model, 75–77
  low labor standards and, 165
  migration and trade, 80–82
  NAFTA case study, 70–72
  outsourcing, 79–80
  overview of, 60
  product cycle model of trade, 73–75
  study questions, 86–87
  summary, 84–85
  United States–China trade, case study, 77–78
  vocabulary, 85
**Comparative advantage**, and gains from trade, 38–59
  absolute productivity advantage, 40–42
  absolute vs. comparative productivity, 50
  attack on economic nationalism, 38–39
  comparative productivity advantage, 44–49
  competitiveness and, 51–53
  economic restructuring and, 53–55
  gains from trade with no absolute advantage, 50–51
  in Republic of Korea (case study), 55–56
  Ricardian model of, 39–40

**Comparative advantage**, beyond
  industrial policies. *See* Industrial policies
  intraindustry trade, 91–96
  overview of, 90–91
  prices and costs with monopolistic competition,
    114–115
  study questions, 113
  summary, 112
  trade and geography, 96–100
  vocabulary, 113
**Comparative productivity advantage**, 44–49, 50
Compensation, for economic restructuring, 54
Competition
  China manufacturing issues, 437
  comparative advantage and, 51–53
  EU agreeing to policies on, 337
  EU benefiting from increased, 346
  impacting wages and jobs, 82–83
**Competitive devaluation**, 341
**Conditionality, IMF**, 294–296
Constitution for Europe, 339, 357
**Consumer surplus**, 117–118, 120
Consumption
  current account deficits in U.S. and, 197–199
  effects of tariffs on, 118–120
  measuring national income, 191–193
  resolving peso crisis of 1994 and 1995 by
    reducing, 281
**Contagion effects**
  Asian crisis of 1997 and 1998, 290–291
  of financial crises, 273
**Contractionary fiscal policy**
  defined, 254
  effect on current account balance, 263–265
  effects of, 262
**Contractionary monetary policy**
  defined, 257
  effect on current account balance, 263–265
  during Great Depression, 259–260
Convention on International Trade in Endangered
    Species, 173
**Convergence criteria**, 351–352
Convertibility Law, Argentina, 234
Coordination, of macroeconomic policies, 268–269
**Core labor standards**, of ILO, 166
Corruption, creating unsustainable debt, 200
Costs
  conditions for adopting single currencies,
    241–242
  EU monetary union, 352–353
  international institutional
    implementation/adjustment, 33–34
  of tariffs and quotas, 139–140
**Council of the European Union**, 338

Countervailing, 307
**Countervailing duties (CVDs)**, 148–149
Court of Auditors, EU, 339
Court of Justice, EU, 339
**Covered interest arbitrage**, 214
**Crawling peg** exchange rate system
  increasing country's vulnerability to crisis,
    276–277, 283–284
  Mexico choosing, 237
  overview of, 232
**Crony capitalism**, 282
Crude oil, 42–43
Cuba, 146, 165
Cultural industries, 145, 308
Currencies. *See also* Supply and demand
  euro. *See* Euro
  exchange rates and trading, 209–211
  institutions participating in foreign, 212–213
  official reserve assets, 184–185
  reasons for holding foreign, 211–212
**Currency board**, 234
**Current account**
  Asian crisis of 1997 and 1998, 288–289
  defined, 178
  financial account relating to, 183–184
  macroeconomy and, 190
  national income and product accounts, 190–192
  trade balance and, 178–179
  in U.S. balance of payments, 182
**Current account balance**
  deficits, curing with austerity, 277
  deficits, harmfulness of, 196–197
  fiscal and monetary policies effecting, 262–265
  interpreting deficits, 196–197
  macro policies for imbalances, 265–267
  measuring national income with, 192–193
  as net foreign investment, 194
  overview of, 179–181
  U.S. deficit in, 180–181, 194–195, 197–199
CUSTA (Canadian–United States Trade
    Agreement), 70, 145, 307–309
**Customs union**, 26
**CVDs (countervailing duties)**, 148–149
Cyprus, 358

**Data dissemination standards**, IMF conditionality,
    296
De Soto, Hernando, 328
**Deadweight losses**, 121–122, 138
Debt, international. *See* International debt
**Debt crisis** of 1980s, Latin American
  causes of, 376–377
  overview of, 311–312
  responses to, 377–380

**Debt service** obligations, 199
**Deep integration**, 8
Deepening, EU cooperation
    defined, 340
    Maastricht Treaty, 350
    Schengen Agreement, 343–344
    Single European Act, 344–349
Defense industry
    commercial aircraft tied to, 110–111
    nations protecting, 144–145
    U.S. industrial policies in, 108–110
Deficits. *See* Current account balance
Deforestation, 159
Deliberation councils, 405, 406
Delors, Jacques, 344–345
**Delors Report**, 344–345
Demand curve, 117–118
**Demand-pull factors**, 81, 320
Democratic Republic of Congo (DRC), odious
    debt of, 202
**Demographic transition**, 401
Demographics
    China and India, 424–425
    DR-CAFTA countries, 326
    East Asian, 395–399
    European Union, 335–336
    European Union population forecast, 360–361
    Latin America and Caribbean, 365–367
    North America, 302–305
De-nationalization, in India, 428
**Deng Xiaoping**, 426–427, 430
**Depreciation**, 211, 226
**Derived demand**, 66
Devaluations, 276–277
Directed credit, in East Asia, 411
**Disintermediation**, 274
Dispute resolution, NAFTA system for, 316
**Doha Development Round**
    comparison of tariff rates, case study, 126–127
    negotiations, case study, 141–142
    overview of, 21
Doing Business Web site, 328, 429
**Dollarization**, 232–233
Dolphin-safe tuna, 169–170
Domestic investment, using national savings for,
    193
Domestic prices, trade price and, 49
Dominican Republic-Central American Free Trade
    Agreement (DR-CAFTA), 325–326
DRC (Democratic Republic of Congo), odious
    debt of, 202
DR-CAFTA (Dominican Republic-Central
    American Free Trade Agreement), 325–326
**Dual track strategy**, 431

**Dumping**, 149–150
Dunning, John, 76–77
DVDs, and intellectual property rights, 132

**EAEC (European Atomic Energy Community)**,
    337
East Asia, 394–422
    Asian model of economic growth, 418–420
    Asian trade blocs, case study, 417–418
    characteristics of growth in HPAEs, 399–403
    export-led growth in, 14
    financial crisis of 1997 and 1998, 2, 187, 277
    HCI in Korea, case study, 413–414
    Indian economy vs. that of, 428
    institutional environment of, 403–407
    measures of income distribution in, 399–400
    openness of, case study, 407–409
    overview of, 394–395
    population, income and economic growth of,
        395–399
    prominent regional trade blocs of, 25
    results of integration with world economy, 10
    role of industrial policies, 410–413
    role of manufactured exports, 414–417
    study questions, 422
    summary, 421
    vocabulary, 421–422
East Asian miracle, 394, 418–420
*The East Asian Miracle: Economic Growth and*
    *Public Policy*, 410
Eastern Europe, joining EU, 356
**EC**. *See* European Community (EC)
ECB (European Central Bank), 355
**ECLA (Economic Commission on Latin America)**,
    370
Economic and Technology Development Zones
    (ETDZ), 431
**Economic Commission on Latin America (ECLA)**,
    370
Economic integration, in North America. *See* North
    America, economic integration in
Economic issues, internation. *See* International
    economy issues
Economic nationalism, 38–39
**Economic populism**, in Latin America, 375–376
Economic reform. *See* Reform process, economic
**Economic restructuring**, 53–55
Economic sanctions. *See* Sanctions
**Economic union**, 26
Economies of scale, 92–94, 346
Economists, vs. business people (on trade issues),
    51–53
**ECSC (European Coal and Steel Community)**
    **Treaty**, 336–337

**Effective rate of protection**, nominal vs., 124–126

**Efficiency loss**, from tariffs, 121–122

"El Pacto", 382

Embraer, 104–105, 110–112

**EMS (European Monetary System)**, 341, 354

EMU (European Monetary Union), 438

Endangered species, 169–170

Endangered Species Act of 1973, 169–170

Entertainment industry, 145

Environment, and income levels, 157–159

Environmental standards, trade and, 167–175
  alternatives to trade measures, 170–173
  issues in China, 440–441
  NAFTA addressing Mexican, 318–320
  study questions, 175
  summary, 173–174
  trade barriers and endangered species, 169–170
  trade negotiations insisting on, 159
  transboundary and non-transboundary effects, 167–169
  vocabulary, 174–175

**EPZ (export processing zone)**, 313–314

**ERM (exchange rate mechanism)**, 341–343, 353–354

**Escape clause relief**, 150–151

ETDZ (Economic and Technology Development Zones), 431

**EU**. *See* European Union (EU)

**Euratom (European Atomic Energy Community)**, 337

**Euro**, 350–355
  costs and benefits of, 352–353
  European Economic Community before, 340–343
  implementation of, 354–355
  Maastricht Treaty calling for, 350
  monetary union and, 351–352
  political economy of single currency, 353–354
  Treaty on European Union leading to creation of, 332

Eurodad (European Network on Debt and Development), 200

**European Atomic Energy Community (EAEC)**, 337

European Central Bank (ECB), 355

**European Coal and Steel Community (ECSC) Treaty**, 336–337

**European Commission**, 338

**European Community (EC)**
  Airbus industry of, 100, 110–112
  dismantling border controls, 343–344
  as former name of EU, 332
  name change from European Economic Community to, 333

prominent regional trade blocs of, 25
  retaliation against U.S. for tariff on pasta, 122
  Single European Act and, 345–349

European Defense Community, 337

**European Economic Community (EEC)**
  former name of European Union, 333
  institutional structure of, 337–340
  Treaty of Rome creating, 336–337

European market, size of, 333–336

**European Monetary System (EMS)**, 341, 354

European Monetary Union (EMU), 438

**European Parliament**, 339

European Political Community, 337

**European Union (EU)**, 332–363
  agricultural subsidies of, 152
  Central and Eastern Europe join, 356–357
  clarifying name of, 333
  composition of world currency trades in 2004, 224
  as customs union, 26
  deepening and widening in 1970s and 1980s, 340–343
  demographic challenges of future, 360–361
  as example of economic union, 26
  financing, 340
  institutional structure of EEC, 337–340
  Maastricht Treaty, 350
  monetary union and euro, 351–355
  overview of, 332–333
  protectionism in, 136–140
  as regional trade agreement, 9
  Schengen Agreement, case study, 343–344
  second wave of deepening, 343–349
  single currency (euros) of, 239–241
  size of European market, 333–336
  Spain switches from emigration to immigration, case study, 358–360
  study questions, 363
  summary, 361–362
  Treaty of Rome creating EEC, 336–337
  Turkey joins, 358
  vocabulary, 362
  World Trade Organization permitting, 22

"Europhoria", 343

"Eurosclerosis", 343

**Exchange rate crisis**, 274–275

**Exchange rate mechanism (ERM)**, 341–343, 353–354

**Exchange rate risk**, 7, 213–214

**Exchange rates**, 209–247
  adjustment process for, 266–267
  alternatives to flexible, 228–229
  Asian crisis of 1997 and 1998, 289
  benefits of EU monetary union, 352

case study, dollarization and currency boards, 232–235

case study, end of Bretton Woods system of, 238–239

case study, NAFTA as optimal currency area, 242–244

choosing right exchange rate system, 235–237

currency trading and, 209–211

domestic policy for, 283–284

fiscal and monetary policies, interest rates and, 261–262

fixed exchange rate systems, 229–232

import substitution industrialization and overvalued, 371–372

institutions for, 212–213

interest rate parity condition, 247

Latin American anti-inflation policies and, 382

in long run, 216–219

in medium and short run, 220–226

most countries using flexible, 211

political economy of single EU currency, 353–354

real exchange rate, 226–228

reasons for holding foreign currencies, 211–212

resolving peso crisis of 1994 and 1995, 281

single currency areas, 239–242

study questions, 245–246

summary, 244–245

supply and demand with flexible, 214–216

vocabulary, 245

Executive body, of EU, 338

**Expansionary fiscal policy**

defined, 254

effect on current account balance, 263–265

effects of, 262

indicators of potential financial crises, 275

populism in Latin America using, 375–376

**Expansionary monetary policy**

defined, 257

effect on current account balance, 263–265

failure to use in Great Depression, 259

populism in Latin America using, 375–376

Expenditure, fiscal policy, 254–255

**Expenditure reducing policies**, 265–266

**Expenditure switching**, 263

**Expenditure switching policies**, 265–266

**Export pessimism**, 370

**Export processing zone (EPZ)**, 313–314

Export targets, 411

Exports. *See also* East Asia

Canadian-U.S. Trade Agreement increasing, 307

China-U.S. trade and, 77–78

China and India patterns of trade, 432–435

comparative advantage in South Korea, 55–56

creating unsustainable debt, 199–200

internal economies of scale and, 94

intraindustry trade and, 94–96

labels for, 171

Latin American export pessimism, 369–370

Lost Decade crisis and, 377

in measuring national income, 192–193

mercantilist thinking on, 38

of pollution, 167–168

in processing industry of Mexico, 313–314

of services, 79–80

U.S. current account balance for, 179–181

U.S. trade balance for, 178–179

voluntary restraint quota for, 128–129

**External debt**, 199–201

**External economies of scale**

interindustry trade and, 92–94

large geographical concentrations of industries and, 97–98

trade and, 98–100

**Externalities**, 101, 144

Factor abundance, 61–62

Factor endowment, 60. *See also* Comparative advantage

Factor scarcity, 61

Fair Labor Standards Act (FLSA), 162, 258

**Fair value**, 149–150

**FDI (foreign direct investment)**. *See* Foreign direct investment (FDI)

Federal Deposit Insurance Corporation, 258

Finance, international. *See* International finance

**Financial account**

Asian crisis of 1997 and 1998, 288–289

defined, 178

limits on financial flows, 188

overview of, 181–184

types of financial flows, 184–187

**Financial crisis**, 274–275. *See also* International financial crises

Financial sector weakness

Asian crisis of 1997 and 1998, 289–290

peso crisis of 1994 and 1995 from, 278–281

**Fiscal policy**

case study, during Great Depression, 257–260

crisis management, 287–288

and current account, 262–265

indicators of potential financial crises, 275–277

interest and exchange rates and, 261–262

overview of, 254–255

stability of HPAE, 404

**Fixed exchange rate system**

avoiding financial crisis using, 284

case study, dollarization and currency boards, 232–235

of China, 438
choosing, 235–237
defined, 228
exchange rate crisis in, 274–275
inability of EU to maintain, 354
overview of, 229–232
**Flexible (floating) exchange rates**
alternatives to, 228–229
avoiding financial crisis using, 284
case study, largest market in world, 224–225
choosing, 235–237
determinants of appreciation or depreciation, 226
EU problems with, 354
exchange rate crisis in, 274–275
in the long run, 216–219
in medium and short run, 220–223
supply and demand with, 214–215
FLSA (Fair Labor Standards Act), 162, 258
**Foreign direct investment (FDI)**
defined, 5
in East Asia, 415
overview of, 186–187
President Zedillo of Mexico encouraging, 189–190
Foreign exchange brokers, 212–213
**Foreign exchange reserves**
directing to targeted industries, 106
IMF handling crises in, 19–20
Foreign investment
in China, 77–78
intra-firm trade model, 75–77
low labor standards as strategy to attract, 164–165
using national savings for, 193–194
**Foreign portfolio investment**, 187
Foreign producers, 129–131
**Foreign trading corporations (FTC)**, 427
Foreigners, in macroeconomy, 249
Formal institutions, 18
**Forward exchange rate**
dealing with exchange rate risk through, 213
in medium and short run, 221–223
**Forward markets**, 213–214
Four Dragons, 394
**Four Tigers**
growth of manufactured exports, 402
overview of, 394
Fox, Vicente
common market and, 26
consideration of single currency for NAFTA region, 243–244
France, openness index for, 5

Free capital issues, of international institutions, 32–33
**Free riding**
concept of, 27–28
international institutions attempting to prevent, 28–29
**Free Trade Agreement of the Americas (FTAA)**, 388
**Free trade areas**
overview of, 23, 26
requiring rules of origin, 327
**FTAA (Free Trade Agreement of the Americas)**, 388
**FTC (foreign trading corporations)**, 427

G8, macroeconomic policy, 268
**Gains from trade.** *See also* Comparative advantage, and gains from trade
absolute productivity advantage and, 40–42
comparative productivity advantage and, 44–49
defined, 38
in Heckscher-Ohlin trade model, 62–65
of intraindustry trade, 94–95
with no absolute advantage, 50–51
GAO (Government Accountability Office), 162
GATS (General Agreement on Trade in Services), 142
**GATT (General Agreement on Tariffs and Trade).** *See* General Agreement on Tariffs and Trade (GATT)
**GDP (gross domestic product).** *See* Gross domestic product (GDP)
**General Agreement on Tariffs and Trade (GATT)**
creation of, 8–9
defined, 17
overview of, 20–21
rounds, case study, 22–23
rules on forming regional trade agreements, 24
on trade barriers and endangered species, 169–170
General Agreement on Trade in Services (GATS), 142
Geography, and trade, 96–97
and external economies, 98–100
external economies of scale, 97–98
forming regional agglomerations, 96–97
Geography, case study on child labor, 161
Germany
as currency trading center, 225
European Community's ERM threatened by reunification of, 341–343
openness index for, 5

**GL (Grubel-Lloyd) index**, 91–92
**GNP (gross national product)**. *See* Gross national product (GNP)
Gold, as reserve asset, 184
**Gold standards**
    end of Bretton Woods system, 238–239
    as form of fixed exchange rates, 229–232
    during Great Depression, 259–260
**Goods and services**
    Chinese and Indian patterns of trade in, 434–435
    current account balance for, 179–181
    EU issues on public procurement of, 349
    main agents in macroeconomy demanding, 249
    trade balance for, 178–179
Government
    business relationships in HPAE, 404–405
    democratic vs. authoritarian, 404
    failure in import substitution industrialization, 371–373
    indicators of potential financial crises, 275–277
    industrial policy tools of, 106
    in macroeconomy, 249
    problems with industrial policy, 107
    reasons to protect industries, 142–146
    use of fiscal policy, 254–255
    use of monetary policy, 255–257
    of widened European Union, 357
Government Accountability Office (GAO), 162
Great Depression
    effects in Latin America, 369–370
    fiscal and monetary policy during, 257–260
    trade policies helping to create, 28–39
**Gross domestic product (GDP)**
    aggregate demand and supply in, 250–254
    Caribbean, 366–367
    child labor and, 162
    China, 424–425
    current account deficits in U.S., 197–199
    defined, 4
    East Asia, 14
    European Union members, 335–336
    export growth and, 414–416
    global capital flows and, 6
    in Great Depression, 258–260
    India, 424–425
    Latin America, 366–367
    measuring national income with, 191–192
**Gross national product (GNP)**
    East Asian income levels, 395–398
    measuring national income with, 191–193
    North America, 302–305
Growth accounting, 419
**Grubel-Lloyd (GL) index**, 91–92

Hard peg exchange rate, 284
**Harmonization of standards**, 156–157
Hatch Act, 109
Heavy and Chemical Industries (HCI)
    defined, 410
    in Korea, 413–414
Heavy Industries Corporation of Malaysia (HICOM), 410
**Heckscher-Ohlin (HO) trade model**
    empirical tests of, 72–73
    gains from trade in, 62–65
    intra-firm trade as extension of, 75–77
    overview of, 61–62
    product cycle model as extension of, 73–75
    specific factors model of, 68–70
    Stolper-Samuelson theorem derived from, 66–68
**Hedging**, 213
**Heterodox model**, of inflation control, 381–382
HICOM (Heavy Industries Corporation of Malaysia), 410
High Technology Development Zones (HTDZ), 431
**High-income countries**
    debt service in, 199
    environment, society and, 157–159
    product cycle in, 73–75
    universal minimum wage standards in, 160
Highly Indebted Poor Countries (HIPC)
    case study, odious debt, 201–202
    debt-relief effort of, 200–201
    overview of, 13–14
**High-performance Asian economies (HPAEs)**
    Asian model of economic growth, 418–420
    Asian trade blocs, case study, 417–418
    characteristics of growth in, 399–403
    export promotion policies of, 414–417
    openness of, case study, 407–409
    overview of, 394–395
    population, income and economic growth of, 395–399
    rapid accumulation of physical and human capital in, 401
    role of industrial policies in, 410–413
    shared growth of, 399–401
History
    of capital flows, 6–7
    of economic globalization, 3
**HO (Heckscher-Ohlin) trade model**. *See* Heckscher-Ohlin (HO) trade model
Home country standards, requiring, 172–173
Hong Kong
    as high-performance Asian economy, 394
    as one of Four Tigers, 394
    separation from China, 397

Hoover, President, 258–259
Households, in macroeconomy, 249
**HPAEs (high-performance Asian economies)**. *See* High-performance Asian economies (HPAEs)
HTDZ (High Technology Development Zones), 431

IBRD (International Bank for Reconstruction and Development), 20. *See also* World Bank
Ideological biases, of international institutions, 32–33
IFS (International Financial Statistics), 207
IIT (India Institute of Technology), 435
**ILO (International Labor Organization)**. *See* International Labor Organziation (ILO)
**IMF (International Monetary Fund)**. *See* International Monetary Fund (IMF)
**IMF conditionality**, 20
Immigration
    bringing workers to home economy through, 80
    migration and trade, 80–82
    Spain switching from emigration to, 358–360
    unauthorized Mexican, 320–322
Implementation costs, criticizing international institutions for, 35
Import licensing requirements, as quota, 128
**Import substitution industrialization (ISI)**, 367–374
    criticisms of, 371–373
    Indian trade policy modeled on, 428–429
    in Mexico, case study, 367–374
    origins and goals of, 369–371
    overview of, 367–369
    policies, 311–312
Imports. *See also* Quotas
    Chinese and Indian patterns of trade, 432–435
    countries eliminating restrictions on, 8
    current account balance for, 179–181
    export production making possible purchase of, 415
    in intraindustry trade, 94–96
    judging importance of international economy by, 3
    limiting through tariffs. *See* Tariffs
    measuring national income, 192–193
    mercantilist thinking on, 38
    openness of East Asian economies and, 407–409
    of services, 79–80
    trade balance and, 178–179
Income distribution effects of trade
    effects of tariffs on, 120–122
    overview of, 65–66
    in product cycle model of trade, 73–75
    in specific factors model, 69–70
    in Stolper-Samuelson theorem, 66–68

Income distribution, in Latin America, 390
Income growth, in HPAEs, 401
Income levels, environment and society and, 157–159
**Index of openness**, 4–5
India, 423–444
    challenges in services, 435–436
    comparing China with, 423–424
    demographics, 424–425
    economic reforms in, 428–429
    future choices, 441–442
    integration into world economy, 14–15
    resource challenges of, 437–438
    study questions, 443–444
    summary, 442–443
    trade patterns, 432–435
    transportation issues, 429
    vocabulary, 443
    in world economy, 432
India Institute of Technology (IIT), 435
Indonesia
    aircraft industry in, 100
    Asian crisis of 1997 and 1998, 288–292
    as high-performance Asian economy, 394
    industrial policies in, 411
    as newly industrializing economy, 395
**Industrial policies**, 100–112
    case study, subsidizing commercial aircraft, 110–112
    East Asia, 410–413
    import substitution industrialization, 369–374
    market failure and, 101–103
    Mexico, 373–374
    overview of, 100–101
    prices and costs with monopolistic competition, 114–115
    problems with, 106–108
    strategic trade and, 103–105
    study questions, 113
    tools, 105–106
    U.S., 108–110
Industry specific councils, Japanese, 405
**Infant industries**, validating protection of, 143–144
Inflation
    indicators of potential financial crises, 276
    Latin American policies to control, 380–383
**Informal economy**, 163
Informal institutions, 18
**Information disclosure**, 283
Innovation, adding to net loss of tariffs, 123
Inputs, 62
    advantages of external economies of scale, 98
    in Heckscher-Ohlin trade model, 61–63
    in product cycle model of trade, 73–75

in Stolper-Samuelson theorem, 66–68
*An Inquiry into the Nature and Causes of the Wealth of Nations* (Smith), 38
Institutional environment, of HPAEs, 403–407
  avoiding rent seeking, 406–407
  business-government relations, 404–406
  fiscal discipline, 404
  open economies of, case study, 407–408
  overview of, 403–404
Institutional Revolutionary Party (PRI), 189–190
Institutions. *See also* International economic institutions
  defining, 17–18
  in foreign currency markets, 212–213
  reform in Latin American, 382
**Intellectual property rights**
  China unable to enforce, 437
  criticizing Uruguay Round agreement on, 33–34
  defining, 131–132
  enforcing with Special 301 trade law, 151
  and trade, 132–133
**Interest parity** , 221–222
**Interest rate arbitrage**, 211
Interest rates
  determining monetary policy, 255–257
  fiscal and monetary policies, exchange rates and, 261–262
  lender of last resort, 293–294
  Lost Decade crisis and, 377
**Interindustry trade**, 91
**Intermediate inputs**, 249–250
**Intermediation**, 274
**Internal economies of scale**
  external economies of scale vs., 98
  interindustry trade and, 92–94
International Bank for Reconstruction and Development (IBRD), 20. *See also* World Bank
*International Country Risk Guide*, 202
International debt
  case study, odious debt, 201–202
  of developing countries, 13–14, 199–201
  settling with reserve assets, 185
International economic institutions, 17–36
  Bretton Woods case study, 29–31
  criticism of, 31–34
  GATT, 20–21
  GATT rounds case study, 22–23
  IMF and World Bank, 19–20
  overview of, 17–18
  regional trade agreements, 23–26
  role of, 8–9, 12–13, 26–29
  study questions, 36
  summary, 31–34

  taxonomy of, 18
  Uruguay Round, 21
  vocabulary, 35
  WTO, 21–22
International economy issues, 11–15
  capital flows, 13–14
  China and India integrated into world economy, 14–15
  debt of developing countries, 13–14
  East Asian export-led growth, 14
  exchange rates and macroeconomy, 13
  financial crises and global contagion, 13
  gains from trade, 11
  Latin American crisis and reform, 14
  regional trade agreements, 12
  resolution of trade conflicts, 12
  role of international institutions, 12–13
  trade deficits, 11–12
  wages, jobs and protection, 11
International finance
  balance of payments. *See* Balance of payments, and trade
  exchange rates. *See* Exchange rates
  instruments of today vs. earlier periods?, 6
  open economy macroeconomics. *See* Open economy macroeconomics
**International financial architecture**, 274
International financial crises, 273–299
  Asian crisis of 1997 and 1998, 288–292
  avoiding with capital controls, 284–286
  avoiding with exchange rate policy, 283–284
  Chilean taxes on capital inflows, 286
  crisis management, Asian crisis, 291–292
  crisis management, overview of, 287–288
  definition of financial crisis, 274–275
  global contagion and, 13
  from macroeconomic imbalances, 275–277
  Mexican peso crisis of 1994 and 1995, 278–281
  moral hazard and financial sector regulation, 282–283
  overview of, 273–274
  reforming international financial architecture, 292–297
  study questions, 299
  summary, 297–298
  vocabulary, 299
  from volatile capital flows, 277–278
International Financial Statistics (IFS), 207
**International investment position**
  measuring, 206–207
  overview of, 203–204
**International Labor Organization (ILO)**
  case study, 165–166
  child labor statistics, 161

increasing international negotiations of, 173
labor standards proposed by, 160
**International Monetary Fund (IMF)**, 2
addressing debt of developing countries, 200–201
creation of, 8–9, 19
criticisms of, 31–34
Highly Indebted Poor Countries program of, 13–14
as lender of last resort, 293–294
overview of, 19–20
publications of, 207–208
resolving peso crisis of 1994 and 1995, 280
International Standards Organization (ISO), 348
International Trade Administration (ITA), 150
International Trade Organization (ITO), 20
Internet, role in economic integration, 3
**Intra-firm trade** model, 75–77
**Intraindustry trade**, 91–96
case study, U.S.-Canada trade, 95–96
characteristics of, 92–94
gains from, 94–95
measures of, 91–92
overview of, 91
Investment
difficulties in changing global standards for, 8
holding foreign currency for, 211
**Investment income**, 179–181
Ireland, EU border controls, 344
**ISI (import substitution industrialization)**. *See* Import substitution industrialization (ISI)
ISO (International Standards Organization), 348
ITA (International Trade Administration), 150
ITO (International Trade Organization), 20

Japan
agricultural subsidies, 152
as currency trading center, 225
growth of manufactured exports, 402
as high-performance Asian economy, 394
openness index for, 5
protectionism in, 136–140
use of deliberation councils, 405
world currency trades in 2004, 224
**J-curve**, 266–267
Jobs
effects of NAFTA on U.S., 322–325
impact of trade on, 82–84
international economic issues, 11
outsourcing issues, 79–80
saved through tariffs and quotas (EU, Japan, and U.S.), 139
Jordan, 159
Jubilee 2000
debt-relief effort of, 200

lobbying for reduction in debt of poor countries, 14
Jubilee Plus, 200

Kennedy Round, 22–23
Kindleburger, Charles, 28–29
Knowledge spillovers, 102–103
Korea
Heavy and Chemical Industries program in, 413–414
industrial policies in, 410
as one of Four Tigers, 394
Kornai, Janos, 432
Kuznets, Simon, 399

Labels on exports, environmental and labor standards on, 171
Labor
advantages of external economies of scale, 98
arguments for national protection of, 143
China's endowment of, 77–78
conditions for adopting single currencies, 242
EU agreeing to policies on, 337
in HO trade model, 61–63
impact of trade on wages and jobs, 11, 82–84
issues in widening European Union, 357
Mexico's export processing industry, 314–315
migration of, 80–82
mobility of, 5–7
NAFTA debate in U.S., 317–318
winners and losers under NAFTA, 70–72
**Labor productivity**
absolute productivity advantage and gains from trade, 40–42
Asian model of economic growth and, 419
comparative productivity advantage and gains from trade, 44–49
Labor standards, 159–166
all trade negotiations insisting on, 159
case study, child labor, 160–162
case study, International Labor Organization, 165–166
defining, 160
increasing international negotiations for, 173
overview of, 159
study questions, 175
summary, 173–174
and trade, 163–165
vocabulary, 174–175
**Large country case,** tariffs, 123–124
Latin America, 364–393
crisis and reform in, 14
debt crisis of 1980s, 376–380
defining economy of, 364–365

dollarization in, 233
economic policy reform, 380–386
import substitution industrialization. *See* ISI
   (import substitution industrialization)
macroeconomic instability and economic
   populism, 375–376
measures of income distribution in, 399–400
newly industrializing economies in, 395
next generation of reforms, 389–391
peso collapse of 1994-1995 effecting, 197
population, income and economic growth of,
   365–367
regional trade blocs in, case study, 386–388
results of non-integration with world economy,
   10
study questions, 392–393
summary, 391–392
vocabulary, 392
Washington Consensus, 388–389
LDCs (less developed countries), impact of trade
   with, 83–84
League of Nations, 165
Legislation, EU
   Council of the European Union, 338
   European Parliament, 339
**Lender of last resort**
   for international financial crises, 293–294
   overview of, 274
Less developed countries (LDCs), impact of trade
   with, 83–84
Licensing requirements, imports, 128
Linguistics, Latin American, 364
Little Dragons, 394
Loans
   acquiring from foreign sources, 187–188
   crony capitalism and, 283
   IMF as lender of last resort, 293–294
   IMF conditionality on, 293–296
   international debt, 199–201
   monetary policy and, 256
Lobbyists
   effect of tariffs on rent seeking, 123
   industrial policies encouraging rent seeking, 108
Local content requirements, NAFTA, 316
Look East policy, 410
**Lost Decade**, in Latin America
   causes of, 376–377
   defined, 14
   overview of, 311–312
   responses to, 377–380
**Low income countries**
   debt service issues of, 199
   environment, society and, 157–159
   external debts of, 200–201

product cycle in, 75
universal minimum wage standards in, 160
**Lower-middle income countries**
   debt service issues of, 199
   environment, society and, 157–159
   external debts of, 200–201


**Maastricht Treaty**, 333, 350
Macroeconomics, 248–272
   adjustment process in U.S., 267–268
   aggregate demand and aggregate supply, 250–254
   crises caused by imbalances in, 275–281
   crisis management, 287
   current account balance and, 260–265
   East Asian stability, 402–403, 411
   economic populism in Latin America and,
      375–376
   fiscal and monetary policy during Great
      Depression, 257–260
   fiscal policy, 254–255
   main agents in, 249
   monetary policy, 255–257
   overview of, 248
   policies for current account imbalances, 265–267
   policies impacting jobs, 82–83
   policy coordination in developed countries,
      268–269
   reforms of Washington Consensus, 388–389
   stability of HPAE, 404
   study questions, 271–272
   summary, 269–270
   vocabulary, 270–271
**Magnification effect**, 68
Malaysia
   Asian crisis of 1997 and 1998, 288–292
   as high-performance Asian economy, 394
   industrial policies in, 410–411
   as newly industrializing economy, 395
   policy during Asian crisis, 285–286
**Managed floats**, 232
Manufacturing
   challenges for China in, 436–439
   forecasts of winners and losers under NAFTA,
      71
   manufactured exports in East Asia, 414–417
   manufactured exports in HPAEs, 402
   in product cycle model of trade, 73–75
   reductions in employment in, 83
*Maquila*, 314
**Maquiladora** industry, 314–315, 319
**Market failures**
   import substitution industrialization and, 371
   industrial policies and, 101–103

...0

...234

...n del Sur (MERCOSUR), 382

...nion, 26

...rade agreement, 9, 387–388

**Mercantilism**, attacked by Adam Smith, 38

MERCOSUR (Mercado Común del Sur). *See*
   Mercado Común del Sur (MERCOSUR)

Mexico. *See also* NAFTA (North American Free
   Trade Agreement)
   anti-inflation policies and, 382
   common market and, 26
   ease of doing business in, 328–329
   economic/demographic characteristics, 302–305
   export processing industry of, 313–314
   forecasting NAFTA winners and losers, 70–72
   free trade controversy with U.S., 68
   import substitution industrialization in, 373–374
   Lost Decade crisis and, 376–377
   NAFTA environmental and labor standards, 159
   openness and outwardness of, 390
   peso crisis of 1994 and 1995, 185, 197, 278–281
   recent economic history of, 310–313
   sexenio crisis, 189–190
   supporting single currency for NAFTA region,
      243–244
   U.S. labor argument against NAFTA, 143

**MFN (most-favored nation) status**, 21–22

Middle East, regional trade blocs, 25

Migration
   European Union population forecast and,
      360–361
   problems of widening European Union, 357
   and trade, 80–82
   U.S.-Mexico relations and, 320–322

Military industry. *See* Defense industry

Minimum wage standards, 160

Ministry of International Trade and Industry
   (MITI), 405

Mission creep, IMF, 295

MITI (Ministry of International Trade and
   Industry), 405

Mobutu, Joseph Desire, 202

**Monetary policy**
   case study, during Great Depression, 257–260
   crisis management, 287–288
   and current account, 262–265
   defined, 254
   indicators of potential financial crises, 275–277
   interest and exchange rates and, 261–262
   overview of, 255–257

**Monopolistic competition**, 94

*Monthly Bulletin of Statistics*, 208

Montreal Protocol, 173

**Moral hazard** problems
   Asian crisis of 1997 and 1998, 292
   financial sector regulation and, 282–283
   with lender of last resort, 293–294

Morality, of low labor standards, 165

Morrill Act, 109

**Most-favored nation (MFN) status**, 21–22

Multiple equilibria, 278

**Multiplier effect**, 253

Mundell, Robert, 240

**Mutual recognition of standards**, 156–157

Myanmar, ILO sanctions against, 166

**NADBank (North American Development Bank)**,
   319–320

NAFTA (North American Free Trade Agreement).
   *See* North American Free Trade Agreement
   (NAFTA)

**National income account**, 190–192

National security, 144–145

**National treatment**, 21

National welfare loss, 138

Nationalism
   case study, economic sanctions, 146–147
   of Latin American countries, 364–365
   populism of Latin America and, 375–376
   protectionism, 142–146
   U.S. protectionist policies, 148–151

Natural disasters, creating unsustainable debt, 200

Natural resources, as source of comparative
   advantage, 42

**Neoliberal model**, 380

**Neoliberalism**, 380

Net foreign investment, 194

Netherlands, 5

New Basel Capital Accord, 282–283

"New Institutionalists", 17–18

New Zealand, 152

**Newly industrializing economies (NIEs)**, 395

Nicaragua, 194

**NIEs (newly industrializing economies)**, 395

**Nominal exchange rate**, 226–228

**Nominal rate of protection**, 124–126

**Nondiminishable**, public goods as, 27

**Nondiscrimination**, 21–22

**Nonexcludable**, public goods as, 27

**Nonrival**, public goods as, 27

**Nontariff barriers (NTBs)**, 131

**Nontariff measures**, 131

**Non-transboundary environmental impacts**,
   167–168

**Nontransparent barriers**, to trade, 116

North, Douglas, 17–18

North America, economic integration in, 302–331
  Canada-U.S. trade relationship, 305–309
  economic/demographic characteristics, 302–305
  Mexico's export processing industry, 313–315
  NAFTA. *See* NAFTA (North American Free
    Trade Agreement)
  overview of, 302
  recent Mexican economic history, 310–313
  study questions, 330–331
  summary, 329–330
  vocabulary, 330
**North American Agreement on Environmental**
  **Cooperation**, 318–320
**North American Agreement on Labor**
  **Cooperation**, 317–318
North American Community, future of NAFTA,
  326–328
**North American Development Bank (NADBank)**,
  319–320
North American Free Trade Agreement (NAFTA)
  common market elements of, 26
  consideration of single currency in, 242–244
  doing business in countries of, 328–329
  environmental and labor standards of, 159
  expansion of, 325–326
  features of, 315–316
  future of, 326–328
  importance of Mexico in, 324–325
  members of, 304
  peso crisis of 1994 and 1995 and, 279–280
  as regional trade agreement, 388
  size of EU market equalling size of, 336
  trade adjustment assistance after, 54–55
  trade within region, 305
  winners and losers in, 70–72
  World Trade Organization permitting, 22
North American Free Trade Agreement (NAFTA),
  debate in U.S., 316–322
  environmental issues, 318–320
  immigration issues, 320–322
  impact on jobs, 322–325
  labor issues, 143, 317–318
North Korea, 146
Norway, 336
**NTBs (nontariff barriers)**, 131

**Odious debt**, 202
**Official reserve assets**
  case study, Mexican sexenio crisis, 190
  overview of, 184–185
**OLI (ownership-location-internalization) theory**,
  76–77
**Oligopoly**, 93
Olson, Mancur, 140

Open economy macroeconomics. *See*
  Macroeconomics
**Open market operations**, 256
Openness index
  Latin America, 384–385
  in world trade, 4–5
**Opportunity costs**
  absolute productivity advantage and, 40
  gains from trade in HO model, 64
  in product cycle model of trade, 75
  and production possibilities curve, 44–45
**Optimal currency area**
  considering if NAFTA region is, 242–244
  overview of, 240–241
Order, maintained by international institutions,
  28–29
**Orthodox model**, of inflation control, 381–382
*The Other Path* (de Soto), 328
Output
  effects of tariffs on, 118–120
  measuring GDP for nation's, 191
  measuring GNP for nation's, 191
  in Stolper-Samuelson theorem, 66–68
**Outsourcing**, 79–80
Overvalued exchange rates, import substitution
  industrialization and, 371–372
**Ownership-location-internalization (OLI) theory**,
  76–77
Oxfam, debt-relief effort, 200

Pacto de Solidarida (Social Solidarity Pact), 382
Partial equilibrium analysis, 116
**Partial trade agreement**, 23
PBOC (People's Bank of China), 438–439
**Pegged exchange rates**
  choosing, 235–237
  exchange rate crisis vulnerability of, 275
  overview of, 231–232
People's Bank of China (PBOC), 438–439
Permitting process, in India, 428
Pharmaceuticals, intellectual property rights and,
  133
Philippines, 288–292
Plaza Accord, 268
Politics
  crony capitalism and, 283
  developing trust through single currencies,
    240–241
  EU monetary union, 353–354
  of environmental and labor standards, 159
  potential of capital inflows and, 203–204
  reform and protest in China, 440–441
  U.S. protectionism, 148–151
**Pollution havens**, 168

Population. *See* Demographics
Populism, in Latin America, 375–376
Portugal, 364
Positive externalities, validating protection of infant industries, 144
Poverty, child labor and, 162
**PPC (production possibilities curve)**. *See* Production possibilities curve (PPC)
Prebisch, Raul, 369–370
Prequalification, for IMF assistance, 295
PRI (Institutional Revolutionary Party), 189–190
**Price line (trade line)**
  gains from trade in HO model, 64–65
  overview of, 46–47
Prices, effects of tariffs on, 118–120
**Private returns**, market failure and, 101–103
Privatization biases, of international institutions, 33
**Producer surplus**
  effects of tariffs on, 120
  impact of EU, Japan and U.S. protection, 138
  overview of, 118
**Product account**, 190–192
**Product cycle model,** of trade
  China exports to U.S. and, 78
  overview of, 73–75
**Product differentiation**, in monopolistic competition, 94
Production, simple model of, 39–40
**Production possibilities curve (PPC)**
  gains from trade in HO model, 63–64
  overview of, 44–45
  price line or trade line and, 46–47
  in Stolper-Samuelson theorem, 67
Productivity
  absolute productivity advantage and gains from trade, 40–42
  case study, current account deficits in U.S. and, 197–199
  comparative productivity advantage and gains from trade, 44–49
  labor argument issues, 143
  in manufacturing vs. services, 83
  measuring East Asian industrial policy, 411–413
Protectionism
  EU, 136–140
  international economic issues, 11
  Japan, 136–140
  nationalism and, 142–146
  quotas as form of, 131
  tariffs as form of, 124–126
  U.S., 148–151
  using labor standards to justify real goal, 164
Public goods
  characteristics of, 27–28

  role of international institutions in providing, 28–29
Public procurement, EU attempts to eliminate discrimination in, 349
Purchases, developing industry through government, 106
**Purchasing power parity**
  in North American countries, 303
  overview of, 218–219

**Qualified majority**, EU legislation, 338
**Quota rents**
  effects of quotas on foreign producers, 129–131
  impact of EU, Japan and U.S., 138
**Quotas**, 128–135
  case study, intellectual property rights and trade, 131–133
  defined, 8
  effect on profits of foreign producers, 129–131
  hidden forms of protection, 131
  impact of EU, Japan and U.S., 137–138
  international institutional issues, 32
  limiting quantity of imports, 116
  for membership to IMF, 19
  study questions, 134–135
  summary, 133
  tariffs vs., 129
  types of, 128–129
  vocabulary, 134

R & D (research and development)
  industrial policy problems, 108
  knowledge spillovers in area of, 103
**Race to the bottom**
  countries with lower standards creating, 159
  defined, 157
  environmental standards and, 167–168
**Real exchange rate**, 226–228
Reform process, economic
  in China, 426–428
  Doing Business index as indicator of, 429
  in India, 428–429
  Latin American inflation control policies, 380–383
  Latin American trade, 383–386
  next generation of, 389–391
  USSR vs. China, 430–432
  Washington Consensus, 388–389
Regional Development Funds, EU, 347, 357
**Regional trade agreements (RTAs)**, 23–26
  international economic issues of, 12
  in Latin America, 385–388

overview of, 9
prominent, 24–25
types of, 23, 26
Regulations, limiting financial flows across borders, 188
**Relative prices**, 45–46
Renminbi, 439–440
Rent seeking
    effect of tariffs on, 123
    HPAEs avoiding, 406
    import substitution industrialization developing widespread, 372–373
    industrial policies encouraging, 107–108
Republic of Korea, 55–56
research and development (R & D)
    industrial policy problems, 108
    knowledge spillovers in area of, 103
Research Triangle, 96
**Reserve assets**
    case study, Mexican sexenio crisis, 190
    overview of, 184–186
Resource allocation, effects of tariffs on, 120–122
Resources, challenges for China, 437–438
Retail customers, participating in foreign currency markets, 212–213
Retaliation
    adding to net loss of tariffs, 122–123
    nations justifying trade barriers through, 145–146
    trade barriers creating potential of, 164
Revenue, EU, 340
Ricardian theory of trade
    empirical tests of, 72
    gains from trade in, 62
    overview of, 40
    trade and income distribution assumptions of, 65–66
Ricardo, David, 40
Roosevelt, President, 258–259
**RTAs (Regional trade agreements)**. *See* Regional trade agreements (RTAs)
"Rule of 72", 398
**Rules of origin**, free trade areas requiring, 327
Russia. *See* USSR

Salinas, President, 279–280, 312–313
Sanctions
    case study, success rate of, 146–147
    imposed by International Labor Organization, 166
    nations justifying retaliation, 145–146
    successful if countries are united on, 165
Savings, in HPAEs, 401
The Schengen Agreement, 343
Schuman, Robert, 336

SDRs (special drawing rights)
    of IMF, 19–20
    as reserve asset, 184
**SEA (Single European Act)**. *See* SEA (Single European Act)
Sea turtles, endangered, 169–170
**Section 301**, U.S. Trade Act of 1974, 151
Securities and Exchange Commission, 258
**Separate standards**, 156–157
Services. *See also* Goods and services
    challenges of India in, 435–436
    outsourcing of, 79–80
    productivity in manufacturing vs., 83
**SEZ (Special Economic Zones)**, 427, 431
**Shallow integration**, 8
Shrimp imports, U.S. prohibitions, 169–170
Signal scrambling, 27
Silicon Valley, 96–97
Singapore
    as currency trading center, 225
    as high-performance Asian economy, 394
    industrial policies in, 411
    as one of Four Tigers, 394
Singer, Hans, 369–370
**Singh, Manmohan**, 428
Single currency areas
    conditions for adopting, 241–242
    overview of, 239–241
**Single European Act (SEA)**
    European Community signs, 332
    forecast of gains from, 345–346
    formation of, 344–345
    Maastricht Treaty, 350
    problems in implementing, 346–349
Smith, Adam, 38–39
**Smithsonian Agreement**, 239
Social Charter, of EU, 337, 350
**Social networks**
    determining migration, 81
    Mexican migrants into the U.S. and, 320
Social programs, opposition to CUSTA in Canada, 308
**Social returns**, market failure and, 101–103
Social Security, 258
*Social Solidarity Pact* (Pacto de Solidaridad Social), 382
Socialism, transition to capitalism, 430
Society
    costs of EU unemployment benefits, 347
    European Union population forecast, 360–361
    income levels, environment and, 157–159
    limitations of GDP to measure well-being of, 191
Solid waste (garbage), deterioration with income growth, 159

South Korea
Asian crisis of 1997 and 1998, 288–292
comparative advantage in, 55–56
as high-performance Asian economy, 394
**Sovereignty** issues, international institutions, 31–32
Spain
from emigration to immigration, 358–360
Latin Americans gaining independence from, 364
macroeconomic policies and unemployment in, 83
**Special 301**, U.S. Trade Act of 1974, 151
Special drawing rights (SDRs)
of IMF, 19–20
as reserve asset, 184
**Special Economic Zones (SEZ)**, 427, 431
Specialization, market size and, 39
**Specific factors model**, 68–70
Speculation, foreign exchange, 211–212
**Spot market**
defined, 213
in medium and short run, 221–223
Standards, 155–176
case study, income, environment and society, 157–159
EU problems with harmonizing, 347–348
options for setting, 156–157
overview of, 155–156
study questions, 175
summary, 173–174
vocabulary, 174–175
Standards, environmental, 167–175
alternatives to trade measures, 170–173
case study, trade barriers and endangered species, 169–170
transboundary and non-transboundary effects, 167–169
Standards, labor, 159–166
case study, child labor, 160–162
case study, International Labor Organization, 165–166
defining, 160
overview of, 159
and trade, 163–165
**Standstills**, IMF conditionality, 296
**Statistical discrepancy**
overview of, 184
in U.S. balance of payments, 182
*Statistical Yearbook*, 208
**Sterilization**, 439
Stiglitz, Joseph, 132
Stock market, role of banks in, 187
**Stolper-Samuelson theorem**
NAFTA debate in U.S., 317
overview of, 66–68
on wage inequality, 83–84

**Strategic trade policy**
overview of, 103–105
problems with, 107
**Structural reform policies**, Latin America, 383–386
**Subsidiarity**, EU, 337
Subsidies
case study, agricultural, 151–152
case study, commercial aircraft, 110–112
directing to targeted industries, 105–106
EU support programs for agriculture, 340
granting countervailing duties to industries hurt by foreign, 148–149
strategic trade policy using, 103–105
Tokyo Round establishing rules for, 22–23
Uruguay Round negotiations, 141
U.S. industrial policies, 108–110
Sulfur dioxide, 159
Sullivan Principles, 173
**Supervisory review**, moral hazard in banking and, 283
Supply and demand
case study, largest market in world, 224–225
exchange rates in long run, 216–219
exchange rates in medium and short runs, 220–223
with flexible exchange rates, 214–215
for foreign exchange, 214
monetary policy and, 255–257
Supply curve, producer surplus and, 118
**Supply-push factors**
determining migration, 80–81
Mexican migrants into the U.S. and, 320
**Swap agreements**, 418
**Swaps**, 418
Switzerland
absence from European Union, 336
composition of world currency trades in 2004, 224
as currency trading center, 225

TAA (trade adjustment assistance), 54–55
Taiwan
as high-performance Asian economy, 394
as one of Four Tigers, 394
Tanzania, 195
**Tariffs**, 116–127
analysis of, 116
average rates in Latin America, 383–384
case study, comparison of tariff rates, 126–127
common external, 26
consumer and producer surplus and, 117–118
effective vs. nominal rates of protection, 124–126
effects on prices, output, and consumption, 118–120

effects on resource allocation and income distribution, 120–122

impact of EU, Japan and U.S., 138

large country case tariff, 123–124

limiting imports through taxes, 116

other potential costs, 122–123

quotas vs., 129

revenues collected for, 142–143

shallow integration and, 8

study questions, 134–135

summary, 133

Uruguay Round negotiations, 141

vocabulary, 134

WTO, Uruguay Round and GATT agreements for, 20–22

Taxation

EU problems with value-added taxes, 348–349

fiscal policy of, 254–255

during Great Depression, 259

special treatments to targeted industries, 106

Technology

challenges for India in, 435–436

Chinese patterns of trade in, 433–434

improvements increase trade and capital flows, 6

India's participation in service trade, 435

large geographical concentrations of industries in, 96–98

Mexico's export processing industry, 315

technological externalities validating protection of infant industries, 144

**Technology transfer**, 203

TED (turtle excluder devices), 169–170

Telecommunications revolution, reducing size of geographical barriers, 96

Tennessee Valley Authority, 258

Tequila effect, 197

**Terms of trade (TOT)**, 370

Terrorism

EU border controls and, 344

effecting Mexican migration into U.S., 321–322

Textile industry

impact of EU, Japan and U.S. protection, 137–140

labels for exports in foreign, 171

**TFP (total factor productivity)**, 419–420

Thailand

Asian crisis of 1997 and 1998, 288–292

as high-performance Asian economy, 394

as newly industrializing economy, 395

Thematic councils, Japanese, 405

Third World debt crisis of 1980s, 275–277

Tokyo Round

accomplishments of, 22–23

allowing production subsidies, 111

**TOT (terms of trade)**, 370

**Total factor productivity (TFP)**, 419–420

Trade

and balance of payments. *See* Balance of payments, and trade

Chinese and Indian patterns of, 432–435

conflict resolution, 12

and economic growth, 9–10

gains from, 11

and geography, 96–100

growth of world, 4–5

modern theory of, 60–65

regional agreements. *See* Regional trade agreements (RTAs)

role in wage inequality, 82–84

Trade adjustment assistance (TAA), 54–55

**Trade balance**

adjustment process in, 266–267

adjustment process in U.S., 267–268

overview of, 178–179

Trade barriers

alternatives to, 170–173

endangered species and, 169–170

European Union programs to address, 347

NAFTA removing most, 316

questioning efficacy of, 163–165

**Trade blocs**. *See also* Regional trade agreements (RTAs)

Asian, 417–418

Latin American, 385

prominent, 24–25

strategic trade policy using, 103–105

Trade deficits

international economic issues, 11–12

United States, 2

Trade price, 49

**Trade Related Aspects Intellectual Property Rights (TRIPS)**

accomplished by Uruguay Round, 142

overview of, 132–133

Trade Related Investment Measures (TRIMS), 142

**Trade rounds**

GATT rounds case study, 22–23

overview of, 21

**Tranches**, 294

**Transaction costs**, for foreign investment, 7

Transatlantic cable, 6

**Transboundary environmental impacts**

overview of, 168–169

of U.S.-Mexico border, 319

**Transition economies**, 430

Transparency issues, of international institutions, 32

**Transparent barriers,** to trade, 116

**Treaty of Rome**, 336–337

**Treaty on European Union**, 332

*Triennial Central Bank Survey of Foreign Exchange and Derivatives Market Activity in April 2004,* 224

TRIMS (Trade Related Investment Measures), 142

**TRIPS (Trade Related Aspects Intellectual Property Rights)**
  accomplished by Uruguay Round, 142
  overview of, 132–133

Tuna, dolphin-safe, 169–170

Turkey
  acquiring from foreign sources, 187
  joining European Union, 358

Turtle excluder devices (TED), 169–170

Twin deficits, 195

Uncertainty, reduced by international institutions, 28–29

Unemployment, impact of trade on, 82–84

**Unilateral transfers**, 179–181

United Farm Workers, 162

United Kingdom
  as currency trading center, 225
  EU border controls of, 344
  openness index for, 5

United Nations (UN)
  creation of, 8–9
  International Labor Organization as part of, 166
  *Statistical Yearbook* and related volumes, 208

United States. *See also* NAFTA (North American Free Trade Agreement)
  adjustment process in, 267–268
  agricultural subsidies of, 152
  Auto Pact agreement with Canada, 95–96, 306–307
  Bretton Woods conference and, 29–31
  case study, current account deficits in, 197–199
  composition of world currency trades in 2004, 224
  as currency trading center, 225
  current account balance, 179–181
  CUSTA, 307–309
  Dominican Republic-Central American Free Trade Agreement, 325–326
  ease of doing business in, 328–329
  economic sanctions of, 146–147
  economic/demographic characteristics, 302–305
  effect of China's savings on, 438–440
  environmental and labor standards, 159
  as example of economic union, 26
  forecasting NAFTA winners and losers, 70–72
  history of speculative excesses and overinvestment in, 7
  industrial policies of, 108–110

interest in joining EU standards process, 348
international investment position of, 203–204
openness index for, 5
protectionism in, 136–140
trade balance, 178–179
on trade barriers and endangered species, 169–170
trade with China, case study, 77–78

United States, in global economy, 1–16
  capital and labor motility, 5–7
  globalization in perspective, 3
  growth of world trade, 4–5
  international economy issues, 11–15
  internationally integrated economies, 2–3
  new issues in trade and investment, 8
  regional trade agreements, 9
  role of international institutions, 8–9
  study questions, 15–16
  trade and economic growth, 9–10
  vocabulary, 15

United States International Trade Commission (USITC)
  filing for antidumping duties with, 150
  filing for escape clause relief with, 151

United States Trade Representative (USTR), 151

**Upper-middle income countries**, 157–159

**Uruguay Round**
  accomplishments of, 22–23
  case study of negotiations, 141–142
  criticisms of, 32–33
  defining prohibited subsidies, 111
  intellectual property rights and, 132
  limiting use of voluntary export restraints, 128
  overview of, 21
  rules for agricultural trade, 151–152
  rules preventing export promotion, 416

U.S. Trade Act of 1974, 151

USA. *See* United States

USITC (United States International Trade Commission)
  filing for antidumping duties with, 150
  filing for escape clause relief with, 151

USSR
  India modeling economic policies on, 428
  transition to capitalism, case study, 430–432

USTR (United States Trade Representative), 151

**Value added**
  defined, 125
  in nominal vs. effective rates of production, 107

Value-added tax (VAT), 348–349

Vernon, Raymond, 73

Volatility, of financial capital across international boundaries, 7

**Voluntary export restraints (VERs)**
    Canadian-U.S. Trade Agreement and, 307
    overview of, 128–129
Voluntary restraint agreement (VRA), 128

Wages
    impact of trade on, 82–84
    international economic issues, 11
**Washington Consensus**, 388–389
Widening, EU boundaries
    Central and Eastern Europe, 356–357
    defined, 340
    overview of, 355–356
    Turkey, 358
Williamson, John, 388
**World Bank**
    addressing debt of developing countries, 200–201
    creation of, 8–9
    criticisms of, 31–34
    defined, 17
    Highly Indebted Poor Countries program of, 13–14
    overview of, 20

*The World Is Flat* (Friedman), 435
**World Trade Organization (WTO)**
    China's accession to, 428, 432
    creation of, 8–9, 141–142
    criticisms of, 31–34
    international environmental negotiations and, 173
    overview of, 21–22
    on production subsidies, 111–112
    resolving trade disputes, 12–13
    studies on regional trade agreements, 24–25
    on trade barriers and endangered species, 169–170
World War II
    economic international organizations after, 8–9
    European Economic Community growing out of, 336–337
    low trade barriers resulting from, 8
    trade and economic growth prior to, 10

Zedillo, President, 189–190
**Zero sum** thinking, 38–39